PRESENTED BY

TIME

THE HAMMOND

WORLD
ATLAS

GAZETTEER-INDEX OF THE WORLD

This alphabetical list of grand divisions, countries, states, colonial possessions, etc., gives page numbers and index references on which they are shown on the largest scale as well as area and population of each unit. The index reference shows the square on the respective map in which the name of the entry may be located. An index of major cities of the United States may be found on pages 175-176.

Country	Page No.	Index Ref.	Area (Sq. Miles)	Population
*Afghanistan	70	A 2	250,000	17,078,263
Africa	54, 57	......	11,682,000	345,000,000
Alabama, U.S.A.	129	......	51,609	3,665,000
Alaska, U.S.A.	130	......	586,412	382,000
*Albania	43	E 5	11,100	2,126,000
Alberta, Canada	114	......	255,285	1,838,037
*Algeria	54	F 6	919,591	16,776,000
American Samoa	89	J 7	83	27,159
Andorra	31	G 1	175	19,000
*Angola	57	K14	481,351	6,761,000
Antarctica	88	......	5,500,000	....
Antigua & Dependencies	125	G 3	171	73,000
*Argentina	93	H10	1,072,070	23,983,000
Arizona, U.S.A.	131	......	113,909	2,270,000
Arkansas, U.S.A.	132	......	53,104	2,109,000
Ascension	5	G 8	34	1,154
Asia	58	......	17,032,000	2,043,997,000
*Australia	86	......	2,967,741	12,630,000
*Austria	38	B 3	32,374	7,419,341
*Bahamas	124	C 1	4,404	168,838
*Bahrain	60	F 4	231	207,000
*Bangladesh	70	F 3	55,126	70,000,000
*Barbados	125	G 4	166	253,620
*Belgium	25	......	11,779	9,660,154
Belize	122	C 2	8,867	122,000
*Benin	54	G10	43,483	3,200,000
Bermuda	125	H 3	21	52,000
*Bhutan	70	G 3	18,000	1,034,774

Country	Page No.	Index Ref.	Area (Sq. Miles)	Population
*Bolivia	90	G 7	424,163	4,804,000
*Botswana	57	L16	224,764	700,000
*Brazil	90	K 6	3,284,426	90,840,000
British Columbia, Canada	117	......	366,255	2,466,608
British Indian Ocean Terr.	58	L10	29	1,400
Brunei	83	E 4	2,226	130,000
*Bulgaria	43	G 4	42,829	8,501,000
*Burma	81	B 2	261,789	31,240,000
*Burundi	57	M12	10,747	4,100,000
California, U.S.A.	133	......	158,693	21,520,000
*Cambodia	81	E 4	69,898	8,110,000
*Cameroon	54	J10	183,568	6,600,000
*Canada	96-97	......	3,851,809	23,388,100
Canal Zone	123	H 6	647	44,650
*Cape Verde	5	F 9	1,557	302,000
Cayman Islands	124	B 3	100	10,652
*Central African Empire	54	K10	236,293	1,800,000
Central America	122-123	......	197,575	20,500,000
*Ceylon (Sri Lanka)	70	E 7	25,332	12,300,000
*Chad	54	K 8	495,752	4,178,000
Channel Islands	11	E 8	74	128,000
*Chile	93	F10	292,257	8,834,820
*China (mainland)	77	......	3,691,506	740,000,000
China (Taiwan)	77	K 7	13,948	14,577,000
*Colombia	90	F 3	439,513	21,117,000
Colorado, U.S.A.	134	......	104,247	2,583,000
*Comoros	57	P14	719	266,000
*Congo	57	J12	132,046	1,400,000

*Members of the United Nations.

Globe shown on cover courtesy of
Replogle Globes, Inc.

GAZETTEER-INDEX OF THE WORLD

Country	Page No.	Index Ref.	Area (Sq. Miles)	Population
Connecticut, U.S.A.	135	.....	5,009	3,117,000
Cook Islands	89	K 7	91	20,000
*Costa Rica	122	E 5	19,575	1,800,000
*Cuba	124	B 2	44,206	8,553,395
*Cyprus	64	E 5	3,473	649,000
*Czechoslovakia	39	C 2	49,370	14,497,000
Delaware, U.S.A.	146	M 3	2,057	582,000
*Denmark	19	.....	16,614	4,912,865
District of Columbia, U.S.A.	146	B 5	67	702,000
*Djibouti	55	P 9	8,880	250,000
Dominica	125	G 4	290	70,302
*Dominican Republic	124	D 3	18,704	4,011,589
*Ecuador	90	E 4	109,483	6,144,000
*Egypt	54	M 6	386,659	37,900,000
*El Salvador	122	C 4	8,260	3,418,455
England, U.K.	11	.....	50,516	46,417,600
*Equatorial Guinea	57	H11	10,831	320,000
*Ethiopia	54, 55	O 9	471,776	27,946,000
Europe	6	.....	4,063,000	652,000,000
Faerøe Islands, Denmark	19	B 2	540	38,000
Falkland Islands	93	H14	6,198	1,950
*Fiji	89	H 8	7,015	519,000
*Finland	16	.....	130,128	4,706,000
Florida, U.S.A.	136	.....	58,560	8,421,000
*France	26	.....	212,841	50,770,000
French Guiana	90	K 3	35,135	48,000
French Polynesia	89	L 8	1,544	109,000
*Gabon	57	J12	103,346	526,000
*Gambia	54	C 9	4,127	524,000
Georgia, U.S.A.	137	.....	58,876	4,970,000
*Germany, East (German Democratic Republic)	20		41,814	17,117,000
*Germany, West (Fed. Rep. of)	20	.....	95,959	61,194,600
*Ghana	54	F10	92,099	9,900,000
Gibraltar	31	D 4	2	27,000
Gilbert Islands	89	J 6	354	47,711
*Great Britain and Northern Ireland (United Kingdom)	8	.....	94,399	56,076,000
*Greece	43	F 6	50,548	8,838,000
Greenland	94	O 2	840,000	55,000
*Grenada	125	G 4	133	96,000
Guadeloupe and Dependencies	124	F 3	687	360,000
Guam	89	E 4	212	84,996
*Guatemala	122	B 3	42,042	5,200,000
*Guinea	54	D 9	94,925	4,500,000
*Guinea-Bissau	54	C 9	13,948	517,000
*Guyana	90	J 2	83,000	763,000
*Haiti	124	D 3	10,694	4,867,190
Hawaii, U.S.A.	130	.....	6,450	887,000
*Holland (Netherlands)	25	.....	13,958	13,077,000
*Honduras	122	D 3	43,277	2,495,000
Hong Kong	77	J 7	398	4,089,000
*Hungary	39	E 3	35,915	10,315,597
*Iceland	19	B 1	39,768	204,578
Idaho, U.S.A.	138	.....	83,557	831,000
Illinois, U.S.A.	139	.....	56,400	11,229,000
*India	70	.....	1,261,483	546,955,945
Indiana, U.S.A.	140	.....	36,291	5,302,000
*Indonesia	83	.....	735,264	119,572,000
Iowa, U.S.A.	141	.....	56,290	2,870,000
*Iran	68	.....	636,293	28,448,000

Country	Page No.	Index Ref.	Area (Sq. Miles)	Population
*Iraq	68	.....	167,924	9,431,000
*Ireland	15	.....	27,136	3,109,000
Ireland, Northern, U.K.	15	G 2	5,452	1,537,200
Isle of Man, U.K.	11	C 3	227	62,000
*Israel	67	.....	7,993	2,911,000
*Italy	32	.....	116,303	54,504,000
*Ivory Coast	54	E10	127,520	6,673,013
*Jamaica	124	C 3	4,411	1,972,000
*Japan	75	.....	143,622	104,665,171
*Jordan	67	.....	37,297	2,300,000
Kansas, U.S.A.	142	.....	82,264	2,310,000
Kentucky, U.S.A.	143	.....	40,395	3,428,000
*Kenya	57	O11	224,960	13,300,000
Korea, North	74	D 3	46,540	13,300,000
Korea, South	74	E 5	38,452	31,683,000
*Kuwait	60	E 4	8,000	733,196
*Laos	81	E 3	91,428	3,500,000
*Lebanon	64	F 6	4,015	2,800,000
*Lesotho	57	M17	11,720	1,100,000
*Liberia	54	E10	43,000	1,600,000
*Libya	54	J 6	679,358	2,500,000
Liechtenstein	37	J 2	61	21,000
Louisiana, U.S.A.	144	.....	48,523	3,841,000
*Luxembourg	25	J 9	999	339,000
Macao	77	H 7	6.2	292,000
*Madagascar	57	R16	226,657	7,700,000
Madeira, Portugal	30	A 2	307	268,700
Maine, U.S.A.	145	.....	33,215	1,070,000
*Malawi	57	N14	45,747	5,100,000
Malaya, Malaysia	81	D 6	50,806	9,000,000
*Malaysia	81, 83	.....	128,308	12,368,000
*Maldives	58	L 9	115	110,770
*Mali	54	F 8	464,873	5,800,000
*Malta	32	E 7	122	321,000
Man, Isle of, U.K.	11	C 3	227	62,000
Manitoba, Canada	110	.....	251,000	1,021,506
Martinique	125	G 4	425	332,000
Maryland, U.S.A.	146	.....	10,577	4,144,000
Massachusetts, U.S.A.	147	.....	8,257	5,809,000
*Mauritania	54	D 8	452,702	1,318,000
*Mauritius	57	S19	790	899,000
Mayotte	57	P14	144	40,000
*Mexico	119	.....	761,601	48,313,438
Michigan, U.S.A.	148	.....	58,216	9,104,000
Midway Islands	130	E 1	1.9	2,220
Minnesota, U.S.A.	149	.....	84,068	3,965,000
Mississippi, U.S.A.	150	.....	47,716	2,354,000
Missouri, U.S.A.	151	.....	69,686	4,778,000
Monaco	26	G 6	368 Acres	23,035
*Mongolia	77	F 2	604,247	1,300,000
Montana, U.S.A.	152	.....	147,138	753,000
Montserrat	125	G 3	40	12,300
*Morocco	54	E 5	241,224	18,000,000
*Mozambique	57	N16	308,641	9,300,000
Namibia (South-West Africa)	57	K16	317,827	883,000
Nauru	89	G 6	8.2	7,000
Nebraska, U.S.A.	153	.....	77,227	1,553,000
*Nepal	70	E 3	54,362	10,845,000
*Netherlands	25	.....	13,958	13,077,000
Netherlands Antilles	124	D 4,F 3	390	220,000
Nevada, U.S.A.	154	.....	110,540	610,000
New Brunswick, Canada	102	.....	28,354	677,250
New Caledonia and Dependencies	89	G 8	8,548	100,579
Newfoundland, Canada	99	.....	156,185	557,725

*Members of the United Nations.

Country	Page No.	Index Ref.	Area (Sq. Miles)	Population
New Hampshire, U.S.A.	155	......	9,304	822,000
New Hebrides	89	G 7	5,700	80,000
New Jersey, U.S.A.	156	......	7,836	7,336,000
New Mexico, U.S.A.	157	......	121,666	1,168,000
New York, U.S.A.	158	......	49,576	18,084,000
*New Zealand	87	......	103,736	2,815,000
*Nicaragua	122	D 4	45,698	1,984,000
*Niger	54	H 8	489,189	4,700,000
*Nigeria	54	H10	379,628	83,800,000
Niue	89	K 7	100	5,323
North America	94	......	9,363,000	314,000,000
North Carolina, U.S.A.	159	......	52,586	5,469,000
North Dakota, U.S.A.	160	......	70,665	643,000
Northern Ireland, U.K.	15	G 2	5,452	1,537,200
Northwest Territories, Canada	96	E 2	1,304,903	42,609
*Norway	16	......	125,181	3,893,000
Nova Scotia, Canada	100	......	21,425	828,571
Oceania	88-89	......	3,292,000	21,800,000
Ohio, U.S.A.	161	......	41,222	10,690,000
Oklahoma, U.S.A.	162	......	69,919	2,766,000
*Oman	60	G 6	82,000	565,000
Ontario, Canada 107-109		......	412,582	8,264,465
Oregon, U.S.A.	163	......	96,981	2,329,000
Pacific Islands, U.S. Trust Terr. of the	88-89	E, F 5	707	98,009
*Pakistan	70	B 3	310,403	60,000,000
*Panama	122	G 6	29,209	1,425,343
*Papua New Guinea	82;89	B 7;E 6	183,540	2,563,610
*Paraguay	93	J 8	157,047	2,314,000
Pennsylvania, U.S.A.	164	......	45,333	11,862,000
*Persia (Iran)	68	......	636,293	28,448,000
*Peru	90	E 5	496,222	13,586,300
*Philippines	83	H 4	115,707	43,751,000
Pitcairn Islands	89	O 8	18	74
*Poland	45	......	120,725	34,364,000
*Portugal	30	......	35,510	9,560,000
Prince Edward Island, Canada	100	E 2	2,184	118,229
Puerto Rico 124-125		G 1	3,435	2,712,033
*Qatar	60	F 4	8,500	100,000
Québec, Canada 104-106		......	594,860	6,234,445
Réunion	57	R20	969	475,700
Rhode Island, U.S.A.	147	H 5	1,214	927,000
Rhodesia (Zimbabwe)	57	M15	150,803	6,600,000
*Rumania	43	F 3	91,699	20,394,000
*Rwanda	57	N12	10,169	4,241,000
Sabah, Malaysia	83	F 4	28,460	633,000
St. Christopher-Nevis- Anguilla	124	F 3	155	71,500
St. Helena and Dependencies	5	H 8	162	6,400
St. Lucia	125	G 4	238	110,000
St-Pierre and Miquelon	99	B 4	93.5	6,000
St. Vincent	125	F 4	150	89,129
San Marino	32	D 3	23.4	19,000
*São Tomé e Príncipe	57	G11	372	80,000
Sarawak, Malaysia	83	E 5	48,050	950,000
Saskatchewan, Canada	113	......	251,700	921,323
*Saudi Arabia	60	D 4	920,000	7,200,000
Scotland, U.K.	13	......	30,414	5,261,000
*Senegal	54	D 9	75,954	5,085,388
*Seychelles	58	J10	145	60,000
*Siam (Thailand)	81	D 3	198,456	35,448,000
*Sierra Leone	54	C10	27,925	3,100,000

Country	Page No.	Index Ref.	Area (Sq. Miles)	Population
*Singapore	81	F 6	226	2,300,000
*Solomon Islands	89	G 6	11,500	161,525
*Somalia	55	R10	246,200	3,170,000
*South Africa	57	L18	472,259	25,900,000
South America	90	......	6,875,000	186,000,000
South Carolina, U.S.A.	165	......	31,055	2,848,000
South Dakota, U.S.A.	166	......	77,047	686,000
South-West Africa (Namibia) ..	57	K16	317,827	883,000
*Spain	31	......	194,896	33,290,000
*Sri Lanka	70	E 7	25,332	12,300,000
*Sudan	54	M 9	967,494	18,347,000
*Surinam	90	J 3	55,144	389,000
*Swaziland	57	N17	6,705	500,000
*Sweden	16	......	173,665	7,978,000
Switzerland	37	......	15,941	6,230,000
*Syria	64	G 5	71,498	5,866,000
*Tanzania	57	N13	363,708	15,506,000
Tennessee, U.S.A.	167	......	42,244	4,214,000
Texas, U.S.A.	168	......	267,339	12,487,000
*Thailand	81	D 3	198,455	42,700,000
*Togo	54	G10	21,622	2,300,000
Tokelau	89	J 6	3.95	2,000
Tonga	89	J 8	270	83,000
*Trinidad and Tobago	125	G 5	1,980	1,040,000
Tristan da Cunha	5	J 8	38	292
*Tunisia	54	H 5	63,170	5,776,000
*Turkey	64	......	301,381	34,375,000
Turks and Caicos Is.	124	D 2	166	6,000
Tuvalu	89	H 6	9.78	5,887
*Uganda	57	N11	91,076	11,400,000
*Ukrainian S.S.R., U.S.S.R.	50	C 5	232,046	47,126,517
*Union of Soviet Socialist Republics	46, 50	......	8,649,498	241,748,000
*United Arab Emirates	60	F 5	31,628	155,881
*United Kingdom	8	......	94,399	56,076,000
*United States of America 126-127		......	3,615,123	217,739,000
*Upper Volta	54	F 9	105,869	6,144,013
*Uruguay	93	J10	72,172	2,900,000
Utah, U.S.A.	169	......	84,916	1,228,000
Vatican City	32	B 6	109 Acres	1,000
*Venezuela	92	......	352,143	10,398,907
Vermont, U.S.A.	155	......	9,609	476,000
*Vietnam	81	E 3	128,405	46,600,000
Virginia, U.S.A.	170	......	40,817	5,032,000
Virgin Islands, British	125	H 1	59	10,484
Virgin Islands, U.S.A.	125	H 1	133	62,468
Wake Island, U.S.A.	89	G 4	2.5	1,647
Wales, U.K.	11	D 5	8,017	2,778,000
Washington, U.S.A.	171	......	68,192	3,612,000
West Indies 124-125		......	91,118	28,500,000
*Western Samoa	89	J 7	1,097	139,810
West Virginia, U.S.A.	172	......	24,181	1,821,000
White Russian S.S.R. (Byelo-russian S.S.R.), U.S.S.R.	50	C 4	80,154	9,002,338
Wisconsin, U.S.A.	173	......	56,154	4,609,000
World	5	......	57,970,000	4,124,000,000
Wyoming, U.S.A.	174	......	97,914	390,000
*Yemen Arab Republic	60	D 7	75,000	5,000,000
*Yemen, Peoples Dem. Rep. of	60	E 7	111,075	1,220,000
*Yugoslavia	43	C 3	98,766	20,586,000
Yukon Territory, Canada	96	C 3	207,076	21,836
*Zaire	57	L12	918,962	25,600,000
*Zambia	57	M14	290,586	4,936,000
Zimbabwe (Rhodesia)	57	M15	150,803	6,600,000

* Members of the United Nations.

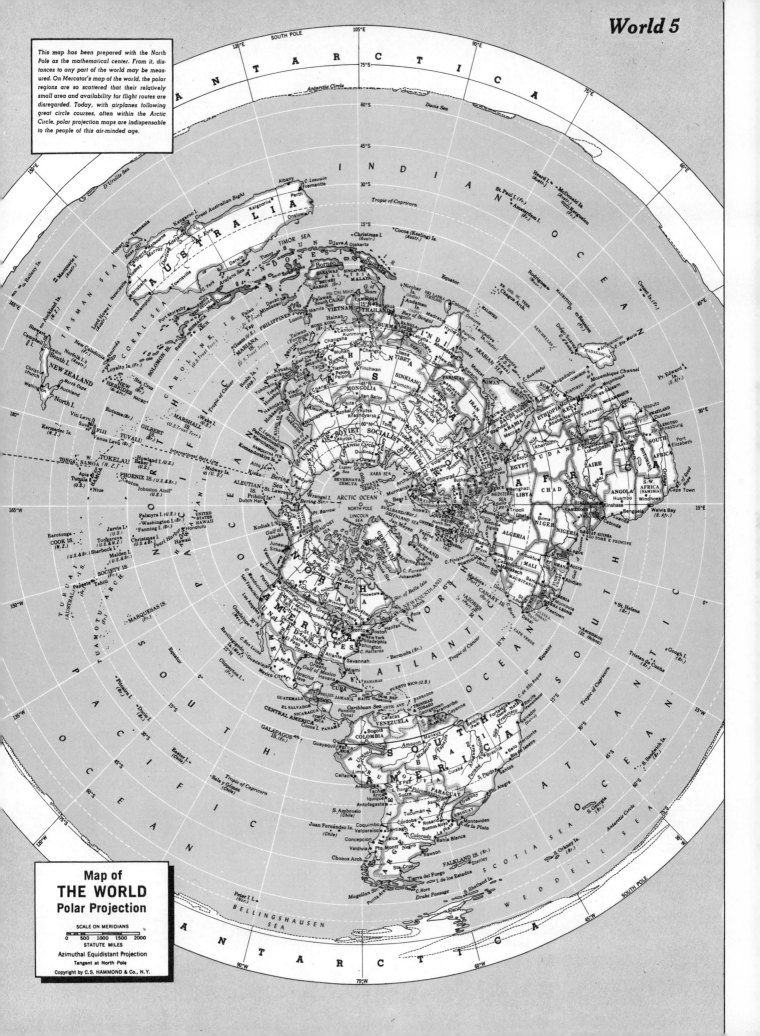

This map has been prepared with the North Pole as the mathematical center. From it, distances to any part of the world may be measured. On Mercator's map of the world, the polar regions are so scattered that their relatively small area and availability for flight routes are disregarded. Today, with airplanes following great circle courses, often within the Arctic Circle, polar projection maps are indispensable to the people of this air-minded age.

Map of
THE WORLD
Polar Projection

SCALE ON MERIDIANS

0 500 1000 1500 2000
STATUTE MILES

Azimuthal Equidistant Projection
Tangent at North Pole

Copyright by C.S. Hammond & Co., N.Y.

AREA 4,063,000 sq. mi.
POPULATION 652,000,000
LARGEST CITY London
HIGHEST POINT El'brus 18,481 ft.
LOWEST POINT Caspian Sea -92 ft.

EUROPE
LAMBERT AZIMUTHAL EQUAL AREA PROJECTION

SCALE OF MILES
0   100   200   300   400   500

SCALE OF KILOMETRES
0   100   200   300   400   500

Capitals of Countries .... ☆
International Boundaries .... -----
Canals .... ----

Copyright by C.S. Hammond & Co., N.Y.

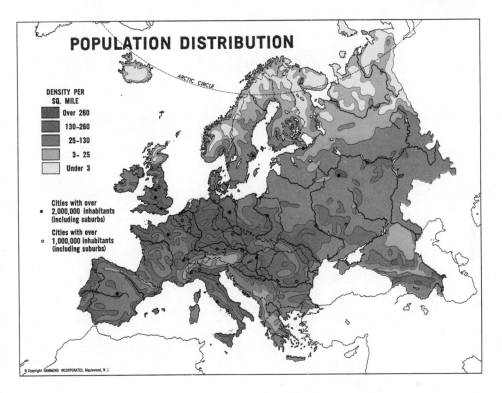

POPULATION DISTRIBUTION

DENSITY PER
SQ. MILE

Over 260
130-260
25-130
3- 25
Under 3

● Cities with over
2,000,000 inhabitants
(including suburbs)

○ Cities with over
1,000,000 inhabitants
(including suburbs)

© Copyright HAMMOND INCORPORATED, Maplewood, N.J.

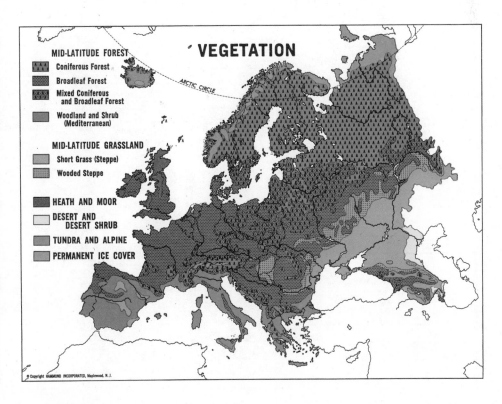

VEGETATION

MID-LATITUDE FOREST

Coniferous Forest
Broadleaf Forest
Mixed Coniferous
and Broadleaf Forest
Woodland and Shrub
(Mediterranean)

MID-LATITUDE GRASSLAND

Short Grass (Steppe)
Wooded Steppe

HEATH AND MOOR
DESERT AND
DESERT SHRUB
TUNDRA AND ALPINE
PERMANENT ICE COVER

© Copyright HAMMOND INCORPORATED, Maplewood, N.J.

Reykjavík (cap.), Iceland ....B 2
Rhine (river) ....E 4
Rhodope (mts.) ....G 4
Rhône (river) ....E 4
Riga, U.S.S.R. ....G 3
Rome (cap.), Italy ....F 4
Rostov, U.S.S.R. ....J 4
Rotterdam, Neth. ....E 3
Rumania ....G 4
Russian S.F.S.R., U.S.S.R. ....J 4
Saint George's (chan.) ....D 3
Salonika, Greece ....G 4
Salzburg, Austria ....F 4
San Marino ....F 4
Saragossa, Spain ....D 4
Sarajevo, Yugoslavia ....F 4
Saratov, U.S.S.R. ....J 3
Sardinia (Sardegna) (isl.),
Italy ....E 5
Sava (river) ....F 4
Scotland ....D 3
Seine (river), France ....E 4
Seville, Spain ....D 5
Shetland (isls.), Scotland ....D 2
Sicily (Sicilia) (isl.), Italy ....F 5
Skagerrak (strait) ....E 3
Sofia (cap.), Bulgaria ....G 4
Sognefjord (fjord), Norway ....E 2
Southampton, England ....D 3
Spain ....D 4
Stockholm (cap.), Sweden ....G 3
Strasbourg, France ....E 4
Stuttgart, W. Germany ....E 4
Sweden ....F 2
Switzerland ....E 4
Szeged, Hungary ....F 4
Tagus (Tajo, Tejo) (riv.) ....D 5

Tampere, Finland ....G 2
Taranto (gulf), Italy ....F 5
Tbilisi, U.S.S.R. ....J 4
Tiber (riv.), Italy ....F 4
Tiranë (cap.), Albania ....F 4
Trieste, Italy ....F 4
Trondheim, Norway ....F 2
Turin (Torino), Italy ....E 4
Turku, Finland ....F 2
Tyrrhenian (sea) ....F 5
Ufa, U.S.S.R. ....K 3
Ukranian, S.S.R., U.S.S.R. ....H 4
Union of Soviet Socialist
Republics ....H 3
United Kingdom ....D 3
Ural (mts.), U.S.S.R. ....L 3
Ural (river), U.S.S.R. ....J 3
Valencia, Spain ....K 5
Varna, Bulgaria ....G 4
Vatican City ....F 4
Venice (Venezia), Italy ....F 4
Vesuvius (mt.), Italy ....F 4
Vienna (cap.), Austria ....F 4
Vistula (riv.), Poland ....F 3
Volga (river), U.S.S.R. ....J 4
Volgograd, U.S.S.R. ....J 4
Wales ....D 3
Warsaw (cap.), Poland ....G 3
Weser (river), Germany ....E 3
West Germany ....E 3
White (sea), U.S.S.R. ....H 2
White Russian S.S.R.,
U.S.S.R. ....G 3
Wrocław, Poland ....F 3
Yugoslavia ....F 4
Zagreb, Yugoslavia ....F 4
Zürich, Switzerland ....E 4

UNITED KINGDOM

AREA 94,399 sq. mi.
POPULATION 56,076,000
CAPITAL London
LARGEST CITY London
HIGHEST POINT Ben Nevis 4,406 ft.
MONETARY UNIT pound sterling
MAJOR LANGUAGES English, Gaelic, Welsh
MAJOR RELIGIONS Protestantism, Roman Catholicism

IRELAND

AREA 27,136 sq. mi.
POPULATION 3,109,000
CAPITAL Dublin
LARGEST CITY Dublin
HIGHEST POINT Carrantuohill 3,415 ft.
MONETARY UNIT Irish pound
MAJOR LANGUAGES English, Gaelic (Irish)
MAJOR RELIGION Roman Catholicism

UNITED KINGDOM

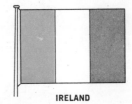

IRELAND

ENGLAND

AREA 50,516 sq. mi.
POPULATION 46,417,600
CAPITAL London
LARGEST CITY London
HIGHEST POINT Scafell Pike 3,210 ft.

WALES

AREA 8,017 sq. mi.
POPULATION 2,778,000
LARGEST CITY Cardiff
HIGHEST POINT Snowdon 3,560 ft.

SCOTLAND

AREA 30,414 sq. mi.
POPULATION 5,261,000
CAPITAL Edinburgh
LARGEST CITY Glasgow
HIGHEST POINT Ben Nevis 4,406 ft.

NORTHERN IRELAND

AREA 5,452 sq. mi.
POPULATION 1,537,200
CAPITAL Belfast
LARGEST CITY Belfast
HIGHEST POINT Slieve Donard 2,796 ft.

ENGLAND

COUNTIES

...on, 920,200	E6
...ffordshire, 491,700	G5
...kshire, 659,000	
...kinghamshire, 512,000	G6
...mbridgeshire, 563,000	G5
...eshire, 916,400	E4
...veland, 567,900	F3
...rnwall, 405,200	C7
...mbria, 473,600	D3
...rbyshire, 887,600	D7
...von, 942,100	
...rset, 575,800	
...rham, 610,400	F3
...st Sussex, 655,600	H7
...sex, 1,426,200	
...oucestershire, 491,500	E6
...eater Manchester, 2,684,100	H2
...ampshire, 1,456,100	
...ereford and Worcester, 594,200	E5
...rtfordshire, 937,300	
...umberside, 848,600	
...le of Wight, 111,300	F7
...les of Scilly, 1,900	A7
...nt, 1,448,100	H6
...ncashire, 1,375,500	E4
...icestershire, 837,900	F5
...ncolnshire, 524,500	G4
...ndon, Greater, 7,028,200	H8
...anchester, Greater, 2,684,100	H2
...erseyside, 1,578,000	G2
...rfolk, 662,500	
...orthamptonshire, 505,900	G5
...orthumberland, 287,300	E2
...orth Yorkshire, 653,000	
...ottinghamshire, 977,500	F4
Oxfordshire, 541,800	F6
Salop, 359,000	E5
Somerset, 404,400	E6
South Yorkshire, 1,318,300	F4
Staffordshire, 997,600	E5
Suffolk, 577,600	H5
Surrey, 1,002,900	H6
Sussex, East, 655,600	H7
Sussex, West, 623,000	G7
Tyne and Wear, 1,182,900	H3
Warwickshire, 471,000	F5
West Midlands, 2,743,300	F5
West Sussex, 623,400	G7
West Yorkshire, 2,072,500	J1
Wiltshire, 512,800	E6
Yorkshire, North, 653,000	F3
Yorkshire, South, 1,318,300	F4
Yorkshire, West, 2,072,500	J1

CITIES and TOWNS

Abingdon, 20,130	F6
Accrington, 36,470	H1
Adwick le Street, 17,650	K2
Aldeburgh, 2,750	J5
Aldershot, 33,750	G8
Aldridge Brownhills, 89,370	E5
Alfreton, 21,560	F4
Alnwick, 7,300	F2
Altrincham, 40,800	H2
Amersham, ⊕17,254	G7
Andover, 27,620	F6
Appleby, 2,240	E3
Arnold, 35,090	F4
Arundel, 2,390	G7
Ashford, 36,380	H6
Ashington, 24,720	F2
Ashton-under-Lyne, 48,500	H2
Axminster, 4,515	D7
Aycliffe, ⊕20,203	F3
Aylesbury, 41,420	G7
Bacup, 14,990	H1
Bakewell, 4,100	J2
Banbury, 31,060	F5
Banstead, 44,100	H8
Barking, 153,800	H8
Barnet, 305,200	H7
Barnsley, 74,730	J2
Barnstaple, 17,820	D6
Barrow-in-Furness, 73,400	D3
Barton-upon-Humber, 7,750	G4
Basildon, 135,720	H8
Basingstoke, 60,910	F6
Bath, 83,100	E6
Batley, 41,630	J1
Battle, ⊕4,987	J1
Bebington, 62,500	G5
Bedford, 74,390	F5
Bedlington, 27,200	F2
Bedworth, 41,600	F5
Beeston and Stapleford, 65,360	F5
Bentfleet, 49,180	J8
Bentley with Arksey, 22,320	F4
Berkhamsted, 15,920	G7
Beverley, 16,920	G4
Bexhill, 34,680	H8
Bexley, 213,500	H8
Biddulph, 18,720	H2
Birkenhead, 135,750	G2
Birmingham, 1,058,800	F5
Bishop Auckland, 32,940	E3
Bishop's Stortford, 21,720	H7
Blackburn, 101,670	H1
Blackpool, 149,000	G1
Blaydon, 31,940	H3
Blyth, 35,390	F2
Bodmin, 10,430	C7
Bognor Regis, 34,620	H8
Bolton, 154,480	H2
Bootle, 71,160	G2
Boston, 26,700	G5
Bournemouth, 144,100	F7
Bracknell, ⊕34,067	G8
Bradford, 458,900	J1
Braintree and Bocking, 26,300	H6
Brent, 256,500	H8
Brentwood, 58,690	J8
Bridgwater, 26,700	E6
Brighouse, 26,920	G3
Bridport, 6,660	E7
Brigg, 4,870	G4
Brighowe, 35,320	J1
Brightlingsea, 7,170	J6
Brighton, 156,500	G7
Broadstairs and Saint Peter's, 21,670	J6
Bromley, 299,100	H8
Bromsgrove, 41,430	E5
Buckfastleigh, 2,870	C7
Buckingham, 5,290	G6
Bude-Stratton, 5,750	C7
Bungay, 4,120	J5
Burgess Hill, 20,030	G7
Burnham-on-Crouch, 4,920	H6
Burnley, 74,300	H1
Burntwood, ⊕23,088	F5
Burton upon Trent, 49,480	F5
Bury, 69,550	H2
Bury Saint Edmunds, 26,800	H5
Bushey, 24,500	H7
Buxton, 20,050	J2
Caister-on-Sea, ⊕6,287	J5
Camborne-Redruth, 43,970	B7
Cambridge, 106,400	G5
Cannock, 56,440	E5
Canterbury, 115,600	J6
Canvey Island, 29,550	J8

Carlisle, 99,600	D3
Carlton, 46,690	F5
Caterham and Warlingham, 35,840	H8
Chatham, 59,550	J8
Cheadle and Gatley, 62,460	H2
Chelmsford, 58,320	J7
Cheltenham, 75,910	E6
Chertsey, 45,070	G8
Chesham, 20,830	G7
Cheshunt, 45,750	H7
Chester, 117,200	G2
Chesterfield, 69,480	J2
Chester-le-Street, 20,720	J3
Chichester, 20,940	G7
Chigwell, 54,220	H8
Chippenham, 18,550	E6
Chorley, 31,800	G2
Christchurch, 31,610	F7
Cirencester, 14,500	E6
Clacton, 39,380	J6
Clay Cross, 9,630	J2
Cleator Moor, ⊕7,686	D3
Cleethorpes, 37,200	H4
Clevedon, 15,140	D6
Clun, ⊕1,261	D6
Coalville, 28,740	F5
Cockermouth, 6,480	D3
Colchester, 79,600	H6
Colne, 19,030	H1
Colne Valley, 21,190	J2
Congleton, 21,500	J2
Consett, 35,080	H3
Corby, 48,850	G5
Coventry, 336,800	F5
Cowes, 19,190	F7
Crawley, 72,600	G6
Crewe and Nantwich, 98,100	E4
Cromer, 5,720	J5
Crook and Willington, 21,120	E3
Crosby, 56,750	G2
Croydon, 330,600	H8
Cuckfield, 26,500	G6
Darlington, 85,120	J8
Dartford, 44,130	J8
Darton, 15,710	J2
Darwen, 29,290	H1
Deal, 26,840	J6
Dearne, 24,780	K2
Denton, 38,110	H2
Derby, 213,700	F5
Dewsbury, 50,560	J1
Didcot, ⊕14,277	F6
Doncaster, 81,530	F4
Dorking, 22,410	G8
Dover, 34,160	J6
Downham Market, 4,120	H5
Droitwich, 13,950	E5
Dronfield, 20,000	J2
Dudley, 187,110	E5
Dunstable, 32,090	G6
Durham, 88,800	J3
Ealing, 293,800	H8
Eastbourne, 73,200	H7
East Grinstead, 19,420	G6
Eastleigh, 46,340	F7
East Retford, 18,260	G4
Egham, 30,320	G8
Egremont, ⊕7,253	D3
Eling, ⊕20,006	F7
Ellesmere, ⊕2,630	D4
Ellesmere Port, 63,870	G2
Enfield, 260,900	H7
Epsom and Ewell, 70,700	G8
Esher, 63,970	H8
Eston, ⊕46,219	F3
Eton, 4,950	G8
Evesham, 14,090	F5
Exeter, 93,300	D7
Exminster, ⊕3,181	D7
Exmouth, 26,840	D7
Falmouth, 17,530	F7
Fareham, 86,300	F7
Farnborough, 43,520	G8
Farnham, 33,140	G8
Farnworth, 26,110	H2
Faversham, 15,010	H6
Felixstowe, 19,460	J6
Felling, 38,990	J3
Filey, 5,660	J3
Fleet, 22,930	G8
Fleetwood, 30,070	D4
Folkestone, 45,610	J6
Formby, 24,850	G2
Framlingham, ⊕2,258	J5
Frimley and Camberley, 47,390	G8
Fareham, 22,910	H1
Gainsborough, 17,440	G4
Gateshead, 91,230	J3
Gillingham, Dorset, ⊕4,050	E6
Gillingham, Kent, 93,900	J8
Glastonbury, 6,580	E6
Glossop, 24,820	J2
Gloucester, 91,600	E6
Godalming, 18,840	G8
Golborne, 28,720	G2
Goole, 17,920	F4
Gosport, 82,300	F7
Grange, 3,520	E3
Grantham, 27,830	G5
Gravesend, 53,500	J8
Great Baddow, ⊕18,755	J7
Great Torrington, 3,430	C7
Great Yarmouth, 49,410	J5
Greenwich, 207,200	H8
Grimsby, 93,800	H4
Guildford, 58,470	G8
Guisborough, 14,860	F3
Hackney, 192,500	H8
Hale, 17,080	H2
Halesowen, 54,120	E5
Halifax, 88,580	J1
Haltemprice, 54,850	G4
Haltwhistle, ⊕3,511	D3
Hammersmith, 170,000	H8
Haringey, 228,200	H8
Harlow, 79,160	H7
Harrogate, 64,620	J1
Harrow, 200,200	H8
Hartlepool, 97,100	F3
Harwich, 15,280	J6
Haslingden, 15,140	H1
Hastings, 74,600	H7
Hatfield, ⊕25,359	H7
Havant and Waterloo, 112,430	G7
Haverhill, 14,550	H5
Havering, 239,200	J8
Hayle, ⊕5,378	B7
Hazel Grove and Bramhall, 40,400	H2
Heanor, 24,590	F4
Hebburn, 23,150	J3
Hedon, 3,010	G4
Hemel Hempstead, 71,150	G7
Hereford, 47,800	E5
Hertford, 20,760	H7
Hetton, 16,810	J3
Hexham, 9,820	E3
Heywood, 31,720	H2
High Wycombe, 61,190	G8
Hillingdon, 230,800	G8
Hinckley, 49,310	F5
Hinderwell, ⊕2,551	J3
Hitchin, 29,190	H7
Hoddesdon, 27,510	H7
Holmfirth, 19,790	J2
Horley, ⊕18,593	H8
Hornsea, 7,280	H4
Horsham, 26,770	G7
Horwich, 16,670	G2
Houghton-le-Spring, 33,150	J3
Hounslow, 199,100	G8
Hove, 72,000	G7
Hoylake, 32,000	G2
Hoyland Nether, 15,500	J2
Hucknall, 27,110	F4
Huddersfield, 130,060	J2
Hugh Town, ⊕1,958	A8
Hull, 276,600	G4
Hunstanton, 4,140	H5
Huntingdon and Godmanchester, 17,200	G5
Huyton-with-Roby, 65,950	G2
Hyde, 37,040	H2
Ilfracombe, 9,350	C6
Ilkeston, 33,690	F4
Immingham, ⊕10,259	G4
Ipswich, 121,500	J5
Islington, 171,600	H8
Jarrow, 28,510	J3
Kendal, 22,440	E3
Kenilworth, 19,730	F5
Kensington and Chelsea, 161,400	G8
Keswick, 4,790	D3
Kettering, 44,480	G5
Keynsham, 18,970	E6
Kidderminster, 49,960	E5
Kingsbridge, 52,690	E4
King's Lynn, 29,990	H5
Kingston upon Thames, 135,600	H8
Kingswood, 30,450	E6
Kirkburton, 20,320	J2
Kirkby, 59,100	G2
Kirkby Lonsdale, ⊕1,506	E3
Kirkby Stephen, ⊕1,539	E3
Knutsford, 14,840	H2
Lambeth, 290,300	H8
Lancaster, 126,300	E3
Leatherhead, 40,830	G8
Leeds, 744,500	J1
Leek, 19,460	H2
Leicester, 289,400	F5
Leigh, 46,390	H2
Leighton-Linslade, 22,590	F7
Letchworth, 31,520	H6
Lewes, 14,170	H7
Lewisham, 237,300	H8
Leyland, 23,690	G1
Lichfield, 23,690	F5
Lincoln, 73,700	G4
Liskeard, 5,360	C7
Litherland, 23,530	G2
Littlehampton, 20,320	G7

(continued on following page)

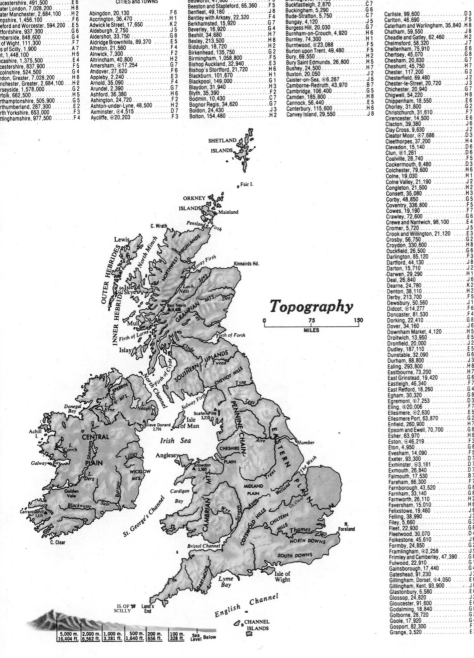

Topography

0 75 150
MILES

5,000 m. 16,404 ft.	2,000 m. 6,562 ft.	1,000 m. 3,281 ft.	500 m. 1,640 ft.	200 m. 656 ft.	100 m. 328 ft.	Sea Level Below

SHETLAND ISLANDS

Fair I.

ORKNEY ISLANDS — Mainland

C. Wrath — Pentland Firth

Lewis

OUTER HEBRIDES

NORTHWEST HIGHLANDS

Kinnairds Hd.

Moray Firth

Skye

INNER HEBRIDES

Loch Ness

GRAMPIAN MTS.

Ben Nevis 4,406

Dee

Mull

Firth of Lorne

Islay

Firth of Clyde

Firth of Forth

North Channel

SOUTHERN UPLANDS

Tweed

CHEVIOT HILLS

Solway Firth

Tyne

Tees

Scafell Pike 3,210

Isle of Man

Irish Sea

PENNINE CHAIN

Humber

CHESHIRE PLAIN

Anglesey

Snowdon 3,560

EASTERN

Aire

MIDLAND PLAIN

Trent

The Wash

Cardigan Bay

CAMBRIAN MTS.

Severn

Avon

Great Ouse

Welland

CHILTERN HILLS

N. Foreland

Bristol Channel

COTSWOLD HILLS

Thames

NORTH DOWNS

SOUTH DOWNS

Isle of Wight

Lyme Bay

IS. OF SCILLY — Land's End

English Channel

CHANNEL ISLANDS

SPERRIN MTS.

Donegal Bay

Neagh

Erne

Slieve Donard 2,796

Achill

CENTRAL PLAIN

L. Corrib

Galway Bay

L. Derg

Shannon

Liffey

WICKLOW MTS.

Barrow

Golden Vale

Blackwater

Carrantuohill 3,415

C. Clear

St. George's Channel

(continued)

Liverpool, 539,700 G 2
Loftus, 7,850 G 3
London (cap.), 7,028,200 H 8
London, ★12,332,900 H 8
Long Eaton, 33,560 F 5
Longbenton, 50,120 J 3
Looe, 4,060 C 7
Loughborough, 49,010 F 5
Lowestoft, 53,260 J 5
Ludlow, ⊙7,466 E 5
Luton, 164,500 G 6
Lydd, 4,670 H 7
Lyme Regis, 3,460 E 7
Lymington, 36,780 F 7
Lynton, 1,770 D 6
Lytham Saint Anne's, 42,120 G 1
Mablethorpe and Sutton, 6,750 H 4
Macclesfield, 45,420 H 2
Maidenhead, 48,210 G 8
Maidstone, 72,110 J 8
Maldon, 14,350 H 6
Malmesbury, 2,550 E 6
Malton, 4,010 G 3
Malvern, 30,420 E 5
Manchester, 490,000 H 2
Mangotsfield, 23,000 E 6
Mansfield, 58,450 K 2
Mansfield Woodhouse, 25,400 F 4
March, 14,560 H 5
Margate, 50,290 J 6
Market Harborough, 15,230 G 5
Marlborough, 6,370 F 6
Matlock, 20,300 J 2
Melton Mowbray, 20,680 G 5
Merton, 169,400 H 8
Middlesbrough, 153,900 F 3
Middleton, 53,340 H 2
Middlewich, 7,600 H 2
Mildenhall, ⊙9,269 H 5
Millom, ⊙7,101 D 3
Milton Keynes, 89,900 F 5
Minehead, 8,230 D 6
Moretonhampstead, ⊙1,440 C 7
Morpeth, 14,450 F 2
Mundesley, ⊙1,536 J 5
Nelson, 31,220 H 1
Neston, 18,210 G 2
Newark, 24,760 G 4
Newbury, 24,850 F 6
Newcastle upon Tyne, 295,800 H 3
Newcastle-under-Lyme, 75,940 E 4
Newham, 228,900 H 8
Newhaven, 9,970 H 7
Newport, 22,430 F 7
New Romney, 3,830 J 7
Newton Abbot, 19,940 D 7
Newton-le-Willows, 21,780 H 2
New Windsor, 29,660 G 8
Northallerton F 3
Northam, 8,310 C 6
Northampton, 128,290 F 5
Northfleet, 27,150 J 8
North Sunderland, ⊙1,725 F 2
Northwich, 17,710 H 2
Norton, 5,580 G 3
Norton-Radstock, 15,900 E 6
Norwich, 119,200 J 5
Nottingham, 280,300 F 5
Nuneaton, 69,210 F 5
Oadby, 20,700 F 5
Oakham, 7,280 G 5
Okehampton, 4,000 D 7
Oldham, 103,690 H 2
Ormskirk, 28,860 G 2
Oswaldtwistle, 14,270 H 1
Oxford, 117,400 F 6
Padstow, ⊙2,802 B 7
Penryn, 5,660 B 7
Penzance, 19,360 B 7
Peterborough, 118,900 G 5
Peterlee, ⊙21,846 J 3
Plymouth, 259,100 C 7
Polperro, ⊙1,491 C 7
Poole, 110,600 E 7
Porlock, ⊙1,290 D 6
Portishead, 9,680 E 6
Portland, 14,860 E 7
Portslade-by-Sea, 18,040 G 7
Portsmouth, 198,500 F 7
Potters Bar, 24,670 H 7
Poulton-le-Fylde, 16,340 G 1
Preston, 94,760 G 1
Prestwich, 32,850 H 2
Queenborough, 31,550 H 6
Radcliffe, 29,630 H 2
Ramsbottom, 16,710 H 2
Ramsgate, 40,090 J 6
Rawtenstall, 20,950 H 1
Rayleigh, 26,740 J 8
Reading, 131,200 G 8
Redbridge, 231,600 H 8
Redcar, ⊙46,325 F 3
Redditch, 44,750 E 5
Reigate, 55,600 H 8
Richmond upon Thames, 166,800 H 8
Rickmansworth, 29,030 G 8
Ripley, 18,060 F 4
Rochdale, 93,780 H 2
Rochester, 56,030 J 8
Rothbury, ⊙1,818 E 2
Rotherham, 84,770 K 2
Royal Leamington Spa, 44,950 F 5
Royal Tunbridge Wells, 44,800 H 6
Rugby, 60,380 F 5
Rugeley, 24,440 E 5
Runcorn, 42,730 G 2
Rushden, 21,840 G 5
Ryde, 23,170 F 7
Rye, 4,530 H 7
Ryton, 15,170 H 3
Saddleworth, 21,340 J 2
Saint Agnes, ⊙4,747 B 7
Saint Albans, 123,800 H 7
Saint Austell-with-Fowey, 32,710 C 7
Saint Columb Major, ⊙3,953 B 7
Saint Helens, 104,890 G 2
Saint Ives, Cornwall, 9,760 B 7
Saint Neots, 17,940 G 5
Salcombe, 2,370 D 7
Sale, 59,060 H 2
Salford, 261,100 H 2
Salisbury, 35,460 F 6
Saltburn and Marske-by-the-Sea, 21,170 G 3
Sandbach, 14,280 H 2
Sandown-Shanklin, 14,800 F 7
Sandwich, 4,420 J 6
Saxmundham, 1,820 J 5
Scarborough, 43,300 G 3
Scunthorpe, 68,100 G 4
Seaford, 18,020 H 7
Seaham, 22,470 J 3
Seascale, ⊙2,106 D 3
Seaton, 4,500 D 7
Seaton Valley, 35,880 J 3
Sedbergh, ⊙2,741 E 3
Selsey, ⊙6,491 G 7
Sevenoaks, 18,160 J 8
Shaftesbury, 4,180 E 7
Sheffield, 558,000 J 2
Sherborne, 9,230 E 7
Sheringham, 4,940 J 5
Shildon, 15,360 F 3
Shoreham-by-Sea, 19,620 G 7
Shrewsbury, 56,120 E 5
Silloth, ⊙2,662 D 3
Sittingbourne and Milton, 32,830 H 6
Skelmersdale, 35,850 G 2
Skelton and Brotton, 15,930 G 3
Sleaford, 8,050 G 5
Slough, 89,060 G 8
Solihull, 108,230 F 5
Southampton, 213,700 F 7
Southend-on-Sea, 159,300 H 6
Southport, 86,030 G 1
South Shields, 96,900 J 3
Southwark, 224,900 H 8
Southwold, 1,960 J 5
Sowerby Bridge, 15,700 H 1
Spalding, 17,040 G 5
Spenborough, 41,460 J 1
Spennymoor, 19,050 F 3
Stafford, 54,860 E 5
Staines, 56,380 G 8
Stamford, 14,980 G 5
Stanley, 42,280 H 3
Staveley, 17,620 K 2
Stevenage, 72,600 G 6
Stockport, 138,350 H 2
Stockton-on-Tees, 165,400 F 3
Stoke-on-Trent, 256,200 E 4
Stourbridge, 56,530 E 5
Stourport-on-Severn, 19,430 E 5
Stowmarket, 9,020 J 5
Stratford-upon-Avon, 20,080 F 5
Stretford, 52,450 H 2
Stroud, 19,600 E 6
Sudbury, 8,860 H 5
Sunbury-on-Thames, 40,070 G 8
Sunderland, 214,820 J 3
Sutton, 166,700 H 8
Sutton Bridge, ⊙3,113 H 5
Sutton in Ashfield, 40,330 K 2
Swadlincote, 21,060 F 5
Swanage, 8,000 E 7
Swindon, 90,680 F 6
Tamworth, 46,960 F 5
Taunton, 37,570 D 6
Tavistock, ⊙7,620 C 7
Telford, ⊙79,451 E 5
Tenbury, ⊙2,151 E 5
Tewkesbury, 9,210 E 6
Thetford, 15,690 H 5
Thirsk, ⊙2,884 F 3
Thornaby-on-Tees, ⊙42,385 F 3
Thorne, ⊙16,694 F 4
Thornton Cleveleys, 27,090 G 1
Thurrock, 127,700 J 8
Tiverton, 16,190 D 7
Todmorden, 14,540 H 1
Tonbridge, 31,410 H 8
Torbay, 109,900 D 7
Torpoint, 6,840 C 7
Tower Hamlets, 146,100 H 8
Tow Law, 2,460 H 4
Trowbridge, 20,120 E 6
Truro, 15,690 B 7
Turton, 22,800 H 2
Tynemouth, 67,090 J 3
Upton upon Severn, ⊙2,048 E 5
Urmston, 44,130 H 2
Uttoxeter, 9,100 E 5
Ventnor, 6,980 F 7
Wainfleet All Saints, ⊙1,116 H 4
Wakefield, 306,500 J 2
Wallasey, 94,520 G 2
Wallsend, 45,490 J 3
Walsall, 182,430 E 5
Waltham Forest, 223,700 H 8
Waltham Holy Cross, 14,810 H 7
Walton and Weybridge, 51,270 G 8
Walton-le-Dale, 27,660 G 1
Wandsworth, 284,600 H 8
Wantage, 8,490 F 6
Ware, 14,900 H 7
Wareham, 4,630 E 7
Warley, 161,260 E 5
Warminster, 14,440 E 6
Warrington, 65,320 G 2
Warwick, 17,870 F 5
Washington, 27,720 J 3
Watchet, 2,980 D 6
Watford, 77,000 H 7
Wellingborough, 39,570 G 5
Wells, 8,960 E 6
Wells-next-the-Sea, 2,450 H 5
Welwyn, 39,900 H 7
Wem, ⊙3,411 E 5
West Bridgford, 28,340 F 5
West Bromwich, 162,740 F 5
West Mersea, 4,730 H 6
Westminster, 216,100 H 8
Weston-super-Mare, 51,960 D 6
Weymouth and Melcombe Regis, 41,080 E 7
Whickham, 29,710 J 3
Whitchurch, ⊙7,142 E 5
Whitehaven, 26,260 D 3
Whitley Bay, 37,010 J 3
Widnes, 58,330 G 2
Wigan, 80,920 G 2
Wigston, 31,650 F 5
Wilmslow, 31,250 H 2
Wilton, 4,090 F 6
Winchester, 88,900 F 6
Windermere, 7,860 E 3
Winsford, 26,920 G 2
Wirral, 27,510 G 2
Wisbech, 16,990 H 5
Witham, 19,730 H 6
Withernsea, 6,300 H 4
Wivenhoe, 5,630 J 6
Woking, 79,300 G 8
Wokingham, 22,390 G 8
Wolverhampton, 266,400 E 5
Wombwell, 17,850 K 2
Woodhall Spa, 2,420 G 4
Woodley and Sandford, ⊙24,581 G 8
Woodstock, 2,070 F 6
Wooler, ⊙1,833 F 2
Worcester, 73,900 E 5
Workington, 28,260 D 3
Worksop, 36,590 F 4
Worsbrough, 15,180 J 2
Worsley, 49,530 H 2
Worthing, 89,100 G 7
Wymondham, 9,390 J 5
Yateley, ⊙16,505 G 8
Yeovil, 26,180 E 7
York, 101,900 F 4

OTHER FEATURES

Aire (riv.) F 4
Atlantic Ocean A 7
Avon (riv.) F 5
Avon (riv.) F 7
Axe Edge (mt.) H 2
Barnstaple (bay) C 6
Beachy (head) H 7
Bigbury (bay) C 7
Blackwater (riv.) H 6
Bristol (chan.) C 6
Brown Willy (mt.) C 7
Cheviot (hills) E 2
Cheviot, The (mt.) E 2
Chiltern (hills) G 6
Cleveland (hills) F 3
Colne (riv.) G 8
Cornwall (cape) B 7
Cotswold (hills) E 6
Cross Fell (mt.) E 3
Cumbrian (mts.) D 3
Dart (riv.) D 7
Dartmoor National Park C 7
Dee (riv.) D 4
Derwent (riv.) G 3
Derwent (riv.) H 3
Don (riv.) F 4
Dorset Heights (hills) E 7
Dove (riv.) J 2
Dover (str.) J 7
Dungeness (prom.) J 7
Dunkery (hill) D 6
Eddystone (rocks) C 7
Eden (riv.) E 3
English (chan.) D 8
Esk (riv.) D 2
Exe (riv.) D 7
Exmoor National Park D 6
Fens, The (reg.) G 5
Flamborough (head) G 3
Formby (head) G 2
Foulness Island (pen.) J 6
Gibraltar (pt.) H 4
Great Ouse (riv.) H 5
Hartland (pt.) C 6
High Willhays (mt.) C 7
Hodder (riv.) H 1
Holderness (pen.), 43,900 G 4
Holy (isl.), 189 F 2
Humber (riv.) G 4
Irish (sea) B 4
Kennet (riv.) F 6
Lake District National Park D 3
Land's End (prom.) B 7
Lea (riv.) G 6
Lincoln Wolds (hills) G 4
Lindisfarne (Holy) (isl.), 189 F 2
Liverpool (bay) D 4
Lizard, The (pen.), 7,371 B 8
Lundy (isl.), 49 C 6
Lune (riv.) E 3
Lyme (bay) D 7
Manacle (pt.) C 7
Medway (riv.) H 6
Mendip (hills) E 6
Mersea (isl.), 4,423 J 6
Mersey (riv.) G 2
Morecambe (bay) D 3
Mounts (bay) B 7
Naze, The (prom.) J 6
Nene (riv.) H 5
New (for.) F 6
North (sea) J 4
North Downs (hills) G 6
North Foreland (prom.) J 6
Northumberland National Park E 2
North York Moors National Park G 3
Orford Ness (prom.) J 5
Ouse (riv.) G 4
Ouse (riv.) G 6
Parrett (riv.) E 6
Peak District National Park F 4
Peak, The (mt.) J 2
Peel Fell (mt.) E 2
Pennine Chain (range) E 3
Plymouth (sound) C 7
Portland, Bill of (pt.) E 7
Prawle (pt.) D 7
Purbeck, Isle of (pen.), 39,500 F 7
Ribble (riv.) E 4
Saint Alban's (head) F 7
Saint Bees (head) D 3
Saint Martin's (isl.), 106 A 8
Saint Mary's (isl.), 1,958 A 8
Scafell Pike (mt.) D 3
Scilly (isls.), 1,900 A 7
Selsey Bill (prom.) G 7
Severn (riv.) E 6
Sheppey (isl.), 31,550 J 6
Sherwood (for.) F 4
Skiddaw (mt.) D 3
Solent (chan.) F 7
Solway (firth) D 3
South Downs (hills) G 7
Spithead (chan.) F 7
Spurn (head) H 4
Stonehenge (ruins) F 6
Stour (riv.) E 7
Stour (riv.) H 6
Stour (riv.) J 6
Swale (riv.) F 3
Tamar (riv.) C 7
Taw (riv.) D 7
Tees (riv.) F 3
Test (riv.) F 6
Thames (riv.) H 6
Tintagel (head) C 7
Torridge (riv.) C 7
Trent (riv.) G 4
Tresco (isl.), 246 A 8
Tweed (riv.) E 2
Tyne (riv.) F 3
Ure (riv.) F 3
Ver (riv.) H 7
Walney, Isle of (isl.), 11,241 D 3
Wash, The (bay) H 5
Weald, The (reg.) H 6
Wear (riv.) F 3
Weaver (riv.) G 2
Welland (riv.) G 5
Wey (riv.) G 6
Wharfe (riv.) E 3
Wirral (pen.), 432,900 G 2
Witham (riv.) G 4
Wolds, The (hills) G 4
Wye (riv.) D 5
Wyre (riv.) G 1
Yare (riv.) J 5
Yorkshire Dales National Park E 3

CHANNEL ISLANDS

CITIES and TOWNS

Saint Anne E 8
Saint Helier (cap.), Jersey, ⊙28,135 E 8
Saint Peter Port (cap.), Guernsey, ⊙16,303 E 8
Saint Sampson's, ⊙6,534 E 8

OTHER FEATURES

Alderney (isl.), 1,686 E 8
Guernsey (isl.), 51,351 E 8
Herm (isl.), 96 E 8
Jersey (isl.), 72,629 E 8
Sark (isl.), 590 E 8

ISLE of MAN

CITIES and TOWNS

Castletown, 2,820 C 3
Douglas (cap.), 20,389 C 3
Laxey, 1,170 C 3
Michael, 408 C 3
Onchan, 4,807 C 3
Peel, 3,081 C 3
Port Erin, 1,714 C 3
Port Saint Mary, 1,508 C 3
Ramsey, 5,048 C 3

OTHER FEATURES

Ayre (pt.) C 3
Calf of Man (isl.) C 3
Langness (prom.) C 3
Snaefell (mt.) C 3
Spanish (head) C 3

WALES

COUNTIES

Clwyd, 376,000 D 4
Dyfed, 323,100 C 6
Gwent, 439,600 D 6
Gwynedd, 225,100 C 4
Mid Glamorgan, 540,400 D 6
Powys, 101,500 D 5
South Glamorgan, 389,200 A 7
West Glamorgan, 371,900 D 6

CITIES and TOWNS

Aberaeron, 1,340 C 5
Abercarn, 18,370 B 6
Aberdare, 38,030 A 6
Abertillery, 20,550 B 6
Amlwch, 3,630 C 4
Bala, 1,650 D 5
Bangor, 16,030 C 4
Barmouth, 2,070 C 5
Barry, 42,780 B 7
Beaumaris, 2,090 C 4
Bedwellty, 25,460 B 6
Bethesda, 4,180 D 4
Betws-y-Coed, 720 D 4
Brecknock (Brecon), 6,460 D 6
Brecon, 6,460 D 6
Bridgend, 14,690 A 7
Brynmawr, 5,970 B 6
Builth Wells, 1,480 D 5
Burry Port, 5,990 C 6
Caernarfon, 8,840 C 4
Caerphilly, 42,190 B 6
Cardiff, 281,500 B 7
Cardigan, 3,830 C 5
Chepstow, 8,260 E 6
Chirk, ⊙3,564 D 5
Colwyn Bay, 25,370 D 4
Criccieth, 1,590 C 5
Cwmamman, 3,950 D 6
Cwmbran, 32,980 B 6
Denbigh, 8,420 D 4
Dolgellau, 2,430 D 5
Ebbw Vale, 25,670 B 6
Ffestiniog, 5,510 D 5
Fishguard and Goodwick, 5,020 B 5
Flint, 15,070 G 2
Gelligaer, 33,820 A 6
Harlech, ⊙332 C 5
Haverfordwest, 8,930 B 6
Hawarden, ⊙20,389 G 2
Hay, 1,200 D 5
Holywell, 8,570 G 2
Kidwelly, 3,090 C 6
Knighton, 2,190 D 5
Llandeilo, 1,780 C 6
Llandovery, 2,040 D 5
Llandrindod Wells, 3,460 D 5
Llandudno, 17,700 D 4
Llanelli, 25,870 C 6
Llanfairfechan, 3,800 D 4
Llangefni, 4,070 C 4
Llangollen, 3,050 D 5
Llanguicke, ⊙15,029 D 6
Llanidloes, 2,390 D 5
Llantrisant, ⊙27,490 A 7
Llanwrtyd Wells, 460 D 5
Llwchwr, 27,530 D 6
Machynlleth, 1,830 D 5
Maesteg, 21,100 D 6
Menai Bridge, 2,730 C 4
Merthyr Tydfil, 61,500 A 6
Milford Haven, 13,960 B 6
Mold, 8,700 G 2
Montgomery, 1,000 D 5
Mountain Ash, 27,710 A 6
Mynyddislwyn, 15,590 B 6
Narberth, 970 C 6
Neath, 27,280 D 6
Nefyn, ⊙2,086 C 5
Newcastle Emlyn, 690 C 5
Newport, Dyfed, ⊙1,062 C 5
Newport, Gwent, 110,090 B 6
New Quay, 760 C 5
Newtown, 6,400 D 5
Neyland, 2,690 B 6
Ogmore and Garw, 19,680 A 6
Pembroke, 14,570 C 6
Penarth, 24,180 B 7
Penmaenmawr, 4,050 C 4
Pontypool, 36,710 B 6
Pontypridd, 34,180 A 6
Porthcawl, 14,980 D 6
Porthmadog, 3,900 C 5
Port Talbot, 58,200 D 6
Prestatyn, 15,480 D 4
Presteigne, 1,330 D 5
Pwllheli, 4,020 C 5
Rhondda, 85,400 A 6
Rhyl, 22,150 D 4
Risca, 15,780 B 6
Ruthin, 4,780 D 4
Saint David's, ⊙1,638 B 6
Swansea, 190,800 C 6
Tenby, 4,930 C 6
Tredegar, 17,450 B 6
Tywyn, 3,850 C 5
Welshpool, 7,370 D 5
Wrexham, 39,530 E 4

OTHER FEATURES

Anglesey (isl.), 64,500 C 4
Aran Fawddwy (mt.) C 5
Bardsey (isl.), 9 C 5
Berwyn (mts.) D 5
Black (mts.) D 6
Braich-y-Pwll (prom.) C 5
Brecon Beacons (mt.) D 6
Brecon Beacons National Park D 6
Caldy (isl.), 70 C 6
Cambrian (mts.) D 5
Cardigan (bay) C 5
Carmarthen (bay) C 6
Cemmaes (head) C 5
Dee (riv.) D 4
Dovey (riv.) D 5
Ely (riv.) B 7
Gower (pen.), 17,220 C 6
Great Ormes (head) C 4
Holy (isl.), 13,715 C 4
Lleyn (pen.), 25,800 C 5
Menai (str.) C 4
Milford Haven (inlet) B 6
Pembrokeshire Coast National Park C 6
Plynlimon (mt.) D 5
Preseli (mts.) C 6
Radnor (for.) D 5
Rhymney (riv.) B 6
Saint Brides (bay) B 6
Saint David's (head) B 6
Saint George's (chan.) B 5
Saint Gowans (head) C 6
Severn (riv.) E 5
Snowdon (mt.) D 4
Snowdonia National Park D 4
Taff (riv.) B 7
Teifi (riv.) C 5
Towy (riv.) D 6
Tremadoc (bay) C 5
Usk (riv.) B 6
Wye (riv.) D 5
Ynys Môn (Anglesey) (isl.), 64,500 C 4

★Population of met. area.
⊙Population of parish.

SCOTLAND

REGIONS

Borders, 99,409 E 5
Central, 269,281 D 4
Dumfries and Galloway, 143,667 E 5
Fife, 336,339 E 4
Grampian, 448,772 F 3
Highland, 182,044 D 3
Lothian, 754,008 E 5
Orkney (islands area), 17,675 E 1
Shetland (islands area), 18,494 F 2
Strathclyde, 2,504,909 C 4
Tayside, 401,987 E 4
Western Isles (islands area), 29,615 A 3

CITIES and TOWNS

Aberchirder, 877 F 3
Aberdeen, 210,362 F 3
Aberdour, 1,576 D 1
Aberfeldy, 1,552 E 4
Aberfoyle, 793 D 4
Aberlady, 737 F 4
Aberlour, 842 E 3
Abernethy, 776 E 4
Aboyne, 1,040 F 3
Acharacle, ⊙764 C 4
Achiltibuie, ⊙1,564 C 3
Achnasheen, ⊙1,078 C 3
Ae, 239 E 5
Airdrie, 38,491 C 2
Alexandria, 9,758 A 1
Alford, 764 F 3
Alloa, 13,558 C 1
Alness, 2,560 D 3
Altnaharra, ⊙1,227 D 2
Alva, 4,593 C 1
Alyth, 1,738 E 4
Ancrum, 266 F 5
Annan, 6,250 E 6
Annat, ⊙550 C 3
Annbank Station, 2,530 D 5
Applecross, ⊙550 C 3
Arbroath, 22,706 F 4
Ardavasar, ⊙449 B 3
Ardersier, 942 E 3
Ardgay, 193 D 3
Ardrishaig, 946 C 4
Ardrossan, 11,072 D 5
Armadale, 7,200 C 2
Arrochar, 543 D 4
Ascog, 230 A 2
Auchenblae, 339 F 4
Auchencairn, 215 E 6
Auchinleck, 4,883 D 5
Auchterarder, 1,738 E 4
Auchtermuchty, 1,426 E 4
Auldearn, 405 E 3
Aviemore, 1,224 E 3
Avoch, 776 D 3
Ayr, 47,990 D 5
Ayton, 410 F 5
Bailivanish, 347 A 3
Baillieston, 7,671 B 2
Balallan, 283 B 2
Balerno, 3,576 D 2
Balfron, 1,149 B 1
Ballantrae, 262 C 5
Ballater, 981 F 3
Ballingry, 4,332 D 1
Ballinluig, 188 E 4
Balloch, Highland, 572 D 3
Balloch, Strathclyde, 1,484 B 1
Baltasound, 246 G 2
Banchory, 2,435 F 3
Banff, 3,832 F 3
Bankfoot, 868 E 4
Bankhead, 1,492 F 3
Bannockburn, 5,889 C 1
Barrhead, 18,736 B 2
Barrhill, 236 D 5
Barvas, 279 B 2
Bathgate, 14,038 C 2
Bayble, 543 B 2
Bearsden, 25,128 B 2
Beattock, 309 E 5
Beauly, 1,141 D 3
Beith, 5,859 D 5
Bellsbank, 3,066 D 5
Bellshill, 18,166 C 2
Berriedale, ⊙1,927 E 2
Bieldside, 1,137 F 3
Biggar, 1,718 E 5
Birnam, 659 E 4
Bishopbriggs, 21,570 B 2
Bishopton, 2,931 B 2
Blackburn, 7,636 C 2
Blackford, 529 E 4
Blair Atholl, 437 E 4
Blairgowrie and Rattray, 5,681 E 4
Blanefield, 835 B 1
Blantyre, 13,992 B 2
Blyth Bridge, ⊙441 E 5
Bo'ness, 12,959 C 1
Boat of Garten, 406 E 3
Boddam, 1,429 G 3
Bonar Bridge, 519 D 3
Bonhill, 4,385 B 1
Bonnybridge, 5,701 C 1
Bonnyrigg and Lasswade, 7,429 D 2
Bowmore, 947 B 5
Braemar, 394 E 3
Breasclete, 234 B 2
Brechin, 6,759 F 4
Bridge of Allan, 4,638 C 1
Bridge of Don, 4,086 F 3
Bridge of Weir, 4,724 A 2
Brightons, 3,106 C 1
Broadford, 310 B 3
Brodick, 630 C 5
Brora, 1,436 E 2
Broxburn, 7,776 D 1
Buchlyvie, 412 B 1
Buckhaven and Methil, 17,930 F 4
Buckie, 8,145 E 3
Bucksburn, 6,567 F 3
Bunessan, ⊙585 B 4
Burghead, 1,321 E 3
Burnmouth, 300 F 5
Burntisland, 5,626 D 1
Cairndow, ⊙874 D 4
Cairnryan, 199 D 6
Callander, 1,805 D 4
Cambuslang, 14,607 B 2
Campbeltown, 6,428 C 5
Cannich, 203 D 3
Canonbie, 234 F 5
Caol, 3,719 C 4
Carbost, ⊙772 B 3
Cardenden, 6,802 D 1
Carloway, 178 B 2
Carluke, 8,864 E 5
Carnoustie, 6,838 F 4
Carnwath, 1,246 E 5
Carradale, 262 C 5
Carrbridge, 416 E 3
Carron, 2,626 C 1
Carsphairn, 186 D 5
Castlebay, 284 A 4
Castle Douglas, 3,384 E 6
Castle Kennedy, 307 D 6
Castletown, 902 E 2
Catrine, 2,681 D 5
Cawdor, 111 E 3
Chirnside, 888 F 5
Chryston, 8,322 C 2
Clackmannan, 3,248 C 1
Clarkston, 8,404 B 2
Closeburn, 225 E 5
Clovulin, ⊙315 C 4
Clydebank, 47,538 B 2
Coalburn, 1,460 E 5
Coatbridge, 50,806 C 2
Cockburnspath, 233 F 5
Cockenzie and Port Seton, 3,539 D 1
Coldingham, 423 F 5
Coldstream, 1,393 F 5
Coll, 305 B 2
Colmonell, 218 D 5
Comrie, 1,119 E 4
Connel, 300 C 4
Cononbridge, 914 D 3
Corpach, 1,296 C 4
Coupar Angus, 2,010 E 4
Cove and Kilcreggan, 1,402 A 1
Cove Bay, 765 F 3
Cowdenbeath, 10,215 D 1
Cowie, 2,751 C 1
Craigellachie, 382 E 3
Craignure, ⊙544 C 4
Crail, 1,033 F 4
Crawford, 384 E 5
Creetown, 769 D 6
Crieff, 5,718 E 4
Crimond, 313 G 3
Crinan, ⊙462 C 4
Cromarty, 492 E 3
Crosshill, 535 D 5
Crossmichael, 317 D 6
Cruden Bay, 528 G 3
Cullen, 1,199 F 3
Culross, 504 C 1
Cults, 3,336 F 3
Cumbernauld, 41,200 C 1
Cumnock and Holmhead, 6,298 D 5
Cupar, 6,607 E 4
Currie, 6,764 D 2
Dailly, 1,258 D 5
Dalbeattie, 3,659 E 6
Daliburgh, 261 A 3
Dalkeith, 9,713 D 2
Dalmally, 283 D 4
Dalmellington, 1,949 D 5
Dalry, 5,833 D 5
Dalrymple, 1,336 D 5
Darvel, 3,177 D 5
Daviot, ⊙513 D 3
Denholm, 581 F 5
Denny and Dunipace, 10,424 C 1
Dervaig, ⊙1,081 B 4
Dingwall, 4,275 D 3
Dollar, 2,573 E 4
Dornoch, 880 D 3
Douglas, 1,843 E 5
Doune, 859 D 4
Drongan, 3,609 D 5
Drumbeg, ⊙833 C 2
Drummore, 336 D 6
Drumnadrochit, 359 D 3
Drymen, 659 B 1
Dufftown, 1,481 E 3
Dumbarton, 25,469 B 1
Dumfries, 29,259 E 5
Dunbar, 4,609 F 4
Dunbeath, 161 E 2
Dunbeg, 939 C 4
Dunblane, 5,222 E 4
Dundee, 194,732 F 4
Dundonald, 2,256 D 5
Dunfermline, 52,098 D 1
Dunkeld, 273 E 4
Dunning, 564 E 4
Dunoon, 8,759 A 2
Dunragit, 323 D 6
Duns, 1,812 F 5
Duntochter, 3,532 B 2
Dunure, 452 D 5
Dunvegan, 301 B 3
Dyce, 2,733 F 3
Eaglesfield, 581 E 5
Eaglesham, 2,788 D 5
Earlston, 1,415 F 5
East Calder, 2,690 D 2
East Kilbride, 71,200 B 2
East Linton, 882 F 5
Eastriggs, 1,455 E 5
Ecclefechan, 844 E 5
Edinburgh (cap.), 470,085 D 1
Edzell, 658 F 4
Elderslie, 5,204 B 2
Elgin, 17,042 E 3
Elie and Earlsferry, 807 F 4
Ellon, 2,855 F 3
Embo, 260 E 3
Errol, 762 E 4
Evanton, 562 D 3
Eyemouth, 2,704 F 5
Fairlie, 1,029 D 5
Falkirk, 36,901 C 1
Falkland, 998 E 4
Fallin, 3,159 C 1
Fauldhouse, 5,247 C 2
Ferness, ⊙287 E 3
Ferryden, 740 F 4
Findhorn, 664 E 3
Findochty, 1,229 E 3
Fintry, 296 B 1
Fochabers, 1,238 E 3
Forfar, 11,179 F 4
Forres, 5,317 E 3
Fort Augustus, 670 D 3
Forth, 2,929 C 2
Fortrose, 1,150 D 3
Fort William, 4,370 C 4
Foyers, 276 D 3
Fraserburgh, 10,930 G 3
Friockheim, 807 F 4
Furnace, 220 C 4
Fyvie, 405 F 3
Gairloch, 125 C 3
Galashiels, 12,808 F 5
Galston, 4,256 D 5
Gardenstown, 892 F 3
Garelochhead, 1,552 A 1
Gargunnock, 457 B 1
Garlieston, 385 D 6
Garmouth, 352 E 3
Garrabost, 307 B 2
Gartmore, 253 B 1
Gatehouse-of-Fleet, 835 D 6
Giffnock, 10,987 B 2
Gifford, 575 F 5
Girvan, 7,597 D 5
Glamis, 190 F 4
Glasgow, 880,617 B 2
Glasgow, ★1,674,789 B 2
Glenbarr, ⊙691 C 5
Glencaple, 275 E 5
Glencoe, 195 C 4
Glenelg, ⊙1,468 C 3
Glenluce, 725 D 6
Glenrothes, 31,400 E 4
Golspie, 1,374 E 3
Gordon, 320 F 5
Gorebridge, 3,426 D 2
Gourock, 11,192 A 1
Grangemouth, 24,430 C 1
Grantown-on-Spey, 1,578 E 3
Greenlaw, 574 F 5
Greenock, 67,275 A 2
Gretna, 1,907 E 5
Gullane, 1,701 F 4
Haddington, 6,767 F 5
Halkirk, 679 E 2
Hamilton, 45,495 C 2
Hamnavoe, 307 G 2
Harthill, 4,712 C 2
Hatton, 315 G 3
Hawick, 16,484 F 5
Heathhall, 1,365 E 5
Helensburgh, 13,327 A 1
Helmsdale, 727 E 2
Hill of Fearn, 233 D 3
Hillside, 692 F 4
Hillswick, ⊙696 G 2
Hopeman, 1,248 E 3
Huntly, 4,078 F 3
Hurlford, 4,294 D 5
Inchnadamph, ⊙833 D 2
Innellan, 922 A 2
Innerleithen, 2,293 E 5
Insch, 881 F 3
Inveraray, 473 C 4
Inverbervie, 853 F 4
Invercassley, ⊙1,067 D 3
Invergordon, 2,385 D 3
Invergowrie, 1,389 E 4
Inverie, ⊙1,468 C 3
Inverkeithing, 6,102 D 1
Inverness, 35,801 D 3
Inverurie, 5,534 F 3
Irvine, 48,500 D 5
Isle of Whithorn, 222 D 6
Jedburgh, 3,953 F 5
John O'Groats, 195 E 2
Johnshaven, 544 F 4
Johnstone, 23,251 B 2
Kames, 230 C 5
Keiss, 344 E 2
Keith, 4,192 F 3
Kelso, 4,934 F 5
Kelty, 6,573 D 1
Kemnay, 1,042 F 3
Kenmore, 211 E 4
Kilbarchan, 2,669 A 2
Kilbirnie, 8,259 A 2
Kilchoan, ⊙764 B 4
Kildonan, ⊙1,105 E 2
Killearn, 1,086 B 1
Killin, 600 D 4
Kilmacolm, 3,348 A 2
Kilmarnock, 50,175 D 5
Kilmaurs, 2,518 D 5
Kilninver, ⊙247 C 4
Kilrenny and Anstruther, 2,951 F 4
Kilsyth, 10,210 B 1
Kilwinning, 8,460 D 5
Kinbrace, ⊙1,105 E 2
Kincardine, 3,278 C 1
Kinghorn, 2,163 D 1
Kingussie, 1,036 D 3
Kinlochewe, ⊙1,794 C 3
Kinlochleven, 1,243 D 4
Kinloch Rannoch, 241 D 4
Kinloss, 2,378 E 3
Kinross, 2,829 E 4
Kintore, 970 F 3
Kippen, 529 B 1
Kirkcaldy, 50,207 D 1
Kirkcolm, 346 C 6
Kirkconnel, 3,318 E 5
Kirkcowan, 354 D 6
Kirkcudbright, 2,690 E 6
Kirkhill, 210 D 3
Kirkintilloch, 26,664 B 2
Kirkmuirhill, 2,575 E 5
Kirkton of Glenisla, ⊙331 E 4
Kirkwall, 4,777 E 2
Kirriemuir, 4,295 E 4
Kyleakin, 268 C 3
Kyle of Lochalsh, 687 C 3
Kylestrome, ⊙745 D 2
Ladybank, 1,216 E 4
Laggan, 393 D 3
Lairg, 572 D 2
Lamlash, 613 C 5
Lanark, 8,842 E 5
Langholm, 2,509 E 5
Larbert, 4,922 C 1
Largs, 9,461 A 2
Larkhall, 15,926 E 5
Lauder, 639 F 5
Laurencekirk, 1,416 F 4

(continued)

ENGLAND and WALES

CONIC PROJECTION

MILES
0 10 20 40 60 80

KILOMETERS
0 10 20 40 60 80

Capitals of Countries..........⊛
Administrative Centers..........◉
Other Capitals..........●
Canals..........

International Boundaries..........
County Boundaries..........
Other Boundaries..........

The administrative centers for MID GLAMORGAN, NORTHUMBERLAND and SURREY are Cardiff, Newcastle upon Tyne and Kingston upon Thames, respectively.

© Copyright HAMMOND INCORPORATED

12 United Kingdom and Ireland
(continued)

Lennoxtown, 3,070	B 1
Lerwick, 6,195	G 2
Leslie, 3,303	E 4
Lesmahagow, 3,906	E 5
Leswalt, 237	C 6
Letham, 804	F 4
Leuchars, 2,482	F 4
Leurbost, 461	B 2
Leven, 9,507	F 4
Leverburgh, 223	B 3
Lhanbryde, 1,184	E 3
Lilliesleaf, 212	F 5
Limekilns, 812	D 1
Linlithgow, 6,098	C 1
Linwood, 10,510	B 2
Lionel, 187	B 2
Livingston, 21,900	C 2
Loanhead, 5,971	D 2
Lochailort, ⊙673	C 4
Lochaline, 213	C 4
Lochans, 355	D 6
Locharbriggs, 2,561	E 5
Lochawe, 200	C 4
Lochboisdale, 382	A 3
Lochcarron, 204	C 3
Lochgelly, 7,754	D 1
Lochgilphead, 1,217	C 4
Lochgoilhead, 216	D 4
Lochinver, 283	C 2
Lochmaben, 1,304	E 5
Lochmaddy, 307	A 3
Lochore, 2,994	D 1
Lochwinnoch, 2,064	A 2
Lockerbie, 3,135	E 5
Lossiemouth and Branderburgh, 5,817	E 3
Lumsden, 248	F 3
Luncarty, 584	E 4
Lybster, 554	E 2
Lyness, ⊙454	E 2
Macduff, 3,682	F 3
Machrihanish, 212	C 5
Maidens, 536	D 5
Mallaig, 903	C 4
Markinch, 2,366	E 4
Mauchline, 3,612	D 5
Maud, 634	F 3
Maybole, 4,703	D 5
Mayfield, 8,232	D 2
Meigle, 357	E 4
Melrose, 2,197	F 5
Melvaig, ⊙1,794	C 3
Methlick, 315	F 3
Methven, 806	E 4
Mid Yell, 220	G 2
Millport, 1,161	A 2
Milnathort, 1,099	E 4
Milngavie, 10,846	B 1
Minnigaff, 658	D 6
Mintlaw, 657	F 3
Moffat, 2,041	E 5
Moniaive, 342	E 5
Monifieth, 7,100	F 4
Montrose, 4,704	F 4
Morar, 184	C 4
Motherwell and Wishaw, 72,991	C 2
Muirkirk, 2,607	E 5
Muir of Ord, 1,339	D 3
Musselburgh, 17,045	D 2
Muthill, 672	E 4
Nairn, 5,821	E 3
Neilston, 4,358	B 2
Nethy Bridge, 431	E 3
New Abbey, 339	E 6
Newarthill, 7,003	C 2
Newburgh, Fife, 2,124	E 4
Newburgh, Grampian, 447	G 3
Newcastleton, 903	F 5
New Cumnock, 5,077	D 5
New Deer, 601	F 3
New Galloway, 337	D 5
Newmains, 6,847	C 2
Newmarket, 613	B 2
Newmill, 449	E 3
Newmilns and Greenholm, 3,509	D 5
New Pitsligo, 1,125	F 3
Newport-on-Tay, 3,762	F 4
New Scone, 3,830	E 4
Newtongrange, 4,555	D 2
Newton Mearns, 6,901	B 2
Newtonmore, 894	D 3
Newton Stewart, 1,983	D 6
Newtown Saint Boswells, 1,101	F 5
Newtyle, 664	E 4
North Berwick, 4,317	F 4
North Tolsta, 527	B 2
Oakley, 3,499	C 1
Oban, 6,515	C 4
Old Kilpatrick, 3,256	B 2
Oldmeldrum, 1,103	F 3
Oykel Bridge, ⊙742	D 3
Paisley, 94,833	B 2
Palnackie, 225	E 6
Patna, 2,867	D 5
Peebles, 6,049	E 5
Penicuik, 10,476	D 2
Penpont, 364	E 5
Perth, 43,098	E 4
Peterculter, 3,226	F 3
Peterhead, 14,846	G 3
Pierowall, ⊙735	E 1
Pitlochry, 2,468	E 4
Pitmedden, 313	F 3
Pittenweem, 1,548	F 4
Plockton, 288	C 3
Poolewe, ⊙1,794	C 3
Port Appin, ⊙2,172	C 4
Port Askaig, ⊙1,795	B 5
Port Bannatyne, 730	A 2
Port Charlotte, 240	B 5
Port Ellen, 932	B 5
Port Glasgow, 22,189	A 2
Portgordon, 814	F 3
Portknockie, 1,217	F 3
Portmahomack, 226	E 3
Portpatrick, 643	C 6
Portree, 1,374	B 3
Portsoy, 1,717	F 3
Port William, 517	D 6
Prestonpans, 3,272	D 1
Prestwick, 13,218	D 5
Queensferry, 5,339	D 1
Reay, 283	E 2
Renfrew, 18,880	B 2
Renton, 3,443	A 1
Rhu, 1,540	A 1
Rhynie, 333	F 3
Rigside, 1,195	E 5
Rosehearty, 1,220	F 3
Rosneath, 946	A 1
Rothes, 1,240	E 3
Rothesay, 6,285	A 2
Rutherglen, 24,091	B 2
Saint Abbs, 203	F 5
Saint Andrews, 12,837	F 4
Saint Combs, 738	G 3
Saint Cyrus, 340	F 4
Saint Margaret's Hope, 210	F 2
Saint Monance, 1,205	F 4
Saline, 831	C 1
Saltcoats, 14,861	D 5
Sandbank, 850	A 1
Sandhead, 248	D 6
Sandwick, 603	B 2
Sanquhar, 2,030	D 5
Sauchie, 6,082	C 1
Scalasaig, ⊙137	B 4
Scalloway, 896	G 2
Scarinish, ⊙875	B 4
Scourie, ⊙745	C 2
Scrabster, 273	E 2
Selkirk, 5,635	F 5
Shader, 258	B 2
Shawbost, 458	B 2
Shieldaig, ⊙550	C 3
Shotts, 9,512	C 2
Skateraw, 674	F 3
Skelmorlie, 1,535	A 2
Skipness, ⊙765	C 5
Slamannan, 1,584	C 2
Spean Bridge, 235	D 4
Springholm, 340	E 5
Stanley, 1,385	E 4
Stenhousemuir, 8,203	C 1
Stevenston, 11,786	D 5
Stewarton, 5,165	D 5
Stirling, 29,799	C 1
Stonehaven, 4,837	F 4
Stonehouse, 7,900	D 5
Stornoway, 5,371	B 2
Stow, 485	F 5
Strachan, ⊙390	F 3
Strachur Bay, ⊙678	C 4
Stranraer, 10,174	C 6
Strathaven, 5,464	D 5
Strathpeffer, 874	D 3
Strichen, 962	F 3
Stromeferry, ⊙1,724	C 3
Stromness, 1,680	E 2
Strontian, ⊙764	C 4
Struan, ⊙772	B 3
Swinton, 235	F 5
Tain, 2,057	D 3
Tarbert, Strathclyde, 1,391	C 5
Tarbert, W. Isles, 479	B 3
Tarbolton, 2,224	D 5
Tarland, 452	F 3
Tayport, 2,848	F 4
Thornhill, Central, 443	D 4
Thornhill, Dumf. & Gall., 1,510	E 5
Thurso, 9,113	E 2
Tillicoultry, 4,320	C 1
Tobermory, 652	B 4
Tolob, ⊙2,033	G 2
Tomatin, 214	D 3
Tomintoul, 306	E 3
Torphins, 499	F 3
Tradespark, 425	E 3
Tranent, 7,212	F 5
Troon, 11,656	D 5
Tullibody, 6,082	C 1
Turriff, 3,051	F 3
Tweedsmuir, ⊙105	E 5
Twynholm, 274	D 6
Tyndrum, ⊙1,153	D 4
Uddingston, 5,278	B 2
Uig, Highland, 103	B 3
Uig, W. Isles, ⊙1,948	A 2
Ullapool, 807	C 3
Uphall, 3,035	C 1
Viewpark, 9,812	C 2
Walkerburn, 842	F 5
Watten, 347	E 2
Wemyss Bay, 323	A 2
West Barns, 659	F 5
West Calder, 2,005	C 2
West Kilbride, 3,883	D 5
West Linton, 705	D 2
Whitburn, 11,647	C 2
Whitehills, 875	F 3
Whithorn, 990	D 6
Whiting Bay, 352	C 5
Wick, 7,804	E 2
Wigtown, 1,118	D 6
Winchburgh, 2,409	D 1
Yetholm, 435	F 5

OTHER FEATURES

A'Chralaig (mt.)	C 3
Ailsa Craig (isl.), 3	C 5
Almond (riv.)	E 4
Annan (riv.)	E 5
Appin (dist.), 2,006	C 4
Ardgour (dist.), 315	C 4
Ardle (riv.)	E 4
Ardnamurchan (pen.), 764	B 4
Argyll (dist.), 4,940	C 4
Arkaig, Loch (lake)	C 4
Arran (isl.), 3,564	C 5
Askival (mt.)	B 4
Assynt (dist.), 833	C 2
Athol (dist.), 1,082	D 4
Atlantic Ocean	B 2
Avon (riv.)	C 1
Avon (riv.)	E 3
Awe, Loch (lake)	C 4
Ayr (riv.)	D 5
Ayr, Heads of (cape)	D 5
Badenoch (dist.), 2,717	D 4
Baleshare (isl.), 64	A 3
Balmoral Castle	E 3
Barra (sound)	A 3
Barra (isl.), 1,005	A 4
Barra (head)	A 4
Barra Isles (isls.), 1,092	A 4
Battock (mt.)	F 4
Beauly (riv.)	D 3
Beinn Dearg (mt.)	D 3
Beinn a Ghlo (mt.)	E 4
Bell Rock (isl.), 3	F 4
Ben Alder (mt.)	D 4
Ben Avon (mt.)	E 3
Benbecula (isl.), 1,355	A 3
Ben Cruachan (mt.)	C 4
Ben Lawers (mt.)	D 4
Ben Lui (mt.)	D 4
Ben Macdhui (mt.)	E 3
Ben Mhor (mt.)	A 3
Ben More (mt.)	B 4
Ben More (mt.)	D 4
Ben More Assynt (mt.)	D 2
Ben Nevis (mt.)	D 4
Bernera (isl.), 276	B 2
Berneray (isl.), 131	A 3
Berneray (isl.), 6	A 4
Bidean nam Bian (mt.)	D 4
Black Isle (pen.), 7,209	D 3
Blackwater (res.)	D 4
Boisdale, Loch (inlet)	A 3
Bracadale, Loch (inlet)	B 3
Braemar (dist.), 7,624	E 3
Breadalbane (dist.), 3,649	D 4
Bressay (isl.), 248	G 2
Broad (bay)	B 2
Broad Law (mt.)	E 5
Broom, Loch (inlet)	C 3
Brough Ness (prom.)	F 2
Buchan (dist.), 40,089	F 3
Buddon Ness (prom.)	F 4
Burray (isl.), 209	F 2
Burrow (head)	D 6
Bute (isl.), 8,423	C 5
Bute (sound)	C 5
Butt of Lewis (prom.)	B 2
Cairn Gorm (mt.)	E 3
Cairngorm (mts.)	E 3
Cairn Toul (mt.)	E 3
Caledonian (canal)	D 3
Canna (isl.), 22	B 3
Carn Ban (mt.)	D 3
Carn Eige (mt.)	C 3
Carrick (dist.), 21,425	D 5
Carron (riv.)	C 1
Carron (riv.)	C 3
Cheviot (hills)	F 5
Cheviot, The (mt.)	F 5
Clisham (mt.)	B 3
Clyde (riv.)	D 5
Clyde (firth)	D 5
Coll (isl.), 144	B 4
Colonsay (isl.), 137	B 4
Copinsay (isl.), 3	F 2
Cowal (dist.), 15,548	C 4
Creag Meagaidh (mt.)	D 4
Cromarty (firth)	D 3
Cuillin (hills)	B 3
Cuillin (sound)	B 3
Dee (riv.)	D 5
Dee (riv.)	F 3
Dennis (head)	F 1
Deveron (riv.)	F 3
Don (riv.)	F 3
Doon (riv.)	D 5
Dornoch (firth)	E 3
Duirinish (dist.), 1,085	B 3
Duncansby (head)	F 2
Dunnet (head)	E 2
Earn (riv.)	E 4
Earn, Loch (lake)	D 4
Eday (isl.), 179	F 1
Eddrachillis (bay)	C 2
Eden (riv.)	F 4
Egilsay (isl.), 39	F 1
Eigg (isl.), 69	B 4
Eil, Loch (lake)	C 4
Eishort, Loch (inlet)	B 3
Enard (bay)	C 2
Eriboll, Loch (inlet)	D 2
Ericht, Loch (lake)	D 4
Eriskay (isl.), 219	A 3
Erisort, Loch (inlet)	B 2
Esk (riv.)	F 5
Etive, Loch (inlet)	C 4
Ewe, Loch (inlet)	C 3
Eye (pen.), 850	B 2
Fair Isle (isl.), 65	F 3
Fetlar (isl.), 88	G 2
Fife Ness (prom.)	F 4
Findhorn (riv.)	E 3
Flannan (isls.), 3	A 2
Formartine (dist.), 10,768	F 3
Forth (riv.)	B 1
Forth (firth)	F 4
Forth and Clyde (canal)	B 2
Foula (isl.), 33	F 2
Fyne, Loch (inlet)	C 5
Galloway (dist.), 54,972	D 5
Galloway, Mull of (prom.)	D 6
Gare Loch (inlet)	A 1
Garioch (dist.), 6,863	F 3
Garry, Loch (lake)	D 3
Gigha (isl.), 174	C 5
Girdle Ness (prom.)	G 3
Glass (riv.)	D 3
Glen More (dist.), 55,035	D 3
Goat Fell (mt.)	C 5
Gometra (isl.), 10	B 4
Grampian (mts.)	D 4
Great Cumbrae (isl.), 1,296	A 2
Gruinard (bay)	C 3
Hallandale (riv.)	E 2
Harris (sound)	A 3
Harris (dist.), 2,175	B 3
Hebrides (sea)	B 3
Hebrides, Inner (isls.), 14,881	B 4
Hebrides, Outer (isls.), 29,615	A 3
Helmsdale (riv.)	E 2
Herma Ness (prom.)	G 2
Holy (isl.), 10	C 5
Holy Loch (inlet)	A 1
Hoy (isl.), 419	E 2
Inchcape (Bell Rock) (isl.), 3	F 4
Inchkeith (isl.), 3	D 1
Indaal, Loch (inlet)	B 5
Inner (sound)	C 3
Inner Hebrides (isls.), 14,881	B 4
Iona (isl.), 145	B 4
Isla (riv.)	E 4
Islay (isl.), 3,816	B 5
Jura (isl.), 210	C 5
Jura (sound)	C 5
Katrine, Loch (lake)	D 4
Kerrera (isl.), 27	C 4
Kilbrannan (sound)	C 5
Kinnairds (head)	G 3
Kintyre (pen.), 10,077	C 5
Kintyre, Mull of (prom.)	C 5
Knapdale (dist.), 4,082	C 5
Kyle of Tongue (inlet)	D 2
Laggan (bay)	B 5
Lammermuir (hills)	F 5
Lennox (hills)	B 1
Leven (lake)	E 4
Leven, Loch (inlet)	D 4
Lewis (dist.), 20,047	B 2
Liddel Water (riv.)	F 5
Linnhe, Loch (inlet)	C 4
Lismore (isl.), 166	C 4
Little Minch (sound)	B 3
Lochaber (dist.), 13,813	D 4
Lochnagar (mt.)	E 4
Lochy, Loch (lake)	D 3
Lomond, Loch (lake)	D 4
Long, Loch (inlet)	D 4
Lorne (dist.), 12,162	C 4
Lorne (firth)	C 4
Loyal, Loch (lake)	D 2
Luce (bay)	D 6
Luing (isl.), 151	C 4
Lyon (riv.)	D 4
Machers, The (pen.), 6,192	D 6
Mainland (isl.), 12,747	E 1
Mainland (isl.), 12,944	G 2
Mar (dist.), 23,931	F 3
Maree, Loch (lake)	C 3
May, Isle of (isl.), 10	F 4
Merrick (mt.)	D 5
Minginish (dist.), 772	B 3
Moidart (dist.), 155	C 4
Monach (sound)	A 3
Monadhliath (mts.)	D 3
Moorfoot (hills)	E 5
Moray (firth)	E 3
Moriston (riv.)	D 3
Morven (dist.), 398	C 4
Morven (mt.)	E 2
Muck (isl.), 24	B 4
Muckle Flugga (isl.), 3	G 2
Mull (isl.), 2,024	C 4
Mull (head)	F 1
Mull (sound)	C 4
Nairn (riv.)	D 3
na Keal, Loch (inlet)	B 4
Naver (riv.)	D 2
Ness, Loch (lake)	D 3
Nevis, Loch (inlet)	C 3
Nith (riv.)	E 5
North (chan.)	C 5
North (sound)	F 1
North (sound)	G 4
North Esk (riv.)	F 4
North Minch (sound)	B 3
North Ronaldsay (isl.), 134	F 1
North Uist (isl.), 1,469	A 3
Oa, Mull of (prom.)	B 5
Ochil (hills)	E 4
Oich (riv.)	D 3
Orchy (riv.)	D 4
Orkney (isls.), 17,675	F 1
Oronsay (isl.), 2	B 4
Outer Hebrides (isls.), 29,615	A 3
Oykel (riv.)	D 3
Pabbay (isl.), 4	A 3
Papa Stour (isl.), 24	F 2
Papa Westray (isl.), 106	F 1
Paps of Jura (mt.)	C 5
Park (dist.), 210	B 2
Peel Fell (mt.)	F 5
Pentland (hills)	D 2
Pentland (firth)	E 2
Pladda (isl.), 2	C 5
Quoich, Loch (lake)	C 3
Raasay (isl.), 163	C 3
Rannoch (dist.), 1,177	D 4
Rannoch, Loch (lake)	D 4
Rhinns, The (pen.), 8,295	C 6
Roag, Loch (inlet)	B 2
Rona (isl.), 3	B 3
Ross of Mull (pen.), 585	B 4
Rousay (isl.), 181	E 1
Rudha Hunish (cape)	B 3
Rudh Re (cape)	C 3
Rum (isl.), 40	B 3
Ryan, Loch (inlet)	C 5
Saint Kilda (isl.), 65	A 2
Saint Magnus (bay)	F 2
Sanda (isl.), 9	C 5
Sanday (isl.), 11	B 3
Sanday (isl.), 592	F 1
Scalpay (isl.), 483	B 3
Scalpay (isl.), 5	C 3
Scapa Flow (chan.)	E 2
Scarp (isl.), 12	A 2
Scridain, Loch (inlet)	B 4
Scurdie Ness (prom.)	F 4
Seaforth, Loch (inlet)	B 3
Seil (isl.), 326	C 4
Sgurr a Choire Ghlais (mt.)	D 3
Sgurr Alasdair (mt.)	B 3
Sgurr Mor (mt.)	C 3
Sgurr na Lapaich (mt.)	C 3
Shapinsay (isl.), 346	F 1
Shetland (isls.), 18,494	G 2
Shiant (sound)	B 3
Shiel, Loch (lake)	C 4
Shin (falls)	D 3
Shin, Loch (lake)	D 2
Shona (isl.), 17	C 4
Sidlaw (hills)	E 4
Sinclair's (bay)	E 2
Skye, Isle of (isl.), 7,183	B 3
Sleat (pt.)	B 4
Sleat (dist.), 449	C 3
Small Isles (isls.), 171	B 4
Snizort, Loch (inlet)	B 3
Soay (isl.), 5	B 3
Solway (firth)	E 6
South Esk (riv.)	F 4
South Ronaldsay (isl.), 776	F 2
South Uist (isl.), 2,281	A 3
Spean (riv.)	D 4
Spey (riv.)	E 3
Start (pt.)	F 1
Stinchar (riv.)	D 5
Strathbogie (dist.), 7,959	F 3
Strathmore (valley)	E 4
Strathspey (dist.), 6,668	E 3
Strathy (pt.)	E 2
Stroma (isl.), 8	E 2
Stronsay (isl.), 436	F 1
Sumburgh (head)	G 2
Sunart, Loch (inlet)	C 4
Swona (isl.), 3	E 2
Taransay (isl.), 5	A 3
Tarbat Ness (prom.)	E 3
Tarbert, East Loch (inlet)	B 3
Tarbert, Loch (inlet)	B 5
Tarbert, West Loch (inlet)	A 3
Tay (riv.)	E 4
Tay (firth)	F 4
Tay, Loch (lake)	D 4
Teith (riv.)	D 4
Teviot (riv.)	F 5
Thurso (riv.)	E 2
Tiree (isl.), 875	B 4
Tolsta (head)	B 2
Tor Ness (prom.)	E 2
Torridon, Loch (inlet)	C 3
Trossachs, The (valley)	D 4
Trotternish (dist.), 1,948	B 3
Tweed (riv.)	F 5
Tyne (riv.)	F 5
Ulva (isl.), 23	B 4
Unst (isl.), 1,124	G 2
Vaternish (dist.), 162	B 3
Vatersay (isl.), 77	A 4
West Burra (isl.), 501	G 2
Westray (firth)	E 1
Westray (isl.), 735	E 1
Whalsay (isl.), 870	G 2
White Coomb (mt.)	E 5
Wigtown (bay)	D 6
Wrath (cape)	C 2
Wyre (isl.), 36	F 1
Yarrow (riv.)	E 5
Yell (isl.), 1,143	G 2
Ythan (riv.)	F 3

★Population of met. area
⊙Population of parish.

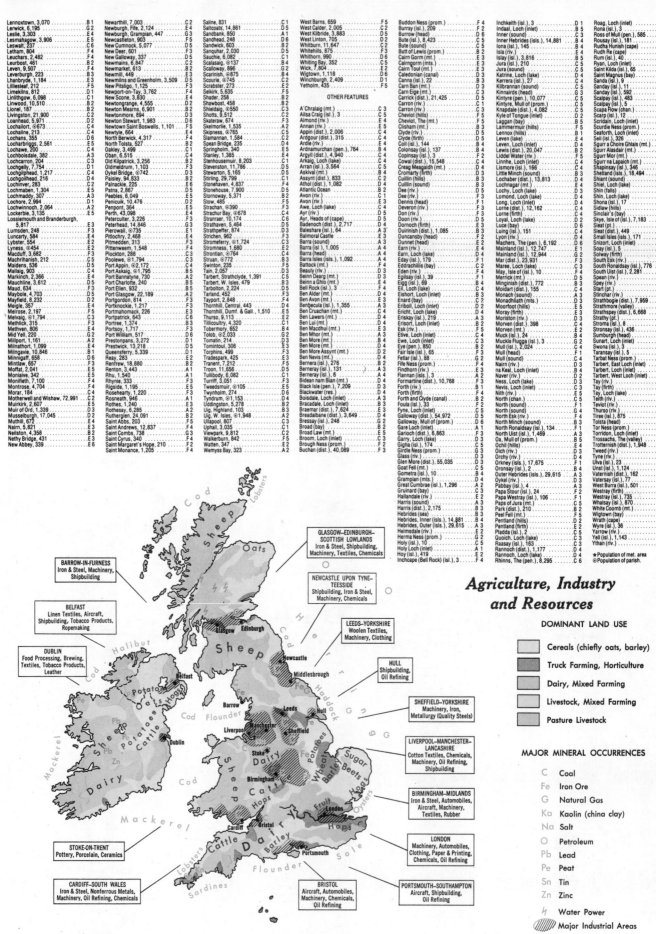

Agriculture, Industry and Resources

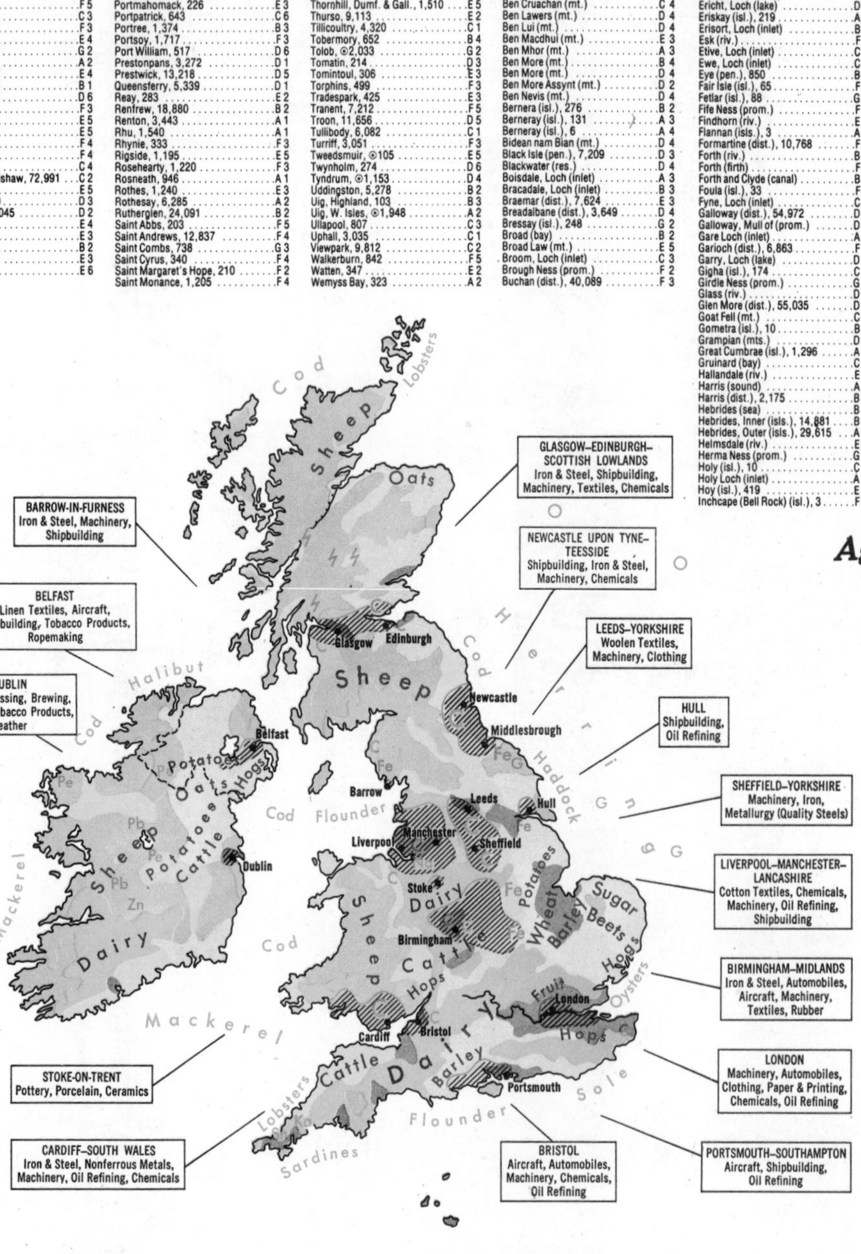

GLASGOW–EDINBURGH–SCOTTISH LOWLANDS
Iron & Steel, Shipbuilding, Machinery, Textiles, Chemicals
BARROW-IN-FURNESS
Iron & Steel, Machinery, Shipbuilding
NEWCASTLE UPON TYNE–TEESSIDE
Shipbuilding, Iron & Steel, Machinery, Chemicals
BELFAST
Linen Textiles, Aircraft, Shipbuilding, Tobacco Products, Ropemaking
LEEDS–YORKSHIRE
Woolen Textiles, Machinery, Clothing
DUBLIN
Food Processing, Brewing, Textiles, Tobacco Products, Leather
HULL
Shipbuilding, Oil Refining
SHEFFIELD–YORKSHIRE
Machinery, Iron, Metallurgy (Quality Steels)
LIVERPOOL–MANCHESTER–LANCASHIRE
Cotton Textiles, Chemicals, Machinery, Oil Refining, Shipbuilding
BIRMINGHAM–MIDLANDS
Iron & Steel, Automobiles, Aircraft, Machinery, Textiles, Rubber
STOKE-ON-TRENT
Pottery, Porcelain, Ceramics
LONDON
Machinery, Automobiles, Clothing, Paper & Printing, Chemicals, Oil Refining
CARDIFF–SOUTH WALES
Iron & Steel, Nonferrous Metals, Machinery, Oil Refining, Chemicals
BRISTOL
Aircraft, Automobiles, Machinery, Chemicals, Oil Refining
PORTSMOUTH–SOUTHAMPTON
Aircraft, Shipbuilding, Oil Refining
Cod
Lobsters
Sheep
Oats
Herring
Haddock
Halibut
Glasgow
Edinburgh
Newcastle
Middlesbrough
Belfast
Potatoes
Oats
Hogs
Barrow
Leeds
Hull
Flounder
Manchester
Liverpool
Sheffield
Dublin
Sheep
Potatoes
Cattle
Mackerel
Stoke
Dairy
Wheat
Barley
Sugar Beets
Hogs
Birmingham
Cattle
Hops
Fruit
London
Oysters
Cardiff
Bristol
Barley
Portsmouth
Sole
Sardines

DOMINANT LAND USE

- Cereals (chiefly oats, barley)
- Truck Farming, Horticulture
- Dairy, Mixed Farming
- Livestock, Mixed Farming
- Pasture Livestock

MAJOR MINERAL OCCURRENCES

- C Coal
- Fe Iron Ore
- G Natural Gas
- Ka Kaolin (china clay)
- Na Salt
- O Petroleum
- Pb Lead
- Pe Peat
- Sn Tin
- Zn Zinc
- Water Power
- Major Industrial Areas

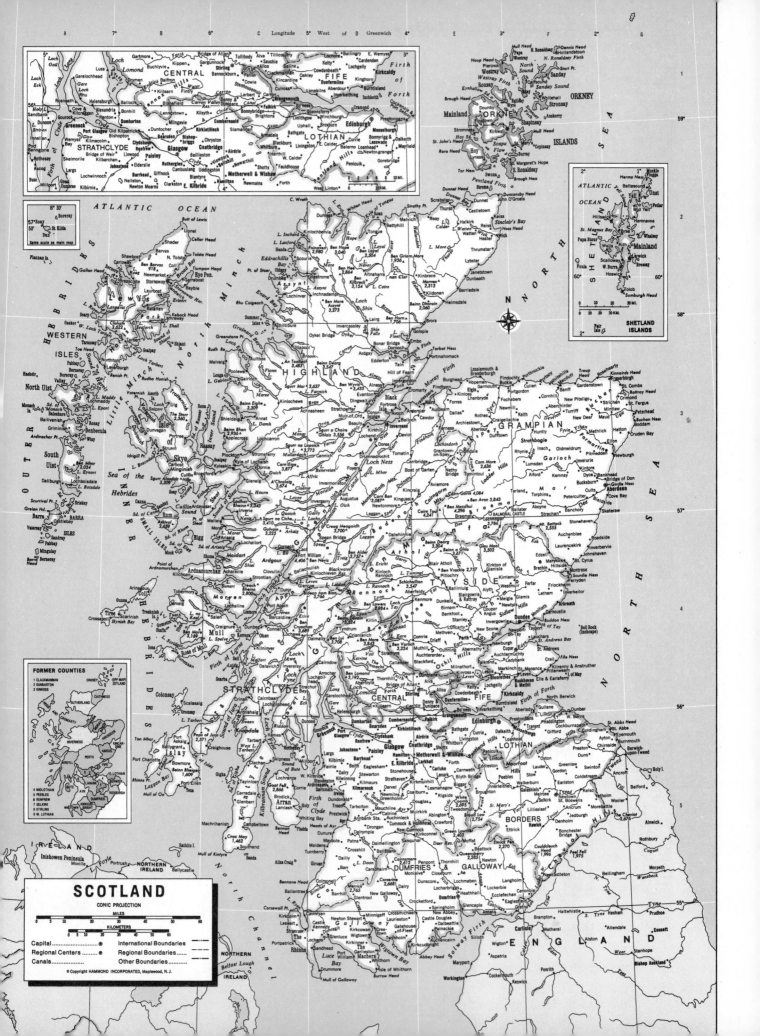

SCOTLAND

CONIC PROJECTION

MILES

KILOMETERS

Capital.............................⊛ International Boundaries_____
Regional Centers.............● Regional Boundaries..............
Canals.............................   Other Boundaries...............

© Copyright HAMMOND INCORPORATED, Maplewood, N.J.

FORMER COUNTIES

1 CLACKMANNAN
2 DUNBARTON
3 KINROSS
4 MIDLOTHIAN
5 PEEBLES
6 RENFREW
7 SELKIRK
8 STIRLING
9 W. LOTHIAN

SHETLAND
ISLANDS

IRELAND

COUNTIES

Carlow, 34,237 H 6
Cavan, 52,618 G 4
Clare, 75,008 D 6
Cork, 352,883 D 7
Donegal, 108,344 K 2
Dublin, 852,219 J 5
Galway, 149,223 D 5
Kerry, 112,772 B 7
Kildare, 71,977 H 5
Kilkenny, 61,473 G 6
Laoighis, 45,259 G 6
Leitrim, 28,360 E 3
Leix (Laoighis), 45,259 G 6
Limerick, 140,459 D 7
Longford, 28,250 F 4
Louth, 74,951 J 4
Mayo, 109,525 C 4
Meath, 71,729 H 4
Monaghan, 46,242 H 3
Offaly, 51,829 F 5
Roscommon, 53,519 E 4
Sligo, 50,275 D 3
Tipperary, 123,565 F 6
Waterford, 77,315 F 7
Westmeath, 53,570 G 5
Wexford, 86,351 H 7
Wicklow, 66,295 J 5

CITIES and TOWNS

Abbeydorney, 188 B 7
Abbeyfeale, 1,337 C 7
Abbeylara, ‡290 F 4
Abbeyleix, 1,033 G 6
Achill Sound, ‡1,163 B 4
Aclare, ‡336 D 3
Adare, 545 D 6
Aghada-Farsid-Rostellan, 461 E 8
Aghadoe, ‡497 B 7
Aghagower, ‡693 C 4
Ahascragh, 221 E 5
Annagry, 201 E 1
Annascaul, 236 B 7
An Uaimh, 4,605 H 4
An Uaimh, *6,665 H 4
Ardagh, Limerick, 213 C 7
Ardagh, Longford, ‡974 F 4
Ardara, 683 E 2
Ardee, *3,183 H 4
Ardee, 3,096 H 4
Ardfert, 286 B 7
Ardfinnan, 510 F 7
Ardmore, 233 F 8
Ardrahan, ‡239 D 5
Arklow, 6,948 J 6
Arthurstown, 1,188 H 7
Arva, 370 F 4
Ashford, 341 J 5
Askeaton, 844 D 6
Athboy, 705 H 4
Athea, 328 C 7
Athenry, 1,240 D 5
Athleague, ‡955 E 4
Athlone, 9,825 F 5
Athlone, *11,611 F 5
Athy, 4,270 H 6
Athy, *4,654 H 6
Aughrim, 451 J 6
Avoca, ‡620 J 6
Bagenalstown (Muinebeag), 2,321 H 6
Baile Átha Cliath (Dublin) (cap.), 567,866 K 5
Bailieborough, 1,293 G 4
Balbriggan, 3,741 J 4
Balla, 293 C 4
Ballaghaderreen, 1,121 E 4
Ballina, Mayo, 6,063 C 3
Ballina, *6,369 C 3
Ballina, Tipperary, 336 E 6
Ballinagh, 459 G 4
Ballinakill, 300 G 6
Ballineen D 8
Ballinamore, 808 F 3
Ballinasloe, 5,969 E 5
Ballincollig-Carrigrohane, 2,110 D 8
Ballindine, 232 C 4
Ballingarry, Limerick, 422 D 7
Ballingarry, Tipperary, ‡574 F 6
Ballinlough, 242 D 4
Ballinrobe, 1,272 C 4
Ballintober, ‡867 E 4
Ballintra, 197 E 2
Ballisodare, 486 E 3
Ballivor, 287 H 4
Ballybay, 754 G 3
Ballybay, *1,159 G 3
Ballybofey-Stranorlar, 2,214 F 2
Ballybunion, 1,287 B 7
Ballycanew, ‡460 J 6
Ballycarney, ‡294 J 6
Ballycastle, ‡724 C 3
Ballyconnell, 421 F 3
Ballycotton, 389 F 8
Ballydehob, 253 C 8
Ballyduff, 406 B 7
Ballygar, 359 E 4
Ballygeary, 725 J 7
Ballyhaise, 274 G 3
Ballyhaunis, 1,093 D 4
Ballyheigue, 450 B 7
Ballyjamesduff, 673 G 4
Ballylanders, 266 E 7
Ballylongford, 504 B 6
Ballymahon, 707 F 4
Ballymakeery, 272 C 8
Ballymore, ‡447 F 5
Ballymore Eustace, 433 J 5
Ballymote, 952 D 3
Ballyporeen, ‡810 E 7
Ballyragget, 519 G 6
Ballyroan, ‡478 G 6
Ballyshannon, 2,325 E 3
Ballytore, ‡580 H 5
Baltimore, 200 C 9
Baltinglass, 909 H 6
Baltray, 236 J 4
Banagher, 1,052 F 5
Bandon, 2,257 D 8
Bandon, *4,071 D 8
Bannow, ‡798 H 7
Bansha, 184 E 7
Bantry, 2,579 C 8
Barna, ‡1,734 C 5
Belmullet, 744 B 3
Belturbet, 1,092 G 3
Bennettsbridge, 367 G 6
Birr, 3,319 F 5
Birr, *3,881 F 5
Blanchardstown, 3,279 H 5
Blarney, 1,128 D 8
Blessington, 637 J 5
Boherbue, 372 C 7
Borris, 430 H 6
Borris-in-Ossory, 276 F 6
Borrisokane, 769 E 6
Borrisoleigh, 471 E 6
Boyle, 1,727 E 4
Boyle, *1,939 E 4
Bray, 14,467 K 5
Bray, *15,841 K 5
Bri Chualann (Bray), 14,467 K 5
Broadford, 226 C 7
Brosna, 250 C 7
Bruff, 547 D 7
Bruree, 243 D 7
Bunbeg-Derrybeg, 878 E 1
Bunclody-Carrickduff, 929 H 6
Buncrana, 2,955 G 1
Buncrana, *3,334 G 1
Bundoran, 1,337 E 3
Burtonport, ‡1,288 E 2
Buttevant, 1,045 D 7
Cahir, 1,747 F 7
Cahirciveen, 1,547 A 8
Callan, 1,283 G 7
Camolin, 306 J 6
Campile, 231 H 7
Cappamore, 567 E 6
Cappawhite, 305 E 6
Cappoquin, 872 F 7
Carbury, ‡894 H 5
Carlingford, 559 J 3
Carlow, 9,588 H 6
Carlow, *10,399 H 6
Carndonagh, 1,146 G 1
Carnew, 570 H 6
Carrickmacross, 2,100 H 4
Carrickmacross, *2,475 H 4
Carrick-on-Shannon, 1,854 F 4
Carrick-on-Suir, 5,006 F 7
Carrigaholt, ‡493 B 6
Carrigaline, 951 E 8
Carrigallen, 230 F 4
Carrigart, ‡753 F 1
Carrigtwohill, 622 E 8
Carrowkeel, ‡326 G 1
Cashel, 2,692 F 7
Castlebar, 5,979 C 4
Castlebar, *6,476 C 4
Castlebellingham, 407 J 4
Castleblayney, 2,118 H 3
Castleblayney, *2,395 H 3
Castlecomer-Donaguile, 1,244 G 6
Castledermot, 583 H 6
Castlefin, 610 F 2
Castlegregory, 216 A 7
Castleisland, 1,929 B 7
Castlemartyr, 491 E 8
Castlepollard, 693 G 4
Castlerea, 1,752 D 4
Castletown, ‡504 F 6
Castletownbere, 812 B 8
Castletownroche, 399 D 7
Castletownshend, 170 C 9
Causeway, 215 B 7
Cavan, 3,273 G 3
Cavan, *4,312 G 3
Ceanannus Mór, 2,391 G 4
Ceanannus Mór, *2,653 G 4
Celbridge, 1,568 H 5
Charlestown-Bellahy, 677 D 4
Charleville (Rathluirc), 2,232 D 7
Clara, 2,156 F 5
Claregalway, ‡594 D 5
Claremorris, 1,718 C 4
Clashmore, ‡379 F 8
Clifden, 790 B 5
Cloghan, 404 F 5
Clogh-Chatsworth, 324 G 6
Clogheen, 530 F 7
Clogherhead, 649 J 4
Clonakilty, 2,430 D 8
Clonaslee, 285 F 5
Clondalkin, 7,009 J 5
Clonegal, 202 H 6
Clones, 2,164 G 3
Clonfert, ‡430 E 5
Clonmany, ‡936 G 1
Clonmel, 11,622 F 7
Clonmel, *12,291 F 7
Clonmellon, 328 H 4
Clonroche, 222 H 7
Clontuskert, 351 E 4
Cloone, ‡460 F 4
Cloughjordan, 480 E 6
Cloyne, 654 E 8
Coachford, 290 D 8
Cóbh, 6,076 E 8
Cóbh, *7,141 E 8
Coill Dubh, 920 H 5
Collon, 262 J 4
Collooney, 546 E 3
Cong, 233 C 4
Convoy, 654 F 2
Coolaney, ‡352 D 3
Coolgreany, ‡603 J 6
Cootehill, 1,415 G 3
Cootehill, *1,542 G 3
Cork, 128,645 E 8
Cork, *134,430 E 8
Corofin, 342 C 6
Courtmacsherry, 210 D 8
Courtown Harbour, 291 J 6
Creeslough, 269 F 1
Crookhaven, ‡400 B 9
Croom, 756 D 6
Crosshaven, 1,222 E 8
Crossmolina, 1,077 C 3
Crusheen, ‡405 D 6
Culdaff, ‡621 G 1
Daingean, 492 G 5
Delvin, 223 G 4
Dingle, 1,401 A 7
Doaghbeg, ‡701 F 1
Donabate, 426 J 5
Donegal, 1,725 F 2
Doneraile, 799 D 7
Dooagh-Keel, 649 A 4
Doon, 387 E 6
Douglas, ‡4,448 D 8
Drimoleague, 415 C 8
Drishane, ‡1,548 C 7
Drogheda, 19,762 J 4
Drogheda, *20,095 J 4
Droichead Nua, 5,053 H 5
Droichead Nua, *6,444 H 5
Dromahair, 177 E 3
Drumcar, ‡1,215 J 4
Drumconrath, ‡1,044 H 4
Drumkeerin, ‡467 E 3
Drumlish, 205 F 4
Drumshanbo, 576 E 3
Dublin (cap.), 567,866 K 5
Dublin, *679,748 K 5
Duleek, 658 J 4
Duncannon, 228 H 7
Dundalk, 21,672 H 3
Dundalk, *23,816 H 3
Dunfanaghy, 303 F 1
Dungarvan, 5,583 F 7
Dungloe, 940 E 2
Dunkineely, 288 E 2
Dún Laoghaire, 53,171 K 5
Dún Laoghaire, *98,379 K 5
Dunlavin, 423 H 5
Dunleer, 855 J 4
Dunmanway, 1,392 C 8
Dunmore, 522 D 4
Dunmore East, 656 G 7
Dunshaughlin, ‡283 H 5
Durrow, Laoighis, 596 G 6
Durrow, Offaly, ‡441 F 5
Easky, 184 D 3
Edenderry, 2,953 G 5
Edenderry, *3,116 G 5
Elphin, 489 E 4
Emyvale, 281 G 3
Ennis, 5,972 D 6
Ennis, *10,840 D 6
Enniscorthy, 5,704 J 7
Enniscorthy, *6,642 J 7
Enniskerry, 772 J 5
Ennistymon, 1,013 C 6
Eyrecourt, 314 E 5
Fahan, ‡1,023 G 1
Falcarragh, 506 E 1
Feakle, ‡398 D 6
Fenit, 360 B 7
Ferbane, 1,064 F 5
Fermoy, 3,237 E 7
Fermoy, *4,033 E 7
Ferns, 712 J 6
Fethard, Tipperary, 1,064 F 7
Fethard, Wexford, ‡637 H 7
Foxford, 868 C 4
Foynes, 624 C 6
Frankford (Kilcormac), 1,089 F 5
Frenchpark, ‡693 E 4
Freshford, 585 G 6
Galbally, 258 E 7
Galway, 27,726 C 5
Galway, *29,375 C 5
Geashill, ‡751 G 5
Glandore, ‡695 C 8
Glanmire-Riverstown, 1,113 E 8
Glanworth, 335 E 7
Glenamaddy, 315 D 4
Glenbeigh, 266 B 7
Glencolumbkille, ‡787 D 2
Glengarriff, 244 C 8
Glenties, 734 E 2
Glenville, ‡264 D 7
Glin, 623 C 6
Golden, ‡640 F 7
Gorey, 2,946 J 6
Gorey, *3,024 J 6
Gormanston, ‡1,384 J 4
Gort, 975 D 5
Gowran, 402 G 6
Graiguenamanagh-Tinnahinch, 1,303 H 6
Granard, 1,054 F 4
Greencastle, 322 H 1
Greenore, 882 J 4
Greystones-Delgany, 4,517 K 5
Gurteen, 165 D 3
Hacketstown, 574 H 6
Headford, 673 C 5
Holycross, ‡902 F 6
Hospital, 525 E 7
Inchigeelagh, ‡516 C 8
Inishannon, 190 D 8
Inistioge, 179 G 7
Inniscrone, 582 C 3
Johnstown, 303 G 6
Kanturk, 2,063 D 7
Keel-Dooagh, 649 A 4
Kells, ‡423 G 6
Kells (Ceanannus Mór), 2,391 G 4
Kenmare, 903 B 8
Kilbaha, ‡471 B 6
Kilbeggan, 635 G 5
Kilcar, 273 D 2
Kilcock, 827 H 5
Kilconnell, ‡629 E 5
Kilcoole, 679 K 5
Kilcormac, 1,089 F 5
Kilcullen, 880 H 5
Kildare, 3,137 H 5
Kildysart, 239 C 6
Kilfenora, ‡441 C 6
Kilfinane, 561 D 7
Kilgarvan, 228 B 8
Kilkee, 1,287 B 6
Kilkelly, 225 D 4
Kilkenny, 9,838 G 6
Kilkenny, *13,306 G 6
Killala, 368 C 3
Killaloe, 871 D 6
Killarney, 7,184 C 7
Killarney, *7,541 C 7
Killavullen, 221 D 7
Killenaule, 592 F 6
Killeshandra, 432 F 3
Killimor, 221 E 5
Killinaboy, ‡297 C 6
Killorglin, 1,150 B 7
Killucan-Rathwire, 290 G 4
Killybegs, 1,094 E 2
Kilmacrennan, 274 F 1
Kilmacthomas, 396 G 7
Kilmallock, 1,170 D 7
Kilmeadan, ‡262 G 7
Kilmihill, 284 C 6
Kilmoganny, 181 G 7
Kilmore Quay, 273 H 7
Kilmurry, ‡387 C 6
Kilnaleck, 273 G 4
Kilronan, 243 B 5
Kilrush, 2,671 C 6
Kilsheelan, ‡665 F 7
Kiltimagh, 978 C 4
Kilworth, 360 E 7
Kingscourt, 1,016 H 4
Kingstown (Dun Laoghaire), 53,171 K 5
Kinlough, 160 E 3
Kinnegad, 362 G 5
Kinnitty, ‡420 F 5
Kinsale, 1,622 D 8
Kinsale, *1,989 D 8
Kinvara, 293 D 5
Knightstown, 236 A 8
Knock, ‡1,202 D 4
Knocklong, 248 D 7
Knocknagashel, 168 C 7
Labasheeda, ‡468 C 6
Laghey, ‡625 E 2
Lahinch, 455 C 6
Lanesborough-Ballyleague, 906 E 4
Laracor, ‡404 H 4
Laytown-Bettystown-Mornington, 1,882 J 4
Leenane, ‡271 B 4
Leighlindridge, 379 H 6
Leitrim, ‡544 F 3
Leixlip, 2,402 H 5
Letterkenny, 4,930 F 2
Letterkenny, *5,207 F 2
Lifford, 1,121 F 2
Limerick, 57,161 D 6
Limerick, *63,002 D 6
Liscarroll, 231 D 7
Lisdoonvarna, 459 C 5
Lismore, 884 F 7
Lismore, *1,041 F 7
Listowel, 3,021 C 7
Littleton, 322 F 6
Longford, 3,876 F 4
Longford, *4,791 F 4
Lorrha, ‡685 E 5
Loughrea, 3,075 E 5
Louisburgh, 310 B 4
Louth, 208 J 4
Lucan-Doddsborough, 4,245 J 5
Luimneach (Limerick), 57,161 D 6
Lusk, 553 J 4
Macroom, 2,256 C 8
Malahide, 3,834 J 5
Malin, ‡552 G 1
Mallow, 5,901 D 7
Mallow, *6,506 D 7
Manorhamilton, 858 E 3
Manulla, ‡660 C 4
Maryborough (Portlaoighise), 3,902 G 5
Maynooth, 1,296 H 5
Meathas Truim, 546 G 4
Midleton, 3,075 E 8
Midleton, *4,666 E 8
Milford, 763 F 1
Millstreet, 1,319 D 7
Milltown, 260 A 7
Miltown-Malbay, 677 C 6
Minard, ‡397 A 7
Mitchelstown, 2,783 E 7
Moate, 1,378 F 5
Mohill, 868 F 4
Monaghan, 5,256 G 3
Monasterevan, 1,619 H 5
Moneygall, 282 F 6
Monivea, ‡405 D 5
Mooncoin, 413 G 7
Mount Bellew, 275 D 5
Mountcharles, 445 E 2
Mountmellick, 2,595 G 5
Mountmellick, *2,864 G 5
Mountrath, 1,098 F 5
Moville, 1,089 G 1
Moycullen, ‡498 C 5
Moynalty, ‡583 H 4
Muff, 240 G 1
Muinebeag, 2,321 H 6
Mullagh, 293 H 4
Mullaghmore, ‡629 D 3
Mullinahone, 262 F 7
Mullinavat, 343 G 7
Mullingar, 6,790 G 4
Mullinger, *9,245 G 4
Naas, 5,078 H 5
Navan (An Uaimh), 4,605 H 4
Nenagh, 5,085 E 6
Nenagh, *5,174 E 6
Newbliss, ‡547 G 3
Newbridge (Droichead Nua), 5,053 H 5
Newcastle, 2,549 D 7
Newcastle, *2,680 D 7
Newmarket, 886 C 7
Newmarket-on-Fergus, 1,052 D 6
New Pallas, ‡1,271 E 6
Newport, Mayo, 420 C 4
Newport, Tipperary, 582 E 6
New Ross, 4,775 H 7
New Ross, *5,153 H 7
Newtownforbes, ‡495 F 4
Newtownmountkennedy, 882 J 5
Newtownsandes, 268 C 6
O'Briensbridge-Montpelier, 237 D 6
Oldcastle, 759 G 4
Old Leighlin, ‡309 G 6
Oola, 348 E 6
Oranmore, 440 D 5
Oughterard, 628 C 5
Passage East, 408 G 7
Passage West, 2,709 E 8
Patrickswell, 415 D 6
Pettigo, 332 F 2
Piltown, 456 G 7
Portarlington, 3,117 G 5
Portlaoighise, 3,902 G 5
Portlaoighise, *6,470 G 5
Portlaw, 1,166 G 7
Portmarnock, 1,726 J 5
Portumna, 913 E 5
Queenstown (Cóbh), 6,076 E 8
Rahan, ‡531 F 5
Ramelton, 807 F 1
Raphoe, 945 F 2
Rathangan, 868 G 5
Rathcoole, 1,740 J 5
Rathcormac, 191 E 7
Rathdowney, 892 F 6
Rathdrum, 1,141 J 6
Rathgormuck, ‡231 F 7
Rathkeale, 1,543 D 7
Rathluirc, 2,232 D 7
Rathmore, 437 J 5
Rathmullen, 486 F 1
Rathnew-Merrymeeting, 954 J 6
Rathowen, ‡294 F 4
Rathvilly, 230 H 6
Ratoath, 300 J 5
Riverstown, 236 E 3
Rockcorry, 233 H 3
Rosapenna, ‡822 F 1
Roscommon, 1,556 E 4
Roscommon, *2,821 E 4
Roscrea, 3,855 F 6
Rosscarbery, 309 C 8
Rosses Point, 464 D 3
Rosslare, 588 J 7
Rosslare Harbour (Ballygeary), 725 J 7
Roundstone, 204 A 5
Roundwood, 260 J 5
Rush, 2,633 J 4
Saint Johnston, 463 F 2
Scarriff, 619 E 6
Schull, 457 B 8
Scotstown, 264 H 3
Shanagolden, 231 C 6
Shannon Airport, 3,657 D 6
Shannon Bridge, 188 F 5
Shercock, 313 G 4
Shillelagh, 246 J 6
Shinrone, 365 F 5
Shrule, 288 C 4
Sixmilebridge, 567 D 6
Skerries, 3,044 J 4
Skibbereen, 2,104 C 8
Slane, 483 H 4
Sligo, 14,080 E 3
Sligo, *14,456 E 3
Sneem, 285 B 8
Spiddal, ‡819 C 5
Stepaside, 748 J 5
Stradbally, Laoighis, 891 G 5
Stradbally, Waterford, 158 F 7
Strokestown, 563 E 4
Swanlinbar, 257 F 3
Swinford, 1,105 C 4
Swords, 4,133 J 5
Taghmon, 369 H 7
Tallaght, 6,174 J 5
Tallow, 883 F 7
Tarbert, 485 C 6
Teltown, ‡739 H 4
Templemore, 2,174 F 6
Templetuohy, 197 F 6
Termonfeckin, 328 J 4
Thomastown, 1,270 G 7
Thurles, 6,840 F 6
Thurles, *7,087 F 6
Timoleague, 257 D 8
Tinahely, 450 H 6
Tipperary, 4,631 E 7
Tipperary, *4,717 E 7
Toomevara, 272 E 6
Tralee, 12,287 B 7
Tralee, *13,263 B 7
Tramore, 3,792 G 7
Trim, 1,700 H 4
Trim, *2,255 H 4
Tuam, 3,808 D 4
Tuam, *4,952 D 4
Tubbercurry, 959 D 3
Tulla, 415 D 6
Tullamore, 6,809 G 5
Tullamore, *7,474 G 5
Tullaroan, ‡301 G 6
Tullow, 1,838 H 6
Tullow, *1,945 H 6
Tynagh, ‡452 E 5
Tyrrellspass, 289 G 5
Urlingford, 652 F 6
Virginia, 583 G 4
Waterford, 31,968 G 7
Waterford, *33,676 G 7
Waterville, 547 A 8
Westport, 3,023 C 4
Wexford, 11,849 H 7
Wexford, *13,293 H 7
Whitegate, 370 E 8
Wicklow, 3,786 K 6
Wicklow, *3,915 K 6
Woodenbridge, ‡620 J 6
Woodford, 198 E 5
Youghal, 5,445 F 8
Youghal, *5,626 F 8

OTHER FEATURES

Achill (isl.), 3,129 A 4
Allen (lake) E 3
Allen, Bog of (marsh) H 5
Aran (isl.), 773 D 2
Aran (isls.), 1,499 B 5
Arklow (bank) K 6
Arrow (lake) E 3
Awbeg (riv.) D 7
Ballinskelligs (bay) A 8
Ballycotton (bay) F 8
Ballyheige (bay) B 7
Ballyhoura (hills) E 7
Ballyteige (bay) H 7
Bandon (riv.) D 8
Bann (riv.) J 6
Bantry (bay) B 8
Barrow (riv.) H 7
Baurtregaum (mt.) A 7
Bear (isl.), 288 B 8
Blacksod (bay) A 3
Blackstairs (mt.) H 6
Blackwater (riv.) D 7
Blackwater (riv.) H 4
Blasket (isls.) A 7
Bloody Foreland (prom.) E 1
Blue Stack (mts.) E 2
Boderg (lake) E 4
Boggeragh (mts.) D 7
Boyne (riv.) J 4
Brandon (head) A 7
Bride (riv.) E 7
Broad Haven (harb.) B 3
Brosna (riv.) F 5
Bull, The (isl.), 5 A 8
Caha (mts.) B 8
Carlingford (inlet) J 3
Carnsore (pt.) J 7
Carrantuohill (mt.) B 7
Clare (riv.) D 5
Clare (isls.), 168 A 4
Clear (cape) B 9
Clear (isl.), 192 C 9
Clew (bay) B 4
Comeragh (mts.) F 7
Conn (lake) C 3
Connacht (prov.), 390,902 C 4
Connemara (dist.), 7,599 B 5
Cork (harb.) E 8
Corrib (lake) C 5
Courtmacsherry (bay) D 8
Curragh, The H 5
Dee (riv.) H 4
Deel (riv.) D 7
Deele (riv.) F 2
Derg (lake) E 6
Derravaragh (lake) G 4
Derryveagh (mts.) E 2
Dingle (bay) A 7
Donegal (bay) D 3
Drum (hills) F 7
Dublin (bay) J 5
Dundalk (bay) J 4
Dunmanus (bay) B 8
Dursey (isl.), 38 A 8
Ennell (lake) G 5
Erne (riv.) E 3
Errigal (mt.) E 1
Erris (head) A 3
Fanad (head) F 1
Fastnet Rock (isl.), 3 B 9
Feale (riv.) C 7
Fergus (riv.) D 6
Finn (riv.) F 2
Finn (riv.) G 3
Flesk (riv.) C 7
Foyle (inlet) G 1
Foyle (riv.) G 2
Galley (head) D 9
Galtee (mts.) E 7
Galtymore (mt.) E 7
Galway (bay) C 5
Gara (lake) D 4
Garadice (lake) F 3
Gill (lake) E 3
Glyde (riv.) H 4
Golden Vale (plain) E 7
Gorumna (isl.), 1,108 B 5
Gowna (lake) G 4
Grand (canal) G 5
Greenore (pt.) J 7
Gweebarra (bay) D 2
Hags (head) B 6
Helvick (head) G 7
Hook (head) H 7
Horn (head) E 1
Iar Connacht (dist.), 10,774 C 5
Inishbofin (isl.), 236 A 4
Inishbofin (isl.), 103 E 1
Inisheer (isl.), 313 B 5
Inishmaan (isl.), 319 C 5
Inishmore (isl.), 864 B 5
Inishowen (head) H 1
Inishowen (pen.), 24,109 G 1
Inishtrahull (isl.), 3 G 1
Inishturk (isls.), 83 A 4
Inny (riv.) A 8
Inny (riv.) F 4
Inver (bay) E 2
Ireland's Eye (isl.) K 5
Irish (sea) K 4
Joyce's Country (dist.), 2,021 B 4
Kenmare (riv.) A 8
Kerry (head) A 7
Key (lake) E 3
Kilkieran (bay) B 5
Killala (bay) C 3
Killary (harb.) A 4
Kinsale (harb.) E 8
Kippure (mt.) J 5
Knockboy (mt.) B 8
Knockmealdown (mts.) F 7
Lady's Island Lake (inlet) J 7
Lambay (isl.), 24 K 4
Laune (riv.) B 7
Leane (lake) B 7
Leane (lake) G 4
Lee (riv.) D 8
Leinster (mt.) H 6
Leinster (prov.), 1,498,140 G 5
Lettermullan (isl.), 221 B 5
Liffey (riv.) H 5
Liscannor (bay) B 6
Long Island (bay) B 9
Loop (head) A 6
Lugnaquillia (mt.) J 5
Macgillicuddy's Reeks (mts.) B 7
Macnean (lake) F 3
Maigue (riv.) D 6
Maine (riv.) C 7
Malin (head) F 1
Mask (lake) C 4
Maumturk (mts.) B 5
Melvin (lake) E 3
Mizen (head) B 9
Moher (cliffs) B 6
Monavullagh (mts.) F 7
Moy (riv.) C 3
Mulkear (riv.) E 6
Mullaghareirk (mts.) C 7
Mulroy (bay) F 1
Munster (prov.), 882,002 D 7
Mweelrea (mt.) B 4
Mweenish (isl.), 198 B 5
Nagles (mts.) E 7
Nenagh (riv.) E 6
Nephin (mt.) C 3
Nore (riv.) G 7
North (sound) B 5
Omey (isl.), 34 A 5
Oughter (lake) G 3
Ovoca (riv.) J 6
Owenmore (riv.) D 3
Owey (isl.), 51 D 1
Paps, The (mt.) C 7
Partry (mts.) C 4
Pollaphuca (res.) J 5
Punchestown H 5
Rathlin O'Birne (isl.), 3 C 2
Ree (lake) F 5
Roaringwater (bay) B 9
Rosses (bay) D 1
Rosskeeragh (pt.) D 3
Royal (canal) G 4
Saint Finan's (bay) A 8
Saint George's (chan.) K 7
Saint John's (pt.) D 2
Saltee (isls.) H 7
Seven (heads) D 8
Seven Hogs, The (isls.) A 7
Shannon (riv.) E 6
Sheeffry (hills) B 4
Sheelin (lake) G 4
Sheep Haven (harb.) F 1
Sheeps (head) B 8
Sherkin (isl.), 82 C 9
Silvermine (mts.) E 6
Slaney (riv.) H 7
Slieve Aughty (mts.) D 5
Slieve Bloom (mts.) F 5
Slieve Gamph (mts.) D 3
Slievenaman (mt.) F 7
Sligo (bay) D 3
Slyne (head) A 5
South (sound) C 5
Stacks (mts.) B 7
Suck (riv.) E 5
Suir (riv.) G 7
Swilly (inlet) F 1
Tara (hill) H 4
Tory (isl.), 273 E 1
Tory (sound) E 1
Tralee (bay) B 7
Trawbreaga (bay) F 1
Ulster (part) (prov.), 207,204 G 2
Valencia (Valentia) (isl.), 770 A 8
Valentia (isl.), 770 A 8
Waterford (harb.) G 7
Wexford (bay) J 7
Wicklow (head) K 6
Wicklow (mts.) J 6
Youghal (bay) F 8

NORTHERN IRELAND

COUNTIES

Antrim, 37,600 J 2
Ards, 52,100 K 2
Armagh, 47,500 H 3
Ballymena, 52,200 J 2
Ballymoney, 22,700 J 1
Bainbridge, 28,800 J 3
Belfast, 368,200 J 2
Carrickfergus, 27,500 K 2
Castlereagh, 63,600 K 2
Coleraine, 44,900 H 1
Cookstown, 27,500 H 2
Craigavon, 71,200 J 3
Down, 48,800 K 3
Dungannon, 43,000 H 3
Fermanagh, 50,900 F 3
Larne, 29,000 K 2
Limavady, 25,000 H 1
Lisburn, 80,800 J 2
Londonderry, 86,600 G 2
Magherafelt, 32,200 H 2
Mourne (Newry and Mourne), 75,300 J 3
Moyle, 13,400 J 1
Newtownabbey, 71,500 J 2
North Down, 59,600 K 2
Omagh, 41,800 G 2
Strabane, 35,500 G 2

CITIES and TOWNS

Ahoghill, ‡1,929 J 2
Annalong, 1,001 K 3
Antrim, 8,351 J 2
Ardglass, 1,052 K 3
Armagh, 13,606 H 3
Armoy, ‡1,051 J 1
Augher, ‡1,986 G
Aughnacloy, ‡1,885 H
Ballycastle, 2,899 J
Ballyclare, 5,155 J
Ballygawley, ‡2,165 G
Ballykelly, 1,116 G
Ballymena, 23,386 J
Ballymoney, 5,697 J
Ballynahinch, 3,485 J
Banbridge, 7,968 J
Bangor, 35,260 K
Belfast (cap.), 353,700 J
Belfast, *551,940 J
Bellaghy, ‡2,265 H
Belleek, ‡2,487 E
Beragh, ‡2,137 G
Bessbrook, 2,619 J
Brookeborough, ‡2,534 G
Broughshane, 1,288 J
Bushmills, 1,288 J
Caledon, ‡1,828 H
Carnlough, 1,416 J
Carrickfergus, 16,603 K
Carrowdore, 2,548 K
Castledawson, 1,162 H
Castlederg, 1,766 F
Castlewellan, 1,488 K
Claudy, ‡2,507 G
Clogher, ‡1,888 G
Coalisland, 3,614 H
Coleraine, 16,354 H
Comber, 5,575 K
Cookstown, 6,965 H
Craigavon, 12,740 J
Crossgar, 1,098 K
Crossmaglen, 1,085 H
Crumlin, 1,450 J
Cullybackey, 1,649 J
Derrygonnelly, ‡2,539 F
Dervock, ‡1,191 J
Donaghadee, 4,008 K
Downpatrick, 7,918 K
Draperstown, ‡2,247 H
Dromore, Bainbridge, 2,848 J
Dromore, Omagh, ‡2,224 G
Drumquin, ‡1,982 F
Dundrum, ‡2,245 K
Dungannon, 8,190 H
Dungiven, 1,536 H
Dunnamanagh, ‡2,242 G
Ederny and Kesh, ‡2,497 F
Enniskillen, 9,679 F
Feeny, ‡1,459 H
Fintona, 1,190 G
Fivemiletown, ‡1,649 G
Garvagh, ‡2,363 H
Gilford, 1,592 J
Glenarm, ‡1,728 J
Glenavy, ‡2,360 J
Glynn, ‡1,872 K
Gortin, ‡2,033 G
Greyabbey, ‡2,646 K
Hillsborough, 1,021 J
Holywood, 9,892 K
Irvinestown, 1,457 F
Keady, 2,145 H
Kells, ‡2,560 J
Kesh, ‡2,497 F
Kilkeel, 4,090 K
Killough, ‡3,295 K
Killyleagh, 2,359 K
Kilrea, 1,196 H
Kircubbin, 1,075 K
Larne, 18,482 K
Limavady, 6,004 H
Lisburn, 31,836 J
Lisnaskea, 1,443 G
Londonderry, 51,200 G
Loughbrickland, ‡2,056 J
Maghera, 2,085 H
Magherafelt, 4,704 H
Markethill, ‡2,352 H
Millisle, 1,172 K
Moneymore, 1,178 H
Moy, ‡2,349 H
Moygashel, 1,086 H
Newcastle, 4,647 J
Newry, 20,279 J
Newtownabbey, 58,114 K
Newtownards, 15,484 K
Newtownbutler, ‡2,663 G
Newtownhamilton, ‡1,936 H
Newtownstewart, 1,433 G
Omagh, 14,594 G
Pomeroy, ‡1,786 H
Portaferry, 1,730 K
Portavogie, 1,310 K
Portglenone, ‡2,061 H
Portrush, 5,376 H
Portstewart, 5,085 H
Randalstown, 2,799 J
Rathfriland, 1,886 J
Rostrevor, 1,617 J
Saintfield, ‡2,198 K
Sion Mills, 1,588 G
Sixmilecross, ‡1,980 G
Stewartstown, ‡1,759 H
Strabane, 9,413 G
Strangford, ‡1,987 K
Tandragee, 1,725 J
Tempo, ‡2,282 G
Trillick, ‡2,167 G
Warrenpoint, 4,291 J
Whitehead, 2,642 K

OTHER FEATURES

Bann (riv.) H
Belfast (inlet) K
Blackwater (riv.) H
Bush (riv.) H
Derg (riv.) F
Divis (mt.) J
Dundrum (bay) K
Erne (lake) F
Foyle (inlet) G
Foyle (riv.) G
Giant's Causeway H
Lagan (riv.) K
Larne (inlet) K
Magee, Island (pen.), 1,581 K
Magilligan (pt.) H
Main (riv.) J
Mourne (mts.) J
Mourne (riv.) G
Neagh (lake) J
North (chan.) K
Rathlin (isl.), 109 J
Red (bay) K
Roe (riv.) H
Saint John's (pt.) K
Slieve Donard (mt.) K
Sperrin (mts.) G
Strangford (inlet) K
Torr (head) K
Ulster (part) (prov.), 1,537,200 G
Upper Lough Erne (lake) F

*City and suburbs.
‡Population of district.

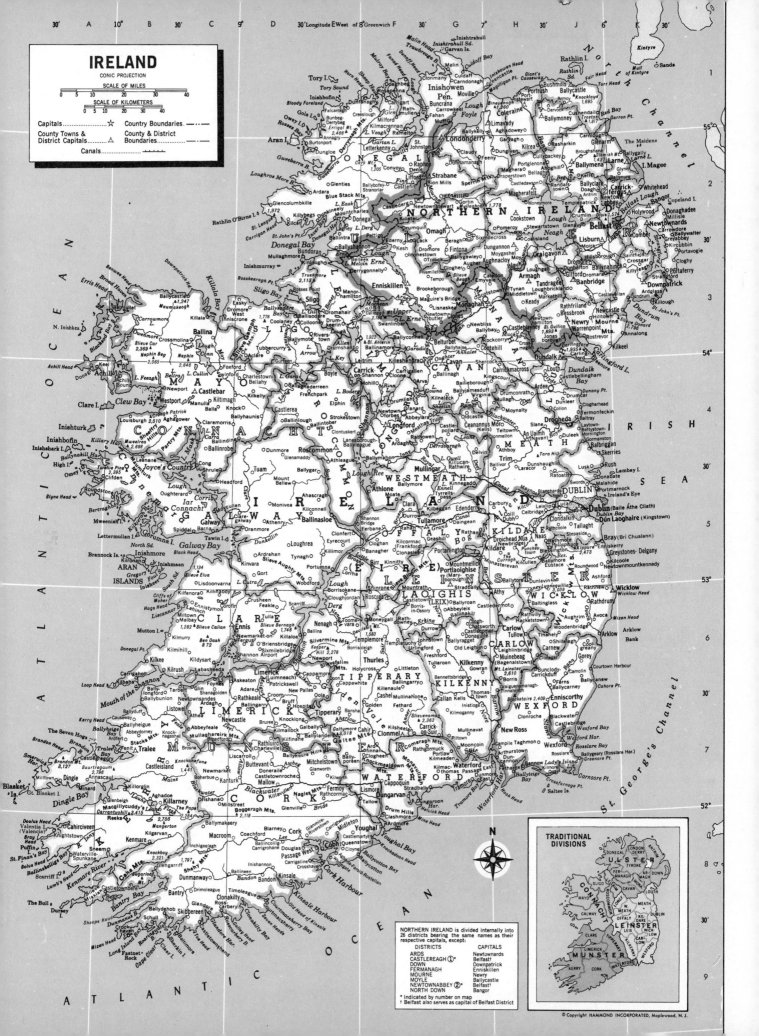

SVALBARD

STOCKHOLM

NORWEGIAN SEA

ATLANTIC OCEAN

ARCTIC OCEAN

BARENTS SEA

NORWAY, SWEDEN,
FINLAND and DENMARK

CONIC PROJECTION

SCALE OF MILES

SCALE OF KILOMETRES

SUBDIVISIONS
indicated by Numbers

Fylker in NORWAY
1 Akershus G6
2 Vestfold G7
3 Østfold G7
4 Oslo G7
5 Bergen D6
Oslo is the administrative
center for Akershus and
Oslo Fylker; Bergen for
Hordaland and Bergen
Fylker.

Län in SWEDEN
6 Göteborg och ... G7
Bohus
7 Västmanland K7
8 Södermanland ... K7
9 Östergötland J7
10 Malmöhus H9
11 Kristianstad J8

Capitals of Countries .... ☆
Administrative Centers .... △
International Boundaries .... ——
Internal Boundaries .... — · —
Canals ....

© C. S. HAMMOND & Co., N. Y.

NORWAY

REA 125,181 sq. mi.
OPULATION 3,893,000
APITAL Oslo
ARGEST CITY Oslo
IGHEST POINT Glittertind 8,110 ft.
ONETARY UNIT krone (crown)
AJOR LANGUAGE Norwegian
AJOR RELIGION Protestantism

SWEDEN

AREA 173,665 sq. mi.
POPULATION 7,978,000
CAPITAL Stockholm
LARGEST CITY Stockholm
HIGHEST POINT Kebnekaise 6,946 ft.
MONETARY UNIT krona (crown)
MAJOR LANGUAGE Swedish
MAJOR RELIGION Protestantism

FINLAND

AREA 130,128 sq. mi.
POPULATION 4,706,000
CAPITAL Helsinki
LARGEST CITY Helsinki
HIGHEST POINT Mt. Haltia 4,343 ft.
MONETARY UNIT Markka (Mark)
MAJOR LANGUAGES Finnish, Swedish
MAJOR RELIGION Protestantism

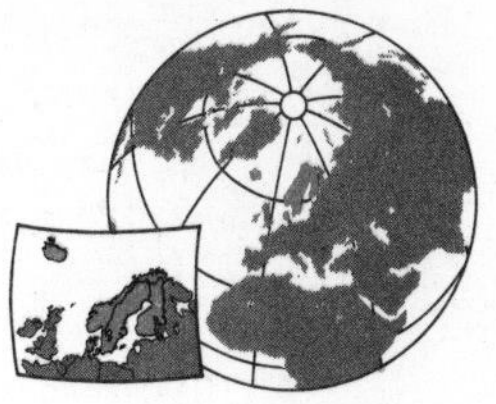

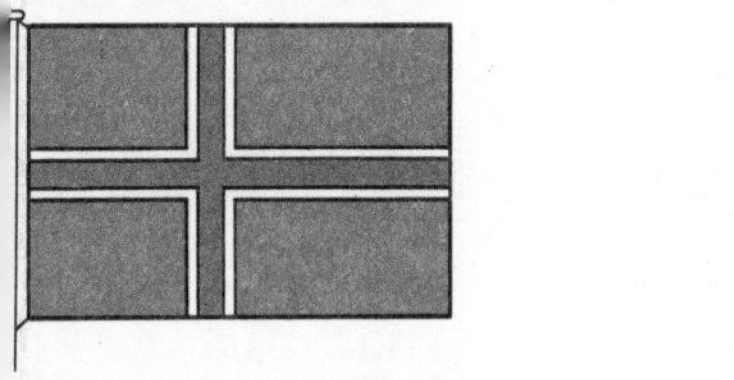

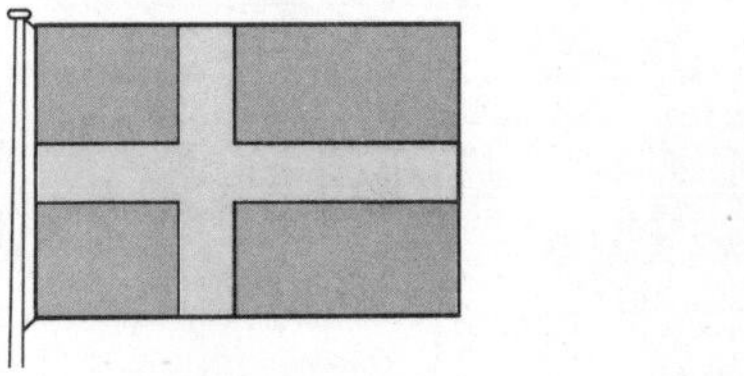

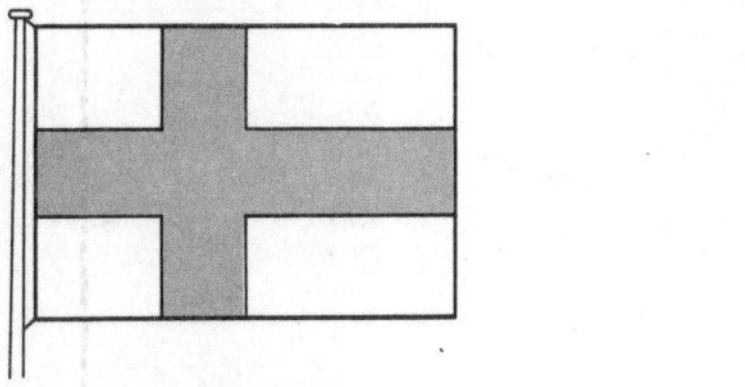

FINLAND

PROVINCES

hvenanmaa, 21,584 ....L 6
äme, 623,756 ....O 6
eski-Suomi, 248,599 ....O 5
uopio, 265,434 ....P 5
ymi, 348,989 ....Q 6
appi, 220,755 ....P 3
likkeli, 225,685 ....P 6
ulu, 422,828 ....P 4
ohjois-Karjala, 193,199 ....Q 5
urku-Pori, 680,713 ....N 6
usimaa, 999,053 ....O 6
aasa, 447,785 ....N 5

CITIES and TOWNS

änekoski, 10,977 ....O 5
bo (Turku), 155,000 ....N 6
Alavus (Alavo), †11,139 ....N 5
Björneborg (Pori), 71,972 ....M 6
Borgå (Porvoo), 15,738 ....O 6
Brahestad (Raahe), 7,637 ....O 4
Ekenäs (Tammisaari), 6,401 ....N 6
Espoo (Esbo), 88,086 ....O 6
Forssa, 15,260 ....N 6
Fredrikshamn (Hamina), 10,872 ....P 6
Gamlakarleby (Kokkola), 20,715 ....N 5
Haapajärvi, 8,943 ....O 5
Haapamäki, 2,200 ....O 5
Hämeenlinna (Tavastehus), 37,333 ....O 6
Hamina, 10,872 ....P 6
Hangö (Hanko), 9,668 ....N 7
Harjavalta, 8,191 ....N 6
Heinola, 13,696 ....P 6
Helsinki (Helsingfors) (cap.), 531,286 ....O 6
Helsinki, *700,000 ....O 6
Himanka, †3,260 ....N 5
Hyrynsalmi, †5,629 ....Q 4
Hyvinkää (Hyvinge), 33,062 ....O 6
Iisalmi, 7,551 ....P 5
Ilomantsi, †12,050 ....R 5
Imatra, 35,054 ....Q 6
Ivalo ....P 2
Jakobstad (Pietarsaari), 19,114 ....N 5
Joensuu, 35,385 ....R 5
Juuka, †9,925 ....Q 5
Jyväskylä, 56,824 ....O 5
Kajaani, 19,131 ....P 4
Kalajoki, †7,314 ....N 4
Karis (Karjaa), 7,940 ....N 6
Karkkila, 8,504 ....N 6
Kaskö (Kaskinen), 1,436 ....M 5
Kauttua ....M 6
Kemi, 30,199 ....O 4
Kemijärvi, 6,546 ....P 3
Kerava (Kervo), 13,322 ....O 6
Kittilä, †8,347 ....O 3
Kokemäki, †10,922 ....N 6
Kokkola (Gamlakarleby), 20,715 ....N 5
Kotka, 33,953 ....P 6
Kouvola, 25,275 ....P 6
Kristiinankaupunki (Kristinestad), 2,726 ....N 5
Kuhmo, †14,847 ....Q 4
Kuopio, 63,800 ....Q 5
Kurikka, 11,373 ....M 5
Kuusamo, †20,324 ....Q 4
Lahti, 87,237 ....O 6
Lappeenranta, 50,543 ....P 6
Lieksa, 4,703 ....R 5
Loimaa, 6,366 ....N 6
Lovisa (Loviisa), 6,695 ....P 6
Maarianhamina (Mariehamn), 8,512 ....M 7
Mänttä, 7,277 ....O 6
Mariehamn (Maarianhamina), 8,512 ....M 7
Mikkeli (Sankt Michel), 24,962 ....P 6
Muonio, †3,226 ....O 3
Naantali (Nådendal), 6,784 ....M 6
Nivala, †10,784 ....O 5
Nokia, 19,200 ....N 6
Nurmes, 2,329 ....Q 5
Nykarleby (Uusikaarlepyy), 1,289 ....N 5
Nyslott (Savonlinna), 17,618 ....Q 6
Nystad (Uusikaupunki), 6,845....M 6
Oulainen, 7,898 ....O 4
Oulu (Uleåborg), 85,094 ....O 4
Outokumpu, 10,862 ....Q 5
Parikkala, †7,052 ....Q 6
Parkano, †8,587 ....N 6
Pello, †7,139 ....O 3
Pieksämäki, 12,821 ....P 5
Pietarsaari (Jakobstad), 19,114 ....N 5
Pori (Björneborg), 71,972 ....M 6
Porvoo (Borgå), 15,738 ....O 6
Posio, †7,454 ....Q 3
Pudasjärvi, †15,622 ....P 4
Raahe (Brahestad), 7,637 ....O 4
Rauma (Raumo), 25,218 ....M 6
Riihimäki, 22,442 ....O 6
Rovaniemi, 28,680 ....O 3
Saarijärvi, †11,586 ....O 5
Salo, 16,715 ....N 6
Sankt Michel (Mikkeli), 24,962..P 6
Savonlinna, 17,618 ....Q 6
Savukoski, †2,392 ....Q 3
Seinäjoki, 19,836 ....N 5
Sodankylä, †11,745 ....P 3
Sotkamo, †14,127 ....Q 4
Suolahti, 5,563 ....O 5
Suomussalmi, †15,507 ....Q 4
Suonenjoki, 10,012 ....P 5
Tammerfors (Tampere), 156,100 ....N 6
Tammisaari (Ekenäs), 6,401 ....N 6
Tampere (Tammerfors), 156,000 ....N 6
Tapiola ....O 6
Tavastehus (Hämeenlinna), 37,333 ....O 6
Teuva, †8,280 ....N 5
Toijala, 7,505 ....N 6
Tornio (Torneå), 7,325 ....O 4
Turku (Åbo), 155,000 ....N 6
Uleåborg (Oulu), 85,094 ....O 4
Ulvila (Ulvsby), †7,800 ....N 6
Utsjoki, †1,436 ....P 2
Uusikaarlepyy (Nykarleby), 1,289 ....N 5
Uusikaupunki (Nystad), 6,845...M 6
Vaala, †6,675 ....P 4
Vaasa (Vasa), 49,109 ....M 5
Valkeakoski, 15,949 ....N 6
Vammala, 5,605 ....N 6
Varkaus, 24,619 ....Q 5
Vasa (Vaasa), 48,262 ....M 5

OTHER FEATURES

Ahvenanmaa (Åland) (isls.), 21,584 ....L 6
Finland (gulf) ....P 7
Haltia (mt.) ....M 2
Hangöudd (prom.) ....N 7
Hauki (lake) ....Q 5
Ii (river) ....O 4
Inari (lake) ....P 2
Juo (lake) ....Q 5
Kala (river) ....O 4
Kalla (lake) ....P 5
Keitele (lake) ....O 5
Kemi (lake) ....Q 3
Kemi (river) ....O 3
Kianta (lake) ....Q 4
Kilpis (lake) ....M 2
Kitinen (river) ....P 3
Kivi (lake) ....O 5
Koitere (lake) ....R 5
Kuusamo (lake) ....Q 4
Längelmä (lake) ....O 6
Lapland (reg.) ....O 2
Lapuan (river) ....N 5
Lesti (lake) ....O 5
Lokka (res.) ....P 3
Muo (lake) ....R 4
Muonio (river) ....M 2
Nasi (lake) ....O 6
Onkivesi (lake) ....P 5
Orihvesi (lake) ....Q 5
Oulu (river) ....O 4
Ounas (river) ....O 3
Päijänne (lake) ....O 6
Pasvik (river) ....Q 2
Pielinen (lake) ....Q 5
Puru (lake) ....Q 6
Puula (lake) ....P 5
Pyhä (lake) ....M 6
Pyhä (lake) ....O 5
Saimaa (lake) ....Q 6
Siika (river) ....O 4
Simo (lake) ....P 3
Simo (river) ....O 4
Tana (Teno) (river) ....P 2
Tornio (river) ....O 3
Vallgrund (isl.), 2,063 ....M 5
Ylikitka (lake) ....Q 3

NORWAY

COUNTIES

Akershus, 282,928 ....D 4
Aust-Agder, 78,184 ....E 7
Bergen, 117,465 ....D 6
Buskerud, 191,789 ....F 6
Finnmark, 75,553 ....O 2
Hedmark, 177,300 ....G 6
Hordaland, 243,545 ....E 6
Møre og Romsdal, 219,384 ....E 5
Nord-Trøndelag, 117,376 ....H 4
Nordland, 244,165 ....J 3
Oppland, 168,819 ....F 6
Oslo (city), 485,200 ....D 3
Østfold, 212,450 ....D 4
Rogaland, 256,501 ....E 7
Sogn og Fjordane, 100,711 ....E 6
Sør-Trøndelag, 224,654 ....G 5
Telemark, 155,834 ....F 7
Troms, 132,407 ....L 2
Vest-Agder, 117,226 ....E 7
Vestfold, 167,778 ....D 4

CITIES and TOWNS

Åfjord, †4,105 ....G 5
Ål, †4,377 ....F 6
Ålesund, 18,558 ....D 5
Åndalsnes, 2,202 ....F 5
Arendal, 11,579 ....F 7
Askim, †9,673 ....E 4
Bamble, †8,338 ....F 7
Barentsburg ....C 2
Bergen, 117,465 ....D 6
Bergen, *270,000 ....D 6
Bodø, 14,048 ....J 3
Borre, 6,636 ....D 4
Drammen, 47,261 ....C 4
Drammen, *48,700 ....C 4
Drøbak, 2,683 ....D 4
Eigersund, 9,730 ....D 7
Elverum, †13,604 ....G 6
Farsund, 7,697 ....E 7
Flekkefjord, 8,616 ....E 7
Flora, 7,836 ....D 6
Fredrikstad, 30,006 ....D 4
Gjøvik, 24,256 ....G 6
Grimstad, 2,610 ....F 7
Gulen, †3,212 ....D 6
Halden, 10,006 ....G 7
Hamar, 14,712 ....G 6
Hammerfest, 6,806 ....N 1
Harstad, 18,892 ....K 2
Haugesund, 27,569 ....D 7
Holmestrand, 6,857 ....C 4
Honningsvåg, 2,813 ....O 1
Horten, 13,387 ....D 4
Kirkenes, 4,433 ....Q 2
Kongsberg, 17,578 ....F 7
Kongsvinger, 13,080 ....H 6
Kragerø, †10,067 ....F 7
Kristiansand, 52,542 ....F 8
Kristiansand, *54,900 ....F 8
Kristiansund, 18,466 ....E 5
Kvinnherad, †9,848 ....E 6
Larvik, 10,728 ....C 4
Lenvik, †10,209 ....L 2
Lesja, †2,755 ....F 5
Lillehammer, 19,808 ....F 6
Lillesand, †4,975 ....F 7
Lillestrøm, 10,547 ....E 3
Løkken, †5,054 ....F 5
Longyearbyen ....D 2
Lysaker, 5,393 ....D 3
Mandal, 10,622 ....E 7
Mo, 8,348 ....J 3
Molde, 17,862 ....E 5
Moss, 23,198 ....D 4
Mysen, 2,500 ....G 7
Namsos, 10,998 ....G 4
Narvik, 13,543 ....K 2
Nesttun, 3,827 ....D 6
Notodden, 13,680 ....F 7
Odda, †10,444 ....E 6
Orkanger, 2,874 ....F 5
Oslo (cap.), 483,196 ....D 3
Oslo, *635,700 ....D 3
Porsgrunn, 28,167 ....G 7
Ringerike, 28,577 ....C 3
Risør, 6,110 ....F 7
Rjukan, 6,308 ....F 7
Røros, †5,259 ....G 5
Sandefjord, 6,085 ....C 4
Sandnes, 28,534 ....D 7
Sandvika, 3,751 ....C 3
Sarpsborg, 13,185 ....D 4
Ski, †12,337 ....D 4
Skien, 47,302 ....F 7
Skjåk, †2,692 ....F 6
Stavanger, 79,700 ....D 7
Stavanger, *80,800 ....D 7
Stavern, 2,148 ....D 4
Steinkjer, 19,874 ....G 4
Stor-Elvdal, †4,151 ....G 6
Sulitjelma, 2,129 ....K 3
Sunndalsøra, 2,376 ....F 5
Svolvaer, 3,812 ....J 2
Tana, †3,286 ....Q 1
Telemark ....C 4
Tønsberg, 11,566 ....D 4
Tromsø, 34,600 ....L 2
Trondheim, 118,703 ....F 5
Trondheim, *123,600 ....F 5
Ullensvang, †4,940 ....E 6
Vadsø, 5,320 ....Q 1
Vardø, 4,185 ....R 1
Volda, 2,647 ....E 5
Voss, †13,473 ....E 6

OTHER FEATURES

Alst (fjord) ....G 3
Alsten (isl.), 4,348 ....H 4
Alta (river) ....N 2
Alte (lake) ....L 2
Ands (fjord) ....K 2
Bardu (river) ....L 2
Barentsöya (isl.) ....D 2
Bellsund (bay) ....C 2
Bjørna (fjord) ....D 6
Bjørnøya (isl.) ....D 3
Bokn (fjord) ....D 7
Bremanger (isl.), 2,028 ....D 6
Dønna (isl.), 1,978 ....H 3
Dovrefjeld (mts.) ....F 5
Edgeøya (isl.) ....E 2
Femund (lake) ....G 5
Folda (fjord) ....G 4
Folda (fjord) ....J 3
Frohavet (bay) ....F 5
Frøya (isl.), 4,034 ....F 5
Glittertind (mt.) ....F 6
Glomma (river) ....G 6
Hadsel (fjord) ....J 2
Hardanger (fjord) ....D 7
Hardanger (mts.) ....E 6
Hinlopen (strait) ....C 1
Hinnøy (isl.), 27,599 ....K 2
Hitra (isl.), 3,134 ....F 5
Hopen (isl.) ....E 2
Hornsund (bay) ....C 2
Hortens (fjord) ....G 4
Is (fjord) ....B 2
Jostedals (glacier) ....E 6
Karmøy (isl.), 19,234 ....D 7
Kob (fjord) ....O 1
Kong Karls Land (isls.) ....E 1
Kvaløy (isl.), 6,869 ....O 1
Lagen (river) ....G 6
Lakse (fjord) ....P 1
Langøy (isl.), 16,500 ....J 2
Lapland (reg.) ....K 2
Lindesnes (cape) ....E 8
Lista (pen.), 7,702 ....E 7
Lofoten (isls.), 28,980 ....H 2
Lopphavet (bay) ....M 1
Magerøy (isl.), 5,545 ....P 1
Mohn (cape) ....E 1
Moskenesøy (isl.), 2,318 ....H 3
Namsen (river) ....H 4
Nord (fjord) ....E 6
Nordaustlandet (isl.) ....D 1
Nordkyn (cape) ....Q 1
North (cape) ....P 1
Norwegian (sea) ....F 3
Ofot (fjord) ....K 2
Otter (river) ....E 7
Pasvik (river) ....Q 2
Platen (cape) ....D 1
Porsanger (fjord) ....O 1
Rana (river) ....J 3
Ran (fjord) ....H 3
Rauma (river) ....F 5
Reisa (river) ....M 2
Ringvassøy (isl.), 1,472 ....L 2
Romsdals (fjord) ....E 5
Salt (fjord) ....J 3
Seiland (isl.), 769 ....N 1
Senja (isl.), 10,541 ....K 2
Skagerrak (strait) ....E 8
Smøla (isl.), 2,840 ....E 5
Snåsa (lake) ....H 4
Sogne (fjord) ....D 6
Sørkapp (cape) ....C 2
Sørøy (isl.), 2,350 ....N 1
South Kvaløy (isl.), 3,444 ....K 2
Spitsbergen (isl.) ....C 2
Steinneset (cape) ....E 2
Stor (fjord) ....D 2
Sunn (fjord) ....D 6
Tana (river) ....P 1
Tjuv (fjord) ....D 2
Tunn (lake) ....H 4
Tyri (fjord) ....C 3
Vågå (lake) ....F 6
Vannøy (isl.), 1,112 ....L 1
Varanger (fjord) ....Q 1
Vega (isl.) ....G 4
Vest (fjord) ....H 3

(continued on following page)

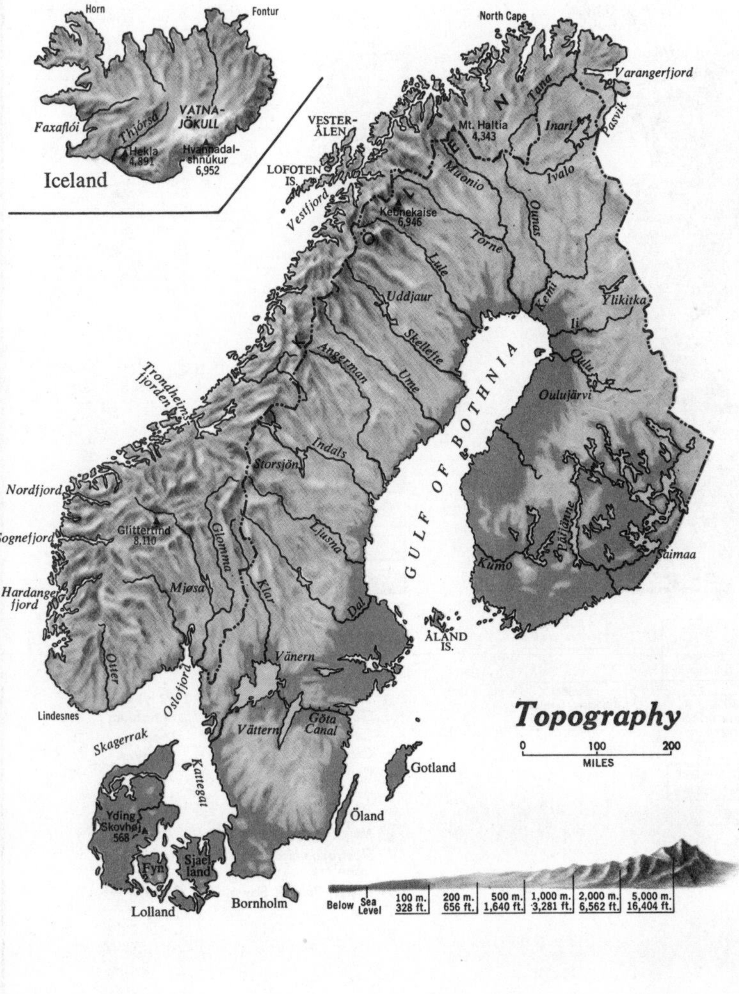
Horn
Fontur
Faxaflói
Thjórsá
VATNAJÖKULL
Hekla 4,891
Hvannadalshnúkur 6,952
Iceland
North Cape
Varangerfjord
Tana
Pasvik
Inari
Mt. Haltia 4,343
Ivalo
Muonio
Ounas
VESTERÅLEN
LOFOTEN IS.
Vestfjord
Kebnekaise 6,946
Torne
Lule
Kemi
Ylikitka
Uddjaur
Ii
Skellefte
Oulu
Ångerman
Ume
GULF OF BOTHNIA
Oulujärvi
Trondheimsfjorden
Indals
Storsjön
Nordfjord
Sognefjord
Glittertind 8,110
Ljusna
Glomma
Klar
Mjøsa
Hardangerfjord
Päijänne
Kumo
Saimaa
Dal
ÅLAND IS.
Vänern
Otter
Lindesnes
Oslofjord
Topography
0 100 200
MILES
Vättern
Göta Canal
Skagerrak
Kattegat
Gotland
Öland
Yding Skovhøj 568
Fyn
Sjælland
Lolland
Bornholm
Below Sea Level
100 m. 328 ft.
200 m. 656 ft.
500 m. 1,640 ft.
1,000 m. 3,281 ft.
2,000 m. 6,562 ft.
5,000 m. 16,404 ft.

NORWAY (continued)

Vesterålen (isls.), 34,385 ....J 2
Vestvågøy (isl.), 11,749 ....H 3
Vikna (isl.), 3,411 ....G 4

SWEDEN

COUNTIES

Älvsborg, 391,851 ....H 7
Blekinge, 150,901 ....J 8
Gävleborg, 294,916 ....K 6
Göteborg och Bohus, 685,449 ....G 7
Gotland, 50,438 ....L 8
Halland, 185,810 ....H 8
Jämtland, 121,552 ....J 5
Jönköping, 292,303 ....H 8
Kalmar, 234,175 ....K 8
Kopparberg, 270,971 ....J 6
Kristianstad, 258,295 ....J 8
Kronoberg, 164,309 ....J 8
Malmöhus, 683,752 ....H 9
Norrbotten, 261,410 ....L 3
örebro, 259,794 ....J 7
östergötland, 369,374 ....J 7
Skaraborg, 248,970 ....H 7
Södermanland, 239,451 ....K 7
Stockholm, 1,406,580 ....L 7
Uppsala, 191,821 ....K 6
Värmland, 273,139 ....H 7
Västerbotten, 235,307 ....K 4
Västernorrland, 277,715 ....K 5
Västmanland, 255,142 ....K 7

CITIES and TOWNS

Åhus, 4,758 ....J 9
Alingsås, 19,810 ....H 7
Älmhult, 6,023 ....H 8
Alvesta, 8,957 ....J 8
Älvsbyn, 4,343 ....M 4
Åmål, 9,397 ....H 7
Anderstorp, 3,960 ....H 8
Ånge, 4,000 ....J 5
Ängelholm, 13,985 ....H 8
Arboga, 12,266 ....J 7
Årjäng, 2,893 ....H 7
Arvidsjaur, 7,767 ....L 4
Arvika, 15,901 ....H 7
Åseda, 3,629 ....J 8
Åsele, 4,727 ....K 4
Åtvidaberg, 9,010 ....K 7
Avesta, 29,232 ....J 6
Båstad, 2,202 ....H 8
Bengtsfors, 3,411 ....H 7
Boden, 24,912 ....M 4
Bollnäs, 17,123 ....K 6
Borås, 70,238 ....H 8
Borlänge, 29,097 ....J 6
Bräcke, 2,658 ....J 5
Brunflo, 2,700 ....J 5
Bureå, 4,583 ....M 4
Burträsk, 6,747 ....M 4
Charlottenberg, 3,112 ....H 6
Danderyd, 15,657 ....H 1
Djursholm, 7,681 ....H 1
Dorotea, 3,964 ....K 4
Edsbyn, 7,132 ....J 6
Eksjö, 9,897 ....J 8
Emmaboda, 3,697 ....J 8
Enköping, 17,684 ....G 1
Eskilstuna, 65,580 ....K 7
Eslöv, 14,737 ....H 9
Fagersta, 16,609 ....J 6
Falkenberg, 12,920 ....H 8
Falköping, 16,032 ....H 7
Falun, 33,840 ....J 6
Filipstad, 7,559 ....H 7
Finspång, 17,616 ....J 7
Flen, 9,112 ....K 7
Forshaga, 4,655 ....H 7
Frösö, 9,520 ....J 5
Frövi, 3,082 ....J 7
Gällivare, 9,718 ....M 3
Gamleby, 3,949 ....K 8
Gävle, 60,868 ....K 6
Gnesta, 3,275 ....G 2
Göteborg, 444,131 ....G 8
Göteborg, *647,122 ....G 8
Gränna, 3,195 ....J 8
Hagfors, 8,964 ....H 6
Hällefors, 12,011 ....J 7
Hallsberg, 12,121 ....J 7
Hallstahammar, 14,099 ....K 7
Halmstad, 46,655 ....H 8
Hälsingborg, 80,801 ....H 8
Haparanda, 9,429 ....N 4
Härnösand, 16,637 ....L 5
Hässleholm, 16,031 ....H 8
Hedemora, 17,744 ....K 6
Hjo, 4,783 ....J 7
Höganäs, 13,846 ....H 8
Holmsund, 5,778 ....M 5
Hudiksvall, 16,057 ....K 6
Hultsfred, 4,979 ....K 8
Huskvarna, 18,198 ....J 8
Järna, 4,591 ....G 2
Järpen, 2,962 ....H 5
Järvsö, 4,850 ....K 6
Jokkmokk, 4,869 ....L 3
Jönköping, 53,774 ....H 8
Jörn, 4,275 ....M 4
Kalmar, 37,938 ....K 8
Karlshamn, 12,351 ....J 8
Karlskoga, 38,284 ....J 7
Karlskrona, 37,358 ....K 8
Karlstad, 54,321 ....H 7
Katrineholm, 21,660 ....K 7
Kinna, 6,386 ....H 8
Kiruna, 29,210 ....L 3
Kisa, 4,353 ....J 8
Köping, 20,807 ....J 7
Kopparberg, 7,985 ....J 7
Kramfors, 11,729 ....K 5
Kristianstad, 27,527 ....J 9
Kristinehamn, 21,925 ....H 7
Kumla, 15,039 ....J 7
Kungälv, 11,213 ....G 8
Kungsbacka, 7,205 ....G 8
Laholm, 3,853 ....H 8
Landskrona, 32,079 ....H 9
Långsele, 4,640 ....K 5
Långshyttan, 3,124 ....K 6
Laxå, 9,498 ....J 7
Leksand, 8,608 ....J 6
Lidingö, 35,400 ....H 1
Lidköping, 19,700 ....H 7
Lindesberg, 6,863 ....J 7
Linköping, 77,881 ....K 7
Ljungby, 11,930 ....J 8
Ljusdal, 10,630 ....J 6
Ljusne, 4,808 ....K 6
Ludvika, 21,989 ....J 6
Luleå, 36,428 ....N 4
Lund, 50,494 ....H 9
Lycksele, 6,333 ....L 4
Lysekil, 8,000 ....G 7
Malmberget, 12,384 ....M 3
Malmköping, 3,450 ....F 1
Malmö, 256,064 ....H 9
Malmö, *428,338 ....H 9
Markaryd, 5,980 ....H 8
Mariefred, 2,502 ....G 1
Mariestad, 15,700 ....H 7
Mellerud, 4,317 ....H 7
Mjölby, 12,790 ....J 7
Mölndal, 31,072 ....H 8
Mönsterås, 6,687 ....K 8
Mora, 13,307 ....J 6
Motala, 27,907 ....J 7
Nacka, 25,798 ....H 1
Nässjö, 20,000 ....J 8
Nora, 9,215 ....J 7
Norberg, 6,160 ....K 6
Norrköping, 94,296 ....K 7
Norrsundet, 4,575 ....K 6
Norrtälje, 11,803 ....L 7
Norsjö, 5,171 ....L 4
Nybro, 10,956 ....J 8
Nyköping, 31,195 ....K 7
Nynäshamn, 10,676 ....L 7
Ockelbo, 5,819 ....K 6
Olofström, 16,218 ....J 8
örbyhus, 2,266 ....K 6
örebro, 86,977 ....J 7
öregrund, 2,026 ....L 6
örnsköldsvik, 16,539 ....L 5
Oskarshamn, 24,873 ....K 8
östersund, 26,600 ....J 5
östhammar, 8,858 ....L 6
övertorneå, 3,589 ....N 3
överum, 2,533 ....K 7
Oxelösund, 14,835 ....K 7
Pajala, 3,871 ....N 3
Piteå, 8,476 ....M 4
Ramnäs, 4,092 ....J 7
Ramsele, 4,547 ....K 5
Rättvik, 7,551 ....J 6
Rimbo, 3,426 ....L 7
Ronneby, 10,125 ....J 8
Ryd, 4,100 ....J 8
Säffle, 12,599 ....H 7
Sala, 11,800 ....K 7
Saltsjöbaden, 6,507 ....J 1
Sandviken, 25,476 ....K 6
Säter, 4,629 ....J 6
Sävsjö, 5,547 ....J 8
Sigtuna, 3,970 ....H 1
Simrishamn, 7,966 ....J 9
Skänninge, 4,482 ....J 7
Skara, 10,376 ....H 7
Skellefteå, 61,880 ....M 4
Skövde, 27,976 ....H 7
Smedjebacken, 10,504 ....J 6
Söderhamn, 13,778 ....K 6
Söderköping, 5,954 ....K 7
Södertälje, 52,601 ....G 1
Sollefteå, 9,715 ....K 5
Sollentuna, 35,038 ....H 1
Solna, 57,707 ....H 1
Sölvesborg, 6,782 ....J 9
Sorsele, 3,550 ....K 4
Stockholm (cap.), 756,697 ....G 1
Stockholm, *1,288,769 ....G 1
Storvik, 2,432 ....K 6
Strängnäs, 9,506 ....F 1
Strömstad, 9,817 ....G 7
Strömsund, 6,058 ....K 5
Sundbyberg, 28,773 ....G 1
Sundsvall, 62,222 ....K 5
Sunne, 11,018 ....H 7
Sveg, 4,975 ....J 5
Svenljunga, 2,925 ....H 8
Täby, 33,694 ....H 1
Tidaholm, 7,250 ....J 7
Tierp, 4,303 ....K 6
Tillberga, 270 ....K 7
Timrå, 12,800 ....K 5
Tomelilla, 6,349 ....J 9
Torsby, 6,796 ....H 6
Torshälla, 7,939 ....K 7
Tranås, 18,845 ....J 7
Trelleborg, 35,249 ....H 9
Trollhättan, 40,945 ....H 7
Uddevalla, 36,510 ....G 7
Ulricehamn, 8,504 ....H 8
Umeå, 51,955 ....M 5
Uppsala, 97,315 ....L 7
Vadstena, 6,893 ....J 7
Vaggeryd, 4,840 ....J 8
Valdemarsvik, 3,590 ....K 7
Vänersborg, 19,975 ....H 7
Vännäs, 4,045 ....L 5
Vansbro, 2,941 ....H 6
Vara, 11,056 ....H 7
Varberg, 18,451 ....G 8
Värnamo, 15,939 ....J 8
Västerås, 110,539 ....J 7
Västerhaninge, 9,814 ....H 1
Västervik, 23,014 ....K 8
Vaxholm, 4,322 ....J 1
Vaxjö, 32,760 ....J 8
Vetlanda, 10,780 ....J 8
Vilhelmina, 9,426 ....K 4
Vimmerby, 7,257 ....J 8
Virserum, 4,650 ....J 8
Visby, 18,338 ....L 8
Vislanda, 2,594 ....H 8
Wallhamn ....G 7
Ystad, 14,002 ....H 9

OTHER FEATURES

Angerman (river) ....K 5
Asnen (lake) ....J 8
Bothnia (gulf) ....M 5
Byske (river) ....L 4
Fårö (isl.), 790 ....L 8
Göta (river) ....H 7
Gotland (isl.), 50,438 ....L 8
Hornslandet (pen.) ....K 6
Kalix (river) ....N 3
Kalmarsund (sound) ....K 8
Kattegat (strait) ....G 8
Kebnekaise (mt.) ....L 3
Lainio (river) ....N 3
Lapland (dist.) ....K 2
Lule (river) ....M 3
Muonio (river) ....M 2
öland (isl.), 20,416 ....K 8
Ornö (isl.), 224 ....J 1
österdal (river) ....H 6
Pite (river) ....M 4
Skellefte (river) ....L 4
Stora Lulevatten (lake) ....L 3
Storuman (lake) ....K 4
Sulitjelma (mt.) ....K 3
Torne (river) ....M 3
Torneträsk (lake) ....L 2
Uddjaur (lake) ....L 4
Ume (river) ....L 4
Vänern (lake) ....H 7
Vättern (lake) ....J 7
Vesterdal (river) ....H 6
Vindel (river) ....L 4
Vojmsjön (lakes) ....J 4

City and suburbs.
†Population of parish or commune.

DENMARK

INTERNAL DIVISIONS

Århus (county), 525,167 ....D 5
Bornholm (county), 47,405 ....F 9
Copenhagen (commune), 634,500 ....F 6
Færøe Islands, 38,000 ....B 2
Frederiksberg (commune), 102,751 ....F 6
Frederiksborg (county), 252,557 ....F 5
Fyn (county), 430,958 ....D 7
København (Copenhagen) (commune), 634,500 ....F 6
København (county), 609,469 .....F 6
Nordjylland (county), 455,062 ....D 4
Ribe (county), 196,894 ....B 6
Ringkøbing (county), 240,014 ....B 5
Roskilde (county), 147,434 ....E 6
Sønderjylland (county), 237,270 ....C 7
Storstrøm (county), 251,815 ......E 7
Vejle (county), 304,358 ....C 6
Vestsjælland (county), 256,997 ....E 6
Viborg (county), 220,214 ....B 4

CITIES and TOWNS

Åbenrå, 15,156 ....C 7
Åbybro, 6,309 ....C 3
Ærøskøbing, 1,228 ....D 8
Agerbæk, 804, ...B 6
Åkirkeby, 1,549 ....F 9
Ålborg, 82,346 ....D 4
Ålborg, *153,307 ....D 4
Ålestrup, 5,228 ....C 4
Allingåbro, 1,352 ....D 5
Allinge-Sandvig, 2,023 ....F 8
Ansager, 1,123 ....B 6
Arden, 1,353 ....C 4
Århus, 109,498 ....D 5
Århus, *232,173 ....D 5
Års, 5,075 ....C 4
Årup, †5,033 ....D 7
Aså, 1,348 ....D 3
Askov, 725 ....C 7
Asnæs, 2,493 ....E 6
Assens, Århus, 1,266 ....D 4
Assens, Fyn, †10,777 ....D 7
Augustenborg, 3,537 ....D 8
Auning, 1,367 ....D 5
Avlum, 3,694 ....B 5
Bælum, 1,922 ....D 4
Bagenkop, 774 ....D 8
Ballerup, †50,128 ....F 6
Bandholm, 1,248 ....E 8
Bested, 1,886 ....B 4
Birkerød, †20,835 ....F 6
Bjerringbro, 6,469 ....C 5
Bogense, †6,450 ....D 6
Bolderslev, 729 ....C 8
Børkop, †9,053 ....C 6
Borup, 2,344 ....E 7
Brabrand, 12,514 ....C 5
Brædstrup, 3,925 ....C 6
Bramminge, 5,937 ....B 7
Brande, 6,814 ....B 6
Bredebro, †3,747 ....B 7
Broager, †5,387 ....C 8
Brønderslev, 10,274 ....C 3
Brøns, 867 ....B 7
Brørup, 4,066 ....C 7
Brovst, †8,086 ....C 3
Christiansfeld, 958 ....C 7
Copenhagen (cap.), 634,500 ....F 6
Copenhagen, 1,346,720 ....F 6
Dronninglund, 9,179 ....D 3
Dybvad, 793 ....D 3
Ebeltoft, 3,168 ....D 5
Egernsund, 1,360 ....C 8
Egtved, 2,857 ....C 6
Ejby, 3,265 ....D 7
Esbjerg, 62,483 ....B 7
Fåborg, 5,630 ....D 7
Fakse, 7,268 ....F 7
Fakse Ladeplads, 1,639 ....F 7
Farsø, 4,126 ....C 4
Farum, †9,583 ....F 6
Fjerritslev, 2,686 ....C 3
Fredensborg, 3,977 ....F 6
Fredericia, 34,464 ....C 6
Frederiksberg, 102,751 ....F 6
Frederikshavn, 24,640 ....D 3
Frederikssund, 7,835 ....E 6
Frederiksværk, 4,385 ....E 6
Fuglebjerg, 5,082 ....E 7
Gedser, 1,195 ....F 8
Gedsted, 1,924 ....C 4
Gelsted, 2,461 ....C 7
Gentofte, †78,641 ....F 6
Gilleleje, 4,300 ....F 5
Give, 8,573 ....C 6
Gjerlev, 1,209 ....D 4
Glamsbjerg, †5,677 ....D 7
Glostrup, †28,169 ....F 6
Glumsø, 819 ....E 7
Glyngøre, 1,047 ....C 4
Gørding, 2,422 ....B 7
Gørlev, 2,437 ....E 6
Græsted, 2,899 ....F 5
Gram, 3,935 ....C 7
Gråsten, †6,336 ....C 8
Grenå, 13,277 ....D 5
Grindsted, 9,345 ....B 6
Gylling, 990 ....D 6
Haderslev, 20,291 ....C 7
Hadsten, 6,919 ....C 5
Hadsund, 6,862 ....D 4
Hals, 3,016 ....D 3
Hammel, 7,456 ....C 5
Hammerum, 2,415 ....C 5
Hanstholm, 3,358 ....B 3
Harboør, 2,224 ....A 4
Hårby, †4,671 ....D 7
Hårlev, 980 ....F 7
Hasle, 1,542 ....F 8
Haslev, 10,173 ....E 7
Havdrup, 5,163 ....F 6
Hedensted, 4,791 ....C 6
Hellebæk, 2,240 ....F 5
Helsinge, 4,707 ....F 6
Helsingør, 30,211 ....F 6
Herning, 32,512 ....B 5
Hillerød, 23,500 ....F 6
Hinnerup, †5,614 ....D 5
Hirtshals, 8,598 ....C 2
Hjallerup, 1,385 ....C 3
Hjerm, 1,421 ....B 5
Hjørring, 15,699 ....C 3
Hobro, 8,845 ....C 4
Højer, 1,407 ....B 8
Højslev, 2,863 ....C 4
Holbæk, 17,892 ....E 6
Holeby, 4,359 ....E 8
Holstebro, 24,009 ....B 5
Holsted, 2,773 ....B 6
Høng, †7,355 ....E 7
Hornslet, 3,371 ....D 5
Horsens, 35,621 ....C 6
Hørsholm, 18,060 ....F 6
Hørve, 2,829 ....E 6
Hov, 607 ....D 6
Humlum, 2,357 ....B 4
Hundested, †6,301 ....E 6
Hurup, 2,560 ....B 4
Hvidbjerg, 2,361 ....B 4
Hvide Sande, 1,775 ....A 6
Hviding, 750 ....B 7
Ikast, 11,110 ....C 5
Jelling, 4,780 ....C 6
Jerslev, 2,672 ....D 3
Juelsminde, 7,245 ....D 6
Jyderup, 3,246 ....E 6
Kalundborg, 11,762 ....D 6
Karby, 2,302 ....B 4
Karise, 1,733 ....F 7
Karup, 1,891 ....C 5
Kastrup ....F 6
Kerteminde, †10,296 ....D 7
Kibæk, 1,179 ....B 5
Kjellerup, 3,506 ....C 5
Klaksvík, Færøe Is., 3,894 ....B 2
København (Copenhagen), (cap.), 634,500 ....F 6
Køge, 17,360 ....F 7
Kolding, 39,609 ....C 7
Kolind, 2,590 ....D 5
Kørsør, 15,550 ....E 7
Kværndrup, 1,963 ....D 7
Langå, 2,801 ....C 5
Lem, 1,060 ....B 5
Lemvig, 6,766 ....B 4
Løgstør, 3,666 ....C 4
Løgumkloster, 2,089 ....B 7
Lohals, 634 ....D 7
Løjt Kirkeby, 2,724 ....C 7
Løkken, 1,388 ....C 3
Løsning, 2,418 ....C 6
Lundby, 2,392 ....E 7
Lunderskov, †4,402 ....C 7
Lyngby, †61,245 ....F 6
Malling, 4,332 ....D 5
Mariager, 3,733 ....D 4
Maribo, 5,235 ....E 8
Marstal, 4,095 ....D 8
Middelfart, 9,015 ....C 7
Møgeltønder, 1,181 ....B 8
Næstved, 24,831 ....E 7
Nakskov, 15,994 ....E 8
Neksø, 3,499 ....F 9
Nibe, 2,786 ....C 4
Nordborg, 3,016 ....C 7
Nordby, 2,353 ....B 7
Nørre Åby, †5,195 ....C 7
Nørre Alslev, 1,939 ....E 8
Nørre Broby, 858 ....D 7
Nørre Nebel, 867 ....B 6
Nørre Snede, 3,019 ....C 6
Nørresundby, 23,848 ....D 3
Nørre Vorupør, 632 ....B 4
Nyborg, 11,698 ....D 7
Nykøbing, Storstrøm, 17,364 ....E 8
Nykøbing, Vestsjælland, 4,905 ....E 6
Nykøbing, Viborg, 8,710 ....B 4
Nysted, 1,211 ....E 8
Odder, 8,144 ....D 6
Odense, 102,698 ....D 7
Odense, *163,593 ....D 7
Ølgod, 7,091 ....B 6
Ørsted, 1,925 ....D 5
Øster Vrå, 931 ....D 3
Otterup, †10,462 ....D 7
Ovtrup, 549 ....B 6
Pandrup, 1,383 ....C 3
Pedersborg, 1,560 ....E 7

Agriculture, Industry and Resources

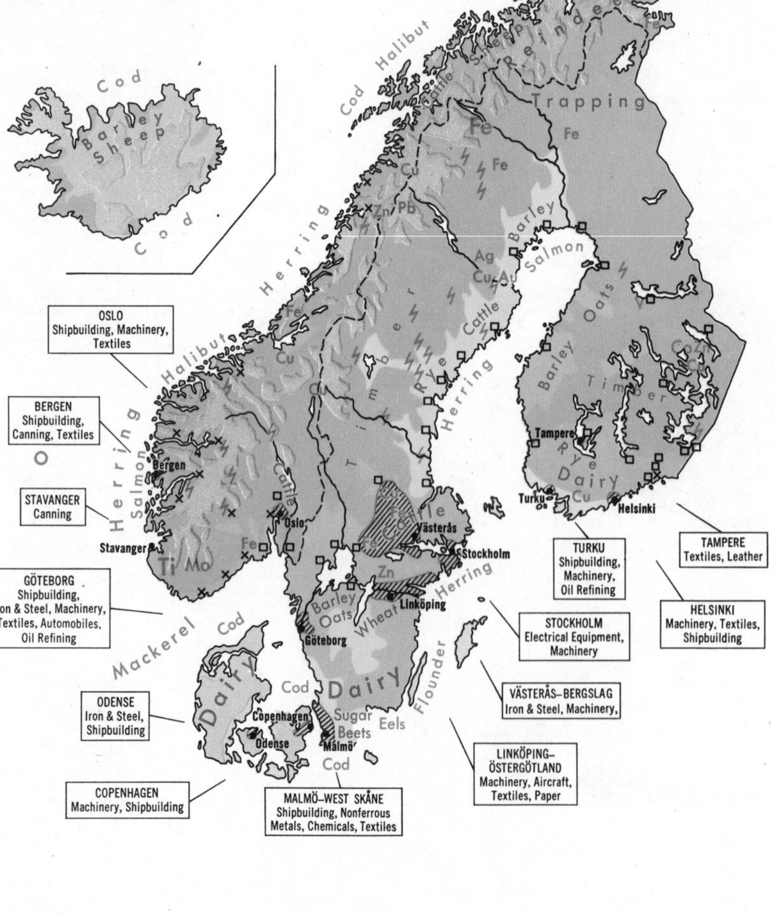
Shrimp
Haddock
Cod
Halibut
Reindeer
Trapping
Fe
Cu
Pb
Barley
Salmon
Ag
Au
Herring
Cattle
Rye
Oats
Timber
Tampere
Turku
Helsinki
Barley
Sheep
OSLO
Shipbuilding, Machinery, Textiles
BERGEN
Shipbuilding, Canning, Textiles
Bergen
STAVANGER
Canning
Stavanger
Ti
Mo
Oslo
Västerås
Stockholm
Zn
Linköping
Wheat
Göteborg
GÖTEBORG
Shipbuilding, Iron & Steel, Machinery, Textiles, Automobiles, Oil Refining
Mackerel
Dairy
Sugar Beets
Eels
Flounder
Copenhagen
Odense
Malmö
ODENSE
Iron & Steel, Shipbuilding
COPENHAGEN
Machinery, Shipbuilding
MALMÖ–WEST SKÅNE
Shipbuilding, Nonferrous Metals, Chemicals, Textiles
LINKÖPING–ÖSTERGÖTLAND
Machinery, Aircraft, Textiles, Paper
VÄSTERÅS–BERGSLAG
Iron & Steel, Machinery,
STOCKHOLM
Electrical Equipment, Machinery
TURKU
Shipbuilding, Machinery, Oil Refining
TAMPERE
Textiles, Leather
HELSINKI
Machinery, Textiles, Shipbuilding

DOMINANT LAND USE

- Cash Cereals, Dairy
- Dairy, Cattle, Hogs
- Dairy, General Farming
- General Farming (chiefly cereals)
- Nomadic Sheep Herding
- Forests, Limited Mixed Farming
- Nonagricultural Land

MAJOR MINERAL OCCURRENCES

- Ag Silver
- Au Gold
- Co Cobalt
- Cu Copper
- Fe Iron Ore
- Mo Molybdenum
- O Petroleum
- Pb Lead
- Ti Titanium
- V Vanadium
- Zn Zinc

- Water Power
- Major Industrial Areas
- × Electrochemical & Electrometallurgical Centers
- □ Paper, Pulp & Sawmilling Centers

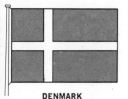

DENMARK

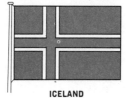

ICELAND

DENMARK

AREA 16,614 sq. mi.
POPULATION 4,912,865
CAPITAL Copenhagen
LARGEST CITY Copenhagen
HIGHEST POINT Yding Skovhøj 568 ft.
MONETARY UNIT krone (crown)
MAJOR LANGUAGE Danish
MAJOR RELIGION Protestantism

ICELAND

AREA 39,768 sq. mi.
POPULATION 204,578
CAPITAL Reykjavík
LARGEST CITY Reykjavík
HIGHEST POINT Hvannadalshnúkur 6,952 ft.
MONETARY UNIT króna (crown)
MAJOR LANGUAGE Icelandic
MAJOR RELIGION Protestantism

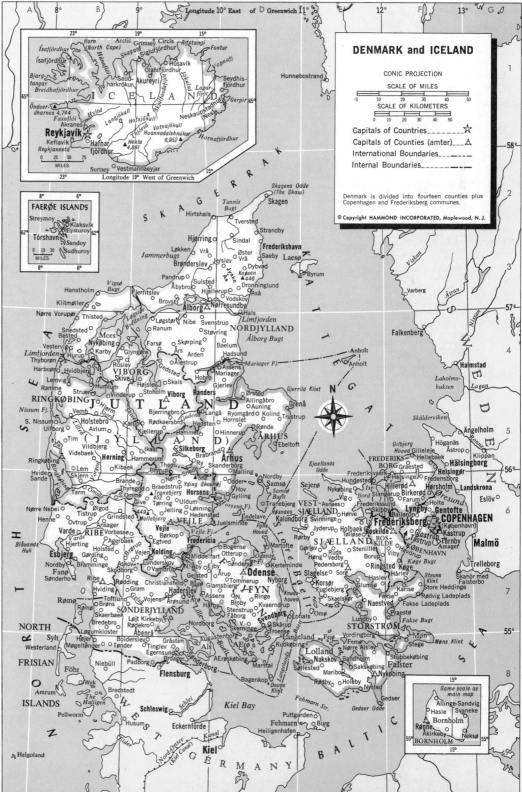

DENMARK and ICELAND

CONIC PROJECTION

SCALE OF MILES

SCALE OF KILOMETERS

Capitals of Countries ★
Capitals of Counties (amter) ▲
International Boundaries
Internal Boundaries

Denmark is divided into fourteen counties plus
Copenhagen and Frederiksberg communes.

© Copyright HAMMOND INCORPORATED, Maplewood, N.J.

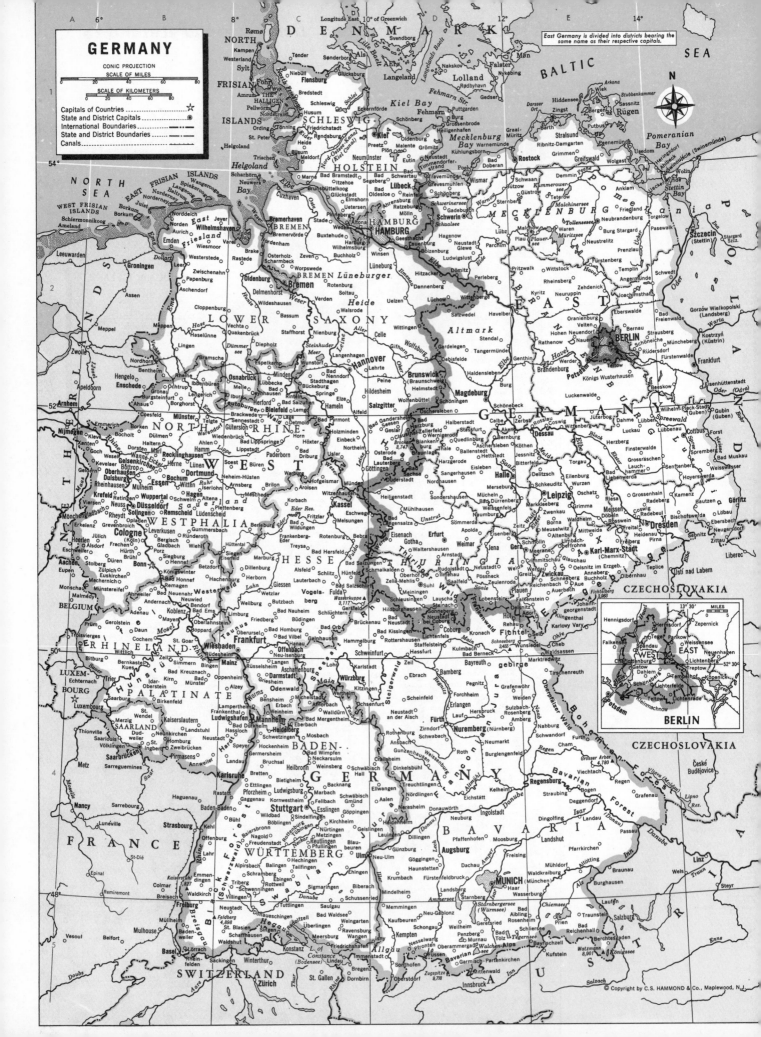

GERMANY

CONIC PROJECTION
SCALE OF MILES
SCALE OF KILOMETERS

Capitals of Countries .... ☆
State and District Capitals .... ◉
International Boundaries ....
State and District Boundaries ......
Canals ....

East Germany is divided into districts bearing the
same name as their respective capitals.

© Copyright by C.S. HAMMOND & Co., Maplewood, N.J.

WEST GERMANY

AREA 95,959 sq. mi.
POPULATION 61,194,600
CAPITAL Bonn
LARGEST CITY Berlin (West)
HIGHEST POINT Zugspitze 9,718 ft.
MONETARY UNIT West German Deutsch mark
MAJOR LANGUAGE German
MAJOR RELIGIONS Protestantism, Roman Catholicism

EAST GERMANY

AREA 41,814 sq. mi.
POPULATION 17,117,000
CAPITAL Berlin (East)
LARGEST CITY Berlin (East)
HIGHEST POINT Fichtelberg 3,983 ft.
MONETARY UNIT East German Deutsch mark
MAJOR LANGUAGE German
MAJOR RELIGIONS Protestantism, Roman Catholicism

Topography

0   50   100
MILES

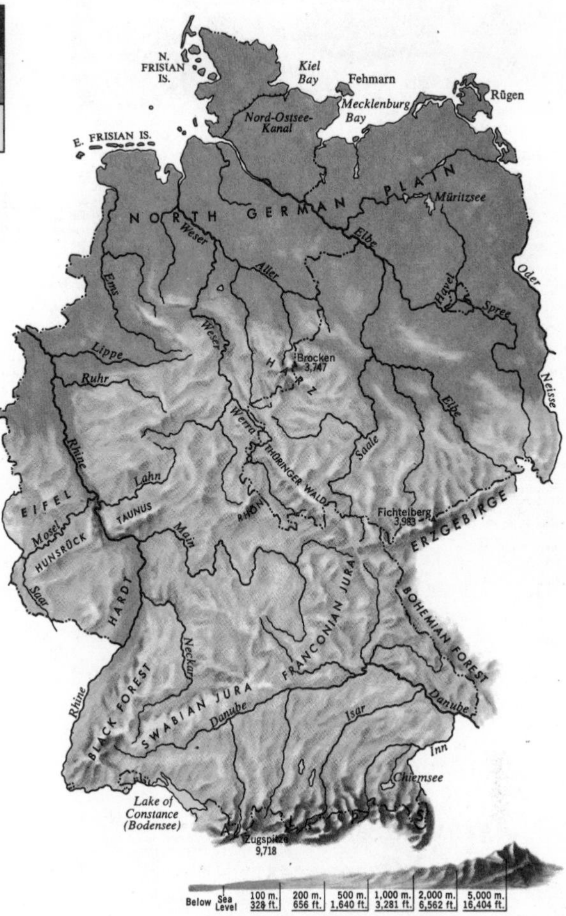

EAST GERMANY

DISTRICTS

Berlin (East), 1,064,000	F 4
Cottbus, 839,133	F 3
Dresden, 1,867,739	E 3
Erfurt, 1,249,540	D 3
Frankfurt, 660,666	F 2
Gera, 735,175	D 3
Halle, 1,932,733	E 3
Karl-Marx-Stadt, 2,082,927	E 3
Leipzig, 1,510,773	E 3
Magdeburg, 1,323,644	D 2
Neubrandenburg, 633,209	E 2
Potsdam, 1,127,498	E 2
Rostock, 842,743	D 1
Schwerin, 594,786	D 2
Suhl, 549,398	D 3

CITIES and TOWNS

Aken, 12,126	D 3
Altenburg, 47,462	E 3
Angermünde, 12,200	E 2
Anklam, 19,436	E 2
Annaberg-Buchholz, 28,663	E 3
Apolda, 29,735	D 3
Arnstadt, 27,674	D 3
Aschersleben, 36,777	D 3
Aue, 31,723	E 3
Auerbach, 19,673	E 3
Bad Doberan, 13,197	D 1
Bad Dürrenberg, 16,500	D 3
Bad Freienwalde, 11,845	F 2
Bad Langensalza, 16,952	D 3
Bad Salzungen, 12,722	C 3
Barth, 12,688	E 1
Bautzen, 44,041	F 3
Bergen, 10,979	E 1
Berlin (East) (capital), 1,084,000	F 4
Bernau, 14,078	E 2
Bernburg, 45,885	D 3
Bischofswerda, 11,345	F 3
Bitterfeld, 30,916	E 3
Blankenburg, 19,595	D 3
Boizenburg, 11,370	D 2
Borna, 20,669	E 3
Brandenburg, 90,753	E 2
Burg, 29,906	D 2
Calbe, 16,464	D 3
Chemnitz (Karl-Marx-Stadt), 295,443	E 3
Coswig, 18,600	E 3
Cottbus, 75,541	F 3
Crimmitschau, 30,752	E 3
Delitzsch, 23,480	E 3
Demmin, 16,755	E 2
Dessau, 95,682	E 3
Döbeln, 499,848	E 3
Dresden, 499,848	E 3
Eberswach, 11,293	E 2
Eberswalde, 33,680	F 2
Eilenburg, 21,366	E 3
Eisenach, 50,234	C 3
Eisenberg, 13,858	D 3
Eisenhüttenstadt, 38,138	F 2
Eisleben, 32,402	D 3
Erfurt, 193,745	D 3
Falkensee, 29,884	E 2
Falkenstein, 15,269	E 3
Finsterwalde, 22,441	F 3
Forst, 29,823	F 3
Frankfurt-an-der-Oder, 58,866	F 2
Freiberg, 49,122	E 3
Freital, 42,675	E 3
Fürstenwalde, 30,527	F 2
Gardelegen, 13,218	D 2
Genthin, 15,619	E 2
Gera, 109,989	E 3
Glauchau, 33,103	E 3
Görlitz, 86,632	F 3
Gotha, 57,692	D 3
Greifswald, 47,402	E 1
Greiz, 39,313	E 3
Grevesmühlen, 10,914	D 2
Grimma, 16,509	E 3
Grimmen, 12,943	E 1
Grossenhain, 19,848	E 3
Grossräschen, 12,737	E 3
Guben (Wilhelm-Pieck-Stadt), 26,586	F 3
Güstrow, 38,185	D 2
Hagenow, 10,434	D 2
Halberstadt, 46,071	D 3
Haldensleben, 20,547	D 2
Halle, 263,928	D 3
Heidenau, 20,161	E 3
Heiligenstadt, 12,627	C 3
Hennigsdorf, 21,398	E 2
Hettstedt, 19,218	D 3
Hoyerswerda, 43,922	F 3
Ilmenau, 19,852	D 3
Jena, 85,032	D 3
Johanngeorgenstadt, 10,801	E 3
Jüterbog, 14,416	E 2
Kamenz, 16,236	F 3
Karl-Marx-Stadt, 295,443	E 3

Kleinmachnow, 13,919	E 4
Klingenthal, 14,748	E 3
Köpenick, 52,294	F 4
Köthen, 38,154	E 3
Kottbus (Cottbus), 75,541	F 3
Lauchhammer, 28,680	E 3
Leipzig, 590,291	E 3
Lichtenberg, 62,841	F 4
Limbach-Oberfrohna, 26,053	E 3
Löbau, 17,066	F 3
Lübben, 12,742	F 3
Lübbenau, 16,976	F 3
Luckenwalde, 29,282	E 2
Ludwigslust, 11,512	D 2
Magdeburg, 268,269	D 2
Markkleeberg, 21,854	E 3
Meerane, 24,262	E 3
Meiningen, 25,025	D 3
Meissen, 47,166	E 3
Merseburg, 55,562	D 3
Meuselwitz, 10,582	E 3
Mittweida, 20,440	E 3
Mücheln, 10,842	D 3
Mühlhausen, 46,155	D 3
Nauen, 12,017	E 2
Naumburg, 37,990	D 3
Neubrandenburg, 38,740	E 2
Neuenhagen, 13,116	F 4
Neugersdorf, 11,889	F 3
Neuruppin, 22,424	E 2
Neustadt, 10,085	D 3
Neustrelitz, 27,624	E 2
Nordhausen, 42,279	D 3
Oelsnitz, 15,954	E 3
Oelsnitz im Erzgebirge, 18,377	E 3
Olbernhau, 14,240	E 3
Oranienburg, 20,401	E 2
Oschatz, 15,582	E 3
Oschersleben, 18,078	D 2
Pankow, 68,785	F 3
Parchim, 19,226	D 2
Pasewalk, 14,086	E 2
Perleberg, 13,707	D 2
Pirna, 42,562	E 3
Plauen, 81,739	D 3
Pössneck, 19,468	D 3
Potsdam, 110,671	E 2
Prenzlau, 20,275	E 2
Quedlinburg, 30,840	D 3
Radeberg, 17,410	E 3
Radebeul, 41,437	E 3
Rathenow, 28,979	E 2
Reichenbach, 29,372	E 3
Ribnitz-Damgarten, 15,301	E 1
Riesa, 43,322	E 3
Rosslau, 16,256	E 3
Rosswein, 10,649	E 3
Rostock, 190,275	E 1
Rüdersdorf, 11,837	F 2
Rudolstadt, 30,433	D 3
Saalfeld, 32,145	D 3
Salzwedel, 19,534	D 2
Sangerhausen, 29,373	D 3
Sassnitz, 13,253	E 1
Schkeuditz, 17,131	E 3
Schmalkalden, 14,569	D 3
Schmölln, 13,992	E 3
Schneeberg, 21,225	E 3
Schönebeck, 44,551	D 3
Schöneiche, 10,101	F 2
Schwedt, 23,359	F 2
Schwerin, 92,356	D 2
Sebnitz, 14,655	F 3
Senftenberg, 24,532	F 3
Sömmerda, 16,061	D 3
Sondershausen, 22,456	D 3
Sonneberg, 29,804	D 3
Spremberg, 23,367	F 3
Stassfurt, 25,622	D 3
Stendal, 36,193	D 2
Stralsund, 68,925	E 1
Strausberg, 17,985	F 2
Suhl, 28,698	D 3
Tangermünde, 12,992	D 2
Teltow, 13,735	E 2
Templin, 11,203	E 2
Teterow, 11,039	E 2
Thale, 17,273	D 3
Torgau, 20,941	E 3
Torgelow, 13,584	F 2
Treptow, 22,302	F 4
Ueckermünde, 11,614	E 2
Waltershausen, 14,250	D 3
Waren, 20,008	E 2
Weida, 11,950	D 3
Weimar, 64,300	D 3
Weissenfels, 47,704	D 3
Weissensee, 50,691	F 4
Weisswasser, 16,016	F 3
Werdau, 23,783	E 3
Wernigerode, 32,579	D 3
Wilhelm-Pieck-Stadt, 26,586	F 3
Wismar, 55,235	D 2
Wittenberg, 46,185	E 3
Wittenberge, 32,621	D 2
Wittstock, 10,358	E 2

Wolgast, 14,955	E 1
Wurzen, 24,349	E 3
Zehdenick, 12,306	E 2
Zeitz, 46,393	E 3
Zella-Mehlis, 17,121	D 3
Zerbst, 19,527	D 3
Zeulenroda, 18,534	D 3
Zittau, 43,259	F 3
Zwickau, 127,688	E 3

OTHER FEATURES

Altmark (reg.), 288,928	D 2
Arkona (cape)	E 1
Baltic (sea)	F 1
Black Elster (riv.)	E 3
Brandenburg (region), 3,726,413	E 2
Brocken (mt.)	D 3
Darsser Ort (point)	E 1
Elbe (riv.)	D 2
Elster (riv.)	E 3
Erzgebirge (Ore) (mts.)	E 3
Fichtelberg (mt.)	E 3
Havel (riv.)	E 2
Kummerowersee (lake)	E 2
Lusatia (reg.)	F 3
Malchinersee (lake)	E 2
Mecklenburg (region), 1,226,685	D 2
Mecklenburg (bay)	D 1
Mulde (riv.)	E 3
Müritzee (lake)	E 2
Neisse (riv.)	F 3
Oder (riv.)	F 2
Ore (Erzgebirge) (mts.)	E 3
Penne (riv.)	E 2
Plauersee (lake)	E 2
Pomerania (region), 711,075	E 2
Pomeranian (bay)	E 1
Rhön (mts.)	D 3
Rügen (isl.), 92,348	E 1
Saale (riv.)	D 3
Saxony (region), 5,318,661	E 3
Schaalsee (lake)	D 2
Schwerinersee (lake)	D 2
Spree (riv.)	F 3
Spreewald (forest)	F 2
Stettin (bay)	F 2
Stubbenkammer (point)	E 1
Thüringer Wald (forest)	D 3
Thuringia (Thüringen) (reg.), 2,017,924	D 3
Tollensee (lake)	E 2
Ucker (riv.)	E 2
Unstrut (riv.)	D 3
Usedom (isl.)	F 1
Warnow (riv.)	D 2
Werra (riv.)	D 3
White Elster (riv.)	E 3

WEST GERMANY

STATES

Baden-Württemberg, 8,909,700	C 4
Bavaria, 10,568,900	D 4
Berlin (West) (free city), 2,134,256	E 2
Bremen, 755,977	C 2
Hamburg, 1,817,122	C 2
Hesse, 5,422,600	C 3
Lower Saxony, 7,100,400	C 2
North Rhine-Westphalia, 17,129,800	B 3
Rhineland-Palatinate, 3,671,300	B 4
Saarland, 1,127,400	B 4
Schleswig-Holstein, 2,557,200	C 1

CITIES and TOWNS

Aachen, 177,642	B 3
Aalen, 35,102	D 4
Ahlen, 50,411	B 3
Ahrensburg, 25,822	C 2
Alfeld, 13,726	C 2
Alsdorf, 31,726	B 3
Altena, 31,164	B 3
Altona	C 2
Alzey, 17,068	C 4
Amberg, 42,141	D 4
Andernach, 22,367	B 3
Ansbach, 30,083	C 4
Arnsberg, 22,577	C 3
Aschaffenburg, 56,236	C 4
Augsburg, 214,376	D 4
Aurich, 12,299	B 2
Backnang, 26,086	C 4
Bad Dürkheim, 15,792	C 4
Baden-Baden, 38,852	C 4
Bad Harzburg, 11,356	D 3
Bad Hersfeld, 23,494	C 3
Bad Homburg vor der Höhe, 41,236	C 3
Bad Honnef am Rhein, 20,649	B 3
Bad Kissingen, 12,572	C 3

Bad Kreuznach, 42,707	B 4
Bad Mergentheim, 12,552	D 4
Bad Nauheim, 15,222	C 3
Bad Oeynhausen, 14,127	C 2
Bad Oldesloe, 18,915	D 2
Bad Pyrmont, 16,527	C 2
Bad Reichenhall, 14,894	E 5
Bad Salzuflen, 49,030	C 2
Bad Schwartau, 16,909	D 2
Bad Segeberg, 12,494	D 2
Bad Tölz, 12,486	D 5
Bad Vilbel, 18,315	C 3
Bad Wildungen, 12,189	C 3
Balingen, 13,693	C 4
Bamberg, 68,713	D 4
Bayreuth, 63,387	D 4
Bendorf, 14,361	B 3
Berchtesgaden, 4,074	E 5
Bergisch Gladbach, 50,095	B 3
Berlin (West), 2,134,256	E 4
Betzdorf, 10,388	B 3
Biberach an der Riss, 25,597	C 4
Bielefeld, 169,347	C 2
Bietigheim, 22,488	C 4
Bingen, 24,452	B 4
Böblingen, 36,644	C 4
Bocholt, 48,134	B 3
Bochum, 346,886	B 3
Bonn, 299,376	B 3
Borken, 30,614	B 3
Borghorst, 17,072	B 2
Bottrop, 108,161	B 3
Brackwede, 40,254	C 2
Brake, 19,388	C 2
Bramsche, 10,733	B 2
Braunschweig (Brunswick), 225,168	D 2
Bremen, 607,184	C 2
Bremerhaven, 148,793	C 2
Brilon, 15,301	C 3
Bruchsal, 27,103	C 4
Brühl, 41,782	B 3
Brunswick, 225,168	D 2
Bückeburg, 13,396	C 2
Burghausen, 16,630	E 4
Burgsteinfurt, 12,554	B 2
Buxtehude, 23,140	C 2
Celle, 56,335	D 2
Charlottenburg	F 4
Clausthal-Zellerfeld, 15,744	D 3
Cloppenburg, 18,162	B 2
Coburg, 41,369	D 3
Coesfeld, 26,565	B 3
Cologne, 866,308	B 3
Crailsheim, 16,687	D 4
Cuxhaven, 45,218	C 2
Dachau, 33,093	D 4
Darmstadt, 141,075	C 4
Deggendorf, 18,601	E 4
Delmenhorst, 63,685	C 2
Detmold, 64,473	C 2
Diepholz, 11,639	C 2
Dillenburg, 10,236	C 3
Dillingen an der Donau, 11,606	D 4
Dingolfing, 10,747	E 4
Donaueschingen, 11,643	C 4
Donauwörth, 11,266	D 4
Dorsten, 39,393	B 3
Dortmund, 648,883	B 3
Duderstadt, 10,421	D 3
Dudweiler, 30,078	B 4
Duisburg, 457,891	B 3
Dülmen, 21,094	B 3
Düren, 54,867	B 3
Düsseldorf, 680,806	B 3
Eberbach, 14,369	C 4
Eckernförde, 21,971	D 1
Ehingen, 12,957	C 4
Eichstätt, 10,040	D 4
Einbeck, 18,618	C 3
Eiserfeld, 22,490	B 1

Ellwangen, 13,128	D 4
Elmshorn, 41,353	D 2
Emden, 48,313	B 2
Emmendingen, 15,986	B 4
Emmerich, 24,512	B 3
Erkelenz, 12,275	B 3
Erlangen, 85,727	D 4
Eschwege, 22,079	C 3
Eschweiler, 39,622	B 3
Espelkamp, 12,309	C 2
Essen, 704,769	B 3
Esslingen am Neckar, 86,497	C 4
Ettlingen, 21,342	C 4
Euskirchen, 41,965	B 3
Eutin, 18,177	D 1
Felibach, 29,343	C 4
Flensburg, 96,778	C 1
Forchheim, 21,582	D 4
Frankenthal, 40,505	C 4
Frankfurt am Main, 660,410	C 3
Frechen, 30,786	B 3
Freiburg im Breisgau, 165,960	B 5
Freising, 30,264	D 4
Freudenstadt, 14,356	C 4
Friedberg, 17,401	C 3
Friedrichshafen, 42,483	C 5
Fulda, 44,262	C 3
Fürstenfeldbruck, 22,495	D 4
Fürth, 94,310	D 4
Füssen, 10,891	D 5
Gaggenau, 14,773	C 4
Garmisch-Partenkirchen, 27,313	D 5
Geesthacht, 23,594	D 2
Geislingen an der Steige, 27,209	C 4
Geldern, 22,602	B 3
Gelsenkirchen, 348,620	B 3
Giessen, 74,731	C 3
Gifhorn, 23,001	D 2
Glückstadt, 10,747	C 2
Goch, 22,721	B 3
Göppingen, 55,840	C 4
Göppingen, 86,899	C 4
Goslar, 41,653	D 3
Göttingen, 115,227	D 3

Grevenbroich, 28,197	B 3
Griesheim, 16,392	C 4
Gronau, 26,596	B 2
Gummersbach, 45,026	B 3
Günzburg, 13,449	D 4
Gütersloh, 76,343	C 2
Haan, 12,388	D 4
Hagen, 203,048	B 3
Haltern, 15,264	B 3
Hamburg, 1,817,122	C 2
Hameln, 47,114	C 2
Hamm, 84,302	B 3
Hanau, 55,674	C 3
Hannover, 517,783	C 2
Harburg-Wilhelmsburg	C 2
Hassloch, 17,852	C 4
Haunstetten, 22,205	D 4
Heide, 23,419	C 1
Heidelberg, 121,929	C 4
Heidenheim an der Brenz, 50,170	D 4
Heilbronn, 99,440	C 4
Helmstedt, 27,161	D 2
Hennef, 26,589	B 3
Herborn, 10,395	C 3
Herford, 67,267	C 2
Herne, 100,798	B 3
Hildesheim, 95,926	D 2
Hockenheim, 15,615	C 4
Hof, 54,805	D 3
Holzminden, 22,273	C 3
Homburg, 32,258	B 4
Höxter, 32,423	C 3
Hürth, 52,011	B 3
Husum, 25,037	C 1
Hüttental, 40,287	C 3
Ibbenbüren, 17,780	B 2
Idar-Oberstein, 32,590	B 4
Immenstadt, 10,775	D 5
Ingolstadt, 71,954	D 4
Iserlohn, 57,792	B 3
Jülich, 20,152	B 3
Kaiserslautern, 99,859	B 4
Karlsruhe, 257,144	C 4
Kassel, 213,494	C 3
Kaufbeuren, 39,940	D 5
Kehl, 15,958	B 4
Kelheim, 11,701	D 4

Kempten, 44,617	D 5
Kevelaer, 20,257	B 3
Kiel, 276,600	C 1
Kirchheim unter Teck, 28,876	C 4
Kitzingen, 18,308	D 4
Kleve, 44,150	B 3
Koblenz, 106,189	B 3
Köln (Cologne), 866,308	B 3
Konstanz, 61,617	C 5
Korbach, 17,324	C 3
Kornwestheim, 28,574	C 4
Krefeld, 228,726	B 3
Kulmbach, 22,768	D 3
Lage, 30,949	C 2
Lahr, 25,028	B 4
Lampertheim, 24,053	C 4
Landau in der Pfalz, 32,318	C 4
Landsberg am Lech, 14,378	D 4
Landshut, 51,393	E 4
Langen, 30,230	C 4
Langenhagen, 37,077	C 2
Lauenburg, 11,445	D 2
Lauf an der Pegnitz, 15,771	D 4
Leer, 29,919	B 2
Lehrte, 21,792	C 2
Lemgo, 38,526	C 2
Lengerich, 21,451	B 2
Leverkusen, 111,588	B 3
Lichtenfels, 11,218	D 3
Limburg an der Lahn, 14,889	C 3
Lindau, 26,260	C 5
Lingen, 25,810	B 2
Lippstadt, 42,859	C 3
Lohr am Main, 11,291	C 4
Lörrach, 32,939	B 5
Lübbecke, 11,433	C 2
Lübeck, 242,191	D 2
Lüdenscheid, 80,096	B 3
Ludwigsburg, 79,538	C 4
Ludwigshafen am Rhein, 174,698	C 4
Lüneburg, 59,944	D 2
Lünen, 72,195	B 3

(continued on following page)

GERMANY Before World War I 1871-1914

DENMARK SWEDEN
NETH. Berlin ☆ RUSSIA
BELG.
LUX.
FRANCE AUSTRIA-
SWITZ. HUNGARY
ITALY

GERMANY Between Wars 1919-1937

DENMARK SWEDEN DANZIG LITH.
NETH. Berlin ☆ POLAND
BELG.
LUX. SAAR (To Germany 1935) CZECHOSLOVAKIA
FRANCE AUSTRIA
SWITZ. ITALY YUGO. HUNG.

Occupied GERMANY 1945-1949

DENMARK SWEDEN U.S.S.R.
NETH. BRITISH ZONE BERLIN RUSSIAN ZONE POLAND
BELG. FRENCH ZONE
LUX. SAAR AMERICAN ZONE CZECHOSLOVAKIA
FRANCE ZONE
SWITZ. ITALY YUGO. HUNG. AUSTRIA

WEST GERMANY (continued)

Mainz, 176,720	C 4
Mannheim, 330,920	C 4
Marburg an der Lahn, 51,382	C 3
Marktredwitz, 15,605	E 3
Marl, 75,779	B 3
Mayen, 18,485	B 3
Memmingen, 35,454	D 5
Meppen, 17,892	B 2
Merzig, 12,443	B 4
Meschede, 16,222	C 3
Metzingen, 14,093	C 4
Minden, 15,307	C 2
Mittenwald, 10,026	D 5
Mölln, 15,307	D 1
Mönchengladbach, 152,172	B 3
Moosburg an der Isar, 11,730	D 4
Mosbach, 13,876	C 4
Mühldorf am Inn, 10,998	E 4
Mülheim an der Ruhr, 191,080	B 3
Münden, 19,111	C 3
Munich (München), 1,326,331	D 4
Münster, 204,571	B 3
Neckarsulm, 18,523	C 4
Neheim-Hüsten, 36,864	C 3
Neuburg an der Donau, 18,530	D 4
Neu-Isenburg, 36,014	C 3
Neumarkt in der Oberpfalz, 18,930	D 4
Neumünster, 84,636	C 1
Neunkirchen, 44,326	B 4
Neuss, 117,599	B 3
Neustadt an der Weinstrasse, 51,058	B 4
Neustadt bei Coburg, 12,496	D 3
Neustadt in Holstein, 16,222	D 1
Neu-Ulm, 27,710	D 4
Neuwied, 31,359	B 3

Nienburg, 22,467	C 2
Norden, 16,355	B 2
Nordenham, 27,368	C 2
Nordhorn, 42,895	B 2
Nördlingen, 14,238	D 4
Northeim, 19,150	C 3
Nuremberg (Nürnberg), 477,108	D 4
Nürtingen, 21,284	C 4
Oberammergau, 4,641	D 5
Oberhausen, 249,045	B 3
Oberlahnstein, 20,131	C 3
Oberursel, 24,933	C 3
Ochtrup, 15,823	B 2
Offenbach am Main, 118,754	C 3
Offenburg, 32,628	B 4
Oldenburg, 131,434	C 2
Opladen, 43,531	B 3
Osnabrück, 141,000	C 2
Osterholz-Scharmbeck, 15,211	C 2
Osterode am Harz, 16,757	D 3
Paderborn, 68,735	C 3
Papenburg, 16,714	B 2
Passau, 31,574	E 4
Peine, 30,882	D 2
Penzberg, 10,784	D 5
Pforzheim, 90,780	C 4
Pfullingen, 15,967	C 4
Pinneberg, 36,439	C 2
Pirmasens, 56,172	B 4
Plettenberg, 30,233	C 3
Plön, 11,142	D 1
Porz am-Rhein, 78,076	B 3
Preetz, 14,653	D 1
Radolfzell, 15,512	C 5
Rastatt, 29,102	C 4
Rastede, 16,851	C 2
Ratingen, 43,420	B 3
Ratzeburg, 12,335	D 1
Ravensburg, 31,819	C 5
Recklinghausen, 125,535	B 3
Regensburg, 128,083	D 4
Rehau, 10,565	D 3

Remscheid, 137,374	B 3
Rendsburg, 35,453	C 1
Reutlingen, 77,853	C 4
Rheine, 51,167	B 2
Rheinfelden, 16,547	B 5
Rheinhausen, 71,698	B 3
Rheydt, 100,633	B 3
Rosenheim, 36,376	D 5
Rotenburg, 16,664	C 2
Roth bei Nürnberg, 11,550	D 4
Rothenburg ob der Tauber, 12,002	D 4
Rottenburg am Neckar, 12,698	C 4
Rottweil, 19,881	C 4
Rüsselsheim, 57,308	C 4
Saarbrücken, 130,765	B 4
Saarlouis (Saarlautern), 36,251	B 4
Säckingen, 12,614	C 5
Salzgitter, 118,020	D 2
Sankt Ingbert, 28,774	B 4
Sankt Wendel, 10,138	B 4
Schleswig, 33,317	C 1
Schöneberg	D 2
Schöningen, 14,551	D 2
Schramberg, 19,050	C 4
Schwabach, 25,774	D 4
Schwäbisch Gmünd, 44,628	C 4
Schwäbisch Hall, 23,765	C 4
Schwandorf in Bayern, 15,995	E 4
Schweinfurt, 59,293	D 3
Schwelm, 34,199	B 3
Schwenningen am Neckar, 35,467	C 4
Schwetzingen, 16,613	C 4
Seesen, 13,027	D 3
Selb, 18,498	E 3
Sennestadt, 20,518	C 3
Siegburg, 34,586	B 3
Siegen, 57,996	C 3
Sindelfingen, 41,029	C 4
Singen, 39,719	C 5

Soest, 40,580	C 3
Solingen, 175,895	B 3
Soltau, 14,981	D 2
Sonthofen, 16,504	D 5
Spandau	E 3
Speyer, 42,323	C 4
Springe, 12,698	C 2
Stade, 31,637	C 2
Stadthagen, 16,876	C 2
Starnberg, 10,622	D 4
Stolberg, 39,589	B 3
Straubing, 36,943	E 4
Stuttgart, 628,412	C 4
Sulzbach-Rosenberg, 18,691	D 4
Tailfingen, 16,787	C 4
Tempelhof	E 2
Traunstein, 14,117	E 5
Trier, 103,412	B 4
Tübingen, 56,008	C 4
Tuttlingen, 26,587	C 5
Überlingen, 12,837	C 5
Uelzen, 23,775	D 2
Uetersen, 16,734	C 2
Ulm, 92,486	C 4
Varel, 12,759	C 2
Vechta, 16,326	C 2
Verden, 16,741	C 2
Viersen, 83,988	B 3
Villingen im Schwarzwald, 37,652	C 4
Völklingen, 39,763	B 4
Waldshut, 10,621	C 5
Walsrode, 13,904	C 2
Wangen im Allgäu, 14,159	C 5
Wanne-Eickel, 99,923	B 3
Warendorf, 18,969	C 3
Wedel, 31,134	C 2
Weiden in der Oberpfalz, 43,097	D 4
Weilheim in Oberbayern, 14,433	D 5
Weingarten, 18,420	C 5
Weinheim, 29,544	C 4
Weissenburg in Bayern, 13,718	D 4

Wertheim, 12,035	C 4
Wesel, 44,710	B 3
Westerstede, 16,387	B 2
Wetzlar, 37,230	C 3
Wiesbaden, 260,614	B 3
Wilhelmshaven, 103,150	B 2
Witten, 97,807	B 3
Wolfenbüttel, 41,225	D 2
Wolfsburg, 89,442	D 2
Worms, 78,004	C 4
Wunstorf, 17,589	C 2
Wuppertal, 414,722	B 3
Würzburg, 120,317	C 4
Zirndorf, 15,363	D 4
Zweibrücken, 32,883	B 4
Zwischenahn, 19,906	B 2

OTHER FEATURES

Aller (riv.)	C 2
Allgäu (reg.), 249,600	C 5
Alz (riv.)	E 4
Ammersee (lake)	D 5
Amrum (isl.), 2,155	C 1
Baltrum (isl.), 924	B 2
Bavarian (forest)	E 4
Bavarian Alps (mts.)	D 5
Black (forest)	C 4
Bodensee (Constance) (lake)	C 5
Bohemian (forest)	E 4
Borkum (isl.), 5,348	B 2
Breisgau (reg.), 675,500	B 5
Chiemsee (lake)	E 5
Constance (lake)	C 5
Danube (Donau) (riv.)	C 4
Dümmer (lake)	C 2
East Friesland (region), 599,700	B 2
East Frisian (isls.), 20,962	B 2
Eder (res.)	C 3
Eider (riv.)	C 1

Eifel (mts.)	B 3
Elbe (riv.)	D 2
Ems (riv.)	B 2
Fehmarn (isl.), 12,586	D 1
Feldberg (mt.)	B 5
Fichtelgebirge (mts.)	D 3
Föhr (isl.), 8,585	C 1
Franconian Jura (mts.)	D 4
Frankenwald (forest)	D 3
Fulda (riv.)	C 3
Grosser Arber (mt.)	E 4
Halligen, The (isls.), 5,112	C 1
Hardt (mts.)	B 4
Harz (mts.)	D 3
Hegau (reg.), 189,900	C 5
Helgoland (isl.), 3,184	B 1
Hunsrück (mts.)	B 3
Iller (riv.)	D 4
Inn (riv.)	E 4
Isar (riv.)	D 4
Jade (bay)	C 2
Juist (isl.), 2,147	B 2
Kaiserstuhl (mt.)	B 4
Kiel (canal)	C 1
Königssee (lake)	E 5
Lahn (riv.)	C 3
Langeoog (isl.), 2,611	B 2
Lech (riv.)	D 4
Leine (riv.)	C 2
Lippe (riv.)	C 3
Lüneburger Heide (reg.)	C 2
Main (riv.)	C 4
Mecklenburg (bay)	D 1
Mosel (riv.)	B 4
Neckar (riv.)	C 4
Nord-Ostsee (Kiel) (canal)	C 1
Norderney (isl.), 8,983	B 2

Nordstrand (isl.), 3,079	C 1
North (sea)	A 1
North Friesland (reg.), 163,800	C 1
North Frisian (islands), 36,259	B 1
Oberpfälzer Wald (forest)	E 4
Odenwald (forest)	C 4
Pellorm (isl.), 2,033	B 1
Regen (riv.)	E 4
Regnitz (riv.)	D 3
Rhine (Rhein) (riv.)	B 3
Rhön (mts.)	D 3
Saar (riv.)	B 4
Salzach (riv.)	E 5
Sauer (riv.)	B 4
Sauerland (reg.)	C 3
Schwarzwald (Black) (forest)	C 4
Spessart (range)	C 4
Spiekeroog (isl.), 823	B 2
Starnbergersee (lake)	D 5
Steigerwald (forest)	D 3
Steinhuder (lake)	C 2
Swabian Jura (mts.)	C 4
Sylt (isl.), 20,407	B 1
Tauber (riv.)	C 4
Taunus (range)	C 3
Tegernsee (lake)	D 5
Teutoburger Wald (forest)	C 3
Vechte (riv.)	B 2
Vogelsberg (mt.)	C 3
Walchensee (lake)	D 5
Wangerooge (isl.), 2,126	B 2
Wasserkuppe (mt.)	D 3
Watzmann (mt.)	E 5
Werra (riv.)	C 3
Weser (riv.)	C 2
Westerwald (forest)	C 3
Wurmsee (Starnbergersee) (lake)	D 5
Zugspitze (mt.)	D 5

Agriculture, Industry and Resources

DOMINANT LAND USE

- Wheat, Sugar Beets
- Cereals (chiefly rye, oats, barley)
- Potatoes, Rye
- Dairy, Livestock
- Mixed Cereals, Dairy
- Truck Farming
- Grapes, Fruit
- Forests

MAJOR MINERAL OCCURRENCES

Ag	Silver		Lg	Lignite
Ba	Barite		Mg	Magnesium
C	Coal		Na	Salt
Cu	Copper		O	Petroleum
Fe	Iron Ore		Pb	Lead
G	Natural Gas		U	Uranium
Gr	Graphite		Zn	Zinc
K	Potash			

⚡ Water Power
 Major Industrial Areas

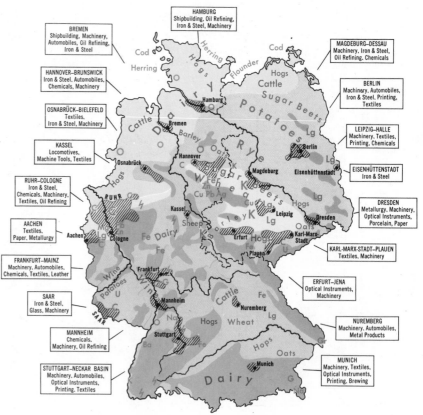

HAMBURG — Shipbuilding, Oil Refining, Iron & Steel, Machinery

BREMEN — Shipbuilding, Machinery, Automobiles, Oil Refining, Iron & Steel

MAGDEBURG–DESSAU — Machinery, Iron & Steel, Oil Refining, Chemicals

HANNOVER–BRUNSWICK — Iron & Steel, Automobiles, Chemicals, Machinery

BERLIN — Machinery, Automobiles, Iron & Steel, Printing, Textiles

OSNABRÜCK–BIELEFELD — Textiles, Iron & Steel, Machinery

LEIPZIG–HALLE — Machinery, Textiles, Printing, Chemicals

KASSEL — Locomotives, Machine Tools, Textiles

EISENHÜTTENSTADT — Iron & Steel

RUHR–COLOGNE — Iron & Steel, Chemicals, Machinery, Textiles, Oil Refining

DRESDEN — Metallurgy, Machinery, Optical Instruments, Porcelain, Paper

AACHEN — Textiles, Paper, Metallurgy

KARL-MARX-STADT–PLAUEN — Textiles, Machinery

FRANKFURT–MAINZ — Machinery, Automobiles, Chemicals, Textiles, Leather

ERFURT–JENA — Optical Instruments, Machinery

SAAR — Iron & Steel, Glass, Machinery

NUREMBERG — Machinery, Automobiles, Metal Products

MANNHEIM — Chemicals, Machinery, Oil Refining

MUNICH — Machinery, Textiles, Optical Instruments, Printing, Brewing

STUTTGART–NECKAR BASIN — Machinery, Automobiles, Optical Instruments, Printing, Textiles

NETHERLANDS

AREA 13,958 sq. mi.
POPULATION 13,077,000
CAPITALS The Hague, Amsterdam
LARGEST CITY Amsterdam
HIGHEST POINT Vaalserberg, 1,056 ft.
MONETARY UNIT guilder
MAJOR LANGUAGE Dutch
MAJOR RELIGIONS Protestantism, Roman Catholicism

BELGIUM

AREA 11,779 sq. mi.
POPULATION 9,660,154
CAPITAL Brussels
LARGEST CITY Brussels (greater)
HIGHEST POINT Botrange 2,277 ft.
MONETARY UNIT Belgian franc
MAJOR LANGUAGES French (Walloon), Flemish
MAJOR RELIGION Roman Catholicism

LUXEMBOURG

AREA 999 sq. mi.
POPULATION 339,000
CAPITAL Luxembourg
LARGEST CITY Luxembourg
HIGHEST POINT Ardennes Plateau, 1,825 ft.
MONETARY UNIT Luxembourg franc
MAJOR LANGUAGES Luxembourgeois (German dialect), French, German
MAJOR RELIGION Roman Catholicism

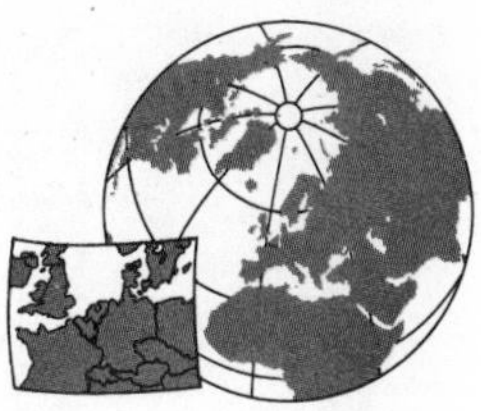

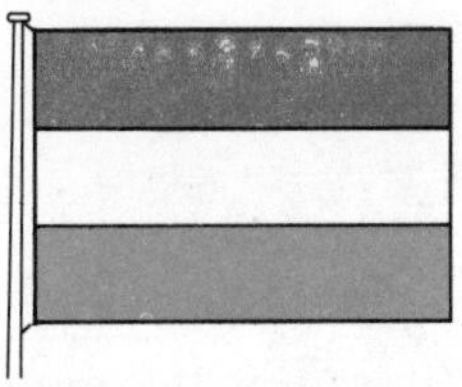

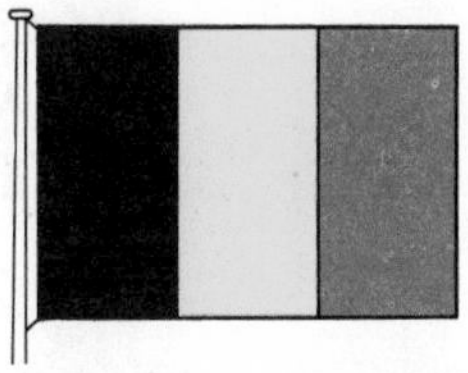

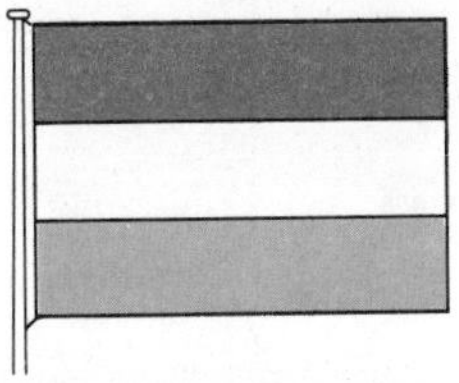

BELGIUM

PROVINCES

Antwerp, 1,529,826 .... F 6
Brabant, 2,166,372 .... F 7
East Flanders, 1,310,638 .... D 7
Hainault, 1,331,810 .... D 7
Liège, 1,016,131 .... H 7
Limburg, 650,338 .... G 7
Luxembourg, 219,369 .... G 9
Namur, 383,618 .... F 8
West Flanders, 1,052,052 .... B 7

CITIES and TOWNS†

Aalst, 45,900 .... D 7
Aalter, 8,569 .... C 6
Aarlen (Arlon), 14,191 .... H 9
Aarschot, 12,329 .... F 7
Aat (Ath), 11,094 .... D 7
Adinkerke, 2,713 .... A 6
Alken, 8,054 .... G 7
Alost (Aalst), 45,900 .... D 7
Amay, 7,561 .... G 7
Andenne, 8,068 .... G 8
Anderlecht, 103,832 .... B 9
Anderlues, 12,930 .... E 8
Antoing, 3,435 .... C 7
Antwerp (Antwerpen), 234,099 .... E 6
Antwerp, *673,259 .... E 6
Ardooie, 7,163 .... C 7
Arendonk, 9,516 .... G 6
Arlon, 14,191 .... H 9
As, 4,087 .... H 6
Asse, 12,631 .... E 7
Assebroek, 15,195 .... C 6
Assesse, 1,138 .... G 8
Ath, 11,094 .... D 7
Athus, 7,185 .... H 9
Audenarde (Oudenaarde), 21,980 .... D 7
Auderghem, 32,782 .... C 9
Autelbas, 1,606 .... H 9
Auvelais, 8,412 .... F 8
Aywaille, 3,813 .... H 8
Baerle-Duc, 2,171 .... F 6
Balen, 14,719 .... G 6
Barvaux, 1,727 .... H 8
Basècles, 4,245 .... D 7
Bastogne (Bastenaken), 6,476 .... H 9
Beaumont, 1,762 .... E 8
Beauraing, 2,703 .... F 8
Berchem, 49,880 .... F 6
Berchem-Sainte-Agathe, 17,689 .... B 9
Bergen (Mons), 27,042 .... E 8
Bertrix, 4,481 .... G 9
Beveren, 15,350 .... E 6
Bilzen, 7,000 .... G 7
Binche, 10,340 .... E 8
Blankenberge, 10,400 .... C 6
Bocholt, 5,582 .... H 6
Boom, 17,280 .... E 6
Borgerhout, 50,226 .... E 6
Borgloon, 3,543 .... G 7
Borgworm (Waremme), 7,623 .... G 7
Bouillon, 3,089 .... G 9
Bourg-Leopold (Leopoldsburg), 9,621 .... G 6
Boussu, 11,626 .... D 8
Bovigny, 1,015 .... H 8
Braine-l'Alleud, 16,028 .... E 7
Braine-le-Comte, 11,343 .... D 7
Bredene, 9,381 .... B 6
Bree, 10,462 .... H 6
Bruges (Brugge), 52,249 .... C 6
Bruges, *112,611 .... C 6
Brussels (Bruxelles) (cap.), *1,073,111 .... C 9
Charleroi, 24,895 .... E 8
Charleroi, *218,089 .... E 8
Châtelet, 15,314 .... F 8
Châtelineau, 20,293 .... F 8
Chièvres, 3,154 .... D 7
Chimay, 3,309 .... E 8
Ciney, 7,431 .... G 8
Comblain-au-Pont, 3,538 .... G 8
Comines, 8,219 .... B 7
Couillet, 15,055 .... E 8
Courcelles, 17,157 .... E 8
Courtrai, 45,310 .... C 7
Couvin, 4,192 .... F 8
Cul-des-Sarts, 993 .... E 9
Deinze, 6,214 .... D 7
Denderleeuw, 9,699 .... E 7
Dendermonde, 9,663 .... E 6
De Panne, 6,792 .... A 6
Dessel, 7,170 .... G 6
Deurne, 75,819 .... F 6
Diegem, 4,760 .... C 9
Diest, 9,587 .... F 7
Diksmuide, 6,557 .... B 6
Dilbeek, 13,620 .... B 9
Dinant, 9,700 .... G 8
Dison, 8,809 .... H 7
Dixmude (Diksmuide), 6,557 .... B 6
Doel, 1,395 .... E 6
Doornik (Tournai), 33,309 .... C 7
Dour, 10,407 .... D 8
Drogenbos, 4,648 .... B 9
Drongen, 8,312 .... D 6
Dudzele, 2,112 .... C 6
Duffel, 13,560 .... F 6
Ecaussinnes d'Enghien, 6,696 .... E 7
Edingen (Enghien), 4,279 .... D 7
Eeklo, 19,007 .... D 6
Eernegem, 5,865 .... B 6
Eigenbrakel (Braine-l'Alleud), 16,028 .... E 7
Ekeren, 24,535 .... E 6
Ellezelles, 3,676 .... D 7
Enghien, 4,279 .... D 7
Ensival, 5,515 .... H 7
Erquelinnes, 4,812 .... E 8
Esneux, 5,923 .... H 7
Essen, 10,515 .... F 6
Étalle, 1,179 .... H 9
Etterbeek, 52,299 .... C 9
Eupen, 14,856 .... J 7
Evere, 24,289 .... C 9
Evergem, 12,329 .... D 6
Flémalle-Haute, 7,800 .... G 7
Fleurus, 8,475 .... F 8
Florennes, 4,070 .... F 8
Florenville, 2,526 .... G 9
Forest, 55,799 .... B 9
Fosses-la-Ville, 3,887 .... F 8
Frameries, 11,624 .... D 8
Frasnes-lez-Buissenal, 2,672 .... D 7
Furnes (Veurne), 7,475 .... B 6
Ganshoren, 19,154 .... B 9
Gaurain-Ramecroix, 3,599 .... D 7
Gedinne, 1,021 .... F 9
Geel, 28,484 .... F 6
Geldenaken (Jodoigne), 4,194 .... F 7
Gembloux, 11,030 .... F 7
Gemmenich, 2,608 .... H 7
Genk, 55,596 .... H 7
Gent (Ghent), 153,301 .... D 6
Gentbrugge, 22,986 .... D 6
Geraardsbergen, 9,201 .... D 7
Ghent, 153,301 .... D 6
Ghent, *229,687 .... D 6
Gilly, 24,155 .... E 8
Gosselies, 10,970 .... E 8
Grammont (Geraardsbergen), 9,201 .... D 7
Haacht, 4,372 .... F 7
Hal (Halle), 20,071 .... E 7
Halen, 5,321 .... G 7
Halle, 20,071 .... E 7
Hamme, 17,083 .... E 6
Hamont, 6,626 .... H 6
Hannut (Hannuit), 3,069 .... G 7
Harelbeke, 17,981 .... C 7
Hasselt, 38,773 .... G 7
Havelange, 1,495 .... G 8
Heer, 578 .... F 8
Heist, 9,289 .... C 6
Heist-op-den-Berg, 13,206 .... F 6
Herbeumont, 590 .... G 9
Herentals, 18,377 .... F 6
Herselt, 7,318 .... F 6
Herstal, 29,602 .... H 7
Herve, 4,357 .... H 7
Hoboken, 31,815 .... E 6
Hoei (Huy), 13,398 .... G 8
Hoeselt, 5,570 .... H 7
Hoogstraten, 4,376 .... F 6
Hornu, 10,905 .... D 8
Houffalize, 1,297 .... H 8
Huy, 13,398 .... G 8
Ieper, 18,461 .... B 7
Ingelmunster, 9,973 .... C 7
Ixelles, 92,532 .... C 9
Izegem, 22,729 .... C 7
Jambes, 14,924 .... F 8
Jemappes, 12,906 .... D 8
Jemeppe, 12,232 .... G 7
Jette, 37,354 .... B 9
Jodoigne, 4,194 .... F 7
Jumet, 28,811 .... E 8
Kain, 4,900 .... C 7
Kalmthout, 12,122 .... F 6
Kapellen, 12,297 .... F 6
Kessel-Lo, 21,351 .... F 7
Knokke, 14,268 .... C 6
Koekelare, 6,423 .... B 6
Koekelberg, 17,348 .... B 9
Koersel, 10,756 .... G 6
Kontich, 13,193 .... E 6
Kortemark, 5,839 .... C 6
Kortrijk (Courtrai), 45,310 .... C 7
Kraainem, 10,560 .... C 9
La Louvière, 23,447 .... E 8
La Louvière, *113,795 .... E 8
La Roche-en-Ardenne, 1,894 .... G 8
Lanaken, 8,216 .... H 7
Landen, 5,247 .... G 7
Langemark, 4,787 .... B 7
Lede, 10,229 .... D 7
Ledeberg, 11,056 .... D 7
Lens, 1,790 .... D 7
Leopoldsburg, 9,621 .... G 6
Lessines (Lessen), 9,047 .... D 7
Leuven (Louvain), 32,125 .... F 7
Leuze, 7,128 .... D 7
Libramont, 2,774 .... G 9
Lichtervelde, 7,372 .... C 6
Liedekerke, 10,273 .... D 7
Liège, 150,127 .... H 7
Liège, *446,990 .... H 7
Lier (Lierre), 28,557 .... F 6
Lierneux, 2,847 .... H 8
Limbourg (Limburg), 3,973 .... J 7
Linkebeek, 4,096 .... C10
Lokeren, 26,654 .... D 6
Lommel, 20,567 .... G 6
Looz (Borgloon), 3,543 .... G 7
Louvain, 32,125 .... F 7
Luik (Liège), 150,127 .... H 7
Maaseik, 8,383 .... H 6
Machelen, 7,331 .... C 9
Maldegem, 14,182 .... C 6
Malines (Mechelen), 65,728 .... F 6
Malmédy, 6,482 .... J 8
Marche-en-Famenne, 4,423 .... G 8
Marchin, 4,361 .... G 8
Marcinelle, 25,992 .... E 8
Mariembourg, 1,776 .... E 8
Martelange, 1,594 .... H 9
Mechelen, 65,728 .... F 6
Meerhout, 8,359 .... G 6
Meerle, 2,809 .... F 6
Melsbroek, 2,034 .... D 9
Menen (Menin), 22,458 .... C 7
Merchtem, 8,772 .... E 7
Merelbeke, 13,755 .... D 7
Merksem, 39,011 .... E 6
Merksplas, 4,950 .... F 6
Messancy, 3,064 .... H 9
Mettet, 3,366 .... F 8
Meulebeke, 10,619 .... C 7
Moeskron (Mouscron), 37,624 .... C 7
Mol, 27,320 .... G 6
Molenbeek-Saint-Jean, 67,271 .... B 9
Mons, 27,042 .... E 8
Montegnée, 11,882 .... G 7
Montignies-sur-Sambre, 24,048 .... F 8
Mortsel, 27,999 .... E 6
Mouscron, 37,624 .... C 7
Namur (Namen), 32,621 .... F 8
Neerlinter, 1,431 .... G 7
Neerpelt, 8,273 .... G 6
Neufchâteau, 2,739 .... G 9
Nieuwpoort (Nieuport), 7,165 .... B 6
Ninove, 12,087 .... D 7
Nivelles (Nijvel), 15,384 .... E 7
Oostende (Ostend), 57,749 .... B 6
Oostkamp, 8,560 .... C 6
Ophoven, 2,487 .... H 6
Opwijk, 9,622 .... E 7
Ostend, 57,749 .... B 6
Oud-Turnhout, 8,219 .... F 6
Oudenaarde, 21,980 .... D 7
Ougrée, 21,152 .... H 7
Overijse, 14,119 .... F 7
Overpelt, 10,002 .... G 6
Peer, 5,882 .... G 6
Péruwelz, 7,814 .... D 8
Perwez (Perwijs), 2,858 .... F 7
Philippeville, 1,822 .... E 8
Poperinge, 12,619 .... B 7
Poppel, 2,246 .... G 6
Putte, 6,856 .... F 6
Quaregnon, 18,289 .... D 8
Quiévrain, 5,685 .... D 8
Raeren, 3,490 .... J 7
Rance, 1,443 .... E 8
Rebecq-Rognon, 3,831 .... E 7
Renaix (Ronse), 25,371 .... D 7
Retie, 6,339 .... G 6
Rièzes, 307 .... E 9
Rochefort, 4,242 .... G 8
Roeselare, 40,077 .... C 7
Roeulx, 2,605 .... E 8
Ronse, 25,371 .... D 7
Roulers (Roeselare), 40,077 .... C 7
Ruisbroek, 5,685 .... B 9
's Gravenbrakel (Braine-le-Comte), 11,343 .... D 7
Saint-Georges, 6,085 .... G 7
Saint-Gérard, 1,626 .... F 8
Saint-Gilles, 57,238 .... B 9
Saint-Hubert, 3,104 .... G 8
Saint-Josse-ten-Noode, 24,335 .... C 9
Saint-Léger, 1,600 .... H 9
Saint-Vith (Sankt-Vith), 2,935 .... J 8
Schaerbeek, 120,650 .... C 9
Schoten, 28,543 .... F 6
Seraing, 40,937 .... G 7
Sint-Amandsberg, 24,778 .... D 6
Sint-Andries, 15,062 .... C 6
Sint-Lenaarts, 4,464 .... F 6
Sint-Niklaas, 48,851 .... E 6
Sint-Pieters-Leeuw, 15,978 .... B 9
Sint-Truiden (Saint-Trond), 21,131 .... G 7
Sivry, 1,384 .... E 8
Soignies, 11,320 .... D 7
Spa, 9,683 .... H 8
Staden, 5,581 .... B 7
Stavelot, 4,661 .... H 8
Steenokkerzeel, 3,877 .... C 9
Stene, 9,304 .... B 6
Stokkem, 3,380 .... H 6
Strombeek-Bever, 10,027 .... C 9
Tamines, 8,139 .... F 8
Tamise (Temse), 14,559 .... E 6
Templeuve, 3,737 .... C 7
Temse, 14,559 .... E 6
Termonde (Dendermonde), 9,663 .... E 6
Tessenderlo, 10,665 .... G 6
Theux, 5,491 .... H 8
Thuin, 5,877 .... E 8
Tielt, Brabant, 3,813 .... F 7
Tielt, West Flanders, 13,887 .... C 7
Tienen (Tirlemont), 22,660 .... F 7
Tongeren (Tongres), 16,880 .... G 7
Torhout, 14,301 .... C 6
Tournai, 33,309 .... C 7
Tronchiennes (Drongen), 8,312 .... D 6
Tubize (Tubeke), 10,269 .... E 7
Turnhout, 37,828 .... F 6
Uccle (Ukkel), 76,579 .... B 9
Verviers, 35,730 .... H 7

(continued on following page)

Agriculture, Industry and Resources

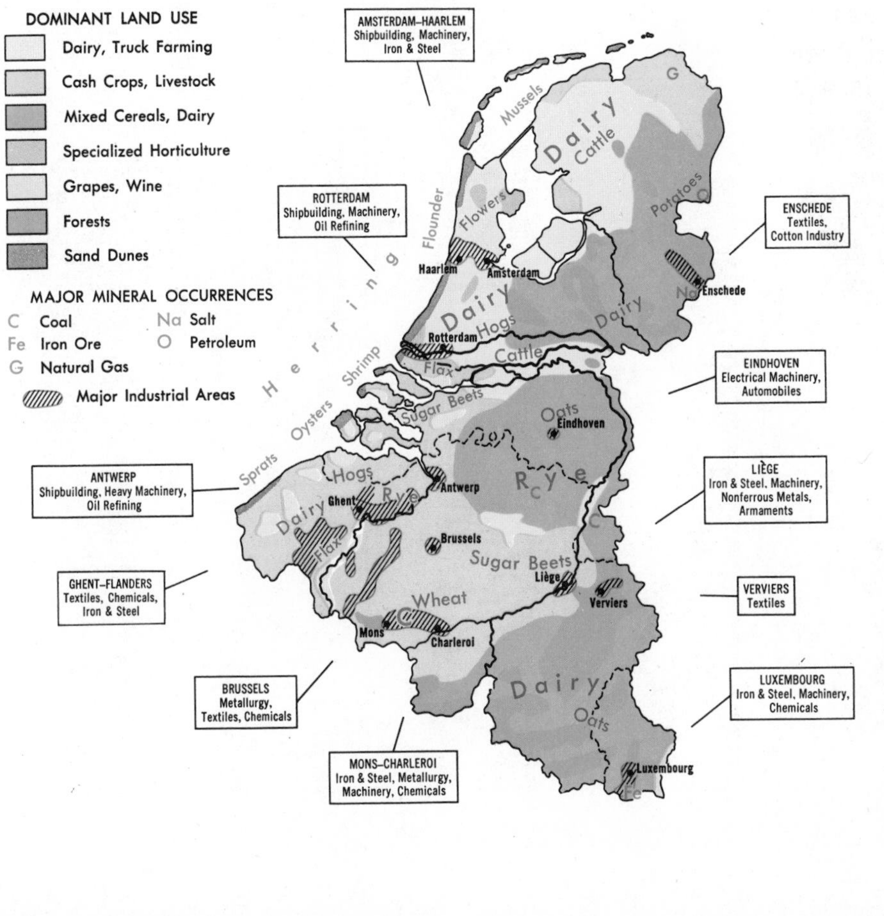

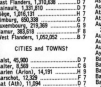

DOMINANT LAND USE
Dairy, Truck Farming
Cash Crops, Livestock
Mixed Cereals, Dairy
Specialized Horticulture
Grapes, Wine
Forests
Sand Dunes
MAJOR MINERAL OCCURRENCES
C Coal
Na Salt
Fe Iron Ore
O Petroleum
G Natural Gas
Major Industrial Areas
AMSTERDAM–HAARLEM
Shipbuilding, Machinery, Iron & Steel
ROTTERDAM
Shipbuilding, Machinery, Oil Refining
ENSCHEDE
Textiles, Cotton Industry
EINDHOVEN
Electrical Machinery, Automobiles
ANTWERP
Shipbuilding, Heavy Machinery, Oil Refining
LIÈGE
Iron & Steel, Machinery, Nonferrous Metals, Armaments
GHENT–FLANDERS
Textiles, Chemicals, Iron & Steel
VERVIERS
Textiles
BRUSSELS
Metallurgy, Textiles, Chemicals
LUXEMBOURG
Iron & Steel, Machinery, Chemicals
MONS–CHARLEROI
Iron & Steel, Metallurgy, Machinery, Chemicals
Mussels
Dairy
Cattle
Potatoes
Flowers
Flounder
Herring
Haarlem
Amsterdam
Enschede
Rotterdam
Hogs
Cattle
Flax
Shrimp
Sugar Beets
Oysters
Oats
Eindhoven
Sprats
Hogs
Rye
Antwerp
Ghent
Flax
Brussels
Sugar Beets
Liège
Verviers
Wheat
Mons
Charleroi
Luxembourg

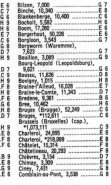

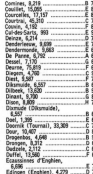

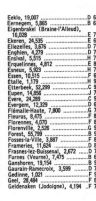

24 Netherlands, Belgium and Luxembourg

(continued)

BELGIUM (continued)

Veurne, 7,475 B 6
Vielsalm, 3,702 J 8
Villers-devant-Orval, 777 G 9
Vilvoorde (Vilvorde), 34,040 F 7
Virton, 3,956 H 9
Visé, 6,595 H 7
Vorst (Forest), 55,799 B 9
Waarschoot, 7,852 D 6
Waasten (Warneton), 3,215 B 7
Waha, 2,664 G 8
Waimes, 2,787 J 8
Walcourt, 2,077 F 8
Wandre, 6,833 H 7
Waregem, 16,928 C 7
Waremme, 7,623 G 7
Warneton, 3,215 B 7
Wasmes, 13,933 D 7
Waterloo, 14,615 E 7
Watermael-Boitsfort, 24,730 C 9
Watervliet, 1,812 D 6
Wavre (Waver), 11,007 F 7
Weismes (Waimes), 2,787 J 8
Wemmel, 11,404 B 9
Wenduine, 1,756 C 6
Wervik, 12,728 B 7
Westende, 2,746 B 6
Westerlo, 7,630 F 6
Wetteren, 20,775 D 7
Wezembeek-Oppem, 10,536 D 9
Wezet (Visé), 6,595 H 7
Willebroek, 15,650 E 6
Wilrijk, 42,109 E 6
Wingene, 7,178 C 6
Woluwe-Saint-Lambert, 44.102 C 9
Woluwe-Saint-Pierre, 37,314 C 9
Wolvertem, 5,326 E 7
Ypres (Ieper), 18,461 B 7
Yvoir, 2,837 F 8
Zaventem, 9,941 C 9
Zeebrugge C 6
Zele, 18,386 E 6
Zellik, 5,165 B 9
Zelzate, 11,751 D 6
Zinnik (Soignies), 11,320 D 7
Zonhoven, 12.910 G 6
Zottegem, 6,905 D 7

OTHER FEATURES

Albert (canal) F 6
Ardennes (plateau) F 9
Botrange (mt.) J 8
Dender (river) D 7
Dyle (river) F 7
Hohe Venn (plateau) H 8
Lesse (river) F 8
Mark (river) F 6
Meuse (river) F 8
Nethe (river) F 6
Ourthe (river) H 8
Rupel (river) F 7
Scheldt (Schelde) (river) C 7
Schnee Eifel (plateau) J 8
Semois (river) G 9
Senne (river) E 7
Vesdre (river) H 7
Weisserstein (mt.) J 8
Yser (river) B 7
Zitterwald (plateau) J 8

LUXEMBOURG

CITIES and TOWNS

Clervaux, 933 J 8
Diekirch, 4,899 J 9
Differdange, 9,808 H 9
Dudelange, 14,849 J10
Echternach, 3,472 J 9
Esch-sur-Alzette, 27,921 J 9
Esch-sur-Sauer, 265 H 9
Ettelbrück, 5,557 J 9
Grevenmacher, 2,850 J 9
Luxembourg (cap.), 77,458 J 9
Mersch, 1,682 J 9
Pétange, 6,251 H 9
Redange, 990 H 9
Remich, 1,958 J 9
Troisvierges, 928 J 8
Vianden, 1,381 J 9
Wasserbillig, 2,047 J 9
Wiltz, 1,538 H 9

OTHER FEATURES

Alzette (river) J 9
Clerf (river) J 8
Eisling (mts.) H 9
Mosel (river) J 9
Our (river) J 9
Sauer (river) J 9

NETHERLANDS

PROVINCES

Drenthe, 366,590 K 3
Friesland, 521,751 H 2
Gelderland, 1,505,760 H 4
Groningen, 517,305 K 2
Limburg, 998,570 H 6
North Brabant, 1,787,783 F 5
North Holland, 2,244,456 F 3
Overijssel, 920,882 J 4
South Holland, 2,968,670 E 5
Utrecht, 801,285 G 4
Zeeland, 305,754 D 6

CITIES and TOWNS

Aalsmeer, †18,166 F 4
Aalst, 4,423 G 6
Aalten, †16,295 K 5
Aardenburg, †3,853 C 6
Akkrum, 2,296 H 2
Alkmaar, †52,091 F 3
Almelo, †58,941 K 4
Amersfoort, †78,189 G 4
Amstelveen, †69,167 B 5
Amsterdam (cap.), 831,463 B 4
Amsterdam, *918,676 B 4
Andijk, †4,602 G 3
Anjum, 939 J 2
Apeldoorn, 123,628 H 4
Apeldoorn, *214,974 H 4
Appelscha, 1,622 J 3
Appingedam, †10,987 K 2
Arnhem, 132,531 H 4
Arnhem, *232,860 H 4
Assen, †38,956 K 3
Asten, †11,209 H 6
Axel, †8,904 D 6
Baarle-Nassau, †4,948 F 6
Baarn, †24,106 G 4
Badhoevedorp, 8,699 B 5
Balkbrug, 2,468 J 3
Barneveld, †30,046 H 4
Bath, 128 E 6
Beilen, †12,289 K 3
Bergeijk (Hof), †7,816 G 6
Bergen, †13,060 F 3
Bergen op Zoom, †39,051 E 5
Bergum, †4,252 H 2
Berkel, †5,936 F 5
Berkhout, †3,941 F 3
Beverwijk, †41,357 F 4
Blerick, 14,593 J 6
Bloemendaal, †19,253 E 4
Blokzijl, †1,375 H 3
Bodegraven, †14,083 F 4
Bolsward, †9,247 H 2
Borculo, †8,510 J 4
Borger, †10,972 K 3
Borne, †15,423 K 4
Boskoop, †11,600 F 4
Boxmeer, †10,850 H 5
Boxtel, †19,080 G 5
Breda, 121,209 F 5
Breda, *233,704 F 5
Breezand, 1,962 F 3
Breskens, †3,857 C 6
Brielle, †8,314 E 5
Broek, †2,260 C 4
Brouwershaven, †3,256 D 5
Brummen, †18,077 J 4
Buiksloot, 23,738 B 4
Bussum, †41,787 G 4
Callantsoog, †1,698 F 3
Coevorden, †12,481 K 3
Colijnsplaat, 1,477 D 5
Culemborg, 11,083 G 5
Cuyk, †12,144 H 5
Dalen, †4,630 K 3
De Bilt, †29,153 G 4
Dedemsvaart, 6,384 J 3
De Koog, 701 F 2
Delft, 83,698 E 4
Delfzijl, †21,990 K 2
Den Burg, 3,579 F 2
Den Helder, †60,612 F 3
Denekamp, †10,919 L 4
Deurne, †23,949 H 6
Deventer, †65,319 J 4
De Wijk, †4,120 J 3
Diemen, †9,558 C 5
Dieren, 8,612 J 4
Diever, †3,180 J 3
Dinxperlo, †6,248 K 5
Dirksland, †6,092 E 5
Doesburg, †9,451 J 4
Doetinchem, †31,097 J 5
Dokkum, †9,886 H 2
Domburg, †3,154 C 5
Dongen, †16.231 F 5
Doorn, †10,084 G 4
Doornspijk, †10,463 H 4
Dordrecht, †88,699 F 5
Dordrecht, *99,284 F 5
Drachten, 16,529 J 2
Driebergen, †15,828 G 4
Druten, †9,761 H 5
Duivendrecht, 2,656 C 5
Durgerdam, 640 C 4
Echt, †15,795 H 6
Edam, †18,184 G 4
Ede, †71,952 H 4
Eefde, 2,396 J 4
Egmond aan Zee, †5,554 E 3
Eindhoven, 188,631 G 6
Eindhoven, *301,049 G 6
Elburg, †5,135 H 4
Elst, †15,182 H 5

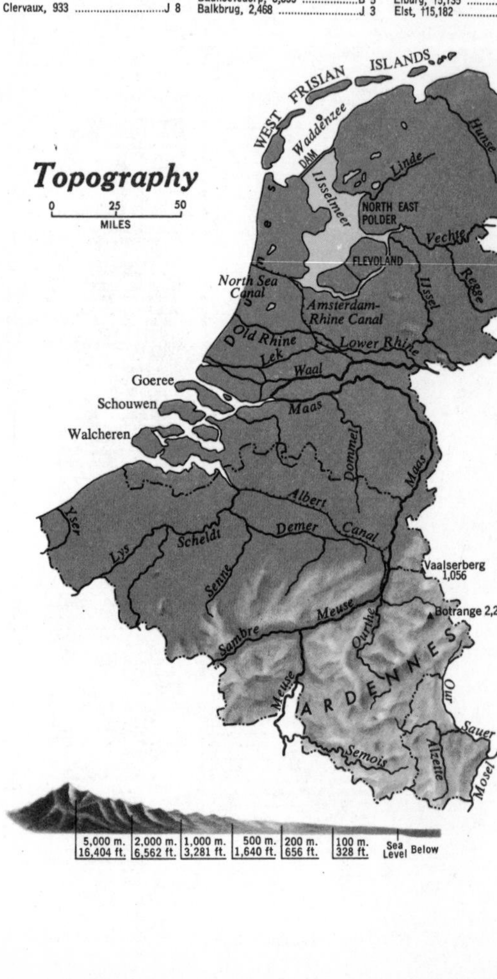

Emmeloord, 7,251 H 3
Emmen, †79,707 K 3
Enkhuizen, †11,502 G 3
Enschede, 139,245 K 4
Epe, †27,515 H 4
Erica, 3,026 K 3
Ermelo, †37,198 H 4
Etten, †19,698 F 5
Flushing, †40,197 C 6
Franeker, †9,575 H 2
Geertruidenberg, †5,575 F 5
Geldermalsen, †7,946 G 5
Geldrop, †26,909 H 6
Geleen, †36,121 H 7
Gemert, †14,329 H 5
Gendringen, †18,028 J 5
Genemuiden, †5,524 H 3
Gennep, †6,922 H 5
Giessendam, †13,588 F 5
Giethoorn, †2,486 J 3
Goes, †25,822 D 6
Goirle, †11,428 G 5
Goor, †9,702 K 4
Gorinchem, †26,380 G 5
Gorredijk, 3,006 J 2
Gouda, †45,990 F 4
Gouda, *84,695 F 4
Graauw, †1,277 E 6
Gramsbergen, †5,431 K 3
Grave, †7,405 H 5
Groenlo, †7,888 K 4
Groesbeek, †17,308 H 5
Groningen, 168,843 K 2
Groningen, *185,757 K 2
Grouw, 3,191 H 2
Haamstede, 1,179 D 5
Haarlem, 172,235 F 4
Haarlemmermeer (Hoofddorp), 4,949 F 4
Hague, The (cap.), 550,613 E 4
Hague, The, *702,296 E 4
Halfweg, 2,171 A 4
Hallum, 1,424 H 2
Hardenberg, †26,011 J 3
Harderwijk, 14,054 H 4
Hardinxveld, †13,588 G 5
Harlingen, †12,552 G 2
Hasselt, †5,005 J 3
Hattem, †9,034 H 4
Heemstede, †26,507 F 4
Heer, †12,217 H 7
Heerde, †15,341 H 4
Heerenveen, †31,434 H 3
Heerlen, †75,147 J 7
Heiloo, †17,736 F 3
Hellendoorn, †29,410 J 4
Hellevoetsluis, †9,653 E 5
Helmond, †57,889 H 6
Helmond, *79,164 H 6
Hengelo, Gelderland, †7,360 J 4
Hengelo, Overijssel, †69,618 K 4
Heusden, †4,587 G 5
Hillegom, †16,963 E 4
Hilvarenbeek, †7,358 G 6
Hilversum, 99,792 G 4
Hindeloopen, †881 G 3
Hippolytushoef, 3,035 G 3
Hoek, †2,817 D 6
Hoek van Holland (Hook of Holland), 5,114 D 5
Hoensbroek, †22,703 H 7
Hof, †7,816 G 6
Holijsloot, 344 C 4
Hollum, 890 H 2
Holwerd, 1,691 H 2
Hoofddorp, 4,949 F 4
Hoogeveen, †37,485 J 3
Hoogezand, †30,189 K 2
Hoogkarspel, †3,681 G 3
Hook of Holland, 5,114 D 5
Hoorn, †18,574 G 3
Horst, †15,310 H 6
Huissen, †9,101 J 5
Huizen, †20,554 G 4
Hulst, †6,699 E 6
IJlst, †1,932 H 2
IJmuiden, 3,587 E 4
IJsselstein, †9,633 F 4
IJzendijke, †2,492 D 6
Ilpendam, †2,955 C 4
Joure, 5,509 H 3
Kampen, †28,902 H 3
Katwijk aan Zee, †36,236 E 4
Kerkbuurt en Thij, †8,244 J 3
Kerkdriel, 3,122 G 5
Kerkrade, †48,150 J 7
Kesteren, †7,290 G 5
Kloosterveen, †7,296 K 3
Kollum, 2,543 J 2
Koog aan de Zaan, †6,114 A 4
Krimpen aan den IJssel, †17,801 F 5
Landsmeer, †6,511 C 4
Laren, †6,528 G 4
Leek, †11,628 J 2
Leerdam, †13,282 F 5
Leeuwarden, 100,006 H 2
Leiden, 101,221 E 4
Lelystad, 716 H 4
Lemmer, 4,399 H 3
Lent, 2,032 H 5
Lisse, †17,049 F 4
Lith, †4,698 G 5
Lochem, †9,452 J 4
Lonneker, 1,599 L 4
Loon op Zand, †16,437 G 5
Losser, 18,713 L 4
Maarssen, †14,734 F 4
Maasbree, †7,676 H 6
Maassluis, †25,878 E 5
Maastricht, †93,927 H 7
Makkum, 2,416 G 2
Margraten, †2,844 H 7
Medemblik, †5,192 G 3
Meerssen, †8,800 H 7
Meppel, †19,364 J 3
Middelburg, †30,211 C 6
Middelharnis, †12,488 E 5
Middenmeer, 1,775 F 3
Millingen aan den Rijn, †4,764 J 5
Moerdijk, 601 F 5
Monnikendam, †6,014 C 4
Montfoort, †2,392 G 4
Muiden, †5,724 G 4
Muntendam, †3,695 K 2
Naaldwijk, †22,306 E 4
Naarden, †17,447 G 4
Nagele, 766 H 3
Neede, †9,739 K 4
Nes, 894 H 2
Nieuw-Buinen, 3,966 K 3
Nieuw-Schoonebeek, 1,602 L 3

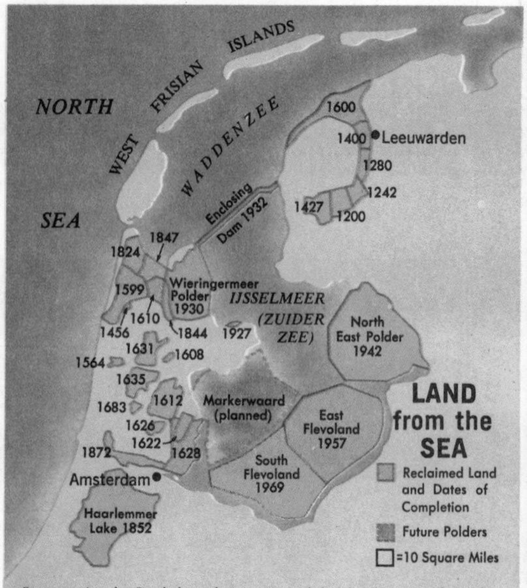

For centuries the Dutch have been renowned for the drainage of marshes and the construction of polders, i.e., arable land reclaimed from the sea. Future projects will convert much of the present IJsselmeer to agricultural land.

Nieuwe Pekela, †5,163 L 2
Nieuwendam, 15,679 C 4
Nieuweschans, †1,846 L 2
Nieuwkoop, †7,835 F 4
Nijkerk, †17,718 H 4
Nijmegen, 148.790 H 5
Nijmegen, *210,865 H 5
Nijverdal, 11,986 J 4
Noordwijk, †20,925 E 4
Norg, †5,386 J 2
Numansdorp, †5,169 E 5
Nunspeet, 7,103 H 4
Odoorn, †11,730 K 3
Oisterwijk, †13,797 G 5
Oldenzaal, †22,604 K 4
Olst, †8,325 J 4
Ommen, †14,712 J 3
Onstwedde, 1,867 K 2
Oostburg, †4,044 C 6
Oosterend, 118 G 2
Oosterhout, †31,826 F 5
Oostmahorn, 131 J 2
Oost-Vlieland, 695 F 2
Oostzaan, †4,869 C 4
Ootmarsum, †3,339 K 4
Oss, †40,085 H 5
Otterlo, 984 H 4
Oud-Beijerland, †10,114 E 5
Ouddorp, †4,226 D 5
Oude-Pekela, †8,085 K 2
Oude-Tonge, 2,459 E 5
Oudenbosch, †9,346 E 5
Oudeschild, 939 F 2
Oudewater, †4,466 F 4
Overloon, 1,007 H 5
Purmerend, †23,288 F 4
Putten, †15,726 H 4
Raalte, †19,885 J 4
Renkum, †33,619 H 5
Reusel, †6,144 G 6
Rheden, †48,713 J 4
Rhenen, †14,860 H 5
Ridderkerk, †41,899 F 5
Rijnsburg, †8,600 F 4
Rijssen, †17,360 J 4
Rijswijk, †50,172 E 4
Roden, †12,444 J 2
Roermond, †35,850 J 6
Roosendaal, †45,935 F 5
Rotterdam, 686,586 E 5
Rotterdam, *1,052,871 E 5
Rutten, 491 H 3
Ruurlo, †6,829 J 4
's Gravendeel, †5,830 E 5
's Gravenhage (The Hague) (cap.), 550,613 E 4
's Gravenhage, *702,296 E 4
's Gravenzande, †12,907 E 4
's Heerenberg, 5,196 J 5
's Hertogenbosch, †81,574 G 5
's Hertogenbosch, *193,356 G 5
Sappemeer, †30,189 K 2
Schagen, †6,772 F 3
Scheveningen, 80,015 E 4
Schiedam, †83,049 E 5
Schiermonnikoog, †814 J 1
Schijndel, †16,362 H 5
Schiphol, 3,368 B 5
Schoonebeek, †7,426 L 3
Schoonhoven, †7,565 F 5
Sint-Annaland, †2,826 E 5
Sint Jacobiparochie, 1,246 H 2
Sittard, †33,887 H 6
Sliedrecht, †19,868 F 5
Slochteren, †12,901 K 2
Sloten, Friesland, †751 H 3
Sloten, North Holland, 1,332 B 5
Sloterdijk, 1,215 B 4
Sluis, †2,810 C 6
Smilde (Kloosterveen), †7,296 K 3
Sneek, †26,244 H 2
Soest, †35,713 G 4
Soesterberg, 4,627 G 4
Stadskanaal, †32.829 L 3
Staphorst, †10,498 J 3
Staveren, †934 G 3
Steenbergen, †12,512 E 5
Steenwijk, †12,226 J 3
Steenwijkerwold (Kerkbuurt en Thij), †8,244 J 3
Stiens, 2,008 H 2
Tegelen, †18,168 J 6
Ter Apel, 2,508 L 3
Termunten, †4,721 K 2
Terneuzen, †22,014 D 6
Tholen, †3,798 E 5
Tiel, †21,789 G 5
Tilburg, 152,589 G 5
Tilburg, *268,395 G 5
Twello, 5,929 J 4
Uden, †23,311 H 5
Uitgeest, †7,151 F 3
Uithoorn, †17,492 F 4
Uithuizen, †4,939 K 2
Ulrum, †3,631 J 2
Urk, 8,027 H 3
Utrecht, 278,966 G 4
Utrecht, *401,981 G 4
Vaals, †10,338 H 7
Valkenswaard, †23,238 H 6
Van Ewijcksluis, 231 F 3
Veendam, †23,709 K 2
Veenendaal, †29,637 G 4
Veenhuizen, †4,097 J 2
Veere, †3,822 D 5
Veghel, †18,374 H 5
Velp, †9,488 J 5
Velsen, †67,580 F 4
Venlo, †62,694 J 6
Venlo, *95,516 J 6
Venraij, †26,056 H 6
Vianen, †8,173 G 5
Vlaardingen, †79,085 E 5
Vlagtwedde, †16,622 L 3
Vlijmen, †12,314 G 5
Vlissingen (Flushing), †40,197 C 6
Volendam, 10,123 G 4
Voorburg, †45,011 E 4
Voorst, †21,379 J 4
Vorden, †6,893 J 4
Vreeswijk, †5,393 G 4
Vrieseveen, †14,658 K 4
Vught, †22,633 G 5
Waalwijk, †23,304 F 5
Wageningen, †26,572 H 5
Wamel, †8,217 H 5
Weert, †35,190 H 6
Weesp, †17,261 C 5
West-Terschelling, †4,294 G 2
Westkapelle, †2,478 C 5
Westzaan, †4,502 A 4
Wierden, †17,653 K 4
Wierum, 628 H 2
Wijhe, †6,225 J 4
Wijk aan Zee, 2,414 E 4
Wijk bij Duurstede, †5,342 G 5
Wijk en Aalburg, †3,583 G 5
Wildervank, 5,280 K 2
Willemstad, †2,306 F 5
Winkel, †2,450 F 3
Winschoten, †18,043 L 2
Winsum, †3,631 K 2
Winterswijk, †26,230 K 5
Woensdrecht, †7,892 E 6
Woerden, †18,448 F 4
Wolvega, 6,620 J 3
Workum, †4,019 G 3
Wormerveer, †14,804 F 4
Yerseke, 4,799 E 6
Zaandam, †63,535 B 4
Zaandijk, †5,696 B 4
Zaltbommel, †7,004 G 5
Zandvoort, †15,451 E 4
Zeist, †55,619 G 4
Zevenbergen, †10,270 E 5
Zierikzee, †7,842 D 5
Zoutkamp, 1,083 J 2
Zundert, †12,124 F 6
Zutphen, †27,610 J 4
Zwanenburg, 6,999 B 4
Zwartsluis, †4,091 H 3
Zwijndrecht, †31,761 F 5
Zwolle, †76,167 J 3

OTHER FEATURES

Alkmaardermeer (lake) F 3
Ameland (isl.), †2,899 H 2
Bergumeer (lake) J 2
Beulaker Wijde (lake) H 3
Borndiep (channel) H 2
De Fluessen (lake) G 3
De Honte (bay) D 6
De Peel (region), 69,356 H 6
De Twente (reg.), 491,403 K 4
De Zaan (river) B 4
Dollart (bay) L 2
Dommel (river) H 6
Duiveland (isl.), 13,317 D 5
Eastern Scheldt (estuary) D 5
Eijerlandsche Gat (strait) F 2
Flevoland Polder, 15,788 G 4
Friesche Gat (channel) J 2
Galgenberg (hill) H 4
Goeree (isl.) D 5
Grevelingen (strait) E 5
Griend (isl.) G 2
Groninger Wad (sound) J 2
Groote IJ Polder, 20 B 4
Haarlemmermeer Polder, 58,966 B 5
Haringvliet (strait) E 5
Het IJ (estuary) C 4
Hoek van Holland (cape) D 5
Hondsrug (hills) K 3
Houtrak Polder, 339 A 4
Hunse (river) K 3
IJmeer (bay) C 4
IJssel (river) J 4
IJsselmeer (lake) G 3
Lauwers (channel) J 1
Lauwers Zee (bay) J 2
Lek (river) F 5
Lemelerberg (hill) J 4
Linde (river) J 3
Lower Rhine (river) H 5
Maas (river) G 5
Mark (river) F 6
Marken (isl.), 1,865 G 4
Markerwaard Polder G 3
Marsdiep (channel) F 3
Noordergat (channel) F 2
North (sea) E 3
North Beveland (isl.), 6,777 D 5
North East Polder, 31,929 H 3
North Holland (canal) C 4
North Sea (canal) F 4
Old Rhine (river) E 4
Ooster Eems (channel) K 1
Oostzaan Polder, 4,869 B 4
Orange (canal) K 3
Overflakkee (isl.), 27,814 E 5
Pinkegat (channel) H 2
Regge (river) K 4
Roer (river) J 6
Rottumeroog (isl.), 3 J 1
Schiermonnikoog (isl.), 814 J 1
Schouwen (isl.), 9,731 D 5
Simonszand (isl.) J 1
Slotermeer (lake) H 3
Sneekermeer (lake) H 2
South Beveland (isl.), 61,968 D 6
Terschelling (isl.), 4,294 G 2
Texel (isl.), 11,394 F 2
Tjeukemeer (lake) H 3
Vaalserberg (mt.) J 7
Vecht (river) J 4
Vechte (river) J 3
Veeregat (channel) D 5
Veluwe (region), 457,834 H 4
Vlie Stroom (strait) G 2
Vlieland (isl.), 933 F 2
Voorne (isl.), 22,742 D 5
Waal (river) G 5
Waddenzee (sound) G 2
Walcheren (isl.), 89,793 C 5
West Frisian (isls.), 18,336 F 2
Wester Eems (channel) K 1
Western Scheldt (De Honte) (bay) D 6
Westgat (channel) F 3
Wieringermeer Polder, 16,562 G 3
Wilhelmina (canal) G 6
Willems (canal) G 5

*City and suburbs.
†Populations of communes.

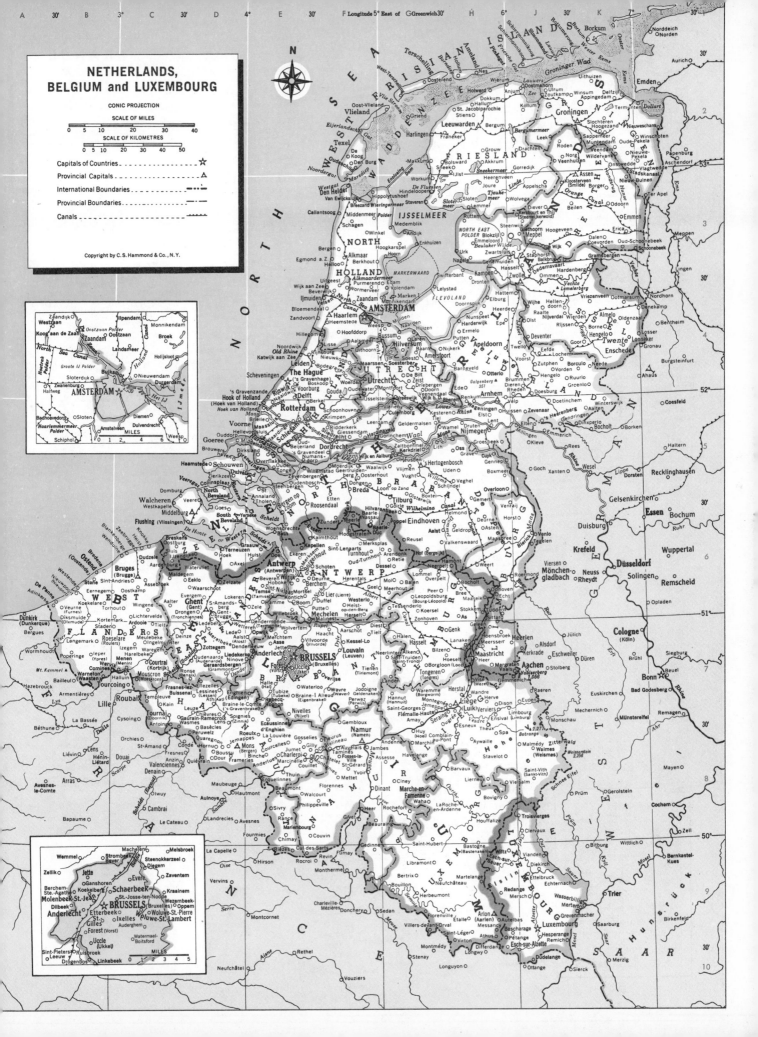

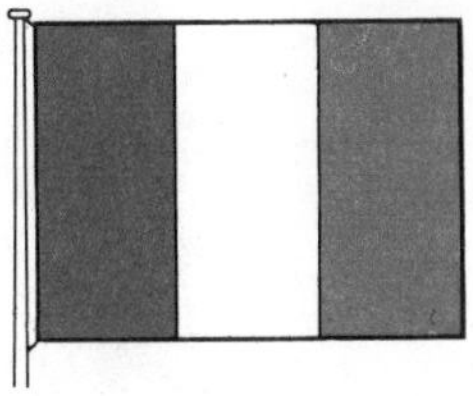

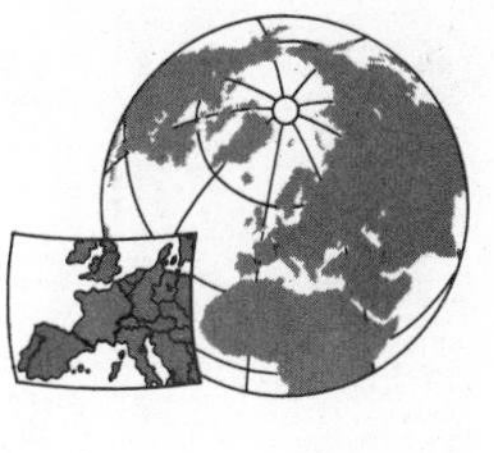

AREA 212,841 sq. mi.
POPULATION 50,770,000
CAPITAL Paris
LARGEST CITY Paris
HIGHEST POINT Mont Blanc 15,771 ft.
MONETARY UNIT franc
MAJOR LANGUAGE French
MAJOR RELIGION Roman Catholicism

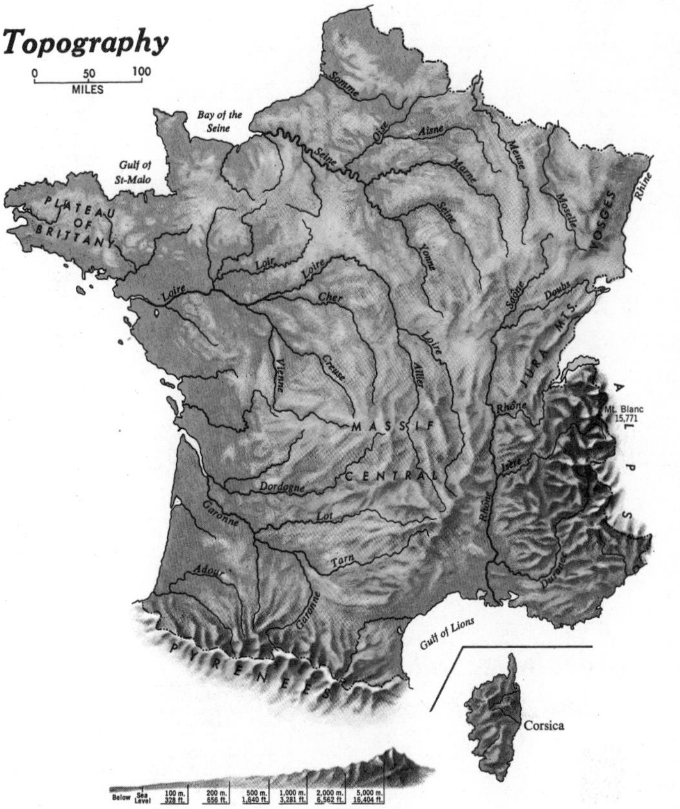
Topography
0 50 100
MILES
Bay of the Seine
Gulf of St-Malo
PLATEAU OF BRITTANY
Somme
Oise
Aisne
Seine
Marne
Meuse
Moselle
Rhine
VOSGES
Loire
Yonne
Saône
Doubs
JURA MTS.
Cher
Vienne
Creuse
Allier
MASSIF CENTRAL
Rhône
Mt. Blanc 15,771
ALPS
Isère
Dordogne
Lot
Garonne
Tarn
Adour
Durance
Gulf of Lions
PYRENEES
Corsica
Below Sea Level
100 m. 328 ft.
200 m. 656 ft.
500 m. 1,640 ft.
1,000 m. 3,281 ft.
2,000 m. 6,562 ft.
5,000 m. 16,404 ft.

DEPARTMENTS

Ain, 339,262	F 4
Aisne, 526,346	E 3
Allier, 386,533	E 4
Alpes-de-Haute-Provence, 104,813	G 5
Alpes-Maritimes, 722,070	G 6
Ardèche, 256,927	F 5
Ardennes, 309,380	F 3
Ariège, 138,478	D 6
Aube, 270,325	E 3
Aude, 278,323	E 6
Aveyron, 281,568	E 5
Bas-Rhin, 827,367	G 3
Belfort (terr.), 118,450	G 4
Bouches-du-Rhône, 1,470,271	F 6
Calvados, 519,695	C 3
Cantal, 169,330	E 5
Charente, 331,016	D 5
Charente-Maritime, 483,622	C 5
Cher, 304,601	E 4
Corrèze, 237,858	D 5
Corsica (Corse), 269,831	B 6
Côte-d'Or, 421,192	F 4
Côtes-du-Nord, 506,102	B 3
Creuse, 156,876	D 4
Deux-Sèvres, 326,462	C 4
Dordogne, 374,073	D 5
Doubs, 426,363	G 4
Drôme, 342,891	F 5
Essonne, 674,157	E 3
Eure, 383,385	D 3
Eure-et-Loir, 302,207	D 3
Finistère, 768,929	A 3
Gard, 478,544	F 6
Gers, 181,577	D 6
Gironde, 1,009,390	C 5
Haut-Rhin, 585,018	G 4
Haute-Garonne, 690,712	D 6
Haute-Loire, 208,337	E 5
Haute-Marne, 214,336	F 3
Haute-Saône, 214,176	G 4
Haute-Savoie, 378,550	G 5
Haute-Vienne, 341,589	D 5
Hautes-Alpes, 91,790	G 5
Hautes-Pyrénées, 225.730	D 6
Hauts-de-Seine, 1,461,619	A 2
Hérault, 591,397	E 6
Ille-et-Vilaine, 652,722	C 3
Indre, 247,178	D 4
Indre-et-Loire, 437,870	D 4
Isère, 768,450	F 5
Jura, 233,547	F 4
Landes, 277,381	C 5
Loir-et-Cher, 267,896	D 4
Loire, 722,383	F 5
Loire-Atlantique, 861,452	C 4
Loiret, 430,629	E 4
Lot, 151,198	D 5
Lot-et-Garonne, 290,592	D 5
Lozère, 77,258	E 5
Maine-et-Loire, 584,709	C 4
Manche, 451,939	C 3
Marne, 485,388	F 3
Mayenne, 252,762	C 3
Meurthe-et-Moselle, 705,413	G 3
Meuse, 209,513	F 3
Morbihan, 540,474	B 4
Moselle, 971,314	G 3
Nièvre, 247,702	E 4
Nord, 2,417,899	E 2
Oise, 540,988	E 3
Orne, 288,524	C 3
Paris, 2,590,771	B 2
Pas-de-Calais, 1,397,159	E 2
Puy-de-Dôme, 547,743	E 5
Pyrénées-Atlantiques, 508,734	C 6
Pyrénées-Orientales, 281,976	E 6
Rhône, 1,325,611	F 5
Saône-et-Loire, 550,362	F 4
Sarthe, 461,839	D 3
Savoie, 288,921	G 5
Seine-et-Marne, 604,340	E 3
Seine-Maritime, 1,113,977	D 3
Seine-Saint-Denis, 1,251,792	B 1
Somme, 512,113	E 3
Tarn, 332,011	E 6
Tarn-et-Garonne, 183,572	D 5
Val-de-Marne, 1,121,340	B 2
Val-d'Oise, 693,269	E 3
Var, 555,926	G 6
Vaucluse, 353,966	F 6
Vendée, 421,250	C 4
Vienne, 340,256	D 4
Vosges, 388,201	G 3
Yonne, 283,376	E 4
Yvelines, 853,386	D 3

CITIES and TOWNS

Abbeville, 23,770	D 2
Agde, 8,812	E 6
Agen, 34,592	D 5
Aix-en-Provence, 74,948	F 6
Aix-les-Bains, 20,594	G 5
Ajaccio, 38,776	B 7
Albert, 10,937	E 2
Albertville, 15,422	G 5
Albi, 38,867	E 6
Alençon, 30,368	D 3
Aléria, 1,000	B 6
Alès, 31,948	E 5
Ambérieu-en-Bugey, 8,570	F 5
Amboise, 8,408	D 4
Amiens, 116,107	D 3
Angers, 127,415	C 4
Angoulême, 46,584	D 5
Annecy, 53,361	G 5
Annonay, 19,591	F 5
Antibes, 47,393	G 6
Antony, 56,556	B 2
Apt, 8,502	F 6
Arcachon, 14,852	C 5
Argentan, 14,418	D 3
Argenteuil, 87,106	A 1
Arles, 33,575	F 6
Armentières, 24,460	E 2
Arras, 48,494	E 2
Asnières, 79,942	A 1
Aubagne, 17,055	F 6
Aubenas, 10,480	F 5
Aubervilliers, 73,559	B 1
Aubusson, 5,641	E 4
Auch, 18,072	D 6
Audincourt, 13,487	G 4
Aulnay-sous-Bois, 61,384	B 1
Auray, 8,180	B 4
Aurignac, 783	D 6
Aurillac, 26,776	E 5
Autun, 17,194	F 4
Auxerre, 33,700	E 4
Avallon, 6,615	E 4
Avesnes-sur-Helpe, 6,253	F 2
Avignon, 78,871	F 6
Avion, 22,390	E 2
Avranches, 9,751	C 3
Bagnères-de-Bigorre, 9,139	D 6
Bagnères-de-Luchon, 4,079	D 6
Bagnolet, 33,607	B 2
Bagnols-sur-Cèze, 15,336	F 5
Bar-le-Duc, 18,874	F 3
Bar-sur-Seine, 2,642	F 3
Barfleur, 825	C 3
Bastia, 48,800	B 6
Bayeux, 11,190	C 3
Bayonne, 39.761	C 6
Beaucaire, 8,820	F 6
Beaune, 16,441	F 4
Beauvais, 46,284	E 3
Bédarieux, 6,929	E 6
Belfort, 53,001	G 4
Belley, 5,958	F 5
Berck, 13,658	D 2
Bergerac, 24,184	D 5
Bernay, 9,298	D 3
Besançon, 107,939	G 4
Bessèges, 5,421	F 5
Béthune, 26,144	E 2
Béziers, 74,517	E 6
Biarritz, 26,628	C 6
Blois, 39,279	D 4
Bobigny, 39,321	B 1
Bolbec, 12,517	D 3
Bondy, 51,555	B 1
Bordeaux, 263,808	C 5
Bordeaux, †648,000	C 5
Boulogne-Billancourt, 108,846	A 2
Boulogne-sur-Mer, 49,064	D 2
Bourg-en-Bresse, 35,064	F 4
Bourges, 67,137	E 4
Bressuire, 8,010	C 4
Brest, 150,696	A 3
Briançon, 7,551	G 5
Briare, 4,725	E 4
Brignoles, 8,010	G 6
Brive-la-Gaillarde, 45,314	D 5
Bruay-en-Artois, 38,608	E 2
Caen, 106,790	C 3
Cahors, 17,775	D 5
Calais, 70,153	D 2
Caluire-et-Cuire, 37,541	F 5
Calvi, 2,523	B 6
Cambrai, 37,290	E 2
Cannes, 66,590	G 6
Carcassonne, 40,580	D 6
Carentan, 5,207	C 3
Carmaux, 13,423	E 5
Carpentras, 18,092	F 5
Castelnaudary, 8,550	E 6
Castelsarrasin, 7,912	D 6
Castres, 35,975	E 6
Cavaillon, 14,815	F 6
Cayeux-sur-Mer, 2,489	D 2
Chalon-sur-Saône, 47,004	F 4
Châlons-sur-Marne, 48,558	F 3
Chambéry, 49,858	F 5
Chambord, 200	D 4
Chamonix-Mont Blanc, 5,907	G 5
Champigny-sur-Marne, 70,353	C 2
Chantilly, 10,156	E 3
Charenton-le-Pont, 22,220	B 2
Charleville-Mézières, 55,230	F 3
Chartres, 34,128	D 3
Château-du-Loir, 5,239	D 4
Château-Gontier, 7,881	C 4
Château-Renault, 5,082	D 4
Château-Thierry, 10,858	E 3
Châteaubriant, 11,196	C 4
Châteaudun, 13,715	D 3
Châteauneuf-sur-Loire, 4,603	E 4
Châteauroux, 48,867	D 4
Châtellerault, 33,491	D 4
Châtillon, 24,468	B 2
Châtillon-sur-Seine, 6,128	F 4
Chatou, 22,495	A 1
Chaumont, 25,602	F 3
Chauny, 13,714	E 3
Chelles, 22,111	C 1
Cherbourg, 37,933	C 3
Chinon, 5,435	D 4
Choisy-le-Roi, 41,080	B 2
Cholet, 40,224	C 4
Clamart, 54,866	A 2
Clermont, 7,119	E 3
Clermont-Ferrand, 145,856	E 5
Clichy, 52,398	B 1
Cluny, 3,552	F 4
Cluses, 12,391	G 4
Cognac, 21,137	C 5
Colmar, 58,623	G 3
Colombes, 80,224	A 1
Commentry, 8,129	E 4
Commercy, 7,043	F 3
Compiègne, 28,881	E 3
Concarneau, 16,458	A 4
Cosne-sur-Loire, 8,931	E 4
Coudekerque-Branche, 22,972	E 2
Coulommiers, 11.182	E 3
Courbevoie, 57,998	A 1
Coutances, 8,599	C 3
Coutras, 4,251	C 5
Creil, 31,792	E 3
Crépy-en-Valois, 8,506	E 3
Créteil, 48,757	B 2
Cusset, 12,286	E 4
Dax, 18,185	C 6
Deauville, 5,103	C 3
Decazeville, 9,581	E 5
Denain, 27,840	E 2
Dieppe, 29,829	D 3
Digne, 11,973	G 5
Digoin, 9,585	F 4
Dijon, 143,120	F 4
Dinan, 12,999	B 3
Dinard, 9,042	B 3
Dôle, 25,620	F 4
Domrémy-la-Pucelle, 184	F 3
Douai, 47,347	E 2
Douarnenez, 18,442	A 3
Draguignan, 16,139	G 6
Drancy, 69,226	B 1
Dreux, 28,156	D 3
Dunkirk (Dunkerque), 26,038	E 2
Elbeuf, 19,110	D 3
Embrun, 3,986	G 5
Épernay, 26,094	E 3
Épinal, 36,219	G 3
Épinay-sur-Seine, 41,538	B 1
Étampes, 15,542	E 3
Étaples, 9,092	D 2
Eu, 7,866	D 3
Évreux, 41,004	D 3
Évry, 7,047	E 3
Falaise, 6,977	C 3
Fécamp, 21,098	D 3
Figeac, 8,462	D 5
Firminy, 24,545	F 5
Flers, 16,677	C 3
Foix, 9,061	D 6
Fontainebleau, 17,565	E 3
Fontenay-le-Comte, 10,884	C 4
Fontenay-sous-Bois, 38,737	C 2
Forbach, 23,062	G 3
Fougères, 25,745	C 3
Fourmies, 14,895	F 2
Fréjus, 22,567	G 6
Gagny, 35,745	C 1
Gap, 22,027	G 5
Gardanne, 12,601	F 6
Gennevilliers, 45,925	B 1
Gentilly, 18,638	B 2
Gex, 3,078	G 4
Gien, 11,655	E 4
Gisors, 7,024	D 3
Givet, 7,697	F 2
Givors, 17,545	F 5
Granville, 12,315	C 3
Grasse, 24,398	G 6
Graulhet, 10,318	E 6
Gray, 7,782	F 4
Grenoble, 161,230	F 5
Guebwiller, 10,684	G 4
Guéret, 12,441	D 4
Guingamp, 9,091	B 3
Guise, 6,732	E 3
Haguenau, 22,335	G 3
Ham, 5,565	E 3
Harfleur, 15,503	D 3
Hautmont, 17,818	F 2
Hayange, 10,218	F 3
Hazebrouck, 16,768	E 2
Hendaye, 7,536	C 6
Hénin-Liétard, 25,067	E 2
Hennebont, 7,605	B 4
Héricourt, 7,376	G 4
Hirson, 11,764	F 3
Honfleur, 9,017	D 3
Hyères, 27,600	G 6
Issoire, 11,745	E 5
Issoudun, 14,559	D 4
Issy-les-Moulineaux, 50,260	A 2
Istres, 8,713	F 6
Ivry-sur-Seine, 60,342	B 2
Joigny, 9,609	E 3
La Baule-Escoublac, 11,962	B 4
La Ciotat, 19,485	F 6
La Courneuve, 42,812	B 1
La Flèche, 9,536	C 4
La Grand-Combe, 8,608	E 5
La Roche-sur-Yon, 32,279	C 4
La Rochelle, 72,075	C 4
La Seyne-sur-Mer, 42,958	F 6
La Tour-du-Pin, 5,649	F 5
L'Aigle, 7,478	D 3
Landerneau, 12,356	B 3
Langeac, 4,584	E 5
Langres, 8,945	F 4
Lannion, 10,066	B 3
Laon, 25,623	E 3
Laval, 45,051	C 3
Lavelanet, 8,512	E 6
Le Blanc-Mesnil, 48,212	B 1
Le Bourget, 9,625	B 1
Le Cateau, 8,922	E 2
Le Chesnay, 13,586	A 2
Le Creusot, 33,581	F 4
Le Croisic, 4,092	B 4
Le Havre, 198,021	C 3
Le Mans, 140,520	C 3
Le Puy, 24,816	F 5
Le Teil, 7,872	F 5
Le Tourquet-Paris-Plage, 4,403	D 2
Le Tréport, 6,194	D 2
Lens, 41,800	E 2
Les Andelys, 6,292	D 3
Les Sables-d'Olonne, 17,856	B 4
Levallois-Perret, 58,890	B 1
Lézignan-Corbières, 7,101	E 6
Libourne, 19,981	C 5
Liévin, 35,733	E 2
Lille, 189,697	E 2
Lille, †1,042,000	E 2
Limoges, 127,605	D 5
Limoux, 9,150	E 6
Lisieux, 23,337	D 3
Livry-Gargan, 32,015	C 1
Lodève, 6,899	E 6
Longwy, 21,052	F 3
Lons-le-Saunier, 18,649	F 4
Lorient, 66,023	B 4
Loudun, 6,118	D 4
Lourdes, 17,627	C 6
Louviers, 15,159	D 3
Lunel, 10,178	E 6
Lunéville, 22,961	G 3
Luxeuil-les-Bains, 9,203	G 4
Lyon, 524,500	F 5
Lyon, †1,305,000	F 5
Mâcon, 33,266	F 4
Maisons-Alfort, 53,118	B 2
Maisons-Laffitte, 24,041	A 1
Malakoff, 36,198	B 2
Manosque, 13,352	G 6
Mantes-la-Jolie, 25,842	D 3
Marmande, 12,145	C 5
Marseille, 880,527	F 6
Marseille, †1,015,000	F 6
Martigues, 17,771	F 6
Maubeuge, 31,992	F 2
Mayenne, 10,010	C 3
Mazamet, 14,650	E 6
Meaux, 29,966	E 3
Melun, 33,345	E 3
Mende, 9,424	E 5
Menton, 23,401	G 6
Metz, 105,533	G 3
Meudon, 30,735	A 2
Millau, 21,420	E 5
Moissac, 7,694	D 5
Mont-de-Marsan, 22,771	C 6
Mont-Dore, 2,045	E 5
Mont-Saint-Michel, 72	C 3
Montargis, 18,087	E 3
Montauban, 33,945	D 5
Montbéliard, 23,402	G 4
Montbrison, 8,733	E 5
Montceau-les-Mines, 18,621	F 4
Montdidier, 5,785	E 3
Montélimar, 23,831	F 5
Montfort, 2,563	C 3
Montigny-les-Metz, 24,417	G 3
Montluçon, 57,638	E 4
Montpellier, 152,105	E 6
Montreuil, 95,420	B 2
Montrouge, 44,788	B 2
Morlaix, 16,750	B 3
Moulins, 25,778	E 4
Moûtiers, 4,066	G 5
Moyeuvre-Grande, 14,559	G 3
Mulhouse, 115,632	G 4
Muret, 10,515	D 6
Nancy, 121,910	G 3
Nanterre, 90,124	A 1
Nantes, 253,105	C 4
Narbonne, 35,236	E 6
Nemours, 8,081	E 3
Neufchâteau, 7,656	F 3
Neufchâtel-en-Bray, 5,734	D 3
Neuilly-sur-Seine, 70,787	B 1
Nevers, 42,092	E 4
Nice, 301,400	G 6
Nîmes, 115,561	F 6
Niort, 46,749	C 4
Nogent-le-Rotrou, 11,040	D 3
Nogent-sur-Seine, 4,271	E 3
Noisy-le-Sec, 34,058	B 1
Noyon, 11,567	E 3
Nyons, 4,311	F 5
Oloron-Sainte-Marie, 12,597	C 6
Orange, 17,582	F 5
Orléans, 94,382	D 3
Orly, 30,151	B 2
Orthez, 8,778	C 6
Oullins, 26,520	F 5
Oyonnax, 19,571	F 4
Pamiers, 13,183	D 6
Pantin, 47,580	B 1
Paray-le-Monial, 10,324	F 4
Paris (cap.), 2,580,010	B 2
Paris, *7,953,065	B 2
Paris, †9,283,000	B 2
Parthenay, 11,177	C 4
Pau, 71,865	C 6
Périgueux, 36,991	D 5
Perpignan, 100,086	E 6
Pessac, 35,343	C 5
Ploërmel, 3,720	B 4
Poitiers, 68,082	D 4
Pont-à-Mousson, 13,283	G 3
Pont-l'Abbé, 6,227	A 4
Pont-l'Évêque, 2,823	D 3
Pontarlier, 16,250	G 4
Pontivy, 9,674	B 3
Pontoise, 16,633	E 3
Port-de-Bouc, 13,447	F 6
Port-Louis, 3,921	B 4

(continued on following page)

HISTORIC PROVINCES

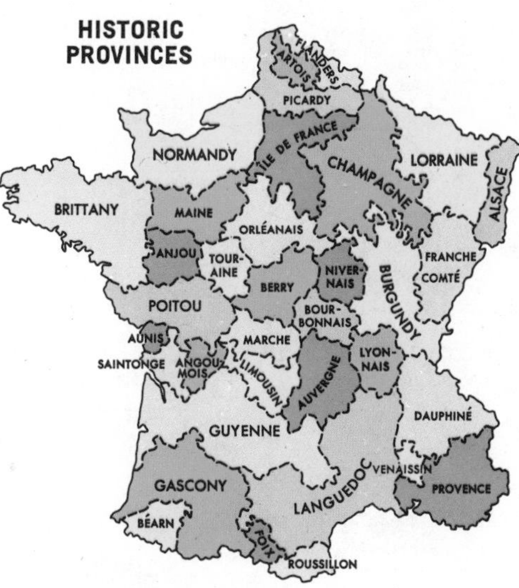
FLANDERS
ARTOIS
PICARDY
NORMANDY
ILE DE FRANCE
CHAMPAGNE
LORRAINE
ALSACE
BRITTANY
MAINE
ORLÉANAIS
ANJOU
TOURAINE
BERRY
NIVERNAIS
BURGUNDY
FRANCHE COMTÉ
POITOU
BOURBONNAIS
AUNIS
MARCHE
SAINTONGE
ANGOUMOIS
LIMOUSIN
LYONNAIS
AUVERGNE
DAUPHINÉ
GUYENNE
GASCONY
LANGUEDOC
VENAISSIN
PROVENCE
BÉARN
FOIX
ROUSSILLON

A resident of the city of Caen thinks of himself as a Norman rather than as a citizen of the modern department of Calvados. In spite of the passing of nearly two centuries, the historic provinces which existed before 1790 command the local patriotism of most Frenchmen.

Port-St-Louis-du-Rhône, 7,194 ....F 6
Port-Vendres, 5,358 ....E 6
Porto-Vecchio, 3,324 ....B 7
Privas, 8,113 ....F 5
Provins, 11,205 ....E 3
Puteaux, 37,801 ....A 1
Quiberon, 4,305 ....B 4
Quimper, 47,811 ....A 3
Quimperlé, 9,701 ....A 4
Rambouillet, 14,043 ....D 3
Redon, 8,767 ....C 4
Reims, 151,988 ....E 3
Remiremont, 9,018 ....G 3
Rennes, 176,024 ....C 3
Rethel, 7,737 ....F 3
Révin, 11,978 ....F 2
Rezé, 31,113 ....C 4
Rive-de-Gier, 15,483 ....F 5
Roanne, 53,178 ....E 4
Rochefort, 26,223 ....C 4
Rodez, 23,041 ....E 5
Romans-sur-Isère, 29,430 ....F 5
Romilly-sur-Seine, 16,867 ....E 3
Romorantin-Lanthenay, 13,516 ....D 4
Roubaix, 114,239 ....E 2
Rouen, 118,323 ....D 3
Royan, 17,187 ....C 5
Ruell-Malmaison, 60,130 ....A 2
Sablé-sur-Sarthe, 8,194 ....C 4
Saint-Affrique, 6,443 ....E 5
Saint-Amand-Mont-Rond, 11,035.E 4
Saint-Brieuc, 49,305 ....B 3
Saint-Céré, 3,682 ....D 5
Saint-Chamond, 35,362 ....F 5
Saint-Claude, 12,344 ....F 4
Saint-Cloud, 28,016 ....A 2
Saint-Denis, 99,027 ....B 1
Saint-Dié, 24,652 ....G 3
Saint-Dizier, 35,742 ....F 3
Saint-Étienne, 212,843 ....F 5
Saint-Florent-sur-Cher, 6,251 ....E 4
Saint-Flour, 5,582 ....E 5
Saint-Gaudens, 9,776 ....D 6
Saint-Germain-en-Laye, 36,251...D 3
Saint-Girons, 7,462 ....D 6
Saint-Jean-d'Angély, 8,883 ....C 4
Saint-Jean-de-Luz, 10,206 ....C 6
Saint-Jean-de-Maurienne, 8,407...G 5
Saint-Jean-Pied-de-Port, 1,677 ...C 6
Saint-Junien, 8,624 ....D 5
Saint-Lô, 17,347 ....C 3
Saint-Malo, 40,252 ....B 3
Saint-Mandé, 22,998 ....B 2
Saint-Maur-des-Fossés, 77,122 ....B 2
Saint-Mihiel, 5,262 ....F 3
Saint-Nazaire, 60,696 ....B 4
Saint-Omer, 17,647 ....E 2
Saint-Ouen, 48,304 ....B 1
Saint-Quentin, 63,932 ....E 3
Saint-Raphaël, 16,117 ....G 6
Saint-Tropez, 5,138 ....G 6
Saint-Vallier, 4,863 ....F 5
Saint-Yrieix-la-Perche, 4,655 ....D 5
Sainte-Mère-Église, 889 ....C 3
Sainte-Savine, 11,616 ....E 3

Saintes, 24,594 ....C 4
Salins-les-Bains, 4,084 ....F 4
Salon-de-Provence, 24,803 ....F 6
Sarrebourg, 11,104 ....G 3
Sarreguemines, 23,074 ....G 3
Sartène, 4,117 ....B 7
Sartrouville, 39,722 ....A 1
Saumur, 21,354 ....C 4
Saverne, 9,432 ....G 3
Sedan, 22,998 ....F 3
Sélestat, 14,558 ....G 3
Senlis, 10,111 ....E 3
Sens, 22,658 ....E 3
Sète, 40,220 ....E 6
Sèvres, 20,025 ....A 2
Soissons, 25,409 ....E 3
Sotteville-lès-Rouen, 33,503 .....D 3
Stiring-Wendel, 13,757 ....G 3
Strasbourg, 247,526 ....H 3
Suresnes, 40,393 ....A 2
Tarare, 12,116 ....F 5
Tarascon, 8,848 ....F 6
Tarbes, 55,200 ....D 6
Thann, 8,108 ....G 3
Thiers, 16,200 ....E 5
Thionville, 35,747 ....G 3
Thonon-les-Bains, 20,095 ....G 4
Thouars, 11,526 ....C 4
Tonnerre, 5,562 ....E 3
Toulon, 169,593 ....F 6
Toulouse, 331,751 ....D 6
Tourcoing, 93,675 ....E 2
Tours, 126,414 ....D 4
Trouville-sur-Mer, 5,718 ....C 3
Troyes, 74,409 ....F 3
Tulle, 17,640 ....D 5
Uckange, 10,326 ....G 3
Uzès, 6,201 ....F 5
Valence, 60,130 ....F 5
Valenciennes, 46,237 ....E 2
Valognes, 5,218 ....C 3
Vannes, 36,380 ....B 4
Vence, 6,450 ....G 6
Vendôme, 15,854 ....D 4
Vénissieux, 47,460 ....F 5
Verdun-sur-Meuse, 21,306 ....F 3
Vernon, 16,983 ....D 3
Versailles, 89,035 ....A 2
Vesoul, 16,079 ....F 4
Vichy, 33,458 ....E 4
Vienne, 26,512 ....F 5
Villefranche, 6,619 ....G 6
Villefranche-de-Rouergue, 9,382..E 5
Villefranche-sur-Saône, 25,995...F 4
Villejuif, 48,737 ....B 2
Villemomble, 28,731 ....C 1
Villeneuve-St-Georges, 30,229 ....B 2
Villeneuve-sur-Lot, 18,612 ....D 5
Villeurbanne, 119,420 ....F 5
Vincennes, 49,116 ....B 2
Vire, 10,819 ....C 3
Vitré, 10,125 ....C 3
Vitry-le-François, 16,409 ....F 3

Vitry-sur-Seine, 77,616 ....B 2
Vittel, 6,343 ....F 3
Voiron, 15,693 ....F 5
Wissembourg, 5,341 ....H 3
Yvetot, 9,208 ....D 3

OTHER FEATURES

Adour (river) ....C 6
Ain (river) ....F 4
Aisne (river) ....E 3
Ajaccio (gulf) ....B 7
Allier (river) ....E 4
Aube (river) ....F 3
Auvergne (mts.) ....E 5
Belle-Île (isl.), 4,442 ....B 4
Biscay (bay) ....B 5
Blanc (mt.) ....G 5
Bonifacio (strait) ....B 7
Calais (strait) ....D 2
Causses (region) ....E 5
Cévennes (mts.) ....E 5
Charente (river) ....C 5
Cher (river) ....D 4
Corse (cape) ....B 6
Corsica (isl.), 269,831 ....B 6
Côte-d'Or (mts.) ....F 4
Cotentin (pen.) ....C 3
Cottian Alps (range) ....G 5
Creuse (river) ....D 4
Dordogne (river) ....C 5
Dore (mts.) ....E 5
Doubs (river) ....G 4
Drôme (river) ....F 5
Dronne (river) ....C 5
Durance (river) ....F 6
English (channel) ....D 3
Eure (river) ....D 3
Forez (mts.) ....E 5
Fréjus (cape) ....G 6
Gard (river) ....F 5
Garonne (river) ....C 5
Gave de Pau (river) ....C 6
Geneva (lake) ....G 4
Gers (river) ....D 6
Gironde (river) ....C 5
Graian Alps (range) ....G 5
Gris-Nez (cape) ....D 2
Groix (isl.), 3,161 ....B 4
Hague (cape) ....C 3
Hérault (river) ....E 6
Hyères (isls.) ....F 6
Indre (river) ....D 4
Isère (river) ....F 5
Isle (river) ....C 5
Jura (mts.) ....F 4
Langres (plateau) ....F 3
Limousin (region) ....D 5
Lions (gulf) ....F 6
Little Saint Bernard (pass) ....G 5
Loir (river) ....C 4
Loire (river) ....D 4
Lot (river) ....D 5
Manche, La (English) (chan.)......B 3
Maritime Alps (range) ....G 5

Marne (river) ....C 2
Mayenne (river) ....C 4
Mediterranean (sea) ....E 7
Médoc (reg.) ....C 5
Meuse (river) ....F 3
Mont Cenis (tunnel) ....G 5
Morvan (plateau) ....E 4
Moselle (river) ....G 3
Noirmoutier (isl.), 8,091 ....B 4
North (sea) ....C 1
Oise (river) ....E 3
Oléron, d' (isl.), 16,355 ....C 5
Omaha (beach) ....C 3
Orb (river) ....E 6
Orne (river) ....D 3
Ouessant (isl.), 1,817 ....A 3
Penmarch (point) ....A 4
Perche (reg.) ....D 3
Puy-de-Dôme (mt.) ....E 5
Pyrenees (range) ....C 6
Ré (isl.), 9,967 ....C 4
Rhine (river) ....G 3
Rhône (river) ....F 5
Risle (river) ....D 3
Riviera (region) ....G 6
Saint-Florent (gulf) ....B 6
Saint-Malo (gulf) ....B 3
Saône (river) ....F 4
Sarthe (river) ....D 4
Sein (isl.), 835 ....A 3
Seine (bay) ....D 3
Seine (river) ....E 3
Sologne (reg.) ....D 4
Somme (river) ....D 2
Tarn (river) ....E 5
Ushant (Ouessant) (isl.), 1,817..A 3
Utah (beach) ....C 3
Vaccarès (lagoon) ....F 6
Vienne (river) ....C 4
Vilaine (river) ....C 4
Vosges (mts.) ....G 3
Yeu, d' (isl.), 4,786 ....B 4
Yonne (river) ....E 3

*City and suburbs.
†Population of metropolitan area.

MONACO
CITIES and TOWNS

Monte Carlo, 9,948 ....G 6

MONACO
AREA 368 acres
POPULATION 23,035

WINE REGIONS

Caen
CALVADOS
(distilled from cider)
Reims
CHAMPAGNE
ALSACE
Colmar
Chablis
Angers
Anjou
Touraine
POUILLY
SANCERRE
QUINCY
REUILLY
Tours
LOIRE VALLEY
BURGUNDY
Côte-d'Or
Beaune
JURA
Mâconnais
Mâcon
Beau-
jolais
COGNAC
Cognac
Bergerac
BORDEAUX
Bordeaux
Médoc
Graves
Sauternois
CÔTES DE DURAS
GAILLAC
LANGUEDOC
Valence
CÔTES
DU
RHÔNE
Avignon
PROVENCE
Toulon
ARMAGNAC
Auch
Béziers
Pau
JURANÇON
LIMOUX
ROUSSILLON

Climate, soil and variety of grape planted determine the quality of wine. Long, hot and fairly dry summers with cool, humid nights constitute an ideal climate. The nature of the soil is such a determining influence that identical grapes planted in Bordeaux, Burgundy and Champagne, will yield wines of widely different types.

Agriculture, Industry and Resources

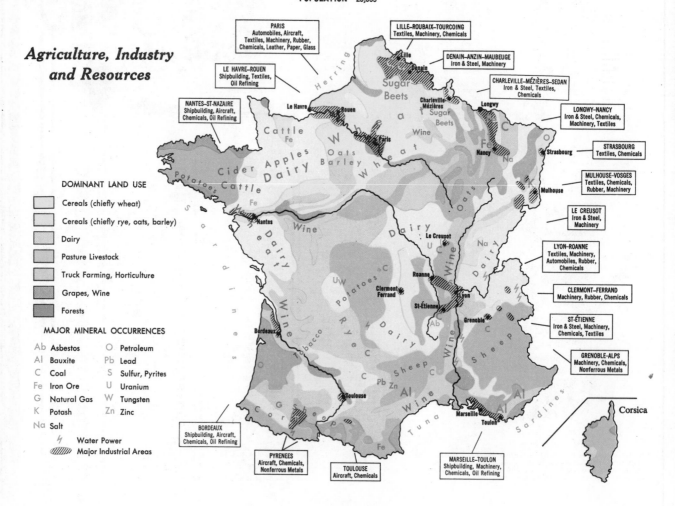

PARIS
Automobiles, Aircraft, Textiles, Machinery, Rubber, Chemicals, Leather, Paper, Glass

LILLE–ROUBAIX–TOURCOING
Textiles, Machinery, Chemicals

DENAIN–ANZIN–MAUBEUGE
Iron & Steel, Machinery

CHARLEVILLE-MÉZIÈRES–SEDAN
Iron & Steel, Textiles, Chemicals

LE HAVRE–ROUEN
Shipbuilding, Textiles, Oil Refining

LONGWY–NANCY
Iron & Steel, Chemicals, Machinery, Textiles

NANTES–ST-NAZAIRE
Shipbuilding, Aircraft, Chemicals, Oil Refining

STRASBOURG
Textiles, Chemicals

MULHOUSE–VOSGES
Textiles, Chemicals, Rubber, Machinery

LE CREUSOT
Iron & Steel, Machinery

LYON–ROANNE
Textiles, Machinery, Automobiles, Rubber, Chemicals

CLERMONT-FERRAND
Machinery, Rubber, Chemicals

ST-ÉTIENNE
Iron & Steel, Machinery, Chemicals, Textiles

GRENOBLE-ALPS
Machinery, Chemicals, Nonferrous Metals

BORDEAUX
Shipbuilding, Aircraft, Chemicals, Oil Refining

PYRENEES
Aircraft, Chemicals, Nonferrous Metals

TOULOUSE
Aircraft, Chemicals

MARSEILLE–TOULON
Shipbuilding, Machinery, Chemicals, Oil Refining

DOMINANT LAND USE

Cereals (chiefly wheat)
Cereals (chiefly rye, oats, barley)
Dairy
Pasture Livestock
Truck Farming, Horticulture
Grapes, Wine
Forests

MAJOR MINERAL OCCURRENCES

Ab Asbestos
Al Bauxite
C Coal
Fe Iron Ore
G Natural Gas
K Potash
Na Salt
O Petroleum
Pb Lead
S Sulfur, Pyrites
U Uranium
W Tungsten
Zn Zinc

⚡ Water Power
▨ Major Industrial Areas

Corsica

ANDORRA

CITIES and TOWNS

Andorra la Vella (cap.), 2,250....G 1

GIBRALTAR

PHYSICAL FEATURES

Europa (point) ....D 4

PORTUGAL

PROVINCES

Algarve, 315,300 ....B 4
Alto Alentejo, 410,200 ....C 3
Baixo Alentejo, 275,000 ....B 3
Beira Alta, 761,500 ....C 2
Beira Baixa, 321,100 ....C 3
Beira Litoral, 1,448,800 ....B 2
Douro Litoral, 1,352,600 ....B 2
Estremadura, 1,998,600 ....B 3
Madeira, 268,700 ....A 2
Minho, 944,800 ....B 2
Ribatejo, 479,400 ....B 3
Trás-os-Montes e Alto Douro, 586,500 ....C 2

CITIES and TOWNS

Águeda, 8,345 ....B 2
Alcácer do Sal, 14,733 ....B 3
Alcântara, 30,625 ....A 1
Alcobaça, 5,166 ....B 3
Aldeia Nova, 7,678 ....C 4
Algés, 14,517 ....A 1
Alhos Vedros, 19,606 ....B 3
Aljezur, 5,333 ....B 4
Aljustrel, 9,913 ....B 4
Almada, 30,688 ....A 1
Almeirim, 8,902 ....B 3
Alpiarça, 7,856 ....B 3
Amadora, 36,331 ....A 1
Amareleja, 4,816 ....C 3
Aveiro, 16,011 ....B 2
Baixa da Banheira, 12,525.................B 3
Barcelos, 5,420 ....B 2
Batalha, 7,053 ....B 3
Beja, 15,702 ....C 3
Belas, 7,509 ....A 1
Belém, 20,416 ....A 1
Benfica, 23,161 ....A 1
Braga, 40,977 ....B 2
Bragança, 8,075 ....C 2
Caldas da Rainha, 10,635 ....B 3
Calheta, 5,404 ....A 2
Campo Maior, 8,807 ....C 3
Cantanhede, 6,630 ....B 2
Caparica, 10,363 ....A 1
Carnaxide, 28,301 ....A 1
Cartaxo, 6,665 ....B 3
Cascais, 10,861 ....B 3
Castelo Branco, 14,838 ....C 3
Castro Marim, 5,347 ....C 4
Chaves, 13,156 ....C 2
Coimbra, 46,313 ....B 2
Cova da Piedade, 15,720 ....A 1
Covilhã, 23,091 ....C 2
Elvas, 11,742 ....C 3
Espinho, 13,503 ....B 2
Estoril, 11,193 ....B 3
Estremoz, 10,122 ....C 3
Évora, 24,144 ....C 3
Fafe, 7,126 ....B 2
Faro, 18,909 ....B 4
Fátima, 5,852 ....B 3
Ferreira do Alentejo, 8,108.................B 3
Figueira da Foz, 10,855 ....B 2
Funchal, 43,301 ....A 2
Gondomar, 11,182 ....B 2
Guarda, 9,094 ....C 2
Guimarães, 23,229 ....B 2
Ilhavo, 12,646 ....B 2
Lagos, 10,008 ....B 4
Lamego, 10,236 ....C 2
Lavos, 5,744 ....B 2
Leiria, 7,477 ....B 3
Lisbon (Lisboa) (cap.), 828,000..A 1
Loulé, 16,152 ....B 4
Louriçal, 5,608 ....B 3
Lourinhã, 8,677 ....B 3
Lousã, 8,191 ....B 2
Machico, 11,608 ....A 2
Marinha Grande, 15,699 ....B 3
Matosinhos, 37,694 ....B 2
Mértola, 5,682 ....C 4
Miranda do Corvo, 5,103 ....B 2
Montargil, 6,357 ....B 3
Montemor-o-Novo, 13,115 ....B 3
Montijo, 17,751 ....B 3
Moscavide, 22,065 ....A 1
Mourão, 12,126 ....C 3
Muge, 5,546 ....B 3
Nazaré, 9,189 ....B 3
Nisa, 5,262 ....C 3
Óbidos, 4,599 ....B 3
Odivelas, 27,423 ....A 1
Oeiras, 6,857 ....B 3
Olhão, 16,017 ....C 4
Olivais, 11,896 ....A 1
Oporto, 324,400 ....B 2
Ovar, 14,128 ....B 2
Peniche, 11,357 ....B 3
Pombal, 9,973 ....B 3
Ponta do Sol, 7,426 ....A 2
Ponte de Sor, 13,010 ....B 3
Portalegre, 11,017 ....C 3
Portimão, 12,129 ....B 4
Porto (Oporto), 324,400 ....B 2
Povoa de Varzim, 17,696 ....B 2
Proença-a-Nova, 6,060 ....B 3
Queluz, 14,703 ....A 1
Ribeira Brava, 8,726 ....A 2
Sacavém, 10,624 ....A 1
Santa Cruz, 9,858 ....A 2
Santarém, 16,449 ....B 3
Santiago do Cacém, 6,939 ....B 3
São Brás de Alportel, 9,058.................C 4
São João da Madeira, 11,921 ....B 2
São Teotónio, 8,183 ....B 4
Serpa, 10,967 ....C 4
Sertã, 6,909 ....B 3
Sesimbra, 16,837 ....B 3
Setúbal, 44,435 ....B 3
Sines, 8,866 ....B 4
Sintra, 19,930 ....B 3
Soure, 9,655 ....B 2
Tavira, 12,046 ....C 4
Tomar, 12,974 ....B 3
Tôrres Novas, 11,974 ....B 3
Tôrres Vedras, 13,091 ....B 3
Vagos, 8,281 ....B 2
Vendas Novas, 9,675 ....B 3
Viana do Castelo, 14,371 ....B 2
Vila do Conde, 12,771 ....B 2
Vila Franca de Xira, 13,404.................B 3
Vila Nova de Gaia, 45,739.................B 2
Vila Real, 10,263 ....C 2
Vila Real de Sto. António, 11,096 ....C 4
Viseu, 16,961 ....C 2

OTHER FEATURES

Carvoeiro (cape) ....B 3
Desertas (isls.) ....A 2
Douro (river) ....C 2
Estrela, Serra da (mts.) ....C 2
Foia (mt.) ....B 4
Guadiana (river) ....C 4
Lima (river) ....B 2
Madeira (isl.), 265,432 ....A 2
Minho (river) ....B 2
Mira (river) ....B 4
Monchique (mts.) ....B 4
Mondego (cape) ....B 3
Mondego (river) ....C 2
Monsanto (hill) ....A 1
Ossa (mts.) ....C 3
Palha, Mar da (bay) ....A 1
Roca (cape) ....B 3
Sado (river) ....B 3
Saint Vincent (cape) ....B 4
Santa María (cape) ....C 4
Setúbal (bay) ....B 3
Tagus (river) ....B 3
Tâmega (river) ....C 2
Tejo (Tagus) (river) ....B 3
Xarrama (river) ....B 3

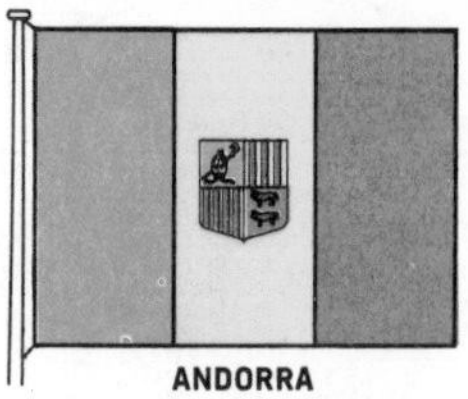

ANDORRA

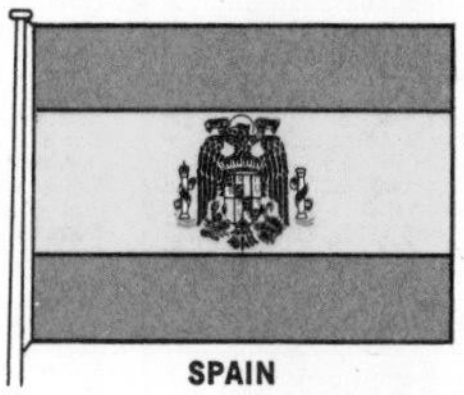

SPAIN

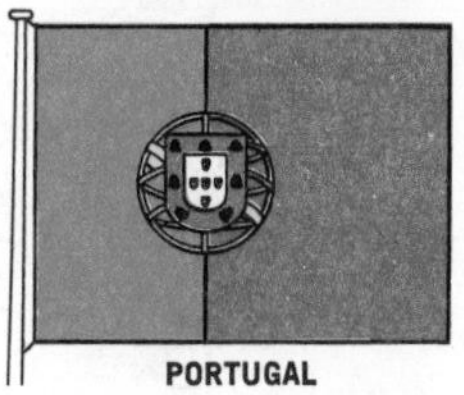

PORTUGAL

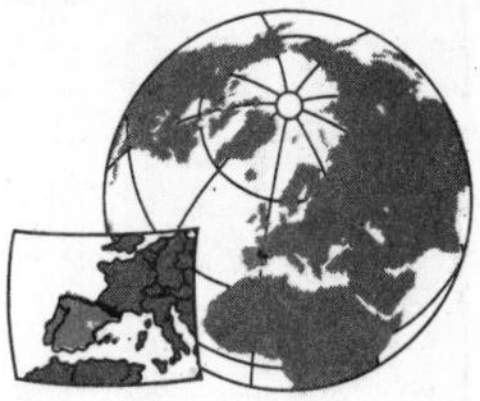

SPAIN

AREA 194,896 sq. mi.
POPULATION 33,290,000
CAPITAL Madrid
LARGEST CITY Madrid
HIGHEST POINT Pico de Teide 12,172 ft. (Canary Is.); Mulhacén 11,411 ft. (mainland)
MONETARY UNIT peseta
MAJOR LANGUAGES Spanish, Catalan, Basque
MAJOR RELIGION Roman Catholicism

PORTUGAL

AREA 35,510 sq. mi.
POPULATION 9,560,000
CAPITAL Lisbon
LARGEST CITY Lisbon
HIGHEST POINT Malhão da Estrêla 6,532 ft.
MONETARY UNIT escudo
MAJOR LANGUAGE Portuguese
MAJOR RELIGION Roman Catholicism

ANDORRA

AREA 175 sq. mi.
POPULATION 19,000
CAPITAL Andorra la Vella
MONETARY UNIT French franc, Spanish peseta
MAJOR LANGUAGE Catalan
MAJOR RELIGION Roman Catholicism

GIBRALTAR

AREA 2 sq. mi.
POPULATION 27,000
CAPITAL Gibraltar
MONETARY UNIT pound sterling
MAJOR LANGUAGES English, Spanish
MAJOR RELIGION Roman Catholicism

SPAIN

PROVINCES

Álava, 148,899 ....E 1
Albacete, 358,290 ....E 3
Alicante, 746,917 ....F 3
Almería, 360,798 ....E 4
Ávila, 231,916 ....D 2
Badajoz, 839,363 ....C 3
Baleares (Balearic Is.), 451,343..H 3
Barcelona, 3,213,212 ....G 2
Burgos, 372,138 ....E 1
Cáceres, 540,060 ....C 3
Cádiz, 874,837 ....D 4
Castellón, 344,350 ....G 2
Ciudad Real, 589,262 ....D 3
Córdoba, 802,633 ....D 3
Cuenca, 305,432 ....E 2
Gerona, 361,250 ....H 1
Granada, 760,210 ....E 4
Guadalajara, 174,572 ....E 2
Guipúzcoa, 532,095 ....E 1
Huelva, 413,459 ....C 4
Huesca, 231,376 ....F 1
Jaén, 720,559 ....E 4
La Coruña, 1,004,149 ....B 1
Las Palmas, 492,466 ....C 4
León, 600,935 ....C 1
Lérida, 336,818 ....G 2
Logroño, 228,922 ....E 1
Lugo, 464,922 ....C 1
Madrid, 2,973,619 ....E 2
Málaga, 783,436 ....D 4
Murcia, 817,545 ....F 4
Navarra, 409,239 ....F 1
Orense, 442,420 ....C 1
Oviedo, 1,034,244 ....C 1
Palencia, 230,426 ....D 1
Pontevedra, 681,295 ....B 1
Salamanca, 401,276 ....C 2
Santa Cruz de Tenerife, 525,095 ....B 5
Santander, 443,113 ....D 1
Saragossa, 670,357 ....F 2
Segovia, 192,229 ....D 2
Seville, 1,295,094 ....D 4
Soria, 140,517 ....E 2
Tarragona, 363,830 ....G 2
Teruel, 205,565 ....F 2
Toledo, 516,870 ....D 3
Valencia, 1,462,005 ....F 3
Valladolid, 368,685 ....D 2
Vizcaya, 852,768 ....E 1
Zamora, 293,489 ....D 2

CITIES and TOWNS

Adra, 10,211 ....E 4
Aguilar, 13,760 ....D 4
Aguilas, 11,970 ....F 4
Alagón, 5,270 ....F 2
Alayor, 4,988 ....J 3
Albacete, 61,635 ....F 3
Albox, 4,036 ....E 4
Alburqerque, 9,540 ....C 3
Alcalá de Chivert, 4,049 ....G 2
Alcalá de Guadaira. 27,378 ....D 4
Alcalá de Henares, 20,572 ....G 4
Alcalá de los Gazules, 7,015 ....D 4
Alcalá la Real, 8,351 ....E 4
Alcanar, 6,332 ....G 2
Alcañiz, 9,489 ....F 2
Alcántara, 3,564 ....C 3
Alcantarilla, 15,748 ....F 4
Alcaudete, 9,280 ....E 4
Alcázar de San Juan, 23,788.................E 3
Alcira, 22,417 ....F 3
Alcoy, 48,712 ....F 3
Alfaro, 8,570 ....F 1
Algeciras, 51,096 ....D 4
Algemesí, 16,683 ....F 3
Alhama de Granada, 6,989 ....E 4
Alhama de Murcia, 7,175 ....F 4
Alicante, 103,289 ....F 3
Almadén, 13,206 ....D 3
Almagro, 9,232 ....E 3
Almansa, 15,391 ....F 3
Almendralejo, 20,867 ....C 3
Almería, 76,643 ....E 4
Almodóvar del Campo, 8,115.................D 3
Almonte, 9,444 ....C 4
Almuñécar, 5,644 ....E 4
Álora, 6,459 ....D 4
Amposta, 11,026 ....G 2
Andújar, 23,897 ....D 3
Antequera, 28,400 ....D 4
Aracena, 5,605 ....C 4
Aranda de Duero, 12,623 ....E 2
Aranjuez, 25,988 ....E 2
Archena, 5,802 ....F 3
Archidona. 7.262 ....D 4
Arcos de la Frontera, 13,536 ....D 4
Arenas de San Pedro, 5,585.................D 2
Arenys de Mar, 6,665 ....H 2
Argamasilla de Alba, 6,411 ....E 3
Arganda, 5,253 ....G 4
Arnedo, 7,958 ....E 1
Aroche, 5,319 ....C 4
Arrecife, 12,748 ....C 4
Arroyo de la Luz, 9,781 ....C 3
Arta, 5,173 ....H 3
Arucas, 10,917 ....B 5
Aspe, 9,742 ....F 3
Astorga, 10,101 ....C 1
Ávila de los Caballeros, 26,738 ....D 2
Avilés, 19,992 ....C 1
Ayamonte, 9,608 ....C 4
Ayora, 5,635 ....F 3
Azpeitia, 8,219 ....E 1
Azuaga, 15,477 ....D 3
Badajoz, 23,715 ....C 3
Badalona, 90,655 ....H 2
Baena, 17,612 ....D 4
Baeza, 13,329 ....E 4
Bailén, 11,144 ....E 3
Balaguer, 8,342 ....G 2
Bañolas, 7,531 ....H 1
Barajas, 9,058 ....F 4
Barbastro, 9,730 ....F 1
Barcarrota, 7,443 ....C 3
Barcelona, 1,555,564 ....H 2
Barruelo de Santullán, 3,761.................D 1
Baza, 13,323 ....E 4
Beas de Segura, 8,194 ....E 3
Béjar, 14,225 ....D 2
Bélmez, 6,907 ....D 3
Benavente, 11,061 ....D 1
Benicarló, 10,627 ....G 2
Berga, 8,923 ....G 1
Berja, 7,989 ....E 4
Bermeo, 12,398 ....E 1
Betanzos, 6,999 ....B 1
Bilbao, 293,939 ....E 1
Blanes, 9,256 ....H 2
Borja, 4,335 ....F 2
Borjas Blancas, 5,086 ....G 2
Brozas, 5,634 ....C 3
Bujalance, 10,465 ....D 4
Bullas, 7,326 ....F 4
Burgos, 79,810 ....E 1
Burriana, 15,670 ....G 3
Cabeza del Buey, 10,734 ....D 3
Cabra, 15,688 ....D 4
Cáceres, 42,903 ....C 3
Cádiz, 117,871 ....C 4
Calahorra, 14,400 ....E 1
Calasparra, 7,543 ....F 3
Calatayud, 15,777 ....F 2
Calella, 7,947 ....H 2
Callosa de Ensarria, 4,617 ....G 3
Calzada de Calatrava, 7,536.................E 3
Campanario, 8,910 ....D 3
Campillos, 8,791 ....D 4
Campo de Criptana, 13,616.................E 3
Candeleda, 6,507 ....D 2
Cangas, 4,059 ....B 1
Caniles, 5,026 ....E 4
Caravaca, 10,016 ....E 3
Carcagente, 15,791 ....F 3
Carmona, 26,368 ....D 4
Cartagena, 42,424 ....F 4
Casar de Cáceres, 4,560 ....C 3
Caspe, 8,251 ....G 2
Castellón de la Plana, 52,868.................G 3
Castro del Río, 11,200 ....D 4
Castro-Urdiales, 7,128 ....E 1
Castuera, 9,905 ....D 3
Caudete, 7,481 ....F 3
Cazalla de la Sierra, 9,414.................D 4
Cazorla, 7,932 ....E 4
Cebreros, 3,898 ....D 2
Ceclavín, 4,778 ....C 3
Cehegín, 10,467 ....F 3
Cervera, 5,215 ....G 2
Cervera del Río Alhama, 3,648.................E 1
Ceuta, 88,000 ....D 5
Chiclana de la Frontera, 19,155..C 4
Chinchón, 4,432 ....G 5
Chiva, 3,978 ....F 3
Ciempozuelos, 9,042 ....F 5
Cieza, 20,620 ....F 3
Ciudadela, 10,872 ....H 2
Ciudad Real, 35,015 ....D 3
Cocentaina, 7,405 ....F 3
Coín, 11,441 ....D 4
Colmenar de Oreja, 5,119 ....G 5
Colmenar Viejo, 8,133 ....F 4
Constantina, 12,015 ....D 4
Consuegra, 10,572 ....E 3
Córdoba, 167,808 ....D 4
Corella, 5,591 ....F 1
Coria del Río, 13,781 ....C 4
Corral de Almaguer, 8,621 ....E 3
Crevillente, 12,025 ....F 3
Cuéllar, 5,703 ....D 2
Cuenca, 26,663 ....E 2
Cúllar de Baza, 3,769 ....E 4
Cullera, 13,040 ....F 3
Daimiel, 19,485 ....E 3
Denia, 8,281 ....G 3
Don Benito, 22,642 ....C 3
Dos Hermanas, 21,517 ....D 4
Durango, 11,882 ....E 1
Écija, 29,262 ....D 4
Eibar, 31,371 ....E 1
Ejea de los Caballeros, 9,000.................F 1
El Arahal, 15,107 ....D 4
El Bonillo, 5,215 ....E 3
Elche, 50,989 ....F 3
Elda, 24,182 ....F 3
El Ferrol del Caudillo, 62,010.................B 1
El Puerto de Santa María, 31,848 ....C 4
Énguera, 4,606 ....F 3
Espejo, 8,006 ....D 4
Estella, 8,142 ....E 1
Estepa, 8,628 ....D 4
Estepona, 11,309 ....D 4
Felanitx, 7,860 ....H 3
Fermoselle, 3,885 ....C 2
Figueras, 16,460 ....H 1
Fraga, 8,264 ....G 2

Agriculture, Industry and Resources

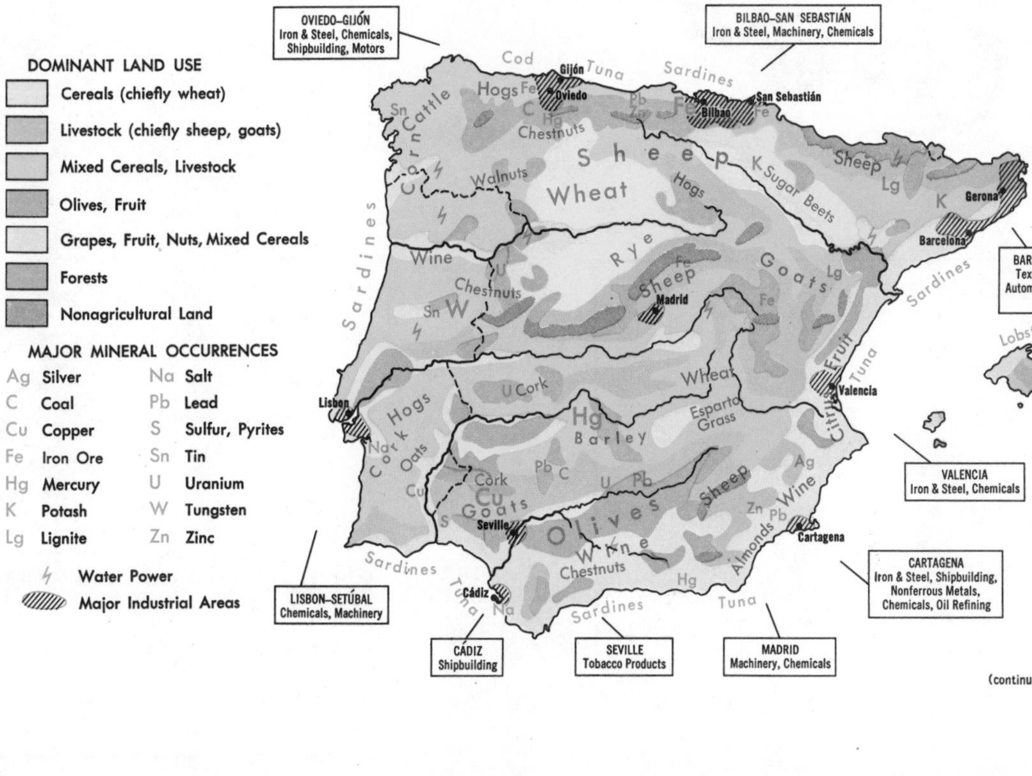

(continued on following page)

SPAIN (continued)

Fregenal de la Sierra, 9,506........C 3
Fuengirola, 5,622 ....D 4
Fuensalida, 4,697 ....D 2
Fuente de Cantos, 8,484 ....C 3
Fuente-Obejuna, 5,353 ....D 3
Fuentes de Andalucía, 8,357.......D 4
Gálvez, 3,828 ....D 3
Gándara, 400 ....C 1
Gandía, 15,940 ....F 3
Garrovillas, 5,665 ....C 3
Gerona, 28,134 ....H 2
Getafe, 21,066 ....F 4
Gijón, 92,020 ....D 1
Granada, 150,186 ....E 4
Granollers, 18,810 ....H 2
Guadalajara, 20,135 ....E 2
Guadalcanal, 5,483 ....D 3
Guadix, 15,897 ....E 4
Guareña, 8.438 ....C 3
Guernica y Luno, 4,855 ....E 1
Haro, 8,375 ....E 1
Hellín, 17,071 ....F 3
Herencia, 8,606 ....E 3
Herrera del Duque, 5,404 ....D 3
Hinojosa del Duque, 14,074.........D 3
Hortaleza, 8,552 ....G 4
Hospitalet, 122,813 ....H 2
Huelma, 5,468 ....E 4
Huelva, 56,548 ....C 4
Huércal-Overa, 4,406 ....F 4
Huesca, 24,338 ....F 1
Huéscar, 5,097 ....E 4
Ibiza, 11,259 ....G 3
Igualada, 19,866 ....G 2
Illora, 5,586 ....E 4
Inca, 13,816 ....H 3
Iniesta, 4,292 ....F 3
Irún, 20,212 ....F 1
Isla Cristina, 9,616 ....C 4
Jaca, 9,821 ....F 1
Jaén, 59,699 ....E 4
Jaraíz, 8,130 ....D 2
Jativa, 19,195 ....F 3
Jávea, 4,929 ....G 3
Jerez de la Frontera, 96,209 ....C 4
Jerez de los Caballeros, 12,349 ....C 3
Jijona, 5,147 ....F 3
Jimena de la Frontera, 3,620......D 4
Jódar, 14,289 ....E 4
Jumilla, 15,703 ....F 3
La Bañeza, 7,869 ....C 1
La Bisbal, 5,194 ....H 1
La Carolina, 10,915 ....E 3
La Coruña, 161,260 ....B 1
La Gineta, 3,237 ....E 3
La Línea, 58,169 ....D 4
La Orotava, 8,019 ....B 4
La Palma del Condado, 8,526......C 4
La Puebla, 9,931 ....H 3
La Puebla de Montalbán, 7,286..D 3
La Rambla, 8,057 ....D 4
Laredo, 6,382 ....E 1
La Roda, 11,739 ....E 3
La Solana, 14,948 ....E 3
Las Palmas, 166,236 ....B 4
Las Pedroñeras, 6,418 ....E 3
La Unión, 9,357 ....F 4
Lavadores, 9,708 ....B 1
Lebrija, 13,663 ....D 4
Ledesma, 2,527 ....C 2
Leganés, 8,064 ....F 4
Lena, Pola de, 3,966 ....D 1
León, 73,483 ....D 1
Lérida, 50,047 ....G 2
Linares, 50,527 ....E 3
Liria, 9,723 ....F 3
Llerena, 7,854 ....C 3
Lluchmayor, 9,827 ....H 3
Logroño, 58,545 ....E 1
Logrosán, 6,595 ....D 3
Loja, 11,441 ....D 4
Lora del Río, 15,086 ....D 4
Lorca, 19,854 ....F 4
Los Navalmorales, 4,686 ....D 3
Los Navalucillos, 4,823 ....D 3
Los Santos de Maimona, 8,910....C 3
Los Yébenes, 6,596 ....E 3
Luarca, 4,070 ....C 1
Lucena, 19,975 ....D 4
Lugo, 45,497 ....C 1
Madrid (cap.), 2,850,631 ....F 4
Madridejos, 9,795 ....E 3
Madroñera, 5,256 ....D 3
Mahón, 14,836 ....J 3
Málaga, 259,245 ....D 4
Malagón, 9,246 ....E 3
Malpartida de Cáceres, 5,751.......C 3
Malpartida de Plasencia, 6,757....C 2
Manacor, 17,544 ....H 3
Mancha Real, 7,587 ....E 4
Manlleu, 8,489 ....H 1
Manresa, 46,105 ....G 2
Manzanares, 16,639 ....E 3
Marbella, 7,302 ....D 4
Marchena, 15,879 ....D 4
Marín, 8,838 ....B 1
Martos, 16,442 ....E 4
Mataró, 29,937 ....H 2
Mazarrón, 3,379 ....F 4
Medina del Campo, 13,640 ....D 2
Medina de Ríoseco, 4,897 ....D 2
Medina-Sidonia, 6,869 ....D 4
Menasalbas, 4,407 ....D 3
Mérida, 28,791 ....C 3
Miajadas, 8,632 ....D 3
Mieres, 19,308 ....D 1
Miranda de Ebro, 22,836 ....E 1
Moguer, 6,776 ....C 4
Monasterio, 7,559 ....C 3
Monforte, 13,737 ....C 1
Monóvar, 7,972 ....F 3
Montánchez, 4,190 ....D 3
Montefrío, 4,917 ....D 4
Montehermoso, 6,006 ....C 2
Montellano, 8,694 ....D 4
Montijo, 12,519 ....C 3
Montilla, 19,830 ....D 4
Montoro, 11,243 ....D 3
Monzón 9,020 ....G 2
Mora, 10,613 ....E 3
Moratalla, 5,675 ....E 3
Morón de la Frontera, 29,096......D 4
Mota del Cuervo, 5,403 ....E 3
Motril, 18,624 ....E 4
Mula, 9,912 ....F 3
Munera, 5,931 ....E 3
Murcia, 83,190 ....F 4
Nava del Rey, 3,815 ....D 2
Navalcarnero, 4,681 ....F 4
Navalmoral de la Mata, 8,978.....D 3
Navalucillos, Los, 4,823.............D 3
Nerja, 5,767 ....E 4
Nerva, 11,974 ....C 4
Novelda, 11,003 ....F 3
Nules, 7,626 ....F 3
Ocaña, 6,592 ....E 3
Oliva, 13,342 ....F 3
Oliva de la Frontera, 11,141.......C 3
Olivenza, 8,304 ....C 3
Olot, 13,099 ....H 1
Olvera, 9,088 ....D 4
Onda, 10,666 ....F 3
Onteniente, 18,787 ....F 3
Orellana la Vieja, 6,925 ....D 3
Orense, 42,371 ....C 1
Orihuela, 15,873 ....F 3
Osuna, 17,671 ....D 4
Oviedo, 91,550 ....C 1
Padul, 6,868 ....E 4
Palafrugell, 7,476 ....H 2
Palamós, 5,481 ....H 2
Palencia, 48,144 ....D 2
Palma, 136,431 ....H 3
Palma del Río, 14,053 ....D 4
Pamplona, 59,227 ....F 1
Paredes de Nava, 4,065 ....D 1
Pego, 8,291 ....F 3
Peñafiel, 5,333 ....E 2
Peñaranda de Bracamonte, 5.943 D 2
Peñarroya-Pueblonuevo, 17,449....D 3
Piedrabuena, 5,453 ....D 3
Pinos-Puente, 8,311 ....E 4
Plasencia, 21,297 ....C 2
Pollensa, 7,370 ....H 3
Ponferrada, 17,042 ....C 1
Pontevedra, 19,739 ....B 1
Porcuna, 9,671 ....D 4
Portugalete, 20,514 ....E 1
Posadas, 8,440 ....D 4
Pozoblanco, 14,728 ....D 3
Priego de Córdoba, 13,469 ....D 4
Puebla de Don Fadrique, 3,771....E 4
Puebla de Montalbán, La, 7,286..D 3
Puente-Genil, 24,836 ....D 4
Puertollano, 48,528 ....D 3
Puerto Real, 12,717 ....D 4
Quesada, 6,503 ....E 4
Quintana de la Serena, 7,160......D 3
Quintanar de la Orden, 9,483......E 3
Reinosa, 10,044 ....D 1
Requena, 8,278 ....F 3
Reus, 32,037 ....G 2
Ripoll, 7,821 ....H 1
Ronda, 17,703 ....D 4
Rota, 14,236 ....C 4
Rute, 8,945 ....D 4
Sabadell, 98,049 ....H 2
Sagunto, 15,210 ....F 3
Salamanca, 90,388 ....D 2
Sallent, 7,462 ....H 2
Sama, 7,149 ....D 1
San Carlos de la Rápita, 6,844....G 2
San Clemente, 6,411 ....E 3
San Felíu de Guixols, 9,077.........H 2
San Fernando, 51,406 ....C 4
San Lorenzo de El Escorial, 7,455 E 2
Sanlucar de Barrameda, 32,580....C 4
Sanlúcar la Mayor, 6,094 ....C 4
San Sebastián, 98,603 ....E 1
Santa Cruz de la Palma, 9,928....B 4
Santa Cruz de la Mudela, 8,724...E 3
Santa Cruz de la Zarza, 5,588.....E 3
Santa Cruz de Tenerife, 82,620....B 4
Santa Eugenia, 5,336 ....B 1
Santafe, 8,212 ....E 4
Santander, 98,784 ....D 1
Santiago, 37,916 ....B 1
Santoña, 7,535 ....E 1
San Vicente de Alcántara, 8,059..C 3
Saragossa, 295,080 ....F 2
Segorbe, 7,136 ....F 3
Segovia, 33,360 ....D 2
Sestao, 24,992 ....E 1
Seville (Sevilla), 423,762............D 4
Sitges, 6,796 ....G 2
Socuéllamos, 14,742 ....E 3
Sóller, 6,011 ....H 3
Sonseca, 5,994 ....D 3
Soria, 18,872 ....E 2
Sueca, 19,005 ....F 3
Tabernes de Valldigna, 12,890.....G 3
Tafalla, 7,320 ....F 1
Talavera de la Reina, 28,107.......D 2
Tarancón, 7,678 ....E 3
Tarazona de Aragón, 11,004.........F 2
Tarazona de la Mancha, 6,850.....F 3
Tarifa, 9,147 ....D 4
Tarragona, 35,689 ....G 2
Tarrasa, 89,128 ....G 2
Tárrega, 7,317 ....G 2
Tauste, 6,544 ....F 2
Telde, 11,761 ....B 5
Teruel, 18,304 ....F 2
Tobarra, 7,029 ....F 3
Toledo, 29,367 ....D 3
Tolosa, 10,980 ....F 1
Tomelloso, 27,715 ....E 3
Toro, 9,123 ....D 2
Torredonjimeno, 12,848 ....D 4

Topography

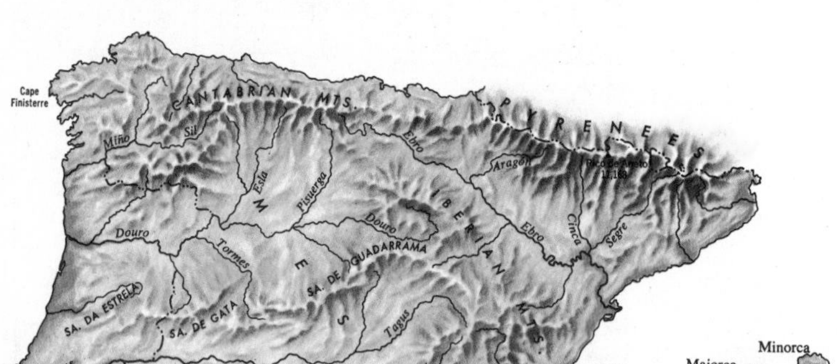

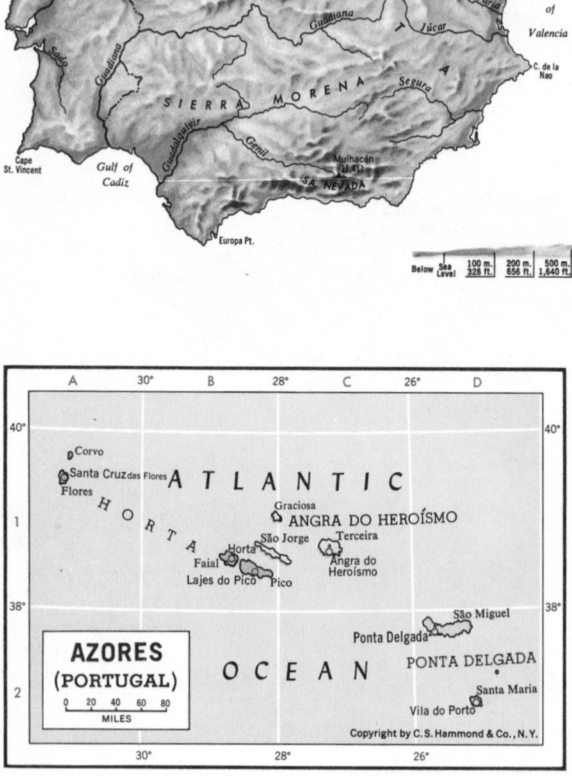

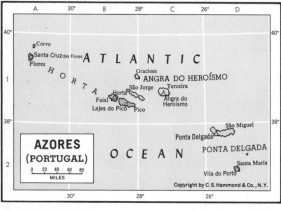

AZORES

DISTRICTS

Angra do Heroísmo, 103,800........C 1
Horta, 44,900 ....A 1
Ponta Delgada, 185,600 ....D 2

CITIES and TOWNS

Angra do Heroísmo, 13,502 ....C 1
Horta, 7,109 ....B 1
Lajes do Pico, 2,508 ....B 1
Ponta Delgada, 22,316 ....C 2
Santa Cruz das Flores, 1,898......A 1
Vila do Porto, 5,373 ....D 2

OTHER FEATURES

Corvo (isl.), 681 ....A 1
Faial (isl.), 20,281 ....B 1
Flores (isl.), 6,583 ....A 1
Graciosa (isl.), 8,669 ....C 1
Pico (isl.), 21,831...........................C 1
Santa Maria (isl.), 13,233 ....D 2
São Jorge (isl.), 15,895 ....B 1
São Miguel (isl.), 168,691 ....D 2
Terceira (isl.), 71,610.....................C 1

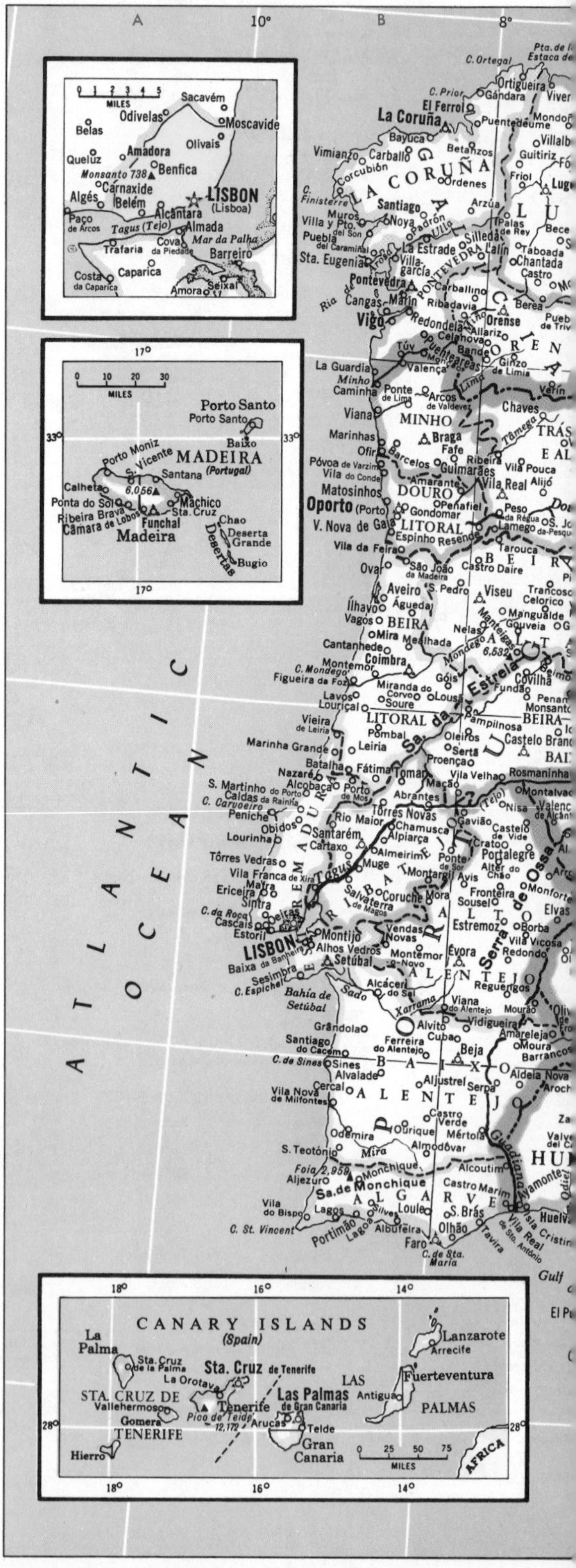

SPAIN and PORTUGAL
CONIC PROJECTION

SCALE OF MILES

SCALE OF KILOMETRES

Capitals of Countries .... ☆
Provincial Capitals .... △
International Boundaries ....
Provincial Boundaries ....

© Copyright by C.S. HAMMOND & Co., Maplewood, N.J.

ITALY

CONIC PROJECTION

SCALE OF MILES

SCALE OF KILOMETERS

Capitals of Countries --------- ☆
Regional Capitals ----------- ⊞
Provincial Capitals ----------- △
International Boundaries -------- ▬ ▬ ▬
Regional Boundaries --------- ▬ ▬ ▬

ITALY is divided for administrative purposes into
20 regions, shown on the map in separate colors.
The regions are subdivided into provinces bearing
the same names as their respective capitals, except:

PROVINCE	CAPITAL
MASSA-CARRARA	Massa
PESARO-URBINO	Pesaro

Copyright by C.S. HAMMOND & Co., N.Y.

VATICAN CITY

SCALE

St. Peter's
Piazza
S. Pietro

ROME and ENVIRONS

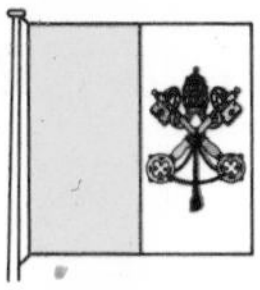

VATICAN CITY
AREA 109 acres
POPULATION 1,000

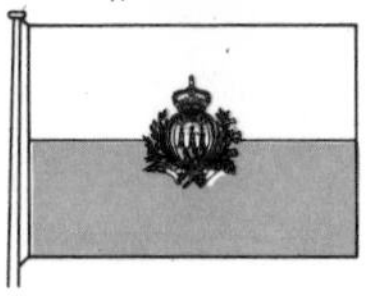

SAN MARINO
AREA 23.4 sq. mi.
POPULATION 19,000

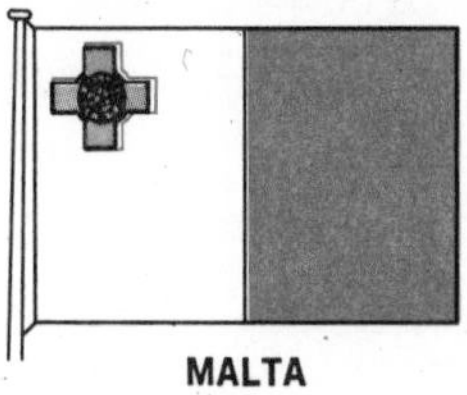

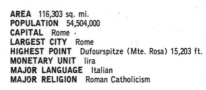

MALTA

AREA 122 sq. mi.
POPULATION 321,000
CAPITAL Valletta
LARGEST CITY Sliema
HIGHEST POINT 787 ft.
MONETARY UNIT Maltese pound
MAJOR LANGUAGES Maltese, English
MAJOR RELIGION Roman Catholicism

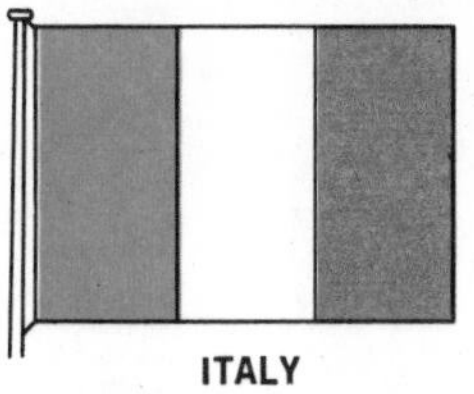

ITALY

AREA 116,303 sq. mi.
POPULATION 54,504,000
CAPITAL Rome
LARGEST CITY Rome
HIGHEST POINT Dufourspitze (Mte. Rosa) 15,203 ft.
MONETARY UNIT lira
MAJOR LANGUAGE Italian
MAJOR RELIGION Roman Catholicism

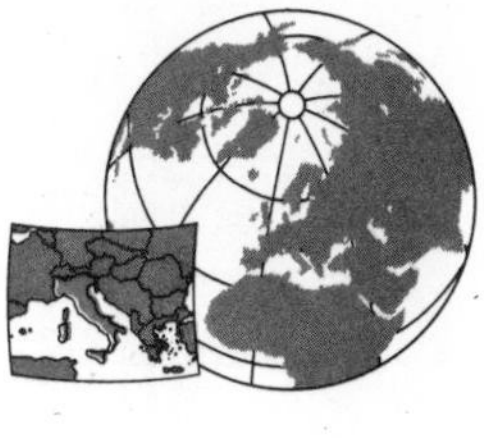

ITALY

REGIONS

Abruzzi, 1,206,266 ....D 3
Aosta, 100,959 ....A 2
Apulia, 3,421,217 ....F 4
Basilicata, 644,297 ....F 4
Calabria, 2,045,047 ....F 5
Campania, 4,760,759 ....E 4
Emilia-Romagna, 3,666,680 ....C 2
Friuli-Venezia Giulia, 1,204,298....D 1
Latium, 3,958,957 ....D 4
Liguria, 1,735,349 ....B 2
Lombardy, 7,406,152 ....B 2
Marche, 1,347,489 ....D 3
Molise, 358,052 ....E 4
Piedmont, 3,914,250 ....A 2
Puglia (Apulia), 3,421,217 ....F 4
Sardinia, 1,419,362 ....B 4
Sicily, 4,721,001 ....E 6
Trentino-Alto Adige, 785,967 ....C 1
Tuscany, 3,286,160 ....C 3
Umbria, 794,745 ....D 3
Venetia, 3,846,562 ....C 2

PROVINCES

Agrigento, 472,945 ....D 6
Alessandria, 478,613 ....B 2
Ancona, 405,709 ....D 3
Aosta, 100,959 ....A 2
Arezzo, 308,964 ....C 3
Ascoli Piceno, 335,627 ....D 3
Asti, 214,604 ....B 2
Avellino, 464,904 ....E 4
Bari, 1,263,245 ....F 4
Belluno, 234,921 ....D 1
Benevento, 313,020 ....E 4
Bergamo, 744,670 ....B 2
Bologna, 841,474 ....C 2
Bolzano, 373,863 ....C 1
Brescia, 882,949 ....C 2
Brindisi, 345,635 ....G 4
Cagliari, 754,965 ....B 5
Caltanissetta, 302,513 ....D 6
Campobasso, 358,052 ....E 4
Caserta, 649,327 ....E 4
Catania, 893,542 ....E 6
Catanzaro, 741,509 ....F 5
Chieti, 373,632 ....E 3
Como, 622,132 ....B 2
Cosenza, 694,398 ....F 5
Cremona, 351,160 ....B 2
Cuneo, 536,356 ....A 2
Enna, 229,126 ....E 6
Ferrara, 403,218 ....C 2
Florence, 1,012,703 ....C 3
Foggia, 665,286 ....E 4
Forlì, 521,128 ....D 2
Frosinone, 438,254 ....D 4
Genoa, 1,031,091 ....B 2
Gorizia, 137,745 ....D 2
Grosseto, 220.305 ....C 3
Imperia, 202,160 ....B 3
L'Aquila, 328,989 ....D 3
La Spezia, 239,256 ....B 2
Latina, 319,056 ....D 4
Lecce, 678,338 ....G 4
Leghorn, 310,210 ....C 3
Lucca, 365,540 ....C 3
Macerata, 291,412 ....D 3
Mantua, 387,255 ....C 2
Massa-Carrara, 202,981 ....C 2
Matera, 200,131 ....F 4
Messina, 685,260 ....E 5
Milan, 3,156,815 ....B 2
Modena, 511,355 ....C 2
Naples, 2,421,243 ....E 4
Novara, 460,190 ....B 2
Nuoro, 283,206 ....B 4
Padua, 694,017 ....C 2
Palermo, 1,111,397 ....D 5
Parma, 389,199 ....C 2
Pavia, 518,193 ....B 2
Perugia, 570,149 ....D 3
Pesaro e Urbino, 314,741 ....D 3
Pescara, 242,958 ....E 3
Piacenza, 291,059 ....B 2
Pisa, 362,396 ....C 3
Pistoia, 232,999 ....C 2
Pordenone, 241,724 ....D 2
Potenza, 444,166 ....E 4
Ragusa, 252,769 ....E 6
Ravenna, 329,559 ....D 2
Reggio di Calabria, 609,140....E 5
Reggio nell'Emilia, 379,688 ....C 2
Rieti, 162,405 ....D 3
Rome, 2,775,380 ....F 6
Rovigo, 277,811 ....C 2
Salerno, 912,265 ....E 4
Sassari, 381,191 ....B 4
Savona, 262,842 ....B 2
Siena, 270,062 ....C 3
Sondrio, 161,450 ....B 1
Syracuse, 345,777 ....E 6
Taranto, 468,713 ....F 4
Teramo, 260,687 ....D 3
Terni, 224,596 ....D 3
Trapani, 427,672 ....D 5
Trento, 412,104 ....C 1
Treviso, 607,616 ....D 2
Trieste, 298,645 ....E 2
Turin, 1,824,254 ....A 2
Udine, 526,184 ....D 1
Varese, 581,528 ....B 2
Venice, 749,173 ....D 2
Vercelli, 400,233 ....B 2
Verona, 667,517 ....C 2
Vicenza, 615,507 ....C 2
Viterbo, 263,862 ....C 3

CITIES and TOWNS

Acireale, 26,744 ....E 6
Acqui Terme, 14,070 ....B 2
Acri, 7,660 ....F 5
Adrano, 31,411 ....E 6
Adria, 11,456 ....D 2
Agira, 13,157 ....E 6
Agrigento, 46,947 ....D 6
Agropoli, 7,200 ....E 4
Alassio, 10,492 ....A 2
Alatri, 5,311 ....D 4
Alba, 16,396 ....B 2
Albano Laziale, 13,007 ....F 7
Albenga, 9,429 ....B 3
Albino, 6,875 ....B 2
Alcamo, 42,974 ....D 6
Alessandria, 65,908 ....B 2
Alghero, 22,139 ....B 4
Altamura, 41,528 ....F 4
Amalfi, 5,183 ....E 4
Amantea, 5,910 ....E 5
Ancona, 77,748 ....D 3
Andria, 69,499 ....F 4
Anzio, 12,102 ....D 4
Aosta, 28,637 ....A 2
Aprilia, 8,784 ....D 4
Aragona, 12,119 ....D 6
Arezzo, 43,868 ....C 3
Ariano Irpino, 11,302 ....E 4
Ascoli Piceno, 33,825 ....D 3
Assisi, 5,302 ....D 3
Asti, 44,455 ....B 2
Augusta, 25,774 ....E 6
Avellino, 31,744 ....E 4
Aversa, 40,245 ....E 4
Avezzano, 24,120 ....D 3
Avigliano, 5,119 ....E 4
Avola, 27,197 ....E 6
Bagheria, 31,435 ....D 5
Barcellona Pozzo di Gotto, 32,147 ....D 5
Bari, 293,963 ....F 4
Barletta, 67,419 ....F 4
Bassano del Grappa, 24,077....C 2
Belluno, 15,400 ....D 1
Benevento, 41,467 ....E 4
Bergamo, 110,666 ....B 2
Biancavilla, 19,858 ....E 6
Biella, 42,994 ....B 2
Bisceglie, 40,520 ....F 4
Bitonto, 34,160 ....F 4
Bitti, 5,623 ....B 4
Bologna, 443,178 ....C 2
Bolzano, 84,685 ....C 1
Bondeno, 6,413 ....C 2
Bonorva, 6,192 ....B 4
Bordighera, 9,045 ....A 3
Borgomanero, 11,843 ....B 2
Borgo San Lorenzo, 6,135 ....C 2
Bosa, 7,890 ....B 4
Bra, 14,472 ....A 2
Bracciano, 6,460 ....C 3
Brescia, 140,518 ....C 2
Bressanone, 10,095 ....C 1
Brindisi, 63,480 ....G 4
Bronte, 19,418 ....E 6
Busto Arsizio, 58,483 ....B 2
Cagliari, 172,925 ....B 5
Caltagirone, 37,634 ....E 6
Caltanissetta, 51,699 ....D 6
Camaiore, 7,130 ....C 3
Campobasso, 27,568 ....E 4
Campo Tures, 1,162 ....C 1
Canicatti, 29,613 ....E 6
Canosa di Puglia, 32,908 ....E 4
Cantù, 17,298 ....B 2
Capua, 13,334 ....E 4
Caravaggio, 9,938 ....B 2
Carbonia, 26,227 ....B 5
Carini, 15,486 ....D 5
Carloforte, 7,153 ....B 5
Carmagnola, 6,583 ....A 2
Carpi, 27,647 ....C 2
Carrara, 37,386 ....C 2
Casale Monferrato, 31,226 ....B 2
Casalmaggiore, 5,995 ....C 2
Cascina-Navacchio, 23,739 ....C 3
Caserta, 36,337 ....E 4
Cassano allo Ionio, 9,250 ....F 5
Cassino, 11,369 ....E 4
Castelfranco Veneto, 9,978 ....D 2
Castel Gandolfo, 2,861 ....F 7
Castellammare del Golfo, 16,581 ....D 5
Castellammare di Stabia, 49,064 ....E 4
Castel San Pietro Terme, 4,824..C 2
Castelvetrano, 30,009 ....D 6
Castrovillari, 13,063 ....F 5
Catania, 358,700 ....E 6
Catanzaro, 44,198 ....F 5
Cava de'Tirreni, 19,883 ....E 4
Cavarzere, 6,109 ....D 2
Cecina, 13,749 ....C 3
Cefalù, 10,360 ....E 5
Ceglie Messapico, 17,891 ....F 4
Celano, 9,743 ....D 3
Cerignola, 43,345 ....E 4
Cernobbio, 6,857 ....B 2
Cesena, 31,153 ....D 2
Cesenatico, 7,684 ....D 2
Chiari, 9,552 ....C 2
Chiavari, 22,835 ....B 2
Chieri, 15,358 ....A 2
Chieti, 31,374 ....E 3
Chioggia, 25,058 ....D 2
Chivasso, 11,806 ....A 2
Ciampino, 10,012 ....F 7
Cittadella, 5,698 ....C 2
Città di Castello, 15,564 ....D 3
Cittanova, 11,567 ....F 5
Cividale del Friuli, 7,698 ....D 1
Civitavecchia, 34,996 ....C 3
Clusone, 5,729 ....C 2
Codriopo, 5,064 ....D 2
Colle di Val d'Elsa, 7,329 ....C 3
Comacchio, 9,743 ....D 2
Comiso, 24,016 ....E 6
Como, 64,301 ....B 2
Conegliano, 16,910 ....D 2
Conversano, 15,543 ....F 4
Corato, 38,774 ....F 4
Cori, 6,930 ....F 7
Corigliano Calabro, 13,526 ....F 5
Corleone, 14,185 ....D 6
Correggio, 8,146 ....C 2
Cortina d'Ampezzo, 4,291 ....D 1
Cosenza, 70,201 ....F 5
Courmayeur, 1,013 ....A 2
Crema, 20,679 ....B 2
Cremona, 64,775 ....B 2
Crotone, 36,516 ....F 5
Cuneo, 32,978 ....A 2
Desenzano del Garda, 8,017 ....C 2
Domodossola, 15,097 ....B 1
Dorgali, 6,976 ....B 4
Eboli, 19,550 ....E 4
Empoli, 22,484 ....C 3
Enna, 26,206 ....E 6
Este, 11,007 ....C 2
Fabriano, 15,127 ....D 3
Faenza, 40,425 ....D 2
Fano, 24,591 ....D 3
Fasano, 17,990 ....F 4
Favara, 27,523 ....D 6
Feltre, 9,446 ....C 1
Fermo, 14,453 ....D 3
Ferrandina, 8,381 ....F 4
Ferrara, 90,419 ....C 2
Fidenza, 13,567 ....B 2
Finale Emilia, 6,711 ....C 2
Finale Ligure, 9,789 ....B 2
Firenze (Florence), 413,455....C 3
Fiumicino, 9,489 ....F 7
Florence, 413,455 ....C 3
Floridia, 16,104 ....E 6
Foggia, 108,682 ....E 4
Foligno, 23,094 ....D 3
Fondi, 14,991 ....D 4
Forlì, 65,376 ....D 2
Formia, 15,048 ....D 4
Fossano, 12,563 ....A 2
Francavilla Fontana, 27,629....F 4
Frascati, 12,602 ....F 6
Frosinone, 20,998 ....D 4
Gaeta, 20,436 ....D 4
Galatina, 19,654 ....G 4
Galatone, 13,487 ....F 4
Gallarate, 34,870 ....B 2
Gallipoli, 15,958 ....F 4
Gela, 54,526 ....E 6
Gemona, 7,698 ....D 1
Genoa (Genova), 747,794....B 2
Genzano di Roma, 11,666 ....F 7
Giarre, 11,859 ....E 6
Gioia del Colle, 23,734 ....F 4
Giovinazzo, 14,189 ....F 4
Giulianova, 11,220 ....E 3
Gorizia, 35,307 ....D 2
Gravina in Puglia, 30,615 ....F 4
Grosseto, 36,558 ....C 3
Grottaferrata, 5,356 ....F 7
Grottaglie, 22,218 ....F 4
Guastalla, 7,511 ....C 2
Gubbio, 9,730 ....D 3
Iesi, 26,018 ....D 3
Iglesias, 20,518 ....B 5
Imola, 32,148 ....C 2
Imperia, 30,522 ....B 3
Isernia, 9,689 ....E 4
Ivrea, 19,344 ....B 2
La Maddalena, 10,414 ....B 4
Lanciano, 15,182 ....E 3
Lanusei, 5,208 ....B 5
L'Aquila, 29,462 ....D 3
La Spezia, 111,768 ....B 2
Latina, 26,171 ....D 4
Lavello, 12,857 ....E 4
Lecce, 68,385 ....G 4
Lecco, 47,468 ....B 2
Leghorn, 152,517 ....C 3
Legnago, 10,126 ....C 2
Lendinara, 6,475 ....C 2
Lentini, 31,788 ....E 6
Leonforte, 17,690 ....E 6
Licata, 38,222 ....D 6
Lido di Ostia, 25,662 ....F 7
Lido di Venezia, 16,581 ....D 2
Lipari, 3,852 ....E 5
Livorno (Leghorn), 152,517....C 3
Lodi, 34,281 ....B 2
Lonigo, 5,774 ....C 2
Lucca, 45,398 ....C 3
Lucera, 24,399 ....E 4
Lugo, 16,550 ....D 2
Macerata, 27,054 ....D 3
Macomer, 7,782 ....B 4
Maglie, 12,205 ....G 4
Manduria, 23,971 ....F 4
Manfredonia, 34,583 ....F 4
Mantua, 55,806 ....C 2
Marino, 9,798 ....F 7
Marsala, 34,294 ....D 6
Martina Franca, 27,588 ....F 4
Massa, 46,992 ....C 2
Massafra, 18.884 ....F 4
Massa Marittima, 6,804 ....C 3
Matera, 36,727 ....F 4
Mazara del Vallo, 35,356 ....D 6
Mazzarino, 17,195 ....E 6
Melfi, 15,122 ....E 4
Menfi, 12,335 ....D 6
Merano, 29,196 ....C 1
Mesagne, 25,042 ....G 4
Messina, 202,095 ....E 5
Mestre, 138,822 ....D 2
Milan, 1,573,009 ....B 2
Milazzo, 14,034 ....E 5
Mirandola, 9,272 ....C 2
Mira Taglio, 8,380 ....D 2
Mistretta, 9,979 ....E 6
Modena, 107,814 ....C 2
Modica, 28,998 ....E 6
Mola di Bari, 22,397 ....F 4
Molfetta, 61,226 ....F 4
Moncalieri, 14,339 ....A 2
Mondovì Breo, 9,893 ....A 2
Monfalcone, 26,708 ....D 2
Monopoli, 25,161 ....F 4
Monreale, 18,881 ....D 5
Monselice, 7,766 ....C 2
Montebelluna, 6,088 ....D 2
Montefiascone, 6,428 ....D 3
Monterotondo, 9,616 ....F 6
Monte Sant'Angelo, 20,512 ....F 4
Montevarchi, 12,413 ....C 3
Monza, 79,715 ....B 2
Mortara, 12,243 ....B 2
Naples, 1,119,392 ....E 4
Nardo, 23,006 ....F 4
Narni, 5,551 ....D 3
Naro, 14,295 ....D 6
Nettuno, 16,187 ....D 4
Nicastro, 21,240 ....F 5
Nicosia, 16,624 ....E 6
Niscemi, 24,468 ....E 6
Nizza Monferrato, 6,229 ....B 2
Nocera Inferiore, 38,690 ....E 4
Noto, 21,586 ....E 6
Novara, 79,188 ....B 2
Novi Ligure, 23,349 ....B 2
Nuoro, 22,559 ....B 4
Olbia, 13,795 ....B 4
Oliena, 6,974 ....B 4
Orbetello, 6,800 ....C 3
Oristano, 16,305 ....B 5
Ortona, 11,315 ....E 3
Orvieto, 9,617 ....D 3
Osimo, 9,406 ....D 3
Ostuni, 25,190 ....F 4
Otranto, 3,510 ....G 4
Ozieri, 10,194 ....B 4
Pachino, 20,645 ....E 6
Padua, 169,298 ....C 2
Palazzolo Acreide, 10,802 ....E 6
Palermo, 531,306 ....D 5
Palestrina, 7,897 ....F 7
Palma di Montechiaro, 20,425....D 6
Palmi, 14,576 ....E 5
Pantelleria, 3,100 ....C 6
Paola, 9,701 ....E 5
Parma, 118,602 ....C 2
Partanna, 12,931 ....D 6
Partinico, 25,924 ....D 6
Paterno, 39,912 ....E 6
Patti, 6,748 ....E 5
Pavia, 69,581 ....B 2
Penne, 5,709 ....D 3
Pergine Valsugana, 4,877 ....C 1
Perugia, 52,534 ....D 3
Pesaro, 47,185 ....D 3
Pescara, 81,697 ....E 3
Pescia, 8,737 ....C 3
Piacenza, 78,905 ....B 2
Piazza Armerina, 23,915 ....E 6
Pietrasanta, 6,785 ....B 3
Pinerolo, 25,262 ....A 2
Piombino, 30,843 ....C 3
Piove di Sacco, 6,230 ....C 2
Pisa, 76,846 ....C 3
Pisticci, 11,469 ....F 4
Pistoia, 41,058 ....C 2
Poggibonsi, 12,932 ....C 3
Pont-Canavese, 4,071 ....A 2
Pontecorvo, 5,845 ....D 4
Pontremoli, 4,839 ....C 2
Popoli, 6,749 ....E 3
Pordenone, 29,461 ....D 2
Porto Civitanova, 18,288 ....D 3
Porto Empedocle, 16,110 ....D 6
Portoferraio, 6,318 ....C 3
Portofino, 735 ....B 2
Portogruaro, 8,913 ....D 2
Portomaggiore, 5,532 ....C 2
Porto Recanati, 4,986 ....D 3
Porto Torres, 10,108 ....B 4
Potenza, 34,216 ....F 4
Pozzallo, 11,862 ....E 6
Pozzuoli, 44,038 ....D 4
Prato, 75,402 ....C 3
Prima Porta, 9,978 ....F 6
Priverno, 9,154 ....D 4
Putignano, 15,976 ....F 4
Quartu Sant'Elena, 22,271 ....B 5
Ragusa, 50,718 ....E 6
Rapallo, 16,628 ....B 2
Ravenna, 56,815 ....D 2
Recanati, 7,242 ....D 3
Reggio di Calabria, 93,964....E 5
Reggio nell'Emilia, 83,073 ....C 2
Rho, 27,586 ....B 2
Riesi, 17,899 ....E 6
Rieti, 21,278 ....D 3
Rimini, 72,720 ....D 2
Rionero in Vulture, 13,567 ....E 4
Riva, 7,626 ....C 2
Rome (cap.), 2,043,055 ....F 6
Rome, *2,656,104 ....F 6
Ronciglione, 5,772 ....C 3
Rossano, 13,323 ....F 5
Rovereto, 20,505 ....C 2
Rovigo, 22,804 ....C 2
Ruvo di Puglia, 23,216 ....F 4
Sala Consilina, 6,742 ....E 4
Salemi, 12,237 ....D 6
Salerno, 103,778 ....E 4
Salsomaggiore Terme, 10,376 ....B 2
Saluzzo, 11,991 ....A 2
Sambiase, 11,551 ....F 5
San Bartolomeo in Galdo, 8,745..E 4
San Benedetto del Tronto, 28,053 ....E 3
San Cataldo, 21,778 ....D 6
San Giovanni in Fiore, 16,528 ....F 5
San Giovanni in Persiceto, 8,692 ....C 2
San Marco in Lamis, 17,933 ....E 4
Sannicandro Garganico, 17,238 ....E 4
San Remo, 40,068 ....A 3
Sansepolcro, 10,063 ....D 3
San Severino Marche, 5,582 ....D 3
San Severo, 47,897 ....E 4
Santa Maria Capua Vetere, 29,925 ....E 4
Santeramo in Colle, 19,587....F 4
San Vito al Tagliamento, 5,278 D 2

(continued on following page)

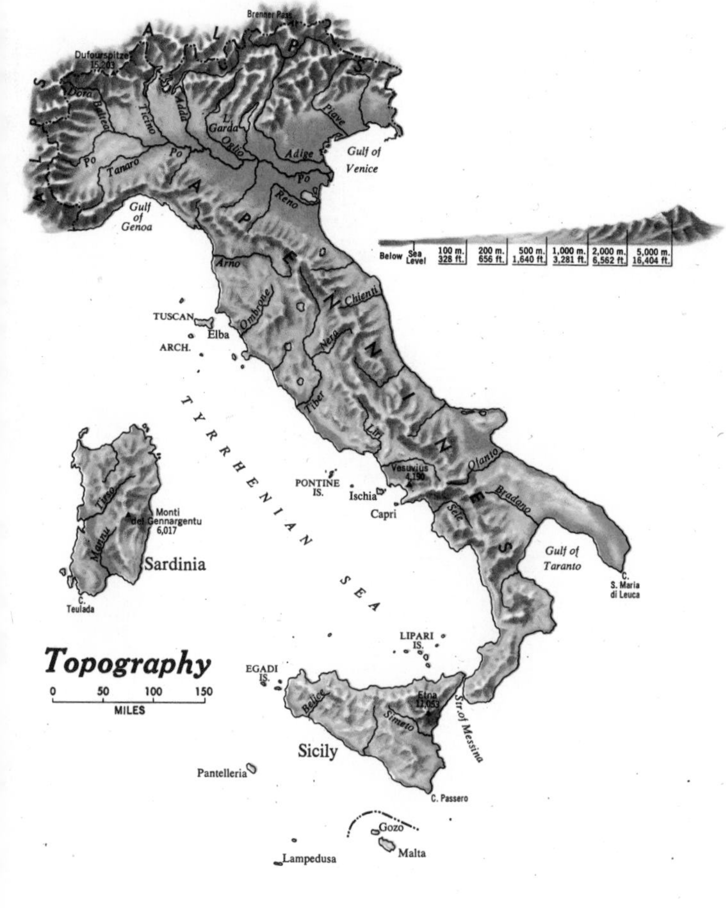
Brenner Pass
Dufourspitze 15,203
A L P S
Dora Baltea
Ticino
Adda
Garda
Oglio
Adige
Piave
Po
Tanaro
Gulf of Venice
Reno
Gulf of Genoa
A P E N N I N E S
Arno
Ombrone
Chienti
Tiber
Nera
Liri
TUSCAN ARCH.
Elba
T Y R R H E N I A N S E A
PONTINE IS.
Ischia
Vesuvius 4,190
Capri
Ofanto
Bradano
Sele
Gulf of Taranto
C. S. Maria di Leuca
Monti del Gennargentu 6,017
Tirso
Sardinia
C. Teulada
LIPARI IS.
EGADI IS.
Etna 11,053
Str. of Messina
Simeto
Belice
Sicily
Pantelleria
C. Passero
Gozo
Malta
Lampedusa
Below Sea Level
100 m. 328 ft.
200 m. 656 ft.
500 m. 1,640 ft.
1,000 m. 3,281 ft.
2,000 m. 6,562 ft.
5,000 m. 16,404 ft.
0 50 100 150
MILES

Topography

Agriculture, Industry and Resources

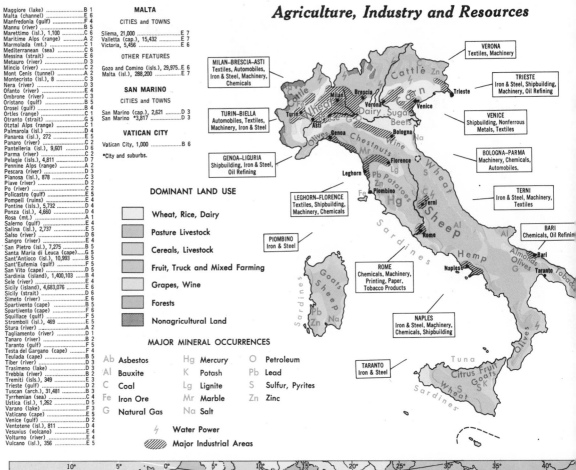

VERONA — Textiles, Machinery

TRIESTE — Iron & Steel, Shipbuilding, Machinery, Oil Refining

VENICE — Shipbuilding, Nonferrous Metals, Textiles

MILAN–BRESCIA–ASTI — Textiles, Automobiles, Iron & Steel, Machinery, Chemicals

TURIN–BIELLA — Automobiles, Textiles, Machinery, Iron & Steel

GENOA–LIGURIA — Shipbuilding, Iron & Steel, Oil Refining

BOLOGNA–PARMA — Machinery, Chemicals, Automobiles.

TERNI — Iron & Steel, Machinery, Textiles

LEGHORN–FLORENCE — Textiles, Shipbuilding, Machinery, Chemicals

PIOMBINO — Iron & Steel

BARI — Chemicals, Oil Refining

ROME — Chemicals, Machinery, Printing, Paper, Tobacco Products

NAPLES — Iron & Steel, Machinery, Chemicals, Shipbuilding

TARANTO — Iron & Steel

DOMINANT LAND USE

- Wheat, Rice, Dairy
- Pasture Livestock
- Cereals, Livestock
- Fruit, Truck and Mixed Farming
- Grapes, Wine
- Forests
- Nonagricultural Land

MAJOR MINERAL OCCURRENCES

Ab Asbestos
Al Bauxite
C Coal
Fe Iron Ore
G Natural Gas

Hg Mercury
K Potash
Lg Lignite
Mr Marble
Na Salt

O Petroleum
Pb Lead
S Sulfur, Pyrites
Zn Zinc

⚡ Water Power
▨ Major Industrial Areas

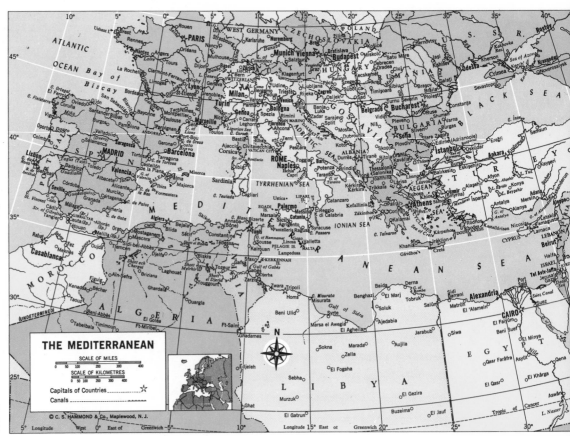

THE MEDITERRANEAN

SCALE OF MILES
0 50 100 200 300 400

SCALE OF KILOMETRES
0 50 100 200 300 400

Capitals of Countries ....☆
Canals ....

© C. S. HAMMOND & Co., Maplewood, N. J.

SWITZERLAND
AREA 15,941 sq. mi.
POPULATION 6,230,000
CAPITAL Bern
LARGEST CITY Zürich
HIGHEST POINT Dufourspitze (Mte. Rosa) 15,203 ft.
MONETARY UNIT Swiss franc
MAJOR LANGUAGES German, French, Italian, Romansch
MAJOR RELIGIONS Protestantism, Roman Catholicism

LIECHTENSTEIN
AREA 61 sq. mi.
POPULATION 21,000
CAPITAL Vaduz
LARGEST CITY Vaduz
HIGHEST POINT Naafkopf 8,445 ft.
MONETARY UNIT Swiss franc
MAJOR LANGUAGE German
MAJOR RELIGION Roman Catholicism

SWITZERLAND

LIECHTENSTEIN

LANGUAGES

Basel · Zürich · St. Gallen
Biel · Lucerne · Chur
★ Bern · Fribourg
Lausanne · St. Moritz
Geneva · Sion · Bellinzona

- German
- French
- Italian
- Romansch

Switzerland is a multilingual nation with four official languages. 70% of the people speak German, 19% French, 10% Italian and 1% Romansch.

SWITZERLAND

CANTONS

Aargau, 397,000	F 2
Appenzell, Ausser-Rhoden, 50,000	H 2
Appenzell, Inner-Rhoden, 13,500	H 2
Baselland, 177,900	E 1
Baselstadt, 237,300	E 1
Bern, 958,000	D 2
Fribourg, 163,000	D 3
Geneva, 304,400	B 4
Glarus, 42,000	H 3
Graubünden (Grisons), 155,000	J 3
Luzern (Lucerne), 274,000	F 2
Neuchâtel, 161,000	C 3
Nidwalden, 25,000	F 3
Obwalden, 25,000	F 3
Sankt Gallen, 363,000	H 2
Schaffhausen, 72,000	G 1
Schwyz, 84,800	G 2
Solothurn (Soleure), 220,000	E 2
Thurgau, 183,000	H 1
Ticino, 220,000	G 4
Uri, 33,000	G 3
Valais, 191,000	E 4
Vaud, 486,000	C 3
Zug, 61,000	G 2
Zürich, 1,048,000	G 2

CITIES and TOWNS

Aadorf, 2,258	G 2
Aarau, 17,400	F 2
Aarau, *47,800	F 2

Aarberg, 2,355	D 2
Aarburg, 5,302	E 2
Adelboden, 2,881	E 3
Aeschi bei Spiez, 1,319	E 3
Affoltern am Albis, 4,904	F 2
Affoltern im Emmental, 1,206	E 2
Aigle, 4,381	C 4
Airolo, 2,023	G 3
Alle, 1,471	C 2
Allschwil, 15,500	D 1
Alpnach, 3,211	F 3
Altdorf, 7,477	G 3
Altstätten, 8,751	J 2
Amriswil, 6,752	H 1
Andermatt, 1,523	G 3
Appenzell, 5,082	H 2
Arbedo-Castione, 1,467	G 4
Ardez, 13,100	H 1
Ardon, 1,432	D 4
Arlesheim, 5,219	E 2
Arosa, 2,600	J 3
Arth, 6,321	G 2
Ascona, 3,053	G 4
Attalens, 1,023	G 4
Aubonne, 1,766	B 4
Avenches, 1,776	D 3
Baar, 9,114	G 2
Baden, 14,900	F 2
Baden, *54,500	F 2
Bad Ragaz, 2,699	H 2
Balerna, 3,040	G 5
Balsthal, 5,735	E 2
Bäretswil, 2,577	G 2
Basel, 213,200	E 1
Basel, *364,800	E 1
Bassecourt, 2,284	D 2
Bätterkinden, 1,916	E 2
Bauma, 3,214	G 2
Beatenberg, 1,303	E 3
Beckenried, 2,042	G 3

Beinwil am See, 2,346	F 2
Bellinzona, 14,900	H 4
Bellinzona, *25,700	H 4
Belp, 4,922	D 3
Bergün-Bravuogn, 551	J 3
Bern (cap.), 166,800	D 3
Bern, *258,000	D 3
Beromünster, 1,443	F 2
Bex, 4,667	D 4
Biasca, 3,349	H 4
Biberist, 7,188	D 2
Biel (Bienne), 67,800	D 2
Biel, *87,000	D 2
Bière, 1,166	B 3
Binningen, 13,800	E 1
Bischofszell, 3,811	H 1
Blumenstein, 1,121	E 3
Bodio, 1,276	G 4
Bolligen, 19,400	E 3
Boltigen, 1,691	D 3
Boncourt, 1,493	C 2
Bönigen, 1,883	E 3
Boswil, 1,663	F 2
Boudry, 3,086	C 3
Bourg-Saint-Pierre, 524	D 5
Breil-Brigels, 1,272	H 3
Breitenbach, 1,851	E 2
Bremgarten, 4,555	F 2
Brienz, 2,864	F 3
Brig, 4,647	E 4
Brissago, 1,845	G 4
Brittnau, 3,070	E 2
Brugg, 6,683	F 2
Brusio, 1,445	K 4
Bubendorf, 1,690	E 2
Bubikon, 2,612	G 2
Buchs, 6,345	H 2
Bülach, 8,188	G 1
Bulle, 5,983	D 3
Buochs, 2,733	F 3
Büren an der Aare, 2,432	D 2
Burgdorf, 15,600	E 2
Bürglen, 3,175	G 3
Bürglen, 1,899	H 1
Bussigny-près-Lausanne, 2,381	B 3
Bütschwil, 3,414	H 2
Carouge, 15,600	B 4
Castagnola, 3,775	G 4
Cazis, 1,553	H 3
Cernier, 1,545	C 2
Chalais, 1,597	E 4
Cham, 6,483	G 2
Chamoson, 2,088	D 4
Charmey, 1,144	D 3
Châteaux-d'Oex, 3,378	D 4
Châtel-Saint-Denis, 2,666	C 3
Chavornay, 1,414	C 3
Chexbres, 1,449	C 3
Chiasso, 7,377	G 5
Chur, 29,100	J 3
Churwalden, 877	J 3
Coire (Chur), 29,100	J 3
Conthey, 3,563	D 4
Coppet, 774	B 4
Corcelles-près-Payerne, 1,253	C 3
Corgémont, 1,414	D 2
Cossonay, 1,284	C 3
Courgenay, 1,666	D 2
Courroux, 1,667	D 2
Court, 1,493	D 2
Courtelary, 1,330	D 2
Courtételle, 1,618	D 2
Couvet, 3,450	C 3
Cully, 1,375	C 3
Därstetten, 900	D 3
Davos (Dorf and Platz), 9,588	J 3
Degersheim, 3,221	H 2
Delémont, 9,542	D 2
Derendingen, 4,463	E 2
Digmtigen, 1,934	D 3
Diessenhofen, 2,222	G 1
Dietikon, 20,600	G 2
Disentis-Mustèr, 2,376	G 3
Dombresson, 1,040	C 2
Dornach, 4,260	E 2
Dübendorf, 17,100	G 2
Düdingen, 4,248	D 3
Dürnten, 4,271	G 2
Dürrenroth, 1,221	E 2
Ebnat-Kappel, 4,979	H 2
Echallens, 1,428	C 3
Egg, 3,018	G 2
Eggiwil, 2,591	E 3
Eglisau, 1,911	G 1
Egnach, 3,483	H 1
Einsiedeln, 8,792	G 2
Elgg, 2,643	G 2
Emmen, 21,400	F 2
Engelberg, 2,646	F 3
Engi, 1,064	H 3
Ennenda, 3,076	H 3
Entlebuch, 3,318	E 3
Erlenbach im Simmental, 1,471	D 3
Ermatingen, 1,857	H 1
Erstfeld, 4,126	G 3
Eschenbach, 2,866	G 2
Escholzmatt, 3,257	E 3
Estavayer-le-Lac, 2,583	C 3
Evolène, 1,786	D 4
Faido, 1,441	G 4

(continued on following page)

Agriculture, Industry and Resources

DOMINANT LAND USE

- Cereals, Dairy
- Pasture Livestock
- General Farming, Livestock
- Fruit, Truck, Mixed Farming
- Forests
- Nonagricultural Land

⚡ Water Power
▨ Major Industrial Areas

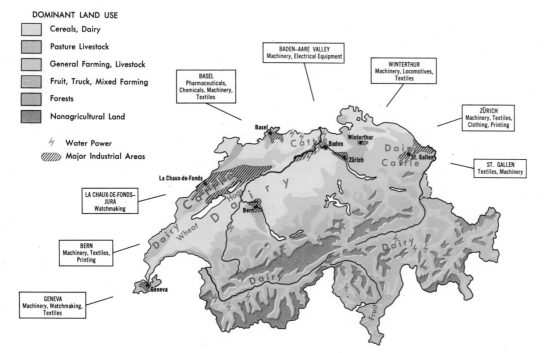

BADEN–AARE VALLEY
Machinery, Electrical Equipment

BASEL
Pharmaceuticals, Chemicals, Machinery, Textiles

WINTERTHUR
Machinery, Locomotives, Textiles

ZÜRICH
Machinery, Textiles, Clothing, Printing

ST. GALLEN
Textiles, Machinery

LA CHAUX-DE-FONDS–JURA
Watchmaking

BERN
Machinery, Textiles, Printing

GENEVA
Machinery, Watchmaking, Textiles

36 Switzerland and Liechtenstein

(continued)

Topography

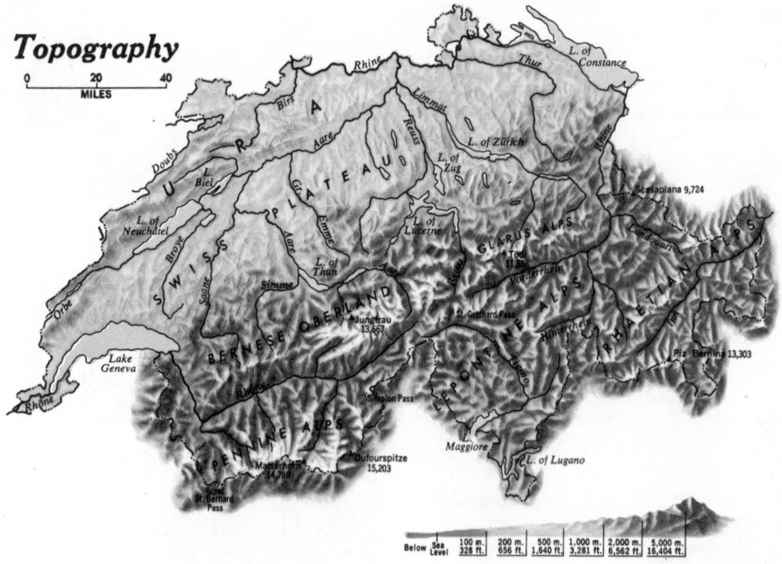

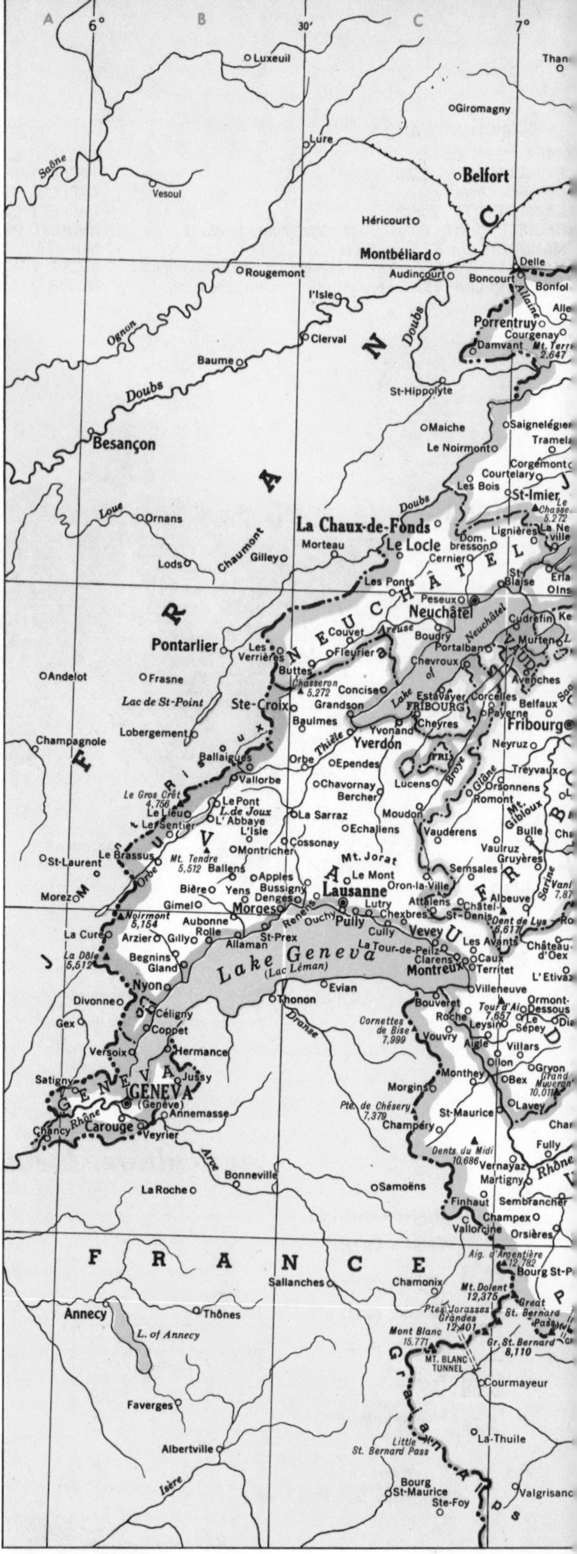

SWITZERLAND (continued)

Flawil, 7,256 ....H 2
Fleurier, 3,814 ....C 3
Flims, 1,444 ....H 3
Flüelen, 1,717 ....G 3
Flums, 4,462 ....H 2
Frauenfeld, 16,800 ....G 1
Fribourg, 38,500 ....D 3
Fribourg, *47,300 ....D 3
Frick, 2,123 ....E 1
Frutigen, 5,565 ....E 3
Fully, 3,419 ....D 4
Gais, 2,488 ....H 2
Gelterkinden, 3,870 ....E 2
Geneva (Genève), 169,500 ....B 4
Geneva, *307,500 ....B 4
Gersau, 1,754 ....G 2
Gimel, 1,091 ....B 3
Giornico, 1,063 ....G 4
Giswil, 2,656 ....F 3
Giubiasco, 4,281 ....H 4
Gland, 1,545 ....B 4
Glarus, 5,852 ....H 2
Glattfelden, 2,426 ....F 1
Gordola, 1,794 ....G 4
Göschenen, 1,284 ....G 3
Gossau, 9,731 ....H 2
Grabs, 4,218 ....H 2
Grandson, 2,091 ....C 3
Gränichen, 4,411 ....F 2
Grenchen, 19,800 ....D 2
Grenchen, *23,400 ....D 2
Grindelwald, 3,244 ....E 3
Grossandelfingen, 1,102 ....G 1
Grosswangen, 2,373 ....F 2
Gruyères, 1,349 ....D 3
Gsteig, 937 ....D 4
Guggisberg, 2,021 ....D 3
Gurtnellen, 1,048 ....G 3
Hallau, 1,966 ....F 1
Heiden, 3,158 ....H 2
Heimberg, 2,125 ....E 3
Hemberg, 1,011 ....H 2
Henau (Uzwil), 7,828 ....H 2
Hérémence, 1,868 ....D 4
Herisau, 15,500 ....H 2
Hermance, 512 ....B 4
Herzogenbuchsee, 4,641 ....E 2
Hinwil, 4,811 ....G 2
Hochdorf, 4,452 ....F 2
Horgen, 15,300 ....G 2
Hospental, 289 ....F 3
Huttwil, 4,664 ....E 2
Igis, 3,902 ....J 3
Ilanz, 1,843 ....H 3
Illnau, 6,160 ....G 2
Ingenbohl, 5,046 ....G 2
Innertkirchen, 1,230 ....F 3
Ins, 2,486 ....D 2
Interlaken, 4,738 ....E 3
Jegenstorf, 1,397 ....D 2
Jenaz, 1,143 ....J 3
Jona, 5,686 ....G 2
Jungfraujoch ....E 3
Kaltbrunn, 2,527 ....H 2
Kandersteg, 937 ....E 4
Kerns, 3,553 ....F 3
Kerzers, 2,228 ....D 3
Kilchberg, 6,784 ....F 2
Kirchberg, 3,304 ....E 2
Kirchberg, 5,554 ....G 2
Kleinlützel, 1,269 ....D 2
Klingnau, 2,192 ....F 1
Klosters, 3,181 ....J 3
Kloten, 8,446 ....G 2
Koblenz, 1,114 ....F 1
Kölliken, 3,007 ....F 2
Köniz, 30,600 ....D 3
Kreuzlingen, 14,900 ....H 1
Kriens, 17,200 ....F 2
Küsnacht, 12,800 ....G 2
Küssnacht, 12,400 ....F 2
Küttigen, 3,457 ....F 2
L'Abbaye, 1,124 ....B 3
La Chaux-de-Fonds, 42,800 ....C 2
Lachen, 3,913 ....G 2
La Neuveville, 3,216 ....D 2
Langenthal, 12,400 ....E 2
Langnau, 9,201 ....E 3
Langnau am Albis, 2,850 ....G 2
La Roche, 1,043 ....D 3
La Sarraz, 1,026 ....C 3
La Tour-de-Peilz, 6,820 ....C 4
Läufelfingen, 1,176 ....E 2
Laufen, 3,955 ....D 2
Laufenburg, 1,850 ....F 1
Laupen, 1,607 ....D 3
Lauperswil, 2,652 ....E 3
Lausanne, 138,300 ....C 3
Lausanne, *214,900 ....C 3
Lauterbrunnen, 3,216 ....E 3
Le Brassus (Le Chenit), 5,242....B 3
Le Châble, 4,237 ....D 4
Le Lieu, 970 ....B 3
Le Locle, 15,100 ....C 2
Le Mont, 1,719 ....C 3
Lengnau, 3,524 ....D 2
Lenk, 1,900 ....D 4
Le Noirmont, 1,559 ....C 2
Lens, 1,743 ....D 4
Lenzburg, 6,378 ....F 2
Les Bois, 1,098 ....C 2
Les Ponts-de-Martel, 1,429 ....C 2
Les Verrières, 1,084 ....B 3
Leuk, 2,546 ....E 4
Leukerbad, 619 ....E 4
Leysin, 2,241 ....C 4
Liestal, 11,300 ....E 2
Linthal, 2,645 ....H 3
Littau, 8,715 ....F 2
Locarno, 12,200 ....G 4
Locarno, *21,000 ....G 4
Lucens, 1,620 ....C 3
Lucerne, 73,000 ....F 2
Lucerne, *148,500 ....F 2
Lugano, 21,100 ....G 4
Lugano, *50,000 ....G 4
Lungern, 1,794 ....F 3
Luthern, 1,801 ....E 2
Lutry, 3,481 ....C 3
Lützelflüh, 3,960 ....E 3
Luzein, 1,013 ....J 3
Luzern (Lucerne), 73,000 ....F 2
Lyss, 5,616 ....D 2
Maienfeld, 1,488 ....J 2
Malans, 1,358 ....J 3
Malters, 4,579 ....F 2
Malvaglia, 1,120 ....H 4
Männedorf, 6,182 ....G 2
Marbach, 1,347 ....E 3
Martigny, 7,593 ....C 4
Meilen, 8,203 ....G 2
Meiringen, 3,749 ....F 3
Melchnau, 1,511 ....E 2
Melide, 1,046 ....G 5
Mellingen, 1,941 ....F 2
Mels, 5,254 ....H 2
Mendrisio, 5,100 ....G 5
Menzingen, 3,340 ....G 2
Menznau, 2,275 ....E 2
Mesocco, 1,324 ....H 4
Minusio, 3,663 ....G 4
Möhlin, 4,681 ....E 1
Mollis, 2,303 ....H 2
Montana-Vermala, 1,543 ....E 4
Monthey, 6,834 ....C 4
Montreux-Le Châtelard, 20,100 ..C 4
Morges, 8,420 ....B 3
Moudon, 2,806 ....C 3
Moutier, 7,472 ....D 2
Müllheim, 1,475 ....G 1
Mümliswil-Ramiswil, 2,714 ....E 2
Münchenbuchsee, 3,652 ....E 2
Münsingen, 6,051 ....E 3
Muotathal, 2,592 ....G 3
Muri, 3,957 ....F 2
Muri bei Bern, 7,855 ....E 3
Murten, 3,330 ....D 3
Müstair, 717 ....K 3
Muttenz, 14,000 ....E 1
Näfels, 3,617 ....H 2
Naters, 3,797 ....E 4
Nebikon, 1,206 ....F 2
Nesslau, 2,002 ....H 2
Netstal, 2,925 ....H 2
Neuchâtel, 36,300 ....C 3
Neuchâtel, *52,600 ....C 3
Neuenegg, 2,921 ....D 3
Neuhausen am Rheinfall, 11,800..G 1
Neunkirch, 1,208 ....F 1
Niederbipp, 3,141 ....E 2
Niederurnen, 3,347 ....G 2
Niederweningen, 1,027 ....F 1
Nunningen, 1,372 ....E 2
Nyon, 7,643 ....B 4
Oberägeri, 2,656 ....G 2
Oberburg, 3,030 ....E 2
Oberdiessbach, 1,927 ....E 3
Oberdorf, 1,132 ....E 2
Oberriet, 5,498 ....J 2
Obersaxen, 710 ....H 3
Oberuzwil, 4,394 ....H 2
Oensingen, 2,907 ....E 2
Ollon, 4,126 ....D 4
Olten, 21,900 ....E 2
Olten, *47,100 ....E 2
Orbe, 3,824 ....C 3
Ormont-Dessous, 996 ....D 4
Orsières, 2,281 ....D 4
Payerne, 6,024 ....C 3
Peseux, 4,933 ....C 3
Pfäffikon, 5,735 ....G 2
Pfaffnau, 2,575 ....E 2
Pieterlen, 2,978 ....D 2
Pontresina, 1,067 ....J 3
Porrentruy, 7,095 ....C 2
Poschiavo, 3,743 ....J 4
Pratteln, 9,492 ....E 1
Pully, 15,900 ....C 4
Quinto, 1,365 ....G 3
Rafz, 1,925 ....G 1
Ramsen, 1,181 ....G 1
Rapperswil, 7,585 ....G 2
Raron, 1,077 ....E 4
Rechthalten, 1,015 ....D 3
Regensdorf, 4,997 ....F 2
Reichenbach, 2,829 ....E 3
Reiden, 2,795 ....F 2
Reigoldswil, 1,192 ....E 2
Reinach, 5,174 ....F 2
Renens, 15,200 ....C 3
Rheinau, 2,363 ....G 1
Rheineck, 3,047 ....J 2
Rheinfelden, 5,197 ....E 1
Richterswil, 5,842 ....G 2
Riehen, 20,100 ....E 1
Riggisberg, 1,949 ....E 3
Riva San Vitale, 1,358 ....G 5
Rivera, 950 ....G 4
Roggwil, 3,420 ....E 2
Rohrbach, 1,534 ....E 2
Rolle, 2,942 ....B 4
Romanshorn, 7,755 ....H 1
Romont, 2,982 ....C 3
Rorschach, 13,400 ....H 2
Rorschach, *24,500 ....H 2
Rosenlaui ....F 3
Rothrist, 5,048 ....E 2
Rougemont, 860 ....D 4
Roveredo, 1,878 ....H 4
Rüeggisberg, 2,035 ....E 3
Rüschegg, 1,628 ....D 3
Ruswil, 4,657 ....F 2
Rüthi, 1,521 ....J 2
Rüti, Glarus, 738 ....H 3
Rüti, Zürich, 8,282 ....G 2
Saanen, 5,649 ....D 4
Saas-Fee, 739 ....E 4
Sachsein, 2,721 ....F 3
Saignelégier, 1,636 ....D 2
Saint-Blaise, 2,412 ....D 2
Sainte-Croix, 6,925 ....B 3
Saint-Imier, 6,704 ....D 2
Saint-Martin, 1,155 ....E 4
Saint-Maurice, 3,196 ....C 4
Saint Moritz, 3,751 ....J 3
Saint Niklaus, 2,071 ....E 4
Saint-Prex, 1,897 ....B 4
Saint-Stephan, 1,227 ....D 3
Saint-Ursanne, 1,304 ....D 2
Samedan, 2,106 ....J 3
Sankt Gallen, 78,900 ....H 2
Sargans, 2,571 ....H 2
Sarnen, 6,554 ....F 3
Satigny, 1,594 ....A 4
Savièse, 3,203 ....D 4
Savognin, 632 ....J 3
Saxon, 2,305 ....D 4
Schaffhausen, 37,400 ....G 1
Schaffhausen, *56,900 ....G 1
Schangnau, 1,031 ....E 3
Schänis, 2,328 ....H 2
Schiers, 2,363 ....J 3
Schinznach-Dorf, 1,081 ....F 2
Schlarigna-Celerina, 868....J 3
Schleitheim, 1,494 ....G 1
Schlieren, 11,600 ....F 2
Schönenwerd, 4,561 ....E 2
Schüpfheim, 3,771 ....F 3
Schwanden, 3,020 ....H 2
Schwyz, 12,200 ....G 2
Scuol-Schuls, 1,429 ....K 3
Sedrun, 1,855 ....G 3
Seewis, 969 ....J 3
Sembrancher, 710 ....D 4
Sempach, 1,345 ....F 2
Semsales, 762 ....C 3
Seon, 3,006 ....F 2
Sevelen, 2,370 ....H 2
Sierre, 8,690 ....D 4
Siggenthal, 7,376 ....F 1
Signau, 2,555 ....E 3
Sigriswil, 3,739 ....E 3
Silenen, 2,261 ....G 3
Sils im Domleschg, 737 ....H 3
Silvaplana, 346 ....J 4
Sins, 2,195 ....F 2
Sion, 18,900 ....D 4
Sirnach, 3,075 ....G 2
Sissach, 4,574 ....E 2
Solothurn (Soleure), 18,900 ....E 2
Solothurn, *36,400 ....E 2
Sonvico, 1,005 ....G 4
Spiez, 8,168 ....E 3
Stäfa, 6,947 ....G 2
Stalden, 1,007 ....E 4
Stammheim, 1,460 ....G 1
Stans, 4,337 ....F 3
Steckborn, 3,514 ....G 1
Steffisburg, 12,100 ....E 3
Stein, 1,060 ....E 1
Stein am Rhein, 2,588 ....G 1
Sulgen, 1,252 ....H 1
Sulz, 1,022 ....F 1
Sumiswald, 5,525 ....E 2
Sursee, 5,324 ....F 2
Tafers, 1,621 ....D 3
Täuffelen, 1,500 ....D 2
Tavannes, 3,939 ....D 2
Thalwil, 13,200 ....G 2
Thayngen, 3,013 ....G 1
Therwil, 1,946 ....E 1
Thun, 33,700 ....E 3
Thun, *56,700 ....E 3
Thusis, 1,998 ....H 3
Trachselwald, 1,269 ....E 2
Tramelan, 5,567 ....D 2
Trogen, 2,101 ....H 2
Trub, 1,981 ....E 3
Trun, 1,583 ....G 3
Turbenthal, 2,685 ....G 2
Turgi, 1,860 ....F 1
Ueberstorf, 1,536 ....D 3
Uetendorf, 2,810 ....E 3
Unterägeri, 3,832 ....G 2
Unterkulm, 2,149 ....F 2
Unterseen, 3,783 ....E 3
Untervaz, 1,142 ....H 3
Urnäsch, 2,330 ....H 2
Uster, 20,800 ....G 2
Utzenstorf, 2,821 ....E 2
Uznach, 3,173 ....H 2
Uzwil, 7,828 ....H 2
Vallorbe, 3,990 ....B 3
Vals, 968 ....H 3
Vaz-Obervaz, 1,568 ....J 3
Vechigen, 3,153 ....E 3
Vernayaz, 1,188 ....D 4
Versoix, 3,426 ....B 4
Vevey, 18,000 ....C 4
Vevey, *29,600 ....C 4
Veyrier, 2,705 ....B 4
Villeneuve, 2,366 ....C 4
Visp, 3,658 ....E 4
Vouvry, 1,368 ....C 4
Wädenswil, 14,300 ....G 2
Wahlern, 4,723 ....D 3
Wald, 7,778 ....G 2
Waldenburg, 1,284 ....E 2
Waldkirch, 2,487 ....H 2
Wallenstadt, 3,296 ....H 2
Walzenhausen, 2,345 ....J 2
Wangen an der Aare, 1,936....E 2
Wängi, 1,681 ....H 1
Wartau, 3,284 ....H 2
Wattwil, 7,480 ....H 2
Weesen, 1,280 ....H 2
Weggis, 2,243 ....F 2
Weinfelden, 6,954 ....H 1
Wettingen, 19,700 ....F 2
Wetzikon, 12,600 ....G 2
Wil, 12,900 ....H 2
Wilchingen, 1,061 ....F 1
Wilderswil, 1,701 ....E 3
Wildhaus, 1,179 ....H 2
Willisau, 2,508 ....F 2
Wimmis, 1,756 ....E 3
Windisch, 5,377 ....F 1
Winterthur, 92,500 ....G 1
Winterthur, *104,600 ....G 1
Wohlen, 8,636 ....F 2
Wohlen bei Bern, 2,985 ....D 3
Wolfenschiessen, 1,647 ....F 3
Wolhusen, 3,446 ....F 2
Wollerau, 2,415 ....G 2
Worb, 5,885 ....E 3
Wynigen, 2,221 ....E 2
Yverdon, 19,200 ....C 3
Yvonand, 1,290 ....C 3
Zäziwil, 1,265 ....E 3
Zell, Luzern, 1,582 ....E 2
Zell, Zürich, 3,347 ....G 2
Zermatt, 2,731 ....E 4
Zizers, 1,290 ....J 3
Zofingen, 1,290 ....F 2
Zollikofen, 6,237 ....E 3
Zollikon, 12,100 ....G 2
Zug, 22,300 ....G 2
Zuoz, 1,001 ....J 3
Zürich, 432,400 ....F 2
Zürich, *671,500 ....F 2
Zurzach, 2,694 ....F 1
Zweisimmen, 2,676 ....D 3

OTHER FEATURES

Aa (river) ....F 3
Aare (river) ....E 3
Ägerisee (lake) ....G 2
Albristhorn (mt.) ....D 4
Aletschhorn (mt.) ....F 4
Allaine (river) ....D 2
Areuse (river) ....C 3
Ault (peak) ....H 3
Baldeggersee (lake) ....F 2
Balmhorn (mt.) ....E 4
Bärenhorn (mt.) ....H 3
Basodino (mt.) ....G 4
Bernese Oberland (region)....E 3
Bernina, Piz (mt.) ....J 4
Bernina (pass) ....K 4
Bernina (river) ....J 4
Beverin (mt.) ....H 3
Biel (lake) ....D 2
Birs (river) ....D 2
Blindenhorn (mt.) ....F 4
Blümlisalp (mt.) ....E 3
Bodensee (Constance) (lake)....H 1
Borgne (river) ....D 4
Breithorn (mt.) ....E 5
Breithorn (mt.) ....E 4
Brienz (lake) ....F 3
Brienzer Rothorn (mt.) ....F 3
Broye (river) ....C 3
Brulé (mt.) ....D 4
Buchegg (mts.) ....D 2
Bürkelkopf (mt.) ....K 3
Bütschelegg (mt.) ....D 3
Calancasca (river) ....H 4
Campo Tencia (peak) ....G 4
Ceneri (mt.) ....G 4
Cheville (pass) ....D 4
Churfirsten (mt.) ....H 2
Claridenstock (mt.) ....G 3
Collon (mt.) ....D 5
Constance (lake) ....H 1
Dammastock (mt.) ....F 3
Davos (valley) ....J 3
Dent Blanche (mt.) ....E 4
Dent de Lys (mt.) ....D 4
Dent de Ruth (mt.) ....D 3
Dent d'Hérens (mt.) ....E 5
Dents du Midi (mt.) ....C 4
Diablerets (mt.) ....D 4
Doldenhorn (mt.) ....E 4
Dolent (mt.) ....C 5
Dom (mt.) ....E 4
Doubs (river) ....C 2
Drance (river) ....D 4
Dufourspitze (mt.) ....E 5
Emmental (valley) ....E 3
Engadine (valley) ....J-K 3-4
Err (mt.) ....J 3
Finsteraarhorn (mt.) ....F 3
Finstermünz (pass) ....K 3
Fletschhorn (mt.) ....F 4
Flüela (pass) ....J 3
Fluhberg (mt.) ....G 2
Fort (mt.) ....D 4
Furka (pass) ....F 3
Generoso (mt.) ....H 5
Geneva (lake) ....C 4
Giacomo (pass) ....G 4
Gibloux (mt.) ....D 3
Glâne (river) ....C 3
Glärnisch (mt.) ....H 2

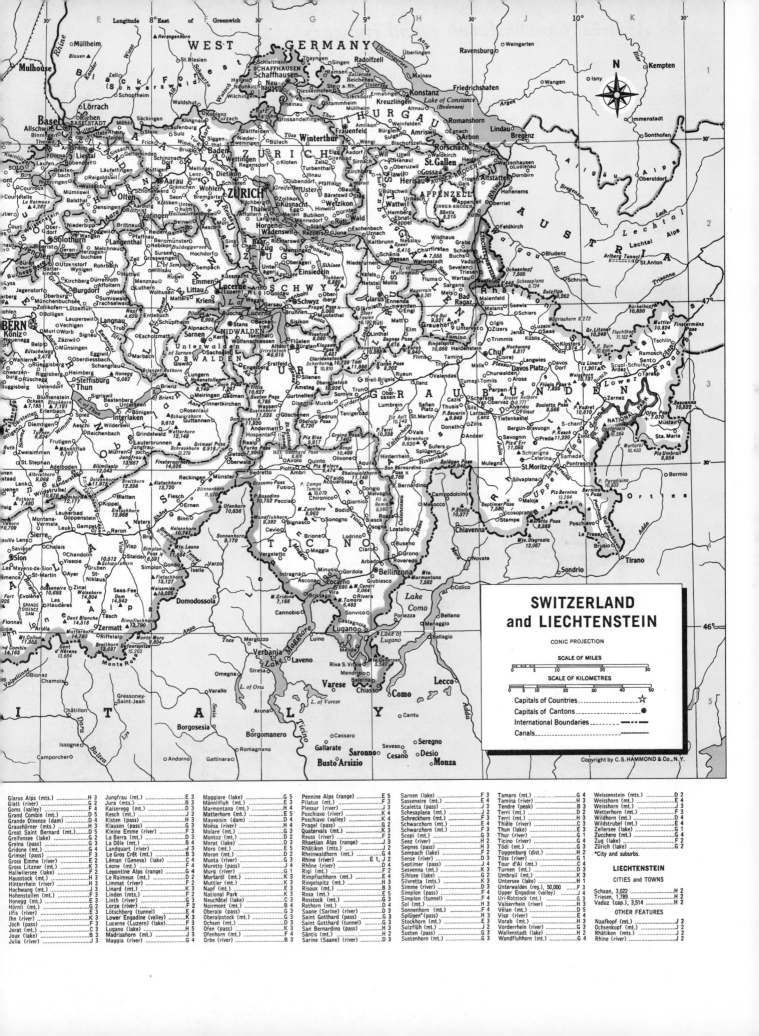

SWITZERLAND and LIECHTENSTEIN

CONIC PROJECTION

SCALE OF MILES

SCALE OF KILOMETRES

Capitals of Countries .... ☆
Capitals of Cantons .... ●
International Boundaries .... ▬ ▬ ▬
Canals .... ∿∿∿∿

Copyright by C.S. HAMMOND & Co., N.Y.

Glarus Alps (mts.)	H 3	Jungfrau (mt.)	E 3
Glatt (river)	F 2	Jura (mts.)	B 3
Goms (valley)	F 4	Kaiseregg (mt.)	D 3
Grand Combin (mt.)	D 5	Kesch (mt.)	J 3
Grande Dixence (dam)	D 4	Kisten (pass)	H 3
Grauehörner (mts.)	H 3	Klausen (pass)	G 3
Great Saint Bernard (mt.)	D 5	Kleine Emme (river)	F 3
Greifensee (lake)	G 2	La Berra (mt.)	D 3
Greina (pass)	G 3	La Dôle (mt.)	B 3
Gridone (mt.)	G 4	Landquart (river)	J 3
Grimsel (pass)	F 3	Le Gros Crêt (mt.)	C 4
Gross Emme (river)	E 3	Léman (Geneva) (lake)	F 4
Gross Litzner (mt.)	K 3	Leone (mt.)	F 4
Hallwilersee (lake)	F 2	Lepontine Alps (range)	G 4
Hausstock (mt.)	H 3	Le Raimeux (mt.)	D 2
Hinterrhein (river)	H 3	Limmat (river)	F 2
Hochwang (mt.)	J 3	Linard (mt.)	K 3
Hohenstollen (mt.)	F 3	Linden (mts.)	K 3
Honegg (mt.)	E 3	Linth (river)	G 2
Hörnli (mt.)	G 2	Lorze (river)	F 2
Ilfis (river)	E 3	Lötschberg (tunnel)	E 3
Ihn (river)	K 3	Lower Engadine (valley)	K 3
Joch (pass)	F 3	Lucerne (Luzern) (lake)	F 3
Jorat (mt.)	C 4	Lugano (lake)	H 5
Joux (lake)	B 3	Madrisahorn (mt.)	J 3
Julia (river)	J 3	Maggia (river)	G 4

Maggiore (lake)	G 5	Pennine Alps (range)	E 5
Männlifluh (mt.)	E 3	Pilatus (mt.)	F 3
Marmontana (mt.)	H 4	Plessur (river)	J 3
Matterhorn (mt.)	D 5	Poschiavo (lake)	K 4
Mauvoisin (dam)	D 4	Poschiavo (valley)	K 4
Moësa (river)	H 4	Pragel (pass)	G 3
Molare (mt.)	G 4	Quatervals (mt.)	K 3
Montoz (mt.)	D 2	Reuss (river)	F 2
Morat (lake)	C 3	Rhaetian Alps (range)	J 4
Moro (mt.)	E 5	Rhätikon (mts.)	J 3
Murg (river)	G 2	Rhine (river)	E 1,2
Murtaröl (mt.)	K 3	Rhône (river)	D 4
Muttier (mt.)	K 3	Rigi (mt.)	F 3
Napf (mt.)	E 3	Rimpfischhorn (mt.)	E 5
National Park	K 3	Ringelspitz (mt.)	H 3
Neuchâtel (lake)	C 3	Risoux (mt.)	B 3
Noirmont (mt.)	B 3	Rosa (mt.)	E 5
Oberalp (pass)	G 3	Rossstock (mt.)	G 3
Oberalpstock (mt.)	G 3	Rothorn (mt.)	J 3
Ofen (pass)	K 3	Saane (Sarine) (river)	D 3
Ofenhorn (mt.)	F 4	Saint Gotthard (pass)	G 3
Orbe (river)	B 3	Saint Gotthard (tunnel)	G 3
		San Bernardino (pass)	H 4
		Säntis (mt.)	H 2
		Sarine (Saane) (river)	D 3

Sarnen (lake)	F 3	Tamaro (mt.)	G 4
Sasseneire (mt.)	D 4	Tamina (river)	H 3
Scaletta (pass)	J 3	Tendre (peak)	B 3
Schesaplana (mt.)	J 3	Terri (mt.)	J 2
Schreckhorn (mt.)	E 3	Terri (mt.)	H 3
Schwarzhorn (mt.)	F 3	Thièle (river)	C 3
Schwarzhorn (mt.)	G 3	Thun (lake)	E 3
Scopi (mt.)	G 3	Thur (river)	G 1
Seez (river)	H 2	Ticino (river)	H 2
Segnes (pass)	H 3	Tödi (mt.)	G 3
Sempach (lake)	F 2	Toggenburg (dist.)	H 2
Sense (river)	D 3	Töss (river)	G 2
Septimer (pass)	J 4	Tour d'Ai (mt.)	C 4
Sesvenna (mt.)	K 3	Turnen (mt.)	D 3
Sihlsee (lake)	G 2	Umbrail (mt.)	K 3
Silvretta (mts.)	K 3	Untersee (lake)	H 1
Simme (river)	D 4	Unterwalden (reg.), 50,000	F 3
Simplon (pass)	F 4	Upper Engadine (valley)	J 4
Simplon (tunnel)	F 4	Uri-Rotstock (mt.)	F 3
Sol (mt.)	H 3	Valserrhein (river)	H 3
Sonnenhorn (mt.)	G 4	Vélan (mt.)	D 5
Splügen (pass)	H 4	Visp (river)	E 4
Stockhorn (mt.)	E 3	Vorab (mt.)	H 3
Sulzfluh (mt.)	J 3	Vorderrhein (river)	G 3
Susten (pass)	G 3	Wallenstadt (lake)	H 2
		Wandfluhhorn (mt.)	G 4

Weissenstein (mts.)	D 2
Weisshorn (mt.)	E 4
Weisshorn (mt.)	J 3
Wetterhorn (mt.)	F 3
Wildhorn (mt.)	D 4
Wildstrubel (mt.)	E 4
Zellersee (lake)	G 1
Zucchero (mt.)	G 4
Zug (lake)	F 2
Zürich (lake)	G 2

*City and suburbs.

LIECHTENSTEIN

CITIES and TOWNS

Schaan, 3,022	H 2
Triesen, 1,789	H 2
Vaduz (cap.), 3,514	H 2

OTHER FEATURES

Naafkopf (mt.)	J 2
Ochsenkopf (mt.)	J 2
Rhätikon (mts.)	J 2
Rhine (river)	J 2

AUSTRIA

PROVINCES

Burgenland, 271,001 ... D 3
Carinthia, 495,226 ... B 3
Lower Austria, 1,374,012 ... C 2
Salzburg, 347,292 ... B 3
Styria, 1,137,865 ... C 3
Tirol, 462,899 ... A 3
Upper Austria 1,131,623 ... B 2
Vienna (city), 1,631,423 ... D 2
Vorarlberg, 226,323 ... A 3

CITIES and TOWNS

Admont, 3,057 ... C 3
Aigen, 1,941 ... B 2
Alt Aussee, 2,026 ... B 3
Altheim, 4,271 ... B 2
Althofen, 3,221 ... C 3
Amstetten, 12,086 ... C 2
Andau, 3,011 ... D 3
Arnoldstein, 6,229 ... B 3
Aspang, 2,359 ... D 3
Attnang-Puchheim, 7,525 ... B 2
Bad Aussee, 5,144 ... B 3
Bad Goisern, 6,028 ... B 3
Bad Hofgastein, 4,700 ... B 3
Bad Ischl, 12,703 ... B 3
Bad Sankt Leonhard, 1,939 ... C 3
Baden, 22,484 ... D 2
Badgastein, 5,742 ... B 3
Berndorf, 8,992 ... C 3
Bischofshofen, 8,287 ... B 3
Bludenz, 11,127 ... A 3
Bramberg, 2,620 ... B 3
Braunau, 14,449 ... B 2
Bregenz, 21,428 ... A 3
Bruck an der Leitha, 6,791 ... D 2
Bruck an der Mur, 16,087 ... C 3
Deutsch Feistritz, 3,427 ... C 3
Deutsch Landsberg, 5,227 ... C 3
Deutsch Wagram, 4,207 ... D 2
Deutschkreutz, 3,901 ... D 3
Dornbirn, 28,075 ... A 3
Ebenfurth, 2,342 ... D 3
Ebensee, 9,602 ... B 3
Eferding, 3,151 ... B 2
Eggenburg, 3,338 ... C 2
Eisenerz, 12,435 ... C 3
Horn, 4,705 ... C 2
Hüttenberg, 2,257 ... C 3
Imst, 5,057 ... A 3
Innsbruck, 113,468 ... A 3
Jenbach, 5,479 ... A 3
Judenburg, 9,869 ... C 3
Kapfenberg, 23,859 ... C 3
Kappl, 1,970 ... A 3
Kaprun, 2,164 ... B 3
Kindberg, 5,766 ... C 3
Kirchdorf an der Krems, 2,964 ... C 3
Kitzbühel, 7,744 ... B 3
Klagenfurt, 69,218 ... C 3
Klosterneuburg, 22,787 ... D 2
Knittelfeld, 14,259 ... C 3
Köflach, 12,367 ... C 3
Königswiesen, 2,707 ... C 2
Korneuburg, 8,276 ... D 2
Kössen, 2,361 ... B 3
Kötschach-Mauthen, 2,763 ... B 3
Krems, 21,046 ... C 2
Kufstein, 11,215 ... B 3
Kundl, 2,508 ... A 3
Laa an der Thaya, 4,925 ... D 2
Laakirchen, 6,722 ... B 3
Lambach, 3,019 ... C 2
Landeck, 6,514 ... A 3
Landskron, 9,058 ... B 3
Längenfeld, 2,314 ... A 3
Langenlois, 4,655 ... C 2
Langenwang, 3,734 ... C 3
Lavamünd, 2,506 ... C 3
Leibnitz, 6,356 ... C 3
Lenzing, 5,372 ... B 3
Leoben, 36,257 ... C 3
Leonfelden, 2,546 ... C 2
Lienz, 11,132 ... B 3
Liezen, 5,444 ... C 3
Lilienfeld, 3,307 ... C 3
Linz, 205,762 ... C 2
Lustenau, 12,582 ... A 3
Mannersdorf, 3,909 ... D 3
Marchegg, 2,159 ... D 2
Mariazell, 2,191 ... C 3
Matrei, 3,430 ... B 3
Mattersburg, 4,270 ... D 3
Mattighofen, 3,919 ... B 2
Mauerkirchen, 2,175 ... B 2
Mautern, 2,365 ... C 3
Mauthausen, 3,836 ... C 2
Mauthen-Kötschach, 2,763 ... B 3
Mayrhofen, 2,523 ... A 3
Schärding, 5,710 ... B 2
Scheibbs, 3,231 ... C 2
Schladming, 3,249 ... B 3
Schrems, 3,080 ... C 2
Schruns, 3,304 ... A 3
Schwarzach, 3,186 ... B 3
Schwaz, 9,455 ... A 3
Schwertberg, 3,369 ... C 2
Sierning, 7,527 ... C 2
Sillian, 1,948 ... B 3
Solbad Hall, 10,750 ... A 3
Spital, 2,421 ... C 3
Spittal, 10,045 ... B 3
Steinach, 2,155 ... A 3
Steyr, 38,306 ... C 2
Stockerau, 11,853 ... D 2
Strassburg, 2,972 ... C 3
Tamweg, 4,431 ... B 3
Telfs, 5,438 ... A 3
Ternitz, 9,032 ... D 3
Traiskirchen, 7,026 ... D 2
Traun, 16,026 ... C 2
Trieben, 4,023 ... C 3
Trofaiach, 6,909 ... C 3
Tulln, 6,306 ... D 2
Velden, 2,039 ... C 3
Vienna (capital), 1,642,072 ... D 2
Villach, 32,971 ... B 3
Vöcklabruck, 9,353 ... B 2
Voitsberg, 6,353 ... C 3
Völkermarkt, 3,678 ... C 3
Vordernberg, 2,896 ... C 3
Waidhofen an der Thaya, 3,748 ... C 2
Waidhofen an der Ybbs, 5,586 ... C 3
Weitensfeld, 2,998 ... B 3
Weiz, 8,146 ... C 3
Wels, 41,060 ... C 2
Weyer, 2,367 ... C 3
Wiener Neustadt, 33,845 ... D 3
Wildon, 2,020 ... C 3
Wilhelmsburg, 6,196 ... C 2
Wolfsberg, 9,470 ... C 3
Wörgl, 6.828 ... A 3
Ybbs, 5,324 ... C 2
Zams, 2,782 ... A 3
Zell am See, 6,455 ... B 3
Zeltweg, 7,340 ... C 3
Zirl, 3,165 ... A 3
Zistersdorf, 3,011 ... D 2
Zwettl, 3,836 ... C 2

OTHER FEATURES

Allgäu Alps (mts.) ... A 3
Atter (lake) ... B 3
Bavarian Alps (mts.) ... A 3
Bodensee (Constance) (lake) ... A 3
Brenner (pass) ... A 3
Carnic Alps (mts.) ... B 3
Coglians (Hohe Warte) (peak) ... B 3
Constance (lake) ... A 3
Danube (river) ... C 2
Donau (Danube) (river) ... D 2
Drau (river) ... C 3
Enns (river) ... C 3
Fertő tó (Neusiedler) (lake) ... D 3
Greiner (forest) ... C 2
Grossglockner (mt.) ... B 3
Gross Höllkogel (mt.) ... B 3
Gross Peilstein (mt.) ... C 2
Hochgolling (mt.) ... B 3
Hohe Tauern (range) ... B 3
Hohe Warte (peak) ... B 3
Inn (river) ... B 2
Kamp (river) ... C 2
Karawanken (mts.) ... C 3
Laufnitz (river) ... D 3
March (river) ... D 2
Mühlviertel (region), 196,037 ... C 2
Mur (river) ... C 3
Mürz (river) ... C 3
Neusiedler (lake) ... D 3
Niedere Tauern (range) ... B 3
Olsa (river) ... C 3
Ötztal Alps (mts.) ... A 3
Parseierspitze (mt.) ... A 3
Raab (river) ... C 3
Rhine (river) ... A 3
Salzach (river) ... B 2
Salzkammergut (region) ... B 3
Semmering (pass) ... C 3
Thaya (river) ... C 2
Traun (lake) ... B 3
Traun (river) ... C 2
Wildspitze (mt.) ... A 3
Zugspitze (mt.) ... A 3

CZECHOSLOVAKIA

REPUBLICS

Czech Soc. Rep., 9,778,000 ... B 1
Slovak Soc. Rep., 4,421,000 ... E 2

REGIONS

Jihočeský, 659,000 ... C 2
Jihomoravský, 1,941,000 ... D 2
Prague (city), 1,025,000 ... C 1
Severočeský, 1,122,000 ... C 1
Severomoravský, 1,695,000 ... C 1
Středočeský, 1,271,000 ... C 2
Středoslovenský, 1,379,000 ... E 2
Východočeský, 1,213,000 ... C 1
Východoslovenský, 1,199,000 ... F 2
Západočeský, 852,000 ... B 2
Západoslovenský, 1,843.000 ... D 2

CITIES and TOWNS

As, 10,000 ... B 1
Austerlitz (Slavkov), 4,869 ... D 2
Bánovce, 3,563 ... E 2
Banská Bystrica, 29,000 ... E 2
Banská Štiavnica, 10,381 ... E 2
Bardejov, 11,000 ... F 2
Bechyně, 2,398 ... C 2
Benešov, 10,000 ... C 2
Beroun, 17,000 ... B 2
Bílina, 12,000 ... B 1
Blansko, 11,000 ... D 2
Blatná, 3,596 ... B 2
Blovice, 2,629 ... B 2
Bojkovice, 2,902 ... D 2
Bor, 2,257 ... B 2
Boskovice, 6,396 ... D 2
Brandýs nad Labem-Stará Boleslav, 13,161 ... C 1
Bratislava, 278,835 ... D 2
Břeclav, 13,000 ... D 2
Březnice, 2,634 ... B 2
Brezno, 11,000 ... E 2
Brno, 333,831 ... D 2
Broumov, 6,370 ... D 1
Brtnice, 2,176 ... C 2
Bruntál, 9,000 ... D 2
Bučovice, 3,381 ... D 2
Budišov, 3,677 ... D 2
Bystřice nad Pernštejnem, 2,653 ... D 2
Bystřice pod Hostýnem, 4,973 ... D 2
Bytča, 4,528 ... E 2
Čadca, 13,000 ... E 2
Čalovo, 4,536 ... D 3
Čáslav, 10,000 ... C 2
Česká Kamenice, 6,084 ... C 1
Česká Lípa, 15,000 ... C 1
Česká Třebová, 14,000 ... D 2
České Budějovice, 70,000 ... C 2
Český Brod, 5,754 ... C 1
Český Krumlov, 10,000 ... C 2
Český Těšín, 16,000 ... E 2
Cheb, 24,000 ... B 1
Chlumec, 4,345 ... C 1
Choceň, 6,789 ... D 1
Chodov, 5,383 ... B 1
Chomutov, 37,000 ... B 1
Chotěboř, 4,846 ... C 2
Chrastava, 3,618 ... C 1
Chrudim, 17,000 ... C 2
Čierny Balog, 5,978 ... E 2
Cukmantl, 2,362 ... D 1
Dačice, 2,810 ... C 2
Děčín, 42,000 ... C 1
Detva, 7,786 ... E 2
Dobřany, 4,905 ... B 2
Dobříš, 4,390 ... C 2
Dobruška, 4,093 ... D 1
Dobšiná, 3,957 ... F 2
Doksy, 3,061 ... C 1
Dolný Kubín, 5,000 ... E 2
Domažlice, 8,000 ... B 2
Dubnica nad Váhom, 11,250 ... E 2
Duchcov, 8,229 ... B 1
Dunajská Streda, 9,000 ... D 3
Dvory, 5,475 ... E 3
Dvůr Králové nad Labem. 16,000 ... C 1
Falknov (Sokolov), 20,000 ... B 1
Fil'akovo, 5,950 ... E 2
Františkovy Lázně, 5,212 ... B 1
Frýdek-Místek, 32,000 ... E 2
Frýdlant nad Ostravicí, 4,178 ... E 2
Frýdlant v čechách, 5,460 ... C 1
Fulnek, 2,765 ... D 2
Galanta, 8,000 ... D 2
Gelnica, 3,240 ... F 2
Golčův Jeníkov, 1,920 ... C 2
Gottwaldov, 63,000 ... D 2
Handlová, 16,000 ... E 2
Havířov, 72,000 ... E 2
Havlíčkův, Brod, 16,000 ... C 2
Hlinsko, 5,189 ... D 2
Hlohovec, 14,000 ... D 2
Hlučín, 11,000 ... E 2
Hodonín, 19,000 ... D 2

(continued)

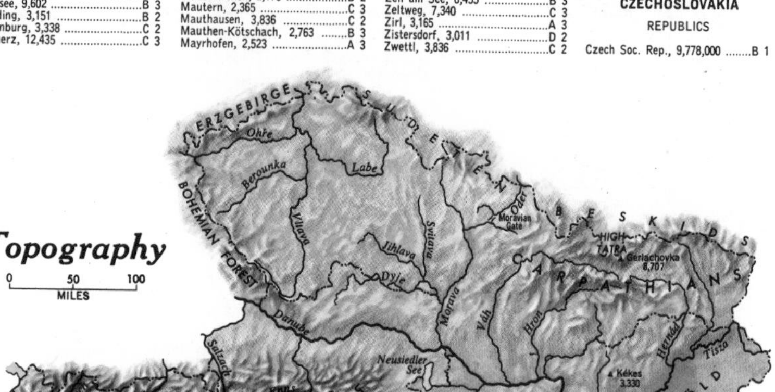
ERZGEBIRGE
SUDETEN
BOHEMIAN FOREST
Ohře
Labe
Berounka
Vltava
Jihlava
Svitava
Dyje
Morava
Oder
Moravian Gate
BESKIDS
HIGH TATRA
Gerlachovka 8,707
CARPATHIANS
Váh
Hron
Danube
Salzach
Enns
Mur
Drau
Neusiedler See
BAKONY
Rába
Balaton
Kapos
Drava
Mura
Tisza
Kékes 3,330
GREAT ALFÖLD
5,000 m. 16,404 ft.
2,000 m. 6,562 ft.
1,000 m. 3,281 ft.
500 m. 1,640 ft.
200 m. 656 ft.
100 m. 328 ft.
Sea Level
Below

Topography

0 50 100
MILES

Eisenstadt, 7,167 ... D 3
Enns, 8,919 ... C 2
Feldbach, 3,687 ... C 3
Feldkirch, 17,343 ... A 3
Feldkirchen in Kärnten, 3,181 ... B 3
Ferlach, 5,672 ... C 3
Fieberbrunn, 3,010 ... B 3
Fohnsdorf, 11,571 ... C 3
Frankenmarkt, 2,565 ... B 3
Frauenkirchen, 2,812 ... D 3
Friesach, 3,388 ... C 3
Freistadt, 5,375 ... C 2
Frohnleiten, 4,969 ... C 3
Fulpmes, 2,282 ... A 3
Fürstenfeld, 6,415 ... C 3
Gaming, 4,218 ... C 3
Gänserndorf, 3,378 ... D 2
Gleisdorf, 4,385 ... C 3
Gloggnitz, 7,228 ... D 3
Gmünd, Carinthia, 2,195 ... B 3
Gmünd, Lower Austria, 6,522 ... C 2
Gmunden, 12,518 ... B 3
Golling an der Salzach, 2,845 ... B 3
Götzis, 7,034 ... A 3
Gratwein, 2,515 ... C 3
Graz, 253,000 ... C 3
Grein, 2,518 ... C 2
Grieskirchen, 4,137 ... B 2
Gross Siegharts, 2,599 ... C 2
Grünburg, 3,609 ... C 3
Güssing, 2,715 ... D 3
Haag, 4,671 ... C 2
Hainburg, 6,437 ... D 2
Hainfeld, 3,883 ... C 2
Hallein, 13,329 ... B 3
Hallstatt, 1,373 ... B 3
Hartberg, 3,629 ... C 3
Haslach an der Mühl, 2,565 ... C 2
Heidenreichstein, 3,653 ... C 2
Heiligenblut, 1,195 ... B 3
Hermagor, 2,778 ... B 3
Herzogenburg, 5,166 ... C 2
Hieflau, 2,003 ... C 3
Hohenau an der March, 3,907 ... D 2
Hohenberg, 2,093 ... C 3
Hohenems, 9,188 ... A 3
Hollabrunn, 5,832 ... D 2
Hopfgarten in Nordtirol, 4,163 ... B 3
Melk, 3,534 ... C 2
Mistelbach an der Zaya, 5,434 ... D 2
Mittersill, 3,502 ... B 3
Mödling, 17,274 ... D 2
Mondsee, 2,050 ... B 3
Murau, 2,755 ... C 3
Mürzzuschlag, 11,586 ... C 3
Nassereith, 1,744 ... A 3
Neuberg an der Mürz, 2,411 ... C 3
Neumarkt, Styria, 1,880 ... C 3
Neumarkt am Wallersee, 2,877 ... B 3
Neunkirchen, 10,027 ... C 3
Neusiedl am See, 3,826 ... D 3
Neustift im Stubaital, 2,195 ... A 3
Ober Grafendorf, 3,825 ... C 2
Oberndorf bei Salzburg, 3,084 ... B 3
Obervellach, 2,371 ... B 3
Oberwart, 4,740 ... D 3
Paternion, 5,581 ... B 3
Perg, 4,106 ... C 2
Peuerbach, 2,105 ... B 2
Pinkafeld, 3,826 ... C 3
Pöchlarn, 2,921 ... C 2
Pörtschach, 2,449 ... C 3
Poysdorf, 2,738 ... D 2
Pregarten, 2,818 ... C 2
Radenthein, 5,651 ... B 3
Radstadt, 3,311 ... B 3
Rankweil, 6,451 ... A 3
Rechnitz, 3,374 ... D 3
Reichenau an der Rax, 4,441 ... C 3
Retz, 2,941 ... D 2
Reutte, 4,285 ... A 3
Ried im Innkreis, 9,471 ... B 2
Rottenmann, 4,139 ... C 3
Saalfelden, 8,901 ... B 3
Salzburg, 120,204 ... B 3
Sankt Aegyd am Neuwalde, 3,206 ... C 3
Sankt Anton am Arlberg, 1,741 ... A 3
Sankt Johann, 4,713 ... B 3
Sankt Michael, 3,433 ... C 3
Sankt Michael im Lungau, 2,422 ... B 3
Sankt Paul, 1,808 ... C 3
Sankt Pölten, 40,112 ... C 2
Sankt Valentin, 7,750 ... C 2
Sankt Veit an der Glan, 10,950 ... C 3
Sankt Wolfgang, 2,234 ... B 3

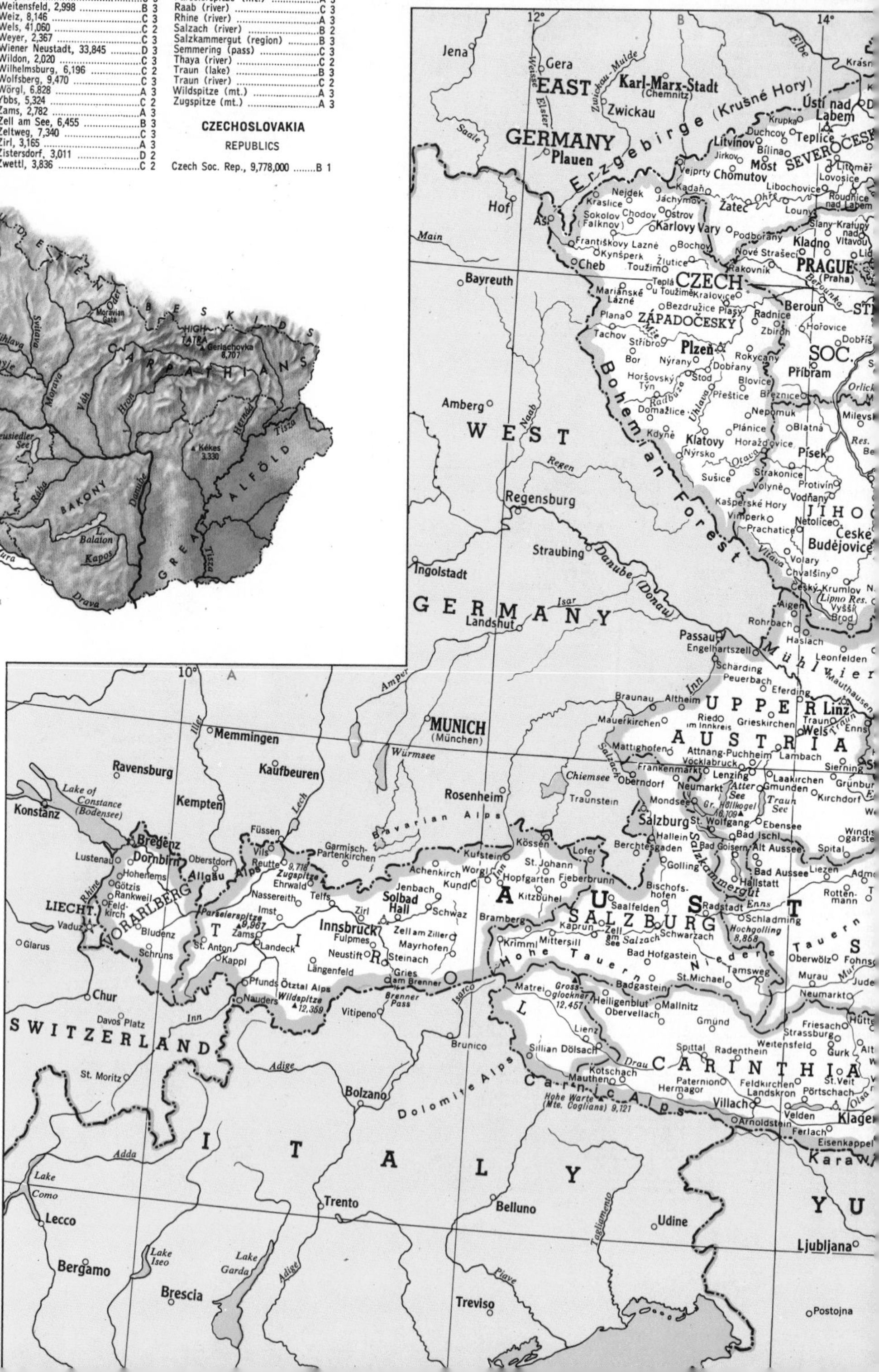
Jena
Gera
EAST
Karl-Marx-Stadt (Chemnitz)
Zwickau
GERMANY
Plauen
Erzgebirge (Krušné Hory)
Ústí nad Labem
Teplice
Most
Chomutov
Karlovy Vary
Cheb
Hof
Bayreuth
Main
CZECH
PRAGUE (Praha)
Beroun
ZÁPADOČESKÝ
Plzeň
Příbram
Domažlice
Klatovy
Písek
Strakonice
Bohemian Forest
České Budějovice
Český Krumlov
Amberg
WEST
Regensburg
Straubing
Danube (Donau)
Ingolstadt
GERMANY
Landshut
Passau
Isar
Inn
MUNICH (München)
Memmingen
Kaufbeuren
Ravensburg
Kempten
Lake of Constance (Bodensee)
Konstanz
Rosenheim
Bavarian Alps
Bregenz
Dornbirn
Allgäu Alps
Füssen
Garmisch-Partenkirchen
Zugspitze
LIECHT.
Vaduz
VORARLBERG
Bludenz
Feldkirch
Innsbruck
Solbad Hall
Kufstein
Kitzbühel
Salzburg
Hallein
Bad Ischl
UPPER AUSTRIA
Linz
Wels
Braunau
SALZBURG
Hohe Tauern
Grossglockner 12,457
Wildspitze 12,359
Brenner Pass
Lienz
Spittal
Villach
CARINTHIA
Klagenfurt
Carnic Alps
Hohe Warte (Mte. Coglians) 9,121
Dolomite Alps
Chur
SWITZERLAND
Davos Platz
St. Moritz
Bolzano
ITALY
Trento
Belluno
Udine
Lake Como
Lecco
Bergamo
Lake Iseo
Lake Garda
Brescia
Treviso
Piave
Adige
Ljubljana
Postojna
Karawanken
Glarus
10°
12°
14°
A
B

AUSTRIA
AREA 32,374 sq. mi.
POPULATION 7,419,341
CAPITAL Vienna
LARGEST CITY Vienna
HIGHEST POINT Grossglockner 12,457 ft.
MONETARY UNIT schilling
MAJOR LANGUAGE German
MAJOR RELIGION Roman Catholicism

CZECHOSLOVAKIA
AREA 49,370 sq. mi.
POPULATION 14,497,000
CAPITAL Prague
LARGEST CITY Prague
HIGHEST POINT Gerlachovka 8,707 ft.
MONETARY UNIT koruna (crown)
MAJOR LANGUAGES Czech, Slovak
MAJOR RELIGIONS Roman Catholicism, Protestantism

HUNGARY
AREA 35,915 sq. mi.
POPULATION 10,315,597
CAPITAL Budapest
LARGEST CITY Budapest
HIGHEST POINT Kékes 3,330 ft.
MONETARY UNIT forint
MAJOR LANGUAGE Hungarian
MAJOR RELIGIONS Roman Catholicism, Protestantism

AUSTRIA

CZECHOSLOVAKIA

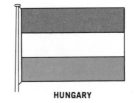

HUNGARY

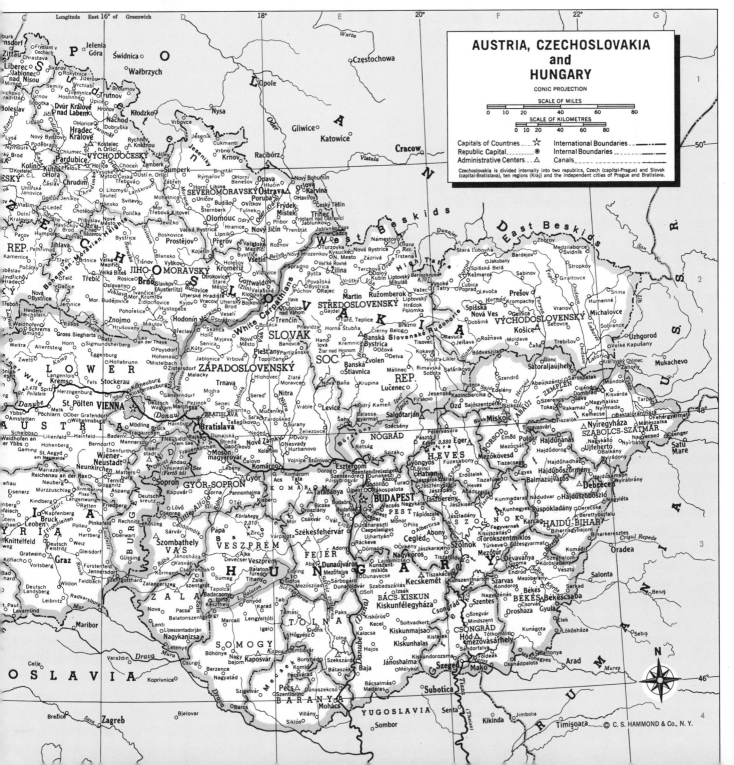

AUSTRIA, CZECHOSLOVAKIA and HUNGARY

CONIC PROJECTION

SCALE OF MILES

0 10 20 40 60 80

SCALE OF KILOMETRES

0 10 20 40 60 80

Capitals of Countries ⭐
Republic Capital ◉
Administrative Centers △
International Boundaries
Internal Boundaries
Canals

Czechoslovakia is divided internally into two republics, Czech (capital-Prague) and Slovak (capital-Bratislava), ten regions (Kraj) and the independent cities of Prague and Bratislava.

© C. S. HAMMOND & Co., N. Y.

CZECHOSLOVAKIA (continued)

Holešov, 6,599 ....D 2
Holíč, 5,881 ....D 2
Holice, 5,695 ....D 1
Horaždovice, 3,098 ....B 2
Hořice, 7,133 ....C 1
Horní Benešov, 3,181 ....D 2
Horní Libina, 4,583 ....D 2
Hořovice, 4,697 ....C 2
Horšovský Týn, 3,475 ....B 2
Hostinné, 4,412 ....C 1
Hradec Králové, 62,000 ....C 1
Hranice, 12,000 ....D 2
Hronov, 11,000 ....D 1
Hrušovany, 3,128 ....D 2
Humenné, 14,000 ....G 2
Humpolec, 5,083 ....C 2
Hurbanovo, 3,578 ....E 3
Hustopeče, 2,698 ....D 2
Ilava, 2,043 ....E 2
Ivančice, 4,742 ....D 2
Jablonec nad Nisou, 33,000 ....C 1
Jablunkov, 4,467 ....E 2
Jáchymov, 6,806 ....B 1
Jaroměř, 12,000 ....C 1
Jelšava, 2,456 ....F 2
Jemnice, 3,383 ....C 2
Jeseník, 5,873 ....D 1
Jesenské, 1,567 ....F 2
Jevičko, 2.881 ....D 2
Jičín, 13,000 ....C 1
Jihlava, 37,000 ....C 2
Jilemnice, 3,362 ....C 1
Jindřichův HraJec, 12,000 ....C 2
Jirkov, 12.000 ....B 1
Kadaň, 5,062 ....B 1
Kamenice, 2,692 ....C 2
Kaplice, 1,931 ....C 2
Karlovy Vary, 45,000 ....B 1
Karviná, 70.000 ....E 2
Kašperské Hory, 2,814 ....B 2
Kdyně, 2,609 ....B 2
Kežmarok, 7,372 ....F 2
Kladno, 55,000 ....B 1
Klatovy, 16,000 ....B 2
Kojetín, 5,292 ....D 2
Kokava, 5,398 ....E 2
Kolárovo, 11,000 ....D 3
Kolín, 25,000 ....C 1
Komárno, 26,000 ....D 3
Košice, 115,332 ....F 2
Kostelec nad Černými, Lesy, 3,616 ....C 2
Kostelec nad Orlicí, 5,539 ....D 1
Králíky, 3,895 ....D 1
Kralovice, 2,268 ....B 2
Král'ovský Chlmec, 3,410 ....G 2
Kralupy nad Vltavou, 14,000 ....C 1
Kraslice, 6,294 ....B 1
Krásna Lípa, 5,041 ....C 1
Kremnica, 4,979 ....E 2
Krnov, 22,000 ....D 1
Kroměříž, 22,000 ....D 2
Krompachy, 3,340 ....F 2
Krupina, 5,418 ....E 2
Krupka, 10,000 ....B 1
Kutná Hora, 17,000 ....C 2
Kúty, 3,348 ....D 2
Kyjov, 5,620 ....D 2
Kynšperk, 5,398 ....B 1
Kysucké Nové Mesto, 2,318 ....E 2
Lanškroun, 6,558 ....D 2
Ledeč, 2,625 ....C 2
Levice, 15,000 ....E 2
Levoča, 7,584 ....F 2
Libáň, 2,261 ....C 1
Liberec, 71,000 ....C 1
Libochovice, 2,879 ....B 1
Lidice, 478 ....C 1
Lipník, 6,887 ....D 2
Liptovský Mikuláš, 14,000 ....E 2
Lišov, 2,691 ....C 2
Litoměřice, 18,000 ....C 1
Litomyšl, 6,384 ....D 2
Litovel, 4,496 ....D 2
Litvínov, 22,000 ....B 1
Lomnice, 2,228 ....C 2
Louny, 13,000 ....B 1
Lovosice, 4,962 ....C 1
L'ubica, 3,335 ....F 2
Lučenec, 18,000 ....E 2
Lysá, 6,500 ....C 1
Malacky, 11,000 ....D 2
Mariánské Lázně, 13,000 ....B 2
Martin, 29,000 ....E 2

Mělník, 15,000 ....C 1
Michalovce, 18,000 ....G 2
Mikulov, 5,220 ....D 2
Milevsko, 3,754 ....C 2
Mimoň, 5,349 ....C 1
Mladá Boleslav, 27,000 ....C 1
Mladá Vožice, 1,732 ....C 2
Mnichovo Hradiště, 4,647 ....C 1
Modra, 6,239 ....D 2
Modrý Kameň, 1,836 ....E 2
Mohelnice, 4,949 ....D 2
Moldava, 2,241 ....F 2
Moravská Třebová, 5,844 ....D 2
Moravské Budějovice, 4,348 ....D 2
Moravský Krumlov, 2,897 ....D 2
Most, 56,000 ....B 1
Mučeníky, 5,207 ....D 2
Myjava, 9,935 ....D 2
Náchod, 18,000 ....D 1
Neded, 4,553 ....D 2
Nejdek, 5,748 ....B 1
Nepomuk, 1,860 ....B 2
Nesvady, 5,070 ....E 3
Netolice, 2.503 ....C 2
Nitra, 39,000 ....E 2
Nová Baňa, 5,113 ....E 2
Nová Bystřice, 2,418 ....C 2
Nové Město na Moravě, 3,250 ....D 2
Nové Město nad Váhom, 14,000 ....D 2
Nové Strašecí, 3,288 ....B 1
Nové Zamky, 24,000 ....D 3
Nový Bohumín, 12,000 ....E 2
Nový Bor, 5,994 ....C 1
Nový Bydžov, 6,120 ....C 1
Nový Hrozenkov, 5,302 ....E 2
Nový Jičín, 17,000 ....E 2
Nymburk, 13,000 ....C 1
Nýřany, 4,420 ....B 2
Nýrsko, 4,124 ....B 2
Odry, 5,340 ....D 2
Olomouc, 77,000 ....D 2
Opava, 46,000 ....E 2
Orlová, 22,000 ....E 2
Oslavany, 3,606 ....D 2
Ostrava, 271,905 ....E 2
Ostrov, 19,000 ....B 1
Otrokovice-Kvítkovice, 11,000 ....D 2
Pacov, 2,775 ....C 2
Pardubice, 65,000 ....C 1
Partizánske, 3,171 ....E 2
Pelhřimov, 8,000 ....C 2
Pezinok, 12,000 ....D 2
Piešťany, 21,000 ....D 2
Písek, 22,000 ....C 2
Planá, 5,216 ....B 2
Plánice, 1,718 ....B 2
Plasy, 1,472 ....B 2
Plzeň, 143,945 ....B 2
Počatky, 2,141 ....C 2
Podbořany, 3,893 ....B 1
Poděbrady, 13,000 ....C 1
Pohořelice, 3,068 ....D 2
Polička, 5,600 ....D 2
Polná, 4,005 ....C 2
Poprad, 18,000 ....F 2
Poruba, 21,179 ....D 2
Považská Bystrica, 13,000 ....E 2
Prachatice, 6,000 ....B 2
Prague (Praha) (capital), 1,031,870 ....C 1
Přelouč, 4,228 ....C 1
Přerov, 35,000 ....D 2
Prešov, 39,000 ....F 2
Přeštice, 4,616 ....B 2
Příbor, 5,491 ....E 2
Příbram, 29,000 ....B 2
Přibyslav, 2,556 ....C 2
Prievidza, 24,000 ....E 2
Prostějov, 35,000 ....D 2
Protivín, 3,217 ....C 2
Púchov, 4,316 ....E 2
Radnice, 2,342 ....B 2
Rajec, 2,753 ....E 2
Rakovník, 12,000 ....B 1
Říčany, 6,376 ....C 2
Rimavská Sobota, 12,000 ....E 2
Rokycany, 13,000 ....B 2
Rokytnice nad Jizerou, 3,893 ....C 1
Rosice, 4,900 ....D 2
Roudnice nad Labem, 11,000 ....C 1
Rožňava, 11,000 ....F 2
Rožnov, 3,989 ....E 2
Rumburk, 6,759 ....C 1
Ružomberok, 20,000 ....E 2
Rychnov nad Kněžnou, 6.000 ....D 1

Rýmařov, 4,328 ....D 2
Sabinov, 3,909 ....F 2
Šafaríkovo, 3,180 ....F 2
Šahy, 4,019 ....E 2
Šal'a, 4,397 ....D 2
Sečovce, 3,354 ....F 2
Sedlčany, 2,083 ....C 2
Semily, 6,549 ....C 1
Senec, 6,184 ....D 2
Senica, 8,000 ....D 2
Sereď, 6,208 ....D 2
Skalica, 5,440 ....D 2
Skuteč, 3,348 ....D 2
Slaný, 12,000 ....C 1
Slavkov, 4,869 ....D 2
Snina, 5,002 ....G 2
Soběslav, 4,643 ....C 2
Sobotka, 2,147 ....C 1
Sokolov, 20.000 ....B 1
Spišská Belá, 3,072 ....F 2
Spišská Nová Ves, 20,000 ....F 2
Stará L'ubovňa, 1,989 ....F 2
Staré Mešto, 6.350 ....D 2
Šternberk, 12,000 ....D 2
Stod, 2,502 ....B 2
Strakonice, 16,000 ....B 2
Strážnice, 5,147 ....D 2
Stříbro, 4,659 ....B 2
Stropkov, 2,506 ....F 2
Štúrovo, 4,082 ....E 3
Šumperk, 22,000 ....D 1
Šurany, 5,381 ....E 2
Sušice, 6,793 ....B 2
Svárov, 3,381 ....C 1
Svitavy, 14,000 ....D 2
Tábor, 21,000 ....C 2
Tachov, 8,000 ....B 2
Tardošked, 6,689 ....E 2
Telč, 4,381 ....C 2
Teplá u Toužimě, 2,500 ....B 2
Teplice, 52,000 ....B 1
Terchová, 4,400 ....E 2
Tišnov, 4,885 ....D 2
Tisovec, 3,988 ....E 2
Topol'čany, 12,000 ....E 2
Třebíč, 21,000 ....C 2
Trebišov, 10,000 ....F 2
Třeboň, 4,663 ....C 2
Trenčin, 26,000 ....E 2
Třešť, 4,900 ....C 2
Trhové Sviny, 2,953 ....C 2
Třinec, 27,000 ....E 2
Trnava, 35,000 ....D 2
Trstená, 2,468 ....E 2
Trutnov, 24,000 ....D 1
Turnov, 12,000 ....C 1
Turzovka, 9,823 ....E 2
Týn, 4,135 ....C 2
Uherské Hradiště, 15,000 ....D 2
Uherský Brod, 6,457 ....D 2
Uhlířské Janovice, 1,979 ....C 2
Uničov, 3,325 ....D 2
Úpice, 5,498 ....C 1
Ústí nad Labem, 72,000 ....C 1
Ústí nad Orlicí, 11,000 ....D 2
Valašské Klobouky, 2,525 ....D 2
Valašské Meziříčí, 15,000 ....D 2
Varnsdorf, 14,000 ....C 1
Važec, 2,747 ....E 2
Vejprty, 5,476 ....B 1
Velká Bíteš, 1,714 ....D 2
Velká Bystřice, 4,459 ....D 2
Vel'ké Kapušany, 2,371 ....G 2
Velké Meziříčí, 6,217 ....D 2
Veselí nad Lužnicí, 4,382 ....C 2
Veselí nad Moravou, 4,636 ....D 2
Vítkov, 2,685 ....D 2
Vizovice, 3,583 ....D 2
Vlašim, 5,066 ....C 2
Vodňany, 5,374 ....C 2
Volary, 5,034 ....B 2
Volyně, 3,019 ....B 2
Votice, 2,191 ....C 2
Vráble, 3,148 ....E 2
Vracov, 4,171 ....D 2
Vranov, 3,964 ....F 2
Vrchlabí, 11,000 ....C 1
Vrútky, 5,927 ....E 2
Vsetín, 20,000 ....D 2
Vyškov, 13,000 ....D 2
Vysoké Mýto, 7,983 ....D 2
Vysoké Tatry, 14,445 ....F 2
Vyšší Brod, 1,905 ....C 2
Zábřeh, 5,847 ....D 2
Žamberk, 4,278 ....D 1
Žatec, 16,000 ....B 1

Zbiroh, 1,718 ....B 2
Zborov, 1,551 ....F 2
Žďár nad Sázavou, 12,000 ....C 2
Želiezovce, 3,748 ....E 2
Žiar nad Hronom, 11,000 ....E 2
Zidlochovice, 2,696 ....D 2
Žilina, 38,000 ....E 2
Zlaté Moravce, 4,003 ....E 2
Zlín (Gottwaldov), 63,000 ....D 2
Žlutice, 2,114 ....B 1
Znojmo, 25.000 ....D 2
Zvolen, 23,000 ....E 2

OTHER FEATURES

Berounka (river) ....C 2
Beskids, East (mts.) ....F 1
Beskids, West (mts.) ....E 2
Bohemia (region), 6,142,000 ....C 2
Bohemian (forest) ....B 2
Bohemian-Moravian Heights ....C 2
Dudváh (river) ....D 2
Dunajec (river) ....F 2
Dyje (river) ....D 2
Erzgebirge (mts.) ....B 1
Gerlachovka (mt.) ....E 2
Hornád (river) ....F 2
Hron (river) ....E 2
Ipel' (river) ....E 2
Jablunka (pass) ....E 2
Jeseniky (mts.) ....D 1
Jihlava (river) ....D 2
Kamýcká (res.) ....C 2
Krušné Hory (Erzgebirge) (mts.) ....B 1
Labe (river) ....C 1
Laborec (river) ....F 2
Lipno (res.) ....C 2
Lužnice (river) ....C 2
Moldau (Vltava) (river) ....C 2
Morava (river) ....D 2
Moravia (region), 3,636,000 ....D 2
Nitra (river) ....E 2
Oder (Odra) (river) ....D 2
Ohře (river) ....B 1
Orava (res.) ....E 2
Orava (river) ....E 2
Orlice (river) ....C 1
Orlická (res.) ....C 2
Otava (river) ....B 2
Poprad (river) ....F 2
Slana (river) ....F 2
Slapská (res.) ....C 2
Slovakia (region), 4,421,000 ....E 2
Slovenske Rudohorie (mts.) ....E 2
Štěchovická (res.) ....C 2
Sudeten (mts.) ....C 1
Tatra, High (mts.) ....E 2
Uh (river) ....G 2
Váh (river) ....D 2
Vltava (river) ....C 2
White Carpathians (mts.) ....E 2

HUNGARY

COUNTIES

Bács-Kiskun, 560,000 ....E 3
Baranya, 280,000 ....E 4
Békés, 440,000 ....F 3
Borsod-Abaúj-Zemplén, 600,000 ....F 2
Budapest (city), 1,990,000 ....E 3
Csongrád, 320,000 ....F 3
Fejér, 390,000 ....E 3
Győr-Sopron, 400,000 ....D 3
Hajdú-Bihar, 360,000 ....F 3
Heves, 340,000 ....F 3
Komárom, 300,000 ....E 3
Nógrád, 240,000 ....E 3
Pest, 870,000 ....E 3
Somogy, 360,000 ....D 3
Szabolcs-Szatmár, 540,000 ....G 3
Szolnok, 440,000 ....F 3
Tolna, 260,000 ....E 3
Vas, 280,000 ....D 3
Veszprém, 420,000 ....D 3
Zala, 260,000 ....D 3

CITIES and TOWNS

Aba, 4.369 ....E 3
Abádszalók, 7,257 ....F 3
Abaújszántó, 4,586 ....F 2
Abony, 16,048 ....E 3
Ács, 8,507 ....E 3
Adony, 4,211 ....E 3
Ajka, 21,000 ....D 3
Albertirsa, 11,490 ....E 3
Aszód, 5,361 ....E 3
Bácsalmás, 9,514 ....E 3
Baja, 34,000 ....E 3
Balassagyarmat, 13,000 ....E 2
Balatonfüred, 7,561 ....D 3
Balkány, 8,224 ....G 3
Balmazújváros, 18,645 ....F 3
Barcs, 7,245 ....D 4
Bátaszék, 7,378 ....E 3
Battonya, 11,019 ....F 3
Békés, 21,296 ....F 3
Békéscsaba, 53,000 ....F 3
Berettyóújfalu, 11,577 ....F 3
Berzence, 3,651 ....D 3
Bicske, 9,106 ....E 3
Biharkeresztes, 4,844 ....F 3
Biharnagybajom, 4,762 ....F 3
Böhönye, 3,809 ....D 3
Bonyhád, 9,354 ....E 3
Budafok, 39,870 ....E 3
Budaörs, 12,682 ....E 3
Budapest (capital), 1,990,000 ....E 3
Cegléd, 37,000 ....S 3
Celldömölk, 9,762 ....D 3
Cigánd, 5,220 ....F 2
Csákvár, 5,135 ....E 3
Csanádpalota, 5,264 ....F 3
Csenger, 4,835 ....G 3
Csepel, 86,287 ....E 3
Csepreg, 4,348 ....D 3
Csongrád, 20,000 ....E 3
Csorna, 9,192 ....D 3
Csorvás, 7,622 ....F 3
Csurgó, 5,400 ....D 3
Debrecen, 160,000 ....F 3
Derecske, 9,980 ....F 3
Dévaványa, 12,137 ....F 3
Devecser, 5,741 ....D 3
Dombóvár, 15,605 ....E 3
Dombrád, 6,868 ....F 2
Dömsöd, 6,532 ....E 3
Dorog, 9,994 ....E 3
Dunaföldvár, 11,039 ....E 3
Dunaharaszti, 13,655 ....E 3
Dunakeszi, 15,636 ....E 3
Dunaújváros, 45,000 ....E 3
Dunavecse, 4,908 ....E 3
Edelény, 6,851 ....F 2
Eger, 45,000 ....F 3
Egyek, 8,678 ....F 3
Elek, 6,325 ....F 3
Emőd, 5,233 ....F 3
Endrőd, 9,263 ....F 3
Enying, 6,406 ....E 3
Ercsi, 7,850 ....E 3
Érd, 25,900 ....E 3
Erdőtelek, 4,634 ....F 3
Esztergom, 26,000 ....E 3
Fegyvernek, 7,835 ....F 3
Fehérgyarmat, 6,024 ....G 3
Földeák, 4,275 ....F 3
Füzesabony, 7,125 ....F 3
Füzesgyarmat, 7,807 ....F 3
Gödöllő, 22,000 ....E 3
Gönc, 3,093 ....F 2
Gyoma, 10,921 ....F 3
Gyöngyös, 32,000 ....E 3
Győnk, 2,684 ....E 3
Győr, 81,000 ....D 3
Gyula, 25,000 ....F 3
Hajdúböszörmény, 30,000 ....F 3
Hajdúdorog, 10,559 ....F 3
Hajdúhadház, 13,030 ....F 3
Hajdúnánás, 17,000 ....F 3
Hajdúsámson, 7,784 ....F 3
Hajdúszoboszló, 22,000 ....F 3
Hajós, 5,584 ....E 3
Hatvan, 21,000 ....E 3
Hercegfalva, 4,951 ....E 3
Heves, 11,349 ....F 3
Hogyesz, 3,501 ....E 3
Hódmezővásárhely, 53,000 ....F 3
Izsák, 8,609 ....E 3
Jánoshalma, 12,897 ....E 3
Jánosháza, 3,468 ....D 3
Jászapáti, 10,495 ....E 3
Jászárokszállás, 10,745 ....E 3
Jászberény, 30,000 ....E 3
Jászfényszaru, 7,542 ....E 3
Jászkarajenő, 4,955 ....E 3
Jászkisér, 7,280 ....F 3
Jászladány, 8.841 ....F 3
Kalocsa, 15,000 ....E 3
Kaposvár, 52.000 ....D 3
Kapuvár, 10,748 ....D 3
Karád, 3,438 ....D 3
Karcag, 24,000 ....F 3
Kazincbarcika, 29,000 ....F 2
Kecel, 10,193 ....E 3
Kecskemét, 76,000 ....E 3
Kemecse, 4,681 ....F 2
Keszthely, 17,000 ....D 3
Kisbér, 4,567 ....D 3
Kiskőrös, 12,954 ....E 3
Kiskundorozsma, 8,679 ....E 3
Kiskunfélegyháza, 33,000 ....E 3
Kiskunhalas, 28,000 ....E 3
Kiskunmajsa, 12,311 ....E 3
Kispest, 66,547 ....E 3
Kistelek, 8,925 ....E 3
Kisújszállás, 13,000 ....F 3
Kisvárda, 13,050 ....G 2
Komádi, 9,850 ....F 3
Komárom, 11,000 ....E 3
Komló, 28,000 ....E 3
Kondoros, 7,462 ....F 3
Körmend, 7,548 ....D 3
Körösladány, 7,302 ....F 3
Kőszeg, 10,000 ....D 3
Kunágota, 5,547 ....F 3
Kunhegyes, 10,792 ....F 3
Kunmadaras, 8,463 ....F 3
Kunszentmárton, 13,383 ....F 3
Kunszentmiklós, 8,198 ....E 3
Lajosmizse, 12,617 ....E 3
Lébény, 3,588 ....D 3
Lengyeltóti, 3,392 ....D 3
Letenye, 4,507 ....D 3
Lökösháza, 2,511 ....F 3
Lőrinci, 11,142 ....E 3
Madaras, 5,177 ....E 3
Makó, 29,000 ....F 3
Mándok, 4,828 ....G 2
Marcali, 7,877 ....D 3
Mátészalka, 11,496 ....G 3
Mélykút, 8,168 ....E 3
Mezőberény, 12,830 ....F 3
Mezőcsát, 6,583 ....F 3
Mezőhegyes, 9,137 ....F 3
Mezőkövesd, 18,160 ....F 3
Mezőszilas, 3,434 ....E 3
Mezőtúr, 22,000 ....F 3
Mindszent, 9,179 ....F 3
Miskolc, 180,000 ....F 2
Mohács, 18,000 ....E 4
Monor, 15,360 ....E 3
Mór, 11,622 ....E 3
Mosonmagyaróvár, 25,000 ....D 3
Nádudvar, 10,006 ....F 3
Nagyatád, 8,791 ....D 3
Nagybajom, 4,972 ....D 3
Nagyecsed, 8,348 ....G 3
Nagyhalász, 6,650 ....F 2
Nagykálló, 11,329 ....F 3
Nagykanizsa, 38,000 ....D 3
Nagykáta, 11,924 ....E 3
Nagykőrös, 26,000 ....E 3
Nagyléta, 6,902 ....G 3
Nagyszénás, 7,439 ....F 3
Nyírábrány, 4,517 ....G 3
Nyírádony, 7,325 ....G 3
Nyírbátor, 10,167 ....G 3
Nyíregyháza, 65,000 ....F 3
Nyírmada, 4,826 ....F 2
örkény, 5,001 ....E 3
Orosháza, 33,000 ....F 3
Oroszlány, 20,000 ....E 3
Ózd, 40,000 ....F 2
Paks, 11,919 ....E 3
Pannonhalma, 3,529 ....D 3
Pápa, 27,000 ....D 3
Pásztó, 8,091 ....E 3
Pécs, 140,000 ....E 3
Pécsvárad, 3,199 ....E 3
Pétervására, 2,727 ....F 3
Pilis, 8,458 ....E 3
Pilisvörösvár, 9,627 ....E 3
Polgár, 9,353 ....F 3
Püspökladány, 15,488 ....F 3
Putnok, 6,440 ....F 2
Ráckeve, 7,456 ....E 3
Rakamaz, 5,381 ....F 2
Rákospalota, 63,344 ....E 3
Sajószentpéter, 12,846 ....F 2
Salgótarján, 37,000 ....E 2
Sándorfalva, 5,815 ....F 3
Sárbogárd, 6,853 ....E 3
Sarkad, 12,169 ....F 3
Sárospatak, 12,799 ....F 2
Sárvár, 11,247 ....D 3
Sátoraljaújhely, 17,000 ....F 2
Siklós, 5,897 ....E 4
Siófok, 10,322 ....E 3
Solt, 7,199 ....E 3
Soltvadkert, 8,244 ....E 3
Sopron, 45,000 ....D 3
Sümeg, 5,925 ....D 3
Szabadszállás, 8,799 ....E 3
Szarvas, 19,000 ....F 3
Szécsény, 4,410 ....E 2
Szeged, 120,000 ....E 3
Szeghalom, 10,093 ....F 3
Szegvár, 6,970 ....F 3
Székesfehérvár, 71,000 ....E 3
Szekszárd, 23,000 ....E 3
Szendrő, 3,773 ....F 2
Szentendre, 12,000 ....E 3
Szentes, 32,000 ....F 3
Szentgotthárd, 5,421 ....D 3
Szerencs, 7,789 ....F 2
Szigetvár, 10,000 ....D 3
Szikszó, 6,110 ....F 2
Szolnok, 61,000 ....F 3
Szombathely, 62,000 ....D 3
Tab, 4,265 ....E 3
Tamási, 7,689 ....E 3
Tápiószele, 5,632 ....E 3
Tapolca, 10,000 ....D 3
Tarpa, 3,966 ....G 2
Tata, 19,000 ....E 3
Tatabánya, 64,000 ....E 3
Tét, 4,861 ....D 3
Tiszacsege, 7,002 ....F 3
Tiszaföldvár, 12,377 ....F 3
Tiszafüred, 11,214 ....F 3
Tiszakécske, 12,834 ....E 3
Tiszalök, 6,125 ....F 2
Tiszavasvári, 12,201 ....F 3
Tokaj, 5,031 ....F 2
Tolna, 8,741 ....E 3
Törökszentmiklós, 24,000 ....F 3
Tótkomlós, 9,368 ....F 3
Tura, 8,169 ....E 3
Túrkeve, 11,000 ....F 3
Újfehértó, 14,386 ....F 3
Újpest, 79,961 ....E 3
Vác, 29,000 ....E 3
Várpalota, 27,000 ....E 3
Vasvár, 4,293 ....D 3
Vecsés, 16,411 ....E 3
Veszprém, 33,000 ....D 3
Vésztő, 10,463 ....F 3
Villány, 2,769 ....E 4
Zahony, 2,117 ....G 2
Zalaegerszeg, 33,000 ....D 3
Zalaszentgrót, 4,470 ....D 3
Zirc, 5,427 ....D 3

OTHER FEATURES

Bakony (mts.) ....D 3
Balaton (lake) ....D 3
Berettyó (river) ....F 3
Börsöny (mts.) ....E 3
Bükk (mts.) ....F 2
Csepelsziget (isl.) ....E 3
Danube (river) ....E 3
Dráva (river) ....D 3
Duna (Danube) (river) ....E 3
Fertö tó (Neusiedler) (lake) ....D 3
Great Alföld (plain) ....F 3
Hernád (river) ....F 2
Ipoly (river) ....E 2
Kapos (river) ....E 3
Kékes (mt.) ....E 3
Kőrishegy (mt.) ....D 3
Körös (river) ....F 3
Little Alföld (plain) ....D 3
Maros (river) ....F 3
Matra (mts.) ....E 3
Mecsek (mts.) ....D 3
Neusiedler (lake) ....D 3
Rába (river) ....D 3
Sajo (river) ....F 2
Sebes Körös (river) ....F 3
Sió (canal) ....E 3
Szentendreisziget (isl.) ....E 3
Tarna (river) ....F 3
Tisza (river) ....F 3
Zala (river) ....D 3

Agriculture, Industry and Resources

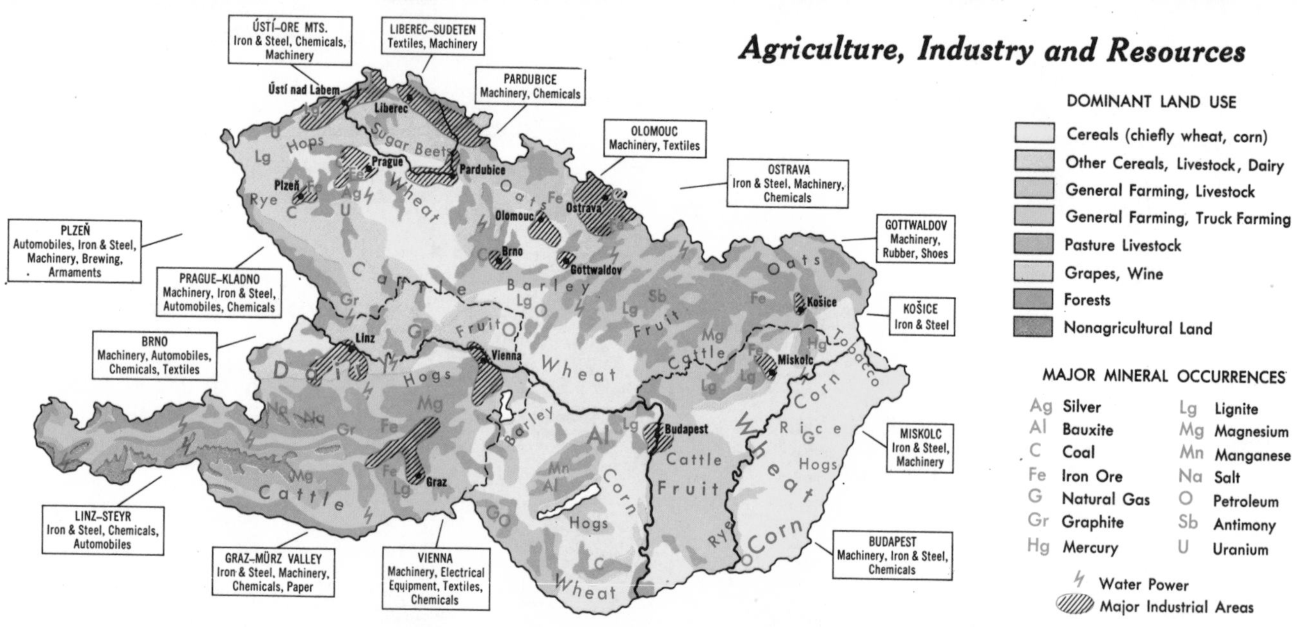

ÚSTÍ–ORE MTS. Iron & Steel, Chemicals, Machinery
LIBEREC–SUDETEN Textiles, Machinery
PARDUBICE Machinery, Chemicals
OLOMOUC Machinery, Textiles
OSTRAVA Iron & Steel, Machinery, Chemicals
GOTTWALDOV Machinery, Rubber, Shoes
KOŠICE Iron & Steel
MISKOLC Iron & Steel, Machinery
BUDAPEST Machinery, Iron & Steel, Chemicals
VIENNA Machinery, Electrical Equipment, Textiles, Chemicals
GRAZ–MÜRZ VALLEY Iron & Steel, Machinery, Chemicals, Paper
LINZ–STEYR Iron & Steel, Chemicals, Automobiles
BRNO Machinery, Automobiles, Chemicals, Textiles
PRAGUE–KLADNO Machinery, Iron & Steel, Automobiles, Chemicals
PLZEŇ Automobiles, Iron & Steel, Machinery, Brewing, Armaments
Ústí nad Labem
Liberec
Prague
Pardubice
Plzeň
Olomouc
Ostrava
Brno
Gottwaldov
Košice
Miskolc
Linz
Vienna
Budapest
Graz
Hops
Sugar Beets
Wheat
Rye
Oats
Barley
Cattle
Fruit
Hogs
Dairy
Corn
Rice
Tobacco
DOMINANT LAND USE
Cereals (chiefly wheat, corn)
Other Cereals, Livestock, Dairy
General Farming, Livestock
General Farming, Truck Farming
Pasture Livestock
Grapes, Wine
Forests
Nonagricultural Land
MAJOR MINERAL OCCURRENCES
Ag Silver
Al Bauxite
C Coal
Fe Iron Ore
G Natural Gas
Gr Graphite
Hg Mercury
Lg Lignite
Mg Magnesium
Mn Manganese
Na Salt
O Petroleum
Sb Antimony
U Uranium
Water Power
Major Industrial Areas

YUGOSLAVIA

AREA 98,766 sq. mi.
POPULATION 20,586,000
CAPITAL Belgrade
LARGEST CITY Belgrade
HIGHEST POINT Triglav 9,393 ft.
MONETARY UNIT Yugoslav dinar
MAJOR LANGUAGES Serbo-Croatian, Slovenian, Macedonian, Albanian
MAJOR RELIGIONS Eastern Orthodoxy, Roman Catholicism, Islam

ALBANIA

AREA 11,100 sq. mi.
POPULATION 2,126,000
CAPITAL Tiranë
LARGEST CITY Tiranë
HIGHEST POINT Korab 9,026 ft.
MONETARY UNIT lek
MAJOR LANGUAGE Albanian
MAJOR RELIGIONS Islam, Eastern Orthodoxy, Roman Catholicism

RUMANIA

AREA 91,699 sq. mi.
POPULATION 20,394,000
CAPITAL Bucharest
LARGEST CITY Bucharest
HIGHEST POINT Moldoveanul 8,343 ft.
MONETARY UNIT leu
MAJOR LANGUAGES Rumanian, Hungarian
MAJOR RELIGION Eastern Orthodoxy

BULGARIA

AREA 42,829 sq. mi.
POPULATION 8,501,000
CAPITAL Sofia
LARGEST CITY Sofia
HIGHEST POINT Musala 9,597 ft.
MONETARY UNIT lev
MAJOR LANGUAGE Bulgarian
MAJOR RELIGION Eastern Orthodoxy

GREECE

AREA 50,548 sq. mi.
POPULATION 8,838,000
CAPITAL Athens
LARGEST CITY Athens
HIGHEST POINT Olympus 9,570 ft.
MONETARY UNIT drachma
MAJOR LANGUAGE Greek
MAJOR RELIGION Eastern (Greek) Orthodoxy

BULGARIA

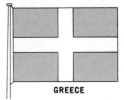

GREECE

YUGOSLAVIA

ALBANIA

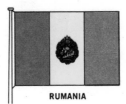

RUMANIA

DOMINANT LAND USE

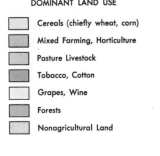

- Cereals (chiefly wheat, corn)
- Mixed Farming, Horticulture
- Pasture Livestock
- Tobacco, Cotton
- Grapes, Wine
- Forests
- Nonagricultural Land

Agriculture, Industry and Resources

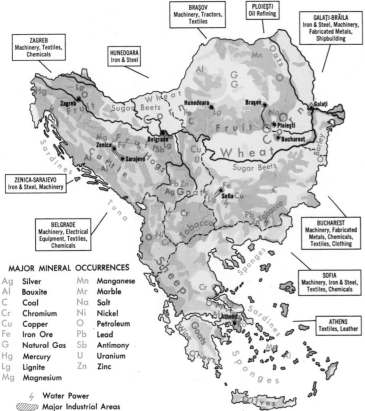

ZAGREB Machinery, Textiles, Chemicals

HUNEDOARA Iron & Steel

BRAŞOV Machinery, Tractors, Textiles

PLOIEŞTI Oil Refining

GALAŢI-BRĂILA Iron & Steel, Machinery, Fabricated Metals, Shipbuilding

ZENICA-SARAJEVO Iron & Steel, Machinery

BELGRADE Machinery, Electrical Equipment, Textiles, Chemicals

BUCHAREST Machinery, Fabricated Metals, Chemicals, Textiles, Clothing

SOFIA Machinery, Iron & Steel, Textiles, Chemicals

ATHENS Textiles, Leather

MAJOR MINERAL OCCURRENCES

Ag	Silver	Mn	Manganese
Al	Bauxite	Mr	Marble
C	Coal	Na	Salt
Cr	Chromium	Ni	Nickel
Cu	Copper	O	Petroleum
Fe	Iron Ore	Pb	Lead
G	Natural Gas	Sb	Antimony
Hg	Mercury	U	Uranium
Lg	Lignite	Zn	Zinc
Mg	Magnesium		

⚡ Water Power
▨ Major Industrial Areas

ALBANIA

CITIES and TOWNS

Berat, 22,000	D	5
Bajram Cur, 1,795	D	4
Burrel, 3,150	D	5
Çorovodë, 1,790	E	5
Delvinë, 5,700	D	6
Durrës, 47,900	D	5
Elbasan, 35,300	E	5
Ersekë, 2,150	E	5
Fier, 17,900	D	5
Gjirokastër, 15,000	D	5
Kavajë, 17,700	D	5
Korcë, 43,700	E	5
Kruë, 6,700	D	5
Kucovë (Stalin), 12,300	D	5
Kukës, 3,900	E	4
Leskovik, 1,625	E	5
Lezh, 3,000	D	5
Lushnje, 16,000	D	5
Pequin, 3,800	D	5
Përmet, 4,000	E	5
Peshkopi, 5,500	E	5
Pogradec, 8,900	E	5
Pukë, 1,700	D	5
Sarandë, 7,700	E	6
Shijak, 5,100	D	5
Shkodër, 47,000	D	5
Stalin, 12,300	D	5
Tepelenë, 2,500	E	5
Tiranë (Tirana) (cap.), 170,000	E	5
Vlorë, 46,900	D	5

OTHER FEATURES

Adriatic (sea)	B	4
Drin (riv.)	E	4
Korab (mt.)	E	5
Ohrid (lake)	E	5
Otranto (str.)	D	5
Prespa (lake)	E	5
Sazan (isl.)	D	5
Scutari (lake)	D	4
Tomor (mt.)	E	5
Vijosë (riv.)	D	5

BULGARIA

CITIES and TOWNS

Alfatar, 3,650	H	4
Akhtopol, 1,058	H	4
Alfatar, 4,042	H	4
Ardino, 2,558	G	5
Asenovgrad, 37,411	G	5
Aytos, 17,769	H	4
Balchik, 8,714	J	4
Bansko, 7,851	F	5
Belogradchik, 5,174	F	4
Berkovitsa, 11,553	F	4
Blagoyevgrad, 32,744	F	5
Botevgrad, 12,051	F	4
Bregovo, 4,725	F	3
Breznik, 4,093	F	4
Burgas, 122,212	H	4
Byala, 9,347	G	4
Byala Slatina, 14,942	F	4
Chirpan, 17,857	G	4
Devin, 4,475	G	5
Dimitrovgrad, 41,787	G	4
Dobrich (Tolbukhin), 55,111	H	4
Dryanovo, 8,187	G	4
Elena, 4,071	G	4
Elin Pelin, 8,074	F	4
Elkhovo, 11,315	H	4
Gabrovo, 57,758	G	4
General Toshevo, 8,251	H	4
Godech, 4,074	F	4
Gorna Dzhumaya (Blagoyevgrad), 32,744	F	5
Gorna Oryakhovitsa, 26,290	G	4
Gotse Delchev, 14,457	F	5
Grudovo, 9,177	H	4
Ikhtiman, 10,325	F	4
Isperikh, 8,445	H	4
Ivaylovgrad, 2,907	H	5
Karapelit, 2,033	H	4
Karlovo (Levskigrad), 20,287	G	4
Karnobat (Polyanovgrad), 18,727	H	4
Kavarna, 8,291	J	4
Kazanlŭk, 44,418	G	4
Kharmanli, 15,478	G	5
Khaskovo, 57,682	G	5
Kolarovgrad (Shumen), 59,362	H	4
Kotel, 7,209	H	4
Krumovgrad, 2,230	G	5
Kubrat, 7,531	H	4
Kula, 6,474	F	4
Kŭrdzhali, 33,319	G	5
Kyustendil, 38,199	F	4
Levskigrad, 20,287	G	4
Lom, 28,189	F	4
Lovech, 30,843	G	4
Lukovit, 9,716	G	4
Mallco Tŭrnovo, 3,744	H	4
Maritsa, 8,532	H	4
Michurin, 2,783	H	4
Mikhaylovgrad, 27,240	F	4
Momchilgrad, 6,084	G	5
Nesebŭr, 2,333	H	4
Nikopol, 5,763	G	4
Nova Zagora, 19,257	G	4
Novi Pazar, 12,476	H	4
Omurtag, 8,148	H	4
Oryakhovo, 7,498	F	4
Panagyurishte, 18,298	G	4
Pazardzhik, 55,410	G	4
Pernik, 75,844	F	4
Peshtera, 14,606	G	4
Petrich, 20,653	F	5
Pirdop, 8,252	G	4
Pleven, 79,234	G	4
Plovdiv, 234,547	G	4
Polyanovgrad, 18,727	H	4
Pomorie, 9,567	H	4
Popina, 2,699	H	3
Popovo, 15,609	H	4
Provadiya, 13,837	H	4
Radomir, 8,458	F	4
Razgrad, 26,297	H	4
Razlog, 10,425	F	5
Rositsa, 1,505	H	4
Ruse, 142,894	H	4
Samokov, 21,585	F	4
Sandanski, 14,590	F	5
Sevlievo, 20,396	G	4
Shabla, 3,788	J	4
Shumen, 59,362	H	4
Silistra, 32,996	H	3
Simeonovgrad (Maritsa), 8,532	H	4
Sliven, 68,331	H	4
Smolyan, 17,479	G	5
Smyadovo, 5,349	H	4
Sofia (cap.), 840,113	F	4
Sofia *923,400	F	4
Sozopol, 3,257	H	4
Stanke Dimitrov, 35,813	F	4
Stara Zagora, 100,565	G	4
Sveti Vlas (Sandanski), 14,590	F	5
Svilengrad, 12,438	G	5
Svishtov, 21,522	G	4
Teteven, 9,807	G	4
Tolbukhin, 55,111	H	4
Topolovgrad, 6,633	G	4
Troyan, 18,982	G	4
Trŭn, 2,922	F	4
Tŭrgovishte, 25,528	H	4
Tutrakan, 9,909	H	4
Varna, 200,827	J	4
Veliko Tŭrnovo, 37,269	G	4
Vidin, 36,820	F	4
Vratsa, 39,052	F	4
Yambol, 58,405	H	4
Zlatograd, 6,508	G	5

OTHER FEATURES

Balkan (mts.)	G	4
Black (sea)	J	4
Danube (Dunav) (riv.)	H	4
Emine (cape)	H	4
Iskŭr (riv.)	G	4
Kaliakra (cape)	J	4
Lom (riv.)	H	4
Maritsa (riv.)	F	5
Mesta (riv.)	F	5
Musala (mt.)	F	4
Osŭm (riv.)	G	4
Rhodope (mts.)	G	5
Ruen (mt.)	F	4
Struma (riv.)	F	5
Timok (riv.)	F	3
Tundzha (riv.)	G	4
Vit (riv.)	G	4

GREECE

REGIONS

Aegean Islands, 477,476	G	6
Áyion Óros (aut. dist.), 2,687	G	5
Central Greece and Euboea, 2,823,658	F	6
Crete, 483,258	G	8
Epirus, 352,604	E	6
Greater Athens, 1,852,709	F	7
Ionian Islands, 212,573	D	6
Macedonia, 1,890,654	F	5
Pelopónnisos, 1,096,390	F	7
Thessalía, 695,385	F	6
Thrace, 356,555	G	5

CITIES and TOWNS

Agrínion, 24,763	E	6
Aíyina, 4,989	F	7
Aíyion, 17,762	F	6
Alexandroúpolis, 18,712	H	5
Alivérion, 3,523	G	6
Almirós, 6,010	F	6
Amaliás, 15,468	E	7
Amfilokhía, 5,408	E	6
Ámfissa, 6,076	F	6
Andíssa, 2,530	H	6
Andravidha, 3,155	E	6
Ándros, 2,032	G	7
Áno Viánnos, 1,820	G	8
Anóyia, 2,461	G	8
Ardhéa, 3,222	F	5
Argalastí, 1,864	F	6
Árgos, 16,712	F	7
Argostólion, 7,322	E	6
Arkhángelos, 2,918	J	7
Arnaía, 2,612	G	5
Árta, 16,899	E	6
Astipálaia, 1,205	H	7
Atalándi, 4,552	F	6
Athens (cap.), 627,564	F	7
Athens, *2,347,000	F	7
Áyios Matthaíos, 1,892	D	6
Áyios Nikólaos, 3,709	G	8
Candia (Iráklion), 63,458	G	8
Canea (Khaniá), 38,467	G	8
Chalcis (Khalkís), 24,745	F	6
Corinth, 15,892	F	7
Delwinákion, 1,076	E	6
Dhidhimótikhon, 7,287	H	5
Dhíkaia, 1,181	H	7
Dhimitsána, 1,300	F	7
Dhomokós, 2,017	F	6
Dráma, 32,195	F	6
Édhessa, 15,534	F	5
Elassón, 6,501	F	6
Eleftheroúpolis, 5,448	G	5
Ermoúpolis, 14,402	G	7
Fársala, 6,356	F	6
Filiátes, 3,065	E	6
Filiatrá, 6,753	E	7
Flórina, 11,833	E	5
Gargaliánoi, 6,637	E	7
Grevená, 6,892	E	5
Ídhra, 2,546	F	7
Ierápetra, 6,488	G	8
Igoumenítsa, 3,235	E	6
Ioánnina, 34,997	E	6
Iráklion, 63,458	G	8
Istiaía, 3,882	F	6
Itháki, 2,632	E	6
Kalámai, 38,211	F	7
Kalampáka, 4,640	E	6
Kalávrita, 2,039	F	6
Kardhítsa, 23,708	E	6
Kariá, 1,739	E	6
Káristos, 4,429	G	6
Karláton, 3,335	E	6
Karpenísion, 3,523	E	6
Kastéllion, 2,071	F	8
Kastéllion, 1,351	G	8
Kastoría, 10,162	E	5
Katerini, 28,046	F	5
Kavála, 44,517	G	5
Kéa, 1,788	G	7
Kérkira, 26,991	D	6
Khalkís, 24,745	F	6
Khaniá, 38,467	G	8
Khíos, 24,053	H	6
Kiáton, 6,069	F	6
Kílkis, 10,963	F	5
Kími, 3,252	F	6
Kiparissía, 4,602	E	7
Kíthira, 469	F	7
Komotiní, 28,355	G	5
Kónitsa, 3,485	E	5
Koropí, 7,862	G	7
Kos, 8,138	H	7

(continued on following page)

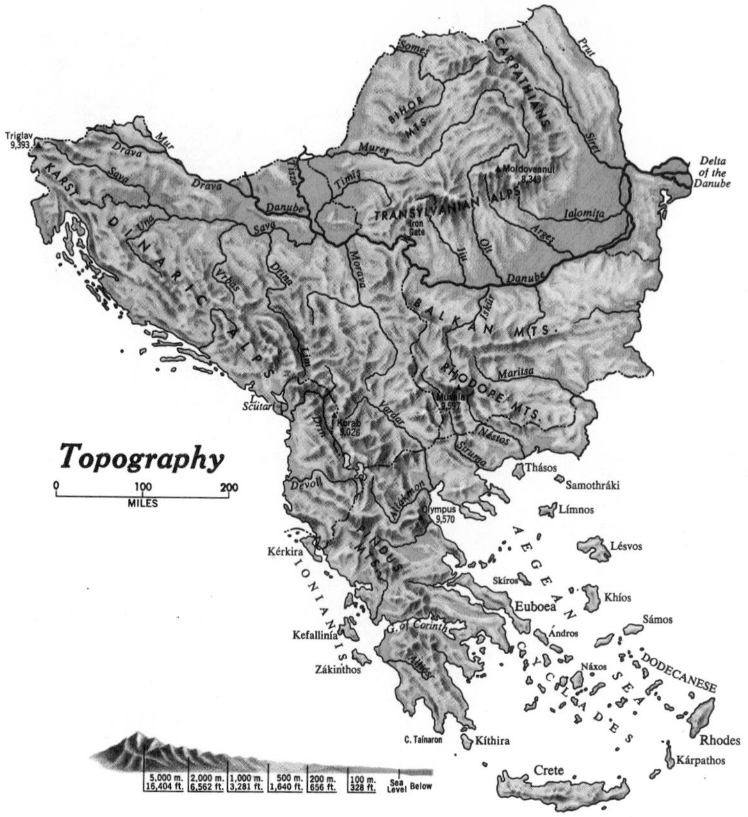

GREECE (continued)

Kozáni, 21,537 F 5
Kranídhion, 3,942 F 7
Lamía, 21,509 F 6
Langadhás, 6,739 F 5
Lárisa, 55,391 F 6
Lávrion, 6,553 G 7
Leonídhion, 3,297 F 7
Levádhia, 12,609 F 6
Levkás, 6,552 E 6
Limenária, 1,999 G 5
Limín Vathéos, 5,469 H 7
Límni, 2,394 F 6
Litókhoron, 5,032 F 5
Lixoúrion, 3,977 E 6
Loutrá Aidhipsoú, 1,859 F 6
Marathón, 2,167 G 6
Megalópolis, 2,235 E 7
Mégara, 15,450 F 6
Meligalá, 1,960 F 7
Mesolóngion, 11,266 E 6
Messíni, 8,249 E 7
Métsovon, 2,976 E 6
Mikínai, 361 F 7
Mílos, 944 G 7
Mírina, 3,460 G 6
Missolonghi (Mesolóngion), 11,266 E 6
Míthimna, 1,828 G 6
Mitilíni, 25,758 H 6
Moláoi, 2,526 F 7
Monólithos, 496 H 7
Moúdhros, 1,236 G 6
Náousa, 15,492 F 5
Návpaktos, 7,080 F 6
Návplion, 8,918 F 7
Náxos, 2,458 G 7
Néa Filippiás, 3,001 E 6
Neápolis, 2,464 F 7
Neméa, 4,720 F 7
Néon Karlóvasi, 5,308 H 7
Nigríta, 9,979 F 5
Olimbía, 771 E 7
Orestiás, 10,281 H 5
Paramithiá, 2,827 E 6
Pátrai, 95,364 E 6
Péta, 2,522 E 6
Pigádhia, 1,281 H 8
Pílos, 2,434 E 7
Piraiévs (Piraeus), 183,877 F 7
Pírgos, 20,558 E 7
Piryí, 1,914 G 6
Píthion, 1,535 H 5
Plomárion, 5,172 H 6
Políkastron, 3,821 F 5
Políkhnitos, 5,131 G 6
Políyiros, 3,541 F 5
Póros, 4,392 F 7
Préveza, 11,172 E 6
Psakhná, 4,433 F 6
Ptolemaïs, 12,747 E 5
Réthimnon, 14,999 G 8
Ródhos (Rhodes), 27,393 J 7
Salamís, 11,161 F 6
Salonika (Thessaloníki), 448,000 F 5
Sámi, 1,065 E 6
Samothráki, 1,555 G 5
Sápai, 2,589 G 5
Sérrai, 40,063 F 5
Sérvia, 4,132 F 5
Siátista, 4,737 E 5
Sidhirókastron, 8,177 F 5
Sími, 2,982 H 7
Sitía, 5,327 H 8
Skíros, 2,411 G 6
Skópelos, 2,955 F 6
Souflíon, 6,693 H 5
Sparta, 10,412 F 7
Spétsai, 3,314 F 7
Stilís, 4,673 F 6
Thebes (Thívai), 15,779 F 6
Thessaloníki, 448,000 F 5
Thásos, 1,875 G 5
Thíra, 1,481 G 7
Thívai, 15,779 F 6
Timbákion, 2,816 G 8
Tínos, 2,888 G 7
Tírnavos, 10,805 F 6
Tríkkala, 27,876 E 6
Trípolis, 18,500 F 7
Vartholomión, 3,244 E 7
Vathí, 3,161 H 7
Velvendós, 4,158 F 5
Vérroia, 25,765 F 5
Vólos, 49,221 F 6
Vólos, *67,424 F 6
Vónitsa, 2,996 E 6
Vrondádhes, 4,685 G 6
Xánthi, 26,377 G 5
Yiannitsá, 19,693 F 5
Yíthion, 4,992 F 7
Zákinthos, 9,506 E 7
Zante (Zúkinthos), 9,506 E 7

OTHER FEATURES

Aegean (sea) G 6
Akrítas (cape) E 7
Aktí (pen.) G 5
Amorgós (isl.), 2,396 G 7
Anáfi (isl.), 471 G 7
Andikíthira (isl.), 178 F 8
Ándros (isl.), 12,928 G 7
Arda (riv.) G 5
Argolís (gulf) F 7
Astipálaia (isl.), 1,539 H 7
Áthos (mt.) G 5
Áyios Evstrátios (isl.), 1,061 G 6
Áyios Yeóryios (cape) G 5
Cephalonia (Kefallinía) (isl.), 39,793 E 6
Chios (Khíos) (isl.), 60,061 G 6
Corfu (Kérkira) (isl.), 99,092 D 6
Corinth (gulf) F 6
Crete (isl.), 483,075 G 8
Crete (sea) G 7
Cyclades (isls.), 99,959 G 7
Dhrépanon (cape) G 6
Dodecanese (isls.), 123,021 H 8
Euboea (isl.), 163,215 G 6
Évros (riv.) H 5
Gávdhos (isl.), 172 F 8
Ikaría (isl.), 9,577 G 7
Ionian (sea) D 7
Íos (isl.), 1,343 G 7
Itháki (Ithaca) (isl.), 5,210 E 6
Kálimnos (isl.), 10,211 H 7
Kafirévs (cape) G 6
6,689 H 8
Kárpathos (isl.), 6,689 H 8
Kásos (isl.), 1,422 H 8
Kassándra (pen.) F 6
Kéa (isl.), 2,361 G 7
Kefallinía (isl.), 39,793 E 6
Kérkira (isl.), 99,092 D 6
Khálki (isl.), 501 H 7
Khani, (gulf) G 8
Khíos (isl.), 60,061 G 6
Kiparissía (gulf) E 7
Kíthira (isl.), 5,340 F 7
Kíthnos (isl.), 2,064 G 7
Kos (isl.), 18,187 H 7
Kriós (cape) F 8
Lakonía (gulf) F 7
Léros (isl.), 6,611 H 7
Lésvos (isl.), 117,371 G 6
Levítha (isl.), 7 H 7
Levkás (isl.), 2,697 E 6
Límnos (isl.), 21,808 G 6
Maléa (cape) F 7
Matapan (Taínaron) (cape) F 7
Merabéllou (gulf) H 8
Mesará (gulf) G 8
Messíni (gulf) E 7
Míkonos (isl.), 3,633 G 7
Mílos (isl.), 4,910 G 7
Mirtóön (sea) F 7
Náxos (isl.), 16,703 G 7
Néstos (riv.) G 5
Nísiros (isl.), 1,788 H 7
Northern Sporades (isls.), 9,810 F 6
Olympus (mt.) F 5
Óssa (mt.) F 6
Parnassus (mt.) F 6
Páros (isl.), 7,830 G 7
Pátmos (isl.), 2,564 H 7
Paxoí (isl.), 2,678 D 6
Pindus (mts.) E 6
Piniós (riv.) E 6
Prespa (lake) E 5
Psará (isl.), 576 G 6
Rhodes (isl.), 63,951 H 7
Rhodope (mts.) G 5
Salonika (Thermaic) (gulf) F 6
Sámos (isl.), 41,124 H 7
Samothráki (isl.), 3,830 G 5
Saría (isl.), 18 H 8
Saronic (gulf) F 7
Sérifos (isl.), 1,878 G 7
Sídheros (cape) H 8
Sífnos (isl.), 2,258 G 7
Sími (isl.), 3,123 H 7
Síros (isl.), 19,570 G 7
Sithoniá (pen.) F 5
Skíros (isl.), 2,882 G 6
Spátha (cape) F 8
Strimón (gulf) G 5
Strofádhes (isls.), 10 E 7
Taínaron (cape) F 7
Thásos (isl.), 15,916 G 5
Thermaic (gulf) F 6
Thíra (isl.), 7,751 G 7
Tílos (isl.), 789 H 7
Tínos (isl.), 9,273 G 7
Toronaic (gulf) F 5
Vardar (riv.) E 5
Voïviïs (lake) F 6
Vólvi (lake) F 5
Voúxa (cape) F 8
Zákinthos (Zante) (isl.), 35,499 E 7

RUMANIA

CITIES and TOWNS

Aiud, 11,886 F 2
Alba Iulia, 22,225 F 2
Alexandria, 21,907 G 3
Anina, 11,837 E 3
Arad, 132,757 E 2
Arad, *137,444 E 2
Babadag, 5,549 J 3
Bacău, 73,481 H 2
Bacău, *87,465 H 2
Baia Mare, 62,769 F 2
Baia Mare, *108,709 F 2
Băileşti, 15,932 F 3
Balş, 6,956 G 3
Beiuş, 6,467 F 2
Bîrlad, 41,061 H 2
Bîrlad, *52,497 H 2
Bistriţa, 25,534 G 2
Blaj, 8,731 F 2
Botoşani, 35,185 H 2
Botoşani, *50,204 H 2
Brad, 9,963 F 2
Brăila, 147,495 H 3
Braşov, 175,264 G 3
Braşov, *264,537 G 3
Bucharest (Bucureşti) (cap.), 1,431,993 G 3
Bucharest, *1,518,725 G 3
Buhuş, 12,382 H 2
Buzău, 56,380 H 3
Buzău, *82,454 H 3
Buziaş, 5,140 E 3
Călafat, 8,069 F 3
Călăraşi, 35,698 H 3
Caracal, 22,715 G 3
Caransebeş, 15,195 F 3
Carei, 16,780 F 2
Cernavodă, 8,802 J 3
Cîmpia Turzii, 11,514 F 2
Cîmpina, 22,862 H 3
Cîmpulung, 24,891 G 3
Cîmpulung Moldovenesc, 13,627 G 2
Cisnădie, 12,246 F 3
Cluj, 193,375 F 2
Cluj, *223,519 F 2
Comaneşti, 12,392 H 2
Constanţa, 165,245 J 3
Constanţa, *202,024 J 3
Corabia, 11,502 G 4
Craiova, 166,249 F 3
Craiova, *174,669 F 3
Curtea de Argeş, 10,764 G 3
Dej, 26,968 F 2
Deva, 26,952 F 3
Deva, *45,836 F 3
Dorohoi, 14,771 H 2
Drăgăşani, 9,963 F 3
Făgăraş, 22,941 G 3
Fălticeni, 13,305 H 2
Feteşti, 21,425 H 3
Focşani, 35,075 H 3
Focşani, *40,701 H 3
Găeşti, 7,179 G 3
Galaţi, 160,097 H 3
Gheorgheni, 11,969 G 2
Gherla, 7,617 G 2
Giurgiu, 39,225 G 3
Giurgiu, *55,471 G 3
Haţeg, 3,853 F 3
Hîrşova, 4,761 J 3
Hunedoara, 68,303 F 3
Hunedoara, *100,953 F 3
Huşi, 20,703 J 2
Iaşi, 173,569 H 2
Iaşi, *196,167 H 2
Isaccea, 5,203 J 3
Jimbolia, 11,281 E 3
Lipova, 10,064 E 2
Lugoj, 35,388 F 3
Lupeni, 29,377 F 3
Mangalia, 4,792 J 4
Medgidia, 27,989 J 3
Mediaş, 46,396 G 2
Miercurea Ciuc, 11,996 G 2
Mizil, 7,460 H 3
Moineşti, 12,934 H 2
Moldova Nouă, 3,582 E 3
Moreni, 11,687 G 3
Năsăud, 5,725 G 2
Ocna Mureş, 10,701 G 2
Odobeşti, 4,977 H 3
Odorhei, 14,162 G 2
Olteniţa, 14,111 H 3
Oradea, 132,266 E 2
Oradea, *136,375 E 2
Orăştie, 10,488 F 3
Oraşul Gheorghe Georghiu-Dej, 35,689 H 2
Oraviţa, 8,175 E 3
Orşova, 6,527 F 3
Panciu, 7,679 H 3
Paşcani, 15,008 H 2
Petrila, 24,804 F 3
Petroşeni, 35,237 F 3
Petroşeni, *130,111 F 3
Piatra Neamţ, 45,925 G 2
Piatra Neamţ, *58,397 G 2
Piteşti, 60,094 G 3
Piteşti, *78,784 G 3
Ploieşti, 156,382 H 3
Ploieşti, *191,663 H 3
Pucioasa, 9,259 G 3
Rădăuti, 15,949 G 2
Reghin, 23,317 G 2
Reşiţa, 58,683 E 3
Reşiţa, *121,458 E 3
Rîmnicu Sărat, 22,325 H 3
Rîmnicu Vîlcea, 23,880 F 3
Roman, 38,990 H 2
Roman, *49,496 H 2
Roşiori de Vede, 21,707 G 3
Săcele, 22,822 G 3
Salonta, 16,276 E 3
Satu Mare, 68,257 F 2
Sebeş, 11,628 F 3
Sfîntu Gheorge, 20,759 G 3
Sibiu, 117,020 G 3
Sighetul-Marmaţiei, 29,768 F 2
Sighişoara, 25,100 G 2
Şimleu Silvaniei, 8,560 F 2
Sinaia, 9,006 G 3
Sînnicolau Mare, 9,956 E 2
Siret, 5,664 G 1
Slănic, 6,842 G 3
Slatina, 13,381 G 3
Slobozia, 9,632 H 3
Solca, 2,384 G 2
Strehaia, 8,545 F 3
Suceava, 37,715 G 2
Suceava, *76,327 G 2
Sulina, 3,622 J 3
Techirghiol, 2,705 J 3
Tecuci, 28,458 H 3
Timişoara, 184,797 E 3
Timişoara, *194,159 E 3
Tîrgovişte, 29,754 G 3
Tîrgovişte, *48,005 G 3
Tîrgu Jiu, 30,837 F 3
Tîrgu Jiu, *33,019 F 3
Tîrgu Mureş, 86,458 G 2
Tîrgu Mureş, *104,922 G 2
Tîrgu Neamţ, 10,373 G 2
Tîrgu Ocna, 11,227 H 2
Tîrgu Secuiesc, 7,500 H 2
Tîrnăveni, 20,354 F 2
Topliţa, 8,944 G 2
Tulcea, 35,552 J 3
Turda, 42,318 G 2
Turda, *69,768 G 2
Turnu Măgurele, 26,409 G 4
Turnu Severin, 45,394 F 3
Turnu Severin, *52,497 F 3
Urlaţi, 8,658 H 3
Urziceni, 6,061 H 3
Vasile Roaită, 3,286 J 3
Vaslui, 14,850 H 2
Vatra Dornei, 10,822 G 2
Vişeu de Sus, 13,956 F 2
Zalău, 13,378 F 2
Zărneşti, 6,673 G 3
Zimnicea, 12,445 G 4

OTHER FEATURES

Argeş (riv.) G 3
Buzău (riv.) H 3
Carpathian (mts.) G 2
Crişul Alb (riv.) F 2
Crişul Repede (riv.) F 2
Danube (river) H 4
Ialomiţa (marshes) J 3
Jiu (riv.) F 3
Moldoveanul (mt.) G 3
Mureş (riv.) E 2
Negoiul (mt.) G 3
Olt (riv.) G 3
Pietrosul (mt.) G 2
Prut (riv.) J 2
Siret (riv.) H 2
Someş (riv.) F 2
Timiş (riv.) E 3
Transylvanian Alps (mts.) G 3

YUGOSLAVIA

INTERNAL DIVISIONS

Bosnia and Hercegovina (rep.), 3,594,000 C 3
Croatia (rep.), 4,281,000 C 3
Kosovo-Mitohiyan (aut. prov.), 1,089,000 E 4
Macedonia (rep.), 1,506,000 E 5
Montenegro (rep.), 471,894 D 4
Serbia (rep.), 7,637,800 E 3
Slovenia (rep.), 1,624,900 B 2
Voyvodina (aut. prov.), 1,880,000 D 3

CITIES and TOWNS

Aleksinac, 8,828 E 4
Apatin, 17,000 D 3
Bačka Topola, 14,000 D 3
Bakar B 3
Banja Luka, 55,000 C 3
Bar, 2,184 D 4
Bečej, 22,000 E 3
Bela Crkva, 11,000 E 3
Belgrade (Beograd) (cap.), 745,000 E 3
Belgrade, *1,050,000 E 3
Bihać, 17,000 B 3
Bijeljina, 19,000 D 3
Bijelo Polje, 5,856 D 4
Bileća, 2,491 D 4
Biograd, 2,418 B 4
Bitola (Bitolj), 52,000 E 5
Bjelovar, 16,000 C 3
Bled, 4,156 A 2
Bor, 19,000 E 3
Bosanska Dubica, 6,259 C 3
Bosanska Gradiška, 6,363 C 3
Bosaska Kostajnica, 2,034 B 3
Bosanska Krupa, 6,191 C 3
Bosanski Brod, 7,350 D 3
Bosanski Novi, 7,023 C 3
Bosanski Petrovac, 3,473 C 3
Bosanski Šamac, 3,654 D 3
Brčko, 20,000 D 3
Brežice, 2,641 B 3
Brod, 30,000 D 3
Bugojno, 5,453 C 3
Buje, 1,955 A 3
Čačak, 30,000 F 4
Čapljina, 3,275 C 4
Caribrod (Dimitrovgrad), 3,665 F 4
Celje, 28,000 B 2
Cetinje, 9,359 D 4
Ćuprija, 12,000 E 4
Debar, 6,323 E 5
Derventa, 9,843 C 3
Dimitrovgrad, 3,665 F 4
Djakovica, 22,000 E 4
Djakovo, 13,000 D 3
Donji Vakuf, 3,764 C 3
Drvar, 3,646 C 3
Dubrovnik, 24,000 C 4
Fiume (Rijeka), 108,000 B 3
Foča, 6,763 D 4
Fojnica, 1,549 C 4
Gacko, 1,368 D 4
Gevgelija, 7,332 F 5
Glamoč, 1,626 C 3
Gnjilane, 14,000 E 4
Gornji Vafuf, 1,860 C 4
Gospić, 6,767 B 3
Gostivar, 14,000 E 5
Gračac, 2,183 B 3
Gračanica, 7,656 D 3
Gradačac, 5,878 D 3
Grubišno Polje, 2,655 C 3
Gusinje, 2,756 D 4
Hercegnovi, 3,797 D 4
Ivangrad, 6,969 E 4
Jajce, 6,853 C 3
Jesenice, 16,000 A 2
Kamnik, 5,062 B 2
Kanjiža, 10,000 D 2
Kardeljevo, 3,267 C 4
Karlovac, 35,000 B 3
Kavadarci, 13,000 E 5
Kičevo, 11,000 E 5
Kikinda, 32,000 E 3
Kladanj, 2,825 D 3
Ključ, 2,320 C 3
Knin, 5,116 C 3
Knjaževac, 7,448 F 4
Kočevje, 5,819 B 3
Konjic, 5,927 D 4
Koper, 12,000 A 3
Koprivnica, 12,000 C 2
Korčula, 2,458 C 4
Kosovska Mitrovica, 29,000 E 4
Kostajnica, 2,080 C 3
Kotor, 4,764 D 4
Kragujevac, 56,000 E 3
Kraljevo (Rankovičevo), 26,000 E 4
Kranj, 23,000 B 2
Križevci, 6,642 C 2
Krk, 1,280 B 3
Krško, 3,518 B 3
Kruševac, 31,000 E 4
Kumanovo, 33,000 E 4
Leskovac, 37,000 E 4
Livno, 5,181 C 4
Ljubljana, 183,000 B 3
Ljubuški, 2,168 C 4
Loznica, 12,000 D 3
Maglaj, 4,556 D 3
Makarska, 3,634 C 4
Maribor, 89,000 B 2
Mladenovac, 12,000 E 4
Modriča, 5,053 D 3
Mostar, 53,000 D 4
Našice, 4,187 C 3
Negotin, 8,635 F 3
Nevesinje, 2,349 D 4
Nikšić, 25,000 D 4
Niš, 92,000 F 4
Nova Gradiška, 9,229 C 3
Novi, 2,075 B 3
Novi Pazar, 23,000 E 4
Novi Sad, 119,000 D 3
Novo Mesto, 6,885 B 3
Novska, 3,844 C 3
Ogulin, 3,522 B 3
Ohrid, 18,000 E 5
Omiš, 2,171 C 4
Opatija, 7,974 A 3
Osijek, 78,000 D 3
Pag, 2,431 B 3
Pančevo, 49,000 E 3
Paraćin, 17,000 E 4
Peć, 30,000 E 4
Petrinja, 7,366 B 3
Piran, 5,474 A 3
Pirot, 20,000 F 4
Plav, 2,535 D 4
Pljevlja, 12,000 D 4
Podgorica (Titograd), 37,000 D 4
Pola (Pula), 40,000 A 3
Poreč, 3,006 A 3
Postojna, 4,857 B 3
Požarevac, 23,000 E 3
Požega, 14,000 C 3
Preševo, 5,680 E 4
Priboj, 5,490 D 4
Prijedor, 13,000 C 3
Prijepolje, 4,566 D 4
Prilep, 40,000 E 5
Priština, 43,000 E 4
Prizren, 29,000 E 4
Prokuplje, 15,000 E 4
Prozor, 1,052 C 4
Ptuj, 7,392 C 2
Pula, 40,000 A 3
Rab, 1,548 B 3
Rača, 1,351 E 3
Radeče, 1,500 B 2
Radoviš, 6,246 F 5
Ragusa (Dubrovnik), 24,000 C 4
Rankovičevo, 26,000 E 4
Raška, 2,278 E 4
Rijeka, 108,000 B 3
Rogatica, 3,040 D 4
Rovinj, 7,155 A 3
Ruma, 21,000 D 3
Šabac, 30,000 D 3
Sanski Most, 5,096 C 3
Sarajevo, 223,000 D 4
Senj, 3,903 B 3
Senta, 22,000 D 3
Šibenik, 27,000 C 4
Sinj, 4,134 C 4
Sisak, 29,000 C 3
Škofja Loka, 3,429 A 2
Skopje, 230,000 E 5
Skradin, 1,118 C 4
Smederevo, 29,000 E 3
Sombor, 31,000 D 3
Split, 106,000 C 4
Srebrenica, 1,859 D 3
Sremska Mitrovica, 22,000 D 3
Sremski Karlovci, 6,390 D 3
Stari Majdan, 1,445 C 3
Štip, 22,000 F 5
Stolac, 2,970 D 4
Struga, 6,857 E 5
Strumica, 17,000 F 5
Subotica, 76,000 D 2
Surdulica, 5,007 F 4
Svetozarevo, 22,000 E 4
Svilajnac, 5,895 E 3
Tešanj, 3,148 C 3
Tetovo, 27,000 E 5
Titograd, 37,000 D 4
Titovo Užice, 26,000 D 4
Titov Veles, 29,000 E 5
Travnik, 12,000 C 3
Trbovlje, 16,000 B 2
Trebinje, 4,073 D 4
Trogir, 5,003 C 4
Tržič, 4,881 B 2
Tuzla, 55,000 D 3
Ulcinj, 5,705 D 5
Valjevo, 27,000 D 3
Varaždin, 28,000 B 2
Vareš, 7,647 D 3
Veliki Bečkerek (Zrenjanin), 56,000 E 3
Vinkovci, 24,000 D 3
Virovitica, 10,000 C 3
Višegrad, 3,309 D 4
Vranje, 18,000 F 4
Vrbas, 19,000 D 3
Vršac, 32,000 E 3
Vukovar, 25,000 D 3
Žabari, 1,984 E 3
Zadar, 28,000 B 3
Zagreb, 503,000 C 3
Zaječar, 18,000 E 4
Zara (Zadar), 28,000 B 3
Zenica, 50,000 C 3
Žepče, 2,709 D 3
Zrenjanin, 56,000 E 3
Zvornik, 5,444 D 3

OTHER FEATURES

Adriatic (sea) B 4
Bobotov Kuk (mt.) D 4
Bosna (riv.) D 3
Brač (isl.), 14,227 C 4
Čazma (riv.) C 3
Cres (isl.), 4,949 B 3
Danube (riv.) E 3
Dinaric Alps (mts.) B 3
Drava (riv.) C 3
Drina (riv.) D 3
Dugi Otok (isl.), 4,873 B 3
Hvar (isl.), 12,147 C 4
Ibar (riv.) E 4
Kamenjak (cape) A 3
Korab (mt.) E 5
Korčula (isl.), 10,245 C 4
Kornat (isl.), 6 B 4
Krk (isl.), 14,548 B 3
Kvarner (gulf) B 3
Lastovo (Lagosta) (isl.), 1,449 C 4
Lim (riv.) D 4
Lošinj (isl.), 5,068 B 3
Mljet (isl.), 1,963 C 4
Morava (riv.) E 3
Mur (riv.) B 2
Neretva (riv.) D 4
Ohrid (lake) E 5
Pag (isl.), 8,017 B 3
Pelagruž (Pelagosa) (isl.) C 4
Prespa (lake) E 5
Rab (isl.), 8,400 B 3
Ruen (mt.) F 4
Sava (riv.) D 3
Scutari (lake) D 4
Solta (isl.), 2,735 C 4
Tara (riv.) D 4
Timok (riv.) F 3
Tisza (riv.) E 4
Triglav (mt.) A 2
Una (riv.) C 3
Vardar (riv.) E 5
Vis (isl.), 7,004 C 4
Vrbas (riv.) C 3
Žirje (isl.), 506 B 4

*City and suburbs.

THE BALKAN STATES

CONIC PROJECTION

SCALE OF MILES

0 25 50 75 100 125 150 175

SCALE OF KILOMETRES

0 25 50 75 100 125 150 175

Capitals of Countries _____ ☆
Administrative Centers _____ △
International Boundaries _____
Major Internal Boundaries _____
Minor Internal Boundaries _____
Canals _____

BULGARIA and GREECE are divided into counties and
departments, respectively. Because of the scale no
attempt has been made to delimit and name these subdivisions; their administrative centers have, however,
been designated.
 The larger divisions named in Greece are well-known
geographical regions, without administrative function.
 RUMANIA consists of thirty-nine counties and
three cities of regional status, Bucharest, Constanţa
and Petroşeni. Scale does not permit delimiting
these counties.
 ALBANIA is divided into twenty-seven districts. Scale
does not permit the delimitation of these divisions.
YUGOSLAVIA is a federation of six republics. The
Serbian republic includes an autonomous province
(Voyvodina), and an autonomous region (Kosovo-
Mitohiyan).

© C. S. HAMMOND & Co., N.Y.

Topography

0   50   100
MILES

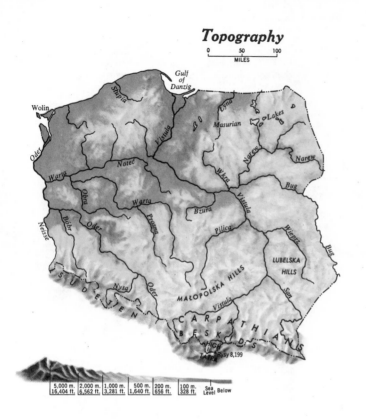

5,000 m. | 2,000 m. | 1,000 m. | 500 m. | 200 m. | 100 m. | Sea | Below
16,404 ft. | 6,562 ft. | 3,281 ft. | 1,640 ft. | 656 ft. | 328 ft. | Level

PROVINCES		
Biała Podlaska, 283,200	F 3
Białystok, 613,800	F 2
Bielsko, 765,500	D 4
Bydgoszcz, 982,100	C 2
Chełm, 221,000	F 3
Ciechanów, 398,500	E 2
Cracow, 1,097,600	E 4
Cracow (city), 651,300	E 4
Częstochowa, 723,200	D 3
Elbląg, 419,800	D 1
Gdańsk, 1,220,500	D 1
Gorzów, 428,700	B 2
Jelenia Góra, 483,400	B 3
Kalisz, 640,300	C 3
Katowice, 3,439,700	D 3
Kielce, 1,030,400	E 3
Konin, 423,700	D 2
Koszalin, 428,500	C 1
Krosno, 418,000	E 4
Legnica, 405,600	C 3
Leszno, 340,600	C 3
Łódź, 1,063,700	D 3
Łódź (city), 777,800	D 3
Łomża, 320,600	F 2
Lublin, 875,300	F 3

Nowy Sącz, 600,300	E 4
Olsztyn, 654,400	E 2
Opole, 961,600	C 3
Ostrołęka, 360,700	E 2
Piła, 414,000	C 2
Piotrków, 581,900	D 3
Płock, 479,700	D 2
Poznań, 1,156,500	C 2
Przemyśl, 373,100	F 4
Radom, 674,400	E 3
Rzeszów, 602,200	F 4
Siedlce, 602,100	F 2
Sieradz, 388,000	D 3
Skierniewice, 388,300	E 3
Słupsk, 352,900	C 1
Suwałki, 412,700	F 1
Szczecin, 841,400	B 2
Tarnobrzeg, 532,200	E 3
Tarnów, 573,900	E 4
Toruń, 580,500	D 2
Wałbrzych, 709,600	C 3
Warsaw, 2,117,700	E 2
Warsaw (city), 1,377,100	E 2
Włocławek, 402,000	D 2
Wrocław, 1,014,600	C 3
Zamość, 472,300	F 3
Zielona Góra, 575,000	B 3

CITIES and TOWNS	
Aleksandrów Łódzki, 14,800	D
Andrespol, 12,500	D
Andrychów, 14,300	D
Augustów, 20,200	F
Bartoszyce, 15,700	E
Będzin, 42,500	D
Bełchatów, 9,230	F
Bełżyce, 5,333	F
Biała Podlaska, 26,700	F
Białogard, 20,800	C
Białystok, 182,300	F
Bielawa, 31,300	C
Bielsk Podlaski, 14,600	F
Bielsko-Biała, 114,200	D
Biłgoraj, 13,600	F
Błonie, 12,500	E
Bochnia, 15,000	E
Bogatynia, 12,300	B
Boguszów-Gorce, 11,900	B
Bolesławiec, 31,400	B
Braniewo, 12,400	D
Brodnica, 17,700	D
Brzeg, 31,500	C
Brzeg Dolny, 10,900	C
Brzesko, 10,800	E

POLAND 1938

0   50   100
MILES

POLAND 1945

0   50   100
MILES

Agriculture, Industry and Resources

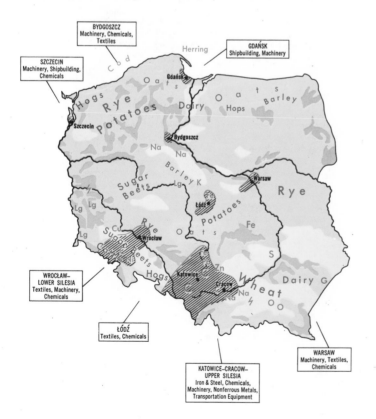

SZCZECIN
Machinery, Shipbuilding, Chemicals

BYDGOSZCZ
Machinery, Chemicals, Textiles

GDAŃSK
Shipbuilding, Machinery

WROCŁAW–
LOWER SILESIA
Textiles, Machinery, Chemicals

ŁÓDŹ
Textiles, Chemicals

KATOWICE–CRACOW–
UPPER SILESIA
Iron & Steel, Chemicals, Machinery, Nonferrous Metals, Transportation Equipment

WARSAW
Machinery, Textiles, Chemicals

DOMINANT LAND USE

- Cereals (chiefly wheat)
- Rye, Oats, Barley, Potatoes
- General Farming, Livestock
- Forests

MAJOR MINERAL OCCURRENCES

C	Coal	Na	Salt
Cu	Copper	Ni	Nickel
Fe	Iron Ore	O	Petroleum
G	Natural Gas	Pb	Lead
K	Potash	S	Sulfur
Lg	Lignite	Zn	Zinc

⚡ Water Power

▨ Major Industrial Areas

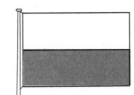

AREA 120,725 sq. mi.
POPULATION 34,364,000
CAPITAL Warsaw
LARGEST CITY Warsaw
HIGHEST POINT Rysy 8,199 ft.
MONETARY UNIT zloty
MAJOR LANGUAGE Polish
MAJOR RELIGION Roman Catholicism

...rozów, 8,591 F 4
...sko-Zdrój, 11,400 E 3
...dgoszcz, 305,500 C 2
...tom, 192,000 A 3
...tów, 10,900 F 3
...heim, 40,000 D 2
...helmno, 18,500 D 2
...helmża, 14,500 C 2
...nojnice, 24,000 C 2
...11,100 B 4
...oszcz, 154,300 B 4
...noszczno, 10,200 B 3
...echanów, 23,500 E 2
...eplice Śląskie-Zdrój, 15,600 B 3
...eszyn, 25,600 D 4
...racow (Kraków), 651,300 E 4
...echowice-Dziedzice, 25,700 D 4
...eladź, 32,700 B 4
...zerwionka, 10,600 A 4
...zęstochowa, 193,400 D 3
...abrowa Górnicza, 62,400 D 3
...abrowa Tarnowska, 9,703 E 4
...arłowo, 11,500 C 1
...ębica, 23,600 E 3
...eblin, 14,900 E 3
...enno, 11,000 D 2
...ziałdowo, 10,500 E 2
...zierżoniów, 33,400 C 3
...lbląg, 91,400 D 1
...k, 27,900 F 2
...gdańsk, 394,000 D 1
...ydnia, 207,600 D 1
...życho, 18,500 F 2
...liwice, 178,300 A 4
...ogów, 22,700 C 3
...łowno, 13,200 D 2
...łubczyce, 11,500 C 3
...łuchołazy, 13,400 C 3
...niezno, 51,300 C 2
...ołdap, 8,886 F 1
...oleniów, 15,000 B 2
...óra, 9,905 C 3
...orlice, 16,600 E 4
...orzów Wielkopolski, 76,200 B 2
...ostyń, 19,800 C 2
...ostynin, 12,200 D 2
...rajewo, 11,400 F 2
...rodzisk, 11,400 C 2
...rodzisk Mazowiecki, 21,000 E 2
...rójec, 10,400 E 3
...rudziądz, 76,600 D 2
...ryfice, 13,600 B 2
...ryfino, 7,446 B 2
...ubin, 15,000 C 3
...ajnówka, 14,600 F 2
...rubieszów, 15,500 F 3
...ława, 17,100 C 3
...lża, 4,419 E 3
...nowrocław, 55,900 D 2
...anów Lubelski, 5,944 F 3
...arocin, 18,300 C 2
...arosław, 29,500 F 4
...asło, 17,800 E 4
...astrzębie-Zdrój, 34,400 D 4
...awor, 15,700 C 3

Jaworzno, 64,500 B 4
Jędrzejów, 13,700 E 3
Jelenia Góra, 56,200 B 3
Kalisz, 82,400 D 3
Kamienna Góra, 21,200 B 3
Kamień Pomorski, 8,725 B 1
Kartuzy, 10,800 C 1
Katowice, 317,700 B 4
Kazimierza Wielka, 8,571 E 3
Kędzierzyn, 34,200 D 3
Kępno, 10,300 C 3
Kętrzyn, 19,600 E 1
Kęty, 12,000 D 4
Kielce, 138,700 E 3
Kłobuck, 12,500 D 3
Kłodzko, 26,300 C 3
Kluczbork, 18,200 D 3
Knurów, 30,600 A 4
Koło, 7,980 D 2
Kołobrzeg, 26,600 B 1
Końskie, 13,700 E 3
Konin, 42,800 D 2
Konstantynów Łódzki, 13,000 D 3
Kościan, 19,000 C 2
Kościerzyna, 15,500 C 1
Kostrzyn, 11,700 B 2
Koszalin, 66,800 C 1
Kowary, 11,400 B 3
Koźle, 13,300 D 3
Krapkowice, 14,200 D 3
Kraśnik, 14,700 F 3
Kraśnik Fabryczny, 13,800 F 3
Krasnystaw, 12,700 F 3
Krosno, 27,200 E 4
Krotoszyn, 22,200 C 3
Krynica, 10,400 E 4
Kutno, 33,900 D 2
Kwidzyn, 23,400 D 2
Łańcut, 12,300 F 4
Łaziska Górne, 10,900 A 4
Łębork, 25,300 C 1
Łęczyca, 13,900 D 2
Lędziny, 12,800 B 4
Legionowo, 21,000 E 2
Legnica, 76,800 C 3
Leszczyny, 12,100 A 4
Leszno, 34,600 C 3
Leżajsk, 9,647 F 4
Libiąż, 10,700 D 4
Lidzbark Warmiński, 13,200 E 1
Lipno, 11,100 D 2
Łobez, 10,300 B 2
Łódź, 777,800 D 3
Łomża, 26,400 F 2
Łosice, 4,197 F 2
Łowicz, 21,100 D 2
Lubaczów, 8,298 F 4
Lubań, 17,500 B 3
Lubartów, 10,300 F 3
Lubin, 31,900 C 3
Lublin, 254,700 F 3
Lubliniec, 20,100 D 3
Luboń, 20,100 C 2
Łuków, 16,300 F 3
Lubsko, 13,800 B 2
Maków Mazowiecki, 7,694 E 2

Międzyrzec Podlaski, 13,800 F 3
Międzyrzecz, 15,200 B 2
Mielec, 27,700 E 3
Mikołów, 21,800 B 4
Mińsk Mazowiecki, 24,900 E 2
Mława, 20,600 E 2
Mońki, 9,560 F 2
Morąg, 9,681 D 1
Mrągowo, 13,700 E 2
Myślenice, 12,400 E 4
Mysłowice, 45,100 B 4
Myszków, 18,300 D 3
Nakło nad Notecią, 17,000 C 2
Namysłów, 11,200 C 3
Nidzica, 10,200 E 2
Nisko, 10,200 F 3
Nowa Ruda, 18,300 C 3
Nowa Sól, 34,000 B 3
Nowy Dwór Gdański, 7,146 D 1
Nowy Dwór Mazowiecki, 17,200 E 2
Nowy Sącz, 42,100 E 4
Nowy Targ, 22,600 E 4
Nysa, 33,100 C 3
Oborniki, 10,300 C 2
Oława, 18,500 C 2
Olecko, 9,510 F 1
Oleśnica, 28,100 C 3
Olkusz, 16,500 D 3
Olsztyn, 104,300 E 2
Opatów, 9,784 E 3
Opoczno, 12,400 E 3
Opole, 87,800 D 3
Ostróda, 21,600 E 2
Ostrołęka, 23,000 E 2
Ostrów Mazowiecka, 15,200 F 2
Ostrów Wielkopolski, 50,300 C 3
Ostrowiec Świętokrzyski, 51,400 E 3
Oświęcim, 40,200 D 3
Otwock, 40,200 E 2
Ozorków, 18,400 D 3
Pabianice, 63,500 D 3
Parczew, 6,952 F 3
Pasłęk, 8,030 D 1
Piaseczno, 20,500 E 2

Piekary Śląskie, 36,600 B 3
Piła, 44,500 C 2
Pińczów, 7,080 E 3
Pionki, 14,000 E 3
Piotrków Trybunalski, 60,800 D 3
Pisz, 11,400 F 2
Pleszew, 13,700 C 3
Płock, 74,100 D 2
Płońsk, 11,900 E 2
Police, 13,200 B 2
Polkowice, 10,600 C 3
Poznań, 495,200 C 2
Prudnik, 20,400 C 3
Pruszcz Gdański, 13,100 D 1
Pruszków, 43,500 E 2
Przasnysz, 11,400 E 2
Przemyśl, 53,800 F 4
Puławy, 36,400 F 3
Pułtusk, 12,800 E 2
Pyskowice, 23,300 A 4
Rabka, 10,800 D 4
Racibórz, 40,600 C 3
Radom, 166,000 E 3
Radomsko, 34,800 D 3
Radziejów, 4,165 D 2
Radzionków, 28,200 A 3
Rawicz, 14,300 C 3
Ruda Śląska, 146,200 A 4
Rumia, 23,800 D 1
Rybnik, 44,000 D 3
Rydułtowy, 19,500 D 3
Rypin, 10,200 D 2
Rzeszów, 83,900 F 4
Sandomierz, 17,300 E 3
Sanok, 22,100 F 4
Siedlce, 39,600 F 2
Siemianowice Śląskie, 67,800 A 4
Sieradz, 19,000 D 3
Sierpc, 12,900 D 2
Skarżysko-Kamienna, 39,700 E 3
Skawina, 16,300 D 4
Skierniewice, 25,800 E 2
Sławno, 10,900 C 1
Słubice, 12,200 B 2

Słupca, 8,634 D 2
Słupsk, 69,900 C 1
Sochaczew, 21,000 E 2
Sokółka, 10,300 F 2
Sokołów Podlaski, 9,569 F 2
Solec Kujawski, 10,800 D 2
Sopot, 48,500 D 1
Sosnowiec, 148,300 B 4
Śrem, 16,400 C 2
Środa Wielkopolska, 15,000 C 2
Stalowa Wola, 31,100 F 3
Starachowice, 43,700 E 3
Stargard Szczeciński, 45,600 B 2
Starogard Gdański, 34,200 D 1
Staszów, 8,449 E 3
Strzegom, 14,400 C 3
Strzelce Opolskie, 15,000 D 3
Strzemieszyce Wielkie, 11,500 B 3
Sulechów, 10,500 B 2
Suwałki, 26,500 F 1
Swarzędz, 12,200 C 2
Świdnica, 48,200 C 3
Świdnik, 23,100 F 3
Świdwin, 12,600 B 2
Świebodzice, 18,200 C 3
Świebodzin, 15,200 B 2
Świecie, 18,300 D 2
Świętochłowice, 57,200 A 4
Świnoujście, 28,800 A 1
Szamotuły, 14,400 C 2
Szczecin, 355,600 B 2
Szczecinek, 29,500 C 2
Szczytno, 17,900 E 2
Szprotawa, 11,500 B 3
Szydłowiec, 6,240 E 3
Tarnobrzeg, 19,700 F 3
Tarnów, 87,200 E 4
Tarnowskie Góry, 35,000 A 3
Tczew, 42,100 D 1
Tomaszów Lubelski, 12,800 F 3
Tomaszów Mazowiecki, 55,600 E 3
Toruń, 139,000 D 2
Trzcianka, 11,200 C 2
Trzebinia-Siersza, 19,600 C 4

Tuchola, 9,439 D 2
Turek, 18,700 D 2
Tychy, 72,800 B 4
Ursus, 30,900 E 2
Wabrzeźno, 11,900 D 2
Wadowice, 12,000 D 4
Wągrowiec, 16,000 C 2
Wałbrzych, 127,400 C 3
Wałcz, 19,200 C 2
Warszawa (Warsaw) (cap.), 1,377,100 E 2
Węgorzewo, 8,522 E 1
Wejherowo, 34,600 C 1
Wieliczka, 14,000 E 3
Wieluń, 14,900 D 3
Wieruszów, 3,650 D 3
Więcbork, 5,910 C 2 (Włocławek, 7,354 D 2)
Wodzisław Śląski, 27,500 D 4
Wołomin, 24,100 E 2
Wołów, 10,100 C 3
Wrocław, 557,200 C 3
Września, 18,400 C 2
Wschowa, 10,100 C 3
Wysokie Mazowieckie, 5,296 F 2
Wyszków, 16,200 E 2
Ząbki, 16,200 E 2
Ząbkowice Śląskie, 14,400 C 3
Zabrze, 200,700 A 4
Zagań, 21,700 B 3
Zagórze, 13,000 B 4
Zakopane, 27,200 E 4
Zambrów, 14,500 F 2
Zamość, 35,600 F 3
Zawiercie, 39,800 D 3
Zduńska Wola, 29,500 D 3
Zgierz, 44,100 D 2
Zgorzelec, 28,600 B 3
Zielona Góra, 75,000 B 3
Złotoryja, 10,400 C 3
Złotów, 12,400 C 2
Złotów, 12,100 C 2
Zwoleń, 5,216 E 3

Żyrardów, 33,300 E 2
Żywiec, 22,900 D 4

OTHER FEATURES

Baltic (sea) B 1
Beskids (mts.) D 4
Brda (river) C 2
Brynica (river) B 3
Bug (river) F 2
Danzig (gulf) D 1
Dukla (pass) E 4
Dunajec (river) E 4
Gwda (river) C 2
Hel (pen.) D 1
High Tatra (mts.) D 4
Kłodnica (river) A 4
Łyna (river) E 1
Mamry (lake) F 1
Masurian (lakes) E 2
Narew (river) E 2
Neisse (river) B 3
Noteć (river) B 2
Nysa Kłodzka (river) C 3
Nysa Łużycka (Neisse) (riv.) B 3
Oder (Odra) (river) C 1
Orava (river) D 4
Pilica (river) D 3
Pomeranian (bay) A 1
Prosna (river) C 3
Przemsza (river) B 4
Rysy (mt.) D 4
San (river) F 3
Słupia (river) C 1
Śniardwy (lake) E 2
Sudeten (mts.) B 3
Uznam (Usedom) (isl.) B 1
Vistula (river) D 1
Warmia (reg.) D 1
Warta (river) D 2
Wieprz (river) F 3
Wisła (Vistula) (river) D 1
Wkra (river) E 2
Wolin (isl.) B 2

POLAND
CONIC PROJECTION
SCALE OF MILES
0 10 20 40 60 80
SCALE OF KILOMETERS
0 10 20 40 60 80

Capitals of Countries............★
Other Capitals....................◉
International Boundaries..........
Internal Boundaries..............
Canals...........................

Poland is divided into 49 provinces (bearing the same name as their capitals) and the autonomous cities of Warsaw, Łódź and Cracow.

UNION REPUBLICS

Armenian S.S.R., 2,491,900 ...... E 6
Azerbaidzhan S.S.R.,
  5,117,100 .... E 5
Estonian S.S.R., 1,356,100 .... C 4
Georgian S.S.R., 4,686,000 .... D 5
Kazakh S.S.R., 12,849,000 .... G 5
Kirgiz S.S.R., 2,932,800 .... H 5
Latvian S.S.R., 2,364,100 .... C 4
Lithuanian S.S.R.,
  3,128,000 .... C 4
Moldavian S.S.R., 3,568,900 ...... C 5
Russian S.F.S.R.,
  130,079,210 .... E 4
Tadzhik S.S.R., 2,900,000 .... H 6
Turkmen S.S.R., 2,158,880 .... F 6
Ukrainian S.S.R.,
  47,126,517 .... D 5
Uzbek S.S.R., 11,960,000 .... G 5
White Russian S.S.R.,
  9,002,338 .... C 4

INTERNAL DIVISIONS

Abkhaz A.S.S.R., 487,000 .... E 5
Adygey Aut. Oblast,
  385,000 .... D 5
Adzhar A.S.S.R., 310,000 .... E 5
Aginsk-Buryat Nat'l Okrug,
  66,000 .... L 4
Bashkir A.S.S.R., 3,818,000 ...... F 4
Buryat A.S.S.R., 812,000 .... M 4
Chechen-Ingush A.S.S.R.,
  1,065,000 .... E 5

Chukchi Nat'l Okrug,
  101,000 .... R 3
Chuvash A.S.S.R.,
  1,224,000 .... F 4
Dagestan A.S.S.R.,
  1,429,000 .... E 5
Evenki Nat'l Okrug,
  13,000 .... K 3
Gorno-Altay Aut. Oblast,
  168,000 .... J 4
Gorno-Badakhshan Aut. Oblast,
  98,000 .... J 6
Jewish Aut. Oblast,
  172,000 .... O 5
Kabardin-Balkar A.S.S.R.,
  588,000 .... E 5
Kalmuck A.S.S.R.,
  268,000 .... E 5
Karachay-Cherkess Aut. Oblast,
  345,000 .... E 5
Karakalpak A.S.S.R.,
  702,000 .... G 5
Karelian A.S.S.R.,
  713,000 .... D 3
Khakass Aut. Oblast,
  446,000 .... J 4
Khanty-Mansi Nat'l Okrug,
  271,000 .... H 3
Komi A.S.S.R., 965,000 .... F 3
Komi-Permyak Nat'l Okrug,
  212,000 .... F 4
Koryak Nat'l Okrug,
  31,000 .... R 3
Mari A.S.S.R., 685,000 .... F 4
Mordvinian A.S.S.R.,
  1,029,000 .... E 4

Nagorno-Karabakh Aut. Oblast,
  150,000 .... E 5
Nakhichevan' A.S.S.R.,
  202,000 .... E 6
Nenets Nat'l Okrug, 39,000 .... F 3
North Ossetian A.S.S.R.,
  552,000 .... E 5
South Ossetian Aut. Oblast,
  99,000 .... E 5
Tatar A.S.S.R., 3,131,000 .... F 4
Taymyr Nat'l Okrug, 38,000 .... K 2
Tuvinian A.S.S.R., 231,000 .... K 4
Udmurt A.S.S.R., 1,418,000 .... F 4
Ust'-Ordynsk-Buryat Nat'l Okrug,
  146,000 .... L 4
Yakut A.S.S.R., 664,000 .... N 3
Yamal-Nenets Nat'l Okrug,
  80,000 .... H 3

CITIES and TOWNS

Abakan, 90,000 .... J 4
Achinsk, 97,000 .... K 4
Adimi .... O 5
Aginskoye, 9,000 .... M 4
Akmolinsk (Tselinograd),
  180,000 .... H 4
Aktyubinsk, 150,000 .... F 4
Aldan, 19,000 .... N 4
Aleksandrovsk-Sakhalinskiy,
  22,000 .... P 5
Aleysk, 32,000 .... J 4
Alga, 17,000 .... F 4
Allakh-Yun' .... O 3
Alma-Ata, 730,000 .... H 5

Ambarchik .... R 3
Amderma .... F 3
Amursk, 15,000 .... O 5
Anadyr', 8,000 .... S 3
Andizhan, 188,000 .... H 5
Angarsk, 203,000 .... L 4
Anzhero-Sudzhensk,
  106,000 .... J 4
Aral'sk, 26,000 .... G 5
Archangel, 343,000 .... E 3
Akalyk, 15,000 .... G 4
Armavir, 145,000 .... E 5
Artem, 61,000 .... O 5
Artemovskiy .... M 4
Arzamas, 67,000 .... E 4
Ashkhabad, 253,000 .... F 6
Ashkhabad, 256,000 .... F 6
Asino, 30,000 .... J 4
Astrakhan', 410,000 .... E 5
Atbasar, 41,000 .... H 4
Atka .... Q 3
Ayaguz, 40,000 .... J 5
Ayan .... O 4
Aykhal .... M 3
Bagdarin .... M 4
Baku, 852,000 .... F 5
Baku, *1,266,000 .... F 5
Balashov, 83,000 .... E 4
Balkhash, 76,000 .... H 5
Balturino, 10,000 .... H 4
Barabinsk, 40,000 .... H 4
Baranovichi, 101,000 .... C 4
Barnaul, 439,000 .... J 4
Batumi, 101,000 .... E 5
Baykit .... K 3
Baykonur .... G 4

Bayram-Ali, 33,000 .... G 6
Belgorod, 151,000 .... D 4
Belogorsk, 57,000 .... N 4
Belomorsk, 18,000 .... D 3
Beloretsk, 67,000 .... F 4
Belovo, 108,000 .... J 4
Berdichev, 71,000 .... C 5
Berdsk, 53,000 .... J 4
Berezniki, 146,000 .... F 4
Berezovo, 6,000 .... G 3
Beringovskiy .... T 3
Bilibino, 13,000 .... R 3
Birobidzhan, 56,000 .... O 5
Biysk, 186,000 .... J 4
Blagoveshchensk,
  128,000 .... N 4
Bobruysk, 138,000 .... C 4
Bodaybo, 19,000 .... M 4
Borisoglebsk, 64,000 .... E 4
Borzya, 28,000 .... M 4
Boshchakul' .... H 4
Bratsk, 155,000 .... L 4
Brest, 122,000 .... C 4
Bryansk, 318,000 .... D 4
Bugul'ma, 72,000 .... F 4
Bukhara, 112,000 .... G 5
Bulun .... N 2
Buzuluk, 67,000 .... F 4
Chagda .... N 4
Chapayevo .... J 5
Chapayevsk, 86,000 .... F 4
Chardzhou, 96,000 .... G 6
Cheboksary, 216,000 .... E 4
Chelkar, 25,000 .... F 5
Chelyabinsk,
  875,000 .... G 4

Cheremkhovo, 99,000 .... L 4
Cherepovets, 188,000 .... D 4
Cherkessk, 67,000 .... E 5
Chernigov, 159,000 .... D 4
Chernovtsy, 159,000 .... C 5
Chernyshevsk, 187,000 .... M 4
Chernyshevskiy,
  10,000 .... M 3
Cherskiy .... R 3
Chimbay, 20,000 .... G 5
Chimkent, 247,000 .... H 5
Chirchik, 107,000 .... H 5
Chita, 241,000 .... M 4
Chokurdakh .... P 2
Chul'man .... N 4
Chumikan .... O 4
Dalnegorsk, 33,500 .... O 5
Dalnerechensk, 30,000 .... O 5
Daugavpils, 100,400 .... C 4
Dikson .... J 2
Dimitrovgrad, 81,000 .... F 4
Dnepropetrovsk,
  862,000 .... D 5
Dolinsk, 18,000 .... P 5
Donetsk, 879,000 .... D 5
Drogobych, 56,000 .... C 5
Druzhina .... P 3
Dudinka, 22,000 .... J 3
Dushanbe, 376,000 .... H 6
Dzerzhinsk, 221,000 .... E 4
Dzhalal-Abad, 44,000 .... H 5
Dzhalinda .... N 4
Dzhambul, 187,000 .... H 5
Dzhetygara, 39,000 .... G 4
Dzhezkazgan, 62,000 .... G 5

Ekibastuz, 46,000 .... H 4
Ekimchan .... N 4
El'dikan .... O 3
Elista, 50,000 .... E 5
Engel's, 130,000 .... F 4
Erivan, 767,000 .... E 5
Evensk .... Q 3
Fergana, 111,000 .... H 5
Fort-Shevchenko,
  12,000 .... F 5
Frolovo, 30,000 .... E 5
Frunze, 430,600 .... H 5
Gasan-Kuli .... F 6
Gizhiga .... Q 3
Gol'chikha .... J 2
Gomel', 272,000 .... D 4
Gor'kiy, 1,170,000 .... E 4
Gorno-Altaysk,
  34,000 .... J 4
Grodno, 132,000 .... C 4
Groznyy, 341,000 .... E 5
Gubakha, 40,000 .... F 4
Gulistan, 31,000 .... H 5
Gur'yev, 114,000 .... F 5
Gusinoozersk, 10,000 .... L 4
Gydy .... J 2
Igarka, 22,000 .... J 3
Ilanskiy, 24,000 .... K 4
Iliysk, 17,000 .... H 5
Indiga .... E 3
Inta, 50,000 .... G 3
Iolotan', 10,000 .... G 6
Irkutsk, 451,000 .... L 4
Ishim, 56,000 .... G 4
Ishimbay, 54,000 .... F 4
Isil'-Kul', 26,000 .... H 4
Ivano-Frankovsk, 105,000 .... C 5

AREA 8,649,498 sq. mi.
POPULATION 241,748,000
CAPITAL Moscow
LARGEST CITY Moscow
HIGHEST POINT Communism Peak 24,590 ft.
MONETARY UNIT ruble
MAJOR LANGUAGES Russian, Ukrainian, White Russian, Uzbek, Azerbaidzhani, Tatar, Georgian, Lithuanian, Armenian, Yiddish, Latvian, Mordvinian, Kirghiz, Tadzhik, Estonian, Kazakh, Moldavian, German, Chuvash, Turkmenian, Bashkir
MAJOR RELIGIONS Eastern (Russian) Orthodoxy, Islam, Judaism, Protestantism (Baltic States)

UNION REPUBLICS

	AREA (sq. mi.)	POPULATION	CAPITAL and LARGEST CITY
RUSSIAN S.F.S.R.	6,592,819	130,079,210	Moscow 6,942,000
KAZAKH S.S.R.	1,048,301	12,849,000	Alma-Ata 730,000
UKRAINIAN S.S.R.	232,046	47,126,517	Kiev 1,632,000
TURKMEN S.S.R.	188,456	2,158,880	Ashkhabad 253,000
UZBEK S.S.R.	173,591	11,960,000	Tashkent 1,385,000
WHITE RUSSIAN S.S.R.	80,154	9,002,338	Minsk 907,000
KIRGIZ S.S.R.	76,641	2,932,800	Frunze 430,600
TADZHIK S.S.R.	55,251	2,900,000	Dushanbe 376,000
AZERBAIDZHAN S.S.R.	33,436	5,117,100	Baku 852,000
GEORGIAN S.S.R.	26,911	4,686,000	Tbilisi 889,000
LITHUANIAN S.S.R.	25,174	3,128,000	Vilna 371,700
LATVIAN S.S.R.	24,595	2,364,100	Riga 731,800
ESTONIAN S.S.R.	17,413	1,356,100	Tallinn 362,706
MOLDAVIAN S.S.R.	13,012	3,568,900	Kishinev 356,900
ARMENIAN S.S.R.	11,500	2,491,900	Erivan 767,000

Topography

(continued on following page)

U.S.S.R. (continued)

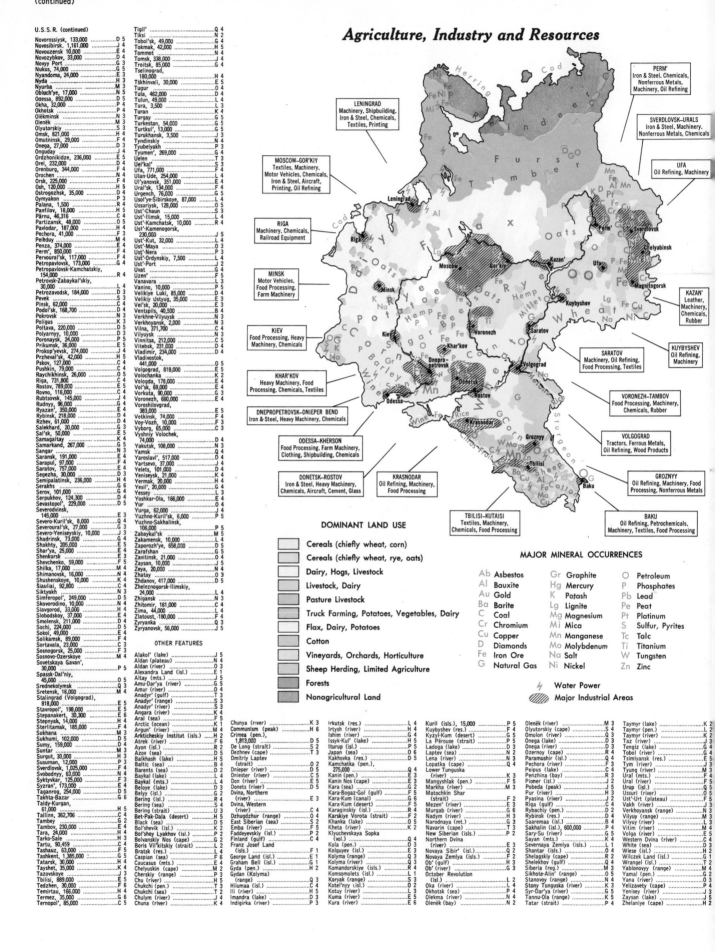

Agriculture, Industry and Resources

PERM'
Iron & Steel, Chemicals, Nonferrous Metals, Machinery, Oil Refining

SVERDLOVSK–URALS
Iron & Steel, Machinery, Nonferrous Metals, Chemicals

UFA
Oil Refining, Machinery

LENINGRAD
Machinery, Shipbuilding, Iron & Steel, Chemicals, Textiles, Printing

MOSCOW–GOR'KIY
Textiles, Machinery, Motor Vehicles, Iron & Steel, Aircraft, Printing, Oil Refining

RIGA
Machinery, Chemicals, Railroad Equipment

MINSK
Motor Vehicles, Food Processing, Farm Machinery

KIEV
Food Processing, Heavy Machinery, Chemicals

KHAR'KOV
Heavy Machinery, Food Processing, Chemicals, Textiles

DNEPROPETROVSK–DNIEPER BEND
Iron & Steel, Heavy Machinery, Chemicals

ODESSA–KHERSON
Food Processing, Farm Machinery, Clothing, Shipbuilding, Chemicals

DONETSK–ROSTOV
Iron & Steel, Heavy Machinery, Chemicals, Aircraft, Cement, Glass

KRASNODAR
Oil Refining, Machinery, Food Processing

TBILISI–KUTAISI
Textiles, Machinery, Chemicals, Food Processing

KAZAN'
Leather, Machinery, Chemicals, Rubber

SARATOV
Machinery, Oil Refining, Food Processing, Textiles

KUYBYSHEV
Oil Refining, Machinery

VORONEZH–TAMBOV
Food Processing, Machinery, Chemicals, Rubber

VOLGOGRAD
Tractors, Ferrous Metals, Oil Refining, Wood Products

GROZNYY
Oil Refining, Machinery, Food Processing, Nonferrous Metals

BAKU
Oil Refining, Petrochemicals, Machinery, Textiles, Food Processing

DOMINANT LAND USE

- Cereals (chiefly wheat, corn)
- Cereals (chiefly wheat, rye, oats)
- Dairy, Hogs, Livestock
- Livestock, Dairy
- Pasture Livestock
- Truck Farming, Potatoes, Vegetables, Dairy
- Flax, Dairy, Potatoes
- Cotton
- Vineyards, Orchards, Horticulture
- Sheep Herding, Limited Agriculture
- Forests
- Nonagricultural Land

MAJOR MINERAL OCCURRENCES

Ab	Asbestos	Gr	Graphite	O	Petroleum
Al	Bauxite	Hg	Mercury	P	Phosphates
Au	Gold	K	Potash	Pb	Lead
Ba	Barite	Lg	Lignite	Pe	Peat
C	Coal	Mg	Magnesium	Pt	Platinum
Cr	Chromium	Mi	Mica	S	Sulfur, Pyrites
Cu	Copper	Mn	Manganese	Tc	Talc
D	Diamonds	Mo	Molybdenum	Ti	Titanium
Fe	Iron Ore	Na	Salt	W	Tungsten
G	Natural Gas	Ni	Nickel	Zn	Zinc

⚡ Water Power
▨ Major Industrial Areas

Agriculture, Industry and Resources

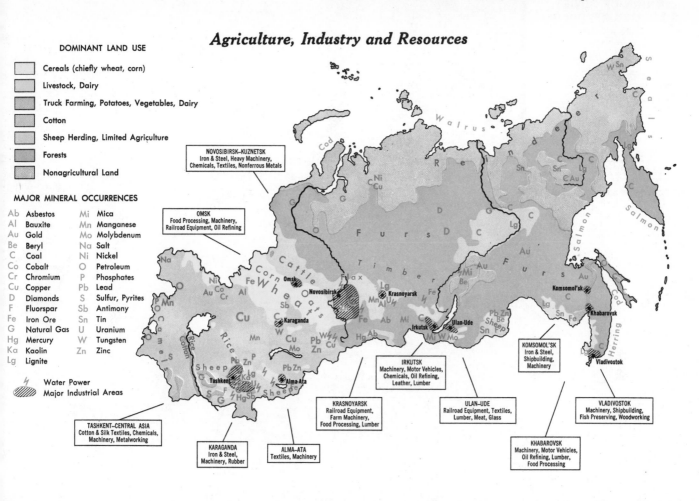

DOMINANT LAND USE

- Cereals (chiefly wheat, corn)
- Livestock, Dairy
- Truck Farming, Potatoes, Vegetables, Dairy
- Cotton
- Sheep Herding, Limited Agriculture
- Forests
- Nonagricultural Land

MAJOR MINERAL OCCURRENCES

Ab	Asbestos	Mi	Mica
Al	Bauxite	Mn	Manganese
Au	Gold	Mo	Molybdenum
Be	Beryl	Na	Salt
C	Coal	Ni	Nickel
Co	Cobalt	O	Petroleum
Cr	Chromium	P	Phosphates
Cu	Copper	Pb	Lead
D	Diamonds	S	Sulfur, Pyrites
F	Fluorspar	Sb	Antimony
Fe	Iron Ore	Sn	Tin
G	Natural Gas	U	Uranium
Hg	Mercury	W	Tungsten
Ka	Kaolin	Zn	Zinc
Lg	Lignite		

⚡ Water Power
▨ Major Industrial Areas

NOVOSIBIRSK–KUZNETSK
Iron & Steel, Heavy Machinery,
Chemicals, Textiles, Nonferrous Metals

OMSK
Food Processing, Machinery,
Railroad Equipment, Oil Refining

KOMSOMOL'SK
Iron & Steel,
Shipbuilding,
Machinery

IRKUTSK
Machinery, Motor Vehicles,
Chemicals, Oil Refining,
Leather, Lumber

ULAN–UDE
Railroad Equipment, Textiles,
Lumber, Meat, Glass

VLADIVOSTOK
Machinery, Shipbuilding,
Fish Preserving, Woodworking

KRASNOYARSK
Railroad Equipment,
Farm Machinery,
Food Processing, Lumber

KHABAROVSK
Machinery, Motor Vehicles,
Oil Refining, Lumber,
Food Processing

TASHKENT–CENTRAL ASIA
Cotton & Silk Textiles, Chemicals,
Machinery, Metalworking

KARAGANDA
Iron & Steel,
Machinery, Rubber

ALMA–ATA
Textiles, Machinery

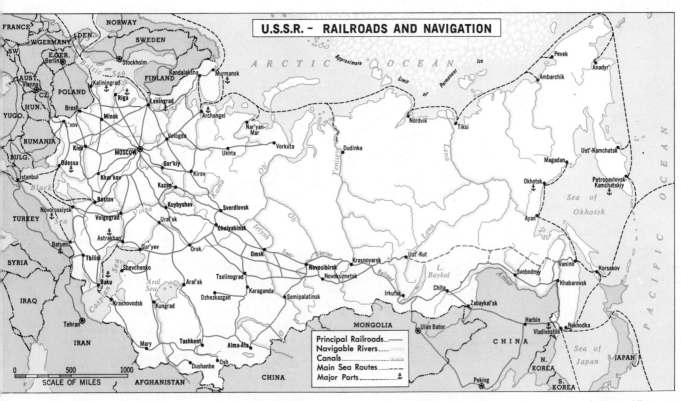

U.S.S.R. - RAILROADS AND NAVIGATION

Principal Railroads
Navigable Rivers
Canals
Main Sea Routes
⚓ Major Ports

0   500   1000
SCALE OF MILES

(continued on following page)

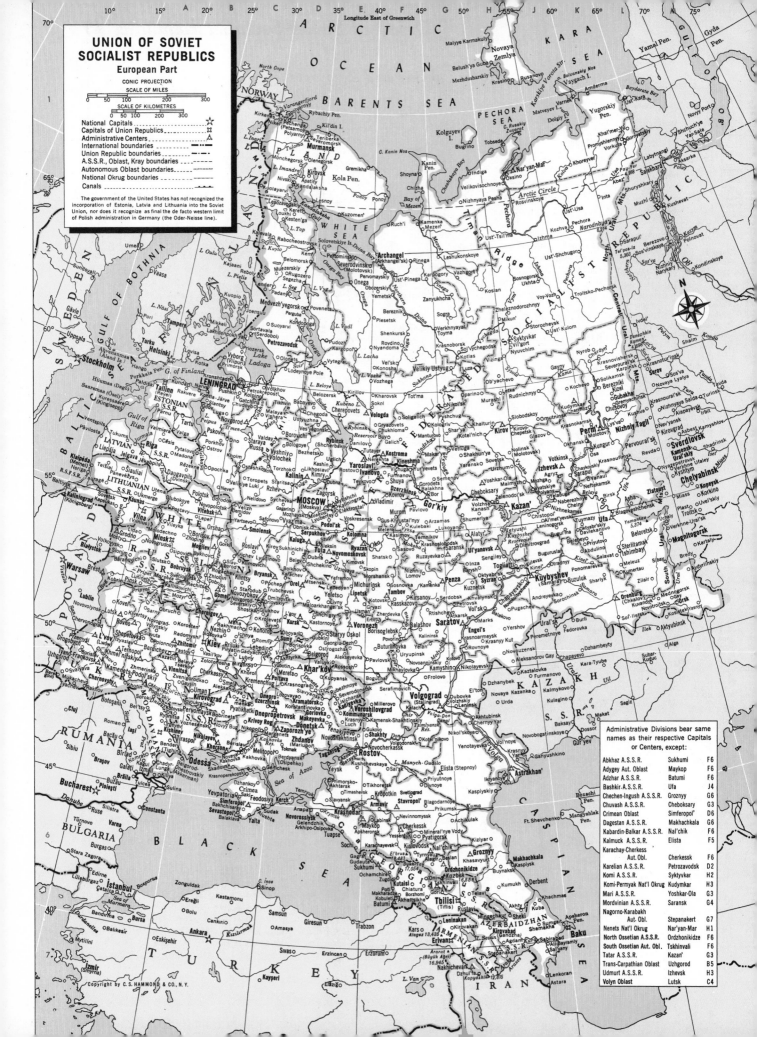

U.S.S.R. - EUROPEAN

UNION REPUBLICS

menian S.S.R., 2,491,900 ....F 6
erbaidzhan S.S.R., 5,117,100 ..G 6
stonian S.S.R., 1,356,100 ....C 3
eorgian S.S.R., 4,686,000 ....F 6
atvian S.S.R., 2,364,100 ....B 3
thuanian S.S.R., 3,128,000 .....B 3
oldavian S.S.R., 3,568,900 ......C 5
ussian S.F.S.R., 130,079,210 ....F 3
krainian S.S.R., 47,126,517 .....D 5
hite Russian S.S.R., 9,002,338..C 4

INTERNAL DIVISIONS

okhaz A.S.S.R., 487,000 ....F 6
dygey Aut. Oblast, 385,000 ......F 6
dzhar A.S.S.R., 310,000 ....F 6
ashkir A.S.S.R., 3,818,000 ... ...J 4
hechen-Ingush A.S.S.R.,
1,065,000 ....G 6
huvash A.S.S.R., 1,224,000 ......G 3
rimean Oblast, 1,813,000 ....D 6
agestan A.S.S.R., 1,429,000 ....G 6
abardin-Balkar A.S.S.R.,
588,000 ....F 6
almuck A.S.S.R., 268,000 ....F 5
arachay-Cherkess Aut. Oblast,
345,000 ....F 6
arelian A.S.S.R., 713,000 ....D 2
omi A.S.S.R., 965,000 ....H 2
omi-Permyak Nat'l Okrug,
212,000 ....H 3
ari A.S.S.R., 685,000 ....G 3
ordvinian A.S.S.R., 1,029,000 ..G 4
agorno-Karabakh Aut. Oblast,
150,000 ....G 7
akhichevan' A.S.S.R., 202,000..F 7
enets Nat'l Okrug, 39,000 ....H 1
orth Ossetian A.S.S.R., 552,000 F 6
outh Ossetian Aut. Oblast,
99,000 ....F 6
atar A.S.S.R., 3,131,000 ....G 3
rans-Carpathian Oblast,
1,057,000 ....B 5
dmurt A.S.S.R., 1,418,000 ......H 3
olyn Oblast, 974,000 ....C 4

CITIES and TOWNS

odulino, 27,000 ....H 4
gdam, 21,300 ....G 6
gryz, 21,000 ....H 3
khaltsikhe, 20,000 ....F 6
khtubinsk, 33,000 ....G 5
khtyrka, 42,000 ....E 4
agir, 18,000 ....F 6
atyr', 47,000 ....G 4
eksandriya, 69,000 ....D 5
ekseyevka, 24,000 ....E 4
eksin, 61,000 ....E 4
i-Bayramly, 33,900 ....G 7
'met'yevsk, 87,000 ....H 3
ushta, 21,000 ....D 6
apa, 25,000 ....E 6
patity, 40,000 ....D 1
osheronsk, 36,000 ....F 6
rchangel (Arkhangel'sk),
343,000 ....F 2
rmavir, 145,000 ....F 5
rzamas, 67,000 ....F 3
strakhan', 410,000 ....G 5
karsk, 30,000 ....G 4
zov, 59,000 ....E 5
akhchisaray, 12,000 ....D 6
akhmach, 14,000 ....D 4
aku, 852,000 ....H 6
aku, *1,266,000 ....H 6
alakhna, 36,000 ....F 3
alaklava, 5,000 ....D 6
alakovo, 103,000 ....G 4
alashoy, 83,000 ....F 4
altiysk, 18,000 ....A 4
aranovichi, 101,000 ....C 4
arysh, 21,000 ....G 4
ataysk, 85,000 ....E 5
atumi, 101,000 ....F 6
elaya Tserkov', 109,000 ....C 5
elebey, 35,000 ....H 4
elev, 18,000 ....E 4
elgorod, 151,000 ....E 4
elgorod-Dnestrovskiy, 30,000 ....D 5
elomorsk, 18,000 ....D 2
eloretsk, 67,000 ....J 4
el'tsy, 101,800 ....C 5
endery, 72,300 ....C 5
erdichev, 71,000 ....C 5
erdyansk, 100,000 ....E 5
eregovo, 30,000 ....B 5
erezniki, 146,000 ....J 3
eslan, 28,000 ....F 6
ezhetsk, 31,000 ....E 3
rsk, 36,000 ....J 3
agoveshchensk, 15,000 ....J 4
obruysk, 138,000 ....C 4
ologoye, 32,000 ....D 3
or, 55,000 ....F 3
orislav, 36,000 ....B 5
orisoglebsk, 64,000 ....F 4
orisov, 84,000 ....C 4
orovichi, 55,000 ....D 3
orzhomi, 17,000 ....F 6
rest, 122,000 ....B 4
ryansk, 318,000 ....D 4
ugul'ma, 72,000 ....H 4
uguruslan, 49,000 ....H 4
uy, 25,000 ....F 3
uynaksk, 41,000 ....G 6
uzuluk, 67,000 ....H 4
ykhov, 16,000 ....C 4
ēsis, 17,700 ....C 3
hadyr-Lunga, 20,200 ....C 5
hapayevsk, 86,000 ....G 4
haykovskiy, 48,000 ....H 3
heboksary, 216,000 ....G 3
herepovets, 188,000 ....E 3
herkassy, 158,000 ....D 5
herkessk, 67,000 ....F 6
hernigov, 159,000 ....D 4
hernovtsy, 187,000 ....C 5
hervonograd, 41,000 ....B 4
hiatura, 30,000 ....F 6
histopol', 60,000 ....H 3
hkalov (Orenburg), 344,000 ....J 4
hortkov, 21,000 ....B 5
husovoy, 58,000 ....J 3
anilov, 17,000 ....E 3
augavpils, 100,400 ....C 3
avlekanovo, 22,000 ....H 4
erbent, 57,000 ....G 6
imitrovgrad, 81,000 ....G 4
neprodzerzhinsk, 227,000 ....D 5
nepropetrovsk, 862,000 ....D 5
obrush, 17,000 ....D 4
onetsk, 879,000 ....E 5
rogobych, 56,000 ....B 5

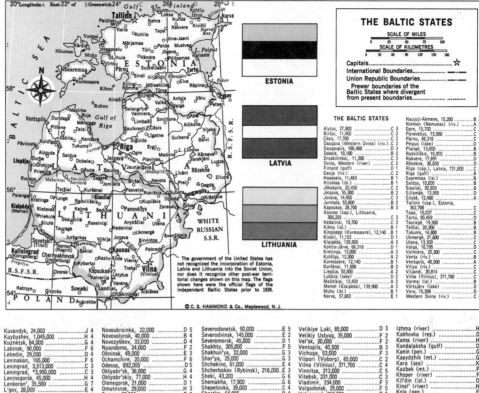

Dubna, 43,700 ....E 3
Dubna, 8,000 ....E 4
Dvinsk (Daugavpils), 100,400 .....C 3
Dzerzhinsk, 221,000 ....F 3
Dzhankoy, 42,000 ....D 5
Elektrostal', 123,100 ....E 3
Elista, 50,000 ....F 5
Engel's, 130,000 ....G 4
Erivan, 767,000 ....F 6
Ertil', 20,000 ....F 4
Fastov, 42,000 ....C 4
Feodosiya, 65,000 ....D 5
Frolovo, 30,000 ....F 5
Furmanov, 44,000 ....F 3
Gagarin, 15,000 ....D 3
Gagra, 23,000 ....E 6
Galich, 20,000 ....F 3
Gandzha (Kirovabad), 189,800 ...G 6
Gatchina, 63,000 ....D 3
Gay, 35,000 ....J 4
Gaysin, 23,000 ....C 5
Gelendzhik, 24,000 ....E 6
Genichesk, 19,000 ....E 5
Georgiu-Dezh, 48,000 ....E 4
Glazov, 68,000 ....H 3
Glukhov, 30,000 ....D 4
Gomel', 272,000 ....D 4
Gori, 45,000 ....F 6
Gorki, 24,000 ....D 4
Gor'kiy, 1,170,000 ....F 3
Gorlovka, 335,000 ....E 5
Gornyatskiy, 30,000 ....K 1
Gorodets, 34,000 ....F 3
Gremyachinsk, 34,000 ....J 3
Grodno, 132,000 ....B 4
Groznyy, 341,000 ....G 6
Gryazi, 40,000 ....F 4
Gubakha, 40,000 ....J 3
Gubkin, 54,000 ....E 4
Gudauta, 14,000 ....F 6
Gukovo, 65,000 ....F 5
Gus'-Khrustal'nyy, 65,000 ....F 3
Ichnya, 14,000 ....D 4
Inta, 50,000 ....K 1
Inza, 20,000 ....G 4
Ishimbay, 54,000 ....J 4
Ivano-Frankovsk, 105,000 ....B 5
Ivanovo, 420,000 ....E 3
Izhevsk, 422,000 ....H 3
Izmail, 70,000 ....C 5
Izyum, 52,000 ....E 5
Jelgava, 55,300 ....B 3
Kadiyevka, 137,000 ....E 5
Kagul, 26,000 ....C 5
Kakhovka, 25,000 ....D 5
Kalach, 23,000 ....F 5
Kalinin, 345,000 ....E 3
Kaliningrad, 297,000 ....B 4
Kaliningrad, 105,900 ....E 3
Kalinkovichi, 22,000 ....C 4
Kaluga, 211,000 ....E 4
Kamenets-Podol'skiy, 57,000 ....C 5
Kamenka, 30,000 ....F 4
Kamensk-Shakhtinskiy,
68,000 ....F 5
Kamyshin, 97,000 ....F 4
Kanash, 45,000 ....G 3
Kandalaksha, 42,000 ....D 1
Kapsukas, 28,700 ....B 4
Kashin, 19,000 ....E 3
Kasimov, 37,000 ....F 4
Kaspiysk, 39,000 ....G 6
Kaunas, 306,200 ....B 4
Kazan', 869,000 ....G 3
Kazatin, 28,000 ....C 5
Kem', 21,000 ....D 2
Kerch', 128,000 ....E 5
Khachmas, 22,300 ....G 6
Khar'kov, 1,223,000 ....E 5
Khasavyurt, 54,000 ....G 6
Kherson, 261,000 ....D 5
Khmel'nitskiy, 113,000 ....C 5
Khorol, 13,000 ....D 5
Khvalynsk, 19,000 ....G 4
Kiev, 1,632,000 ....D 4
Kiliya, 26,000 ....C 5
Kimovsk, 44,000 ....E 4
Kimry, 53,000 ....E 3
Kinel', 38,000 ....H 4
Kineshma, 96,000 ....F 3
Kirov, 30,000 ....D 4
Kirov, 333,000 ....G 3
Kirovabad, 189,800 ....G 6
Kirovakan, 107,000 ....G 6
Kirovo-Chepetsk, 51,000 ....H 3
Kirovograd, 189,000 ....D 5
Kirovsk, 48,000 ....D 1
Kirsanov, 24,000 ....F 4
Kishinev, 356,900 ....C 5
Kislovodsk, 90,000 ....F 6
Kizel, 49,000 ....J 3
Kizlyar, 30,000 ....G 6
Klaipėda, 139,900 ....B 3
Klimovichi, 13,000 ....D 4
Klintsy, 58,000 ....D 4
Kobrin, 25,000 ....B 4
Kobuleti, 18,000 ....F 6
Kohtla-Järve, 68,318 ....C 3
Kolomna, 135,900 ....E 4
Kolpino, 70,000 ....D 3
Kommunarsk, 123,000 ....E 5
Komrat, 21,400 ....C 5
Kondopoga, 25,000 ....D 2
Königsberg (Kaliningrad),
297,000 ....B 4
Konotop, 68.000 ....D 4
Konstantinovka, 105,000 ....E 5
Korosten', 56,000 ....C 4
Kostroma, 223,000 ....F 3
Kotel'nich, 30,000 ....G 3
Kotel'nikovo, 21,000 ....F 5
Kotlas, 56,000 ....G 2
Kotovo, 20,000 ....G 4
Kotovsk, 38,000 ....C 5
Kotovsk, 32,000 ....F 4
Kovel', 35,000 ....C 4
Kovrov, 123,000 ....F 3
Kramatorsk, 150,000 ....E 5
Krasnoarmeysk, 21,000 ....G 4
Krasnodar, 464,000 ....E 6
Krasnograd, 18,000 ....E 5
Krasnokamsk, 55,000 ....H 3
Krasnovishersk, 16,000 ....J 2
Krasnyy Kut, 17,000 ....G 4
Krasnyy Luch, 103,000 ....E 5
Kremenchug, 148,000 ....D 5
Krichev, 26,000 ....D 4
Krivoy Rog, 573,000 ....D 5
Krolevets, 18,000 ....D 4
Kropotkin, 68,000 ....F 5
Krymsk, 44,000 ....E 6
Kuba, 18,900 ....G 6
Kudymkar, 20,000 ....H 3
Kulebaki, 48,000 ....F 3
Kumertau, 42,000 ....J 4
Kungur, 74,000 ....J 3
Kupyansk, 28,000 ....E 5
Kursk, 284,000 ....E 4
Kutaisi, 161,000 ....F 6

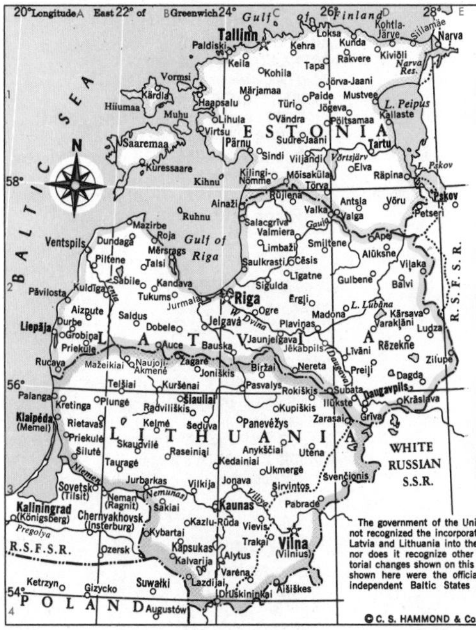

THE BALTIC STATES

SCALE OF MILES 0 25 50 75 100
SCALE OF KILOMETRES 0 30 60 90 120 150 180

Capitals.. ☆
International Boundaries........................ —··—
Union Republic Boundaries..................... —·—
Prewar boundaries of the Baltic States where divergent from present boundaries........................ ....

THE BALTIC STATES

Alytus, 27,900 ....C 3
Biržai, 11,400 ....C 2
Cēsis, 17,700 ....C 2
Daugava (Western Dvina) (riv.)..C 2
Daugavpils, 100,400 ....D 3
Dobele, 10,100 ....B 2
Druskininkai, 11,200 ....C 3
Dvina, Western (river) ....C 2
Finland (gulf) ....D 1
Gauja (riv.) ....C 2
Haapsalu, 11,483 ....B 1
Hiiumaa (isl.) ....B 1
Jēkabpils, 22,400 ....C 2
Jelgava, 55,300 ....B 2
Jonava, 14,400 ....C 3
Jurmala, 53,800 ....B 2
Kapsukas, 28,700 ....B 3
Kaunas (cap.), Lithuania,
306,200 ....C 3
Kedainiai, 19,700 ....C 3
Kihnu (isl.) ....B 1
Kingisepp (Kuressaare), 12,140 ..B 1
Kivioli, 11,153 ....D 1
Klaipėda, 139,900 ....A 3
Kohtla-Järve, 68,318 ....D 1
Kretinga, 13,000 ....A 3
Kuldīga, 12,300 ....A 2
Kuressaare, 12,140 ....B 1
Kuršėnai, 11,500 ....B 2
Liepāja, 92,800 ....A 2
Lubāna (lake) ....D 2
Mažeikiai, 13,400 ....A 2
Memel (Klaipėda), 139,900 ....A 3
Muhu (isl.) ....B 1
Narva, 57,863 ....E 1
Naujoji-Akmene, 10,200 ....B 2
Niemen (Nemunas) (riv.) ....A 3
Ogre, 15,700 ....C 2
Panevėžys, 73,500 ....C 3
Pärnu, 46,316 ....C 1
Peipus (lake) ....D 1
Plungė, 13,600 ....B 3
Radviliškis, 16,900 ....B 3
Rakvere, 17,891 ....D 1
Rēzekne, 30,800 ....D 2
Riga (cap.), Latvia, 731,800 ....C 2
Riga (gulf) ....B 2
Saaremaa (isl.) ....B 1
Saldus, 10,000 ....B 2
Šiauliai, 92,800 ....B 3
Sillamäe, 13,505 ....D 1
Silutė, 12,400 ....A 3
Tallinn (cap.), Estonia,
362,706 ....C 1
Tapa, 10,037 ....C 1
Tartu, 90,459 ....D 1
Tauragė, 19,500 ....B 3
Telšiai, 20,200 ....B 2
Tukums, 14,800 ....B 2
Ukmergė, 21,600 ....C 3
Utena, 13,300 ....C 3
Valga, 16,795 ....D 2
Valmiera, 20,300 ....C 2
Venta (riv.) ....B 2
Ventspils, 40,500 ....A 2
Viliya (riv.) ....C 3
Viljandi, 20,814 ....C 1
Vilna (Vilnius), 371,700 ....C 3
Vormsi (isl.) ....B 1
Võrtsjärv (lake) ....D 1
Voru, 15,398 ....D 2
Western Dvina (riv.) ....C 2

Kuvandyk, 24,000 ....J 4
Kuybyshev, 1,045,000 ....H 4
Kuznetsk, 84,000 ....G 4
Labinsk, 50,000 ....F 6
Lebedin, 29,000 ....D 4
Leninakan, 165,000 ....F 6
Leningrad, 3,513,000 ....C 3
Leningrad, *3,950,000 ....C 3
Leninogorsk, 45,000 ....H 4
Lenkoran', 35,500 ....G 7
L'gov, 28,000 ....E 4
Lida, 48,000 ....C 4
Liepāja, 92,800 ....B 3
Lipetsk, 289,000 ....E 4
Lisichansk, 118,000 ....E 5
Livny, 37,000 ....E 4
Lodeynoye Pole, 20,000 ....D 2
Lozovaya, 34,000 ....E 5
Lubny, 39,000 ....D 4
Luga, 30,000 ....C 3
Lutsk, 94,000 ....B 4
L'vov (Lwów), 553,000 ....B 5
Lys'va, 73,000 ....J 3
Lyubertsy, 139,400 ....E 3
Lyubotin, 38,000 ....E 4
Lyudinovo, 33,000 ....D 4
Makeyevka, 392,000 ....E 5
Makhachkala, 186,000 ....G 6
Makharadze, 24,000 ....F 6
Manturovo, 21,000 ....F 3
Marganets, 47,000 ....E 5
Mariupol' (Zhdanov), 417,000 ....E 5
Marks, 18,000 ....G 4
Maykop, 110,000 ....F 6
Mednogorsk, 41,000 ....J 4
Medvezh'yegorsk, 18,000 ....D 2
Melenki, 19,000 ....F 3
Meleuz, 28,000 ....J 4
Melitopol', 137,000 ....D 5
Memel (Klaipėda), 139,900 ....B 3
Merefa, 32,000 ....E 5
Michurinsk, 94,000 ....F 4
Mikhaylovka, 50,000 ....F 4
Millerovo, 38,000 ....F 5
Mineralnye Vody, 55,000 ....F 6
Mingechaur, 43,100 ....G 6
Minsk, 907,000 ....C 4
Minsk, *917,000 ....C 4
Mirgorod, 28,000 ....D 5
Mogilev, 202,000 ....C 4
Mogilev-Podol'skiy, 27,000 ....C 5
Molodechno, 50,000 ....C 4
Molotov (Perm'), 850,000 ....J 3
Monchegorsk, 49,000 ....D 1
Morshansk, 45,000 ....F 4
Moscow (Moskva) (cap.),
6,942,000 ....E 3
Moscow, *7,061,000 ....E 3
Mozhaysk, 20,300 ....E 3
Mozhga, 34,000 ....H 3
Mozyr', 49,000 ....C 4
Mtsensk, 24,000 ....E 4
Mukachevo, 57,000 ....B 5
Murmansk, 309,000 ....D 1
Murom, 99,000 ....F 3
Mytishchi, 118,700 ....E 3
Naberezhnye Chelny, 38,000 ....H 3
Nakhichevan', 33,200 ....F 7
Nal'chik, 146,000 ....F 6
Narva, 57,863 ....C 3
Nar'yan-Mar, 15,000 ....H 1
Neftekamsk, 35,000 ....J 3
Nelidovo, 30,000 ....D 3
Nerekhta, 28,000 ....F 3
Nevinnomyssk, 85,000 ....F 6
Nezhin, 56,000 ....D 4
Nikel', 17,000 ....C 1
Nikolayev, 331,000 ....D 5
Nikopol', 125,000 ....D 5
Nizhnekamsk, 49,000 ....H 3
Nizhniy Lomov, 19,000 ....F 4
Nosovka, 23,000 ....D 4
Novaya Kakhovka, 40,000 ....D 5
Novgorod, 128,000 ....D 3
Novoanninskiy, 21,000 ....F 4
Novocherkassk, 162,000 ....F 5
Novograd-Volynskiy, 36,000 ....C 4
Novogrudok, 20,000 ....C 4
Novokuybyshevsk, 104,000 ....G 4
Novomoskovsk, 134,000 ....E 4
Novopolotsk, 40,000 ....C 3
Novorossiysk, 133,000 ....E 6
Novoshakhtinsk, 102,000 ....E 5
Novotroitsk, 83,000 ....J 4

Novoukrainka, 22,000 ....D 5
Novovolynsk, 40,000 ....B 4
Novozybkov, 33,000 ....D 4
Nyandoma, 24,000 ....F 2
Obninsk, 49,000 ....E 3
Ochamchire, 20,000 ....F 6
Odessa, 892,000 ....D 5
Oktyabr'sk, 36,000 ....G 4
Oktyabr'skiy, 77,000 ....H 4
Olenegorsk, 21,000 ....D 1
Omutninsk, 29,000 ....H 3
Onega, 27,000 ....E 2
Ordzhonikidze, 236,000 ....F 6
Orel, 232,000 ....E 4
Orenburg, 344,000 ....J 4
Orgeyev, 25,800 ....C 5
Orsha, 101,000 ....C 4
Orsk, 225,000 ....J 4
Osipenko (Berdyansk), 100,000....E 5
Osipovichi, 19,000 ....C 4
Ostashkov, 22,000 ....D 3
Ostrogozhsk, 35,000 ....E 4
Ostrov, 19,000 ....C 3
Otradnyy, 46,000 ....H 4
Panevėžys, 73,500 ....B 3
Pärnu, 46,316 ....C 3
Pavlovo, 63,000 ....F 3
Pechora, 41,000 ....J 1
Penza, 374,000 ....F 4
Perm', 850,000 ....J 3
Pervomaysk, 59,000 ....D 5
Pervomayskiy, 18,000 ....F 2
Petrovsk, 32,000 ....G 4
Petrozavodsk, 184,000 ....D 2
Pinsk, 62,000 ....C 4
Piryatin, 18,000 ....D 4
Pochep, 16,000 ....D 4
Podol'sk, 168,700 ....E 3
Polonnoye, 23,000 ....C 4
Polotsk, 64,000 ....C 3
Poltava, 220,000 ....D 5
Postavy, 13,000 ....C 3
Poti, 48,000 ....F 6
Povorino, 22,000 ....F 4
Prikumsk, 36,000 ....F 6
Priluki, 57,000 ....D 4
Primorsko-Akhtarsk, 30,000 ....E 5
Priyutovo, 20,000 ....H 4
Promyshlennyy, 22,000 ....K 1
Pskov, 127,000 ....C 3
Pugachev, 38,000 ....G 4
Pushkin, 79,000 ....C 3
Pyatigorsk, 93,000 ....F 6
Pyatikhatki, 20,000 ....D 5
Radomyshl', 12,000 ....C 4
Rakhov, 11,000 ....B 5
Rakvere, 17,891 ....C 3
Rasskazovo, 40,000 ....F 4
Rechitsa, 48,000 ....C 4
Revel (Tallinn), 362,706 ....B 3
Rēzekne, 30,800 ....C 3
Riga, 731,800 ....B 3
Rogachev, 12,000 ....D 4
Romny, 48,000 ....D 4
Roslavl', 48,000 ....D 4
Rossosh', 36,000 ....E 4
Rostov, 32,000 ....E 3
Rostov, 789,000 ....F 5
Rovno, 116,000 ....C 4
Rtishchevo, 40,000 ....F 4
Rubezhnoye, 58,000 ....E 5
Rustavi, 98,000 ....G 6
Ruzayevka, 38,000 ....F 4
Ryazan', 350,000 ....E 4
Rybinsk, 218,000 ....E 3
Rybnitsa, 32,400 ....C 5
Rzhev, 61,000 ....D 3
Safonovo, 44,000 ....D 3
Saki, 23,000 ....D 5
Salavat, 114,000 ....H 4
Sal'sk, 50,000 ....F 5
Sal'yany, 24,200 ....G 7
Samara (Kuybyshev), 1,045,000..H 4
Saransk, 191,000 ....G 4
Sarapul, 97,000 ....H 3
Saratov, 757,000 ....G 4
Sarny, 10,000 ....C 4
Sasovo, 28,000 ....F 4
Segezha, 30,000 ....D 2
Semenov, 25,000 ....F 3
Serdobel (Sortavala), 23,000 ....D 2
Serdobsk, 33,000 ....F 4
Serpukhov, 124,300 ....E 4
Sevastopol', 229,000 ....D 6

Severodonetsk, 90,000 ....E 5
Severodvinsk, 145,000 ....E 2
Severomorsk, 45,000 ....D 1
Shakhty, 205,000 ....F 5
Shakhun'ya, 22,000 ....G 3
Shar'ya, 25,000 ....G 3
Shchekino, 61,000 ....E 4
Shcherbakov (Rybinsk), 218,000..E 3
Sheki, 43,200 ....G 6
Shemakha, 17,900 ....G 6
Shepetovka, 39,000 ....C 4
Shostka, 64,000 ....D 4
Shumerlya, 33,000 ....G 3
Shuya, 69,000 ....F 3
Šiauliai, 92,800 ....B 3
Sibay, 42,000 ....J 4
Simferopol', 249,000 ....D 6
Skopin, 23,000 ....F 4
Slantsy, 40,000 ....C 3
Slavuta, 24,000 ....C 4
Slavyansk, 124,000 ....E 5
Slavyansk-na-Kubani, 52,000 ....E 5
Slobodskoy, 37,000 ....H 3
Slonim, 30,000 ....B 4
Slutsk, 36,000 ....C 4
Smela, 55,000 ....D 5
Smolensk, 211,000 ....D 4
Sochi, 224,000 ....E 6
Sokol, 49,000 ....F 3
Solikamsk, 89,000 ....J 3
Sol'-Iletsk, 25,000 ....J 4
Sorochinsk, 25,000 ....H 4
Soroki, 21,700 ....C 5
Sortavala, 23,000 ....D 2
Sosnogorsk, 25,000 ....H 2
Sovetsk, 38,000 ....B 4
Sovetsk, 19,000 ....G 3
Stalingrad (Volgograd),
818,000 ....F 5
Staraya Russa, 34,000 ....D 3
Staryy Oskol, 52,000 ....E 4
Stavropol', 198,000 ....F 5
Stepanakert, 30,300 ....G 7
Stepnoy (Elista), 50,000 ....G 5
Sterlitamak, 185,000 ....J 4
Stupino, 59,300 ....E 4
Sukhumi, 102,000 ....F 6
Sumgait, 124,400 ....G 6
Sumy, 159,000 ....E 4
Svetlogorsk, 40,000 ....C 4
Svetlograd, 30,000 ....F 5
Syktyvkar, 125,000 ....H 2
Syzran', 173,000 ....G 4
Taganrog, 254,000 ....E 5
Tallinn, 362,706 ....B 3
Tambov, 230,000 ....F 4
Tartu, 90,459 ....C 3
Tauragė, 19,500 ....B 3
Tbilisi, 889,000 ....F 6
Telavi, 23,000 ....G 6
Telšiai, 20,200 ....B 3
Temryuk, 28,000 ....E 5
Ternopol', 85,000 ....C 5
Teykovo, 34,000 ....E 3
Tiflis (Tbilisi), 889,000 ....F 6
Tighina (Bendery), 72,300 ....C 5
Tikhoretsk, 60,000 ....F 5
Tikhvin, 29,000 ....D 3
Timashevsk, 35,000 ....E 5
Tiraspol', 105,700 ....D 5
Togliatti, 251,000 ....G 4
Tokmak, 39,000 ....E 5
Torzhok, 47,000 ....D 3
Tskhinvali, 30,000 ....F 6
Tuapse, 51,000 ....E 6
Tula, 462,000 ....E 4
Tul'chin, 14,000 ....C 5
Tuymazy, 35,000 ....H 4
Tyrnyauz, 19,000 ....F 6
Uchaly, 18,000 ....J 4
Ufa, 771,000 ....J 4
Uglich, 36,000 ....E 3
Ukhta, 63,000 ....H 2
Ukmergė, 21,600 ....C 3
Ul'yanovsk, 351,000 ....G 4
Uman', 63,000 ....D 5
Uryupinsk, 37,000 ....F 4
Usman', 19,000 ....E 4
Uzhgorod, 65,000 ....B 5
Uzlovaya, 62,000 ....E 4
Valga, 16,795 ....C 3
Valmiera, 20,300 ....C 3
Valuyki, 29,000 ....E 4
Vasil'kov, 27,000 ....D 4

Velikiye Luki, 85,000 ....D 3
Velikiy Ustyug, 35,000 ....F 2
Vel'sk, 20,000 ....F 2
Ventspils, 40,500 ....B 3
Vichuga, 53,000 ....F 3
Viipuri (Vyborg), 65,000 ....C 2
Vilna (Vilnius), 371,700 ....C 4
Vinnitsa, 212,000 ....C 5
Vitebsk, 231,000 ....C 3
Vladimir, 234,000 ....F 3
Volgodonsk, 25,000 ....F 5
Volgograd, 818,000 ....F 5
Volkhov, 46,000 ....D 3
Volkovysk, 22,000 ....B 4
Vologda, 178,000 ....F 3
Vol'sk, 69,000 ....G 4
Volzhsk, 44,000 ....G 3
Volzhskiy, 142,000 ....G 5
Vorkuta, 90,000 ....K 1
Voronezh, 660,000 ....E 4
Voroshilovgrad, 383,000 ....F 5
Voskresensk, 66,900 ....E 3
Votkinsk, 74,000 ....H 3
Voznesensk, 36,000 ....D 5
Vyatskiye Polyany, 33,000 ....H 3
Vyaz'ma, 42,000 ....D 3
Vyborg, 65,000 ....C 2
Vyksa, 46,000 ....F 3
Vyshniy Volochek, 74,000 ....D 3
Yalta, 62,000 ....D 6
Yanaul, 18,000 ....J 3
Yaroslavl', 517,000 ....E 3
Yartsevo, 37,000 ....D 3
Yefremov, 47,000 ....E 4
Yelabuga, 36,000 ....H 3
Yelets, 101,000 ....E 4
Yenakiyevo, 92,000 ....E 5
Yershov, 20,000 ....G 4
Yessentuki, 65,000 ....F 6
Yevpatoria, 79,000 ....D 5
Yeysk, 64,000 ....E 5
Yoshkar-Ola, 166,000 ....G 3
Yur'yevets, 23,000 ....F 3
Zagorsk, 92,400 ....E 3
Zaporozh'ye, 658,000 ....E 5
Zelenodol'sk, 77,000 ....G 3
Zhdanov, 417,000 ....E 5
Zherdevka, 20,000 ....F 4
Zhigulevsk, 52,000 ....G 4
Zhitomir, 161,000 ....C 4
Zhlobin, 25,000 ....D 4
Zhmerinka, 34,000 ....C 5
Zhodino, 17,000 ....C 4
Znamenka, 30,000 ....D 5
Zolotonosha, 27,000 ....D 5
Zugdidi, 39,000 ....F 6
Zvenigorodka, 21,000 ....D 5

OTHER FEATURES

Apsheron (pen.) ....H 6
Araks (river) ....G 7
Azov (sea) ....E 5
Baltic (sea) ....B 3
Barents (sea) ....E 1
Belaya (river) ....H 3
Beloye (lake) ....E 2
Berezina (river) ....C 4
Black (sea) ....D 6
Bug (river) ....B 4
Bug (river) ....D 5
Caspian (sea) ....G 6
Caucasus (mts.) ....F 6
Central Ural (mts.) ....J 2
Chir (river) ....F 5
Crimea (pen.), 1,813,000 ....D 5
Dagö (Hiiumaa) (isl.) ....B 3
Denezhkin Kamen' (mt.) ....K 2
Desna (river) ....D 4
Dnieper (river) ....D 5
Dniester (river) ....C 5
Don (river) ....F 5
Donets (river) ....E 5
Dvina (bay) ....E 2
Dvina, Northern (river) ....F 2
Dvina, Western (river) ....C 3
Dykh-Tau (mt.) ....F 6
El'brus (mt.) ....F 6
Finland (gulf) ....C 3
Goryn' (river) ....C 4
Hiiumaa (isl.) ....B 3
Ilek (river) ....J 4
Il'men (lake) ....D 3
Izhma (river) ....H 2
Kakhovka (res.) ....D 5
Kama (river) ....H 3
Kandalaksha (gulf) ....D 1
Kanin (pen.) ....G 1
Kapydzhik (mt.) ....G 7
Kara (sea) ....K 1
Kazbek (mt.) ....F 6
Khoper (river) ....F 4
Kil'din (isl.) ....D 1
Kinel' (river) ....H 4
Kola (pen.) ....E 1
Kolguyev (isl.) ....G 1
Kolva (river) ....J 1
Kuban' (river) ....E 5
Kubeno (lake) ....E 3
Kura (river) ....G 6
Kuyto (lake) ....D 2
Ladoga (lake) ....D 2
Lapland (reg.) ....C 1
Lovat' (river) ....D 3
Mansel'ka (mts.) ....C 1
Manych-Gudilo (lake) ....F 5
Matveyev (isl.) ....J 1
Medveditsa (river) ....F 4
Mezen' (river) ....G 1
Mezhdusharskiy (isl.) ....G 1
Moksha (river) ....F 4
Moskva (river) ....E 3
Msta (river) ....D 3
Niemen (river) ....B 4
North Ural (mts.) ....K 1
Northern Dvina (river) ....F 2
Novaya Zemlya (isls.) ....H 1
Oka (river) ....F 4
Onega (bay) ....E 2
Onega (lake) ....E 2
Ösel (Saaremaa) (isl.) ....B 3
Pay-Yer (mt.) ....K 1
Pechora (river) ....H 1
Pechora (sea) ....H 1
Peipus (lake) ....C 3
Pinega (river) ....G 2
Ponoy (river) ....E 1
Pripet (marsh) ....C 4
Pripyat' (river) ....C 4
Prut (river) ....C 5
Psel (river) ....D 4
Riga (gulf) ....B 3
Russkiy Zavorot (cape) ....H 1
Rybachiy (pen.) ....D 1
Saaremaa (isl.) ....B 3
Samara (river) ....H 4
Seg (lake) ....D 2
Sevan (lake) ....G 6
Seym (river) ....D 4
Solovetskiye (isls.) ....E 1
South Ural (mts.) ....J 4
Suda (river) ....E 3
Sukhona (river) ....F 2
Sura (river) ....G 4
Svir' (river) ....D 2
Sysola (river) ....H 2
Tel'pos-Iz (mt.) ....K 2
Timan Ridge (mts.) ....H 1
Top (lake) ....D 1
Tuloma (river) ....D 1
Ufa (river) ....J 3
Undzha (river) ....F 3
Ural (mts.) ....J 2
Ural (river) ....J 4
Usa (river) ....K 1
Vaga (river) ....F 2
Valday (hills) ....D 3
Vaygach (isl.) ....K 1
Velikaya (river) ....C 3
Vetluga (river) ....G 3
Vodl (lake) ....E 2
Volga (river) ....G 5
Volga-Don (canal) ....F 5
Volkhov (river) ....D 3
Vorona (river) ....F 4
Vorskla (river) ....E 4
Vozhe (lake) ....F 2
Vyatka (river) ....H 3
Vychegda (river) ....G 2
Vyg (lake) ....E 2
Vym' (river) ....H 2
Western Dvina (river) ....C 3
White (sea) ....E 1
Yamantau (mt.) ....J 4
Yug (river) ....G 2
Yugorskiy (pen.) ....K 1

*City and suburbs.

ALGERIA
AREA 919,591 sq. mi.
POPULATION 16,776,000
CAPITAL Algiers
LARGEST CITY Algiers
HIGHEST POINT Tahat 9,850 ft.
MONETARY UNIT Algerian dinar
MAJOR LANGUAGES Arabic, Berber, French
MAJOR RELIGION Islam

ANGOLA
AREA 481,351 sq. mi.
POPULATION 6,761,000
CAPITAL Luanda
LARGEST CITY Luanda
HIGHEST POINT Mt. Moco 8,593 ft.
MONETARY UNIT kwanza
MAJOR LANGUAGES Mbundu, Kongo, Lunda, Portuguese
MAJOR RELIGIONS Tribal religions, Roman Catholicism

BENIN
AREA 43,483 sq. mi.
POPULATION 3,200,000
CAPITAL Porto-Novo
LARGEST CITY Cotonou
HIGHEST POINT Atakora Mts. 2,083 ft.
MONETARY UNIT CFA franc
MAJOR LANGUAGES Fon, Somba, Yoruba, Bariba, French, Mina, Dendi
MAJOR RELIGIONS Tribal religions, Islam, Roman Catholicism

BOTSWANA
AREA 224,764 sq. mi.
POPULATION 700,000
CAPITAL Gaborone
LARGEST CITIES Selebi-Pikwe
HIGHEST POINT Tsodilo Hill 5,922 ft.
MONETARY UNIT pula
MAJOR LANGUAGES Setswana, Shona, Bushman, English, Afrikaans
MAJOR RELIGIONS Tribal religions, Protestantism

BURUNDI
AREA 10,747 sq. mi.
POPULATION 4,100,000
CAPITAL Bujumbura
LARGEST CITY Bujumbura
HIGHEST POINT 8,858 ft.
MONETARY UNIT Burundi franc
MAJOR LANGUAGES Kirundi, French, Swahili
MAJOR RELIGIONS Tribal religions, Roman Catholicism, Islam

CAMEROON
AREA 183,568 sq.mi.
POPULATION 6,600,000
CAPITAL Yaoundé
LARGEST CITY Douala
HIGHEST POINT Cameroon 13,350 ft.
MONETARY UNIT CFA franc
MAJOR LANGUAGES Fang, Bamileke, Fulani, Duala, French, English
MAJOR RELIGIONS Tribal religions, Christianity, Islam

CAPE VERDE
AREA 1,557 sq. mi.
POPULATION 302,000
CAPITAL Praia
LARGEST CITY Praia
HIGHEST POINT 9,281 ft.
MONETARY UNIT Cape Verde escudo
MAJOR LANGUAGE Portuguese
MAJOR RELIGION Roman Catholicism

CENTRAL AFRICAN EMPIRE
AREA 236,293 sq. mi.
POPULATION 1,800,000
CAPITAL Bangui
LARGEST CITY Bangui
HIGHEST POINT Gao 4,659 ft.
MONETARY UNIT CFA franc
MAJOR LANGUAGES Banda, Gbaya, Sangho, French
MAJOR RELIGIONS Tribal religions, Christianity, Islam

CHAD
AREA 495,752 sq. mi.
POPULATION 4,178,000
CAPITAL N'Djamena
LARGEST CITY N'Djamena
HIGHEST POINT Emi Koussi 11,204 ft.
MONETARY UNIT CFA franc
MAJOR LANGUAGES Arabic, Bagirmi, French, Sara, Massa, Moudang
MAJOR RELIGIONS Islam, Tribal religions

COMOROS
AREA 719 sq. mi.
POPULATION 266,000
CAPITAL Moroni
LARGEST CITY Moroni
HIGHEST POINT Karthala 8,399 ft.
MONETARY UNIT CFA franc
MAJOR LANGUAGES Arabic, French, Swahili
MAJOR RELIGION Islam

CONGO
AREA 132,046 sq. mi.
POPULATION 1,400,000
CAPITAL Brazzaville
LARGEST CITY Brazzaville
HIGHEST POINT Leketi Mts. 3,412 ft.
MONETARY UNIT CFA franc
MAJOR LANGUAGES Kikongo, Bateke, Lingala, French
MAJOR RELIGIONS Christianity, Tribal religions, Islam

DJIBOUTI
AREA 8,880 sq. mi.
POPULATION 250,000
CAPITAL Djibouti
LARGEST CITY Djibouti
HIGHEST POINT Moussa Ali 6,768 ft.
MONETARY UNIT Djibouti franc
MAJOR LANGUAGES Arabic, Somali, Afar, French
MAJOR RELIGIONS Islam, Roman Catholicism

EGYPT
AREA 386,659 sq. mi.
POPULATION 37,900,000
CAPITAL Cairo
LARGEST CITY Cairo
HIGHEST POINT Jeb. Katherina 8,651 ft.
MONETARY UNIT Egyptian pound
MAJOR LANGUAGE Arabic
MAJOR RELIGIONS Islam, Coptic Christianity

EQUATORIAL GUINEA
AREA 10,831 sq. mi.
POPULATION 320,000
CAPITAL Malabo
LARGEST CITY Malabo
HIGHEST POINT 9,868 ft.
MONETARY UNIT ekuele
MAJOR LANGUAGES Fang, Bubi, Spanish, English, Ibo
MAJOR RELIGIONS Tribal religions, Christianity

ETHIOPIA
AREA 471,776 sq. mi.
POPULATION 27,946,000
CAPITAL Addis Ababa
LARGEST CITY Addis Ababa
HIGHEST POINT Ras Dashan 15,157 ft.
MONETARY UNIT Ethiopian dollar
MAJOR LANGUAGES Amharic, Gallinya, Tigrinya, Somali, Sidamo, Arabic, Ge'ez, Italian
MAJOR RELIGIONS Coptic Christianity, Islam

GABON
AREA 103,346 sq. mi.
POPULATION 526,000
CAPITAL Libreville
LARGEST CITY Libreville
HIGHEST POINT Ibounzi 5,165 ft.
MONETARY UNIT CFA franc
MAJOR LANGUAGES Fang and other Bantu languages, French
MAJOR RELIGIONS Tribal religions, Christianity, Islam

GAMBIA
AREA 4,127 sq. mi.
POPULATION 524,000
CAPITAL Bathurst
LARGEST CITY Bathurst
HIGHEST POINT 100 ft.
MONETARY UNIT dalasi
MAJOR LANGUAGES Mandingo, Fulani, Wolof, English, Malinke
MAJOR RELIGIONS Islam, Tribal religions, Christianity

GHANA
AREA 92,099 sq. mi.
POPULATION 9,900,000
CAPITAL Accra
LARGEST CITY Accra
HIGHEST POINT Togo Hills 2,900 ft.
MONETARY UNIT new cedi
MAJOR LANGUAGES Twi, Fante, Dagbani, Ewe, Ga, English, Hausa, Akan
MAJOR RELIGIONS Tribal religions, Christianity, Islam

GUINEA
AREA 94,925 sq. mi.
POPULATION 4,500,000
CAPITAL Conakry
LARGEST CITY Conakry
HIGHEST POINT Nimba Mts. 6,070 ft.
MONETARY UNIT syli
MAJOR LANGUAGES Fulani, Mandingo, Susu, French
MAJOR RELIGIONS Islam, Tribal religions

GUINEA-BISSAU
AREA 13,948 sq. mi.
POPULATION 517,000
CAPITAL Bissau
LARGEST CITY Bissau
HIGHEST POINT 689 ft.
MONETARY UNIT Guinea-Bissau peso
MAJOR LANGUAGES Balante, Fulani, Crioulo, Mandingo, Portuguese
MAJOR RELIGIONS Islam, Tribal religions, Roman Catholicism

IVORY COAST
AREA 127,520 sq. mi.
POPULATION 6,673,013
CAPITAL Abidjan
LARGEST CITY Abidjan
HIGHEST POINT Nimba Mts. 5,745 ft.
MONETARY UNIT CFA franc
MAJOR LANGUAGES Bale, Bete, Senufu, French, Dioula
MAJOR RELIGIONS Tribal religions, Islam

KENYA
AREA 224,960 sq. mi.
POPULATION 13,300,000
CAPITAL Nairobi
LARGEST CITY Nairobi
HIGHEST POINT Kenya 17,058 ft.
MONETARY UNIT Kenya shilling
MAJOR LANGUAGES Kikuyu, Luo, Kavirondo, Kamba, Swahili, English
MAJOR RELIGIONS Tribal religions, Christianity, Hinduism, Islam

LESOTHO
AREA 11,720 sq. mi.
POPULATION 1,100,000
CAPITAL Maseru
LARGEST CITY Maseru
HIGHEST POINT 11,425 ft.
MONETARY UNIT South African rand
MAJOR LANGUAGES Sesotho, English
MAJOR RELIGIONS Tribal religions, Christianity

LIBERIA
AREA 43,000 sq. mi.
POPULATION 1,600,000
CAPITAL Monrovia
LARGEST CITY Monrovia
HIGHEST POINT Wutivi 5,584 ft.
MONETARY UNIT Liberian dollar
MAJOR LANGUAGES Kru, Kpelle, Bassa, Vai, English
MAJOR RELIGIONS Christianity, Tribal religions, Islam

LIBYA
AREA 679,358 sq. mi.
POPULATION 2,500,000
CAPITAL Tripoli
LARGEST CITY Tripoli
HIGHEST POINT Bette Pk. 7,500 ft.
MONETARY UNIT Libyan dinar
MAJOR LANGUAGES Arabic, Berber, Italian
MAJOR RELIGION Islam

MADAGASCAR
AREA 226,657 sq. mi.
POPULATION 7,700,000
CAPITAL Antananarivo
LARGEST CITY Antananarivo
HIGHEST POINT Maromokotro 9,436 ft.
MONETARY UNIT Malagasy franc
MAJOR LANGUAGES Malagasy, French
MAJOR RELIGIONS Tribal religions, Roman Catholicism, Protestantism

MALAWI
AREA 45,747 sq. mi.
POPULATION 5,100,000
CAPITAL Lilongwe
LARGEST CITY Blantyre
HIGHEST POINT Mlanje 9,843 ft.
MONETARY UNIT Malawi kwacha
MAJOR LANGUAGES Chichewa, Yao, English, Nyanja, Tumbuka, Tonga, Ngoni
MAJOR RELIGIONS Tribal religions, Islam, Christianity

MALI
AREA 464,873 sq. mi.
POPULATION 5,800,000
CAPITAL Bamako
LARGEST CITY Bamako
HIGHEST POINT Hombori Mts. 3,789 ft.
MONETARY UNIT Mali franc
MAJOR LANGUAGES Bambara, Senufu, Fulani, Soninke, French
MAJOR RELIGIONS Islam, Tribal religions

MAURITANIA
AREA 452,702 sq. mi.
POPULATION 1,318,000
CAPITAL Nouakchott
LARGEST CITY Nouakchott
HIGHEST POINT 2,972 ft.
MONETARY UNIT ouguiya
MAJOR LANGUAGES Arabic, French,
Wolof, Tukolor
MAJOR RELIGION Islam

MAURITIUS
AREA 790 sq. mi.
POPULATION 899,000
CAPITAL Port Louis
LARGEST CITY Port Louis
HIGHEST POINT 2,711 ft.
MONETARY UNIT Mauritian rupee
MAJOR LANGUAGES English, French,
French Creole, Hindi, Urdu
MAJOR RELIGIONS Hinduism,
Christianity, Islam

AFRICA
AREA 11,682,000 sq. mi.
POPULATION 345,000,000
LARGEST CITY Cairo
HIGHEST POINT Kilimanjaro 19,304 ft.
LOWEST POINT Qattara Depression -436 ft.

MOROCCO
AREA 241,224 sq. mi.
POPULATION 18,000,000
CAPITAL Rabat
LARGEST CITY Casablanca
HIGHEST POINT Jeb. Toubkal 13,665 ft.
MONETARY UNIT dirham
MAJOR LANGUAGES Arabic, Berber, French
MAJOR RELIGIONS Islam, Judaism,
Christianity

MOZAMBIQUE
AREA 308,641 sq. mi.
POPULATION 9,300,000
CAPITAL Maputo
LARGEST CITY Maputo
HIGHEST POINT Mt. Binga 7,992 ft.
MONETARY UNIT Mozambique escudo
MAJOR LANGUAGES Makua, Thonga,
Shona, Portuguese
MAJOR RELIGIONS Tribal religions,
Roman Catholicism, Islam

NIGER
AREA 489,189 sq. mi.
POPULATION 4,700,000
CAPITAL Niamey
LARGEST CITY Niamey
HIGHEST POINT Banguezane 6,234 ft.
MONETARY UNIT CFA franc
MAJOR LANGUAGES Hausa, Songhai, Fulani,
French, Tamashek, Djerma
MAJOR RELIGIONS Islam, Tribal religions

NIGERIA
AREA 379,628 sq.mi.
POPULATION 83,800,000
CAPITAL Lagos
LARGEST CITY Lagos
HIGHEST POINT Vogel 6,700 ft.
MONETARY UNIT naira
MAJOR LANGUAGES Hausa, Yoruba, Ibo, Ijaw,
Fulani, Tiv, Kanuri, Ibibio, English, Edo
MAJOR RELIGIONS Islam, Christianity,
Tribal religions

RHODESIA (ZIMBABWE)
AREA 150,803 sq. mi.
POPULATION 6,600,000
CAPITAL Salisbury
LARGEST CITY Salisbury
HIGHEST POINT Mt. Inyangani 8,517 ft.
MONETARY UNIT Rhodesian dollar
MAJOR LANGUAGES English, Shona,
Ndebele
MAJOR RELIGIONS Tribal religions,
Protestantism

RWANDA
AREA 10,169 sq. mi.
POPULATION 4,241,000
CAPITAL Kigali
LARGEST CITY Kigali
HIGHEST POINT Karisimbi 14,780 ft.
MONETARY UNIT Rwanda franc
MAJOR LANGUAGES Kinyarwanda, French,
Swahili
MAJOR RELIGIONS Tribal religions, Roman
Catholicism, Islam

SÃO TOMÉ E PRÍNCIPE
AREA 372 sq. mi.
POPULATION 80,000
CAPITAL São Tomé
LARGEST CITY São Tomé
HIGHEST POINT Pico 6,640 ft.
MONETARY UNIT São Tomean escudo
MAJOR LANGUAGES Bantu
languages, Portuguese
MAJOR RELIGIONS Tribal
religions, Roman Catholicism

SENEGAL
AREA 75,954 sq. mi.
POPULATION 5,085,388
CAPITAL Dakar
LARGEST CITY Dakar
HIGHEST POINT Futa Jallon 1,640 ft.
MONETARY UNIT CFA franc
MAJOR LANGUAGES Wolof, Peul (Fulani),
French, Mende, Mandingo, Dida
MAJOR RELIGIONS Islam, Tribal religions,
Roman Catholicism

SEYCHELLES
AREA 145 sq. mi.
POPULATION 60,000
CAPITAL Victoria
LARGEST CITY Victoria
HIGHEST POINT Morne Seychellois 2,970 ft.
MONETARY UNIT Seychellois rupee
MAJOR LANGUAGES English, French, Creole
MAJOR RELIGION Roman Catholicism

SIERRA LEONE
AREA 27,925 sq. mi.
POPULATION 3,100,000
CAPITAL Freetown
LARGEST CITY Freetown
HIGHEST POINT Loma Mts. 6,390 ft.
MONETARY UNIT leone
MAJOR LANGUAGES Mende, Temne,
Vai, English, Krio (pidgin)
MAJOR RELIGIONS Tribal religions,
Islam, Christianity

SOMALIA
AREA 246,200 sq. mi.
POPULATION 3,170,000
CAPITAL Mogadishu
LARGEST CITY Mogadishu
HIGHEST POINT Surud Ad 7,900 ft.
MONETARY UNIT Somali shilling
MAJOR LANGUAGES Somali, Arabic,
Italian, English
MAJOR RELIGIONS Islam

SOUTH AFRICA
AREA 458,179 sq. mi.
POPULATION 24,400,000
CAPITALS Cape Town, Pretoria
LARGEST CITY Johannesburg
HIGHEST POINT Injasuti 11,182 ft.
MONETARY UNIT rand
MAJOR LANGUAGES Afrikaans,
English, Xhosa, Zulu, Sesotho
MAJOR RELIGIONS Protestantism,
Roman Catholicism, Islam, Hinduism

SOUTH-WEST AFRICA (NAMIBIA)
AREA 317,827 sq. mi.
POPULATION 883,000
CAPITAL Windhoek
LARGEST CITY Windhoek
HIGHEST POINT Brandberg 8,550 ft.
MONETARY UNIT S. African rand
MAJOR LANGUAGES Ovambo,
Hottentot, Herero, Afrikaans, English
MAJOR RELIGIONS Tribal religions,
Protestantism

SUDAN
AREA 967,494 sq. mi.
POPULATION 18,347,000
CAPITAL Khartoum
LARGEST CITY Khartoum
HIGHEST POINT Jeb. Marra 10,073 ft.
MONETARY UNIT Sudanese pound
MAJOR LANGUAGES Arabic, Dinka, Nubian,
Beja, Nuer, English
MAJOR RELIGIONS Islam, Tribal religions

SWAZILAND
AREA 6,705 sq. mi.
POPULATION 500,000
CAPITAL Mbabane
LARGEST CITY Mbabane
HIGHEST POINT Emlembe 6,109 ft.
MONETARY UNIT lilangeni
MAJOR LANGUAGES siSwati, English
MAJOR RELIGIONS Tribal religions,
Christianity

TANZANIA
AREA 363,708 sq. mi.
POPULATION 15,506,000
CAPITAL Dar es Salaam
LARGEST CITY Dar es Salaam
HIGHEST POINT Kilimanjaro 19,340 ft.
MONETARY UNIT Tanzanian shilling
MAJOR LANGUAGES Nyamwezi-Sukuma,
Swahili, English
MAJOR RELIGIONS Tribal religions,
Christianity, Islam

TOGO
AREA 21,622 sq. mi.
POPULATION 2,300,000
CAPITAL Lomé
LARGEST CITY Lomé
HIGHEST POINT Agou 3,445 ft.
MONETARY UNIT CFA franc
MAJOR LANGUAGES Ewe, French, Twi, Hausa
MAJOR RELIGIONS Tribal religions, Roman
Catholicism, Islam

TUNISIA
AREA 63,170 sq. mi.
POPULATION 5,776,000
CAPITAL Tunis
LARGEST CITY Tunis
HIGHEST POINT Jeb. Chambi 5,066 ft.
MONETARY UNIT Tunisian dinar
MAJOR LANGUAGES Arabic, French
MAJOR RELIGION Islam

UGANDA
AREA 91,076 sq. mi.
POPULATION 11,400,000
CAPITAL Kampala
LARGEST CITY Kampala
HIGHEST POINT Margherita 16,795 ft.
MONETARY UNIT Ugandan shilling
MAJOR LANGUAGES Luganda, Acholi, Teso,
Nyoro, Soga, Nkole, English, Swahili
MAJOR RELIGIONS Tribal religions, Christianity,
Islam

UPPER VOLTA
AREA 105,869 sq. mi.
POPULATION 6,144,013
CAPITAL Ouagadougou
LARGEST CITY Ouagadougou
HIGHEST POINT 2,352 ft.
MONETARY UNIT CFA franc
MAJOR LANGUAGES Mossi, Lobi, French,
Samo, Gourounsi
MAJOR RELIGIONS Islam, Tribal religions,
Roman Catholicism

ZAIRE
AREA 918,962 sq. mi.
POPULATION 25,600,000
CAPITAL Kinshasa
LARGEST CITY Kinshasa
HIGHEST POINT Margherita 16,795 ft.
MONETARY UNIT zaire
MAJOR LANGUAGES Tshiluba, Mongo, Kikongo,
Kingwana, Zande, Lingala, Swahili, French
MAJOR RELIGIONS Tribal religions, Christianity

ZAMBIA
AREA 290,586 sq. mi.
POPULATION 4,936,000
CAPITAL Lusaka
LARGEST CITY Lusaka
HIGHEST POINT Sunzu 6,782 ft.
MONETARY UNIT Zambian kwacha
MAJOR LANGUAGES Bemba, Tonga,
Lozi, Luvale, Nyanja, English, Afrikaans
MAJOR RELIGIONS Tribal religions

MAYOTTE
AREA 144 sq. mi.
POPULATION 40,000
CAPITAL Mamoutzou

RÉUNION
AREA 969 sq. mi.
POPULATION 475,700
CAPITAL St-Denis

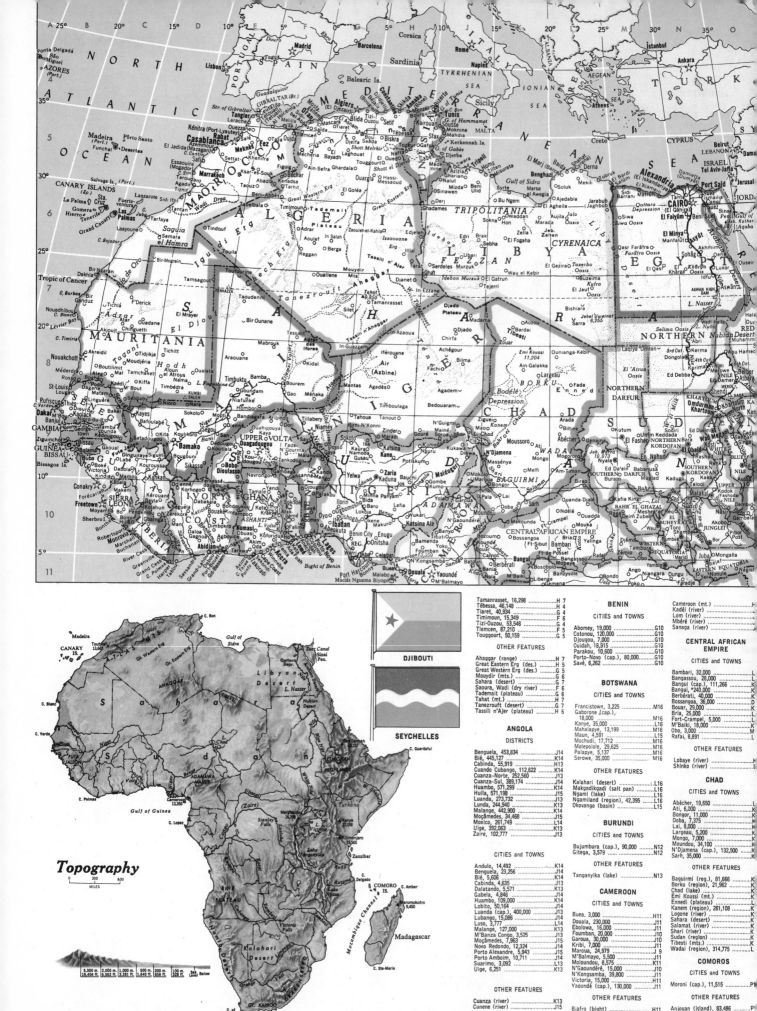

Topography

5,000 m. / 2,000 m. / 1,000 m. / 500 m. / 200 m. / 100 m. / Sea Level Below
16,404 ft. / 6,562 ft. / 3,281 ft. / 1,640 ft. / 656 ft. / 328 ft.

0   300   400
MILES

DJIBOUTI

SEYCHELLES

Tamanrasset, 16,298	H 7
Tébessa, 46,148	H 4
Tiaret, 40,934	G 4
Timimoun, 15,349	F 6
Tizi-Ouzou, 53,546	G 4
Tlemcen, 87,210	F 5
Touggourt, 50,159	G 5

OTHER FEATURES

Ahaggar (range)	H 7
Great Eastern Erg (des.)	H 5
Great Western Erg (des.)	F 5
Mouydir (mts.)	G 6
Sahara (desert)	G 7
Saoura, Wadi (dry river)	F 6
Tademait (plateau)	G 6
Tahat (mt.)	H 7
Tanezrouft (desert)	G 7
Tassili n'Ajer (plateau)	H 6

ANGOLA

DISTRICTS

Benguela, 453,834	J14
Bié, 445,127	K14
Cabinda, 55,919	H13
Cuando Cubango, 112,622	K14
Cuanza-Norte, 252,560	J13
Cuanza-Sul, 389,174	J14
Huambo, 571,299	K14
Huíla, 571,198	J14
Luanda, 273,732	J13
Lunda, 244,340	K14
Malange, 442,900	K14
Moçâmedes, 34,468	J15
Moxico, 261,749	L14
Uíge, 392,063	J13
Zaire, 102,777	J13

CITIES and TOWNS

Andulo, 14,492	K14
Benguela, 23,256	J14
Bié, 5,606	K14
Cabinda, 4,635	J13
Dalatando, 5,571	K13
Gabela, 4,846	J14
Huambo, 109,000	K14
Lobito, 50,164	J14
Luanda (cap.), 400,000	J13
Lubango, 15,086	J14
Luso, 3,777	L14
Malange, 127,000	K14
M'Banza Congo, 3,525	J13
Moçâmedes, 7,963	J15
Novo Redondo, 12,324	J14
Porto Alexandre, 5,943	J15
Porto Amboim, 10,711	J14
Suarimo, 3,092	L13
Uíge, 6,251	K13

OTHER FEATURES

Cuanza (river)	K13
Cunene (river)	J15

BENIN

CITIES and TOWNS

Abomey, 19,000	G10
Cotonou, 120,000	G10
Djougou, 7,000	G10
Ouidah, 18,915	G10
Parakou, 10,600	G10
Porto-Novo (cap.), 80,000	G10
Savé, 6,262	G10

BOTSWANA

CITIES and TOWNS

Francistown, 3,225	M16
Gaborone (cap.), 18,000	M16
Kanye, 35,000	L16
Mahalapye, 13,199	M16
Maun, 4,591	L16
Mochudi, 17,712	M16
Molepolole, 29,625	M16
Palapye, 5,137	M16
Serowe, 35,000	M16

OTHER FEATURES

Kalahari (desert)	L16
Makgadikgadi (salt pan)	L16
Ngami (lake)	L16
Ngamiland (region), 42,395	L16
Okovango (basin)	L15

BURUNDI

CITIES and TOWNS

Bujumbura (cap.), 90,000	N12
Gitega, 3,579	N12

OTHER FEATURES

Tanganyika (lake)	N13

CAMEROON

CITIES and TOWNS

Buea, 3,000	H11
Douala, 230,000	H11
Ebolowa, 16,000	J11
Foumban, 20,000	J10
Garoua, 30,000	J10
Kribi, 7,000	J11
Maroua, 24,979	J10
M'Balmayo, 5,500	J11
Mouloundou, 8,575	K11
N'Gaoundéré, 15,000	J10
N'Kongsamba, 39,800	J11
Victoria, 15,000	J11
Yaoundé (cap.), 130,000	J11

OTHER FEATURES

Biafra (bight)	H11

Cameroon (mt.)	H...
Kadéi (river)	K...
Lom (river)	J...
Mbéré (river)	K...
Sanaga (river)	J...

CENTRAL AFRICAN EMPIRE

CITIES and TOWNS

Bambari, 32,000	L...
Bangassou, 28,000	L...
Bangui (cap.), 111,266	K...
Bangui, *240,000	K...
Berbérati, 40,000	K...
Bossangoa, 36,000	D...
Bouar, 25,000	K...
Bria, 25,000	L...
Fort-Crampel, 5,000	K...
M'Baiki, 18,000	K...
Obo, 3,000	M...
Rafai, 8,891	L...

OTHER FEATURES

Lobaye (river)	K...
Shinko (river)	L...

CHAD

CITIES and TOWNS

Abécher, 19,650	K...
Ati, 6,000	K...
Bongor, 11,000	K...
Doba, 7,375	K...
Lai, 8,000	K...
Largeau, 5,200	K...
Mongo, 7,000	K...
Moundou, 34,100	K...
N'Djamena (cap.), 132,500	K...
Sarh, 35,000	K...

OTHER FEATURES

Baguirmi (reg.), 81,666	K...
Borku (region), 21,962	K...
Chad (lake)	K...
Emi Koussi (mt.)	K...
Ennedi (plateau)	K...
Kanem (region), 261,108	K...
Logone (river)	K...
Sahara (desert)	K...
Salamat (river)	K...
Sudan (region)	K...
Tibesti (mts.)	K...
Wadai (region), 314,775	K...

COMOROS

CITIES and TOWNS

Moroni (cap.), 11,515	P...

OTHER FEATURES

Anjouan (island), 83,486	P...

FLAGS OF AFRICA

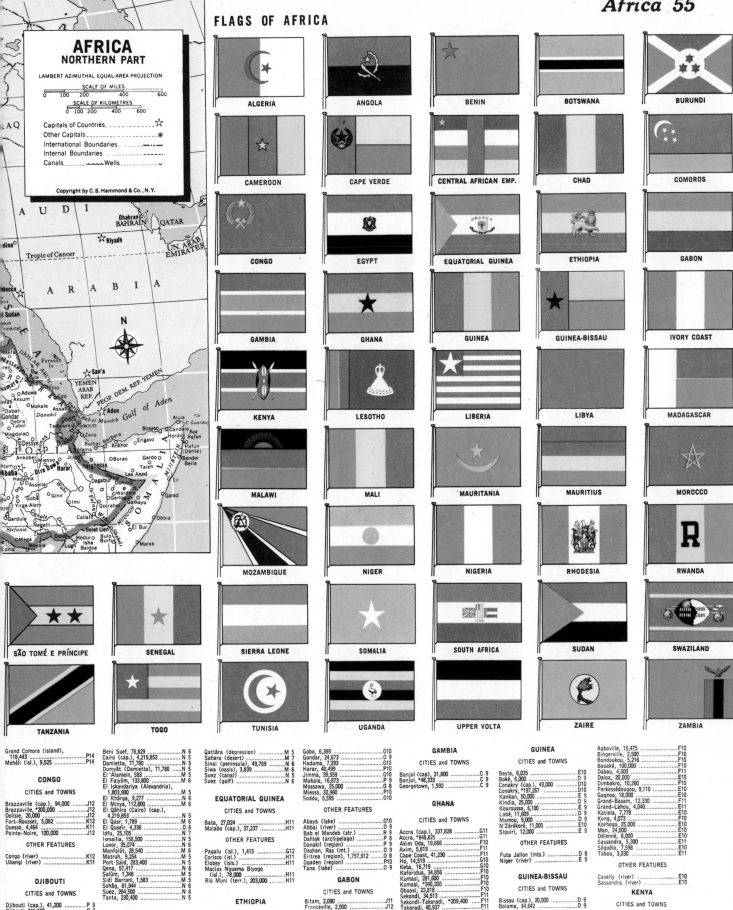

ALGERIA · ANGOLA · BENIN · BOTSWANA · BURUNDI
CAMEROON · CAPE VERDE · CENTRAL AFRICAN EMP. · CHAD · COMOROS
CONGO · EGYPT · EQUATORIAL GUINEA · ETHIOPIA · GABON
GAMBIA · GHANA · GUINEA · GUINEA-BISSAU · IVORY COAST
KENYA · LESOTHO · LIBERIA · LIBYA · MADAGASCAR
MALAWI · MALI · MAURITANIA · MAURITIUS · MOROCCO
MOZAMBIQUE · NIGER · NIGERIA · RHODESIA · RWANDA
SÃO TOMÉ E PRÍNCIPE · SENEGAL · SIERRA LEONE · SOMALIA · SOUTH AFRICA · SUDAN · SWAZILAND
TANZANIA · TOGO · TUNISIA · UGANDA · UPPER VOLTA · ZAIRE · ZAMBIA

AFRICA
NORTHERN PART
LAMBERT AZIMUTHAL EQUAL-AREA PROJECTION

SCALE OF MILES
0 100 200 400 600

SCALE OF KILOMETRES
0 100 200 400 600

Capitals of Countries..............☆
Other Capitals.....................◉
International Boundaries...........
Internal Boundaries...............
Canals...........Wells...........

Copyright by C.S. Hammond & Co., N.Y.

Grand Comoro (island), 118,443 .....P14	
Mohéli (isl.), 9,525 .....P14	

CONGO

CITIES and TOWNS

Brazzaville (cap.), 94,000 .....J12
Brazzaville, *200,000 .....J12
Dolisie, 20,000 .....J12
Fort-Rousset, 5,082 .....K12
Ouesso, 4,464 .....K11
Pointe-Noire, 100,000 .....J12

OTHER FEATURES

Congo (river) K12
Ubangi (river) K11

DJIBOUTI

Djibouti (cap.), 41,200 .....P 9
Djibouti, *61,500 .....P 9
Tadjoura, 2,000 .....P 9

EGYPT

CITIES and TOWNS

Akhmim, 41,580 .....N 6
Alexandria, 1,803,900 .....M 5
Aswân, 127,700 .....N 7
Asyût, 154,100 .....N 6
Beni Suef, 78,829 .....N 6
Cairo (cap.), 4,219,853 .....N 5
Damietta, 71,780 .....N 5
Dumyât (Damietta), 71,780 .....N 5
El 'Alamein, 593 .....M 5
El Faiyûm, 133,800 .....N 6
El Iskandariya (Alexandria), 1,803,900 .....M 5
El Khârga, 9,277 .....N 6
El Minya, 112,800 .....N 6
El Qâhira (Cairo) (cap.), 4,219,853 .....N 5
El Qasr, 1,789 .....N 6
El Quseir, 4,336 .....O 6
Idfu, 25,105 .....N 7
Ismailia, 156,500 .....N 5
Luxor, 35,074 .....N 6
Manfalût, 28,540 .....N 6
Matruh, 9,254 .....M 5
Port Said, 283,400 .....N 5
Qena, 57,417 .....N 6
Salûm, 1,348 .....M 5
Sidi Barrani, 1,583 .....M 5
Sohâg, 61,944 .....N 6
Suez, 264,500 .....N 5
Tanta, 230,400 .....N 5

OTHER FEATURES

'Aqaba (gulf) .....O 6
Arabian (desert) .....N 6
Aswân High (dam) .....N 7
Bânâs, Ras (cape) .....O 7
Katherina, Jebel (mt.) .....N 6
Khârga (oasis) 12,346 .....N 6
Libyan (desert) .....M 6
Nasser (lake) .....N 7
Nile (river) .....N 7
Qattâra (depression) .....M 5
Sahara (desert) .....M 7
Sinai (peninsula), 49,769 .....M 6
Hadama, 7,293 .....O10
Siwa (oasis), 3,839 .....M 5
Suez (canal) .....N 5
Suez (gulf) .....N 6

EQUATORIAL GUINEA

CITIES and TOWNS

Bata, 27,024 .....H11
Malabo (cap.), 37,237 .....H11

OTHER FEATURES

Pagalu (isl.), 1,415 .....G12
Corisco (isl.) H11
Elobey (isls.) H11
Macias Nguema Biyogo (isl.), 78,000 .....H11
Río Muni (terr.), 203,000 .....H11

ETHIOPIA

CITIES and TOWNS

Addis Ababa (cap.), 644,120 .....O10
Addis Alam, 7,789 .....O10
Aksum, 11,094 .....O 9
Ankober, 12,871 .....O10
Asmara, 190,500 .....O 9
Asselle, 9,523 .....O10
Debra Markos, 20,096 .....O 9
Dessye, 40,000 .....O 9
Dire Dawa, 40,000 .....P10
Gambela, 9,955 .....N10

OTHER FEATURES

Abaya (lake) O10
Abbai (river) .....O 9
Bab el Mandeb (str.) .....R 9
Dahlak (archipelago) .....P 9
Danakil (region) .....P 9
Dashan, Ras (mt.) .....O 9
Eritrea (region), 1,757,912 .....O 9
Ogaden (region) P10
Tana (lake) .....O 9

GABON

CITIES and TOWNS

Bitam, 2,080 .....J11
Franceville, 2,000 .....J12
Koula-Moutou, 3,170 .....J12
Lambaréné, 7,000 .....H12
Lastoursville, 2,000 .....J12
Libreville (cap.), *57,000 .....H11
Oyem, 3,050 .....J11
Port-Gentil, 30,000 .....H12
Tchibanga, 2,080 .....J12

OTHER FEATURES

Lopez (cape) H12
Ogooué (river) J12

GAMBIA

CITIES and TOWNS

Banjul (cap), 31,800 .....C 9
Banjul, *48,333 .....C 9
Georgetown, 1,592 .....C 9

GHANA

CITIES and TOWNS

Accra (cap.), 337,828 .....G11
Accra, *848,825 .....G11
Akim Oda, 19,666 .....F10
Axim, 5,619 .....F11
Cape Coast, 41,230 .....F11
Ho, 14,519 .....G10
Keta, 16,719 .....G10
Koforidua, 34,856 .....F10
Kumasi, 281,600 .....F10
Kumasi, *340,200 .....F10
Obuasi, 22,818 .....F10
Sekondi, 34,513 .....F11
Sekondi–Takoradi, *209,400 .....F11
Takoradi, 40,937 .....F11
Tamale, 40,443 .....F10
Tarkwa, 13,545 .....F11
Wa, 14,342 .....F 9
Winneba, 25,376 .....F11
Yendi, 16,096 .....F10

OTHER FEATURES

Volta (lake) F10
Volta (river) F10

GUINEA-BISSAU

CITIES and TOWNS

Bissau (cap.), 20,000 .....D 9
Bolama, 4,642 .....D 9

OTHER FEATURES

Bijagós (isls.), 9,332 .....C 9

IVORY COAST

CITIES and TOWNS

Abidjan (cap.), 180,000 .....E10
Abidjan, *425,000 .....E10

GUINEA

CITIES and TOWNS

Beyla, 6,035 .....E10
Boké, 6,000 .....D10
Conakry (cap.), 43,000 .....D10
Conakry, *197,267 .....D10
Kankan, 50,000 .....E 9
Kindia, 25,000 .....D 9
Kouroussa, 6,100 .....E 9
Labé, 11,609 .....D 9
Mamou, 9,000 .....D 9
N'Zérékoré, 11,000 .....E 9
Siguiri, 12,000 .....E 9

OTHER FEATURES

Futa Jallon (mts.) .....D 9
Niger (river) .....E 9

Agboville, 15,475 .....F10
Bingerville, 2,500 .....F10
Bondoukou, 5,216 .....F10
Bouaké, 100,000 .....E10
Dabou, 4,500 .....F11
Daloa, 20,000 .....E10
Dimbokro, 10,260 .....F10
Ferkessédougou, 9,110 .....E10
Gagnoa, 18,000 .....E10
Grand-Basam, 12,330 .....F11
Grand-Lahou, 4,040 .....E11
Katiola, 7,778 .....E10
Kong, 4,073 .....E10
Korhogo, 25,000 .....E10
Man, 24,000 .....E10
Odienné, 6,000 .....E10
Sassandra, 5,300 .....E11
Séguéla, 7,598 .....E10
Tabou, 3,030 .....E11

OTHER FEATURES

Cavally (river) E10
Sassandra (river) E10

KENYA

CITIES and TOWNS

Eldoret, 16,900 .....L11
Fort Hall, 5,389 .....O12
Kisumu, 30,700 .....N12
Kitale, 11,500 .....O11
Lamu, 5,828 .....P12
Malindi, 5,818 .....P12
Mombasa, 234,400 .....P12
Nairobi (cap.), 477,600 .....O12
Nakuru, 47,800 .....O11
Nanyuki, 11,200 .....O12
Nyeri, 9,900 .....O12
(continued on following page)

Agriculture, Industry and Resources

DOMINANT LAND USE

- Cereals, Horticulture, Livestock
- Cash Crops, Mixed Cereals
- Cotton, Cereals
- Diversified Tropical Crops
- Plantation Agriculture
- Oases
- Pasture Livestock
- Nomadic Livestock Herding
- Forests
- Nonagricultural Land

MAJOR MINERAL OCCURRENCES

Ab	Asbestos	Mi	Mica
Ag	Silver	Mn	Manganese
Al	Bauxite	Na	Salt
Au	Gold	O	Petroleum
Be	Beryl	P	Phosphates
C	Coal	Pb	Lead
Co	Cobalt	Pt	Platinum
Cr	Chromium	Sb	Antimony
Cu	Copper	Sn	Tin
D	Diamonds	So	Soda Ash
Fe	Iron Ore	Ti	Titanium
G	Natural Gas	U	Uranium
Gp	Gypsum	V	Vanadium
Gr	Graphite	W	Tungsten
K	Potash	Zn	Zinc

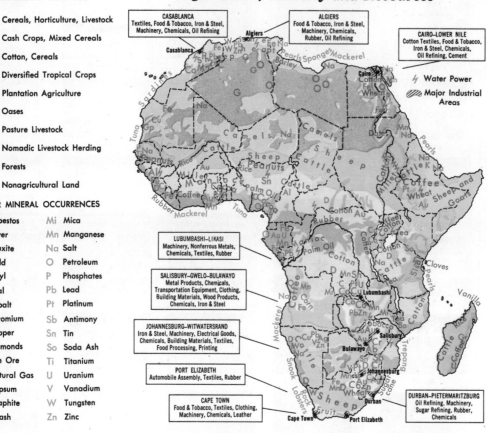

CASABLANCA — Textiles, Food & Tobacco, Iron & Steel, Machinery, Chemicals, Oil Refining

ALGIERS — Food & Tobacco, Iron & Steel, Machinery, Chemicals, Rubber, Oil Refining

CAIRO–LOWER NILE — Cotton Textiles, Food & Tobacco, Iron & Steel, Chemicals, Oil Refining, Cement

LUBUMBASHI–LIKASI — Machinery, Nonferrous Metals, Chemicals, Textiles, Rubber

SALISBURY–GWELO–BULAWAYO — Metal Products, Chemicals, Transportation Equipment, Clothing, Building Materials, Wood Products, Chemicals, Iron & Steel

JOHANNESBURG–WITWATERSRAND — Iron & Steel, Machinery, Electrical Goods, Chemicals, Building Materials, Textiles, Food Processing, Printing

PORT ELIZABETH — Automobile Assembly, Textiles, Rubber

CAPE TOWN — Food & Tobacco, Textiles, Clothing, Machinery, Chemicals, Leather

DURBAN–PIETERMARITZBURG — Oil Refining, Machinery, Sugar Refining, Rubber, Chemicals

⚡ Water Power

▨ Major Industrial Areas

- ngklip (cape) G20
- x River (mts.) J18
- eks (river) H19
- asteel (mts.) G18
- mpopo (river) N16
- aclear (cape) F20
- ange (river) K17
- bben (isl.) F19
- aint Helena (bay) K18
- ndown (bay) G20
- al (isl.) G20
- angkop (point) F20
- eeuwkop (mt.) H20
- ble (bay) F19
- ble (mt.) F19
- al (river) M17
- alker (bay) H20
- nderend (mts.) J19
- nderend (river) H20
- luland (district), 570,160 .... N17

SOUTH-WEST AFRICA (NAMIBIA)

CITIES and TOWNS

- thanie, 1,142 .... K17
- babis, 4,326 .... K16
- ootfontein, 1,919 .... K15
- rasburg, 2,234 .... K17
- ribib, 1,398 .... K16
- eetmanshoop, 8,064 .... K17
- ideritz, 3,633 .... J17
- altahöhe, 1,048 .... K16
- ariental, 3,498 .... K16
- kahandja, 2,977 .... K16
- maruru, 2,698 .... K16
- anjemund, 3,125 .... K17
- avi, 1,303 .... K15
- jiwarongo, 6,368 .... K16
- tjo, 2,963 .... K15
- hoboth, 2,973 .... K16
- vakopmund, 4,701 .... J16
- umeb, 7,823 .... K15
- sakos, 4,278 .... K16
- indhoek (cap.), 36,050 .... K16

OTHER FEATURES

- aprivi Strip (reg.), 15,871 .... L15
- unene (river) J15
- amaraland (reg.) K16
- tosha (salt pan) J15
- sh (river) K17
- ia (cape) J15
- reat Namaland (reg.) K17
- aokoveld (mts.) J15
- amib (desert) J15
- kovango (river) K15
- ange (river) K17
- vamboland (reg.), 203,862 .... K15

SUDAN

PROVINCES

- ahr el Ghazal, 813,000 .... M10
- lue Nile, 216,000 .... N 9
- astern Equatoria, 507,000 .... N11
- l Buheyrat, 574,000 .... M10
- l Gezira, 1,775,000 .... N 9
- unglei, 202,000 .... N10
- assala, 1,113,000 .... O 8
- hartoum, 1,160,000 .... N 8
- ile, 552,000 .... N 8
- orthern, 416,000 .... M 7
- orthern Darfur, 1,013,000 .... L 8
- orthern Kordofan, 1,266,000 .... M 9
- ed Sea, 446,000 .... O 7
- outhern Darfur, 1,160,000 .... L 9
- outhern Kordofan, 951,000 .... N 9
- pper Nile, 621,000 .... N 9
- estern Equatoria, 251,000 .... M10
- hite Nile, 1,122,000 .... N 9

CITIES and TOWNS

- tbara, 36,000 .... N 8
- erber, 10,977 .... N 8
- or, 5,000 .... N10
- ongola, 3,350 .... M 8
- d Damazin, 12,000 .... N 9
- d Damer, 5,458 .... N 8
- d Dueim, 12,319 .... N 9
- l Fasher, 26,161 .... M 9
- l Obeid, 53,000 .... N 9
- n Nahud, 16,499 .... M 9
- r Roseires, 3,927 .... O 9
- ashoda (Kodok), 9,100 .... N10
- edaref, 17,537 .... O 9
- eneina, 11,817 .... L 9
- uba, 10,660 .... N10
- adugli, 4,716 .... M 9
- arima, 5,989 .... N 8
- assala, 40,000 .... O 8
- hartoum (cap.), 194,000 .... N 8
- hartoum North, 40,000 .... N 8
- odok, 9,100 .... N10
- osti, 22,688 .... N 9
- Malakal, 9,680 .... N10
- Nyala, 12,278 .... L 9
- Omdurman, 206,000 .... N 8
- Port Sudan, 110,000 .... O 8
- Rumbek, 17,000 .... M10
- Sennar, 8,093 .... N 9
- Shendi, 11,031 .... N 8
- Singa, 9,436 .... N 9
- Suakin, 4,228 .... O 8
- Tokar, 16,802 .... O 8

- Wadi Halfa, 11,006 .... N 7
- Wad Medani, 48,000 .... N 9

OTHER FEATURES

- Abu Shagara, Ras (cape) .... O 7
- Atbara (river) .... O 8
- Bahr el 'Arab (river) M10
- Blue Nile (river) .... N 9
- Cataract, 3rd (rapids) .... M 8
- Cataract, 4th (rapids) .... N 8
- Cataract, 5th (rapids) .... N 8
- Cataract, 6th (rapids) .... N 8
- Gezira, El (region) .... N 9
- Lol (dry river) M10
- Meroe (ruins) .... N 8
- Naqa (ruins) .... N 8
- Nasser (lake) .... N 7
- Nile (river) .... N 8
- Nubia (lake) .... N 7
- Nuri (ruins) .... N 8
- Sahara (desert) .... M 7
- Sobat (river) N10
- Sudan (region) .... M 9
- Sudd (swamp) N10
- White Nile (river) N10
- Yei (river) N10

SWAZILAND

CITIES and TOWNS

- Mbabane (cap.), 13,803 .... N17

TANZANIA

CITIES and TOWNS

- Arusha, 32,452 .... O12
- Bagamoyo, 5,112 .... O13
- Bukoba, 8,141 .... N12
- Chake Chake, 4,862 .... P13
- Chunya, 2,398 .... N13
- Dar es Salaam (cap.), 272,821 .... P13
- Dodoma, 23,559 .... O13
- Geita, 3,066 .... N12
- Iringa, 21,746 .... O13
- Kasanga, ‡10,462 .... N13
- Kigoma-Ujiji, 21,369 .... N12
- Kilosa, 4,458 .... O13
- Kilwa Kivinje, 2,790 .... P13
- Kondoa, 4,514 .... O12
- Lindi, 13,352 .... O14
- Liwale, ‡22,205 .... O13
- Mahenge, ‡32,047 .... O13
- Manyoni, 14,362 .... N13
- Mbeya, 12,479 .... N13
- Morogoro, 25,262 .... O13
- Moshi, 26,864 .... O12
- Mtwara-Mikindani, 20,413 .... P14
- Musoma, 15,412 .... N12
- Mwadui, 7,383 .... N12
- Mwanza, 34,861 .... N12
- Nachingwea, 3,751 .... O14
- Pangani, 2,955 .... O13
- Shinyanga, 5,135 .... N12
- Singida, 9,478 .... N12
- Songea, 5,430 .... O14
- Tabora, 21,012 .... N12
- Tanga, 61,058 .... O12
- Zanzibar, 68,490 .... P13
- Zanzibar, *95,047 .... P13

OTHER FEATURES

- Eyasi (lake) O12
- Great Ruaha (river) O13
- Juani (island), 696 .... P13
- Kilimanjaro (mt.) O12
- Mafia (island), 15,459 .... P13
- Natron (lake) O12
- Nyasa (lake) N14
- Pangani (river) O12
- Pemba (island), 164,321 .... P13
- Rufiji (river) O13
- Rukwa (lake) N13
- Ruvuma (river) O14
- Tanganyika (lake) N13
- Victoria (lake) N12
- Zanzibar (island), 190,494 .... P13

TOGO

CITIES and TOWNS

- Anécho, †11,040 .... G10
- Atakpamé, †18,008 .... G10
- Lome (cap.), 90,600 .... G10
- Lomé, *149,879 .... G10
- Palimé, †20,331 .... G10
- Sansanné-Mango .... G 9
- Sokodé, †30,271 .... G10

TUNISIA

CITIES and TOWNS

- Bizerte, 51,700 .... J 4
- Gabès, 32,300 .... H 5
- Gafsa, 32,400 .... H 5
- Kairouan, 46,200 .... H 4
- Mahdia, 10,000 .... J 4
- Médenine, 8,000 .... J 5
- Menzel Bourguiba, 36,700 .... H 4
- Moknine, 18,500 .... J 4
- Nefta, 15,000 .... H 5
- Sfax, 65,000 .... J 5
- Sousse, 48,200 .... J 4
- Tozeur, 11,820 .... H 5
- Tunis (cap.), 662,000 .... J 4
- Tunis, *800,000 .... J 4

OTHER FEATURES

- Bon (cape) .... J 4
- Djerba (isl.), 62,445 .... J 5
- Gabès (gulf) .... J 5
- Hammamet (gulf) .... J 4
- Kerkennah (islands), 13,704 .... J 5
- Tunis (gulf) .... J 4

UGANDA

CITIES and TOWNS

- Arua, 4,645 .... N11
- Butiaba, 1,216 .... N11
- Entebbe, 10,941 .... N12
- Fort Portal, 8,317 .... N11
- Jinja, 29,741 .... N11
- Kabale, 10,919 .... N12
- Kampala (cap.), 330,000 .... N11
- Masindi, 1,571 .... N11
- Mbarara, 3,844 .... N12
- Soroti, 6,645 .... N11

OTHER FEATURES

- Kioga (lake) N11
- Ruwenzori (mt.) N11
- Victoria (lake) N12

UPPER VOLTA

CITIES and TOWNS

- Bobo-Dioulasso, 56,100 .... F 9
- Dédougou, 3,680 .... F 9
- Dori, 3,500 .... G 9
- Fada-N'Gourma, 4,867 .... G 9
- Gaoua, 5,907 .... F 9
- Kaya, 10,304 .... F 9
- Koudougou, 7,940 .... F 9
- Ouagadougou (cap.), 77,500 .... F 9
- Ouagadougou, *100,000 .... F 9
- Ouahigouya, 12,960 .... F 9
- Tenkodogo, 6,561 .... G 9

OTHER FEATURES

- Black Volta (river) .... F 9
- Red Volta (river) .... F 9
- Sudan (region) .... F 9
- White Volta (river) .... F 9

ZAIRE

CITIES and TOWNS

- Aketi, 15,339 .... L11
- Banana J13
- Bandundu, 74,467 .... K12
- Banzyville, 6,608 .... L11
- Basankusu, 5,613 .... L11
- Bikoro, 6,491 .... K12
- Boma, 33,143 .... J13
- Bukavu, 134,861 .... M12
- Bumba, 5,182 .... L11
- Bunia, 12,410 .... N11
- Buta, 10,845 .... M11
- Butembo, 9,980 .... M11
- Elisabethville (Lubumbashi), 318,000 .... M14
- Gemena, 8,135 .... L11
- Goma, 14,115 .... M12
- Ingende, 6,730 .... K12
- Isiro, 17,430 .... M11
- Kalemie, 29,934 .... M13
- Kambove (with Shinkolobwe), 14,517 .... M14
- Kamina, 20,915 .... L13
- Kikwit, 111,960 .... K13
- Kindu-Port Empain, 19,385 .... L12
- Kinshasa (cap.), 1,323,039 .... K12
- Kipushi, 22,602 .... M14
- Kisangani, 229,596 .... M11
- Kolwezi, 45,192 .... L14
- Kongolo, 10,434 .... M13
- Léopoldville (Kinshasa) (cap.), 1,323,039 .... K12
- Likasi, 80,075 .... M14
- Lodja, 7,227 .... L12
- Lubumbashi, 318,000 .... M14
- Luluabourg, 428,960 .... L13
- Lusambo, 9,395 .... L12
- Manono, 12,234 .... M13
- Matadi, 110,436 .... J13
- Mbandaka, 107,910 .... K11
- Mbuji-Mayi, 256,154 .... L13
- Mushie, 12,118 .... K12
- Paulis (Isiro), 17,430 .... M11
- Shinkolobwe (with Kambove), 14,517 .... M14
- Thysville, 16,369 .... K13
- Watsa, 6,077 .... M11
- Yangambi, 18,849 .... L11

OTHER FEATURES

- Albert (lake) M11
- Bomu (river) L11
- Congo (river) K12
- Edward (lake) M12
- Kasai (region), 4,306,092 .... L12
- Kasai (river) K12
- Katanga (region), 2,753,714 .... M13
- Kivu (lake) M12
- Kivu (region), 3,361,883 .... M12
- Kwilu (region) K13
- Leopold II (lake) K12
- Lomami (river) M12
- Lualaba (river) M13
- Luapula (river) M14
- Mweru (lake) M13
- Ruwenzori (mt.) N11
- Stanley (falls) M11
- Stanley (pool) K12
- Tanganyika (lake) N13
- Ubangi (river) K11
- Uele (river) L11
- Zaire (Congo) (river) K12

ZAMBIA

CITIES and TOWNS

- Chipata, †13,300 .... N14
- Choma, †11,300 .... M15
- Kabwe, †67,200 .... M14
- Kalomo, 2,560 .... M15
- Kasama, †8,900 .... N13
- Livingstone, †43,000 .... L15
- Lusaka (cap.), †238,200 .... M15
- Mankoya, 1,600 .... L14
- Mansa, †5,700 .... M14
- Mazabuka, †9,400 .... M15
- Mbala, †5,200 .... N13
- Mongu, †10,700 .... L15
- Monze, †4,300 .... M15
- Ndola, †150,800 .... M14
- Nkana, 54,500 .... M14
- Serenje, 1,650 .... N14
- Solwezi, 1,930 .... M14

OTHER FEATURES

- Bangweulu (lake) N14
- Barotseland (region), 417,000 .... L15
- Kafue (river) M15
- Kariba (lake) M15
- Mweru (lake) M13
- Tanganyika (lake) N13
- Victoria (falls) M15
- Zambezi (river) M15

*City and suburbs.

†Population of urban area.

‡Population of sub-division.

◉Population of municipality.

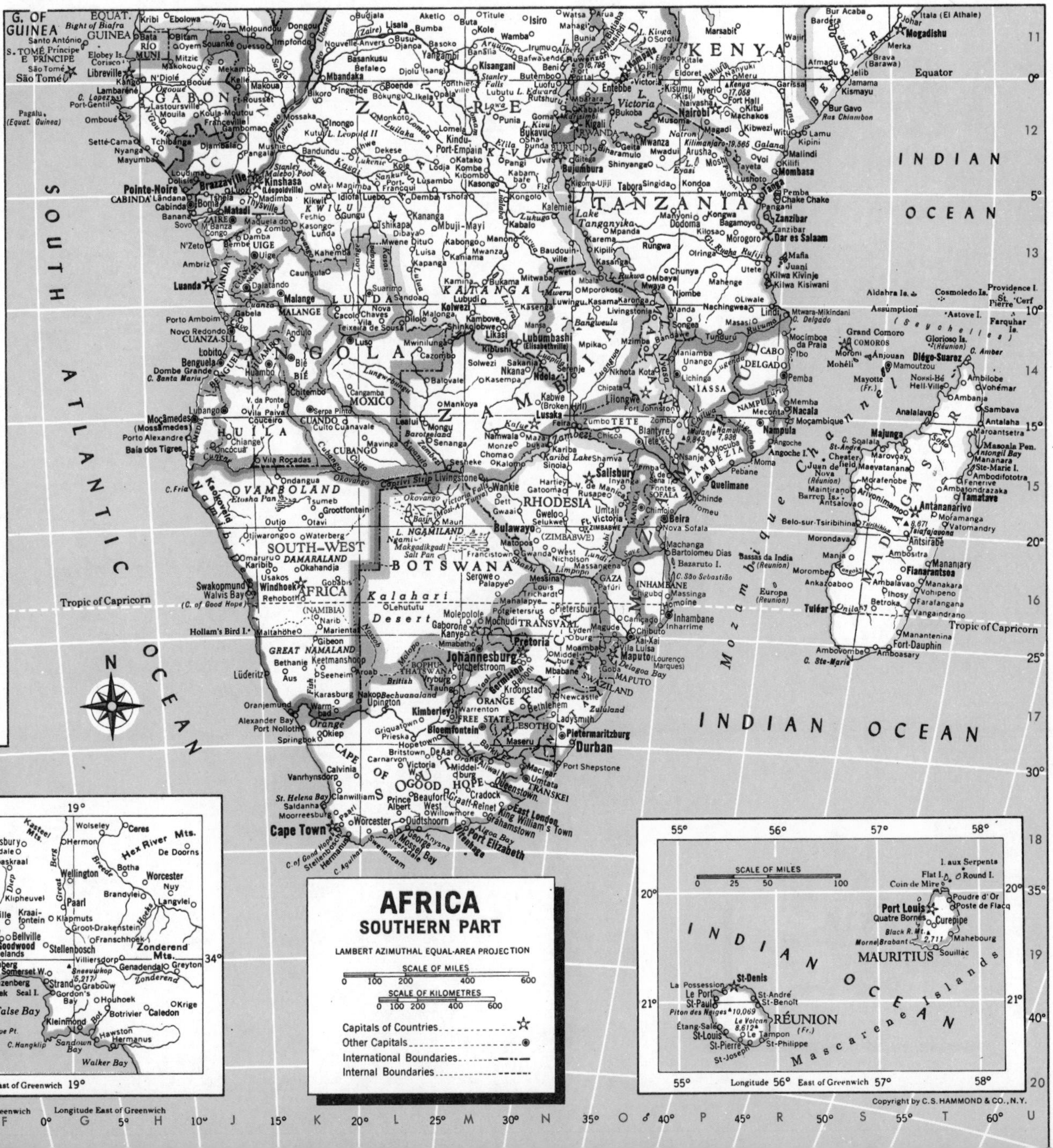

AFRICA
SOUTHERN PART
LAMBERT AZIMUTHAL EQUAL-AREA PROJECTION
SCALE OF MILES
SCALE OF KILOMETRES
Capitals of Countries
Other Capitals
International Boundaries
Internal Boundaries
SOUTH ATLANTIC OCEAN
INDIAN OCEAN
MAURITIUS
RÉUNION
Mascarene Islands

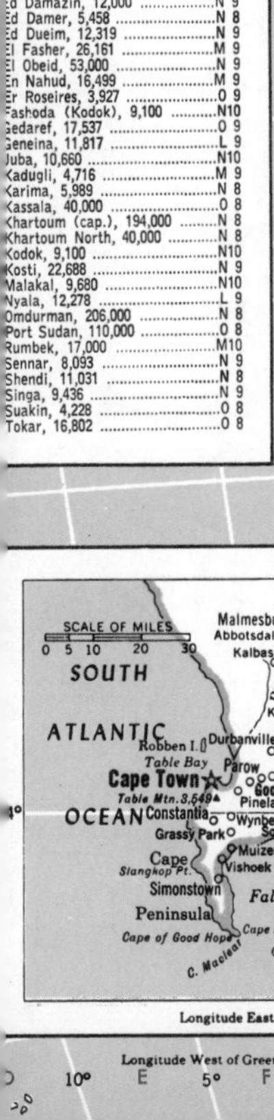

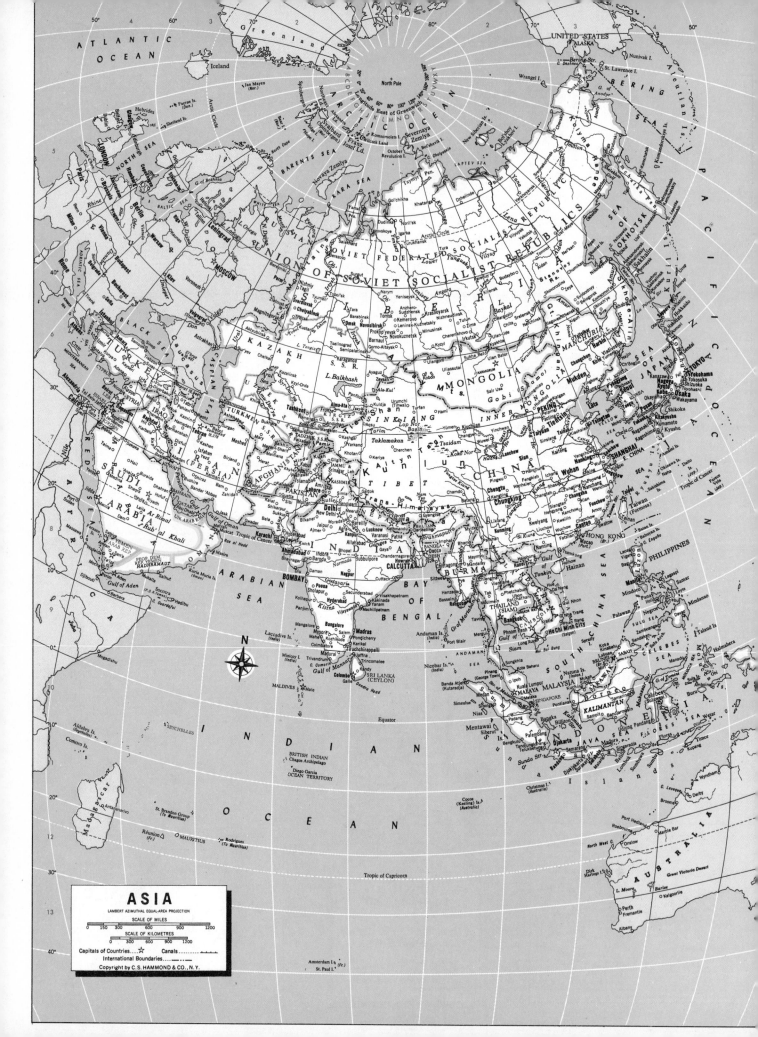

ASIA

LAMBERT AZIMUTHAL EQUAL-AREA PROJECTION

SCALE OF MILES

0 150 300 600 900 1200

SCALE OF KILOMETRES

0 300 600 900 1200

Capitals of Countries.... ☆   Canals.......
International Boundaries.........
Copyright by C. S. HAMMOND & CO., N.Y.

POPULATION DISTRIBUTION

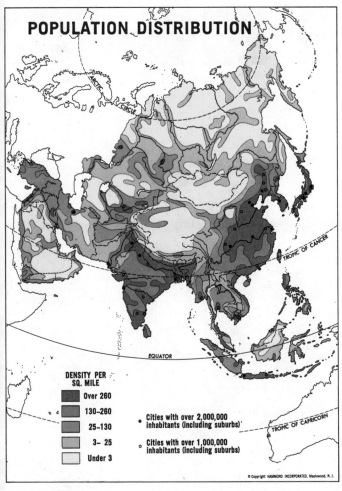

DENSITY PER SQ. MILE

- Over 260
- 130–260
- 25–130
- 3– 25
- Under 3

● Cities with over 2,000,000 inhabitants (including suburbs)

○ Cities with over 1,000,000 inhabitants (including suburbs)

© Copyright HAMMOND INCORPORATED, Maplewood, N. J.

AREA 17,032,000 sq. mi.
POPULATION 2,043,997,000
LARGEST CITY Tokyo
HIGHEST POINT Mt. Everest 29,028 ft.
LOWEST POINT Dead Sea -1,290 ft.

VEGETATION

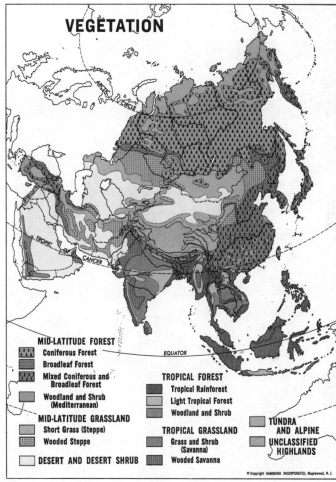

MID-LATITUDE FOREST
- Coniferous Forest
- Broadleaf Forest
- Mixed Coniferous and Broadleaf Forest
- Woodland and Shrub (Mediterranean)

MID-LATITUDE GRASSLAND
- Short Grass (Steppe)
- Wooded Steppe

DESERT AND DESERT SHRUB

TROPICAL FOREST
- Tropical Rainforest
- Light Tropical Forest
- Woodland and Shrub

TROPICAL GRASSLAND
- Grass and Shrub (Savanna)
- Wooded Savanna

TUNDRA AND ALPINE

UNCLASSIFIED HIGHLANDS

© Copyright HAMMOND INCORPORATED, Maplewood, N. J.

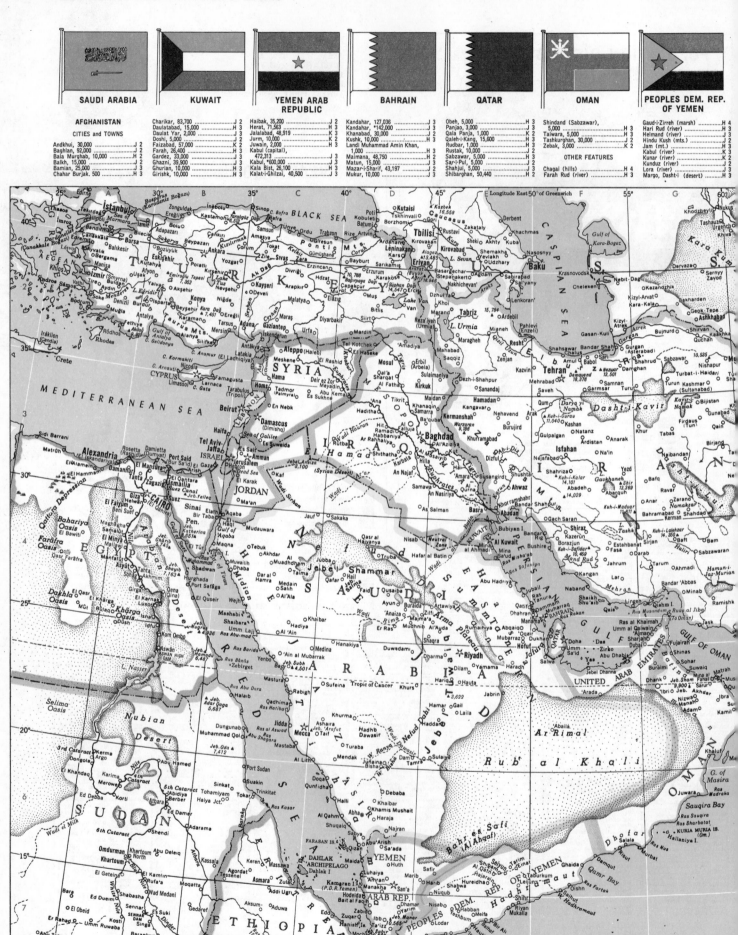

SAUDI ARABIA | **KUWAIT** | **YEMEN ARAB REPUBLIC** | **BAHRAIN** | **QATAR** | **OMAN** | **PEOPLES DEM. REP. OF YEMEN**

AFGHANISTAN
CITIES and TOWNS

Andkhui, 30,000	J 2
Baghlan, 92,000	H 2
Bala Murghab, 10,000	H 2
Balkh, 15,000	H 2
Bamian, 25,000	J 3
Chahar Burjak, 500	H 3

Charikar, 83,700	J 2
Daulatabad, 15,000	H 2
Daulat Yar, 2,000	J 3
Doshi, 5,000	J 2
Faizabad, 57,000	K 2
Farah, 26,400	H 3
Gardez, 33,000	J 3
Ghazni, 39,900	J 3
Ghurian, 10,000	H 3
Girishk, 10,000	H 3

Haibak, 35,200	J 2
Herat, 71,563	H 3
Jalalabad, 48,919	K 3
Jurm, 10,000	K 2
Juwain, 2,000	H 3
Kabul (capital), 472,313	J 3
Kabul, *600,000	J 3
Kala Bist, 26,100	H 3
Kalat-i-Ghilzai, 40,500	J 3

Kandahar, 127,036	J 3
Kandahar, *142,000	J 3
Khanabad, 30,000	J 2
Kushk, 10,000	H 2
Landi Muhammad Amin Khan, 1,000	K 3
Malmana, 48,750	H 2
Matun, 15,000	J 3
Mazar-i-Sharif, 43,197	H 2
Mukur, 10,000	J 3

Obeh, 5,000	H 3
Panjao, 3,000	J 3
Qala Panja, 1,000	K 2
Qaleh-i-Kang, 15,000	H 3
Rudbar, 1,000	H 3
Rustak, 10,000	J 2
Sabzawar, 5,000	H 3
Sar-i-Pul, 5,000	J 2
Shahjui, 50,440	H 2

Shindand (Sabzawar), 5,000	H 3
Taiwara, 5,000	H 3
Tashkurghan, 30,000	J 2
Zebak, 3,000	K 2

OTHER FEATURES

Chagai (hills)	H 4
Farah Rud (river)	H 3

Gaud-i-Zirreh (marsh)	H 4
Hari Rud (river)	J 3
Helmand (river)	J 3
Hindu Kush (mts.)	J 2
Jam (mt.)	J 3
Kabul (river)	K 2
Kunar (river)	K 2
Kunduz (river)	J 2
Lora (river)	J 3
Margo, Dasht-i (desert)	H 3

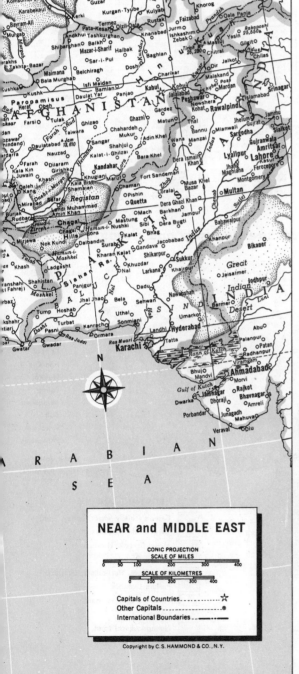

(continued on following page)

SAUDI ARABIA
AREA 920,000 sq. mi.
POPULATION 7,200,000
CAPITALS Riyadh, Mecca
MONETARY UNIT riyal
MAJOR LANGUAGE Arabic
MAJOR RELIGION Islam

KUWAIT
AREA 8,000 sq. mi.
POPULATION 733,196
CAPITAL Al Kuwait
MONETARY UNIT Kuwaiti dinar
MAJOR LANGUAGE Arabic
MAJOR RELIGION Islam

YEMEN ARAB REPUBLIC
AREA 75,000 sq. mi.
POPULATION 5,000,000
CAPITAL San'a
MONETARY UNIT bakcha
MAJOR LANGUAGE Arabic
MAJOR RELIGION Islam

PEOPLES DEMOCRATIC REPUBLIC OF YEMEN
AREA 111,075 sq. mi.
POPULATION 1,220,000
CAPITAL Aden
MONETARY UNIT East African shilling
MAJOR LANGUAGE Arabic
MAJOR RELIGION Islam

BAHRAIN
AREA 231 sq. mi.
POPULATION 207,000
CAPITAL Manama
MONETARY UNIT Bahrain dinar
MAJOR LANGUAGE Arabic
MAJOR RELIGION Islam

QATAR
AREA 8,500 sq. mi.
POPULATION 100,000
CAPITAL Doha
MONETARY UNIT Qatar-Dubai riyal
MAJOR LANGUAGE Arabic
MAJOR RELIGION Islam

UNITED ARAB EMIRATES
AREA 31,628 sq. mi.
POPULATION 155,881
CAPITAL Abu Dhabi
MONETARY UNIT rupee, Bahrain dinar, Qatar-Dubai riyal
MAJOR LANGUAGE Arabic
MAJOR RELIGION Islam

OMAN
AREA 82,000 sq. mi.
POPULATION 565,000
CAPITAL Muscat
MONETARY UNIT rial saidi
MAJOR LANGUAGE Arabic
MAJOR RELIGION Islam

Topography

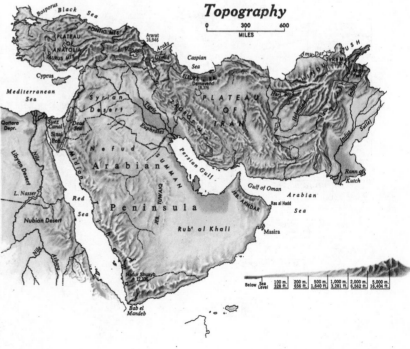

MILES
0   300   600

Below Sea Level | 100 m. 328 ft. | 200 m. 656 ft. | 500 m. 1,640 ft. | 1,000 m. 3,281 ft. | 2,000 m. 6,562 ft. | 5,000 m. 16,404 ft.

NEAR and MIDDLE EAST
CONIC PROJECTION
SCALE OF MILES
0 50 100   200   300   400
SCALE OF KILOMETRES
0   100   200   300   400

Capitals of Countries .... ☆
Other Capitals .... ◉
International Boundaries _____

(continued)

IRAN (continued)

Enzeli (Pahlevi), 41,785 ......E 2
Estahbanat, 18,187 ......F 4
Fahrej (Iranshahr), 5,000 ......H 4
Fasa, 19,000 ......F 4
Firdaus, 11,000 ......G 3
Gach Saran ......F 3
Garmsar, 4,723 ......F 2
Gulpaigan, 20,515 ......F 3
Gunabad, 8,000 ......G 3
Gurgan, 51,181 ......F 2
Hamadan, 124,167 ......E 3
Iranshahr, 5,000 ......H 4
Isfahan, 424,045 ......F 3
Jahrum, 38,236 ......F 4
Juimand (Gunabad), 8,000 ......G 3
Kangavar, 9,414 ......E 3
Kashan, 58,468 ......F 3
Kashmar, 17,000 ......G 2
Kazerun, 39,758 ......F 4
Kazvin, 88,106 ......E 2
Kerman, 85,404 ......G 3
Kermanshah, 187,930 ......E 3
Khaf, 5,000 ......H 3
Khoi, 47,648 ......E 2
Khorramshahr, 88,536 ......E 3
Khur, 2,912 ......G 3
Khurramabad, 59,578 ......E 3
Lar, 22,000 ......F 4
Mahabad, 28,610 ......E 2
Maragheh, 54,106 ......E 2
Marand, 24,000 ......E 2
Meshed, 409,616 ......H 2
Mianeh, 28,447 ......E 2
Mirjawa, 11,000 ......H 4
Na'in, 5,925 ......F 3
Naishapur (Nishapur), 33,482 ......G 2
Nasratabad (Zabul), 20,000 ......H 3
Natanz, 4,370 ......F 3
Nehavend, 24,000 ......E 3
Nejafabad, 43,384 ......F 3
Nishapur, 33,482 ......G 2
Pahlevi, 41,785 ......E 2
Qain, 6,000 ......G 3
Quchan, 29,133 ......G 2
Qum, 134,292 ......F 3
Ravar, 7,000 ......G 3
Resht, 143,557 ......E 2
Reza'iyeh, 110,749 ......D 2
Sabzawar, 42,415 ......G 2
Sabzawaran, 7,000 ......G 4
Samnan, 31,058 ......F 2
Sanandaj, 54,578 ......E 2
Saqqiz, 17,000 ......E 2
Sari, 44,547 ......F 2
Saveh, 17,565 ......F 2
Shahr-i-Tajan (Sari), 44,547 ......F 2
Shahriza, 34,220 ......F 3
Shahrud, 30,767 ......G 2
Shahsawar, 12,000 ......F 2
Shiraz, 269,865 ......F 4
Shirvan, 11,000 ......G 2
Shushtar, 24,000 ......E 3
Sirjan, 12,160 ......G 4
Sultanabad (Arak), 71,925 ......E 3
Sultanabad (Kashmar), 17,000 ......G 2
Susangird, 21,000 ......E 3
Tabas (Tabas-Masina), 10,000 ......H 3
Tabriz, 403,413 ......E 2
Tehran (capital), 2,719,730 ......F 2
Tun (Firdaus), 11,000 ......G 3
Turbat-i-Haidari, 30,106 ......G 2
Turbat-i-Shaikh Jam, 13,000 ......H 2
Turshiz (Kashmar), 17,000 ......G 2
Turun ......G 2
Urmia (Reza'iyeh), 110,749 ......D 2
Yezd, 93,241 ......F 3
Zabul, 20,000 ......H 3
Zahidan, 39,732 ......H 4
Zarand, 5,000 ......G 3
Zenjan, 58,714 ......E 2

OTHER FEATURES

Araks (river) ......E 2
Atrek (river) ......G 2
Bazman, Kuh-i-(mt.) ......H 4
Demavend (mt.) ......F 2
Diz, Ab-i- (river) ......E 3
Elburz (mts.) ......F 2
Galvkhaneh (lake) ......F 3
Gurgan (river) ......F 2
Haliri (river) ......G 4
Jaz Murian, Hamun-i- (marsh) ......G 4
Karun (river) ......E 3
Kavir, Dasht-i- (salt desert) ......G 3
Kavir-i-Namak (salt desert) ......G 3
Lut, Dasht-i- (desert) ......G 3
Maidani, Ras (cape) ......G 4
Mand Rud (river) ......F 4
Mashkel (river) ......H 4
Mehran (river) ......F 4
Namak, Darya-i- (salt lake) ......F 3
Namaksar (salt lake) ......H 3
Namakzar (marsh) ......G 3
Nezwar (mt.) ......F 2
Oman (gulf) ......G 5
Persian (gulf) ......F 4
Qais (isl.) ......F 4
Qishm (isl.) ......G 4
Qizil Uzun (river) ......E 2
Safidar, Kuh-i- (mt.) ......F 4
Shaikh Shu'aib (isl.) ......F 4
Shir (mt.) ......F 3
Taftan (mt.) ......H 4
Talab (river) ......H 4
Tashk (lake) ......F 4
Urmia (lake) ......E 2
Zagros (mts.) ......E 3

IRAQ

CITIES and TOWNS

Al 'Aziziya, 7,450 ......E 3
Al Falluja, 38,072 ......D 3
Al Musaiyib, 15,955 ......D 3
Al Qurna, 5,638 ......E 3
'Amadiya, 2,578 ......D 2
'Amara, 64,847 ......E 3
An Najaf, 128,096 ......D 3
An Nasiriya, 60,405 ......E 3
'Ana, 6,884 ......D 3
Ar Rahhaliya ......D 3
Arbela (Erbil), 90,320 ......D 2
As Salman, 1,789 ......E 3
Baghdad (capital), 502,503 ......E 3
Baghdad, *1,745,328 ......E 3
Ba'quba, 34,575 ......D 3
Basra, 313,327 ......E 3
Erbil, 90,320 ......D 2
Habbaniya, 14,405 ......D 3
Haditha, 6,870 ......D 3
Hai, 16,988 ......E 3
Hilla, 84,717 ......D 3
Hit, 9,131 ......D 3
Karbala', 83,301 ......D 3
Khanaqin, 23,522 ......D 3
Kirkuk, 167,413 ......D 2
Kut, 42,116 ......E 3
Maidan, 354 ......E 3
Mosul, 315,157 ......D 2
Qal'a Sharqat, 2,434 ......D 2
Ramadi, 28,723 ......D 3
Rutba, 5,091 ......D 3
Samarra, 24,746 ......D 3
Samawa, 33,473 ......D 3
Shithatha, 2,326 ......D 3
Sulaimaniya, 86,822 ......E 2
Tikrit, 9,921 ......D 3

OTHER FEATURES

Al Batin, Wadi (river) ......E 4
'Aneiza, Jebel (mt.) ......C 3
'Ar'ar, Wadi (dry river) ......D 3
El Hamad (desert) ......D 3
Euphrates (river) ......E 3
Hauran, Wadi (dry river) ......D 3
Mesopotamia (reg.) ......D 3
Tigris (river) ......E 3

KUWAIT

CITIES and TOWNS

Al Kuwait (capital), 80,008 ......E 4
Al Kuwait, *217,364 ......E 4
Mina al-Ahmadi ......E 4

OTHER FEATURES

Bubiyan (isl.) ......E 4
Persian (gulf) ......F 4

OMAN

CITIES and TOWNS

Adam ......G 5
Buraimi ......G 5
Dhank ......G 5
Ibra ......G 5
'Ibri ......G 5
Juwara ......G 6
Kamil ......G 5
Khaluf ......G 5
Khasab ......G 4
Manah ......G 5
Matrah, 15,000 ......G 5
Mina al Fahal ......G 5
Murbat ......G 6
Muscat (capital), 7,500 ......G 5
Nizwa ......G 5
Quryat ......G 5
Risut ......F 6
Salala, 4,000 ......F 6
Sarur ......G 5
Shinas ......G 5
Sohar ......G 5
Sur ......G 5
Suwaiq ......G 5

OTHER FEATURES

Akhdar, Jebel (range) ......G 5
Arabian (sea) ......H 5
Batina (reg.) ......G 5
Dhofar (reg.), 120,000 ......F 6
Hadd, Ras al (cape) ......G 5
Hallaniya (isl.), 78 ......G 6
Jibsh, Ras (cape) ......G 5
Kuria Muria (isls.), 78 ......G 6
Madraka, Ras (cape) ......G 6
Masira (gulf) ......G 6
Masira (isl.) ......G 5
Musandam, Ras (cape) ......G 4
Nus, Ras (cape) ......G 6
Oman (gulf) ......G 5
Oman (reg.) ......G 5
Ruus al Jibal (dist.) ......G 4
Sauqira (bay) ......G 6
Sauqira, Ras (cape) ......G 6
Sham, Jebel (mt.) ......G 5
Sharbatat, Ras (cape) ......G 6

QATAR

CITIES and TOWNS

Doha (capital), 45,000 ......F 4
Dukhan, 2,500 ......F 4
Umm Sa'id, 3,500 ......F 5

OTHER FEATURES

Persian (gulf) ......F 4
Rakan, Ras (cape) ......F 4

SAUDI ARABIA

PROVINCES

'Asir, 900,000 ......D 6
Eastern, 2,250,000 ......E 4
Hejaz, 1,250,000 ......C 4
Nejd, 1,500,000 ......D 4

CITIES and TOWNS

Abha ......D 6
Abqaiq ......E 4
Abu 'Arish ......D 6
Abu Hadriya ......E 4
'Ain al Mubarrak ......C 5
Al 'Ain ......C 4
Al 'Ala ......C 4
Al 'Auda ......E 4
Al Lith ......C 5
Al Muadhdham ......C 4
Al Qahm ......D 6
'Anaiza ......D 4
Artawiya ......E 4
Badr ......C 5
Buraida ......D 4
Buraimi ......G 5
Dam ......D 5
Dammam, 3,000 ......F 4
Dar al Hamra ......C 4
Dhaba ......C 4
Dhahran, 12,500 ......E 4
Dharma ......E 5
Dilam ......E 5
Doqa ......D 6
Duwadami ......D 5
Er Ras ......D 4
Faid ......D 4
Haddar ......E 5
Hadiya ......C 4
Hafar al Batin ......E 4
Hail, 20,000 ......D 4
Halli ......D 6
Hamar ......E 5
Hanakiya ......D 5
Haql ......C 4
Haradh ......E 5
Haraja ......D 6
Hariq ......E 5
Hauta ......E 5
Hofuf, 83,000 ......E 4
Jabrin ......E 5
Jauf, 5,000 ......C 4
Jidda, 194,000 ......C 5
Jubail ......F 4
Jubba ......D 4
Junaina ......D 5
Kaf ......C 3
Khaibar ......D 6
Khamis Mushait ......D 6
Khurma ......D 5
Khurs ......D 5
Laila ......E 5
Majma'a ......D 4
Maqna ......C 4
Mastaba ......C 5
Mastura ......C 5
Mecca (capital), 185,000 ......C 5
Medain Salih ......C 4
Medina, 72,000 ......D 5
Mendak ......D 5
Mina Sa'ud ......E 4
Mubarraz ......E 4
Mudhnib ......D 4
Muwailih ......C 4
Najran ......D 6
Nisab ......D 4
Oqair ......E 4
Qadhima ......C 5
Qafar ......D 4
Qasr al Haiyanya ......D 4
Qatif ......E 4
Qizan ......D 6
Qunfidha ......D 6
Qusaiba ......D 4
Rabigh ......C 5
Ras Tanura ......F 4
Riyadh (capital), 225,000 ......E 5
Rumaihiya ......E 4
Sabya ......D 6
Sakaka ......D 4
Salwa ......F 5
Shaqra ......D 4
Shuqaiq ......D 6
Sufeina ......D 5
Sulaiyil ......E 5
Taif, 54,000 ......D 5
Taima ......C 4
Tamra ......D 5
Tebuk ......C 4
Truba ......D 4
Turaba ......D 5
Umm Lajj ......C 4
Wejh ......C 4
Yamama ......E 5
Yenbo ......C 5
Zilfi ......E 4

OTHER FEATURES

Abu-mad (cape) ......C 5
'Ar'ar, Wadi (dry river) ......D 3
Al Ahqaf (Bahr es Safi) (desert) ......E 6
'Aneiza, Jebel (mt.) ......C 3
'Aqaba (gulf) ......C 4
Arafat, Jebel (mt.) ......D 5
Ar'ar, Wadi (dry river) ......D 3
Arma (plateau) ......E 4
Aswad, Ras al (cape) ......C 5
Bahr es Safi (desert) ......E 6
Barida, Ras (cape) ......C 5
Bisha, Wadi (dry river) ......D 5
Dahana (desert) ......E 4
Dawasir, Wadi (dry river) ......E 5
Dawasir, Hadb (range) ......D 5
Farasan (isls.) ......D 6
Hasa (reg.) ......E 4
Hatiba, Ras (cape) ......C 5
Jafura (desert) ......F 5
Mashabi (isl.) ......C 4
Midian (district) ......C 4
Misha'ab, Ras (cape) ......E 4
Nefud (desert) ......D 4
Nefud Dahi (desert) ......D 5
Persian (gulf) ......F 4
Ranya, Wadi (dry river) ......D 5
Red (Nefud) (desert) ......D 4
Red (sea) ......C 5
Rima, Wadi (river) ......D 4
Rimal, Ar (desert) ......F 5
Rub' al Khali (desert) ......F 5
Safaniya, Ras (cape) ......E 4
Salma, Jebel (mts.) ......D 4
Shaibara (isl.) ......C 4
Shammar, Jebel (plateau) ......D 4
Sirhan, Wadi (dry river) ......C 3
Subh, Jebel (mt.) ......C 5
Summan (plateau) ......E 4
Tihama (reg.) ......C 5
Tiran (isl.) ......B 4
Tiran (str.) ......B 4
Tuwaiq, Jebel (range) ......E 5

UNITED ARAB EMIRATES

CITIES and TOWNS

Abu Dhabi (capital), 22,000 ......F 5
Abu Dhabi, *35,000 ......F 5
'Ajman, 3,725 ......G 4
'Arada ......F 5
Buraimi ......G 5
Dubai, 13,092 ......F 4
Dubai, *57,400 ......F 4
Fujairah, 761 ......G 4
Jebel Dhauna ......F 5
Ras al Khaimah, 5,244 ......F 4
Sharjah, 19,198 ......F 4
Sharjah, *20,621 ......F 4
Umm al Qaiwain, 2,928 ......F 4

OTHER FEATURES

Das (isl.) ......F 4
Persian (gulf) ......F 4
Yas (isl.) ......F 5
Zirko (isl.) ......F 5

YEMEN ARAB REP.

CITIES and TOWNS

'Amran ......D 6
Bait al Faqih ......D 7
Dhamar ......D 7
Harib ......E 6
Hodeida, 40,000 ......D 7
Huth ......D 6
Ibb ......D 7
Luhaiya (Loheia) ......D
Maida, 2,500 ......D
Manakha ......D
Marib ......D
Mocha ......D
Sa'ada ......D
Safir ......E
San'a (capital), 100,000 ......D
Sheikh Sa'id ......D
Ta'izz, 80,000 ......D
Yarim, 5,000 ......D
Zabid, 8,000 ......D

OTHER FEATURES

Hanish (isls.) ......D
Manar, Jebel (mt.) ......D
Red (sea) C
Sabir, Jebel (mt.) ......D
Tihama (reg.) C
Zuqar (isl.) ......D

YEMEN, PEOPLES DEM. REPUBLIC OF

CITIES and TOWNS

Aden (capital), 150,000 ......E
Aden, *225,000 ......E
Ahwar ......E
Al Qatn ......E
Balhaf ......E
Bir 'Ali ......E
Damqut ......F
'Einat ......E
Ghaida ......F
Hadibu ......F
Hajarain ......E
Haura ......E
Hureidha ......E
'Irqa ......E
Lahej ......E
Leijun ......E
Lodar ......E
Madinat ash Sha'b, 29,897 ......E
Maqatin ......E
Meifa ......E
Mukalla, 30,000 ......E
Nisab ......E
Nuqub ......E
Qishn ......F
Riyan ......E
Saihut, 10,000 ......F
Seiyun ......E
Shabwa ......E
Shibam, 6,000 ......E
Shihr ......E
Shuqra ......E
Taburkum ......E
Tarim ......E
Yeshbum ......E
Zinjibar ......E

OTHER FEATURES

Fartak, Ras (cape) ......F
Hadhramaut (dist.), 350,000 ......E
Hadhramaut, Wadi (dry river) ......F
Kamaran (island), 2,200 ......D
Mandeb, Bab el (strait) ......D
Perim (isl.), 381 ......D
Socotra (island), 14,000 ......F

*City and suburbs.

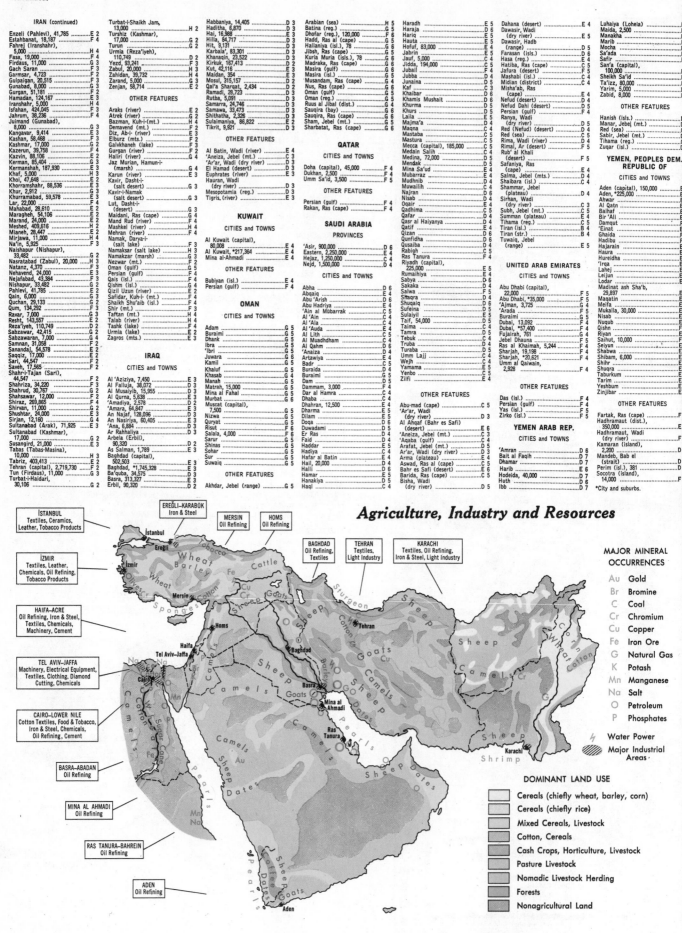

Agriculture, Industry and Resources

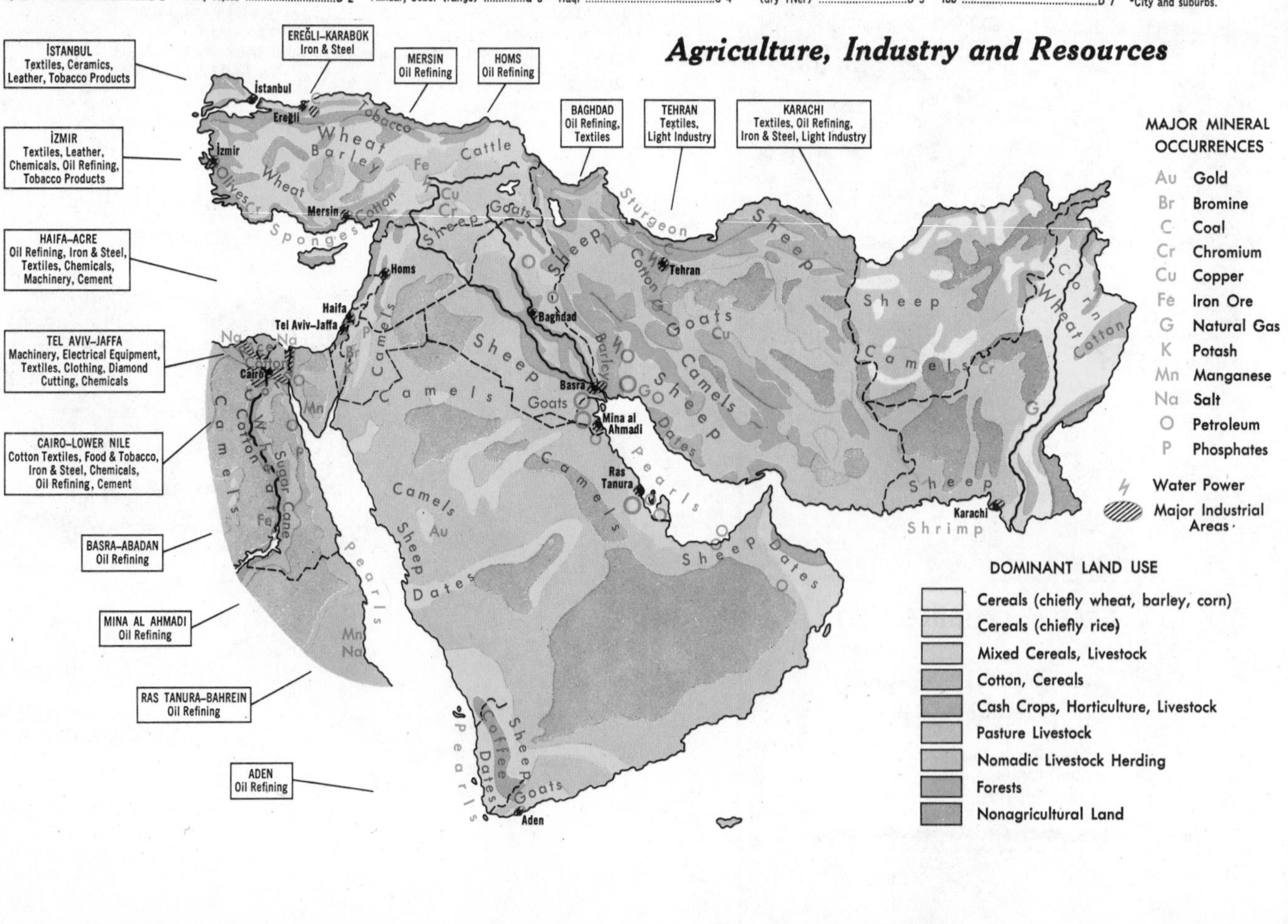

İSTANBUL Textiles, Ceramics, Leather, Tobacco Products
EREĞLI–KARABÜK Iron & Steel
MERSIN Oil Refining
HOMS Oil Refining
BAGHDAD Oil Refining, Textiles
TEHRAN Textiles, Light Industry
KARACHI Textiles, Oil Refining, Iron & Steel, Light Industry
İZMIR Textiles, Leather, Chemicals, Oil Refining, Tobacco Products
HAIFA–ACRE Oil Refining, Iron & Steel, Textiles, Chemicals, Machinery, Cement
TEL AVIV–JAFFA Machinery, Electrical Equipment, Textiles, Clothing, Diamond Cutting, Chemicals
CAIRO–LOWER NILE Cotton Textiles, Food & Tobacco, Iron & Steel, Chemicals, Oil Refining, Cement
BASRA–ABADAN Oil Refining
MINA AL AHMADI Oil Refining
RAS TANURA–BAHREIN Oil Refining
ADEN Oil Refining
İstanbul
Ereğli
İzmir
Mersin
Homs
Haifa
Tel Aviv–Jaffa
Cairo
Baghdad
Tehran
Basra
Mina al Ahmadi
Ras Tanura
Karachi
Aden
Wheat
Barley
Tobacco
Cattle
Olives
Cotton
Sponges
Sheep
Goats
Camels
Sturgeon
Corn
Sugar Cane
Dates
Pearls
Shrimp
MAJOR MINERAL OCCURRENCES
Au Gold
Br Bromine
C Coal
Cr Chromium
Cu Copper
Fe Iron Ore
G Natural Gas
K Potash
Mn Manganese
Na Salt
O Petroleum
P Phosphates
Water Power
Major Industrial Areas
DOMINANT LAND USE
Cereals (chiefly wheat, barley, corn)
Cereals (chiefly rice)
Mixed Cereals, Livestock
Cotton, Cereals
Cash Crops, Horticulture, Livestock
Pasture Livestock
Nomadic Livestock Herding
Forests
Nonagricultural Land

TURKEY

SYRIA

LEBANON

CYPRUS

TURKEY
AREA 301,381 sq. mi.
POPULATION 34,375,000
CAPITAL Ankara
LARGEST CITY Istanbul (greater)
HIGHEST POINT Ararat 16,914 ft.
MONETARY UNIT Turkish pound (lira)
MAJOR LANGUAGE Turkish
MAJOR RELIGION Islam

SYRIA
AREA 71,498 sq. mi.
POPULATION 5,866,000
CAPITAL Damascus
LARGEST CITY Damascus
HIGHEST POINT Hermon 9,232 ft.
MONETARY UNIT Syrian pound
MAJOR LANGUAGES Arabic, Kurdish, Armenian
MAJOR RELIGIONS Islam, Christianity

LEBANON
AREA 4,015 sq. mi.
POPULATION 2,800,000
CAPITAL Beirut
LARGEST CITY Beirut
HIGHEST POINT Qurnet es Sauda 10,131 ft.
MONETARY UNIT Lebanese pound
MAJOR LANGUAGE Arabic
MAJOR RELIGIONS Christianity, Islam

CYPRUS
AREA 3,473 sq. mi.
POPULATION 649,000
CAPITAL Nicosia
LARGEST CITY Nicosia
HIGHEST POINT Troodos 6,406 ft.
MONETARY UNIT Cypriot pound
MAJOR LANGUAGES Greek, Turkish
MAJOR RELIGIONS Eastern (Greek) Orthodoxy, Islam

CYPRUS

CITIES and TOWNS

Famagusta, 38,000 ... F 5
Famagusta, *41,000 ... F 5
Kyrenia, 3,500 ... E 5
Kyrenia, *4,500 ... E 5
Larnaca, 20,000 ... E 5
Larnaca, *21,000 ... E 5
Lefka, 3,673 ... E 5
Lefkara, 2,075 ... E 5
Limassol, 46,500 ... E 5
Limassol, *50,000 ... E 5
Morphou, 6,642 ... E 5
Nicosia (capital), 47,000 ... E 5
Nicosia, *112,000 ... E 5
Paphos, 10,000 ... E 5
Paphos, *11,500 ... E 5
Yialousa, 2,541 ... F 5

OTHER FEATURES

Andreas (cape) ... F 5
Arnauti (cape) ... E 5
Famagusta (bay) ... F 5
Gata (cape) ... F 5
Greco (cape) ... F 5
Klides (isls.) ... F 5
Kormakiti (cape) ... E 5
Larnaca (bay) ... E 5
Morphou (bay) ... E 5
Sovereign Base Area, 3,602 ... E 5
Troodos (mt.) ... E 5

LEBANON

CITIES and TOWNS

*Aleih, 18,630 ... F 6
Amyun, 7,926 ... F 5
Ba'albek, 15,560 ... G 5
Batrun, 5,976 ... F 5
Beirut (capital), 700,000 ... F 6
Beirut, *840,000 ... F 6
En Naqura, 967 ... F 6
Hermil, 2,652 ... G 5

Merj 'Uyun, 9,318 ... F 6
Rashelya, 6,731 ... F 6
Rayak, 1,480 ... G 6
Saida, 32,200 ... F 6
Sidon (Saida), 32,200 ... F 6
Sur, 16,483 ... F 6
Tarabulus (Tripoli), 127,611 ... F 5
Tyre (Sur), 16,483 ... F 6
Zahle, 53,121 ... G 6
Zegharta, 18,210 ... G 5

OTHER FEATURES

Hermon (mt.) ... F 6
Lebanon (range) ... F 6
Litani- (Leontes) (river) ... F 6
Sauda, Qurnet es (mt.) ... G 5

SYRIA

GOVERNORATES

Aleppo, 1,131,854 ... G 4
Damascus, 1,060,484 ... G 6
Damascus (municipality), 630,063 ... G 6
Deir ez Zor, 286,010 ... H 5
Der'a, 221,275 ... G 6
El Quneitra, 6,396 ... F 6
Es Suweida, 151,500 ... G 6
Hama, 390,084 ... G 5
Haseke, 309,279 ... J 4
Homs, 504,098 ... G 5
Idlib, 374,751 ... G 5
Latakia, 625,473 ... G 5
Rashid, 124,876 ... H 5

CITIES and TOWNS

Abu Kemal, 6,907 ... J 5
Aleppo, 566,770 ... G 4
A'zaz, 13,923 ... G 4
Baniyas, 8,537 ... F 5
Damascus (cap.), 789,840 ... G 6
Deir ez Zor, 60,335 ... H 5
Der'a, 20,465 ... G 6

Dimishq (Damascus) (capital), 789,840 ... G 6
Duma, 30,050 ... G 6
El Bab, 27,366 ... G 4
El Haseke, 23,074 ... J 4
El Ladhiqiya (Latakia), 72,378 ... F 5
El Quneitra, 206 ... F 6
El Rashid, 11,998 ... H 5
En Nebk, 16,334 ... G 5
Es Suweida, 17,592 ... G 6
Haleb (Aleppo), 566,770 ... G 4
Hama, 196,224 ... G 5
Harim, 6,837 ... G 4
Homs, 231,877 ... G 5
Idlib, 37,501 ... G 5
Jeble, 15,715 ... F 5
Jerablus, 8,610 ... H 4
Jisr esh Shughur, 13,131 ... G 5
Latakia, 72,378 ... F 5
Masyaf, 7,058 ... G 5
Membij, 13,796 ... G 4
Meyadin, 12,515 ... J 5
Palmyra (Tadmor), 10,670 ... H 5
Qamishliye, 31,448 ... J 4
Quteife, 4,993 ... G 6
Raqqa (El Rashid), 11,998 ... H 5
Safita, 9,650 ... G 5
Selemiya, 25,728 ... G 5
Tadmor, 10,670 ... H 5
Tartus, 39,137 ... F 5
Zebdani, 10,010 ... G 6

OTHER FEATURES

'Abdul 'Aziz, Jebel (mts.) ... J 4
Abu Rujmein, Jebel (mts.) ... H 5
'Asi (river) ... G 5
Druz, Jebel ed (mts.) ... G 6
Euphrates (El Furat) (river) ... H 4
Furat, El (river) ... H 4
Hermon (mt.) ... F 6
Khabur (river) ... J 5
Orontes ('Asi) (river) ... G 5
Ruad (island) ... F 5
Sharqi, Jebel esh (range) ... G 5
Tigris (river) ... K 4

TURKEY

PROVINCES

Adana, 902,712 ... F 4
Adıyaman, 267,288 ... H 4
Afyon-Karahisar, 502,248 ... D 3
Ağrı, 246,961 ... K 3
Amasya, 285,729 ... G 2
Ankara, 1,644,302 ... E 3
Antalya, 486,910 ... D 4
Artvin, 210,065 ... J 2
Aydın, 524,918 ... C 4
Balıkesir, 708,342 ... C 3
Bilecik, 139,041 ... D 2
Bitlis, 154,069 ... J 3
Bolu, 383,939 ... D 2
Burdur, 194,950 ... D 4
Bursa, 755,504 ... C 3
Çanakkale, 350,317 ... B 2
Çankırı, 250,706 ... E 2
Çorum, 485,567 ... F 2
Denizli, 463,369 ... C 4
Diyarbakır, 475,916 ... H 4
Edirne, 303,234 ... B 2
Elâzığ, 322,727 ... H 3
Erzincan, 258,586 ... H 3
Erzurum, 628,001 ... J 3
Eskişehir, 415,101 ... D 3
Gaziantep, 511,026 ... G 4
Giresun, 428,015 ... H 2
Gümüşhane, 262,731 ... H 2
Hakkâri, 83,937 ... K 4
Hatay, 506,154 ... G 4
İçel, 511,273 ... F 4
Isparta, 266,240 ... D 4
İstanbul, 2,293,823 ... C 2
İzmir, 1,234,667 ... B 3
Kars, 606,313 ... K 2
Kastamonu, 441,638 ... E 2
Kayseri, 536,206 ... F 3
Kırklareli, 258,386 ... B 2
Kırşehir, 196,836 ... F 3
Kocaeli, 335,518 ... D 2
Konya, 1,122,622 ... E 4
Kütahya, 398,081 ... C 3

Malatya, 452,624 ... H 3
Manisa, 748,545 ... B 3
Maraş, 438,423 ... G 4
Mardin, 397,880 ... J 4
Muğla, 334,973 ... C 4
Muş, 198,716 ... J 3
Nevşehir, 203,316 ... F 3
Niğde, 362,044 ... F 4
Ordu, 543,863 ... G 2
Rize, 281,099 ... J 2
Sakarya, 404,078 ... D 2
Samsun, 755,946 ... G 2
Siirt, 264,832 ... J 4
Sinop, 266,069 ... F 2
Sivas, 705,186 ... G 3
Tekirdağ, 287,381 ... B 2
Tokat, 495,352 ... G 3
Trabzon, 595,782 ... H 2
Tunceli, 154,175 ... H 3
Urfa, 450,798 ... H 4
Uşak, 190,536 ... C 3
Van, 266,840 ... K 3
Yozgat, 437,883 ... F 3
Zonguldak, 650,191 ... D 2

CITIES and TOWNS

Abana, 2,455 ... F 1
Acıgol, 3,265 ... F 3
Acıpayam, 4,118 ... C 4
Adalia (Antalya), 71,833 ... D 4
Adana, 289,919 ... F 4
Adapazarı, 86,124 ... D 2
Adilcevaz, 6,148 ... K 3
Adıyaman, 22,153 ... H 4
Afşin, 8,069 ... G 3
Afyon, 44,026 ... D 3
Ağlasun, 3,730 ... D 4
Ağlı, 3,425 ... E 2
Ağri (Karaköse), 24,168 ... K 3
Ahlat, 5,879 ... K 3
Akçaabat, 7,600 ... H 2
Akçadağ, 5,995 ... G 3
Akçakale, 4,526 ... H 4
Akçakoca, 7,179 ... D 2
Akdağmadeni, 4,321 ... F 3
Akhisar, 46,167 ... B 3
Aksaray, 24,414 ... F 3

Akşehir, 25,269 ... D 3
Akseki, 2,505 ... D 4
Akviran, 3,786 ... E 4
Akyazı, 9,090 ... D 2
Alaca, 8,288 ... F 2
Alaçam, 7,833 ... F 2
Alanya, 12,436 ... D 4
Alaşehir, 16,012 ... C 3
Alexandretta (İskenderun), 69,382 ... G 4
Aliağa, 3,087 ... B 3
Alibeyköyü, 15,199 ... C 5
Almus, 4,110 ... G 3
Alpu, 2,709 ... D 3
Altındağ, 89,838 ... C 5
Altınova, 6,368 ... K 3
Altıntaş, 2,361 ... C 3
Amasya, 34,168 ... G 2
Anadoluhisarı, 13,959 ... D 6
Anamur, 11,246 ... E 4
Andırın, 3,695 ... G 4
Ankara (capital), 905,660 ... E 3
Antâkya, 57,855 ... G 4
Antalya, 71,833 ... D 4
Araç, 2,820 ... E 2
Aralık, 2,879 ... L 3
Arapkir, 7,056 ... H 3
Ardahan, 9,117 ... K 2
Ardeşen, 5,488 ... J 2
Arhavi, 4,510 ... J 2
Arnavutköy, 22,468 ... D 6
Arsin, 4,028 ... H 2
Artova, 2,863 ... G 2
Artvin, 9,847 ... J 2
Aşkale, 6,943 ... J 3
Aslanköy, 3,656 ... F 4
Avanos, 5,675 ... F 3
Ayancık, 5,320 ... F 2
Ayaş, 3,873 ... E 2
Aybastı, 7,450 ... G 2
Aydın, 43,483 ... B 4
Ayvacık, 2,277 ... B 3
Ayvalık, 16,283 ... B 3
Babadağ, 5,511 ... C 4
Babaeski, 13,879 ... B 2
Bafra, 26,239 ... F 2
Bahçe, 2,264 ... G 4
Bakırköy, 65,285 ... D 6

Baklan, 2,680 ... C 4
Balâ, 3,646 ... E 3
Balıkesir, 69,341 ... B 3
Banaz, 3,495 ... C 3
Bandırma, 33,116 ... B 2
Barak, 3,117 ... E 2
Bartın, 14,259 ... E 2
Başkale, 4,007 ... K 3
Başmakçı, 5,093 ... D 4
Batman, 24,990 ... J 4
Bayburt, 15,184 ... H 2
Bayındır, 11,273 ... B 3
Bayramiç, 4,607 ... B 3
Bergama, 24,121 ... B 3
Beşiktaş, 58,814 ... D 6
Besni, 11,625 ... G 4
Beykoz, 37,730 ... D 5
Beylerbeyi, 21,741 ... D 6
Beyoğlu, 39,984 ... D 6
Beypazarı, 9,860 ... D 2
Beyşehir, 7,456 ... D 4
Biga, 12,063 ... B 2
Bigadiç, 4,820 ... C 3
Bilecik, 9,722 ... C 2
Bingöl (Çapakçur), 11,727 ... J 3
Birecik, 15,317 ... H 4
Bismil, 4,444 ... J 4
Bitlis, 18,725 ... J 3
Bodrum, 5,136 ... B 4
Boğazlıyan, 7,925 ... F 3
Bolu, 21,700 ... D 2
Bolvadin, 20,139 ... D 3
Bor, 14,309 ... F 4
Borçka, 3,763 ... J 2
Bornova, 30,445 ... B 3
Boyabat, 9,418 ... F 2
Bozdoğan, 6,739 ... C 4
Bozkır, 3,112 ... E 4
Bozkurt, 2,954 ... F 2
Bozova, 3,425 ... H 4
Bozüyük, 10,842 ... D 3
Bucak, 10,094 ... D 4
Bulancak, 9,342 ... H 2
Bulanık, 6,186 ... K 3
Buldan, 9,813 ... C 3
Bünyan, 8,467 ... F 3
Burdur, 29,268 ... D 4
Burhaniye, 12,597 ... B 3

(continued on following page)

Agriculture, Industry and Resources

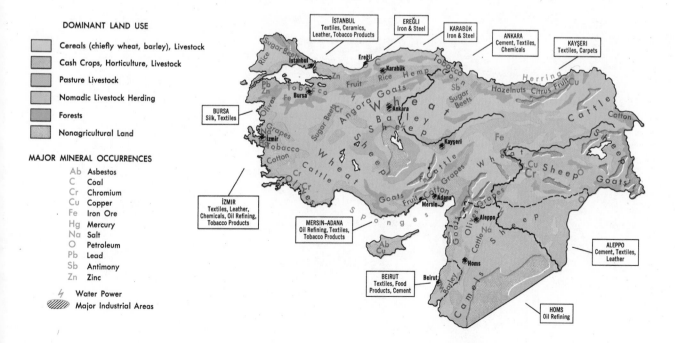

DOMINANT LAND USE

Cereals (chiefly wheat, barley), Livestock
Cash Crops, Horticulture, Livestock
Pasture Livestock
Nomadic Livestock Herding
Forests
Nonagricultural Land

MAJOR MINERAL OCCURRENCES

Ab Asbestos
C   Coal
Cr Chromium
Cu Copper
Fe Iron Ore
Hg Mercury
Na Salt
O   Petroleum
Pb Lead
Sb Antimony
Zn Zinc

⚡ Water Power
▨ Major Industrial Areas

ISTANBUL — Textiles, Ceramics, Leather, Tobacco Products
EREĞLI — Iron & Steel
KARABÜK — Iron & Steel
ANKARA — Cement, Textiles, Chemicals
KAYSERI — Textiles, Carpets
BURSA — Silk, Textiles
İZMIR — Textiles, Leather, Chemicals, Oil Refining, Tobacco Products
MERSIN–ADANA — Oil Refining, Textiles, Tobacco Products
ALEPPO — Cement, Textiles, Leather
BEIRUT — Textiles, Food Products, Cement
HOMS — Oil Refining

TURKEY (continued)

Bursa, 211,644	C 2
Büyükada, 5,261	D 6
Büyükdere	C 2
Çal, 2,325	C 3
Çalköy, 2,232	C 3
Çamlıdere, 3,132	E 2
Can, 5,826	B 2
Çanakkale, 22,789	B 6
Çandır, 4,619	F 3
Çankaya, 161,804	E 3
Çankırı, 21,450	E 2
Çapakçur, 11,727	J 3
Çardak, 2,410	C 6
Çarşamba, 18,003	F 1
Çatalca, 5,811	D 2
Çay, 9,761	D 3
Çaydeli, 11,496	F 2
Çayıralan, 4,357	F 3
Cebeci, 204,592	E 2
Çekerek, 3,286	F 2
Çelikhan, 3,305	H 4
Çemişgezek, 2,235	H 3
Çerkeş, 2,865	D 2
Çerkezköy, 5,355	C 2
Çermik, 5,420	H 3
Çeşme, 4,068	B 3
Çetinkaya, 2,525	G 3
Cevizli, 2,580	D 4
Ceyhan, 41,124	F 4
Çeylanpınar, 12,508	H 4
Cide, 2,130	D 1
Çifteler, 5,901	D 3
Cihanbeyli, 6,739	E 3
Çıldır, 2,040	K 2
Çine, 8,271	B 4
Çivril, 5,780	C 3
Cizre, 8,662	K 4
Çölemerik, -6,129	K 4
Çorlu, 27,187	C 2
Çorum, 41,574	F 2
Çubuk, 8,857	E 2
Çukur, 4,045	J 3
Çumra, 10,299	E 4
Darende, 7,643	G 3
Demirci, 10,050	C 3
Demirköy, 3,309	C 2
Denizli, 64,331	C 3
Derik, 6,684	J 4
Derinkuyu, 4,056	F 3
Develi, 13,411	F 3
Devrek, 5,058	D 2
Dicle, 3,577	J 3
Dikili, 5,805	B 3
Dinar, 11,298	C 3
Dirmil, 2,736	C 4
Divriği, 9,160	H 3
Diyadin, 2,934	K 3
Diyarbakır, 102,653	H 4
Doğanbey, 3,058	J 3
Doğanhisar, 5,966	D 3
Doğanşehir, 4,944	G 3
Döğer, 2,913	D 3
Doğubayazıt, 8,523	K 3
Dörtyol, 11,595	F 4
Dumlu, 3,416	J 2
Dursunbey, 6,533	C 3
Düzce, 22,274	D 2
Eceabat, 2,842	B 6
Edirne, 46,091	B 2
Edremit, 25,003	B 3
Eğridir, 8,912	D 3
Eğriköy, 76,605	H 3
Elbistan, 13,492	G 3
Eldivan, 3,344	E 2
Eleşkirt, 6,019	K 3
Elmalı, 8,482	C 4
Emet, 4,815	C 3
Emirdağ, 10,914	D 3
Emirgazi, 3,509	E 3
Enez, 1,808	A 2
Erbaa, 13,168	G 2
Erciş, 14,072	K 3
Erdek, 7,813	B 2
Erdemli, 10,304	E 4
Ereğli, 38,362	D 2
Ereğli, 18,978	E 3
Erenköy, 35,980	D 6
Ergani, 10,528	H 3
Erkilet, 3,223	F 3
Ermenak, 8,017	E 4
Erzin, 3,298	G 4
Erzincan, 10,257	H 3
Erzincan, 45,197	H 3
Erzurum, 105,317	J 3
Eskimalatya, 4,244	G 3
Eskişehir, 173,882	D 3
Esme, 5,035	C 3
Espiye, 5,318	H 2
Eynesil, 5,210	H 2
Eyüp, 58,244	D 6
Ezbider, 3,185	H 2
Ezine, 7,819	B 3
Fakılı, 3,377	F 3
Fatih, 71,965	D 6
Fatsa, 9,738	G 2
Feke, 3,030	F 4
Fethiye, 8,386	C 4
Fevzipaşa, 3,917	G 4
Fındıklı, 3,928	J 2
Finike, 4,352	D 4
Foça, 2,953	B 3
Gallipoli, 12,945	B 2
Gaziantep, 160,152	G 4
Gazipaşa, 3,524	E 4
Gebze, 9,269	C 2
Gediz, 7,486	C 3
Gelemerk, 4,660	J 2
Gemlik, 15,716	C 2
Genç, 3,114	J 3
Genezin, 4,691	G 3
Gerçüş, 2,593	J 4
Gerede, 6,677	D 2
Germencik, 7,344	B 3
Gerze, 5,387	F 1
Gevaş, 4,019	K 3
Geyve, 5,001	D 2
Giresun, 25,331	H 2
Gökşun, 4,511	G 3
Gölbaşı, 5,886	G 4
Gölcük, 21,544	C 2
Gölköy, 3,826	H 2
Gölhisar, 5,562	C 4
Gölköy, 5,852	G 2
Gölmarmara, 8,301	B 3
Gölpazarı, 3,960	D 2
Gördes, 11,666	C 3
Gördes, 5,665	C 3
Görele, 5,887	H 2
Göynük, 2,084	D 2
Gülşehir, 3,549	E 3
Gümüş, 2,949	F 2
Gümüşacıköy, 10,199	F 2
Gümüşhane, 8,092	H 2
Güney, 7,416	C 3
Gürün, 6,374	G 3
Hacıbektaş, 3,739	F 3
Hacılar, 10,149	F 3
Hadim, 7,176	D 4
Hafik, 2,634	G 3
Hakkâri (Çölemerik), 6,129	K 4
Halfeti, 2,822	G 4
Hani, 4,802	H 3
Harput, 2,205	H 3
Haruniye, 5,198	G 4
Hatay (Antakya), 57,855	G 4
Havran, 7,205	B 3
Havza, 10,338	F 2
Haymana, 5,396	E 3
Hayrabolu, 9,444	C 2
Hazro, 3,483	H 3
Hekimhan, 4,288	G 3
Helete, 3,636	G 3
Hendek, 10,788	D 2
Hilvan, 3,390	H 4
Hınıs, 5,263	J 3
Hisarönü, 3,730	D 2
Hopa, 5,703	J 2
Horasan, 5,236	J 3
Hozat, 4,540	H 3
İçel (Mersin), 86,692	E 4
İçme, 2,680	H 3
İdil, 2,109	K 4
Iğdir, 15,701	K 3
Ilgaz, 2,824	E 2
Ilgın, 10,196	D 3

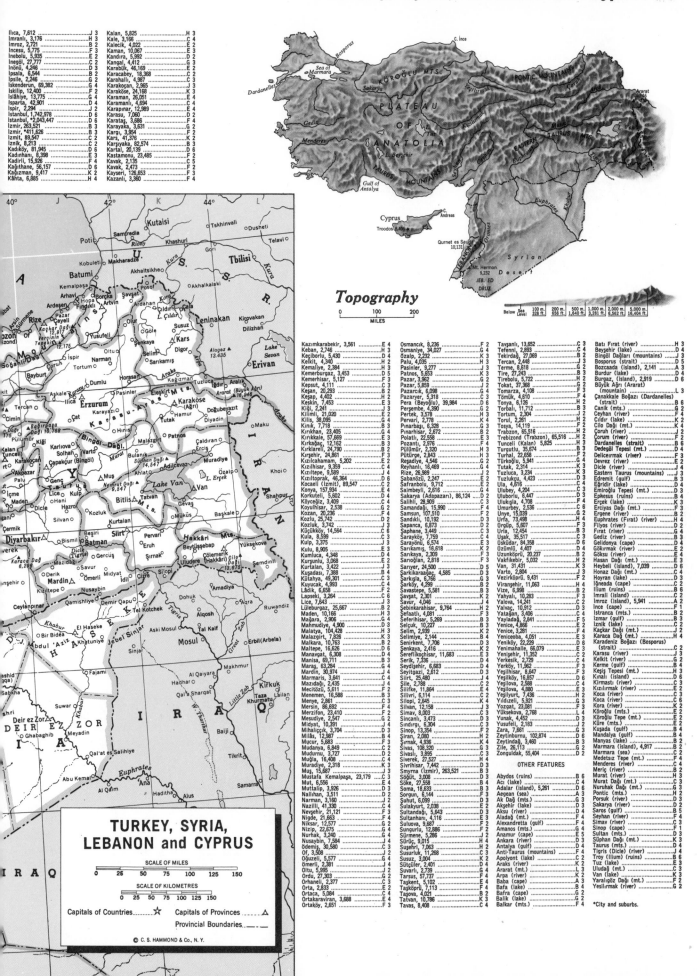

Ilıca, 7,612 .... J 3	Kalan, 5,825 .... H 3
İmranlı, 3,176 .... H 3	Kale, 3,166 .... C 4
İmroz, 2,721 .... B 2	Kalecik, 4,022 .... E 2
İncesu, 5,775 .... F 3	Kaman, 10,067 .... E 3
İnebolu, 5,935 .... E 1	Kandıra, 5,992 .... D 2
İnegöl, 27,777 .... C 2	Kangal, 4,412 .... G 3
İnönü, 4,246 .... D 3	Karabük, 46,169 .... E 2
İpsala, 6,544 .... B 2	Karacabey, 18,368 .... C 2
İpsile, 2,246 .... J 2	Karahallı, 4,987 .... C 3
İskenderun, 69,382 .... G 4	Karakoçan, 2,965 .... J 3
İskilip, 12,400 .... F 2	Karaköse, 24,168 .... K 3
İslâhiye, 13,775 .... G 4	Karaman, 26,051 .... E 4
Isparta, 42,901 .... C 4	Karamanlı, 4,694 .... C 4
İspir, 2,294 .... J 2	Karapınar, 12,989 .... E 4
İstanbul, 1,742,978 .... D 6	Karasu, 7,060 .... D 2
İstanbul, *2,043,447 .... D 2	Karataş, 3,686 .... F 4
İzmir, 263,521 .... B 3	Karayaka, 3,631 .... G 2
İzmir, *411,626 .... C 2	Kargı, 3,954 .... F 2
İznik, 89,547 .... C 2	Kars, 41,376 .... K 2
İznik, 8,213 .... C 2	Karşıyaka, 82,574 .... B 3
Kadıköy, 81,945 .... F 4	Kartal, 20,139 .... D 6
Kadınhanı, 8,398 .... E 3	Kastamonu, 23,485 .... E 2
Kadirli, 15,926 .... F 4	Kavak, 2,135 .... C 5
Kağıthane, 56,157 .... D 6	Kavak, 2,473 .... F 2
Kağızman, 9,417 .... K 2	Kayseri, 126,653 .... F 3
Kâhta, 6,885 .... H 4	Kazanlı, 3,360 .... F 4

Topography

Below Sea Level | 100 m. 328 ft. | 200 m. 656 ft. | 500 m. 1,640 ft. | 1,000 m. 3,281 ft. | 2,000 m. 6,562 ft. | 5,000 m. 16,404 ft.

Kazımkarabekir, 3,561 .... E 4	Osmancık, 8,236 .... F 2	Tavşanlı, 13,652 .... C 3	Batı Fırat (river) .... H 3
Keban, 2,746 .... H 3	Osmaniye, 34,027 .... G 4	Tefenni, 2,893 .... C 4	Beyşehir (lake) .... D 4
Keçiborlu, 5,430 .... D 4	Özalp, 2,232 .... K 3	Tekirdağ, 27,069 .... B 2	Bingöl Dağları (mountains) .... J 3
Kelkit, 4,340 .... H 2	Palu, 4,035 .... H 3	Tercan, 2,448 .... J 3	Bosporus (strait) .... D 5
Kemaliye, 2,384 .... C 3	Pasinler, 9,277 .... J 2	Terme, 6,818 .... G 2	Bozcaada (island), 2,141 .... A 3
Kemerburgaz, 3,453 .... D 5	Patnos, 5,653 .... K 3	Tire, 27,243 .... B 3	Burdur (lake) .... C 4
Kemerhisar, 5,127 .... E 3	Pazar, 3,962 .... G 2	Tirebolu, 5,722 .... H 2	Burgaz, (island), 2,919 .... D 6
Kepsut, 4,111 .... C 3	Pazar, 5,859 .... J 2	Tokat, 37,368 .... F 2	Büyük Ağrı (Ararat)
Keşan, 20,293 .... B 2	Pazarcık, 6,098 .... G 4	Tomarza, 4,108 .... F 3	(mountain) .... L 3
Keşap, 4,402 .... H 2	Pazaryer, 5,318 .... C 3	Tömük, 4,610 .... H 2	Çanakkale Boğazı (Dardanelles)
Keskin, 7,453 .... E 3	Pera (Beyoğlu) 39,984 .... D 6	Tonya, 6,126 .... H 2	(strait) .... B 6
Kiği, 2,241 .... J 3	Perşembe, 4,390 .... G 2	Torbalı, 11,712 .... B 3	Canik (mts.) .... G 2
Kilimli, 11,020 .... D 2	Pertek, 3,578 .... H 3	Tortum, 2,304 .... J 2	Ceyhan (river) .... F 4
Kilis, 38,095 .... G 4	Pervari, 2,778 .... K 4	Torul, 2,261 .... H 2	Çıldır (lake) .... K 2
Kırıkhan, 23,405 .... G 4	Pınarbaşı, 6,328 .... G 3	Tosya, 14,119 .... F 2	Cilo Dağı (mt.) .... K 4
Kırıkkale, 57,669 .... E 3	Pınarhisar, 2,672 .... B 2	Trabzon, 65,516 .... H 2	Çoruh (river) .... J 2
Kırkağaç, 12,162 .... C 3	Polatlı, 22,558 .... E 3	Trabzon (Trabzon), 65,516 .... H 2	Çorum (river) .... F 2
Kırklareli, 24,790 .... B 2	Pozantı, 2,976 .... F 4	Tunceli (Kalan), 5,825 .... H 3	Dardanelles (strait) .... B 6
Kırşehir, 24,861 .... F 3	Pülümür, 2,320 .... H 3	Turgutlu, 35,674 .... B 3	Dedegöl Tepesi (mt.) .... D 4
Kızılcahamam, 5,202 .... E 2	Pütürge, 2,843 .... H 3	Turhal, 22,658 .... F 2	Delicerrmak (river) .... E 2
Kızılhisar, 9,359 .... C 4	Reşadiye, 4,546 .... G 2	Türkoğlu, 5,941 .... G 4	Devrez (river) .... E 2
Kızıltepe, 5,589 .... J 4	Reyhanlı, 16,469 .... G 4	Tutak, 2,314 .... K 3	Dicle (river) .... J 3
Kızıltoprak, 46,364 .... D 6	Rize, 26,989 .... J 2	Tuzluca, 3,234 .... K 2	Eastern Taurus (mountains) .... J 3
Kocaeli (İzmit), 89,547 .... C 2	Sabanözü, 2,247 .... E 2	Tuzlukçu, 4,423 .... D 3	Edremit (gulf) .... B 3
Konya, 157,934 .... E 4	Safranbolu, 9,712 .... E 2	Ula, 4,976 .... C 4	Eğridir (lake) .... D 4
Korkuteli, 5,602 .... D 4	Saimbeyli, 2,616 .... G 4	Ulubey, 4,204 .... C 3	Emiroğlu Tepesi (mt.) .... D 3
Köyceğiz, 3,409 .... C 4	Sakarya (Adapazarı), 86,124 .... D 2	Uluborlu, 6,447 .... D 4	Ephesus (ruins) .... B 3
Koyulhisar, 2,538 .... G 2	Salihli, 28,909 .... C 3	Ulukışla, 4,706 .... F 4	Erçek (lake) .... K 3
Kozan, 20,236 .... F 4	Samandağı, 15,990 .... F 4	Umurbey, 2,538 .... C 6	Erciyas Dağı (mt.) .... F 3
Kozlu, 25,742 .... D 2	Samsun, 107,510 .... F 2	Unye, 15,009 .... G 2	Ergene (river) .... B 2
Kozluk, 3,742 .... J 3	Sandıklı, 10,192 .... D 3	Urfa, 73,498 .... H 4	Euphrates (Fırat) (river) .... H 4
Küçükköy, 14,564 .... C 6	Sapanca, 6,873 .... D 2	Ürgüp, 5,607 .... F 3	Filyos (river) .... D 2
Kula, 8,599 .... C 3	Şaphane, 3,449 .... C 3	Urla, 12,454 .... B 3	Fırat (river) .... G 4
Kula, 3,375 .... B 3	Sarayköy, 7,759 .... C 3	Üsküdar, 84,358 .... D 6	Gediz (river) .... C 3
Kulu, 8,905 .... E 3	Sarayönü, 6,574 .... E 3	Üzümlü, 4,407 .... D 3	Gelidonya (cape) .... D 4
Kuluncak, 4,348 .... H 3	Sarıkamış, 16,618 .... K 2	Uzunköprü, 20,237 .... B 2	Gökırmak (river) .... E 2
Kurşunlu, 3,068 .... E 2	Sarıkaya, 2,309 .... F 3	Vakfıkebir, 5,032 .... H 2	Göksu (river) .... E 3
Kurtalan, 3,422 .... J 3	Sarıoğlan, 2,818 .... F 3	Van, 31,431 .... K 3	Hasan Dağı (mt.) .... E 3
Kuşadası, 7,388 .... B 3	Sarıyer, 24,500 .... D 5	Varto, 2,804 .... J 3	Heybeli (island), 7,039 .... D 6
Kütahya, 49,301 .... C 3	Şarkikaraağaç, 4,585 .... J 4	Verirköprü, 9,431 .... F 2	Honaz Dağı (mt.) .... C 3
Kuyucak, 4,993 .... C 3	Şarkışla, 6,766 .... G 3	Viranşehir, 11,063 .... H 4	Hoyran (lake) .... D 3
Ladik, 6,658 .... F 2	Şarköy, 4,299 .... B 2	Vize, 6,998 .... B 2	İğneada (cape) .... B 6
Lapseki, 3,969 .... B 2	Savaştepe, 5,581 .... B 3	Yahyalı, 10,283 .... F 4	Ilium (ruins) .... A 3
Lice, 7,643 .... J 3	Şavşat, 2,301 .... J 2	Yalova, 14,241 .... C 2	İmralı (island) .... C 2
Lüleburgaz, 25,667 .... B 2	Savur, 4,046 .... J 4	Yalvaç, 10,912 .... D 3	İmroz (island), 5,941 .... A 2
Maden, 10,166 .... H 3	Şebinkarahisar, 9,764 .... H 2	Yaşlıdağ, 3,406 .... D 3	İnce (cape) .... F 1
Mağara, 7,906 .... G 4	Şefaatli, 4,081 .... F 3	Yayladağ, 2,841 .... F 5	İstranca (mts.) .... B 2
Mahmudiye, 4,900 .... D 3	Selçuk, 10,227 .... B 3	Yenice, 4,866 .... C 3	İzmar (gulf) .... B 3
Malatya, 104,428 .... H 3	Selim, 2,939 .... K 2	Yenice, 3,281 .... C 3	Kaçkar Dağı (mt.) .... J 2
Malazgirt, 7,826 .... J 3	Selimiye, 2,144 .... B 3	Yenicekoca, 4,051 .... D 3	Karaca Dağ (mt.) .... H 4
Malkara, 10,763 .... B 2	Şenirkent, 7,706 .... D 3	Yeniköy, 22,229 .... C 6	Karadeniz Boğazı (Bosporus)
Maltepe, 16,626 .... D 6	Şenkaya, 2,416 .... J 2	Yenimahalle, 66,079 .... E 3	(strait) .... D 5
Manavgat, 6,308 .... D 4	Şereflikoçhisar, 11,883 .... E 3	Yenişehir, 11,352 .... C 2	Karasu (river) .... J 3
Manisa, 69,711 .... B 3	Serik, 7,336 .... D 4	Yerkesik, 2,392 .... C 4	Kelkit (river) .... G 2
Maraş, 63,284 .... G 4	Seydişehir, 6,683 .... D 4	Yerköy, 11,962 .... F 3	Kerme (gulf) .... B 4
Mardin, 30,974 .... J 4	Seyitgazi, 2,612 .... D 3	Yeşilhisar, 8,647 .... F 3	Keşiş Tepesi (mt.) .... H 3
Marmaris, 3,641 .... C 4	Siirt, 25,480 .... J 4	Yeşilköy, 16,857 .... D 6	Kınalı (island) .... D 6
Mazıdağı, 2,435 .... J 4	Silifke, 11,864 .... E 4	Yeşilova, 2,388 .... C 4	Kırmastı (river) .... C 2
Mecitözü, 5,611 .... F 2	Silivri, 6,114 .... C 2	Yeşilova, 4,880 .... B 3	Kızılırmak (river) .... E 3
Menemen, 16,588 .... B 3	Silopi, 2,645 .... K 4	Yığılçar, 7,436 .... H 2	Koca (river) .... B 2
Menye, 2,861 .... C 3	Silvan, 12,158 .... J 3	Yıldızeli, 5,921 .... G 3	Koca (river) .... C 3
Mersin, 86,692 .... F 4	Simav, 8,003 .... C 3	Yozgat, 23,081 .... F 3	Köroğlu (mts.) .... E 2
Merzifon, 23,410 .... F 2	Sincanlı, 3,473 .... D 3	Yüksekova, 2,768 .... L 4	Köroğlu Tepe (mt.) .... E 2
Mesudiye, 2,547 .... G 2	Sındırgı, 6,304 .... C 3	Yunak, 4,452 .... D 3	Küre (mts.) .... E 2
Midyat, 10,391 .... J 4	Sinop, 13,354 .... F 2	Yusufeli, 2,183 .... J 2	Kuşada (gulf) .... B 3
Mihalıççık, 3,704 .... D 3	Şiran, 2,868 .... H 2	Zara, 7,661 .... G 3	Mandalya (gulf) .... B 4
Milâs, 6,587 .... B 3	Şırnak, 4,936 .... K 4	Zeytinburnu, 102,874 .... D 6	Manyas (lake) .... B 2
Mucur, 5,683 .... F 3	Sivas, 108,320 .... G 3	Zeytindağ, 3,460 .... B 3	Marmara (island), 4,917 .... C 2
Mudanya, 6,849 .... C 2	Siverek, 27,527 .... H 4	Zonguldak, 55,404 .... D 2	Marmara (Sea) .... C 2
Mudurnu, 3,727 .... D 2	Sivrihisar, 7,442 .... D 3		Medetsize Tepe (mt.) .... F 4
Muğla, 16,408 .... C 4	Smyrna (İzmir), 263,521 .... B 3		Meriç (river) .... B 2
Muradiye, 2,318 .... K 3	Söğüt, 3,008 .... D 3		Murat (river) .... J 3
Muş, 15,687 .... J 3	Söke, 27,558 .... B 3	**OTHER FEATURES**	Murat Dağı (mt.) .... C 3
Mustafa Kemalpaşa, 23,179 .... C 2	Soma, 18,633 .... B 3		Nurhak Dağı (mt.) .... G 4
Mut, 6,556 .... E 4	Sorgun, 6,144 .... F 3		Pontic (mts.) .... G 2
Muttalip, 3,926 .... D 3	Suhut, 6,099 .... D 3	Abydos (ruins) .... B 6	Porsuk (river) .... D 3
Nalıhan, 3,511 .... D 2	Sulakyurt, 2,038 .... E 3	Acı (lake) .... C 4	Sakarya (river) .... D 2
Narman, 3,160 .... J 2	Sultandağı, 5,643 .... D 3	Adalar (island), 5,261 .... D 6	Saros (gulf) .... B 5
Nazilli, 41,330 .... C 3	Sultanhanı, 4,116 .... E 3	Aegean (sea) .... A 3	Seyhan (river) .... F 4
Nevşehir, 21,121 .... F 3	Sungurlu, 12,886 .... F 2	Ak Dağ (mts.) .... G 3	Simav (river) .... C 3
Niğde, 21,663 .... F 4	Sungurlu, 5,286 .... J 2	Akşehir (lake) .... D 3	Sinop (cape) .... F 1
Niksar, 12,577 .... G 2	Sürüç, 9,015 .... H 4	Aksu (river) .... D 4	Süphan Dağı (mt.) .... K 3
Nizip, 22,675 .... G 4	Suşehri, 7,063 .... H 2	Aladağ (mt.) .... F 4	Taurus (mts.) .... E 4
Nurhak, 3,240 .... H 4	Susurluk, 11,268 .... C 3	Alexandretta (gulf) .... F 4	Süphan Dağı (mt.) .... K 3
Nusaybin, 7,584 .... J 4	Susuz, 3,004 .... K 2	Amanos (mts.) .... G 4	Taurus (mts.) .... E 4
Ödemiş, 30,580 .... B 3	Süçüler, 2,401 .... D 4	Anamur (cape) .... E 5	Tigris (Dicle) (river) .... J 4
Of, 3,508 .... H 2	Suvarlı, 2,739 .... G 4	Ankara (river) .... E 3	Troy (Ilium) (ruins) .... A 3
Öğüzeli, 5,577 .... G 4	Tarsus, 57,737 .... F 4	Antalya (gulf) .... D 4	Tuz (lake) .... E 3
Ömerli, 2,381 .... J 4	Taşkent, 5,102 .... E 4	Anti-Taurus (mountains) .... G 3	Uludağ (mt.) .... C 3
Oltu, 5,995 .... J 2	Taşköprü, 7,113 .... F 2	Apolyont (lake) .... C 2	Van (lake) .... K 3
Ordu, 27,303 .... G 2	Taşova, 5,084 .... G 2	Araks (river) .... K 2	Yaralıgöz Dağı (mt.) .... F 2
Orhaneli, 2,377 .... C 3	Ortakaraviran, 3,688 .... E 4	Ararat (mt.) .... L 3	Yeşilırmak (river) .... G 2
Orta, 2,833 .... E 2	Ortaköy, 2,651 .... F 3	Arpa (river) .... K 2	
Ortaca, 5,084 .... C 4	Tatvan, 10,798 .... K 3	Baba (cape) .... A 3	
Ortakaraviran, 3,688 .... E 4	Tavas, 8,408 .... C 4	Bafa (lake) .... B 3	*City and suburbs.
Ortaköy, 2,651 .... F 3		Bafra (cape) .... G 2	
		Balık (lake) .... G 2	
		Balkar (mts.) .... F 4	

TURKEY, SYRIA, LEBANON and CYPRUS

SCALE OF MILES
0 25 50 75 100 125 150

SCALE OF KILOMETRES
0 25 50 75 100 125 150

Capitals of Countries .... ☆   Capitals of Provinces .... △

Provincial Boundaries ....

© C. S. HAMMOND & Co., N.Y.

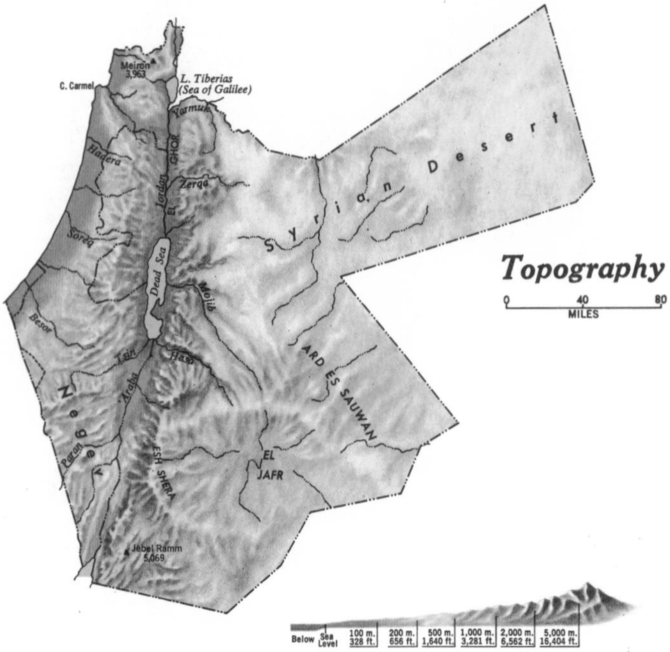

Topography
0 40 80
MILES
Meiron 3,963
C. Carmel
L. Tiberias (Sea of Galilee)
Yarmuk
Hadera
GHOR
Jordan
Zerqa
Soreq
Dead Sea
Mojib
Besor
Syrian Desert
Hasa
Lain
Araba
Negev
Paran
ARD ES SAUWAN
ESH SHERA
EL JAFR
Jebel Ramm 5,069
Below Sea Level
100 m. 328 ft.
200 m. 656 ft.
500 m. 1,640 ft.
1,000 m. 3,281 ft.
2,000 m. 6,562 ft.
5,000 m. 16,404 ft.

ISRAEL

DISTRICTS

Central, 426,454 .... B 3
Haifa, 391,380 .... C 2
Jerusalem, 201,749 .... B 4
Northern, 363,159 .... C 2
Southern, 213,283 .... B, D 5
Tel Aviv, 735,776 .... B 3

CITIES and TOWNS

Acre, 28,100 .... C 2
Afiqim, 1,243 .... D 2
Afula, 15,000 .... C 2
Ahuzzam, 407 .... B 4
Akko (Acre), 28,100 .... C 2
Arad .... C 5
'Arrabe, 3,636 .... C 2
Ashdod, 11,700 .... B 4
Ashdot Ya'aqov, 1,197 .... D 2
Ashqelon, 28,400 .... A 4
Atlit, 1,516 .... B 2
Avihayil, 579 .... B 3
Azor, 3,687 .... B 3
Bat Shelomo, 218 .... B 2
Bat Yam, 39,100 .... B 3
Beer Ora .... D 5
Be'er Tuveya, 602 .... B 4
Be'eri, 390 .... A 5
Beersheba, 51,600 .... D 4
Bene Beraq, 51,700 .... B 3
Bet Dagan, 2,932 .... B 4
Bet Hagaddi, 566 .... B 5
Bet Qama, 228 .... B 5
Bet She'an, 10,900 .... D 3
Bet Shemesh, 8,200 .... B 4
Binyamina, 2,950 .... B 2
Carmiel .... C 2
Dafna, 577 .... D 1
Dalyat al-Karmel, 4,124 .... B 2
Dan, 498 .... D 1
Dimona, 12,100 .... D 4
Dor, 195 .... B 2
'Ein Harod, 1,372 .... C 2
El 'Auja .... D 5
Elath (Elat), 7,000 .... D 5
Elyakim, 568 .... C 2
Elyashiv, 435 .... B 3
Even Yehuda, 3,464 .... B 3
Gal'on, 356 .... B 4
Gan Yavne, 2,668 .... B 4
Gat, 430 .... B 4
Gedera, 4,561 .... B 4
Gesher, 360 .... D 2
Gesher Haziv, 238 .... C 1
Gevar'am, 283 .... B 4
Gilat, 561 .... B 5
Ginnosar, 473 .... D 2
Giv'atayim, 30,932 .... B 3
Giv'at Brenner, 1,505 .... B 4
Giv'at Hayyim, 1,360 .... B 3
Gosh Halav (Jish), 1,498 .... C 1
Habonim, 189 .... B 2
Hadera, 27,200 .... B 3
Haifa, 212,200 .... B 2
Haifa, *447,800 .... B 2
Hazerim, 127 .... B 5
Helez, 466 .... B 4
Herzeliyya, 30,000 .... B 3
Hod Hasharon .... B 3
Hodiyya, 400 .... B 4
Holon, 55,200 .... B 3
Iksal, 2,156 .... C 2
Jerusalem (capital), 275,000 .... C 4
Jish, 1,498 .... C 1
Kafar Kanna, 3,549 .... C 2
Kafar Yasif, 2,975 .... C 2
Karkur, 2,856 .... C 3
Kefar Atta, 16,300 .... C 2
Kefar Blum, 565 .... D 1
Kefar Gil'adi, 701 .... D 1
Kefar Ruppin, 306 .... D 3
Kefar Sava, 19,000 .... B 3
Kefar Vitkin, 808 .... B 3
Kefar Yona, 2,372 .... B 3
Kefar Zekhariya, 420 .... B 4
Kinneret, 909 .... D 2
Kurnub .... C 5
Lod (Lydda), 21,000 .... B 4
Lydda, 21,000 .... B 4
Magen, 149 .... A 5
Malkiya .... D 1
Mash' Abbe Sade, 238 .... B 6
Mavqi'im, 177 .... B 4
Megiddo .... C 2
Me'ona, 317 .... C 1
Metula, 261 .... D 1
Migdal, 688 .... C 2
Mikhmoret, 608 .... B 3
Mishmar Hanegev, 336 .... B 5
Mishmar Hayarden .... D 1
Mivtahim, 398 .... A 5
Mizpe Ramon, 331 .... D 5
Moza Illit, 219 .... C 4
Mughar, 4,010 .... C 2
Muqeible, 459 .... C 2
Nahariyya, 15,900 .... C 1
Nazareth, 26,400 .... C 2
Negba, 453 .... B 4
Nes Ziyyona, 11,200 .... B 4
Nesher, 8,450 .... C 2
Netanya, 46,200 .... B 3
Nevatim, 436 .... B 5
Newe Yam, 211 .... B 2
Nir Am, 331 .... B 4
Nir Yitzhaq, 209 .... A 5
Nizzanim, 479 .... B 4
'Omer .... B 5
Oron .... C 6
Pardes Hanna, 8,200 .... B 2
Peduyim, 361 .... B 5
Petah Tiqwa, 58,700 .... B 3
Qadima, 2,937 .... B 3
Qedma, 157 .... B 4
Qiryat Bialik, 10,400 .... C 2
Qiryat Gat, 10,111 .... B 4
Qiryat Haayin, 9,256 .... B 2
Qiryat Motzkin, 10,300 .... C 2
Qiryat Shemona, 13,900 .... C 1
Qiryat Tiv'on, 9,650 .... C 2
Qiryat Yam, 11,600 .... C 2
Ra'anana, 10,000 .... B 3
Ramat Gan, 109,400 .... B 3
Ramat Hasharon, 11,100 .... B 3
Rame, 2,986 .... C 2
Ramla, 23,900 .... B 4
Rehovot, 30,400 .... B 4
Re'im, 155 .... A 5
Revadim, 175 .... B 4
Revivim, 258 .... D 5
Rishon Le Ziyyon, 30,000 .... B 4
Rosh Pinna, 700 .... D 2
Ruhama, 497 .... B 4
Sa'ad, 418 .... B 5
Safad (Zefat), 11,500 .... C 2
Sakhnin, 5,500 .... C 2
Sede Boqer .... D 5
Sedom .... D 5
Sedot Yam, 511 .... B 3
Shave Ziyyon, 269 .... B 2
Shefar'am, 7,650 .... C 2
Shefayim, 614 .... B 3
Shoval, 393 .... B 5
Tayibe, 8,100 .... C 3
Tel Aviv-Jaffa, 384,700 .... B 3
Tel Aviv-Jaffa, *838,000 .... B 3
Tiberias, 22,300 .... C 2
Tirat Hakarmel, 11,300 .... B 2
Tirat Zevi, 353 .... D 3
Tur'an, 2,304 .... C 2
Umm el Fahm, 8,100 .... C 2
Urim, 203 .... B 5
Uzza, 487 .... B 4
Yad Mordekhai, 416 .... A 1
Yagur, 1,266 .... C 2
Yavne, 6,200 .... B 4
Yavne'el, 1,580 .... C 2
Yehud, 7,000 .... B 3
Yeroham, 1,574 .... B 6
Yesodot, 293 .... B 4
Yesud Hama'ala, 428 .... D 1
Yiftah .... D 1
Yirka, 2,715 .... C 2
Yoqne'am, 2,884 .... C 2
Yotvata .... D 5
Zavdi'el, 396 .... B 4
Ze'elim, 148 .... A 5
Zefat, 11,500 .... C 2
Zikhron Ya'aqov, 4,393 .... B 2
Zippori, 241 .... C 2

OTHER FEATURES

'Araba, Wadi (dry river) .... D 5
Beer Ef'e (well) .... C 5
Beer Sheva', Wadi (dry river) .... B 4
Besor (river) .... B 5
Borot Kidod (well) .... C 5
Carmel (cape) .... B 2
Carmel (mt.) .... C 2
Dead (sea) .... C 4
Dimona (mt.) .... C 5
'Ein Gedi (well) .... C 5
'Ein Netafim (well) .... D 5
Galilee (region) .... C 2
Galilee, Sea of (sea) .... D 2
Gerar, Wadi (dry river) .... B 5
Hadera (river) .... B 3
Haifa (bay) .... C 2
Hatira (mt.) .... B 6
Hemar, Wadi (dry river) .... C 5
Judaea (region) .... B 5
Lakhish, Wadi (dry river) .... B 4
Meiron (mt.) .... C 1
Negev (region) .... D 5
Paran, Wadi (dry river) .... D 5
Qarn (river) .... C 1
Qishon (river) .... C 2
Ramon (mt.) .... D 5

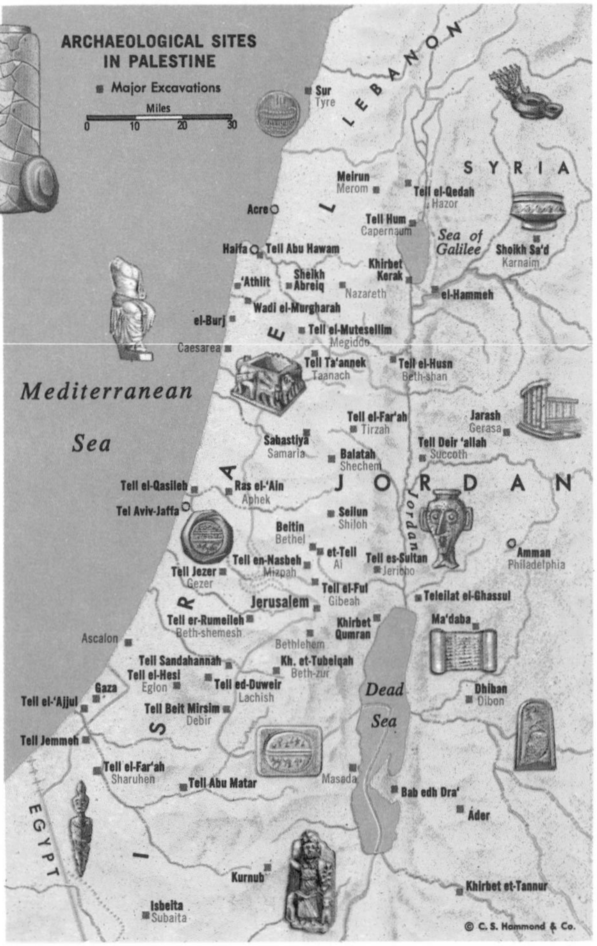

ARCHAEOLOGICAL SITES IN PALESTINE
Major Excavations
Miles
0 10 20 30
Sur
Tyre
LEBANON
SYRIA
Meirun
Merom
Tell el-Qedah
Hazor
Acre
Tell Hum
Capernaum
Sea of Galilee
Haifa
Tell Abu Hawam
Sheikh Sa'd
Karnaim
'Athlit
Sheikh Abreiq
Khirbet Kerak
Nazareth
el-Hammeh
Wadi el-Murgharah
el-Burj
Tell el-Mutesellim
Megiddo
Caesarea
Tell Ta'annek
Taanach
Tell el-Husn
Beth-shan
Mediterranean
Sea
Tell el-Far'ah
Tirzah
Jarash
Gerasa
Sebastiya
Samaria
Balatah
Shechem
Tell Deir 'allah
Succoth
Tell el-Qasileh
Ras el-'Ain
Aphek
JORDAN
Tell Aviv-Jaffa
Seilun
Shiloh
Beitin
Bethel
et-Tell
Ai
Jordan
Amman
Philadelphia
Tell en-Nasbeh
Mizpah
Tell es-Sultan
Jericho
Tell Jezer
Gezer
Tell el-Ful
Gibeah
Teleilat el-Ghassul
Jerusalem
Tell er-Rumeileh
Beth-shemesh
Khirbet Qumran
Ma'daba
Ascalon
Bethlehem
Tell Sandahannah
Kh. et-Tubeiqah
Beth-zur
Tell el-Hesi
Eglon
Gaza
Tell ed-Duweir
Lachish
Dead Sea
Dhiban
Dibon
Tell el-'Ajjul
Tell Beit Mirsim
Debir
Tell Jemmeh
Tell el-Far'ah
Sharuhen
Tell Abu Matar
Masada
Bab edh Dra'
Áder
EGYPT
ISRAEL
Kurnub
Khirbet et-Tannur
Isbeita
Subaita
© C. S. Hammond & Co.

Agriculture, Industry and Resources

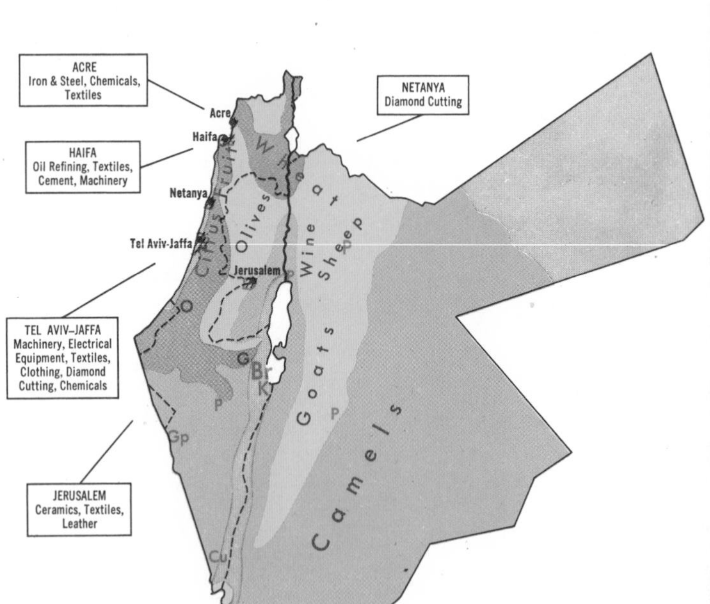

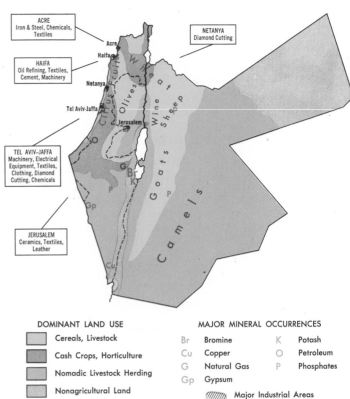

ACRE
Iron & Steel, Chemicals, Textiles
NETANYA
Diamond Cutting
HAIFA
Oil Refining, Textiles, Cement, Machinery
Acre
Haifa
Netanya
Tel Aviv-Jaffa
Jerusalem
Citrus Fruit
Olives
Wheat
Wine
Sheep
Goats
Camels
TEL AVIV–JAFFA
Machinery, Electrical Equipment, Textiles, Clothing, Diamond Cutting, Chemicals
JERUSALEM
Ceramics, Textiles, Leather
G
Br
K
P
Gp
Cu
O

DOMINANT LAND USE

- Cereals, Livestock
- Cash Crops, Horticulture
- Nomadic Livestock Herding
- Nonagricultural Land

MAJOR MINERAL OCCURRENCES

Br	Bromine	K	Potash
Cu	Copper	O	Petroleum
G	Natural Gas	P	Phosphates
Gp	Gypsum		

Major Industrial Areas

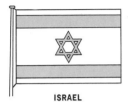

ISRAEL

JORDAN

ISRAEL
AREA 7,993 sq. mi.
POPULATION 2,911,000
CAPITAL Jerusalem
LARGEST CITY Tel Aviv-Jaffa
HIGHEST POINT Meiron 3,963 ft.
MONETARY UNIT Israeli pound
MAJOR LANGUAGES Hebrew, Arabic
MAJOR RELIGIONS Judaism, Islam,
Christianity

JORDAN
AREA 37,297 sq. mi.
POPULATION 2,300,000
CAPITAL Amman
LARGEST CITY Amman
HIGHEST POINT Jeb. Ramm 5,069 ft.
MONETARY UNIT Jordanian dinar
MAJOR LANGUAGE Arabic
MAJOR RELIGION Islam

Rubin, Wadi
  (dry river) .... B 4
Shiqma (river) .... B 4
Tiberias (Galilee) (sea) .. D 2
Tseelim, Wadi
  (dry river) .... C 5
Tsin, Wadi
  (dry river) .... D 5
Yarmuk (river) .... D 2
Yarqon (river) .... B 3

JORDAN

GOVERNORATES

El Asima, 526,000 .... C 3
El Balqa, 95,000 .... D 4
El Karak, 81,000 .... E 5
Hebron, 145,000 .... C 4
Irbid, 334,000 .... D 3
Jerusalem, 418,000 .... C 4
Ma'an, 58,000 .... D 5
Nablus, 414,000 .... C 3

CITIES and TOWNS

'Ajja, 1,322 .... C 3
'Ajlun, 5,390 .... D 3
Amman (capital),
  330,220 .... D 4
'Anabta, 4,018 .... C 3
Anin, 914 .... C 3
'Anjara, 3,163 .... D 3
'Anza, 807 .... D 3
'Aqaba, 8,908 .... D 6
Ariha (Jericho), 5,312 ... C 4
'Arraba, 4,231 .... C 3
Arura, 849 .... C 4
Attil, 3,808 .... C 3
Bal'ama, 769 .... E 3
Baqura, 3,042 .... D 2
Beit Fajjar, 2,474 ...... C 4
Beit Hanina, 3,067 ..... C 4
Beit Khalil (Bethlehem),
  14,439 .... C 4
Beit Nuba, 1,350 .... B 4
Beit Sahur, 5,380 ...... C 4
Bethlehem, 14,439 ...... C 4
Biddu, 1,259 .... C 4
Bir Zeit, 2,311 .... C 4
Birqin, 2,036 .... C 3
Burqa, 2,477 .... C 3
Damiya, 483 .... D 4
Dana, 844 .... E 5
Deir Abu Sa'id, 1,927 .. D 3
Deir Ballut, 1,058 ..... C 3
Deir Sharaf, 973 .... C 3
Dhahiriya, 4,875 .... B 5
Dhira', 214 .... D 4
Duma, 524 .... D 3
Dura, 4,954 .... C 4
El 'Al, 492 .... D 4
El Bira, 9,674 .... C 4
El Husn, 3,728 .... D 3
El Karak, 7,422 ...... E 4
El Khalil (Hebron),
  38,309 .... C 4
El Kitta, 987 .... D 3
El Madwar, 164 ...... E 3
El Mafraq, 9,499 ..... E 3
El Majdal, 259 ...... D 3
El Quweira, 268 ..... E 5
El Yaduda, 251 ...... D 4
Er Ramtha, 10,791 ... E 2
Er Rihiya, 555 ...... C 4
Er Ruseifa, 6,200 ... E 3
Es Sahab, 2,580 ..... E 3
Es Salt, 16,176 ..... D 4
Es Sukhna, 649 ..... E 3
Et Shaubak .... D 5
Et Tafila, 4,506 .... D 5
Et Taiyiba, 2,606 ... D 2
Ez Zababida, 1,474 .. C 3
Ez Zarqa', 121,303 .. E 3
Falama, 162 .... C 3
Halhul, 6,041 .... C 4
Harima, 635 .... D 2
Haris, 667 .... C 3
Hawara, 2,342 ...... D 3
Hebron, 38,309 ..... C 4
Hisban, 718 .... D 4
'Ibbin, 1,364 ...... D 3
Idna, 3,713 .... C 4
'Imwas, 1,955 ...... C 4
Irbid, 44,685 ...... D 3
Jaba', 2,817 .... C 3
Jabir, 135 .... E 2
Jalama, 784 .... C 3
Jalbun, 914 .... D 3
Jalud, 221 .... D 3
Jarash, 3,796 ...... D 3
Jenin, 8,346 .... C 3
Jericho, 5,312 ..... C 4
Jerusalem (old city),
  60,488 .... C 4
Jifna, 655 .... C 4

Kharas, 1,364 .... C 4
Kitim, 1,026 .... D 3
Kuraiyima .... D 3
Ma'ad, 125 .... D 2
Ma'an, 6,643 .... E 5
Ma'daba, 11,224 ..... D 4
Ma'in, 1,271 .... D 4
Manja, 353 .... D 4
Mazra'a, 1,194 ...... D 4
Nablus, 41,709 ...... C 3
Nablus (Nablus), 41,709 C 3
Nahhalin, 1,109 ..... C 4
Na'ur, 2,382 .... D 4
Ni'lin, 1,227 .... C 4
Nitil, 348 .... D 4
Qabalan, 1,970 ...... C 3
Qabatiya, 6,005 ..... C 3
Qaffin, 2,480 .... C 3
Qalqiliya, 8,926 .... C 3
Qibya, 926 .... C 3
Qumeim, 955 .... D 2
Rafidiya, 1,123 ..... C 3
Ramallah, 12,134 .... C 4
Rammun, 1,198 .... C 4
Rantis, 897 .... C 3
Ra's en Naqb, 225 ... E 5
Safi, 3,468 .... D 5
Safut, 421 .... D 3
Salfit, 3,201 ...... C 3
Samar, 716 .... D 2
Samu, 3,784 .... C 4
Sarih, 3,390 .... D 3
Shu'fat, 2,732 ..... C 4
Shunat Nimrin, 109 .. D 4
Shuweika, 2,332 ..... C 3
Silat Dhahr, 3,566 .. C 3
Sinjil, 1,823 ...... C 4
Siris, 1,285 .... C 3
Subeihi, 514 .... C 3
Suf, 3,259 .... D 3
Suweilih, 3,457 .... D 3
Suweima, 315 .... D 3
Tammun, 2,952 ...... C 3
Tarqumiya, 2,412 ... C 4
Tubas, 5,262 .... C 3
Tulkarm, 10,255 .... C 3
Tur, 4,289 .... C 4
Um Jauza, 863 ...... D 3
Wadi es Sir, 4,455 . D 4
Wadi Musa, 654 ..... E 5
Waqqas, 2,321 ...... D 2
Ya'bad, 4,857 ...... C 3
Yabrud, 277 .... C 4
Yamun, 4,173 .... C 3
Yatta, 7,281 .... C 4
Zububa, 633 .... C 3
Zuweiza, 126 .... D 4

OTHER FEATURES

'Ajlun (range) ...... D 3
Anabta (mt.) .... D 3
'Aqaba (gulf) ...... D 6
'Araba, Wadi
  (dry river) ...... D 5
Dead (sea) .... D 4
Ebal (mt.) .... C 3
El Ghor (reg.) .... C 5
El Lisan (pen.) ... C 5
Hasa, Wadi
  (dry river) ...... E 5
Hebron (mt.) ...... C 4
Jordan (river) .... D 3
Judaea (region) ... C 4
Khirbet Qumran
  (site) .... D 4
Kufrinja (mt.) .... D 3
Kufrinja, Wadi
  (dry river) ...... D 3
Mashash, Wadi
  (dry river) ...... D 4
Nebo (mt.) .... D 4
Petra (ruins) ..... D 5
Samaria (region) .. C 3
Shallala, Wadi
  (dry river) ...... D 2
Shu'eib, Wadi
  (dry river) ...... D 4
Tell 'Asur (mt.) .. C 4
Tur (mt.) .... C 3
Yabis, Wadi
  (dry river) ...... D 3
Yamun (mt.) .... D 3
Zarqa' (river) .... D 3

GAZA STRIP
Total Population, 480,000

CITIES and TOWNS

'Abasan, 1,481 ...... A 5
Bani Suheila, 7,561 . A 5
Beit Hanun, 4,756 ... A 4
Deir el Balah, 10,854 A 5
Gaza, 87,793 .... A 5
Gaza, *118,272 ..... A 5
Jabaliya, 10,508 ... A 5
Khan Yunis, 29,522 . A 5
Rafah, 10,812 ...... A 5

*City and suburbs.

IRAN

INTERNAL DIVISIONS

Bakhtiari (governorate), 298,448 .... F 4
Boyer Ahmedi and Kahkiluye (governorate), 24,717 .... G 5
Central (province), 4,979,081 .... G 3
East Azerbaijan (province), 2,596,439 .... E 1
Fars (province), 1,429,804 .... H 6
Gilan (province), 1,752,504 .... F 2
Hamadan (governorate), 889,988 .... F 3
Ilam (governorate), 1,703,701 .... H 4
Isfahan (province), 1,703,701 .... H 4
Kerman (province), 761,851 .... K 5
Kermanshah (prov.), 924,717 .... E 3
Khurasan (prov.), 2,497,381 .... K 3
Khuzistan (prov.), 1,578,079 .... F 5
Kurdistan (prov.), 619,573 .... E 3
Luristan (governorate), 686,307 .... F 4
Mazanderan (province), 1,841,637 .... H 2
Ports and Islands (province), 346,410 .... H 7
Samnan (governorate), 207,786 .... J 3
Seistan and Baluchistan (prov.), 454,996 .... M 6
Southern Coast (province), 251,921 .... G 6
West Azerbaijan (province), 1,087,182 .... D 1
Yezd (governorate), 366,712 .... J 4
Zenjan (governorate) .... F 2

CITIES and TOWNS

Abadan, 272,962 .... F 5
Abadeh, 16,000 .... H 5
Abarquh, 8,000 .... F 2
Ahar, 24,000 .... F 1
Ahwaz, 206,375 .... F 5
Amul, 2,038 .... H 2
Anarak, 4,076 .... H 3
Andimeshk, 16,000 .... F 4
Aradan, 18,978 .... F 3
Arak, 71,925 .... F 3
Ardebil, 83,596 .... F 1
Ardistan, 6,645 .... H 4
Asadabad, 7,000 .... F 3
Asterabad (Gurgan), 17,000 .... H 2
Azarshahr, 6,000 .... E 1
Azna, 5,000 .... F 4
Babol, 49,973 .... H 2
Babulsar, 12,000 .... H 2
Bafq, 5,000 .... J 4
Baft, 6,000 .... K 6
Bahramabad, 21,000 .... K 5
Bam, 22,000 .... L 6
Bandar 'Abbas, 34,627 .... J 7
Bandar Ma'shur, 17,000 .... G 5
Bandar Shah, 13,000 .... H 2
Bandar Shahpur, 6,000 .... H 2
Behbehan, 39,874 .... G 5
Behshahr, 26,032 .... H 2
Bijar, 12,000 .... E 3
Birjand, 25,854 .... L 4
Borazjun, 20,000 .... G 6
Bujnurd, 31,248 .... L 2
Bukan, 9,000 .... D 2
Burujird, 71,476 .... F 3

Bushire, 26,032 .... G 6
Chalus, 15,000 .... G 2
Dalijan, 6,000 .... G 3
Damghan, 13,000 .... J 3
Darab, 13,000 .... J 6
Daran, 4,609 .... G 3
Darreh Gaz, 11,000 .... L 2
Daulatabad (Malayer), 28,434 .... F 3
Deh Haqq, 4,115 .... H 3
Demavend, 5,391 .... H 3
Dizful, 84,499 .... F 4
Duzdab (Zahidan), 40,000 .... M 6
Enzeli (Pahlevi), 41,785 .... F 2
Estahbanat, 18,187 .... H 6
Fahrej (Iranshahr), 5,000 .... M 7
Fariman, 8,000 .... L 3
Farrashband, 3,532 .... H 6
Fasa, 19,000 .... H 6
Firdaus, 11,000 .... K 3
Firuzabad, 8,718 .... H 6
Firuzkuh, 4,684 .... H 3
Fumen, 9,000 .... F 2
Gach Saran, 9,000 .... G 5
Ganaveh, 9,000 .... G 5
Garmsar, 4,723 .... H 3
Golshan (Tabas), 10,000 .... K 4
Gulpaigan, 20,515 .... G 3
Gumishan, 6,000 .... H 2
Gunabad, 8,000 .... L 3
Gunbad-i-Qabus, 40,667 .... J 2
Gurgan, 51,181 .... H 2
Haft Kel, 10,000 .... F 5
Hamadan, 124,167 .... F 3
Hashtgar, 5,000 .... G 3
Homayunshahr, 46,836 .... G 3
Ilam, 15,000 .... E 4
Iranshahr, 8,000 .... M 7
Isfahan, 424,045 .... G 3
Jahrum, 38,236 .... H 6

Kangavar, 9,414 .... F 3
Karaj, 44,243 .... G 3
Kashan, 44,303 .... G 3
Kashmar, 17,000 .... L 3
Kazerun, 39,758 .... G 6
Kazvin, 88,106 .... F 2
Kerman, 85,404 .... K 5
Kermanshah, 187,930 .... E 3
Khaf, 5,000 .... L 3
Khoi, 47,648 .... D 1
Khorramshahr, 88,536 .... F 5
Khunsar, 10,947 .... G 3
Khur, 2,912 .... J 3
Khurramabad, 59,578 .... F 4
Lahijan, 25,725 .... F 2
Lar, 22,000 .... J 7
Mahabad, 28,610 .... D 2
Mahallat, 12,000 .... G 3
Mahan, 8,000 .... K 5
Maibud, 15,000 .... J 4
Maku, 7,000 .... D 1
Malayer, 26,434 .... F 3
Maragheh, 54,106 .... E 2
Marand, 24,000 .... D 1
Marvdasht, 25,498 .... H 6
Masjid-i-Sulaiman, 64,488 .... F 5
Meshed, 409,616 .... L 3
Meshed-i-Sar (Babulsar), 12,000 .... H 2
Meshkinshahr, 9,000 .... E 1
Mianeh, 28,447 .... E 2
Mirjawa, 11,000 .... M 6
Miyanduab, 16,000 .... D 2
Nafti-Shah, 3,043 .... E 4
Na'in, 5,925 .... H 4
Nasratabad (Zabul), 20,000 .... M 5
Natanz, 4,370 .... H 3
Naushahr, 8,000 .... H 2
Nehavend, 24,000 .... F 3

Nejafabad, 43,384 .... G 4
Niriz, 16,114 .... J 6
Nishapur, 33,482 .... L 3
Pahlevi (Enzeli), 41,785 .... L 2
Qain, 6,000 .... L 4
Qasr-i-Shirin, 15,904 .... E 3
Quchan, 29,133 .... L 2
Qum, 134,292 .... G 3
Rafsenjan (Bahramabad), 21,000 .... K 5
Rai, 102,825 .... G 3
Ram Hormuz, 9,000 .... F 5
Ramsar, 12,000 .... G 2
Ravar, 7,000 .... K 5
Reza'iyeh, 110,749 .... D 2
Resht, 143,557 .... F 2
Sabzawar, 42,415 .... L 3
Sabzawaran, 7,000 .... K 6
Saidabad (Sirjan), 20,000 .... K 6
Samnan, 31,058 .... J 3
Sanandaj, 54,578 .... E 3
Sang-i-Sar, 9,000 .... J 3
Saqqiz, 17,000 .... E 2
Sarab, 16,000 .... E 2
Sardasht, 6,000 .... D 2
Sari, 44,547 .... H 2
Savanat (Estahbanat), 18,187 .... H 6

Shushtar, 24,000 .... F 4
Sinneh (Sanandaj), 54,578 .... E 3
Sirjan, 20,000 .... K 6
Sultanabad (Kashmar), 17,000 .... L 3
Sunqur, 10,433 .... E 3
Susangird, 21,000 .... F 5
Tabas, 10,000 .... K 4
Tabriz, 403,413 .... D 2
Taft, 7,000 .... J 4
Tajrish, 157,486 .... G 3
Takistan, 13,485 .... F 2
Tehran (capital), 2,719,730 .... G 3
Tuiserkan, 12,000 .... F 3
Tun (Firdaus), 11,000 .... K 3
Turbat-i-Haidari, 30,106 .... L 3
Turbat-i-Shaikh Jam, 13,000 .... M 3
Urmia (Reza'iyeh), 110,749 .... D 2
Ushnuiyeh, 5,000 .... D 2
Veramin, 11,183 .... G 3
Yezd, 93,241 .... J 5
Zabul, 34,220 .... M 5
Zahidan, 39,732 .... M 6
Zarand, 5,000 .... K 5
Zarghan, 7,000 .... H 6
Zenjan, 58,714 .... F 2

OTHER FEATURES

Abi-Diz (river) .... F 4
Aji Chai (river) .... E 1
Arabi (isl.) .... G 7
Aras (Araks) (river) .... E 1
Atrek (river) .... L 2
Bakhtegan (lake) .... J 6
Baluchistan (region) .... M 7
Bampur (river) .... M 7
Behistun (ruins) .... E 3
Caspian (sea) .... F 1

Darya-yi-Namak (salt lake) .... H 3
Dasht-i-Kavir (salt desert) .... J 3
Dasht-i-Lut (desert) .... L 5
Demavend (mt.) .... H 3
Dez (Ab-i-Diz) (river) .... F 4
Elburz (range) .... G 2
Farsi- (isl.) .... G 6
Hamun-i-Helmand (marsh) .... M 6
Hamun-i-Jaz-Murian (marsh) .... L 6
Hamun-i-Sabari (lake) .... M 5
Hanjam (isl.) .... J 7
Hari Rud (river) .... M 3
Hashtadan (reg.) .... M 4
Hormuz (strait) .... J 7
Kalar, Kuh-i- (mt.) .... G 3
Karkheh (river) .... F 4
Karun (river) .... F 5
Kashaf Rud (river) .... L 3
Kharg (isl.), 647 .... G 6
Kuh, Ras el (cape) .... K 7
Kuh-i-Aladagh (mts.) .... L 2
Kuh-i-Bagraband (mts.) .... L 3
Kuh-i-Bazqush (mts.) .... E 2
Kuh-i-Dinar (mts.) .... G 5
Kuh-i-Gugird (mts.) .... J 3
Kuh-i-Jagatai (mts.) .... L 3
Kuh-i-Shah Jehan (mts.) .... L 3
Kur Rud (river) .... H 6
Kurang (river) .... G 4
Laristan (region) .... J 7
Maidani (cape) .... M 7
Makran (region) .... M 7
Mand Rud (river) .... H 6
Mashkel (river) .... M 7
Mehran (river) .... J 7
Mura, Qal'eh-i- (river) .... M 5
Namaksar (lake) .... M 4

IRAN and IRAQ
CONIC PROJECTION

SCALE OF MILES
0 25 50 100 200

SCALE OF KILOMETRES
0 25 50 100 150 200

Capitals of Countries .... ★
Capitals of Provinces .... △
Capitals of Governorates .... ◉
International Boundaries .... —
Provincial Boundaries .... —
Governorate Boundaries .... —

Copyright by C.S. HAMMOND & CO., N.Y.

Iran consists of fifteen provinces called ostans. Attached to seven of these provinces are eight governorates.

Namakzar (dry lake)	L 3	Babil	D 4
Nezwar (mt.)	H 3	Baghdad	D 4
Nihing (river)	N 7	Basra	E 5
Oman (gulf)	M 8	Dhi Qar	D 4
Pasargadae (ruins)	H 5	Diyala	D 3
Persepolis (ruins)	H 6	Dohuk	C 2
Persian (gulf)	F 6	Erbil	C 3
Pusht-i-Kuh (mts.)	E 4	Karbala'	B 4
Qais (isl.)	J 7	Maysan	D 4
Qarajeh Dagh (mts.)	E 1	Muthanna	D 5
Qara Su (river)	G 3	Ninawa	B 3
Qara Su (river)	E 2	Qadisiya	D 4
Qaranqu (river)	E 2	Salahuddin	C 3
Qishm (isl.)	J 7	Sulaimaniya	D 3
Qizil Uzun (river)	F 2	Tamim	C 3
Sefid Rud (river)	H 7	Wasit	D 4
Shaikh Shu'aib (island)	M 5		
Shelagh (river)	M 5	**CITIES and TOWNS**	
Shirvan (river)	E 3		
Shur (river)	J 7	Ad Diwaniya, 60,553	D 5
Siah Kuh (mts.)	L 3	'Afaq, 5,390	D 4
Silop (river)	M 8	Al 'Azair, 2,255	E 5
Susa (ruins)	F 4	Al 'Aziziya, 7,450	D 4
Talab (river)	N 6	Al Falluja, 38,072	C 4
Tashk (lake)	J 6	Al Kufa, 30,862	D 4
Urmia (lake)	D 2	Al Kumait, 2,225	E 4
Yezd (region)	J 5	Al Musaiyib, 15,955	D 4
Zagros (mts.)	E 4	Al Qa'im, 3,372	A 3
Zaindeh Rud (river)	H 4	Al Qaiyara, 3,060	C 3
Zarineh (river)	E 2	Al Qosh, 3,863	C 2
Zilbir Chai (river)	D 1	Al Qurna, 5,638	E 5
Zuhreh Rud (river)	F 5	'Ali Gharbi, 5,735	E 4
		'Ali Sharqi, 1,980	E 4
IRAQ		Al'maniya, 11,943	D 4
PROVINCES		Qal'a Sharqat, 2,434	C 3
		Qal'at Diza, 6,250	D 2
Anbar	B 4	Ramadi, 28,723	C 4
An Najaf	C 5	Rania, 4,090	D 2

Ar Rahhaliya	C 4
Arbela (Erbil), 90,320	D 2
As Salman, 1,789	D 5
Az Zubair, 41,408	E 5
Badra, 3,564	D 4
Baghdad (capital), 502,503	D 4
Baghdad, *1,745,328	D 4
Baiji, 6,785	C 3
Ba'quba, 34,575	D 4
Basra, 313,327	E 5
Dohuk, 16,998	C 2
Erbil, 90,320	D 2
Fao, 15,399	F 6
Habbaniya, 14,405	C 4
Hadhar, 1,019	C 3
Haditha, 6,870	C 4
Hai, 16,988	E 4
Halabja, 11,206	D 3
Hilla, 84,717	D 4
Hindiya, 16,436	D 4
Hit, 9,131	C 4
Karbala', 83,301	D 4
Khanaqin, 23,522	D 3
Kifri, 8,500	D 3
Kirkuk, 167,413	D 3
Kut, 42,116	D 4
Lailan, 1,526	D 3
Maidan, 354	C 3
Makhmur, 2,556	C 3
Mandali, 11,262	D 4
Mosul, 315,157	C 2
Muqdadiyah, 12,181	D 4
Na'maniya, 11,943	D 4
Qal'a Sharqat, 2,434	C 3
Qal'at Diza, 6,250	D 2
Ramadi, 28,723	C 4
Rania, 4,090	D 2
Refa'i, 7,681	D 5
Rumaitha, 10,222	D 5
Rutba, 5,091	B 4
Sa'diya, 5,285	D 3
Samarra, 24,746	C 3
Samawa, 33,473	D 5
Shaikh Sa'ad, 2,958	E 4
Shaqlawa, 6,814	D 2
Shatra, 18,822	E 5
Shithatha, 2,326	C 4
Sinjar, 7,942	B 2
Sulaimaniya, 86,822	D 3
Tal Kaif, 7,482	C 2
Tauq, 845	D 3
Taza Khurmatu, 2,681	D 3
Tikrit, 9,921	C 3
Tuz Khurmatu, 13,860	D 3
Zakho, 14,790	C 2
Zorbatiya, 1,602	D 4

OTHER FEATURES

Adhaim (river)	D 3
Al Hajara (plain)	D 5
'Aneiza, Jebel (mt.)	A 4
'Arab, Shatt-al- (river)	F 5
'Arar, Wadi (dry river)	B 5
Babylon (ruins)	C 4
Bahr al Milh (lake)	C 4
Batin, Wadi al (dry river)	E 6
Ctesiphon (ruins)	D 4
Darbandikhan (dam)	D 3
Euphrates (river)	C 4
Great Zab (river)	C 2
Hajara, Al (plain)	D 5
Haji Ibrahim (mt.)	D 2
Hammar, Hor al (lake)	E 5
Hauran, Wadi (dry river)	B 4
Ibrahim, Haji (mt.)	D 2
Little Zab (river)	C 3
Mesopotamia (region)	D 4
Nineveh (ruins)	C 2
Sa'diya, Hor (lake)	E 4
Saniya, Hor (lake)	E 5
Sha'ib Hisb, Wadi (dry river)	C 5
Shatt-al-'Arab (river)	F 5
Sinjar, Jebel (mts.)	B 2
Siyah Kuh (mts.)	B 4
Syrian (desert)	B 4
Tigris (river)	D 4
Ubaiyidh, Wadi (dry river)	B 5
Ur (ruins)	D 5

*City and suburbs.
†Population of sub-district.

IRAN

IRAQ

IRAN

AREA 636,293 sq. mi.
POPULATION 28,448,000
CAPITAL Tehran
LARGEST CITY Tehran
HIGHEST POINT Demavend 18,376 ft.
MONETARY UNIT rial
MAJOR LANGUAGES Persian, Azerbaijani, Kurdish
MAJOR RELIGIONS Islam, Zoroastrianism

IRAQ

AREA 167,924 sq. mi.
POPULATION 9,431,000
CAPITAL Baghdad
LARGEST CITY Baghdad
HIGHEST POINT Haji Ibrahim 11,811 ft.
MONETARY UNIT Iraqi dinar
MAJOR LANGUAGES Arabic, Kurdish
MAJOR RELIGION Islam

Topography

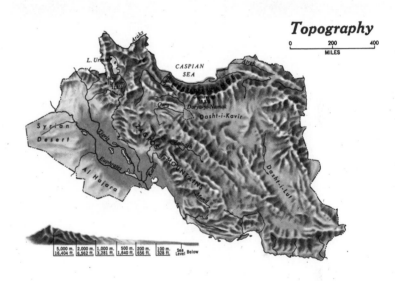

Agriculture, Industry and Resources

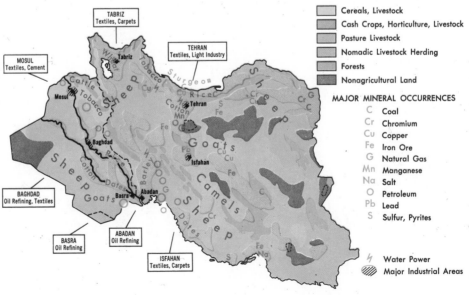

DOMINANT LAND USE

Cereals, Livestock
Cash Crops, Horticulture, Livestock
Pasture Livestock
Nomadic Livestock Herding
Forests
Nonagricultural Land

MAJOR MINERAL OCCURRENCES

C Coal
Cr Chromium
Cu Copper
Fe Iron Ore
G Natural Gas
Mn Manganese
Na Salt
O Petroleum
Pb Lead
S Sulfur, Pyrites

Water Power
Major Industrial Areas

TABRIZ — Textiles, Carpets
TEHRAN — Textiles, Light Industry
MOSUL — Textiles, Cement
BAGHDAD — Oil Refining, Textiles
BASRA — Oil Refining
ABADAN — Oil Refining
ISFAHAN — Textiles, Carpets

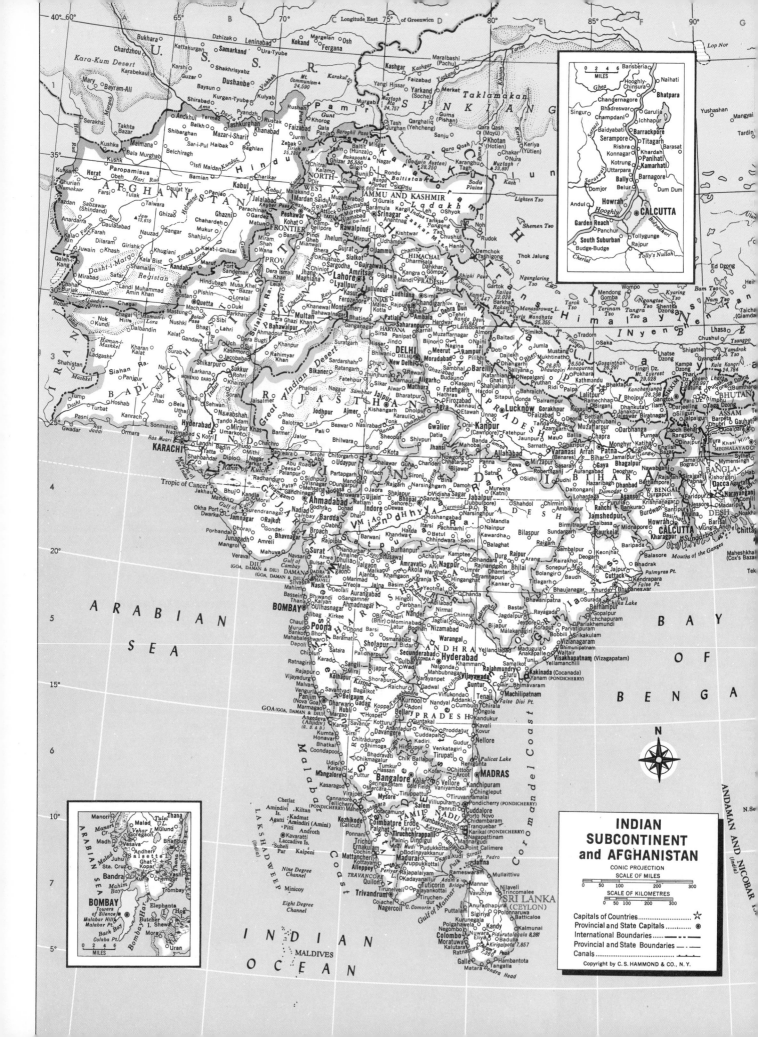

INDIAN SUBCONTINENT and AFGHANISTAN

CONIC PROJECTION

SCALE OF MILES

0   50   100   200   300

SCALE OF KILOMETRES

0   50   100   200   300

Capitals of Countries .... ☆
Provincial and State Capitals .... ◉
International Boundaries ....
Provincial and State Boundaries _._._
Canals ....

Copyright by C.S. HAMMOND & CO., N.Y.

BOMBAY

CALCUTTA

INDIA

PAKISTAN

SRI LANKA (CEYLON)

AFGHANISTAN

BANGLADESH

BHUTAN

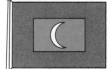

MALDIVES

NEPAL

INDIA

AREA 1,261,483 sq. mi.
POPULATION 546,955,945
CAPITAL New Delhi
LARGEST CITY Calcutta (greater)
HIGHEST POINT K2 (Godwin Austen) 28,250 ft.
MONETARY UNIT Indian rupee
MAJOR LANGUAGES Hindi, English, Bihari, Telugu, Marathi,
 Bengali, Tamil, Gujarati, Rajasthani, Kanarese, Malayalam,
 Oriya, Punjabi, Assamese, Kashmiri
MAJOR RELIGIONS Hinduism, Islam, Christianity, Sikhism,
 Buddhism, Jainism, Zoroastrianism, Animism

AFGHANISTAN

AREA 250,000 sq. mi.
POPULATION 17,078,263
CAPITAL Kabul
LARGEST CITY Kabul
HIGHEST POINT Hindu Kush 24,556 ft.
MONETARY UNIT afghani
MAJOR LANGUAGES Pushtu, Dari,
 Uzbek
MAJOR RELIGION Islam

MALDIVES

AREA 115 sq. mi.
POPULATION 110,770
CAPITAL Male
LARGEST CITY Male
HIGHEST POINT 20 ft.
MONETARY UNIT Indian &
 Ceylonese rupee
MAJOR LANGUAGE Divehi
MAJOR RELIGION Islam

PAKISTAN

AREA 310,403 sq. mi.
POPULATION 60,000,000
CAPITAL Islamabad
LARGEST CITY Karachi
HIGHEST POINT Tirich Mir 25,230 ft.
MONETARY UNIT Pakistani rupee
MAJOR LANGUAGES Urdu, English,
 Punjabi, Pushtu, Sindhi, Baluchi
MAJOR RELIGIONS Islam, Hinduism,
 Sikhism, Christianity

SRI LANKA (CEYLON)

AREA 25,332 sq. mi.
POPULATION 12,300,000
CAPITAL Colombo
LARGEST CITY Colombo
HIGHEST POINT Pidurutalagala
 8,281 ft.
MONETARY UNIT Ceylonese rupee
MAJOR LANGUAGES Singhalese,
 Tamil, English
MAJOR RELIGIONS Buddhism,
 Hinduism, Christianity

BANGLADESH

AREA 55,126 sq. mi.
POPULATION 70,000,000
CAPITAL Dacca
LARGEST CITY Dacca
HIGHEST POINT Mowdok Mual
 3,292 ft.
MONETARY UNIT taka
MAJOR LANGUAGES Bengali,
 English
MAJOR RELIGIONS Islam,
 Hinduism, Christianity

NEPAL

AREA 54,362 sq. mi.
POPULATION 10,845,000
CAPITAL Kathmandu
LARGEST CITY Kathmandu
HIGHEST POINT Mt. Everest 29,028 ft.
MONETARY UNIT Nepalese rupee
MAJOR LANGUAGES Nepali, Maithili,
 Tamang, Newari, Tharu
MAJOR RELIGIONS Hinduism, Buddhism

BHUTAN

AREA 18,000 sq. mi.
POPULATION 1,034,774
CAPITAL Thimphu
LARGEST CITY Thimphu
HIGHEST POINT Chomo Lhari 23,997 ft.
MONETARY UNIT Indian rupee
MAJOR LANGUAGES Tibetan dialects,
 Nepali
MAJOR RELIGIONS Buddhism, Hinduism

AFGHANISTAN

CITIES and TOWNS

Andkhui, 30,000 .... B 1
Baghlan, 92,000 .... B 1
Balkh, 15,000 .... B 2
Bamian, 25,000 .... B 2
Charikar, 83,700 .... B 1
Faizabad, 57,000 .... C 1
Farah, 26,400 .... A 2
Gardez, 33,000 .... B 2
Ghazni, 39,900 .... B 2
Haibak, 35,000 .... B 1
Herat, 71,563 .... A 2
Jalalabad, 48,919 .... B 2
Kabul (cap.), 472,313 .... B 2
Kabul, *600,000 .... B 2
Kala Bist, 26,100 .... A 2
Kalat-i-Ghilzai, 40,500 .... B 2
Kandahar, 127,036 .... B 2
Kandahar, *142,000 .... B 2
Khanabad, 30,000 .... B 1
Maimana, 48,750 .... A 1
Mazar-i-Sharif, 43,197 .... B 1
Shibarghan, 50,440 .... B 1
Tashkurghan, 30,000 .... B 1

OTHER FEATURES

Hari Rud (river) .... A 1
Helmand (river) .... B 2
Hindu Kush (mts.) .... B 1
Kabul (river) .... C 2
Kunar (river) .... C 1
Kunduz (river) .... B 1
Paropamisus (range) .... A 2
Registan (desert) .... B 2

BANGLADESH

CITIES and TOWNS

Barisal, 69,936 .... G 4
Bogra, 33,784 .... F 4
Chittagong, 364,205 .... G 4
Chittagong, *437,000 .... G 4
Comilla, 54,504 .... G 4
Dacca (cap.), 556,712 .... G 4
Dacca, *829,000 .... G 4
Dinajpur, 37,711 .... F 3
Faridpur, 28,333 .... F 4
Jessore, 46,366 .... F 4
Khulna, 127,970 .... F 4
Khulna, *320,000 .... F 4
Mymensingh, 53,256 .... G 4
Narayanganj, 162,054 .... G 4
Narayanganj, *327,000 .... G 4
Noakhali, 19,874 .... G 4
Pabna, 40,792 .... F 4
Rajshahi, 56,885 .... F 4
Rangamati, 6,416 .... G 4
Rangpur, 40,634 .... F 3
Sylhet, 37,740 .... G 4

OTHER FEATURES

Bengal (bay) .... F 5
Brahmaputra (riv.) .... G 3
Ganges (river) .... F 3
Sundarbans (swamp) .... F 4

BHUTAN

CITIES and TOWNS

Bumthang, 10,000 .... G 3
Paro Dzong, 35,000 .... F 3
Punakha, 12,000 .... G 3
Taga Dzong, 18,000 .... G 3
Thimphu (cap.), 50,000 .... G 3
Tongsa Dzong .... G 3

OTHER FEATURES

Chomo Lhari (mt.) .... F 3
Kula Kangri (mt.) .... G 3

INDIA

INTERNAL DIVISIONS

Andaman and Nicobar Islands
 (terr.), 115,092 .... G 6
Andhra Pradesh (state),
 43,394,951 .... D 5
Arunachal Pradesh (terr.),
 381,000 .... G 3
Assam (state), 14,630,422 .... G 4
Bihar (state), 56,387,296 .... F 4
Chandigarh (terr.), 150,000 .... D 2
Dadra and Nagar Haveli (terr.),
 69,000 .... C 4
Delhi (terr.), 4,044,281 .... D 3
Goa, Daman and Diu (terr.),
 675,000 .... C 5
Gujarat (state), 25,189,000 .... C 4
Haryana (state), 9,914,145 .... D 3
Himachal Pradesh (state),
 3,432,000 .... D 2
Jammu and Kashmir (state),
 4,615,025 .... D 2
Karnataka (state), 27,985,000 .... D 6
Kerala (state), 20,296,000 .... D 6
Lakshadweep (terr.), 27,000 .... C 6
Madhya Pradesh (state),
 41,449,729 .... D 4
Maharashtra (state), 50,295,081 .... C 5
Manipur (state), 1,035,000 .... G 4
Meghalaya (state), 983,336 .... G 3
Mizoram (terr.), 321,686 .... G 4
Nagaland (state), 515,551 .... G 3
Orissa (state), 20,674,000 .... E 5
Pondicherry (terr.), 430,000 .... E 6
Punjab (state), 13,935,000 .... D 2
Rajasthan (state), 25,724,595 .... C 3
Sikkim (state), 191,000 .... F 3
Tamil Nadu (state),
 33,886,863 .... D 6
Tripura (state), 1,424,000 .... G 4
Uttar Pradesh (state),
 88,299,453 .... D 3
West Bengal (state), 44,440,095 . F 4

CITIES and TOWNS

Achalpur, 36,538 .... D 4
Achalpur, *54,028 .... D 4
Adoni, 69,951 .... D 5
Agartala, 54,878 .... G 4
Agra, 610,328 .... D 3
Agra, *658,781 .... D 3
Ahmadabad, 1,507,921 .... C 4
Ahmadabad, *1,746,111 .... C 4
Ahmadnagar, 131,973 .... C 5
Aizwal, 31,436 .... G 4
Ajmer, 265,156 .... C 3
Akola, 143,919 .... D 4
Aligarh, 232,278 .... D 3
Allahabad, 521,568 .... E 3
Allahabad, *537,047 .... E 3
Alleppey, 161,279 .... D 7
Alwar, 72,707 .... D 3
Amalner, 46,963 .... C 4
Ambala, 87,750 .... D 2
Ambala, *200,576 .... D 2
Amravati, 177,066 .... D 4
Amreli, 34,699 .... C 4
Amritsar, 424,961 .... C 2
Amritsar, *459,179 .... C 2
Anakapalle, 46,402 .... E 5
Anantapur, 52,280 .... D 5
Andheri, 122,401 .... B 7
Arcot, 25,526 .... D 6
Arrah, 76,766 .... E 3

Balasore, 33,931 .... F 4
Ballia, 38,216 .... E 3
Bally, 247,844 .... F 1
Balrampur, 31,776 .... E 3
Banda, 37,744 .... E 3
Bandra, 36,099 .... B 7
Bangalore, 1,027,327 .... D 6
Bangalore, *1,648,232 .... D 6
Bankura, 62,833 .... F 4
Bansberia, 45,463 .... F 1
Bagalkot, 39,934 .... D 5
Barasat, *61,621 .... F 1
Baidyabati, 44,312 .... F 1

Bareilly, *343,559 .... D 3
Baripada, 20,301 .... F 4
Barmer, 27,600 .... C 4
Barnagore, 143,621 .... F 1
Baroda, 400,725 .... C 4
Barrackpore, 63,778 .... F 1
Barrackpore, *158,244 .... F 1
Barsi, 50,389 .... D 5
Basirhat, 53,943 .... F 4
Bassein, 22,598 .... C 5
Bassein, *28,238 .... C 5
Batala, 51,300 .... D 2
Beawar, 53,931 .... C 3

Belgaum, 156,105 .... C 5
Belgaum, *176,857 .... C 5
Bellary, 85,673 .... D 5
Belur, 29,737 .... F 1
Benares (Varanasi), 619,822 .... E 3
Berhampore, 62,317 .... F 4
Berhampur, 76,931 .... F 5
Bettiah, 39,990 .... E 3
Bhadrak, 25,285 .... F 4
Bhadreswar, 35,489 .... F 1
Bhagalpur, 174,538 .... F 3
Bhandara, 27,710 .... D 4
Bhandup, 33,020 .... B 7

Bharatpur, 49,776 .... D 3
Bhatinda, 52,253 .... C 2
Bhatpara, 159,219 .... F 1
Bhavnagar, 217,533 .... C 4
Bhilai, 86,116 .... E 4
Bhilwara, 43,499 .... C 3
Bhimavaram, 43,281 .... E 5
Bhir (Bir), 33,066 .... D 5
Bhiwandi, 47,630 .... C 5
Bhiwani, 58,194 .... D 3
Bhopal, 310,733 .... D 4
Bhopal, *441,939 .... D 4
Bhubaneswar, 38,211 .... F 4

(continued on following page)

Balasore, 33,931 .... F 4
Aruppukkottai, 50,200 .... D 7
Aruppukkottai, *55,977 .... D 7
Asansol, 134,056 .... F 4
Asansol, *278,350 .... F 4
Aurangabad, Bihar, 14,154 .... F 4
Aurangabad, Maharashtra,
 87,579 .... D 5
Azamgarh, 32,391 .... E 3
Azadpara, 43,908 .... C 3

OTHER FEATURES (left map area — Burma / islands)

(Andaman and Nicobar area)
Preparis North Channel
Preparis I.
Preparis South Channel
Little Coco Great Coco (Burma)
Coco Channel
N. Andaman (India)
ANDAMAN
Middle Andaman
Baratang Barren I.
Ritchies Arch.
S. Andaman
Rutland I. ISLANDS
Duncan Passage
Little Andaman
Toibalawe
Ten Degree Channel
Sawi Car Nicobar
Batti Malv
NICOBAR Tillanchong
Teressa Camorta
Katchall Nancowry
Sombrero Channel
ISLANDS Little Nicobar
Laful
Great Nicobar
Great Channel
Web
Banda Atjeh
Sumatra
INDONESIA

Map labels (topographic map)

Amu-Darya
HINDU KUSH
Hari Rud
Helmand
K2 (Godwin Austen) 28,250
Khyber Pass
SULAIMAN RA.
Indus
Kabul
Sutlej
Great Indian Desert
ARAVALLI RA.
Ganges
Jumna
HIMALAYA
Brahmaputra
NAGA HILLS
INDO-GANGETIC PLAIN
Rann of Kutch
Gulf of Kutch
VINDHYA RANGE
CHOTA NAGPUR PLATEAU
Mahanadi
Kathiawar Peninsula
SATPURA RANGE
Narmada
DECCAN
G. of Cambay
WESTERN GHATS
PLATEAU
Godavari
Arabian Sea
Krishna
EASTERN GHATS
Bay of Bengal
Malabar Coast
Coromandel Coast
ANDAMAN ISLANDS
LACCADIVE ISLANDS
C. Comorin
Gulf of Mannar
Ceylon
Pidurutalagala 8,281
Dondra Head
NICOBAR ISLANDS

Topography

| 5,000 m. 16,404 ft. | 2,000 m. 6,562 ft. | 1,000 m. 3,281 ft. | 500 m. 1,640 ft. | 200 m. 656 ft. | 100 m. 328 ft. | Sea Level | Below |

0   200   400
MILES

Bhuj, 38,953 ....B 4
Bhuj, *40,180 ....B 4
Bhusawal, 73,994 ....D 4
Bhusawal, *79,121 ....D 4
Bidar, 32,420 ....D 5
Bihar, 78,581 ....F 3
Bijapur, 78,854 ....D 5
Bijnor, 33,821 ....D 3
Bikaner, 186,560 ....C 3
Bilaspur, 86,706 ....E 4
Bir, 33,066 ....D 5
Bodhan, 30,929 ....D 5
Bodinayakkanur, 44,914 ....D 6
Bombay, *5,931,989 ....B 7
Broach, 73,639 ....C 4
Budaun, 58,770 ....D 3
Budge-Budge, 39,824 ....F 2
Bulsar, 35,028 ....C 4
Burdwan, 147,528 ....F 4
Burhanpur, 82,090 ....D 4
Calcutta, 7,040,345 ....F 2
Calicut (Kozhikode), 315,786 ....D 6
Cambay, 51,291 ....C 4
Cannanore, 46,101 ....C 6
Cawnpore (Kanpur), 1,163,524 ....E 3
Champdani, 42,129 ....F 1
Chanda, 51,484 ....D 5
Chandernagore, 67,105 ....F 1
Chandigarh, 89,321 ....D 2
Chandigarh, *110,614 ....D 2
Chapra, 75,580 ....F 3
Chembur, 85,582 ....B 7
Chhindwara, 37,244 ....D 4
Chidambaram, 40,694 ....E 6
Chikmagalur, 30,253 ....D 6
Chingleput, 25,977 ....E 6
Chirala, 45,410 ....E 5
Chitradurga, 33,336 ....D 6
Chittoor, 47,876 ....D 6
Churu, 41,727 ....D 3
Cocanada (Kakinada), 146,332 ....E 5
Cochin, 35,076 ....D 6
Coimbatore, 393,145 ....D 6
Cooch Behar, 41,922 ....F 3
Cuddalore, 79,168 ....E 6
Cuddapah, 49,027 ....D 6
Cuttack, 198,405 ....F 4
Dabhoi, 30,841 ....C 4
Daltonganj, 25,270 ....E 4
Damoh, 46,656 ....D 4
Darbhanga, 121,438 ....F 3
Darjeeling, 40,651 ....F 3
Datia, 29,430 ....D 3
Davangere, 78,124 ....D 6
Dehra Dun, 136,469 ....D 2
Dehra Dun, *167,297 ....D 2
Delhi, *3,629,842 ....D 3
Deoghar, 35,105 ....F 4
Deolali, 37,264 ....C 5
Deoria, 28,407 ....E 3
Dewas, 34,577 ....D 4
Dhamtari, 31,552 ....E 4
Dhanbad, 57,400 ....F 4
Dhar, 28,325 ....C 4
Dharwar, 77,163 ....C 5
Dhoraji, 48,951 ....C 4
Dhubri, 28,355 ....G 3
Dhulia, 98,893 ....C 4
Dibrugarh, 58,480 ....G 3
Dindigul, 92,947 ....D 6
Dispur, 1,725 ....G 3
Dohad, 35,483 ....C 4
Dohad, *50,434 ....C 4
Domjor, 8,670 ....F 1
Dum Dum, 20,041 ....F 1
Dum Dum, *174,177 ....F 1
Durg, 64,132 ....E 4
Durg, *204,784 ....E 4
Durgapur, *41,696 ....F 4
Eluru, 130,166 ....E 5
Ernakulam, 203,493 ....D 6
Ernakulam, *474,187 ....D 6
Erode, 73,762 ....D 6
Erode, *96,528 ....D 6
Etawah, 69,681 ....D 3
Faizabad, 83,717 ....E 3
Faizabad, *88,296 ....E 3
Fatehgarh, 87,793 ....D 3
Fatehgarh, *94,591 ....D 3
Fatehpur, 27,039 ....C 3
Fatehpur, 28,323 ....E 3
Ferozepore, 47,060 ....C 2
Ferozepore, *97,932 ....C 2
Firozabad, 98,611 ....D 3
Gadag, 76,614 ....D 5
Gandhinagar, 24,049 ....C 4
Ganganagar, 63,854 ....C 3
Gangtok, 6,848 ....F 3
Garden Reach, 152,347 ....F 2
Garulia, 29,041 ....F 1
Gauhati, 210,561 ....G 3
Gaya, 167,500 ....F 4
Ghat Kopar, 34,256 ....B 7
Ghaziabad, 63,190 ....D 3
Ghaziabad, *70,438 ....D 3
Ghazipur, 37,147 ....E 3
Godhra, 52,167 ....C 4
Gonda, 43,496 ....E 3
Gondal, 45,069 ....C 4
Gorakhpur, 234,497 ....E 3
Gudur, 25,618 ....D 6
Gulbarga, 97,069 ....D 5
Guna, 31,031 ....D 4
Guntakal, 48,083 ....D 5
Guntur, 264,138 ....D 5
Gwalior, 361,780 ....D 3
Harda, 22,279 ....D 4
Hardoi, 36,725 ....E 3
Hardwar, 58,513 ....D 2
Hardwar, *59,960 ....D 2
Hassan, 32,172 ....D 6
Hathras, 64,045 ....D 3
Hazaribagh, 40,958 ....F 4
Hindupur, 32,445 ....D 6
Hinganghat, 36,890 ....D 4
Hingoli. 23,407 ....D 5
Hissar, 60,222 ....D 3
Hooghly-Chinsura, 83,104 ....F 1
Hospet, 53,242 ....D 5
Howrah, 590,385 ....F 2
Hubli, 217,284 ....C 5
Hubli, *303,696 ....C 5
Hyderabad, 1,294,800 ....D 5
Hyderabad, *1,798,910 ....D 5
Imphal, 67,717 ....G 4
Indore, 483,969 ....D 4
Itanagar ....G 3
Jabalpur, 406,214 ....D 4
Jabalpur, *497,946 ....D 4
Jaipur, 533,151 ....D 3
Jalgaon, 80,351 ....D 4
Jalna, 67,158 ....D 4
Jalpaiguri, 48,738 ....F 3
Jamalpur, 57,039 ....F 3
Jammu, 102,738 ....D 2
Jammu, *108,257 ....D 2
Jamnagar, 200,918 ....B 4
Jamshedpur, 402,462 ....F 4
Jamshedpur, *465,740 ....F 4
Jaunpur, 61,851 ....E 3
Jhansi, 177,456 ....D 3
Jhansi, *216,736 ....D 3
Jodhpur, 270,404 ....C 3
Jorhat, 24,953 ....G 3
Jubbulpore (Jabalpur), 406,214 ....D 4
Jullundur, 281,623 ....D 2
Jullundur, *333,938 ....D 2
Junagadh, 74,298 ....B 4
Kadayanallur, 41,249 ....D 7
Kakinada, 146,332 ....E 5
Kalyan, 73,482 ....C 5
Kalyan, *194,334 ....C 5
Kamarhati, 190,695 ....F 1
Kamptee, 40,859 ....D 4
Kanchipuram, 92,714 ....E 6
Kannauj, 24,646 ....D 3
Kanpur, 1,163,524 ....E 3
Kanpur, *1,273,042 ....E 3
Karad, 33,772 ....C 5
Karaikudi, 43,698 ....D 7
Karanja, 26,440 ....D 4
Karikal, 22,252 ....E 6
Karnal, 72,109 ....D 3
Karur, 50,564 ....D 6
Karwar, 23,906 ....C 6
Kasaragod, 27,635 ....C 6
Kasganj, 37,559 ....D 3
Katihar, 46,837 ....F 3
Katihar, *59,344 ....F 3
Katni (Murwara), 46,169 ....E 4
Kavaratti, 2,828 ....C 6
Khamgaon, 44,432 ....D 4
Khamman, 35,888 ....D 5
Khandwa, 63,505 ....D 4
Kharagpur, 163,929 ....F 4
Khardah, 28,362 ....F 1
Kirkee, 58,496 ....C 5
Kishangarh, 25,244 ....D 3
Kolar, 32,587 ....D 6
Kolar Gold Fields, 167,610 ....D 6
Kolhapur, 245,206 ....C 5
Kolhapur, *259,482 ....C 5
Konnagar, 29,443 ....F 1
Kota, 205,429 ....D 3
Kotrung, 31,031 ....F 1
Kottayam, 52,685 ....D 7
Kozhikode, 315,786 ....D 6
Kozhikode, *381,096 ....D 6
Krishnanagar, 70,440 ....F 4
Kumbakonam, 92,581 ....D 6
Kumbakonam, *96,746 ....D 6
Kurla, 98,018 ....B 7
Kurnool, 157,448 ....D 5
Latur, 40,913 ....D 5
Lucknow, 763,604 ....E 3
Lucknow, *830,298 ....E 3
Ludhiana, 363,403 ....D 2
Machilipatnam, 126,855 ....E 5
Madhubani, 28,229 ....F 3
Madras, 2,047,735 ....E 6
Madras, *2,470,288 ....E 6
Madurai, 486,480 ....D 7
Mahbubnagar, 35,588 ....D 5
Mahuva, 31,668 ....C 4
Mahuva, *32,732 ....C 4
Malad, 88,287 ....B 6
Malegaon, 243,474 ....C 4
Maler-Kotla, 39,543 ....D 2
Malkapur, 29,687 ....D 4
Mandsaur, 41,876 ....C 4
Mandvi, 26,609 ....B 4
Mangalore, 168,646 ....C 6
Mangalore, *234,680 ....C 6
Mangrol, 21,089 ....B 4
Manmad, 23,570 ....C 4
Manmad, *31,551 ....C 4
Mannargudi, 33,558 ....E 6
Mathura, 135,166 ....D 3
Mathura, *144,485 ....D 3
Mattancheri, 83,896 ....D 7
Mau, 48,785 ....E 3
Mayuram, 51,393 ....D 6
Meerut, 244,824 ....D 3
Meerut, *335,565 ....D 3
Mehsana, 32,577 ....C 4
Mhow, 48,032 ....D 4
Midnapore, 59,532 ....F 4
Miraj, 53,345 ....D 5
Mirzapur, 113,177 ....E 4
Monghyr, 89,768 ....F 3
Moradabad, 205,509 ....D 3
Moradabad, *221,433 ....D 3
Morvi, 50,192 ....C 4
Mulund, 56,430 ....B 6
Murwara, 46,169 ....E 4
Murwara, *60,472 ....E 4
Muzaffarnagar, 87,622 ....D 3
Muzaffarpur, 152,831 ....E 3
Mysore, 262,136 ....D 6
Nadiad, 78,952 ....C 4
Nagapattinam, 59,063 ....E 6
Nagapattinam, *61,305 ....E 6
Nagaur, 24,296 ....C 3
Nagercoil, 136,264 ....D 7
Nagina, 30,247 ....D 3
Nagpur, 876,020 ....D 4
Nagpur, *933,344 ....D 4
Naihati, 58,457 ....F 1
Nander, 81,087 ....D 5
Nandurbar, 41,055 ....C 4
Nandyal, 42,927 ....D 5
Nasik, 169,451 ....C 4
Nasik, *282,782 ....C 4
Navsari, 51,300 ....C 4
Nellore, 134,404 ....E 6
New Delhi (cap.), 324,283 ....D 3
Nimach, 36,287 ....D 4
Nizamabad, 79,093 ....D 5
Nova Goa (Panjim), †79,437 ....C 5
Ongole, 35,804 ....E 5
Ootacamund, 50,140 ....D 6
Palayankottai, 51,002 ....D 7
Palghat, 77,620 ....D 6
Palni, 39,832 ....D 6
Pandharpur, 45,421 ....D 5
Panihati, 93,749 ....F 1
Panipat, 67,026 ....D 3
Panjim, †79,437 ....C 5
Parbhani, 36,795 ....D 5
Parlakhemundi, 22,708 ....E 5
Parvatipuram, 25,281 ....E 5
Patan, 50,264 ....C 4
Patiala, 154,414 ....D 2
Patna, 449,471 ....F 3
Patna, *451,520 ....F 3
Pilibhit, 57,527 ....D 3
Pondicherry, 40,421 ....E 6
Poona, 718,220 ....C 5
Poona, *1,123,399 ....C 5
Porbandar, 74,476 ....B 4
Porbandar, *75,081 ....B 4
Port Blair, 14,075 ....G 6
Proddatur, 50,616 ....D 6
Pudukkottai, 50,488 ....D 6
Puri, 60,815 ....F 5
Purnea, 40,602 ....F 3
Purulia, 48,134 ....F 4
Quilon, 91,018 ....D 7
Raichur, 63,329 ....D 5
Raigarh, 36,933 ....E 4
Raipur, 204,632 ....E 4
Rajahmundry, 155,450 ....E 5
Rajapalaiyam, 71,203 ....D 7
Rajkot, 270,186 ....C 4
Rajnandgaon, 44,678 ....E 4
Rajpipla, 21,426 ....C 4
Rajpur, 24,812 ....F 2
Rampur, 136,349 ....D 3
Ranchi, 137,280 ....F 4
Ranchi, *176,789 ....F 4
Ratangarh, 26,631 ....C 3
Ratlam, 87,472 ....C 4
Ratnagiri, 31,091 ....C 5
Raurkela, 90,287 ....F 4
Rewa, 43,065 ....E 4
Rewari, 36,994 ....D 3
Rishra, 38,535 ....F 1
Sagar, 97,556 ....D 4
Sagar, *120,262 ....D 4
Saharanpur, 223,459 ....D 3
Salem, 297,168 ....D 6
Samalkot, 31,924 ....E 5
Sambalpur, 38,915 ....E 4
Sambhal, 68,940 ....D 3
Sangli, 88,753 ....C 5
Sangli, *150,407 ....C 5
Santa Cruz, 101,232 ....B 7
Santipur, 51,190 ....F 4
Sardarshahr, 32,072 ....C 3
Sasaram, 37,782 ....E 4
Satara, 44,353 ....C 5
Satara, *48,709 ....C 5
Satna, 38,046 ....E 4
Savanur, 16,930 ....D 6
Secunderabad, 187,471 ....D 5
Sehore, 28,489 ....D 4
Seoni, 30,274 ....D 4
Serampore, 91,521 ....F 1
Shahjahanpur, 121,107 ....E 3
Shahjahanpur, *129,737 ....E 3
Sheo, †56,033 ....C 3
Shillong, 84,269 ....G 3
Shillong, *130,195 ....G 3
Shimoga, 63,764 ....D 6
Shivpuri, 28,681 ....D 3
Sholapur, 398,996 ....D 5
Sidhpur, 33,850 ....C 4
Sikar, 50,636 ....D 3
Silchar, 41,062 ....G 4
Siliguri, 65,471 ....F 3
Simla, 42,597 ....D 2
Sirsa, 33,363 ....D 3
Sitapur, 53,884 ....E 3
South Suburban, 307,471 ....F 2
South Suburban, *513,337 ....F 2
Srikakulam, 35,071 ....E 5
Srinagar, 285,257 ....D 2
Surat, 368,917 ....C 4
Surendranagar, 48,602 ....C 4
Tanda, 32,687 ....E 3
Tellicherry, 44,763 ....C 6
Tenali, 78,525 ....E 5
Thana, 154,770 ....B 6
Thana, *164,896 ....B 6
Thanjavur, 120,681 ....D 6
Tinsukia, 28,468 ....H 3
Tiruchchirappalli, 279,283 ....D 6
Tirunelveli, 87,988 ....D 7
Tirupati, 35,845 ....D 6
Tiruvannamalai, 46,441 ....D 6
Titagarh, 76,429 ....F 1
Tonk, 43,413 ....D 3
Trichur, 73,038 ....D 6
Trivandrum, 336,757 ....D 7
Trivandrum, *435,566 ....D 7
Trombay, 17,258 ....B 7
Tumkur, 47,277 ....D 6
Tuni, 22,452 ....E 5
Tuticorin, 150,784 ....D 7
Tuticorin, *157,943 ....D 7
Udaipur, 133,368 ....C 4
Udipi, 24,610 ....C 6
Ujjain, 157,435 ....D 4
Ulhasnagar, 137,636 ....C 5
Umrer, 22,682 ....D 4
Unnao, 29,780 ....E 3
Uttarpara, 21,132 ....F 1
Vaniyambadi, 42,048 ....D 6
Varanasi, 619,822 ....E 3
Varanasi, *643,720 ....E 3
Vellore, 120,643 ....D 6
Vellore, *138,914 ....D 6
Veraval, 46,637 ....C 4
Veraval, *60,857 ....C 4
Vidisha, 27,718 ....D 4
Vijayawada, 312,822 ....D 5
Villupuram, 43,496 ....D 6
Viramgam, 38,955 ....C 4
Visakhapatnam, 285,837 ....E 5
Visnagar, 25,982 ....C 4
Vizagapatam (Visakhapatnam), 285,837 ....E 5
Vizianagaram, 76,808 ....E 5
Warangal, 178,559 ....D 5
Wardha, 49,113 ....D 4
Wun, 18,176 ....D 5
Yeola, 21,039 ....C 4
Yeotmal, 45,587 ....D 4
Ziro ....G 3

OTHER FEATURES

Adam's Bridge (shoals) ....D 7
Agatti (isl.), 2,411 ....C 6
Amindivi (isls.), 7,854 ....C 6
Amini (isl.), 3,530 ....C 6
Andaman (isls.) ....G 6
Andaman (sea) ....G 6
Androth (isl.), 4,183 ....C 6
Arabian (sea) ....B 5
Baltistan (region) ....D 1
Bengal (bay) ....F 5
Berar (region), 4,580,302 ....D 4
Brahmaputra (river) ....G 3
Cambay (gulf) ....C 4
Chenab (river) ....D 2
Chetlat (isl.), 953 ....C 6
Comorin (cape) ....D 7
Coromandel Coast (reg.) ....E 6
Daman (dist.), 22,390 ....C 4
Damodar (river) ....F 4
Deccan (plateau) ....D 6
Diu (dist.), 14,280 ....C 4
Eastern Ghats (mts.) ....D 6
Elephanta (isl.) ....B 7
Ganges (Ganga) (river) ....F 3
Goa (dist.), 589,997 ....C 5
Godavari (river) ....D 5
Godwin Austen (K2) (mt.) ....D 1
Golconda (ruins) ....D 5
Great Indian (des.) ....C 3
Himalaya (mts.) ....D 2
Hooghly (river) ....F 2
Indravati (river) ....E 5
Indus (river) ....D 2
Jhelum (river) ....C 2
Jumna (river) ....E 3
K2 (mt.) ....D 1
Kadmat (isl.), 1,851 ....C 6
Kalpeni (isl.), 2,613 ....C 7
Kamet (mt.) ....D 2
Kanchenjunga (mt.) ....F 3
Karakoram (mts.) ....D 1
Kiltan (isl.), 1,520 ....C 6
Kistna (Krishna) (river) ....D 5
Kunlun (range) ....D 1
Kutch (gulf) ....B 4
Kutch, Rann of (salt marsh) ....B 4
Laccadive (isls.), 12,115 ....C 6
Ladakh (region), 88,651 ....D 2
Mahanadi (river) ....E 4
Malabar (hill) ....B 7
Malabar Coast (reg.) ....C 6
Mannar (gulf) ....D 7
Minicoy (isl.), 4,139 ....C 7
Nanda Devi (mt.) ....D 2
Nanga Parbat (mt.) ....D 1
Narmada (river) ....D 4
Nicobar (isls.) ....G 7
Palk (strait) ....D 7
Penganga (river) ....D 5
Pitti (isl.), 80 ....C 6
Rakaposhi (mt.) ....C 1
Salsette (isl.), 1,566,572 ....B 7
Saraswati (river) ....F 1
Satpura (range) ....D 4
Shipki (pass) ....D 2
Sundarbans (swamp) ....F 4
Sutlej (river) ....C 3
Towers of Silence ....B 7
Travancore (region) ....D 7
Tungabhadra (river) ....D 5
Vindhya (range) ....D 4
Western Ghats (mts.) ....C 5
Yamuna (Jumna) (river) ....E 3

MALDIVES

Maldives, 110,770 ....C 7

NEPAL

CITIES and TOWNS

Bhaktapur, 33,877 ....F 3
Biratnagar, 35,355 ....F 3
Birganj, 10,769 ....F 3
Kathmandu (capital), 121,019 ....E 3
Lalitpur, 47,713 ....E 3
Nepalganj, 15,817 ....E 3

OTHER FEATURES

Annapurna (mt.) ....E 3
Dhaulagiri (mt.) ....E 3
Everest (mt.) ....F 3
Himalaya (mts.) ....F 3
Kanchenjunga (mt.) ....F 3

PAKISTAN

PROVINCES

Baluchistan, 1,400,000 ....B 3
Federal Capital (terr.), 50,000 ....C 2
North-West Frontier, 9,500,000 ....C 2
Punjab, 36,290,000 ....C 2
Sind, 11,900,000 ....B 3

CITIES and TOWNS

Abbottabad, 31,036 ....C 2
Ahmadpur East, 20,423 ....C 3
Bahawalnagar, 36,290 ....C 2
Bahawalpur, 84,377 ....C 3
Bahawalpur, *147,000 ....C 3
Dera Ghazi Khan, 47,105 ....C 3
Dera Ismail Khan, 46,140 ....C 2
Gujranwala, 196,154 ....C 2
Gujranwala, *289,000 ....C 2
Gujrat, 59,608 ....C 2
Hyderabad, 434,537 ....B 3
Hyderabad, *698,000 ....B 3
Islamabad (capital), 50,000 ....C 2
Jhang-Maghiana, 94,971 ....C 2
Jhang-Maghiana, *118,000 ....C 2
Jhelum, 52,585 ....C 2
Karachi, 1,912,598 ....B 4
Karachi, *3,060,000 ....B 4
Khairpur, 34,144 ....B 3
Kohat, 49,854 ....C 2
Lahore, 1,296,477 ....C 2
Lahore, *1,823,000 ....C 2
Larkana, 48,008 ....B 3
Lyallpur, 425,248 ....C 2
Lyallpur, *854,000 ....C 2
Mardan, 77,932 ....C 2
Mirpur Khas, 60,861 ....B 3
Multan, 358,201 ....C 2
Multan, *597,000 ....C 2
Nawabshah, 45,651 ....B 3
Peshawar, 218,691 ....C 2
Peshawar, *296,000 ....C 2
Quetta, 106,633 ....B 2
Quetta, *130,000 ....B 2
Rahimyar Khan, 43,548 ....C 3
Rawalpindi, 340,175 ....C 2
Rawalpindi, *445,000 ....C 2
Sargodha, 129,291 ....C 2
Sargodha, *194,000 ....C 2
Sialkot, 164,346 ....C 2
Sialkot, *167,000 ....C 2
Sukkur, 103,216 ....B 3
Sukkur, *131,000 ....B 3

OTHER FEATURES

Arabian (sea) ....B 5
Chagai (hills) ....A 3
Chenab (river) ....C 2
Hindu Kush (mts.) ....C 1
Indus (river) ....B 3
Jhelum (river) ....C 2
Kabul (river) ....C 2
Khyber (pass) ....C 2
Kutch, Rann of (salt marsh) ....B 4
Mohenjo Daro (ruins) ....B 3
Ravi (river) ....C 2
Sulaiman (range) ....C 3
Sutlej (river) ....C 3
Taxila (ruins) ....C 2
Tirich Mir (mt.) ....C 1

SRI LANKA (CEYLON)

CITIES and TOWNS

Anuradhapura, 29,397 ....E 7
Badulla, 27,088 ....E 7
Batticaloa, 22,957 ....E 7
Colombo (cap.), 551,200 ....D 7
Galle, 64,942 ....D 7
Jaffna, 94,248 ....E 7
Kalutara, 25,286 ....D 7
Kandy, 67,768 ....E 7
Kurunegala, 21,293 ....E 7
Matara, 32,284 ....E 7
Moratuwa, 77,632 ....D 7
Negombo, 47,026 ....D 7
Nuwara Eliya, 19,988 ....E 7
Ratnapura, 21,582 ....D 7
Trincomalee, 34,872 ....E 7

OTHER FEATURES

Adam's Bridge (shoals) ....D 7
Dondra (head) ....E 7
Mannar (gulf) ....D 7
Palk (strait) ....D 7
Pidurutalagala (mt.) ....E 7

*City and suburbs.
†Population of sub-division.
‡Population of district.

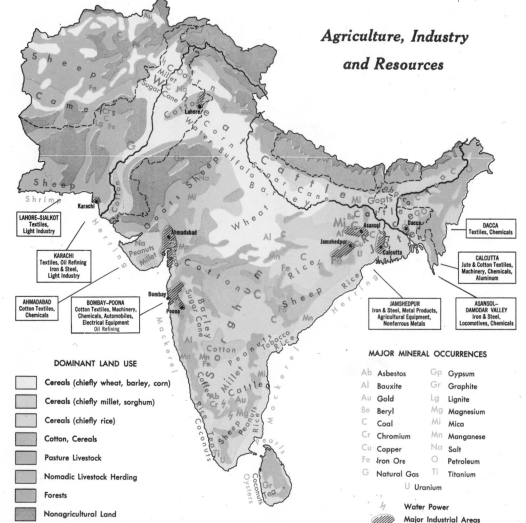

Agriculture, Industry and Resources
LAHORE–SIALKOT Textiles, Light Industry
KARACHI Textiles, Oil Refining Iron & Steel, Light Industry
AHMADABAD Cotton Textiles, Chemicals
BOMBAY–POONA Cotton Textiles, Machinery, Chemicals, Automobiles, Electrical Equipment Oil Refining
JAMSHEDPUR Iron & Steel, Metal Products, Agricultural Equipment, Nonferrous Metals
ASANSOL–DAMODAR VALLEY Iron & Steel, Locomotives, Chemicals
CALCUTTA Jute & Cotton Textiles, Machinery, Chemicals, Aluminum
DACCA Textiles, Chemicals
DOMINANT LAND USE
Cereals (chiefly wheat, barley, corn)
Cereals (chiefly millet, sorghum)
Cereals (chiefly rice)
Cotton, Cereals
Pasture Livestock
Nomadic Livestock Herding
Forests
Nonagricultural Land
MAJOR MINERAL OCCURRENCES
Ab Asbestos
Al Bauxite
Au Gold
Be Beryl
C Coal
Cr Chromium
Cu Copper
Fe Iron Ore
G Natural Gas
Gp Gypsum
Gr Graphite
Lg Lignite
Mg Magnesium
Mi Mica
Mn Manganese
Na Salt
O Petroleum
Ti Titanium
U Uranium
Water Power
Major Industrial Areas

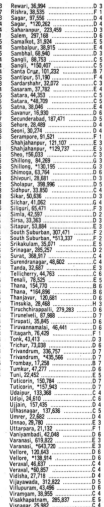

JAPAN
AREA 143,622 sq. mi.
POPULATION 104,665,171
CAPITAL Tokyo
LARGEST CITY Tokyo
HIGHEST POINT Fuji 12,389 ft.
MONETARY UNIT yen
MAJOR LANGUAGE Japanese
MAJOR RELIGIONS Buddhism, Shintoism

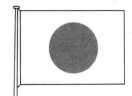

NORTH KOREA
AREA 46,540 sq. mi.
POPULATION 13,300,000
CAPITAL P'yŏngyang
LARGEST CITY P'yŏngyang
HIGHEST POINT Paektu 9,003 ft.
MONETARY UNIT won
MAJOR LANGUAGE Korean
MAJOR RELIGIONS Confucianism, Buddhism, Christianity

SOUTH KOREA
AREA 38,452 sq. mi.
POPULATION 31,683,000
CAPITAL Seoul
LARGEST CITY Seoul
HIGHEST POINT Halla 6,398 ft.
MONETARY UNIT won
MAJOR LANGUAGE Korean
MAJOR RELIGIONS Confucianism, Buddhism, Chondogyo, Christianity

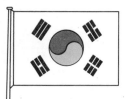

JAPAN
PREFECTURES

Aichi, 4,798,653 .... H 6
Akita, 1,279,835 .... J 4
Aomori, 1,416,591 .... K 3
Chiba, 2,701,770 .... P 2
Ehime, 1,446,384 .... F 7
Fukui, 750,557 .... G 5
Fukuoka, 3,964,611 .... D 7
Fukushima, 1,983,754 .... K 5
Gifu, 1,700,365 .... H 6
Gumma, 1,605,584 .... J 5
Hiroshima, 2,281,146 .... E 6
Hokkaido, 5,171,800 .... K 2
Hyogo, 4,309,944 .... H 7
Ibaraki, 2,056,154 .... K 5
Ishikawa, 980,499 .... H 5
Iwate, 1,411,118 .... K 4
Kagawa, 900,845 .... G 6
Kagoshima, 1,853,541 .... E 8
Kanagawa, 4,430,743 .... O 2
Kochi, 812,714 .... F 7
Kumamoto, 1,770,736 .... E 7
Kyoto, 2,102,808 .... J 7
Mie, 1,514,467 .... H 6
Miyagi, 1,753,126 .... F 4
Miyazaki, 1,080,692 .... E 8
Nagano, 1,958,007 .... J 5
Nagasaki, 1,641,245 .... D 7
Nara, 826,965 .... J 8
Niigata, 2,398,931 .... J 5
Oita, 1,187,480 .... E 7
Okayama, 1,645,135 .... F 6
Okinawa, 1,108,271 .... N 6
Osaka, 6,657,189 .... J 8
Saga, 871,886 .... E 7
Saitama, 3,014,983 .... O 2
Shiga, 853,385 .... J 7

Shimane, 821,620 .... F 6
Shizuoka, 2,912,521 .... H 6
Tochigi, 1,521,656 .... K 5
Tokushima, 815,115 .... G 7
Tokyo, 10,869,244 .... O 2
Tottori, 579,853 .... G 6
Toyama, 1,025,465 .... H 5
Wakayama, 1,026,975 .... G 6
Yamagata, 1,263,103 .... K 4
Yamaguchi, 1,543,573 .... E 6
Yamanashi, 763,194 .... J 6

CITIES and TOWNS

Abashiri, 44,195 .... M 1
Ageo, 54,776 .... O 2
Aizuwakamatsu, 104,000 .... J 5
Ajigasawa, 20,504 .... J 3
Akabira, 46,646 .... K 2
Akashi, 187,000 .... H 8
Aki, 26,605 .... F 7
Akita, 233,000 .... J 4
Akkeshi, 19,039 .... M 2
Akune, 36,026 .... E 8
Amagasaki, 532,000 .... H 8
Amagi, 44,060 .... E 7
Amaha, 18,062 .... G 7
Anan, 59,105 .... G 7
Aomori, 252,000 .... K 3
Asahi, 31,063 .... K 6
Asahikawa, 293,000 .... L 2
Ashibetsu, 52,123 .... L 2
Ashikaga, 153,000 .... J 5
Ashiya, 63,195 .... H 8
Atami, 54,540 .... J 6
Atsugi, 61,833 .... O 2
Awaji, 9,972 .... H 8
Hakodate, 249,000 .... K 3
Hakui, 29,090 .... H 5
Bibai, 63,051 .... L 2

Biratori, 12,930 .... L 2
Chiba, 407,000 .... P 2
Chichibu, 60,330 .... O 2
Chigasaki, 119,000 .... O 3
Chitose, 51,243 .... K 2
Chofu, 145,000 .... O 2
Choshi, 91,492 .... Q 3
Sht, 57,107 .... G 6
Ebetsu, 44,510 .... K 2
Esashi, Hokkaido, 15,380 .... J 3
Esashi, Hokkaido, 11,401 .... L 1
Esashi, Iwate, 42,666 .... K 4
Fuchu, Hiroshima, 45,341 .... F 6
Fuchu, Tokyo, 148,000 .... O 2
Fuji, 173,000 .... J 6
Fujieda, 70,789 .... J 6
Fujisawa, 211,000 .... O 3
Fukuchiyama, 58,223 .... G 6
Fukue, 36,876 .... D 7
Fukui, 193,000 .... G 5
Fukuoka, 812,000 .... E 7
Fukushima, 225,000 .... K 5
Fukuyama, 233,000 .... F 6
Funabashi, 281,000 .... P 2
Furukawa, 52,853 .... K 4
Futtsu, 16,445 .... O 3
Gifu, 398,000 .... H 6
Gobo, 30,040 .... G 7
Gose, 35,788 .... J 8
Gosen, 38,113 .... J 5
Goshogawara, 47,433 .... J 3
Gotsu, 30,209 .... F 6
Habikino, 50,333 .... J 8
Haboro, 30,266 .... K 1
Hachinohe, 209,000 .... K 3
Hachioji, 229,000 .... O 2
Hagi, 53,905 .... E 6
Hamada, 44,439 .... E 6

Hamamatsu, 420,000 .... H 6
Hanamaki, 62,710 .... K 4
Hanawa, 20,507 .... K 3
Hanno, 47,825 .... O 2
Haramachi, 40,643 .... K 5
Hayama, 17,617 .... O 3
Higashiosaka, 454,000 .... H 8
Hikone, 62,740 .... H 6
Himeji, 403,000 .... G 7
Himi, 62,452 .... H 5
Hirakata, 164,000 .... J 7
Hirara, 32,591 .... N 6
Hirata, 33,128 .... F 6
Hiratsuka, 151,000 .... O 3
Hiroo, 13,598 .... L 2
Hirosaki, 162,000 .... K 3
Hiroshima, 542,000 .... E 6
Hitachi, 184,000 .... K 5
Hitachiota, 36,974 .... K 5
Hitoyoshi, 44,831 .... E 7
Hofu, 94,342 .... E 6
Hondo, 39,790 .... E 7
Honjo, 38,361 .... J 4
Hyuga, 43,678 .... E 8
Ibaraki, 143,000 .... J 7
Ichihara, 134,000 .... P 2
Ichikawa, 236,000 .... P 2
Ichinohe, 25,165 .... K 3
Ichinomiya, 210,000 .... H 6
Ichinoseki, 57,238 .... K 4
Ide, 8,199 .... J 7
Iida, 79,145 .... H 6
Iizuka, 82,033 .... E 7
Ikeda, Hokkaido, 15,529 .... L 2
Ikeda, Osaka, 82,478 .... J 7
Ikuno, 9,466 .... G 7
Imabari, 109,000 .... F 6
Imari, 67,316 .... D 7
Imazu, 11,245 .... G 6

Ina, 51,944 .... H 6
Isahaya, 63,886 .... D 7
Ise, 104,000 .... H 6
Ishigaki, 41,315 .... L 7
Ishige, 18,481 .... O 2
Ishinomaki, 106,000 .... K 4
Ishioka, 36,789 .... K 5
Itami, 141,000 .... H 7
Ito, 55,404 .... J 6
Itoigawa, 39,332 .... H 5
Itoman, 34,065 .... N 6
Iwaizumi, 24,846 .... L 3
Iwaki, 337,000 .... K 5
Iwakuni, 106,000 .... E 6
Iwami, 18,024 .... G 6
Iwamisawa, 65,508 .... L 2
Iwanai, 25,405 .... J 2
Iwasaki, 5,432 .... J 3
Iwata, 58,940 .... H 6
Iwatsuki, 41,946 .... O 2
Iyo, 28,611 .... F 7
Izuhara, 21,989 .... D 6
Izumi, 84,771 .... J 8
Izumiotsu, 53,312 .... J 8
Izumisano, 66,521 .... J 8
Izumo, 68,765 .... F 6
Joyo, 20,038 .... J 7
Kadoma, 137,000 .... J 7
Kaga, 54,860 .... H 5
Kagoshima, 406,000 .... E 8
Kaizuka, 69,365 .... J 8
Kakogawa, 115,000 .... G 8
Kamaishi, 82,104 .... L 4
Kamakura, 136,000 .... O 3
Kameoka, 43,335 .... J 7
Kaminoyama, 38,679 .... J 4
Kamiyaku, 12,458 .... E 8
Kamo, 9,034 .... J 7
Kanazawa, 344,000 .... H 5
Kanonji, 44,200 .... F 6

Kanoya, 70,518 .... E 8
Kanuma, 77,240 .... J 5
Karatsu, 73,999 .... D 7
Kaseda, 28,565 .... E 8
Kashiwa, 133,000 .... P 2
Kashihara, 57,065 .... J 8
Kashiwazaki, 71,465 .... J 5
Kasugai, 141,000 .... H 6
Kasukabe, 42,460 .... O 2
Katsuta, 52,625 .... K 5
Katsuura, 29,133 .... K 6
Kawachi, 91,853 .... J 8
Kawachinagano, 40,109 .... J 8
Kawagoe, 148,000 .... O 2
Kawaguchi, 284,000 .... O 2
Kawanishi, 61,282 .... H 7
Kawasaki, 910,000 .... O 2
Kazanawa, 12,787 .... P 3
Kazusa, 12,567 .... P 3
Kembuchi, 8,013 .... L 1
Kesennuma, 59,884 .... K 4
Kikonai, 11,353 .... K 3
Kiryu, 132,000 .... J 5
Kisarazu, 54,928 .... P 3
Kishiwada, 156,000 .... J 8
Kitaibaraki, 55,334 .... K 5
Kitakata, 40,424 .... J 5
Kitakyushu, 1,042,319 .... E 7
Kitami, 74,841 .... L 2
Kizu, 10,814 .... J 7
Kobayashi, 41,922 .... E 8
Kobe, 1,288,754 .... H 7
Kodaira, 125,000 .... O 2
Kofu, 185,000 .... J 6
Kokubu, 31,249 .... E 8
Komagane, 28,327 .... H 6
Komatsu, 91,163 .... H 5
Koriyama, 240,000 .... K 5
Koshigaya, 112,000 .... P 2
Koza, 55,923 .... N 6

Kuji, 38,374 .... K 3
Kuki, 26,773 .... O 2
Kumagaya, 119,000 .... J 5
Kumamoto, 432,000 .... E 7
Kumano, 30,041 .... H 7
Kumiyama, 7,231 .... J 7
Kurashiki, 332,000 .... F 6
Kurayoshi, 50,114 .... F 6
Kure, 237,000 .... E 6
Kurume, 188,000 .... E 7
Kushikino, 31,781 .... E 8
Kushima, 36,425 .... E 8
Kushimoto, 20,252 .... H 7
Kushiro, 195,000 .... M 2
Kutchan, 19,738 .... K 2
Kyonan, 13,980 .... O 3
Kyoto, 1,418,933 .... J 7
Machida, 154,000 .... O 2
Maebashi, 225,000 .... J 5
Maibara, 13,415 .... G 6
Maizuru, 96,641 .... G 6
Mashike, 13,063 .... K 2
Masuda, 52,729 .... E 6
Matsubara, 71,406 .... H 8
Matsudo, 206,000 .... P 2
Matsue, 118,000 .... F 6
Matsumae, 19,111 .... J 3
Matsumoto, 159,000 .... H 5
Matsunaga, 34,610 .... F 6
Matsusaka, 104,000 .... H 6
Matsuto, 29,649 .... H 5
Matsuyama, 310,000 .... F 7
Mihara, 82,175 .... F 6
Miki, 38,542 .... H 7
Mikuni, 22,135 .... H 5
Minamata, 45,577 .... E 7
Minobu, 12,250 .... J 6
Minoo, 43,851 .... J 7
Misawa, 36,326 .... K 3
Mitaka, 146,000 .... O 2
Mito, 167,000 .... P 2
Mitsukaido, 36,584 .... O 2
Miura, 42,601 .... O 3
Miyako, 56,575 .... L 4
Miyakonojo, 121,000 .... E 8
Miyazaki, 212,000 .... E 8
Miyazu, 33,285 .... G 6
Miyoshi, 37,871 .... F 6
Mizusawa, 45,985 .... K 4
Mobara, 42,486 .... P 3
Mombetsu, 40,389 .... L 1
Mooka, 38,117 .... K 5
Mori, 18,330 .... K 2
Moriguchi, 164,000 .... J 7
Morioka, 191,000 .... K 4
Motobu, 15,068 .... N 6
Muko, 20,730 .... J 7
Murakami, 32,651 .... J 4
Muroran, 181,000 .... K 2
Muroto, 28,746 .... G 7
Musashino, 135,000 .... O 2
Mutsu, 39,282 .... K 3
Nachikatsuura, 24,889 .... H 7
Nagahama, Ehime, 16,193 .... F 7
Nagahama, Shiga, 49,871 .... H 6
Nagaoka, 159,000 .... J 5
Nagaoka, 27,522 .... J 7
Nagaoka, 159,000 .... J 7
Nagasaki, 422,000 .... D 7
Nagato, 29,246 .... E 6
Nago, 19,601 .... N 6
Nagoya, 2,036,022 .... H 6
Naha, 294,000 .... N 6
Nakaminato, 33,620 .... K 5
Nakamura, 35,717 .... F 7
Nakasato, 15,898 .... K 3
Nakatsu, 58,371 .... E 7
Nakoso, 46,731 .... K 5
Nanao, 48,715 .... H 5
Nankoku, 41,237 .... F 7
Naoetsu, 45,650 .... H 5
Nara, 191,000 .... J 8
Narashino, 64,897 .... P 2
Nayoro, 36,106 .... L 1
Naze, 44,111 .... M 2
Nemuro, 45,149 .... M 2
Neyagawa, 174,000 .... J 7
Nichinan, 57,612 .... E 8
Niigata, 379,000 .... J 5
Niihama, 130,000 .... F 7
Niimi, 34,063 .... F 6
Niitsu, 56,594 .... J 5
Nikko, 32,031 .... J 5
Nishinomiya, 357,000 .... H 8
Nishinoomote, 30,490 .... E 8
Nobeoka, 134,000 .... E 8
Noboribetsu, 39,101 .... K 2
Noda, 59,799 .... P 2
Nogata, 57,839 .... E 7
Nose, 9,306 .... J 7
Noshiro, 61,921 .... J 3
Noto, 17,719 .... H 5
Numata, 44,347 .... J 5
Numazu, 186,000 .... J 6
Obama, 35,160 .... G 6
Obihiro, 129,000 .... L 2
Oda, 42,322 .... F 6
Odate, 59,662 .... K 3
Odawara, 151,000 .... O 3
Ofunato, 38,347 .... K 4
Oga, 43,333 .... J 3
Ogaki, 134,000 .... H 6

(continued on following page)

Agriculture, Industry and Resources

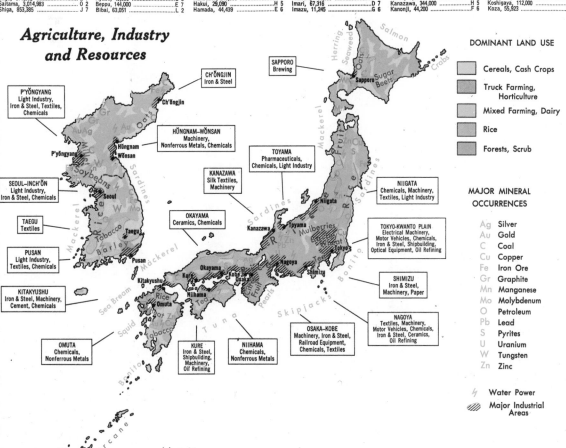

DOMINANT LAND USE

- Cereals, Cash Crops
- Truck Farming, Horticulture
- Mixed Farming, Dairy
- Rice
- Forests, Scrub

MAJOR MINERAL OCCURRENCES

Ag Silver
Au Gold
C Coal
Cu Copper
Fe Iron Ore
Gr Graphite
Mn Manganese
Mo Molybdenum
O Petroleum
Pb Lead
S Pyrites
U Uranium
W Tungsten
Zn Zinc

⚡ Water Power
▨ Major Industrial Areas

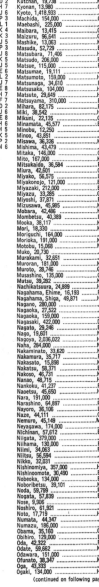

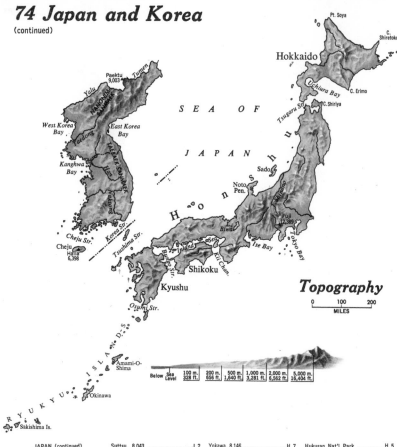

Topography

0   100   200
MILES

Below Sea Level	100 m. 328 ft.	200 m. 656 ft.	500 m. 1,640 ft.	1,000 m. 3,281 ft.	2,000 m. 6,562 ft.	5,000 m. 16,404 ft.

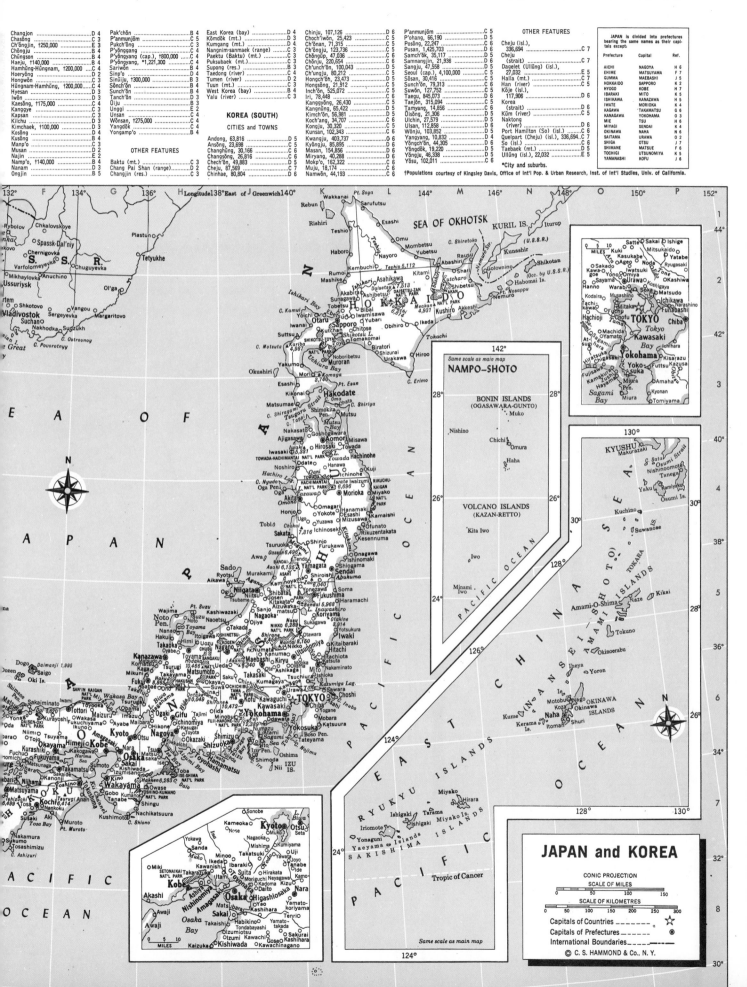

Changjon		D 4
Chasong		C 3
Ch'ongjin, 1,250,000		E 3
Chongju		C 3
Chunggon		C 3
Haeju, 1,140,000		B 4
Hamhung-Hungnam, 1,200,000		D 3
Hoeryong		D 2
Hongwon		D 3
Hungnam-Hamhung, 1,200,000		D 3
Hyesan		D 3
Iwon		D 3
Kaesong, 1,175,000		C 4
Kanggye		C 3
Kapsan		D 3
Kilchu		D 3
Kimchaek, 1,100,000		D 3
Kosong		B 4
Manp'o		C 3
Musan		D 2
Najin		E 2
Namp'o, 1,140,000		B 4
Nanam		D 3

OTHER FEATURES

Baktu (mt.)		C 3
Chang Pai Shan (range)		D 2
Changjin (res.)		C 3

Pak'chon		B 4
P'anmunjom		C 5
Pukch'ong		C 3
P'yonggang		C 4
P'yongyang (cap.), †800,000		C 4
P'yongyang, *1,221,300		B 4
Sariwon		B 4
Sinp'o		D 3
Sinuiju, †300,000		B 3
Sonch'on		B 4
Sunch'on		B 4
Tanch'on		D 3
Oiju		C 3
Unggi		E 2
Unsan		C 4
Wonsan, †275,000		C 4
Yangdok		C 4
Yongamp'o		B 4

KOREA (SOUTH)
CITIES and TOWNS

Andong, 63,816		C 5
Ansong, 23,698		C 5
Changhung, 30,166		C 6
Changsong, 26,816		C 5
Chech'on, 49,883		D 5
Cheju, 87,569		C 7
Chinhae, 80,804		D 6

East Korea (bay)		D 4
Komdok (mt.)		D 3
Kumgang (mt.)		C 4
Nangnim-sanmaek (range)		C 3
Paektu (Baktu) (mt.)		C 3
Puksubaek (mt.)		C 3
Supong (res.)		B 3
Taedong (river)		C 4
Tumen (river)		D 2
Tuun (river)		D 2
West Korea (bay)		B 4
Yalu (river)		C 3

Chinju, 107,126		D 6
Choch'iwon, 25,423		C 5
Posong, 22,247		C 6
Ch'onan, 71,315		C 5
Ch'ongju, 123,736		C 5
Chongup, 47,036		C 6
Chonju, 220,654		C 6
Ch'unch'on, 100,043		C 5
Ch'ungju, 80,212		C 5
Hongch'on, 23,473		C 5
Hongsong, 21,912		C 5
Inch'on, 525,072		C 5
Iri, 78,448		C 6
Kanggyong, 26,430		C 5
Kangnung, 65,422		D 5
Kimch'on, 56,981		C 5
Koch'ang, 34,707		C 6
Kongju, 30,320		C 5
Kunsan, 102,343		C 6

P'anmunjom		C 5
P'ohang, 66,190		D 6
Posong, 22,247		C 6
Pusan, 1,425,703		D 6
Samch'ok, 35,117		D 5
Samnangjin, 21,936		D 6
Sangju, 47,558		C 5
Seoul (cap.), 4,100,000		C 5
Sosan, 30,416		C 5
Sunch'on, 79,313		C 6
Suwon, 127,752		C 5
Taegu, 845,073		D 6
Taejon, 315,094		C 5
Tamyang, 14,856		C 6
Oisong, 21,306		D 5
Ulchin, 27,579		D 5
Ulsan, 112,858		D 6
Wonju, 103,852		C 5
Kwangju, 403,737		C 6
Kyongju, 85,895		D 6
Masan, 154,856		D 6
Miryang, 40,288		D 6
Mokp'o, 162,322		C 6
Muju, 18,174		C 6
Namwon, 44,193		C 6

OTHER FEATURES

Cheju (isl.), 336,694		C 7
Cheju (strait)		C 7
Dagelet (Ulung) (isl.), 27,032		E 5
Halla (mt.)		C 7
Han (river)		C 5
Koje (isl.), 117,906		D 6
Korea (strait)		D 6
Kum (river)		C 5
Naktong (river)		D 6
Port Hamilton (So) (isl.)		C 6
Quelpart (Cheju) (isl.), 336,694		C 7
So (isl.)		C 6
Taebaek (mt.)		D 5
Ulung (isl.), 22,032		E 5

JAPAN is divided into prefectures bearing the same names as their capitals except:

Prefecture	Capital	Ref.
AICHI	NAGOYA	H 6
EHIME	MATSUYAMA	F 7
GUMMA	MAEBASHI	J 5
HOKKAIDO	SAPPORO	K 2
HYOGO	KOBE	H 7
IBARAKI	MITO	K 5
ISHIKAWA	KANAZAWA	H 5
IWATE	MORIOKA	K 3
KAGAWA	TAKAMATSU	G 6
KANAGAWA	YOKOHAMA	J 6
MIE	TSU	H 6
MIYAGI	SENDAI	K 4
OKINAWA	NAHA	N 6
SAITAMA	URAWA	O 2
SHIGA	OTSU	J 7
SHIMANE	MATSUE	F 6
TOCHIGI	UTSUNOMIYA	J 6
YAMANASHI	KOFU	J 6

*City and suburbs.

†Populations courtesy of Kingsley Davis, Office of Int'l Pop. & Urban Research, Inst. of Int'l Studies, Univ. of California.

JAPAN and KOREA
CONIC PROJECTION
SCALE OF MILES
SCALE OF KILOMETRES

Capitals of Countries ☆
Capitals of Prefectures ◉
International Boundaries

© C. S. HAMMOND & Co., N. Y.

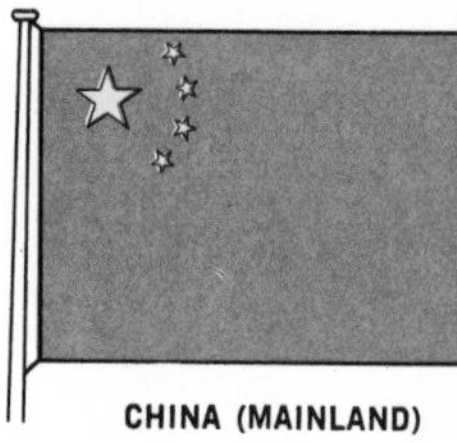
CHINA (MAINLAND)

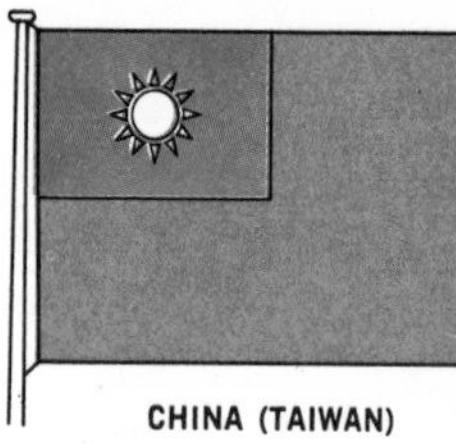
CHINA (TAIWAN)

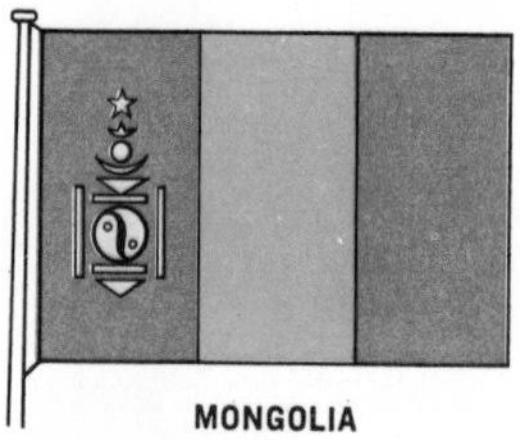
MONGOLIA

CHINA (MAINLAND)

AREA 3,691,506 sq. mi.
POPULATION 740,000,000
CAPITAL Peking
LARGEST CITY Shanghai
HIGHEST POINT Mt. Everest 29,028 ft.
MONETARY UNIT yüan
MAJOR LANGUAGES Chinese, Chuang, Uigur, Yi, Tibetan, Miao, Mongol
MAJOR RELIGIONS Confucianism, Buddhism, Taoism, Islam

Topography

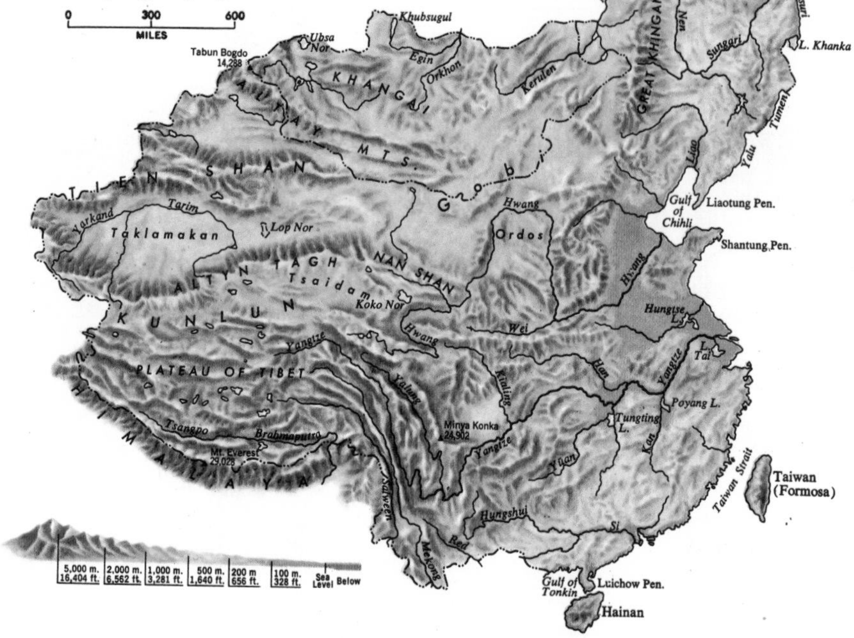

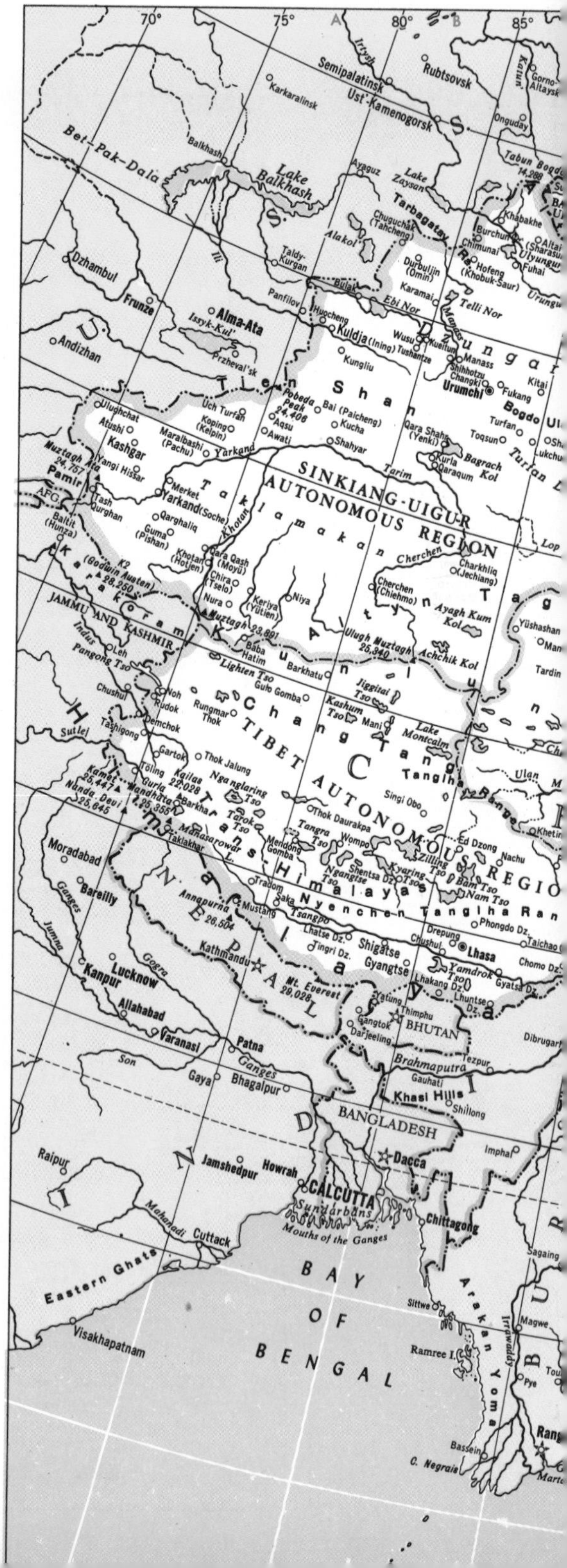

CHINA

PROVINCES

Anhwei, 33,560,000 .... J 5
Chekiang, 25,280,000 .... J 6
Fukien, 14,650,000 .... J 6
Heilungkiang, 14,860,000 .... L 2
Honan, 48,670,000 .... H 5
Hopei, 44,720,000 .... J 4
Hunan, 36,220,000 .... H 6
Hupei, 30,790,000 .... H 5
Inner Mongolian Autonomous Region, 9,200,000 .... G 3
Kansu, 12,800,000 .... F 4
Kiangsi, 18,610,000 .... J 6
Kiangsu, 45,230,000 .... K 5
Kirin, 12,550,000 .... L 3
Kwangsi Chuang Autonomous Region, 19,390,000 .... G 7
Kwangtung, 37,960,000 .... H 7
Kweichow, 16,890,000 .... G 6
Liaoning, 24,090,000 .... K 3
Ningsia Hui Autonomous Region, 1,810,000 .... G 4
Shansi, 15,960,000 .... H 4
Shantung, 54,030,000 .... J 4
Shensi, 18,130,000 .... G 5
Sinkiang-Uigur Autonomous Region, 5,640,000 .... B 3
Szechwan, 72,160,000 .... F 5
Taiwan, 14,577,000 .... K 7
Tibet Autonomous Region, 1,270,000 .... C 5
Tsinghai, 2,050,000 .... E 4
Yünnan, 19,100,000 .... F 7

CITIES and TOWNS†

Ahpa .... F 5
Aicheng .... G 8
Aigun .... L 1
Aihui (Aigun) .... L 1
Aliho .... K 1
Altai .... C 2
Amoy, 400,000 .... J 7
Ankang .... G 5
Anking, 160,000 .... J 5
Anshan, 1,500,000 .... K 3
Anshun, 40,000 .... G 6
Ansi .... E 3
Antung (Tantung), 450,000 .... K 3
Anyang, 225,000 .... H 4
Aqsu .... B 3
Atushi, 5,000 .... A 4
Awati .... B 3
Baba Hatim .... B 4
Bai .... B 3
Barkha .... B 5
Barkhatu .... B 4
Barkol .... D 3
Batang .... E 6
Bayinhot .... F 4
Canton, 2,300,000 .... H 7
Chalainor .... J 2
Chamdo .... E 5
Changchih, 300,000 .... H 4
Changchow, 400,000 .... J 5
Changchow, 81,200 .... J 7
Changchun, 1,500,000 .... K 3
Changsha, 850,000 .... H 6
Changteh, 225,000 .... H 6
Changyeh, 45,000 .... E 4
Chankiang, 220,000 .... H 7
Chaoan (Chaochow), 101,000 .... J 7
Chaochow, 101,000 .... J 7
Chaotung, 50,000 .... F 6
Chaoyang, 30,000 .... J 3
Charkhliq .... C 4
Chefoo, 180,000 .... K 4
Chengchow, 1,500,000 .... H 5
Chengteh, 200,000 .... J 3
Chengtu, 2,000,000 .... F 5
Chenpa .... G 5
Cherchen .... C 4
Chiai, 221,817 .... K 7
Chiehmo (Cherchen) .... C 4
Chihfeng, 49,000 .... J 3
Chinchow, 750,000 .... J 3
Chinkiang, 250,000 .... K 5
Chinsi, 45,000 .... K 3
Chinwangtao, 400,000 .... K 4
Chomo Dzong .... D 6
Chüanchow, 130,000 .... J 7
Chuchow, 350,000 .... H 6
Chuguchak .... B 2
Chumatien, 45,000 .... H 5
Chungking, 3,500,000 .... G 6
Chungning .... G 4
Chungshan, 135,000 .... H 7
Chushul .... D 6
Dairen (in Lüta) .... K 4
Denchin .... E 5
Drepung .... D 6
Durbuljin .... B 2
Ed Dzong .... D 5
Fatshan, 120,000 .... H 7
Fengfeng, 45,000 .... H 4
Fenyang, 25,000 .... H 4
Foochow, 900,000 .... J 6
Fowyang, 75,000 .... J 5
Fuchin .... M 2
Fuhai .... C 2
Fushun, 1,700,000 .... K 3
Fusin, 350,000 .... K 3
Fusingchen, 20,000 .... F 7
Fuyü, 62,969 .... L 2
Gartok .... B 5
Giamda Dzong (Taichao) .... D 5
Guma .... A 4
Gyangtse .... C 6
Gyatsa Dzong .... D 6
Haikow (Hoihow), 500,000 .... H 7
Hailar, 60,000 .... J 2
Hailun .... L 2
Hailung, 20,000 .... L 3
Hami .... D 3
Hanchung, 120,000 .... G 5
Hangchow, 1,100,000 .... J 5
Hankow (in Wuhan) .... H 5
Hantan, 500,000 .... H 4
Hanyang (in Wuhan) .... H 5
Harbin, 2,750,000 .... L 2
Hengshui .... J 4
Hengyang, 310,000 .... H 6
Hochwan, 75,000 .... G 5
Hofei, 400,000 .... J 5
Hofeng .... C 2
Hoihow, 500,000 .... H 7
Hokang, 350,000 .... M 2
Hoppo, 80,000 .... G 7
Hotien (Khotan) .... A 4
Hsüchang, 58,000 .... H 5
Huhehot, 700,000 .... H 3
Huma .... L 1
Hunchun, 13,246 .... M 3
Hwainan, 350,000 .... J 5
Hwaiteh, 60,000 .... K 3
Hwangchung .... F 4
Hwangling .... G 4
Hwangshih, 200,000 .... J 5
Hwangyüan .... F 4
Hwohsien .... H 4
Ichang, 150,000 .... H 5
Ichun, 200,000 .... L 2
Ierhsieh .... J 2
Ining (Kuldja), 160,000 .... B 3
Ipin, 275,000 .... F 6
Ishan .... G 7
Jechiang (Charkhliq) .... C 4
Jyekundo .... E 5
Kaifeng, 330,000 .... J 5
Kalgan, 1,000,000 .... J 3
Kanchow, 135,000 .... H 6
Kangting .... F 6
Kaohsiung, 719,899 .... J 7
Karamai, 43,000 .... B 2
Kashgar, 175,000 .... A 4
Kashing, 132,000 .... K 5
Keelung, 304,740 .... K 6
Kelpin (Koping) .... A 3
Keriya .... B 4
Khabakhe .... C 2
Khetinsiring .... D 5
Khobuk-Saur (Hofeng) .... C 2
Khotan .... A 4
Kiamusze, 275,000 .... L 2
Kian, 100,000 .... J 6
Kiayükwan .... E 4
Kienow .... J 6
Kienyang, 50,000 .... H 6
Kinghung .... E 7
Kingku .... F 7
Kingtehchen, 300,000 .... J 6
Kinhwa, 46,200 .... J 6
Kirin, 1,200,000 .... L 3
Kisi, 350,000 .... M 2
Kitai .... C 3
Kiuchüan, 50,000 .... E 4
Kiukiang, 120,000 .... J 6
Kokiu, 250,000 .... F 7
Kongmoon, 150,000 .... H 7
Koping .... A 3
Kucha .... B 3
Kulang .... F 4
Kuldja, 160,000 .... B 3
Kungju .... B 3
Kunming, 1,700,000 .... F 6
Kwanghwa .... H 5
Kweilin, 225,000 .... G 6
Kweisui (Huhehot), 700,000 .... H 3
Kweiyang, 1,500,000 .... G 6
Lanchow, 1,500,000 .... F 4
Lantsang .... E 7
Lhakang Dzong .... D 6
Lhasa, 175,000 .... D 6
Lhatse Dzong .... C 6
Lhuntse Dzong .... D 6
Liaoyang, 250,000 .... K 3
Liaoyüan, 300,000 .... L 3
Lienyünkang, 300,000 .... J 5
Likiang .... F 6
Linchwan, 45,000 .... J 6
Linsia, 75,000 .... F 4
Lintsing, 45,000 .... J 4
Liuchow, 250,000 .... G 7
Loho, 55,000 .... H 5
Loshan, 250,000 .... F 6
Loyang, 750,000 .... H 5
Luchow, 225,000 .... F 6
Lungchen, 14,000 .... L 2
Lüshun (Port Arthur) (in Lüta) .... K 4
Lüta, ‡4,000,000 .... K 4
Mahai .... D 4
Manass .... C 3
Manchouli, 30,000 .... J 2
Mani .... C 5
Manning (Wanning) .... H 8
Maralbashi .... A 4
Markham Dzong .... E 6
Mato .... E 4
Mendong Gomba .... C 5
Merket .... A 4
Minhsien .... F 5
Mowming, 15,000 .... H 7
Moyü (Qara Qash) .... B 4
Mukden, 3,750,000 .... K 3
Muli .... F 6
Mutankiang, 400,000 .... M 3
Nachü .... D 5
Nanchang, 900,000 .... H 6
Nancheng, 50,000 .... J 6
Nanchung, 275,000 .... G 5
Nanking, 2,000,000 .... J 5
Nanning, 375,000 .... G 7
Nanping, 53,445 .... J 6
Nanyang, 75,000 .... H 5
Neikiang, 240,000 .... F 6
Ningpo, 350,000 .... K 6
Ningsia (Yinchwan), 175,000 .... F 4
Omin (Durbuljin) .... B 2
Pachen .... D 5
Pachu (Maralbashi) .... A 4
Paicheng, 75,000 .... K 2
Paiyin, 50,000 .... F 4
Paiyü .... E 5
Pakhoi, 175,000 .... G 7
Paoki, 275,000 .... G 5
Paoting, 350,000 .... J 4
Paotow, 800,000 .... G 3
Pehan, 130,000 .... L 2
Peihai (Pakhoi), 175,000 .... G 7

(continued on following page)

CHINA (TAIWAN)
AREA 13,948 sq. mi.
POPULATION 14,577,000
CAPITAL Taipei
LARGEST CITY Taipei
HIGHEST POINT Hsinkao Shan 12,959 ft.
MONETARY UNIT new Taiwan dollar
MAJOR LANGUAGES Chinese, Formosan
MAJOR RELIGIONS Confucianism, Buddhism, Taoism, Christianity, Tribal religions

MONGOLIA
AREA 604,247 sq. mi.
POPULATION 1,300,000
CAPITAL Ulan Bator
LARGEST CITY Ulan Bator
HIGHEST POINT Tabun Bogdo 15,266 ft.
MONETARY UNIT tugrik
MAJOR LANGUAGES Mongolian, Kazakh
MAJOR RELIGION Buddhism

HONG KONG
AREA 398 sq. mi.
POPULATION 4,089,000
CAPITAL Victoria
MONETARY UNIT Hong Kong dollar
MAJOR LANGUAGES Chinese, English
MAJOR RELIGIONS Confucianism, Buddhism, Christianity

MACAO
AREA 6.2 sq. mi.
POPULATION 292,000
CAPITAL Macao
MONETARY UNIT pataca
MAJOR LANGUAGES Chinese, Portuguese
MAJOR RELIGIONS Confucianism, Buddhism, Taoism, Christianity

CHINA and MONGOLIA
CONIC PROJECTION

SCALE OF MILES
0 100 200 300 400 500

SCALE OF KILOMETRES
0 100 200 300 400 500

Capitals of Countries.... ☆   International Boundaries ___ . ___
Provincial Capitals........ ◉   Provincial Boundaries...... ___ . . ___
Canals ....   Walls .... ⌒⌒⌒

© Copyright by C.S. HAMMOND & CO., N.Y.

*Wuhan municipality consists of Hankow, Hanyang and Wuchang.

Agriculture, Industry and Resources

DOMINANT LAND USE
- Cereals (chiefly wheat, millet)
- Cereals (chiefly wheat, rice, barley)
- Cereals (chiefly rice, barley)
- Livestock Herding, Limited Agriculture
- Forests
- Nonagricultural Land

MAJOR MINERAL OCCURRENCES
- Ab Asbestos
- Ag Silver
- Al Bauxite
- Au Gold
- C Coal
- Cu Copper
- F Fluorspar
- Fe Iron Ore
- G Natural Gas
- Gp Gypsum
- Hg Mercury
- J Jade
- Mg Magnesium
- Mn Manganese
- Mo Molybdenum
- Na Salt
- O Petroleum
- Pb Lead
- Sb Antimony
- Sn Tin
- Tc Talc
- U Uranium
- W Tungsten
- Zn Zinc

- Water Power
- Major Industrial Areas

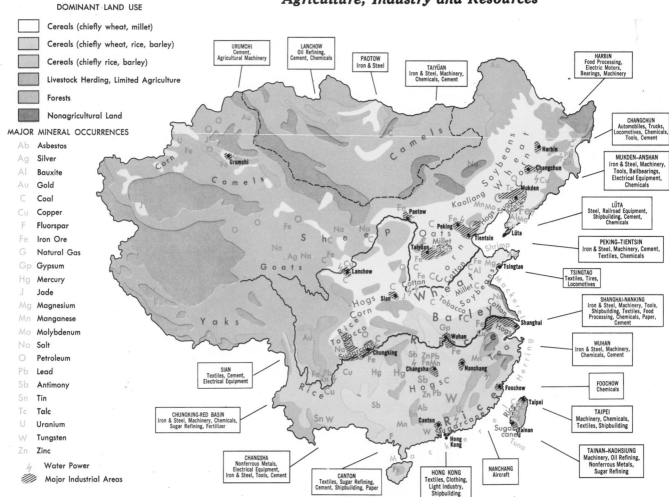

URUMCHI — Cement, Agricultural Machinery

LANCHOW — Oil Refining, Cement, Chemicals

PAOTOW — Iron & Steel

TAIYÜAN — Iron & Steel, Machinery, Chemicals, Cement

HARBIN — Food Processing, Electric Motors, Bearings, Machinery

CHANGCHUN — Automobiles, Trucks, Locomotives, Chemicals, Tools, Cement

MUKDEN–ANSHAN — Iron & Steel, Machinery, Tools, Ballbearings, Electrical Equipment, Chemicals

LÜTA — Steel, Railroad Equipment, Shipbuilding, Cement, Chemicals

PEKING–TIENTSIN — Iron & Steel, Machinery, Cement, Textiles, Chemicals

TSINGTAO — Textiles, Tires, Locomotives

SHANGHAI–NANKING — Iron & Steel, Machinery, Tools, Shipbuilding, Textiles, Food Processing, Chemicals, Paper, Cement

WUHAN — Iron & Steel, Machinery, Chemicals, Cement

FOOCHOW — Chemicals

TAIPEI — Machinery, Chemicals, Textiles, Shipbuilding

TAINAN–KAOHSIUNG — Machinery, Oil Refining, Nonferrous Metals, Sugar Refining

SIAN — Textiles, Cement, Electrical Equipment

CHUNGKING–RED BASIN — Iron & Steel, Machinery, Chemicals, Sugar Refining, Fertilizer

CHANGSHA — Nonferrous Metals, Electrical Equipment, Iron & Steel, Tools, Cement

CANTON — Textiles, Sugar Refining, Cement, Shipbuilding, Paper

HONG KONG — Textiles, Clothing, Light Industry, Shipbuilding

NANCHANG — Aircraft

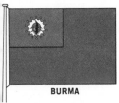

BURMA

THAILAND

LAOS

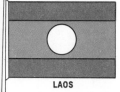

CAMBODIA

VIETNAM

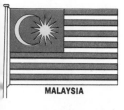

MALAYSIA

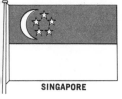

SINGAPORE

BURMA
AREA 261,789 sq. mi.
POPULATION 31,240,000
CAPITAL Rangoon
LARGEST CITY Rangoon
HIGHEST POINT Hkakabo Razi 19,296 ft.
MONETARY UNIT kyat
MAJOR LANGUAGES Burmese, Karen, Shan, Kachin, Chin, Kayah, English
MAJOR RELIGIONS Buddhism, Tribal religions

THAILAND
AREA 198,455 sq. mi.
POPULATION 42,700,000
CAPITAL Bangkok
LARGEST CITY Bangkok
HIGHEST POINT Doi Inthanon 8,452 ft.
MONETARY UNIT baht
MAJOR LANGUAGES Thai, Lao, Chinese, Khmer, Malay
MAJOR RELIGIONS Buddhism, Tribal religions

LAOS
AREA 91,428 sq. mi.
POPULATION 3,500,000
CAPITAL Vientiane
LARGEST CITY Vientiane
HIGHEST POINT Phu Bia 9,252 ft.
MONETARY UNIT kip
MAJOR LANGUAGES Lao, French
MAJOR RELIGIONS Buddhism, Tribal religions

CAMBODIA
AREA 69,898 sq. mi.
POPULATION 8,110,000
CAPITAL Phnom Penh
LARGEST CITY Phnom Penh
HIGHEST POINT 5,948 ft.
MONETARY UNIT riel
MAJOR LANGUAGES Khmer (Cambodian), French
MAJOR RELIGION Buddhism

VIETNAM
AREA 128,405 sq. mi.
POPULATION 46,600,000
CAPITAL Hanoi
LARGEST CITY Ho Chi Minh City (Saigon)
HIGHEST POINT Fan Si Pan 10,308 ft.
MONETARY UNIT dong
MAJOR LANGUAGES Vietnamese, Thai, Muong, Meo, Yao, Khmer, French, Chinese, Cham
MAJOR RELIGIONS Buddhism, Taoism, Confucianism, Roman Catholicsm, Cao-Dai

MALAYSIA
AREA 128,308 sq. mi.
POPULATION 12,368,000
CAPITAL Kuala Lumpur
LARGEST CITY Kuala Lumpur
HIGHEST POINT Mt. Kinabalu 13,455 ft.
MONETARY UNIT Malaysian dollar
MAJOR LANGUAGES Malay, Chinese, English, Tamil, Dayak, Kadazan
MAJOR RELIGIONS Islam, Confucianism, Buddhism, Tribal religions, Hinduism, Taoism, Christianity, Sikhism

SINGAPORE
AREA 226 sq. mi.
POPULATION 2,300,000
CAPITAL Singapore
LARGEST CITY Singapore
HIGHEST POINT Bukit Timah 581 ft.
MONETARY UNIT Singapore dollar
MAJOR LANGUAGES Chinese, Malay, Tamil, English, Hindi
MAJOR RELIGIONS Confucianism, Buddhism, Taoism, Hinduism, Islam, Christianity

Topography

0   200   400
MILES

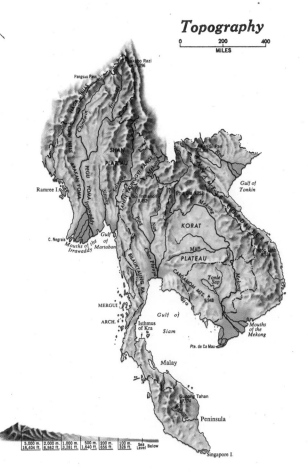

5,000 m. 2,000 m. 1,000 m. 500 m. 200 m. 100 m. Sea Level Below
16,404 ft. 6,562 ft. 3,281 ft. 1,640 ft. 656 ft. 328 ft.

BURMA

INTERNAL DIVISIONS

Arakan (div.) ....B 3
Chin Hills (special div.) ....B 2
Irrawaddy (div.) ....B 3
Kachin (state) ....C 1
Kawthoolei (state) ....C 3
Kayah (state) ....C 3
Magwe (div.) ....B 2
Mandalay (div.) ....B 2
Pegu (div.) ....C 3
Sagaing (div.) ....B 1
Shan (state) ....C 2
Tenasserim (div.) ....C 4

CITIES and TOWNS

Allanmyo, 15,580 ....B 3
Amarapura, 11,268 ....B 2
Amherst, 6,000 ....C 3
Athok, 4,819 ....B 3
Bassein, ‡105,000 ....B 3
Bhamo, 9,821 ....C 1
Bilin, 5,248 ....C 3
Chauk, 24,464 ....B 2
Danubyu, 9,833 ....B 3
Falam ....B 2
Fort Hertz (Putao) ....C 1
Gangaw, 3,800 ....B 2
Gyobingauk, 9,922 ....B 3
Henzada, ‡100,000 ....B 3
Insein, 27,030 ....C 3
Kalemyo, 3,158 ....B 2
Kalewa, 2,230 ....B 2
Kama, 3,523 ....B 3
Kamayut, 23,032 ....C 3
Kanbalu, 3,281 ....B 2
Kani, 2,600 ....B 2
Katha, 7,648 ....C 1
Kawlin, 3,735 ....B 2
Kyaikto, 13,154 ....C 3
Kyangin, 6,073 ....B 3
Kyaukpadaung, 5,480 ....B 2
Kyaukpyu, 7,335 ....B 3
Kyaukse, 8,659 ....C 2
Kywebwe, 3,150 ....C 3
Labutta, 12,982 ....B 3
Lashio ....C 2
Letpadan, 15,896 ....C 3
Loi-kaw ....C 3
Madauk, 4,618 ....C 3
Magwe, 13,270 ....B 2
Mahlaing, 6,543 ....C 2
Mandalay, ‡300,000 ....C 2
Martaban, 5,661 ....C 3
Ma-ubin, 23,362 ....B 3
Maungdaw, 3,772 ....B 2
Mawlaik, 2,993 ....B 2
Maymyo, 22,287 ....C 2
Meiktila, 19,474 ....B 2
Mergui, 33,697 ....C 4
Minbu, 9,096 ....B 2
Minbya, 5,783 ....B 3
Minhla, 6,470 ....B 3
Mogaung, 2,920 ....C 1
Mogok, 8,334 ....C 2
Monywa, 26,297 ....B 2
Moulmein, ‡175,000 ....C 3
Mudon, 20,136 ....C 3
Myanaung, 11,155 ....B 3
Myaungmya, 24,532 ....B 3
Myebon, 3,499 ....B 2
Myingyan, 36,439 ....B 2
Myinhla, 6,470 ....B 3
Myitkyina, 12,382 ....C 1
Myitnge, 3,888 ....B 2
Myohaung, 6,534 ....B 2
Nyaunglebin, 12,155 ....C 3
Pa-an, 4,139 ....C 3
Pagan, 2,824 ....B 2
Pakokku, 30,943 ....B 2
Palaw, 5,596 ....C 4
Papun ....C 3
Paungde, 17,286 ....B 3
Pegu, 47,378 ....C 3

Putao ....C 1
Pyapon, 19,174 ....B 3
Pye, 36,997 ....A 3
Pyinmana, 22,025 ....C 3
Pyu, 10,443 ....C 3
Rangoon (capital), *1,700,000...C 3
Rathedaung, 2,969 ....B 2
Sagaing, 15,382 ....B 2
Sandoway, 5,172 ....B 3
Shwebo, 17,827 ....B 2
Shwegyin, 5,439 ....C 3
Shwenyaung ....C 2
Singkaling Hkamti ....B 1
Singu, 4,027 ....C 2
Sittwe, 42,329 ....A 3
Syriam, 15,296 ....C 3
Taungdwingyi, 16,233 ....C 2
Taunggyi ....C 2
Taungup, 4,065 ....B 3
Tavoy, 40,312 ....C 4
Tenasserim, 1,086 ....C 5
Tharrawaddy, 8,977 ....C 3
Thaton, 38,047 ....C 3
Thayetmyo, 11,649 ....B 2
Thazi, 7,531 ....C 2
Thongwa, 10,829 ....C 3
Thonze, 14,443 ....B 3
Toungoo, 31,589 ....C 3
Victoria Point, 1,520 ....C 5
Wakema, 20,716 ....B 3
Yamethin, 11,167 ....C 2
Yandoon, 15,245 ....B 3
Ye, 12,852 ....C 4
Yenangyaung, 24,416 ....B 2
Yesagyo, 7,880 ....B 2
Ye-u, 5,307 ....B 2

OTHER FEATURES

Amya (pass) ....C 4
Andaman (sea) ....C 4
Arakan Yoma (mts.) ....B 3
Bengal (bay) ....B 3
Bilauktaung (range) ....C 4
Chaukan (pass) ....C 1
Cheduba (isl.), 2,621 ....B 3
Chin (hills) ....B 2
Chindwin (river) ....B 2
Coco (chan.) ....B 3
Combermere (bay) ....B 3
Dawna (range) ....C 3
Great Coco (isl.) ....B 4
Great Tenasserim (river) .....C 4
Hkakabo Razi (mt.) ....C 1
Indawgyi (lake) ....C 1
Inle (lake) ....C 2
Irrawaddy (river) ....B 3
Irrawaddy, Mouths of the (delta) ....B 4
Kaladan (river) ....B 2
Khao Luang (mt.) ....C 5
Loi Leng (mt.) ....C 2
Manipur (river) ....B 2
Martaban (gulf) ....C 4
Mekong (river) ....D 2
Mergui (arch.) ....C 5
Mon (river) ....B 2
Mu (river) ....B 2
Nam Hka (river) ....C 2
Nam Pawn (river) ....C 2
Nam Teng (river) ....C 2
Negrais (cape) ....B 3
Pakchan (river) ....C 5
Pangsau (pass) ....B 1
Pegu Yoma (mts.) ....B 3
Preparis (isl.) ....B 4
Ramree (isl.), 11,133 ....B 3
Salween (river) ....C 2
Shan (plateau) ....C 2
Sittang (river) ....C 3
Taungthonton (mt.) ....B 1
Tavoy (point) ....C 4
Tenasserim (isl.) ....C 4
Three Pagodas (pass) ....C 3
Victoria (mt.) ....B 2

(continued on following page)

(continued)

CAMBODIA

CITIES and TOWNS

Banam, †87,048 ... E 5
Battambang, 38,846 ... D 4
Cheom Ksan ... E 4
Chhlong, †46,108 ... E 4
Chong Kal, †16,918 ... D 4
Kampot, 12,558 ... E 5
Kep, 7,565 ... E 5
Khemarak Phouinville ... D 5
Kohnieh ... E 4
Kompong Cham, 28,534 ... E 4
Kompong Chhnang, 12,847 ... D 4
Kompong Kleang ... E 4
Kompong Som, 6,578 ... D 5
Kompong Speu, 7,453 ... E 5
Kompong Thom, 9,682 ... E 4
Kompong Trabek, †108,227 ... E 5
Koulen ... E 4
Kratie, 11,908 ... E 4
Krauchmar, †63,262 ... E 4
Moung, †88,321 ... D 4
Pailin, †15,536 ... D 4
Phnom Penh (capital), *500,000 ... E 5
Phsar Babau ... D 4
Phsar Oudong, †50,456 ... E 5
Phum Rovieng, †21,151 ... E 4
Phum Troun ... E 4
Poipet ... D 4
Prek Po ... E 5
Prey Veng, 8,792 ... E 5
Pursat, 14,329 ... D 4
Ream ... D 5
Sambor, †11,213 ... E 4
Siem Pang, †8,959 ... E 4
Siem Reap, 10,230 ... D 4
Sisophon, †29,581 ... D 4
Sre Khtum ... E 4
Stung Treng, 3,369 ... E 4
Suong ... E 5
Svay Rieng, 11,184 ... E 5
Takeo, 11,312 ... E 5
Virachei, †16,912 ... E 4

OTHER FEATURES

Angkor Wat (ruins) ... E 4
Dang Raek, Phanom (mts.) ... D 4
Joncs (plain) ... E 5
Kas Kong (isl.) ... D 5
Kas Tang (isl.) ... D 5
Kong, Kas (isl.) ... D 5
Mekong (river) ... E 4
Phanom Dang Raek (mts.) ... D 4
Preapatang (rapids) ... E 4
Rong, Koh (isl.) ... D 5
Samit (point) ... D 5
Se Khong (river) ... E 4
Se San (river) ... E 4
Siam (gulf) ... D 5
Srepok (river) ... E 4
Stung Sen (river) ... E 4
Tang, Kas (isl.) ... D 5
Tonle Sap (lake) ... D 4

LAOS

CITIES and TOWNS

Attopeu, 2,750 ... E 4
Ban Bung Sai ... E 4
Borikhane ... D 3
Botene ... D 3
Boun Neua, 2,500 ... D 2
Boun Tai, †1,681 ... D 2
Champassak, 3,500 ... E 4
Houei Sai, 1,500 ... D 2
Hua Muong ... D 2
Keng Kok, 2,000 ... E 3
Kham Keut, †31,206 ... E 3
Khone ... E 4
Khong, 1,750 ... E 4
Khong Sédone, 2,000 ... E 4
Luang Prabang, 7,596 ... D 3
Mahaxay, 2,000 ... E 3
Muong Beng, †2,305 ... D 2
Muong Bo ... D 3
Muong Hai, †476 ... D 2
Muong Hôm ... D 3
Muong Lan, †836 ... D 3
Muong May ... E 4
Muong Phalane ... E 3
Muong Phine ... E 3
Muong Phong ... D 3
Muong Sai, 2,000 ... D 2
Muong Sing, 1,091 ... D 2
Muong Son ... D 2
Muong Song Khone, 2,000 ... E 3
Muong Wapi ... E 4
Muong Yo ... D 2
Nam Tha, 1,459 ... D 2
Napé ... E 3
Nong Het ... D 3
Ou Neua, †4,300 ... D 2
Pak Beng, †2,964 ... D 3
Pak Hin Boun, 1,750 ... E 3
Pak Sane, 2,500 ... D 3
Paklay, 2,000 ... D 3
Pakse, 8,000 ... E 4
Phiafay, †17,216 ... E 4
Phon Tiou ... E 3
Phong Saly, 2,500 ... D 2
Sam Neua, 3,000 ... E 2
Saravane, 2,350 ... E 4
Savannakhet, 8,500 ... E 3
Sayaboury, 2,500 ... D 3
Tchepone, 1,250 ... E 3
Tha-deua ... D 3
Thakhek, 5,500 ... E 3
Tourakom ... D 3
Vang Vieng, 1,250 ... D 3
Vien Phou Kha ... D 2
Vientiane (capital), 132,253 ... D 3
Vientiane, *162,297 ... D 3
Xieng Khouang, 3,500 ... D 3

OTHER FEATURES

Bolovens (plateau) ... E 4
Hou, Nam (river) ... D 2
Jars (plain) ... D 3
Mekong (river) ... D 3
Nam Hou (river) ... D 2
Nam Tha (river) ... D 2
Phu Bia (mt.) ... D 3
Phu Co Pi (mt.) ... E 3
Phu Loi (mt.) ... D 2
Rao Co (mt.) ... E 3
Se Khong (river) ... E 4
Tha, Nam (river) ... D 2
Tran Ninh (plateau) ... D 3

MALAYSIA★

STATES

Federal Territory ... D 7
Johor, 1,236,412 ... D 7
Kedah, 885,775 ... D 6
Kelantan, 645,200 ... D 6
Melaka, 391,003 ... D 7
Negeri Sembilan, 488,318 ... D 7
Pahang, 405,156 ... D 7
Perak, 1,568,024 ... D 6
Perlis, 113,350 ... D 6
Pinang, 724,169 ... D 6
Selangor, 1,339,142 ... D 7
Terengganu, 360,388 ... D 6

CITIES and TOWNS

Alor Gajah, 2,135 ... D 7
Alor Setar, 52,915 ... D 6
Baling, 4,121 ... D 6
Bandar Maharani, 39,046 ... D 7
Bandar Penggaram, 39,294 ... D 7
Batu Gajah, 10,143 ... D 6
Bentong, 18,845 ... D 7
Butterworth, 42,504 ... D 6
Cameron Highlands ... D 6
Chukai, 10,803 ... D 6
Gemas, 4,873 ... D 7
George Town (Pinang), 234,903 ... C 6
Ipoh, 125,770 ... D 6
Johor Baharu, 74,909 ... F 5
Kampar, 24,602 ... D 6
Kangar, 6,064 ... D 6
Kelang, 75,649 ... D 7
Keluang, 31,181 ... D 7
Kota Baharu, 38,103 ... D 6
Kota Tinggi, 7,475 ... F 5
Kuala Dungun, 12,515 ... D 6
Kuala Lipis, 8,753 ... D 6
Kuala Lumpur (cap.), 325,000 ... D 7
Kuala Pilah, 12,024 ... D 7
Kuala Selangor, 2,285 ... D 7
Kuala Terengganu, 29,446 ... D 6
Kuantan, 23,034 ... D 7
Kulai, 7,759 ... F 5
Lumut, 2,947 ... D 6
Melaka (Malacca), 69,848 ... D 7
Mersing, 7,228 ... E 7
Pekan, 2,070 ... D 7
Pekan Nanas, 7,129 ... E 5
Pinang, 234,903 ... C 6
Pontian Kechil, 8,459 ... E 5
Port Dickson, 4,416 ... D 7
Port Swettenham, 16,925 ... D 7
Port Weld, 2,260 ... D 6
Raub, 15,363 ... D 7
Segamat, 18,445 ... D 7
Seremban, 52,091 ... D 7
Shah Alam ... D 7
Sungei Petani, 22,916 ... C 6
Taiping, 48,206 ... D 6
Tanah Merah, 775 ... D 6
Telok Anson, 37,042 ... D 6
Tumpat, 8,946 ... D 6

OTHER FEATURES

Aur, Pulau (isl.), 415 ... E 7
Belumut, Gunong (mt.) ... D 7
Gelang, Tanjong (point) ... D 6
Johor (river) ... F 5
Johore (str.) ... E 6
Kelantan (river) ... D 6
Langkawi, Palau (isl.), 16,535 ... C 6
Ledang, Gunong (mt.) ... D 7
Lima, Pulau (isl.) ... F 6
Malacca (str.) ... D 7
Malaya (region), 9,000,000 ... E 6
Pahang (river) ... D 7
Pangkor, Pulau (isl.), 2,580 ... D 6
Perak, Gunong (mt.) ... D 6
Perhentian (isls.), 447 ... D 6
Pulai (river) ... E 5
Pinang, Pulau (isl.), 338,898 ... C 6
Ramunia, Tanjong (point) ... F 6
Redang, Pulau (isl.), 470 ... D 6
Sedili Kechil, Tanjong (point) ... F 5
Tahan, Gunong (mt.) ... D 6
Temiang, Bukit (mt.) ... D 6
Tenggol, Pulau (isl.), 2,386 ... D 6
Tinggi, Pulau (isl.), 440 ... E 7

SINGAPORE

CITIES and TOWNS

Jurong ... E 6
Nee Soon, 6,043 ... F 6
Paya Lebar, 45,440 ... F 6
Serangoon, 3,798 ... F 6
Singapore (cap.), *1,987,900 ... F 6
Woodlands, 737 ... F 6

OTHER FEATURES

Johore (str.) ... E 6
Keppel (harb.) ... F 6
Main (str.) ... F 6
Singapore (str.) ... F 6
Tekong Besar, Pulau (isl.), 4,074 ... F 6

THAILAND (SIAM)

CITIES and TOWNS

Amnat, 11,335 ... E 4
Ang Thong, 6,458 ... C 4
Ayutthaya, 24,597 ... D 4
Ban Aranyaprathet, 11,112 ... D 4
Ban Kantang, 5,076 ... C 6
Ban Khlong Yai, 3,815 ... D 5
Ban Pak Phanang, 11,963 ... D 5
Ban Pua, 12,317 ... D 3
Ban Sattahip, 22,942 ... D 4
Ban Tha Uthen, 7,297 ... D 3
Bang Lamung, 9,087 ... D 4
Bang Saphan, 6,959 ... C 5
Bangkok (capital), 1,299,528 ... D 4
Bangkok, *2,000,000 ... D 4
Banphot Phisai, 6,036 ... C 3
Buriram, 12,579 ... D 4
Chachoengsao, 19,809 ... G 4
Chai Badan, 6,158 ... D 4
Chai Buri, †31,135 ... D 3
Chainat, 4,652 ... D 4
Chaiya, 3,607 ... C 5
Chaiyaphum, 9,633 ... D 4
Chang Khoeng, 6,037 ... C 3
Chanthaburi, 10,780 ... D 4
Chiang Dao, 8,017 ... C 3
Chiang Khan, 5,810 ... D 3
Chiang Rai, 11,663 ... C 3
Chiang Saen, 5,443 ... C 2
Chiengmai, 65,600 ... C 3
Chon Buri, 32,496 ... D 4
Chumphon, 9,342 ... C 5
Dan Sai, 6,710 ... D 3
Den Chai, 12,732 ... C 3
Hat Yai, 35,504 ... C 6
Hua Hin, 17,078 ... D 4
Kabin Buri, 3,703 ... D 4
Kalasin, 11,043 ... D 3
Kamphaeng Phet, 7,171 ... C 3
Kanchanaburi, 12,957 ... C 4
Khemmarat, 5,426 ... E 4
Khon Kaen, 19,591 ... D 3
Khorat (Nakhon Ratchasima), 41,037 ... D 4
Khu Khan, †122,206 ... E 4
Kra Buri, 3,717 ... C 5
Krung Thep (Bangkok) (cap.), 1,299,528 ... D 4
Kumphawapi, 20,759 ... D 3
Lae, 5,743 ... D 3
Lampang, 36,488 ... C 3
Lamphun, 10,602 ... C 3
Lang Suan, 4,108 ... C 5
Loei, 7,301 ... D 3
Lom Sak, 8,386 ... D 3
Lop Buri, 21,244 ... D 4
Maha Sarakham, 15,680 ... D 3
Mukdahan, 17,738 ... E 3
Nakhon Nayok, 8,048 ... D 4
Nakhon Pathom, 28,426 ... C 4
Nakhon Phanom, 14,799 ... D 3
Nakhon Ratchasima, 41,037 ... D 4
Nakhon Sawan, 34,947 ... D 4
Nakhon Si Thammarat, 25,919 ... D 5
Nan, 13,843 ... D 3
Nang Rong, 15,623 ... D 4
Narathiwat, 17,508 ... D 6
Ngao, †32,643 ... D 3
Nong Khai, 21,120 ... D 3
Pattani, 16,804 ... D 6
Phanat Nikhom, 9,307 ... D 4
Phangnga, 4,782 ... C 5
Phatthalung, 10,420 ... D 6
Phayao, 17,959 ... C 3
Phet Buri, 24,654 ... C 4
Phetchabun, 5,947 ... D 3
Phichai, 5,258 ... D 3
Phichit, 9,258 ... D 3
Phitsanulok, 30,364 ... D 3
Phon Phisai, 6,745 ... D 3
Phrae, 16,005 ... D 3
Phuket, 28,163 ... C 6
Phutthaisong, 9,315 ... D 4
Prachin Buri, 13,420 ... D 4
Prachuap Khiri Khan, 6,303 ... D 5
Pran Buri, 7,795 ... D 4
Rahaeng (Tak), 13,274 ... C 3
Ranong, 5,993 ... C 5
Rat Buri, 20,383 ... C 4
Rayong, 9,680 ... D 4
Roi Et, 12,930 ... D 4
Rong Kwang, †39,375 ... D 3
Sakon Nakhon, 16,457 ... E 3
Samut Prakan, 21,769 ... D 4
Samut Sakhon, 27,802 ... D 4
Samut Songkhram, 12,801 ... C 4
Sara Buri, 17,572 ... D 4
Satun, 4,369 ... C 6
Sawankhalok, 7,880 ... C 3
Selaphum, 10,395 ... E 3
Sing Buri, 8,384 ... D 4
Singora (Songkhla), 31,014 ... D 6
Sisaket, 9,519 ... E 4
Songkhla, 31,014 ... D 6
Sukhothai, 8,627 ... D 3
Suphan Buri, 13,859 ... C 4
Surat Thani, 19,738 ... C 5
Surin, 13,860 ... D 4
Suwannaphum, 15,731 ... D 4
Tak, 13,274 ... C 3
Takua Pa, 6,308 ... C 5
Thoen, 17,283 ... C 3
Thonburi, 403,818 ... D 4
Thonburi, *460,000 ... D 4
Trang, 17,158 ... C 6
Trat, 3,813 ... D 4
Ubon, 27,092 ... E 4
Udon Thani, 29,965 ... D 3
Uthai Thani, 10,729 ... C 4
Uttaradit, 9,120 ... D 3
Warin Chamrap, 7,067 ... E 4
Yala, 18,083 ... D 6
Yasothon, 9,717 ... D 4

OTHER FEATURES

Amya (pass) ... C 4
Bilauktaung (range) ... C 4
Chao Phraya, Mae Nam (river) ... D 4
Chi, Mae Nam (river) ... D 3
Chong Pak Phra (cape) ... C 5
Dang Raek, Phanom (mts.) ... D 4
Doi Inthanon (mt.) ... C 3
Doi Pha Hom Pok (mt.) ... C 2
Doi Pia Fai (mt.) ... D 4
Kao Prawa (mt.) ... C 3
Khao Luang (mt.) ... C 5
Khwae Noi, Mae Nam (river) ... C 4
Ko Chang (isl.) ... D 4
Ko Kut (isl.) ... D 5
Ko Lanta (isl.), 9,486 ... C 6
Ko Phangan (isl.) ... D 5
Ko Phuket (isl.), 75,652 ... C 5
Ko Samui (isl.), 30,818 ... D 5
Ko Tao (isl.) ... C 5
Ko Terutao (isl.) ... C 6
Ko Thalu (isls.) ... C 5
Kra (isthmus) ... C 5
Laem Pho (cape) ... D 6
Laem Talumphuk (cape) ... D 5
Luang (mt.) ... C 5
Mae Klong, Mae Nam (river) ... C 4
Mekong (river) ... E 3
Mulayit Taung (mt.) ... C 3
Mun, Mae Nam (river) ... D 4
Nan, Mae Nam (river) ... D 3
Nong Lahan (lake) ... D 3
Pa Sak, Mae Nam (river) ... D 4
Pakchan (river) ... C 5
Phanom Dang Raek (mts.) ... D 4
Ping, Mae Nam (river) ... C 3
Samui (str.) ... D 5
Siam (gulf) ... D 5
Tapi, Mae Nam (river) ... C 5
Tha Chin, Mae Nam (river) ... C 4
Thale Luang (lagoon) ... D 6
Three Pagodas (pass) ... C 4
Wang, Mae Nam (river) ... C 3

VIETNAM

CITIES and TOWNS

An Khe ... F 4
An Loc, 15,276 ... E 5
Bac Can ... E 2
Bac Lieu (Vinh Loi), 53,841 ... E 5
Bac Ninh, 22,560 ... E 2
Ba Don ... E 3
Bai Thuong ... E 3
Ban Me Thuot, 68,771 ... F 4
Bao Ha ... D 2
Bao Lac ... E 2
Bien Hoa, 87,135 ... E 5
Binh Dinh ... F 4
Binh Son ... F 4
Bong Son ... F 4
Bu Dop ... E 4
Cam Ranh, 84,281 ... F 5
Can Tho, 92,132 ... E 5
Cao Bang ... E 2
Cao Lanh, 16,482 ... E 5
Cap Saint-Jacques (Vung Tau), 79,270 ... E 5
Chau Phu, 37,175 ... E 5
Cheo Reo ... E 4
Chu Lai ... F 4
Co Lieu ... E 3
Con Cuong ... E 3
Cua Rao ... E 3
Dak Bla ... E 4
Da Lat, 83,992 ... F 5
Dam Doi ... E 5
Da Nang, 363,343 ... E 3
Dien Bien Phu ... D 2
Di Linh ... F 5
Dong Hoi ... E 3
Duong Dong ... D 5
Go Cong, 33,191 ... E 5
Go Quao ... E 5
Ha Giang ... D 2
Haiphong, 182,496 ... E 2
Haiphong, ‡*600,000 ... E 2
Ham Tan, 19,323 ... E 5
Hanoi (capital), 414,620 ... E 2
Hanoi, ‡*1,400,000 ... E 2
Ha Tien ... E 5
Ha Tinh ... E 3
Hoa Binh ... E 2
Hoa Da ... F 5
Ho Chi Minh City, 1,706,869 ... E 5
Hoi An, 45,059 ... F 4
Hoi Xuan ... E 2
Hon Chong ... E 5
Hon Gay, ‡100,000 ... E 2
Hue, 170,884 ... E 3
Huong Khe ... E 3
Ke Bao ... E 2
Khanh Hoa ... F 4
Khanh Hung, 59,015 ... E 5
Kontum, 33,554 ... E 4
Lai Chau ... D 2
Lang Mo ... E 3
Lang Son, 15,071 ... E 2
Lao Cai ... E 2
Loc Chou ... E 3
Loc Ninh ... E 5
Long Xuyen, 72,658 ... E 5
Luc An Chau ... E 2
Moc Hoa, 3,191 ... E 5
Mo Duc ... F 4
Mon Cay ... E 2
Muong Khuong ... E 2
My Tho, 109,967 ... E 5
Nam Dinh, ‡125,000 ... E 2
Nghia Lo ... D 2
Nha Trang, 103,184 ... F 4
Ninh Binh ... E 2
Phan Rang, 33,377 ... F 5
Phan Ri ... F 5
Phan Thiet, 80,122 ... F 5
Phoc Tuy, 16,419 ... E 5
Phuc Loi ... E 3
Phu Cuong, 28,267 ... E 5
Phu Dien ... E 3
Phu Lang Thuong ... E 2
Phu Loc ... E 3
Phuly ... E 2
Phu My ... F 4
Phu Qui ... E 3
Phu Rieng ... E 5
Phu Tho, 10,888 ... E 2
Phu Vinh (Tra Vinh), 48,485 ... E 5
Pleiku, 23,720 ... E 4
Pleime ... E 4
Quang Nam ... E 4
Quang Khe ... E 3
Quang Ngai, 14,119 ... F 4
Quang Tri, 15,874 ... E 3
Quang Yen ... E 2
Quan Long, 59,331 ... E 5
Qui Nhon, 116,821 ... F 4
Rach Gia, 66,745 ... E 5
Ron ... E 3
Sa Dec, 51,867 ... E 5
Saigon (Ho Chi Minh City), 1,706,869 ... E 5
Song Cau ... F 4
Son Ha ... F 4
Son La ... D 2
Son Tay, 19,213 ... E 2
Tam Ky, 38,532 ... F 4
Tam Quan ... F 4
Tan An, 38,082 ... E 5
Tay Ninh, 22,957 ... E 5
Thai Binh, 14,739 ... E 2
Thai Nguyen, ‡110,000 ... E 2
Thanh Hoa, 31,211 ... E 3
That Khe ... E 2
Tien Yen ... E 2
Tra Vinh, 48,485 ... E 5
Truc Giang, 68,629 ... E 5
Trung Khanh Phu ... E 2
Tuyen Quang ... E 2
Tuy Hoa, 63,552 ... F 4
Van Gia ... F 4
Van Hoa ... E 2
Van Yen ... E 2
Vinh, 43,954 ... E 3
Vinh Loi, 53,841 ... E 5
Vinh Long, 30,667 ... E 5
Vinh Yen ... E 2
Vo Dat ... E 5
Vu Liet ... E 3
Vung Tau, 79,270 ... E 5
Yen Bai ... E 2
Yen Minh ... E 2

OTHER FEATURES

Bach Long Vi, Dao (isl.) ... F 2
Batangan (cape) ... F 4
Bến Gôi (bay) ... F 4
Black (river) ... D 2
Ca Mau (Mui Bai Bung) (pt.) ... E 5
Cam Ranh (bay) ... F 5
Cat Ba, Dao (isl.) ... E 2
Chon May (bay) ... F 3
Chu Yang Sin (mt.) ... F 4
Con Son (isls.), 3,147 ... E
Cu Lao Hon (isls.) ... F
Dama, Poulo (isls.) ... D
Dao Bach Long Vi (isl.) ... F
Dao Phu Quoc (isl.) ... D
Darlac (plateau) ... F
Dent du Tigre (mt.) ... E
Deux Frères, Les (isls.) ... E
Fan Si Pan (mt.) ... D
Hon Khoai (isl.) ... E
Hon Panjang (isl.) ... D
Ia Drang (riv.) ... E
Joncs (plain) ... E
Ke Ga (point) ... F
Kontum (plateau) ... E
Lang Bian (mts.) ... E
Lay (cape) ... E
Mekong, Mouths of the (delta) ... E
Mui Bai Bung (pt.) ... E
Mui Dinh (cape) ... F
Mui Duong (cape) ... E
Nam Tram (cape) ... F
Nightingale (Bach Long Vi) (isl.) ... F
Nui Ba Den (mt.) ... E
Phu Quoc, Dao (isl.) ... D
Poulo Dama (isls.) ... D
Poulo Way (isls.) ... D
Rao Co (mt.) ... E
Red (river) ... E
Se San (river) ... E
Siam (gulf) ... D
Sip Song Chau Thai (mts.) ... D
Song Ba (river) ... F
Song Bo (Black) (river) ... D
Song Ca (river) ... E
Song Cai (river) ... F
Song Coi (Red) (river) ... E
South China (sea) ... F
Tigre (isl.) ... E
Tonkin (gulf) ... E
Varella (cape) ... F
Way, Poulo (isls.) ... D

★See page 84 for other Malaysian entries.
*City and suburbs.
†Population of district.

‡City populations courtesy of Kingsley Davis, Office of Int'l Pop. & Urban Research, Inst. of Int'l Studies, Univ. of California.

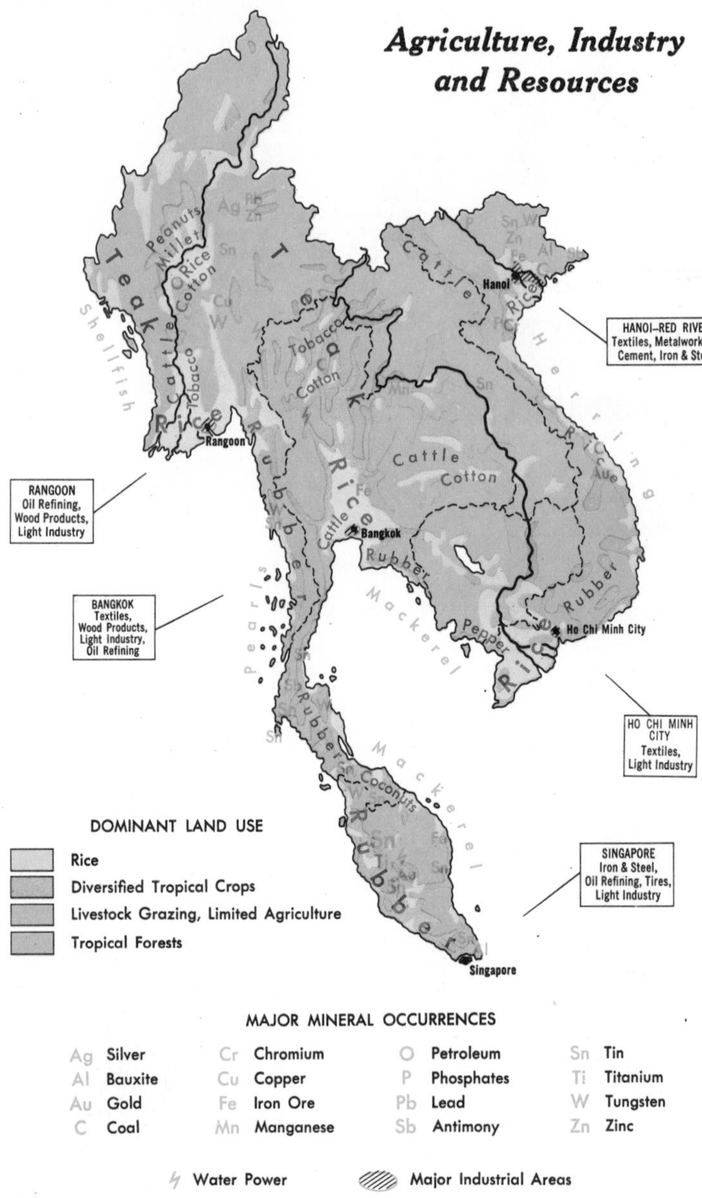

Agriculture, Industry and Resources
HANOI–RED RIVER Textiles, Metalworking, Cement, Iron & Steel
RANGOON Oil Refining, Wood Products, Light Industry
BANGKOK Textiles, Wood Products, Light Industry, Oil Refining
HO CHI MINH CITY Textiles, Light Industry
SINGAPORE Iron & Steel, Oil Refining, Tires, Light Industry
Hanoi
Rangoon
Bangkok
Ho Chi Minh City
Singapore
Teak
Rice
Rubber
Cattle
Cotton
Tobacco
Peanuts
Millet
Coconuts
Pepper
Shellfish
Pearls
Mackerel
Herring
DOMINANT LAND USE
Rice
Diversified Tropical Crops
Livestock Grazing, Limited Agriculture
Tropical Forests
MAJOR MINERAL OCCURRENCES
Ag Silver
Al Bauxite
Au Gold
C Coal
Cr Chromium
Cu Copper
Fe Iron Ore
Mn Manganese
O Petroleum
P Phosphates
Pb Lead
Sb Antimony
Sn Tin
Ti Titanium
W Tungsten
Zn Zinc
Water Power
Major Industrial Areas

BURMA, THAILAND,
INDOCHINA
and MALAYA

CONIC PROJECTION

SCALE OF MILES

SCALE OF KILOMETRES

International Boundaries _____
Division and State Boundaries _____
Capitals of Countries _____ ☆
Division and State Capitals _____ ■

Copyright by C.S. HAMMOND & Co., N.Y.

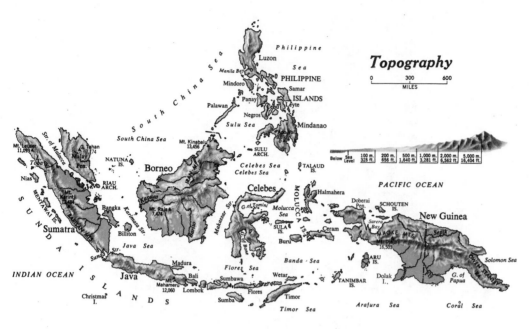

Topography

0 300 600
MILES

| Below Sea Level | 100 m. 328 ft. | 200 m. 656 ft. | 500 m. 1,640 ft. | 1,000 m. 3,281 ft. | 2,000 m. 6,562 ft. | 5,000 m. 16,404 ft. |

PHILIPPINES

AREA 115,707 sq. mi.
POPULATION 43,751,000
CAPITAL Manila
LARGEST CITY Manila
HIGHEST POINT Apo 9,692 ft.
MONETARY UNIT piso
MAJOR LANGUAGES Pilipino (Tagalog), English, Spanish, Bisayan, Ilocano, Bikol
MAJOR RELIGIONS Roman Catholicism, Islam, Protestantism, Tribal religions

BRUNEI

CITIES and TOWNS

Bandar Seri Begawan (cap.), 37,000 ....E 4

INDONESIA

CITIES and TOWNS

Agats, 300 ....K 7
Amahai, 18,017 ....H 6
Amboina, 70,000 ....H 6
Ambon (Amboina), 70,000 ...H 6
Balikpapan, 113,000 ....F 6
Banda Atjeh, 49,000 ....A 4
Bandanaira, 13,686 ....H 6
Bandjarmasin, 264,000 ....E 6
Bandung, 1,006,000 ....J 2
Bangil, 34,112 ....K 2
Bangkalan, 129,536 ....K 2
Banjuwangi, 53,576 ....L 2
Bantul, 30,572 ....J 2
Barabai, 9,366 ....F 6
Barus, †35,716 ....B 5
Batang, 57,561 ....J 2
Batavia (Djakarta) (cap.), 3,429,000 ....H 1
Baturadja, 126,706 ....C 6
Batusangkar, 10,437 ....C 6
Bekasi, 32,012 ....H 2
Bengkajang, †17,029 ....E 5
Bengkalis, 136,433 ....C 5
Bengkulu, 31,000 ....C 6
Benteng, 7,035 ....H 7
Bindjai, 56,000 ....B 5
Bitung, 15,249 ....H 5
Blitar, 78,000 ....K 2

Blora, 49,296 ....K 2
Bodjonegoro, †61,749 ....J 2
Bogor, 172,000 ....H 2
Bondowoso, 144,215 ....L 2
Bonthain, 140,289 ....F 7
Brebes, †72,971 ....J 2
Bukittinggi, 62,000 ....B 6
Bula, 3,116 ....J 6
Bulukumba, 14,137 ....G 7
Bumiaju, †52,790 ....J 2
Buntok, 3,884 ....F 6
Demak, †42,915 ....J 2
Denpasar, 152,000 ....F 7
Djailolo, 110,170 ....H 5
Djajapura, 14,462 ....K 6
Djakarta (cap.), 3,429,000 ..H 1
Djakarta, †5,692,000 ....H 1
Djambi (Telanaipura) 139,000 ....C 6
Djeponto, 10,350 ....F 7
Djepara, †54,025 ....J 2
Djokjakarta, 385,000 ....J 2
Djombang, 157,370 ....K 2
Dompu, 8,886 ....F 7
Fakfak, 2,430 ....J 6
Galela, †7,384 ....H 5
Garut, 167,542 ....H 2
Gorontalo, 88,000 ....G 5
Gresik, 36,790 ....K 2
Gunungsitoli, †44,712 ....B 5
Hollandia (Djajapura), 14,462 ....K 6
Indramaju, †56,117 ....H 2
Isimu, 4,304 ....G 5
Kaimana, 1,128 ....J 6
Kajuagung, 15,000 ....D 6
Kalianda, †31,073 ....D 7
Kampung Baru (Tolitoli), 8,333 ....G 5
Karangasem, 16,022 ....F 7
Kau, 17,497 ....H 5
Kebumen, †64,874 ....J 2

Kediri, 196,000 ....K 2
Kendal, 23,129 ....J 2
Kendari, 191,065 ....G 6
Kendawangan, 6,845 ....D 6
Klaten, 33,400 ....J 2
Kolaka, 118,671 ....G 6
Kotaagung, †25,314 ....C 7
Kragan, 23,786 ....K 2
Krawang, 49,867 ....H 2
Kualakurun, 111,489 ....E 6
Kudus, 62,130 ....J 2
Kumai, 8,835 ....E 6
Kuningan, †77,181 ....H 2
Kupang, 17,171 ....G 8
Kutaradja (Banda Atjeh), 49,000 ....A 4
Kutoardjo, 44,962 ....J 2
Labuan, †22,259 ....C 6
Lahat, †25,781 ....C 6
Lamongan, †34,825 ....K 2
Langsa, 147,044 ....B 5
Lawang, 140,239 ....K 2
Longiram, 7,776 ....F 5
Longnawan, 116,234 ....F 5
Lubuklinggau, 14,890 ....C 6
Lubuksikaping, 11,778 ....B 5
Lumadjang, 55,700 ....K 2
Madiun, 152,000 ....K 2
Madjalengka, 147,055 ....H 2
Madjene, †37,727 ....F 6
Magelang, 119,000 ....J 2
Magetan, †54,159 ....K 2
Makassar (Udjung Pandang), 473,000 ....F 7
Malang, 419,000 ....K 2
Malili, 5,735 ....G 6
Malinau, 9,677 ....F 5
Mamudju, †47,309 ....F 6
Manado, 160,000 ....G 5
Manokwari, 10,461 ....J 6

Marabahan, 8,893 ....E 6
Martapura, †53,216 ....F 6
Masamba, †15,152 ....G 6
Medan, 590,000 ....B 5
Menggala, 20,343 ....D 6
Meulaboh, 6,544 ....A 5
Merak, †36,293 ....G 1
Merauke, 5,989 ....K 7
Mindiptana, 1,577 ....L 7
Modjokerto, 64,000 ....K 2
Muarabungo, 10,706 ....C 6
Muarateweh, 6,135 ....F 6
Muntok, 125,883 ....C 6
Namlea, 16,018 ....H 6
Nangapinoh, †24,836 ....E 6
Nangatajap, 18,285 ....E 6
Negara, 10,161 ....E 7
Ngabang, †24,516 ....D 5
Ngawi, 29,220 ....K 2
Padang, 178,000 ....B 6
Padangsidimpuan, †71,704 ..B 5
Painan, 12,060 ....C 6
Pajakumbuh, †74,393 ....C 6
Pakanbaru, 87,000 ....C 5
Palangkaraja, 9,000 ....E 6
Paleleh, 5,466 ....G 5
Palembang, 585,000 ....D 6
Pamangkat, †51,871 ....D 5
Pamekasan, †42,650 ....L 2
Pameungpeuk, †24,662 ......H 2
Panarukan, 6,846 ....L 2
Pandeglang, †24,823 ....G 1
Pangkalanberandan, †23,806 ..B 5
Pangkalpinang, 74,000 ....D 6
Pare, 185,528 ....K 2
Parepare, 84,000 ....F 6
Pariaman, †45,812 ....B 6
Pasuruan, 78,000 ....K 2
Pati, †56,749 ....J 2

Patjitan, 44,383 ....J 2
Pekalongan, 125,000 ....J 2
Pemalang, 193,608 ....J 2
Pematangsiantar, 142,000 ...B 5
Perahubumulih, 41,951 ......C 6
Pinrang, 23,818 ....F 6
Piru, †23,633 ....H 6
Ponorogo, 49,993 ....J 2
Pontianak, 185,000 ....D 5
Poso, †41,292 ....G 6
Praja, 26,729 ....F 7
Prapat, 5,552 ....B 5
Probolinggo, 85,000 ....K 2
Purbolinggo, 31,719 ....J 2
Purwakarta, 188,680 ....H 2
Purwodadi, 154,648 ....J 2
Purwokerto, 22,623 ....J 2
Purworedjo, 23,209 ....J 2
Putussibau, 18,357 ....E 5
Rangkasbitung, 151,176 .....G 2
Rantauprapat, 25,707 ....C 5
Rembang, 39,939 ....K 2
Rengat, †22,982 ....C 6
Ruteng, 15,814 ....G 7
Sabang, 6,747 ....B 4
Salatiga, 72,000 ....J 2
Samarinda, 87,000 ....F 6
Sambas, †53,290 ....D 5
Sampang, 47,596 ....K 2
Sanana, 23,388 ....H 6
Sangkapura, 128,039 ....E 5
Sangkulirang, 6,108 ....F 5
Saparua, 53,390 ....H 6
Saumlaki, †22,732 ....J 7
Sawahlunto, 15,000 ....C 6
Semarang, 619,000 ....J 2
Semitau, 19,255 ....E 5
Sengkang, †17,948 ....F 6
Serang, †43,661 ....G 1
Serui, 2,743 ....J 2

(continued on following page)

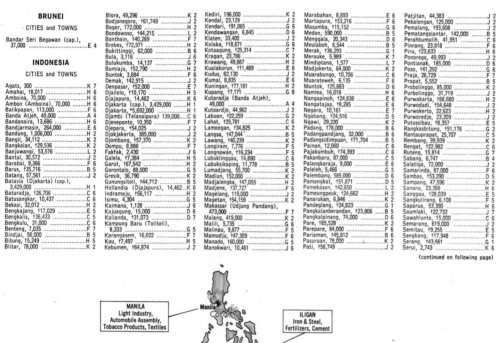

Agriculture, Industry and Resources

MANILA,
Light Industry,
Automobile Assembly,
Tobacco Products, Textiles

ILIGAN,
Iron & Steel,
Fertilizers, Cement

SINGAPORE
Iron & Steel, Oil Refining,
Tires, Light Industry

DJAKARTA
Textiles, Light Industry

DOMINANT LAND USE

Cereals (chiefly rice, corn)
Diversified Tropical Crops
Forests

MAJOR MINERAL OCCURRENCES

Al Bauxite
Au Gold
C Coal
Cr Chromium
Fe Iron Ore
Mn Manganese
Ni Nickel
O Petroleum
Sn Tin
Major Industrial Areas

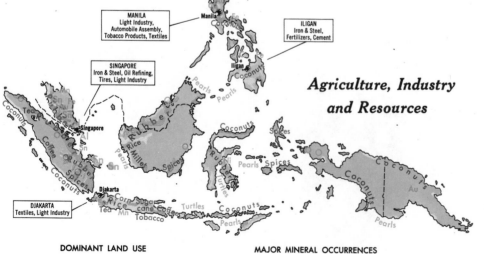

(continued on following page)

INDONESIA

AREA 735,264 sq. mi.
POPULATION 119,572,000
CAPITAL Djakarta
LARGEST CITY Djakarta
HIGHEST POINT Mt. Djaja 16,400 ft.
MONETARY UNIT rupiah
MAJOR LANGUAGES Bahasa Indonesian, local
   Indonesian languages, Papuan languages
MAJOR RELIGIONS Islam, Tribal religions,
   Christianity, Hinduism

PAPUA NEW GUINEA

AREA 183,540 sq. mi.
POPULATION 2,563,610
CAPITAL Port Moresby
LARGEST CITY Port Moresby
HIGHEST POINT Mt. Wilhelm 15,400 ft.
MONETARY UNIT kina
MAJOR LANGUAGES Pidgin English,
   Motuan, English
MAJOR RELIGIONS Tribal religions,
   Christianity

BRUNEI

AREA 2,226 sq. mi.
POPULATION 130,000
CAPITAL Bandar Seri Begawan

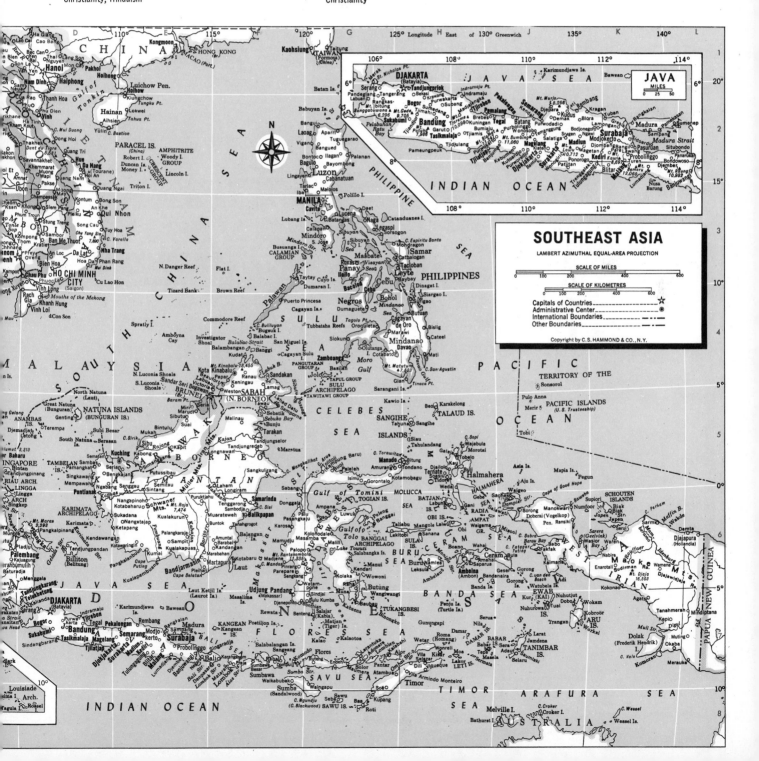

*City and suburbs.
†Population of district.
‡Population of sub-district.
▲Population of municipality.
★See page 80 for other Malaysian entries.

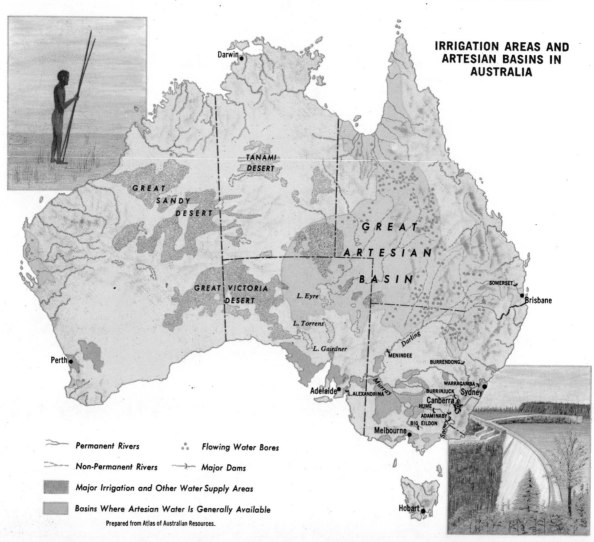

IRRIGATION AREAS AND ARTESIAN BASINS IN AUSTRALIA

Darwin

TANAMI DESERT

GREAT SANDY DESERT

GREAT ARTESIAN BASIN

GREAT VICTORIA DESERT

L. Eyre
L. Torrens
L. Gairdner

SOMERSET

Brisbane

Perth

Darling
Murray
MENINDEE
BURRENDONG
WARRAGAMBA
BURRINJUCK
Sydney
Canberra
HUME
ADAMINABY
BIG EILDON
Snowy
Adelaide
L. ALEXANDRINA
Melbourne

Hobart

Permanent Rivers

Non-Permanent Rivers

Flowing Water Bores

Major Dams

Major Irrigation and Other Water Supply Areas

Basins Where Artesian Water Is Generally Available

Prepared from Atlas of Australian Resources.

AUSTRALIA

AREA 2,967,741 sq. mi.
POPULATION 12,630,000
CAPITAL Canberra
LARGEST CITY Sydney (greater)
HIGHEST POINT Mt. Kosciusko 7,316 ft.
LOWEST POINT Lake Eyre -39 ft.
MONETARY UNIT Australian dollar
MAJOR LANGUAGE English
MAJOR RELIGIONS Protestantism, Roman Cath.

NEW ZEALAND

AREA 103,736 sq. mi.
POPULATION 2,815,000
CAPITAL Wellington
LARGEST CITY Auckland
HIGHEST POINT Mt. Cook 12,349 ft.
MONETARY UNIT New Zealand dollar
MAJOR LANGUAGES English, Maori
MAJOR RELIGION Protestantism

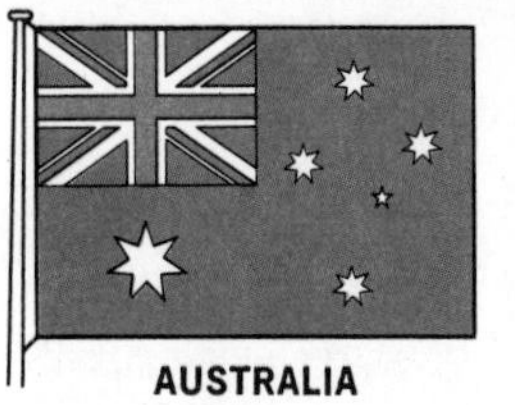
AUSTRALIA

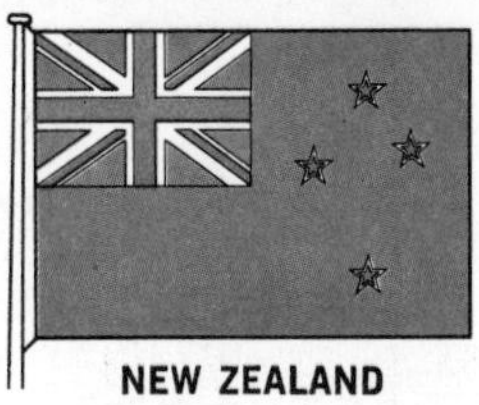
NEW ZEALAND

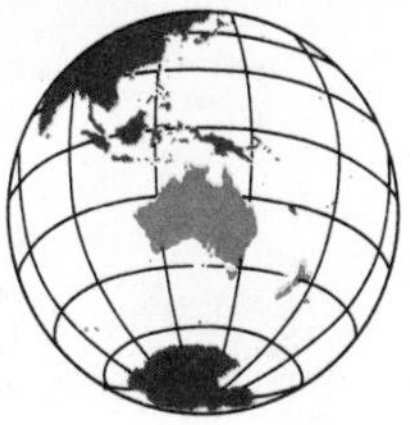

AUSTRALIA

STATES and TERRITORIES

Australian Capital Terr., 136,300 ....J 7
Coral Sea Islands Terr., 3 ....J 3
New South Wales, 4,595,400 ....H 6
Northern Territory, 73,000 ....E 3
Queensland, 1,810,000 ....G 4
South Australia, 1,169,600 ....F 6
Tasmania, 393,700 ....H 8
Victoria, 3,461,400 ....G 7
Western Australia, 991,300 ....C 5

CITIES and TOWNS

Adelaide (capital), S.A., †727,916 ....D 7
Adelaide River, N.T., ‡300 ....E 2
Albany, W.A., 11,419 ....B 6
Albury, N.S.W., 25,112 ....H 7
Alice Springs, N.T., 6,037 ....E 4
Aramac, Q. ....H 4
Ararat, V., 8,233 ....G 7
Armadale, W.A., 3,463 ....B 2
Armidale, N.S.W., 14,984 ....J 6
Augathella, Q. ....H 5
Ayr, Q., 8,674 ....H 3
Bacchus Marsh, V., 3,707 ....K 1
Bairnsdale, V., 7,785 ....H 7
Balhannah, S.A. ....E 8
Ballarat, V., *56,290 ....G 7
Ballina, N.S.W., 4,931 ....J 5
Balranald, N.S.W., 1,490 ....G 6
Bankstown, N.S.W., 159,981 ....L 3
Barcaldine, Q., 1,779 ....G 4
Bargo, N.S.W. ....K 4
Barraba, N.S.W., 1,425 ....J 6
Bathurst, N.S.W., 17,222 ....H 6
Beachport, S.A., ‡1,903 ....F 7
Bega, N.S.W., 3,925 ....J 7
Bendigo, V., *42,208 ....G 7
Beverley, W.A., ‡1,773 ....B 2
Bingara, N.S.W., 1,504 ....H 5
Blackall, Q., 2,004 ....G 4
Blacktown, N.S.W., 111,488 ....K 3
Blair Athol, Q. ....H 4
Blue Mts., N.S.W., 30,731 ....H 6
Bombala, N.S.W., 1,495 ....H 7
Bordertown, S.A., 1,758 ....G 7
Botany, N.S.W., 31,871 ....L 3
Boulder, W.A., 5,234 ....C 6
Bourke, N.S.W., 3,262 ....H 6
Bowen, Q., 5,144 ....H 3
Brewarrina, N.S.W., 1,255 ....H 5
Bridgetown, W.A., 1,569 ....B 6
Bright, V., 747 ....H 7
Brighton, V., 40,617 ....L 2
Brisbane (capital), Q., †718,822 ....J 5
Broken Hill, N.S.W., 30,014 ....G 6
Brookton, W.A., ‡1,341 ....B 2
Broome, W.A., 1,570 ....C 3
Bullfinch, W.A. ....B 6
Bulli, N.S.W. ....L 4
Bunbury, W.A., 15,459 ....A 6
Bundaberg, Q., 25,402 ....J 5
Burnie, T., 15,806 ....H 8
Busselton, W.A., 4,278 ....A 6
Cairns, Q., 29,326 ....H 3
Camberwell, V., 99,908 ....L 2
Camden, N.S.W., 3,427 ....K 4
Camooweal, Q. ....F 4
Campbelltown, N.S.W., 25,695 ....L 3
Canberra, A.C.T. (cap.), Australia, *136,300 ....H 7
Cardwell, Q. ....H 3
Carnarvon, W.A., 2,956 ....A 4
Casino, N.S.W., 8,502 ....J 5
Casterton, V., 2,492 ....G 7
Caulfield, V., 76,119 ....L 2
Ceduna, S.A., 1,406 ....E 6
Cessnock, N.S.W., *34,515 ....J 6
Charleville, Q., 4,871 ....H 5
Charters Towers, Q., 7,602 ....G 4
Chelsea, V., 24,789 ....L 2
Clermont, Q., 1,649 ....H 4
Cloncurry, Q., 2,149 ....G 4
Cobar, N.S.W., 2,348 ....H 6
Coburg, V., 68,568 ....L 1
Coffs Harbour, N.S.W., 7,667 ....J 6
Coleraine, V., 1,518 ....G 7
Collie, W.A., 7,628 ....B 6
Collinsville, Q., 1,887 ....H 4
Condobolin, N.S.W., 3,571 ....H 6
Coober Pedy, S.A. ....E 5
Cooktown, Q. ....H 3
Coolgardie, W.A., ‡762 ....C 6
Cooma, N.S.W., 9,103 ....H 7
Coonamble, N.S.W., 3,396 ....H 6
Cootamundra, N.S.W., 6,219 ....H 6
Corio, V. ....K 2
Corrigin, W.A., ‡2,099 ....B 5
Corrimal, N.S.W. ....L 4
Cowra, N.S.W., 7,076 ....H 6
Cudgewa, V. ....H 7
Cue, W.A., ‡430 ....B 5
Culcairn, N.S.W., 1,019 ....H 7
Cunnamulla, Q., 1,980 ....H 5
Cygnet, T. ....H 8
Dalby, Q., 8,860 ....J 5
Daly Waters, N.T., ‡265 ....E 3
Dandenong, V., 31,698 ....L 2
Darwin (capital), N.T., 18,042 ....E 2
Daylesford, V., 2,664 ....G 7
Deloraine, T., 1,793 ....H 8
Deniliquin, N.S.W., 6,239 ....H 7
Derby, W.A., 1,424 ....C 3
Devonport, T., 14,874 ....H 8
Dirranbandi, Q. ....H 5
Dubbo, N.S.W., 15,561 ....H 6
Echuca, V., 7,043 ....G 7
Echunga, S.A. ....E 7
Eidsvold, Q. ....J 5
Elizabeth, S.A., 32,949 ....D 7
Emerald, Q., 2,193 ....H 4
Esperance, W.A., 2,677 ....C 6
Essendon, V., 58,258 ....K 2
Footscray, V., 58,823 ....K 2
Forbes, N.S.W., 7,369 ....H 6
Frankston, V., 38,718 ....L 2
Fremantle, W.A., 25,284 ....B 2
Gawler, S.A., 5,703 ....D 7
Geelong, V., *105,059 ....K 2
Geraldton, W.A., 12,125 ....A 5
Gingin, W.A., ‡1,021 ....B 1
Gladstone, Q., 12,426 ....J 4
Glen Innes, N.S.W., 5,737 ....J 5
Glenmorgan, Q. ....H 5
Gold Coast, Q., 49,481 ....J 5
Goomalling, W.A., ‡1,567 ....B 1
Goondiwindi, Q., 3,529 ....H 5
Goulburn, N.S.W., 20,871 ....J 7
Grafton, N.S.W., 15,951 ....J 5
Griffith, N.S.W., 9,537 ....H 6
Gunnedah, N.S.W., 7,507 ....H 6
Gympie, Q., 11,279 ....J 5
Halls Creek, W.A., ‡577 ....D 3
Hamilton, V., 10,054 ....G 7
Hay, N.S.W., 2,952 ....H 6
Heidelberg, V. 63,929 ....L 1
Helensburgh, N.S.W., 2,334 ....L 4
Henley and Grange, S.A., 14,146 ....D 7
Hillston, N.S.W., 1,034 ....G 6
Hindmarsh, S.A., 11,352 ....D 7
Hobart (capital), T., †119,469 ....H 8
Home Hill, Q., 3,507 ....H 3
Horsham, V., 10,562 ....G 7
Hughenden, Q., 2,033 ....G 4
Hurstbridge, V. ....L 1
Hurstville, N.S.W., 64,851 ....L 3
Ingham, Q., 5,354 ....H 3
Injune, Q. ....H 5
Innisfail, Q., 7,432 ....H 3
Inverell, N.S.W., 8,413 ....J 5
Ipswich, Q., 54,531 ....J 5
Iron Knob, S.A. ....F 6
Ivanhoe, N.S.W. ....G 6
Jamestown, S.A. 1,282 ....F 6
Jandowae, Q. ....J 5
Jericho, Q. ....H 4
Junee, N.S.W., 3,904 ....H 6
Kadina, S.A., 1,865 ....F 6
Kalgoorlie, W.A., *19,908 ....C 6
Katanning, W.A., 3,506 ....B 6
Katherine, N.T., 1,302 ....E 2
Kelmscott, W.A., 914 ....B 2
Kempsey, N.S.W., 8,181 ....J 6
Kensington and Norwood, S.A., 11,928 ....D 8
Kerang, V., 4,164 ....G 7
Kew, V., 32,816 ....L 1
Kingaroy, Q., 5,080 ....J 5
Kingscote, S.A., 1,071 ....F 7
Kingston, S.A., 1,065 ....F 7
Kogarah, N.S.W., 47,654 ....L 3
Kwinana, W.A., 1,272 ....B 2
Lake Cargelligo, N.S.W., 1,128 ....H 6
Larrimah, N.T., ‡88 ....E 3
Launceston, T., 37,217 ....H 8
Laverton, W.A., ‡206 ....C 5
Leigh Creek, S.A., 1,014 ....F 6
Leonora, W.A., 623 ....C 5
Lismore, N.S.W., 19,734 ....J 5
Lithgow, N.S.W., 13,165 ....J 6
Liverpool, N.S.W., 68,959 ....K 3
Longford, T., 1,688 ....H 8
Longreach, Q., 3,871 ....G 4
Loxton, S.A., 2,418 ....G 6
Mackay, Q., 24,578 ....H 4
Maitland, N.S.W., 28,428 ....J 6
Mandurah, W.A., 2,730 ....B 2
Manilla, N.S.W., 1,761 ....J 6
Manly, N.S.W., 38,141 ....L 3
Maralinga and Woomera, S.A., 4,745 ....E 5
Marble Bar, W.A., ‡567 ....C 4
Mareeba, Q., 4,799 ....H 3
Marion, S.A., 66,950 ....D 8
Maryborough, Q., 20,393 ....J 5
Maryborough, V., 7,707 ....G 7
Mataranka, N.T., ‡114 ....E 2
Meekatharra, W.A., ‡1,011 ....B 5
Melbourne (cap.), V., †2,110,168 ....L 1
Merredin, W.A., 3,599 ....B 6
Midland, W.A., 9,335 ....B 2
Mildura, V., 12,931 ....G 6
Miles, Q., 1,485 ....H 5
Mingenew, W.A., ‡978 ....B 5
Mitchell, Q., 1,704 ....H 5
Moonta, S.A., 1,122 ....F 6
Moora, W.A., 1,185 ....B 6
Morawa, W.A., ‡1,718 ....B 5
Mordialloc, V., 28,076 ....L 2
Moree, N.S.W., 8,031 ....H 5
Mornington, V., 7,349 ....L 2
Mossman, Q., 1,614 ....G 3
Mount Barker, S.A., 1,934 ....E 8
Mount Gambier, S.A., 17,251 ....F 7
Mount Garnet, Q. ....G 3
Mount Isa, Q., 16,877 ....F 4
Mount Lofty, S.A. ....D 8
Mount Magnet, W.A. ....B 5
Mount Morgan, Q., 4,055 ....H 4
Mount Pleasant, S.A., ‡1,433 ....E 7
Mount Torrens, S.A. ....E 7
Mudgee, N.S.W., 5,372 ....J 6
Mullewa, W.A., ‡1,825 ....B 5
Murray Bridge, S.A., 5,957 ....F 7
Murwillumbah, N.S.W., 7,311 ....J 5
Muswellbrook, N.S.W., 6,312 ....J 6
Nanango, Q., 1,300 ....J 5
Nannup, W.A., ‡1,272 ....B 6
Naracoorte, S.A., 4,378 ....F 7
Narembeen, W.A., ‡1,590 ....B 6
Narrabri, N.S.W., 5,953 ....H 6
Narrandera, N.S.W., 4,905 ....H 6
Narrogin, W.A., 4,861 ....B 6
Narromine, N.S.W., 2,465 ....H 6
Nedlands, W.A., 23,320 ....B 2
New Norfolk, T., 5,770 ....H 8
Newcastle, N.S.W., *233,936 ....J 6
Normanton, Q. ....G 3
Norseman, W.A., 1,863 ....C 6
Northam, W.A., 7,400 ....B 2
Northampton, W.A., ‡2,021 ....A 5
Nowra, N.S.W., 9,633 ....J 6
Nyngan, N.S.W., 2,584 ....H 6
Orange, N.S.W., 22,196 ....H 6
Orbost, V., 2,797 ....H 7
Parkes, N.S.W., 8,438 ....H 6
Parramatta, N.S.W., 106,996 ....K 3
Penrith, N.S.W., 46,357 ....K 3
Perth (capital), W.A., †499,969 ....B 2
Peterborough, S.A., 3,117 ....F 6
Picton, N.S.W., 1,327 ....K 4
Pine Creek, N.T., ‡577 ....E 2
Pingelly, W.A., ‡1,453 ....B 2
Pinnaroo, S.A., ‡1,717 ....G 7
Port Adelaide, S.A., 39,823 ....D 7
Port Albert, V. ....H 7
Portarlington, V., 1,224 ....K 2
Port Augusta, S.A., 10,103 ....F 6
Port Fairy, V., 2,579 ....G 7
Port Hedland, W.A., 1,778 ....B 3
Port Kembla, N.S.W. ....J 6
Portland, V., 6,690 ....G 7
Port Lincoln, S.A., 8,888 ....E 6
Port Macquarie, N.S.W., 7,063 ....J 6
Port Melbourne, V., 12,591 ....K 2
Port Pirie, S.A., 15,566 ....F 6
Port Wakefield, S.A., ‡1,020 ....F 6
Proserpine, Q., 2,951 ....H 4
Queenstown, T., 4,295 ....G 8
Quirindi, N.S.W., 2,730 ....H 6
Quorn, S.A., 588 ....F 6
Radium Hill, S.A. ....G 6
Randwick, N.S.W., 113,634 ....L 3
Ravensthorpe, W.A., ‡782 ....C 6
Renmark, S.A., 6,275 ....G 6
Reynella-Port Noarlunga, 11,818 ....D 8
Richmond, V., 32,530 ....L 2
Ringwood, V., 29,141 ....L 1
Rockdale, N.S.W., 81,463 ....L 3
Rockhampton, Q., 46,083 ....J 4
Rockingham, W.A., 3,767 ....B 2
Roebourne, W.A., ‡1,782 ....B 4
Roma, Q., 5,996 ....H 5
Ryde, N.S.W., 81,291 ....L 3
Saint Arnaud, V., 3,004 ....G 7
Saint George, Q., 2,233 ....H 5
Saint Kilda, V., 58,129 ....L 2
Sale, V., 8,640 ....H 7
Salisbury, S.A., 35,762 ....D 7
Sandgate, Q., 22,621 ....J 5
Sandringham, V., 36,671 ....L 2
Sarina, Q., 2,422 ....H 4
Scone, N.S.W., 2,915 ....J 6
Singleton, N.S.W., 6,188 ....J 6
Spalding, S.A., ‡705 ....F 6
Stanthorpe, Q., 3,641 ....J 5
Stawell, V., 5,909 ....G 7
Strathalbyn, S.A., 1,449 ....D 8
Strathfield, N.S.W., 26,704 ....L 3
Streaky Bay, S.A., ‡2,134 ....E 6
Subiaco, W.A., 16,621 ....B 2
Sunbury, V., 3,526 ....K 1
Swan Hill, V., 7,381 ....G 7
Sydney (cap.), N.S.W., †2,446,345 ....L 3
Tamworth, N.S.W., 21,680 ....J 6
Taree, N.S.W,. 10,560 ....J 6
Temora, N.S.W., 4,536 ....H 6
Tennant Creek, N.T., 1,001 ....E 3
Tenterfield, N.S.W., 3,270 ....J 5
Theodore, Q. ....H 4
Thursday Island, Q., 2,551 ....G 2
Toowoomba, Q., 55,799 ....J 5
Townsville, Q., 58,847 ....H 3
Truro, S.A., ‡588 ....F 6
Tully, Q., 2,860 ....H 3
Tumbarumba, N.S.W., 1,443 ....H 7
Tumut, N.S.W., 4,277 ....H 7
Ulverstone, T., 6,842 ....H 8
Unley, S.A., 39,727 ....D 8
Victor Harbor, S.A., 2,160 ....F 7
Wagga Wagga, N.S.W., 25,819 ....H 7
Wagin, W.A., 1,750 ....B 6
Walcha, N.S.W., 1,544 ....J 6
Walgett, N.S.W., 1,985 ....H 6
Wallaroo, S.A., 2,094 ....F 6
Wandoan, Q. ....H 5
Wangaratta, V., 15,175 ....H 7
Waroona, W.A., 1,013 ....B 2

(continued on following page)

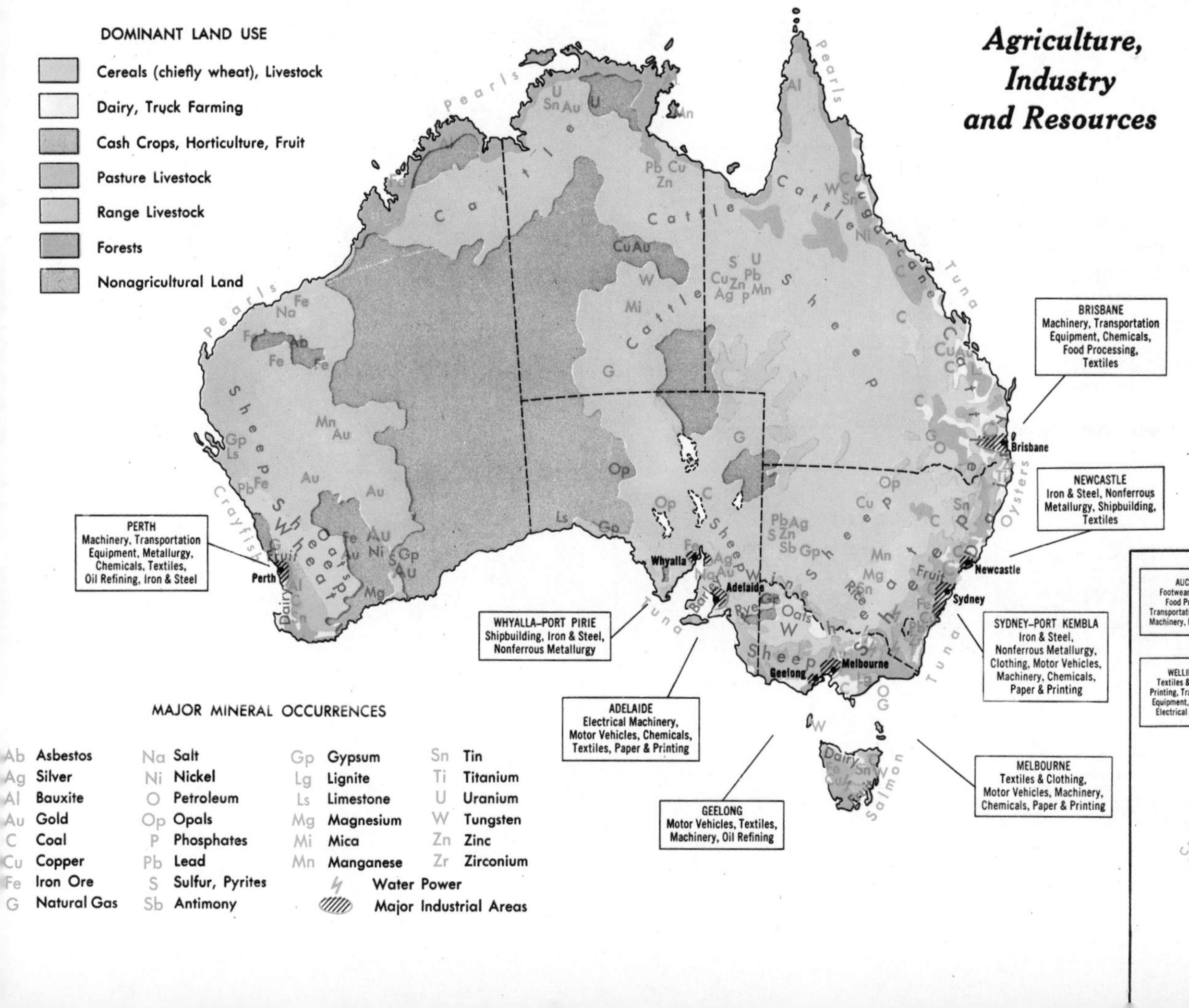

DOMINANT LAND USE
Cereals (chiefly wheat), Livestock
Dairy, Truck Farming
Cash Crops, Horticulture, Fruit
Pasture Livestock
Range Livestock
Forests
Nonagricultural Land
Agriculture, Industry and Resources
BRISBANE
Machinery, Transportation Equipment, Chemicals, Food Processing, Textiles
NEWCASTLE
Iron & Steel, Nonferrous Metallurgy, Shipbuilding, Textiles
PERTH
Machinery, Transportation Equipment, Metallurgy, Chemicals, Textiles, Oil Refining, Iron & Steel
WHYALLA–PORT PIRIE
Shipbuilding, Iron & Steel, Nonferrous Metallurgy
SYDNEY–PORT KEMBLA
Iron & Steel, Nonferrous Metallurgy, Clothing, Motor Vehicles, Machinery, Chemicals, Paper & Printing
ADELAIDE
Electrical Machinery, Motor Vehicles, Chemicals, Textiles, Paper & Printing
MELBOURNE
Textiles & Clothing, Motor Vehicles, Machinery, Chemicals, Paper & Printing
GEELONG
Motor Vehicles, Textiles, Machinery, Oil Refining
Perth
Whyalla
Adelaide
Geelong
Melbourne
Sydney
Newcastle
Brisbane
Pearls
Cattle
Sheep
Tuna
Oysters
Crayfish
Salmon
Dairy
Sugarcane
MAJOR MINERAL OCCURRENCES
Ab Asbestos
Ag Silver
Al Bauxite
Au Gold
C Coal
Cu Copper
Fe Iron Ore
G Natural Gas
Na Salt
Ni Nickel
O Petroleum
Op Opals
P Phosphates
Pb Lead
S Sulfur, Pyrites
Sb Antimony
Gp Gypsum
Lg Lignite
Ls Limestone
Mg Magnesium
Mi Mica
Mn Manganese
Sn Tin
Ti Titanium
U Uranium
W Tungsten
Zn Zinc
Zr Zirconium
Water Power
Major Industrial Areas

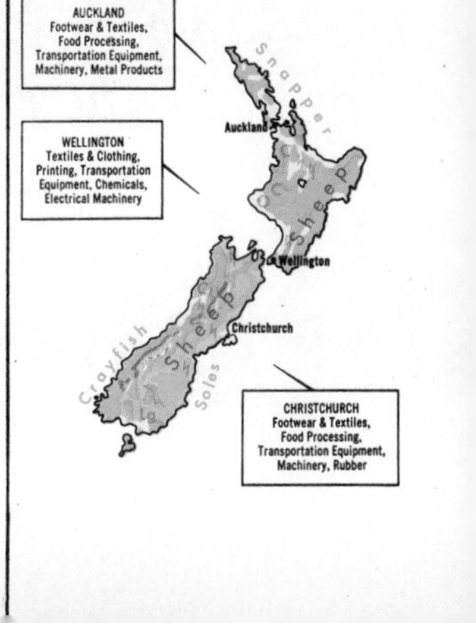

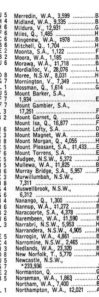

AUCKLAND
Footwear & Textiles, Food Processing, Transportation Equipment, Machinery, Metal Products
WELLINGTON
Textiles & Clothing, Printing, Transportation Equipment, Chemicals, Electrical Machinery
CHRISTCHURCH
Footwear & Textiles, Food Processing, Transportation Equipment, Machinery, Rubber
Auckland
Wellington
Christchurch
Snapper
Sheep
Crayfish
Soles

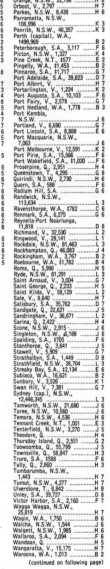

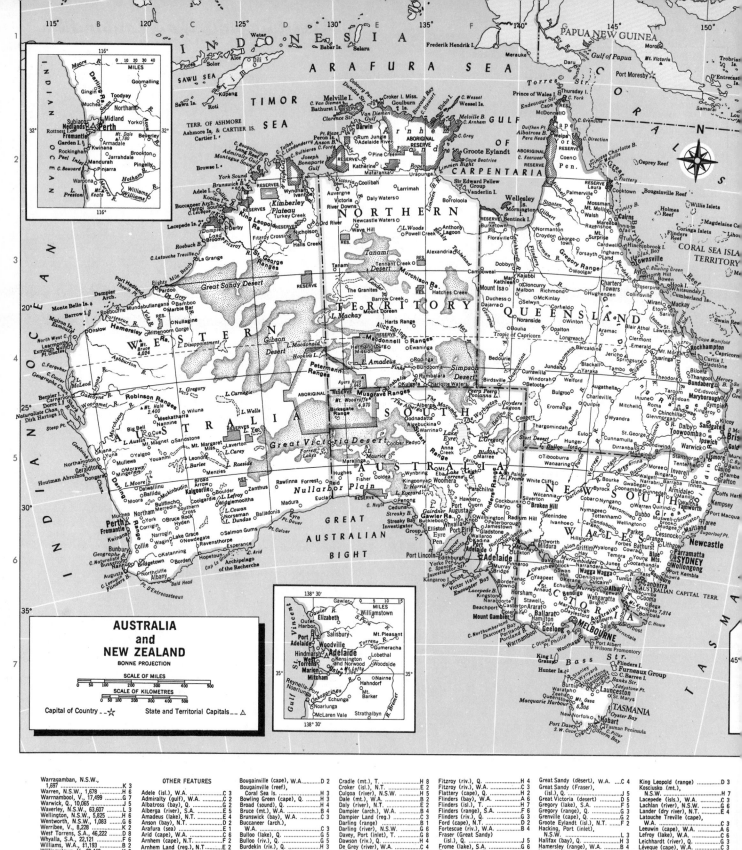

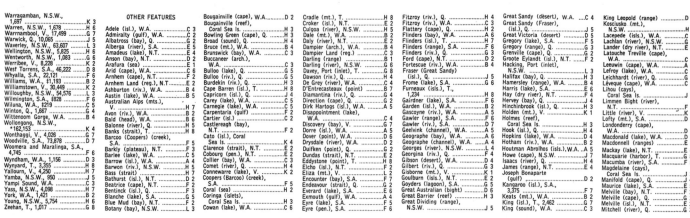

AUSTRALIA and NEW ZEALAND
BONNE PROJECTION

SCALE OF MILES

SCALE OF KILOMETRES

Capital of Country ☆   State and Territorial Capitals △

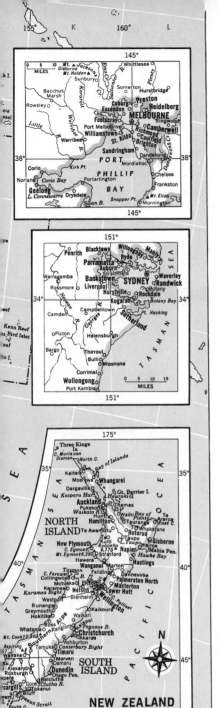

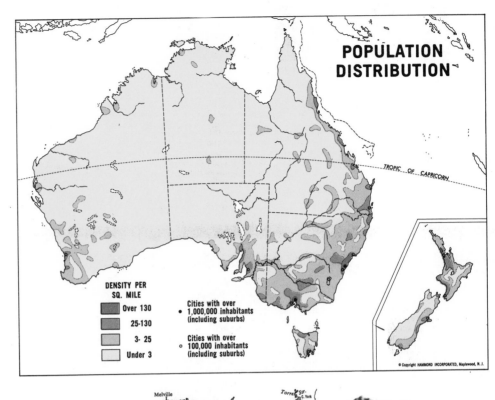

POPULATION DISTRIBUTION

DENSITY PER SQ. MILE
- Over 130
- 25-130
- 3- 25
- Under 3

● Cities with over 1,000,000 inhabitants (including suburbs)

○ Cities with over 100,000 inhabitants (including suburbs)

© Copyright HAMMOND INCORPORATED, Maplewood, N. J.

Topography

5,000 m. 16,404 ft. | 2,000 m. 6,562 ft. | 1,000 m. 3,281 ft. | 500 m. 1,640 ft. | 200 m. 656 ft. | 100 m. 328 ft. | Sea Level Below

NEW ZEALAND — Same scale as main map

Copyright by C. S. Hammond & Co., N. Y.

Montague (sound), W.A. ...C 2	Plenty (river), V. ...L 1	Swan (river), W.A. ...B 2
Monte Bello (isls.), W.A. ...A 4	Port Philip (bay), V. ...K 2	Talbot (cape), W.A. ...D 2
Moore (lake), W.A. ...B 5	Portland (bay), V. ...G 7	Tasman (pen.), T. ...H 8
Moore (river), W.A. ...B 1	Preston (lake), W.A. ...D 2	Thomson (river), Q. ...G 4
Moreton (isl.), Q. ...J 5	Prince of Wales (isl.), Q. ...G 2	Timor (sea) ...C 2
Mornington (isl.), Q. ...G 3	Princess Charlotte (bay), Q. ...G 2	Torrens (lake), S.A. ...F 5
Murchison (range) ...E 4	Recherche (arch.), W.A. ...C 6	Torres (strait) ...G 2
Murchison (river), W.A. ...B 5	Roebuck (bay), W.A. ...C 3	Trinity (bay), Q. ...H 3
Murray (river), V. ...G 6	Roper (river), N.T. ...E 2	Van Diemen (cape), N.T. ...D 2
Murray (river), W.A. ...B 2	Rottnest (isl.), W.A. ...A 2	Van Diemen (gulf), N.T. ...E 2
Murrumbidgee (river), N.S.W. ...G 6	Ruhieres (cape), W.A. ...D 3	Victoria (river), N.T. ...E 3
Musgrave (range) ...E 5	Saint George (ranges), W.A. ...D 3	Warrego (river), N.S.W. ...H 5
Naturaliste (cape), W.A. ...A 6	Saint Vincent (gulf), S.A. ...D 7	Wellesley (isls.), Q. ...F 3
Naturaliste (channel), W.A. ...A 5	Saltwater (river), V. ...K 1	Wells (lake), W.A. ...C 5
Nepean (river), N.S.W. ...K 3	Sandy (cape), Q. ...J 4	Werribee (river), V. ...K 2
Norman (river), Q. ...G 3	Shark (bay), W.A. ...A 5	Wessel (cape), N.T. ...F 2
North West (cape), W.A. ...A 4	Simpson (desert), N.T. ...F 5	Wessel (isls.), N.T. ...F 2
Northumberland (cape), S.A. ...F 7	Sir Edward Pellew (isls.), N.T. ...F 3	Whitsunday (isl.), Q. ...H 4
Nullarbor (plain) ...D 6	South Para (river), S.A. ...E 6	Wilberforce (cape), N.T. ...F 2
Onkaparinga (river), S.A. ...D 3	South West (cape), T. ...G 8	Williams (river), N.S.W. ...B 3
Ord (river), W.A. ...D 3	Spencer (cape), S.A. ...F 7	Willis (islets) ...J 3
Ossa (mt.) ...H 8	Spencer (gulf), S.A. ...F 6	Wilsons (promontory), W.A. ...H 7
Oyster (bay), T. ...H 8	Steep (point), W.A. ...A 5	Wooramel (river), W.A. ...A 5
Paroo (river), N.S.W. ...G 5	Stewart (cape), N.T. ...E 2	York (cape), Q. ...G 2
Peel (inlet), W.A. ...B 2	Storm (bay), T. ...H 8	York (sound), W.A. ...C 2
Peera Peera Poolanna (lake), S.A. ...F 5	Stuart (range), S.A. ...E 5	Yorke (pen.), S.A. ...F 7
Pera (head), Q. ...G 2	Sturt (desert) ...F 5	Yule (river), W.A. ...B 4
Peron (islands), N.T. ...D 2	Swain (reefs), Q. ...J 4	
Pillar (cape), T. ...H 8	Swan (bay), V. ...K 2	

NEW ZEALAND

CITIES and TOWNS

Alexandra, 3,160 ...K 7	Picton, 2,610 ...L 6	Whakatane, 9,080 ...M 5
Ashburton, 12,950 ...L 7	Pukekohe, 6,800 ...L 5	Whangarei, †31,600 ...L 5
Auckland, †588,400 ...L 5	Rangiora, 4,270 ...L 7	
Balclutha, 4,570 ...L 7	Rotorua, †35,300 ...M 6	**OTHER FEATURES**
Blenheim, 13,950 ...L 6	Runanga, 1,683 ...L 7	
Bluff, 3,300 ...L 7	Stratford, 5,470 ...L 6	Aspiring (mt.) ...K 7
Christchurch, 1,256,300 ...L 7	Tauranga, †33,500 ...M 5	Canterbury (bight) ...L 7
Dannevirke, 5,780 ...M 6	Te Awamutu, 6,780 ...L 6	Cook (mt.) ...L 7
Dargaville, 3,910 ...L 5	Te Kuiti, 4,830 ...L 6	Cook (strait) ...L 6
Dunedin, †109,800 ...L 7	Temuka, 3,190 ...L 7	East (cape) ...M 5
Feilding, 9,360 ...L 6	Thames, 5,680 ...L 6	Egmont (cape) ...L 6
Gisborne, †28,500 ...M 6	Timaru, †28,400 ...L 7	Egmont (mt.) ...L 6
Gore, 8,380 ...L 7	Tuatapere, 954 ...K 7	Farewell (cape) ...L 6
Greymouth, 8,590 ...L 7	Waihi, 3,170 ...L 6	Foveaux (strait) ...K 7
Hamilton, 168,000 ...L 6	Wairoa, 5,190 ...M 6	Great Barrier (isl.), 272 ...M 5
Hastings, †39,200 ...M 6	Wanganui, 138,500 ...L 6	Hauraki (gulf) ...L 5
Hawera, 8,210 ...L 6	Wellington (capital), †175,500 ...L 6	Hawke (bay) ...M 6
Hokitika, 3,310 ...L 7	Westport, 5,230 ...L 6	Islands (bay) ...L 5
Invercargill, †47,800 ...K 7		Karamea (bight) ...K 6
Kaiapoi, 3,610 ...L 7		
Kaitaia, 3,110 ...L 5		Maria van Diemen (cape) ...L 5
Lower Hutt, 58,700 ...L 6		North (isl.), 1,956,411 ...L 6
Marton, 4,780 ...L 6		Otago (pen.) ...L 7
Masterton, 17,950 ...M 6		Pegasus (bay) ...L 7
Motueka, 3,840 ...L 6		Plenty (bay) ...M 5
Napier, †39,900 ...M 6		Ruapehu (vol.) ...L 6
Nelson, 25,100 ...L 6		South (cape) ...L 8
New Plymouth, †35,800 ...L 6		South (isl.), 798,681 ...L 7
Oamaru, 13,350 ...L 7		Southern Alps (mts.) ...L 7
Palmerston North, †50,900 ...M 6		Stewart (isl.), 332 ...K 8
		Tasman (bay) ...L 6
		Tasman (sea) ...L 6
		Taupo (lake) ...M 6
		Te Anau (lake) ...K 7
		Waikato (river) ...L 6

*City and suburbs.
†Population of metropolitan area.
‡Population of district or sub-division.

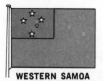

WESTERN SAMOA   **SOLOMON ISLANDS**   **TONGA**   **FIJI**

WESTERN SAMOA
AREA 1,133 sq. mi.
POPULATION 159,000
CAPITAL Apia
LARGEST CITY Apia
HIGHEST POINT Mt. Silisili 6,094 ft.
MONETARY UNIT tala
MAJOR LANGUAGES Samoan, English
MAJOR RELIGIONS Protestantism,
Roman Catholicism

TONGA
AREA 270 sq. mi.
POPULATION 102,000
CAPITAL Nuku'alofa
LARGEST CITY Nuku'alofa
HIGHEST POINT 3,389 ft.
MONETARY UNIT pa'anga
MAJOR LANGUAGES Tongan, English
MAJOR RELIGION Protestantism

NAURU
AREA 7.7 sq. mi.
POPULATION 8,000
CAPITAL Yaren (district)
MONETARY UNIT Australian dollar
MAJOR LANGUAGES Nauruan, English
MAJOR RELIGION Protestantism

SOLOMON ISLANDS
AREA 11,500 sq. mi.
POPULATION 196,708
CAPITAL Honiara
HIGHEST POINT Mount Popomanatseu 7,647
MONETARY UNIT Solomon Islands dollar
MAJOR LANGUAGES English, Pidgin English,
Melanesian dialects
MAJOR RELIGIONS Tribal religions, Protestantism,
Roman Catholicism

FIJI
AREA 7,055 sq. mi.
POPULATION 569,468
CAPITAL Suva
LARGEST CITY Suva
HIGHEST POINT Tomaniivi 4,341 ft.
MONETARY UNIT Fijian dollar
MAJOR LANGUAGES Fijian, Hindi, English
MAJOR RELIGIONS Protestantism, Hinduism

TUVALU
AREA 9.78 sq. mi.
POPULATION 5,887
CAPITAL Fongafale
MONETARY UNIT Australian dollar
MAJOR LANGUAGES English, Tuvaluan
MAJOR RELIGION Protestantism

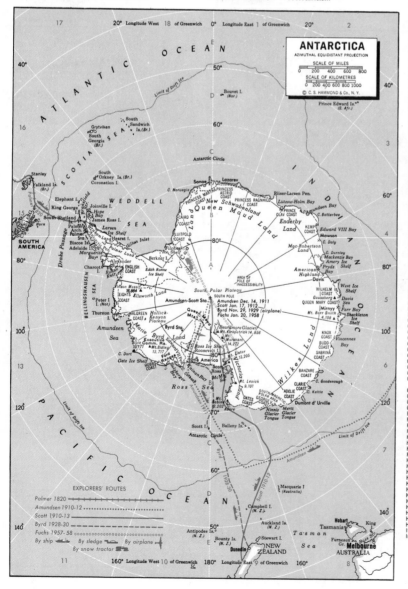

ANTARCTICA
AZIMUTHAL EQUIDISTANT PROJECTION
SCALE OF MILES
0 200 400 600 800
SCALE OF KILOMETRES
0 200 400 600 800 1000
© C. S. HAMMOND & Co., N.Y.

EXPLORERS' ROUTES
Palmer 1820
Amundsen 1910-12
Scott 1910-13
Byrd 1928-30
Fuchs 1957-58
By ship   By sledge   By airplane
By snow tractor

Index columns:

Name	Grid
Abaing (atoll), 3,271	H 5
Abemama (atoll), 2,126	H 5
Adamstown, 74	N 8
Adelaide, 1727,916	D 9
Admiralty (isls.), 21,588	E 6
Agaña, 2,131	E 4
Agrihan (isl.), 64	E 3
Ahau, 414	H 7
Ailinglapalap (atoll), 1,281	G 5
Ailuk (atoll), 371	H 4
Aitutaki (isl.), 2,579	K 7
Alamagan (isl.), 48	E 4
Albany, 11,419	A 9
Albury, 25,172	H 9
Alice Springs, 6,037	D 8
Alofi, 1,117	K 7
Amanu (atoll), 117	N 7
Ambrym (atoll), 4,200	G 7
American Samoa, 30,000	J 7
Anaa (atoll), 360	M 7
Anatahan (isl.), 23	E 4
Aneityum (isl.), 300	H 8
Angaur (isl.), 533	D 5
Apataki (atoll), 108	M 7
Apia, 27,000	J 7
Armidale, 18,984	H 9
Arnhem Land (reg.)	D 7
Arno (atoll), 1,198	H 5
Arorae (atoll), 1,830	H 6
Atafu (atoll), 615	J 6
Atiu (isl.), 1,327	L 8
Atuona, 663	M 7
Auckland, 152,200	H 9
Auki, 600	G 6
Austral (isls.), 5,053	L 8
Australia, 13,684,900	
Australian Cap. Terr., 204,200	H 9
Avarua, 4,100	L 8
Babelthuap (isl.), 5,222	D 5
Bairiki, 1,300	H 6
Baker (isl.)	J 5
Ballarat, *56,290	G 9
Banks (isls.), 3,250	G 7
Belep (isls.), 551	G 8
Bendigo, *42,208	G 9
Beru (atoll), 2,412	H 6
Bikini (atoll)	G 4
Bismarck (arch.), 209,051	E 6
Blackall, 2,004	H 8
Blue Mountains, 30,731	E 8
Bora-Bora (isl.), 2,071	L 7
Bougainville (isl.), 72,661	F 6
Boulder, 5,234	C 9
Bourail, 672	G 8
Bowen, 5,144	H 7
Brisbane, 1718,822	J 8
Broken Hill, 30,014	G 9
Broome, 1,570	C 7
Bunbury, 15,459	B 9
Bundaberg, 25,402	J 8
Butaritari (atoll), 2,714	H 5
Cairns, 29,326	H 7
Canberra, *204,200	H 9
Canton (isl.), 421	J 6
Carnarvon, 2,956	A 8
Caroline (isls.), 54,563	E 5
Charleville, 4,871	H 8
Charters Towers, 7,602	H 7
Chatham (isls.), 520	J 10
Chichi (isl.), 203	E 3
Choiseul (isl.), 6,600	F 6
Christchurch, 165,000	H10
Christmas (isl.), 367	L 5
Cloncurry, 2,149	G 7
Collie, 7,628	B 9
Cook (isls.), 17,046	K 7
Coral (sea)	F 6
Cunnamulla, 1,980	H 8
Daito (isls.), 3,896	D 3
Daly Waters, 1265	D 7
Danger (Pukapuka) (atoll), 684	K 7
Daru, 3,663	D 7
Darwin, 18,042	D 6
D'Entrecasteaux (isls.), 32,288	F 6
Derby, 1,424	C 7
Devonport, 16,757	E10
Dunedin, 77,800	H10
Easter (isl.), 1,598	Q 8
Eauripik (atoll), 158	E 5
Ebon (atoll), 731	H 6
Efate (isl.), 10,000	G 7
Elato (atoll), 35	E 5
Enderbury (isl.)	J 6
Eniwetok (atoll)	G 4
Erromanga (isl.), 600	H 7
Esperance, 2,677	C 9
Espíritu Santo (isl.), 10,000	G 7
Fais (isl.), 230	E 5
Fakaofo (isl.), 740	J 6
Fakarava (atoll), 230	M 7
Fanning (isl.), 376	L 5
Faraulep (atoll), 178	E 5
Fatuhiwa (isl.), 459	N 7
Fiji, 569,468	H 8
Fly (riv.)	E 6
Fongafale, 826	H 6
Fremantle, 25,284	B 9
French Polynesia, 135,000	L 8
Funafuti (atoll), 826	H 6
Furneaux Group (isls.), 1,234	E 9
Gambier (isls.), 516	N 8
Garapan, 4,100	E 4
Gardner (isl.), 230	J 6
Geelong, *105,059	G 9
Geraldton, 12,125	A 8
Gilbert (isls.), 44,205	H 6
Gilbert Islands, 47,711	H 6
Gisborne, 25,600	H 9
Grafton, 15,951	J 9
Great Barrier (reef)	E 7
Greenwich (Kapingamarangi) (atoll), 411	F 5
Greymouth, 8,590	H10
Guadalcanal (isl.), 23,922	F 7
Guam, 111,000	E 4
Gympie, 11,279	J 8
Ha'apai Group (isls.), 10,591	J 7
Halls Creek, 5577	D 7
Hamilton, 67,700	H 9
Hao (atoll), 448	N 7
Hastings, 28,100	J 9
Hawaii (isl.), 63,468	L 3
Hawaii (state), 769,913	L 4
Hawaiian (isls.), 772,133	J 3
Hikeru (atoll), 115	M 7
Hilo, 26,353	L 4
Hivaoa (isl.), 1,027	N 6
Hobart, 53,257	E 10
Honiara, 14,942	F 6
Honolulu, 324,871	J 4
Honolulu, *630,528	J 4
Hoorn (isls.), 3,000	J 7
Howland (isl.)	J 5
Huahine (isl.), 2,814	L 7
Hughenden, 2,213	G 7
Hull (isl.), 583	J 6
Ifalik (atoll), 321	E 5
Invercargill, 45,300	H10

Name	Grid
Ipswich, 54,531	F 8
Iwo (isl.)	E 3
Jaluit (atoll), 932	G 5
Jarvis (isl.)	K 6
Johnston (atoll), 1,007	L 4
Kalgoorlie, *19,908	B 9
Kandavu (isl.), 6,600	H 7
Kangaroo (isl.), 3,375	F 9
Kapingamarangi (atoll), 411	F 5
Katherine, 1,302	D 7
Kauai (isl.), 29,524	J 3
Kavieng, 2,142	E 6
Kermadec (isls.), 9	J 8
Kieta, 755	F 6
Kili (atoll), 320	G 5
Koror, 5,541	D 5
Kolonia, 7,201	E10
Kusaie (isl.), 3,648	G 5
Kwajalein (atoll), 3,841	G 5
Lae, 12,392	F 6
Lamotrek (atoll), 203	E 5
Lanai (isl.), 2,204	L 3
Lau Group (isls.), 15,988	J 7
Launceston, 37,217	E10
Laverton, *206	C 8
Lavongai (isl.), 7,829	E 6
Levuka, 1,685	H 7
Lifu (isl.), 6,837	G 8
Line (isls.), 1,180	K 5
Lismore, 19,734	J 8
Lithgow, 13,165	F 9
Little Makin (isl.), 1,387	H 5
Longreach, 3,871	G 7
Lord Howe (isl.), 267	G 9
Lord Howe (Ontong Java)	F 6
Loyalty (isls.), 12,248	G 8
Luganville, 3,500	G 7
Mackay, 24,578	H 7
Madang, 6,601	E 6
Maitland, 28,428	F 9
Majuro (atoll), 5,957	H 5
Makatea (isl.), 55	L 7
Makin (Butaritari) (atoll), 2,714	H 5
Malaita (isl.), 54,000	G 6
Malekula (isl.), 11,200	G 7
Maloelap (atoll), 494	H 5
Mangaia (isl.), 2,002	L 8
Mangareva (isl.), 516	N 8
Manihiki (atoll), 584	K 7
Manra (Sydney) (isl.), 7	K 6
Manua (isls.), 2,112	K 7
Manuae (atoll), 15	L 8
Manus (isl.), 11,088	E 6
Maré (isl.), 3,410	G 8
Mariana (isls.), 11,827	E 4
Mariana Trench	E 4
Marquesas (isls.), 5,174	N 6
Marshall (isls.), 19,328	G 4
Marutea (atoll)	N 8
Maryborough, 20,393	J 8
Matautu 566	J 7
Maui (isl.), 38,691	L 3
Mauke (isl.), 671	L 8
Meekatharra, ±1,011	B 8
Mehetia (isl.)	M 7
Melanesia (reg.)	E 5
Melbourne, 2,110,168	G 9
Micronesia (reg.)	E 4
Midway (isls.), 2,220	J 3
Mili (atoll), 360	F 5

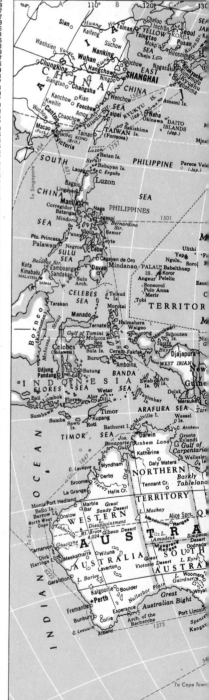

Mitiaro (isl.), 293 ....L 7
Moen (isl.), 4,966 ....F 5
Moerai; 684 ....L 8
Mokil (atoll), 393 ....G 5
Molokai (isl.), 5,089 ....L 3
Moorea (isl.), 4,370 ....L 7
Morobe, 12,132 ....E 6
Mount Gambier, 17,251 ....D 9
Mururoa (isl.) ....M 8
Namatanai, 22,221 ....F 6
Namonuito (atoll) ....E 5
Namorik (atoll), 490 ....G 5
Nandi, 2,542 ....H 7
Nanumea (atoll), 1,076 ....H 6
Napier, 36,700 ....H 9
Nassau (isl.), 167 ....K 7
Nauru, 8,000 ....G 6
Ndeni (isl.) ....G 7
Nelafu, 3,593 ....H 7
Nelson, 27,900 ....H10
New Britain (isl.), 138,689 ....F 6
New Caledonia, 136,000 ....G 8
New Caledonia (isl.), 86,802 ....G 8
Newcastle, 233,936 ....E 6
New Georgia (isls.) ....F 6
New Guinea (isl.) ....E 6
New Hebrides (isls.), 97,468 ....G 7
New Ireland (isl.), 48,774 ....F 6
New South Wales (state), 4,847,800 ...E 9
New Zealand, 3,121,904 ....H10
Ngatik (atoll), 442 ....F 5
Ngulu (atoll), 43 ....D 5
Niihau (isl.), 237 ....K 3
Nikumaroro (Gardner) (isl.), 230 ...J 6
Ninigo Group (isls.), 1,051 ....E 6

Niuafo'ou (isl.), 599 ....J 7
Niuatoputapu (isl.), 1,294 ....J 7
Niue (isl.), 2,992 ....K 7
Niutao (atoll), 796 ....H 6
Norfolk (isl.), 1,870 ....G 8
North (isl.), 1,956,411 ....H 9
Northern Territory (terr.), 98,400 ...D 7
Nouméa, 41,853 ....G 8
Nouméa, *47,966 ....G 8
Nui (atoll), 569 ....H 6
Nuku'alofa, 15,685 ....J 8
Nukuhiva (isl.), 1,351 ....M 6
Nukulaelae (atoll), 354 ....H 6
Nukumanu (atoll), 675 ....F 6
Nukunono (atoll), 528 ....J 6
Nukuoro (atoll), 408 ....F 5
Oahu (isl.), 629,176 ....L 2
Ocean (isl.), 2,192 ....G 6
Oeno (isl.) ....O 8
Onotoa (atoll), 1,960 ....H 6
Ontong Java (atoll), 900 ....G 6
Orange, 22,196 ....E 9
Orona (Hull) (isl.), 583 ....J 6
Pacific Islands, Terr. of, 120,000 ...F 5
Pagan (isl.), 62 ....E 4
Pago Pago, 2,481 ....J 7
Palau (isls.), 12,291 ....D 5
Palmerston (atoll), 86 ....K 7
Palmerston North, 49,200 ....H10
Palmyra (isl.) ....K 5
Pangai, 1,870 ....J 8
Papeete, 22,278 ....M 7
Papeete, *37,485 ....M 7
Papua New Guinea, 2,800,000 ....E 6
Peleliu (isl.), 810 ....D 5

Penrhyn (Tongareva) (atoll) 545 ....L 6
Perth, 1,499,969 ....B 9
Phoenix (isls.), 1,018 ....H 6
Pines, Isle of (isl.), 978 ....G 8
Pingelap (atoll), 815 ....G 5
Pitcairn (isl.), 67 ....O 8
Polynesia (reg.) ....K 7
Ponape (isl.), 13,976 ....F 5
Port Augusta, 10,103 ....D 9
Port Hedland, 1,778 ....B 8
Port Lincoln, 8,888 ....D 9
Port Moresby, 56,206 ....E 6
Port Pirie, 15,566 ....D 9
Puka-Puka (atoll), 98 ....N 7
Pukapuka (atoll), 684 ....K 7
Pulap (atoll), 302 ....E 5
Pulo Anna (isl.), 13 ....D 5
Pulusuk (atoll), 305 ....E 5
Puluwat (atoll), 412 ....E 5
Queensland (state), 2,015,300 ....E 8
Rabaul, 8,737 ....F 6
Raiatea (isl.), 6,187 ....L 7
Raivavae (isl.), 995 ....M 8
Rakahanga (atoll), 323 ....K 7
Ralik Chain (isls.), 9,268 ....G 5
Rangiroa (atoll), 868 ....M 7
Rapa (isl.), 363 ....M 8
Rapa Nui (Easter) (isl.), 1,598 ....Q 8
Raroia (atoll), 52 ....M 7
Rarotonga (isl.), 9,571 ....K 8
Ratak Chain (isls.), 10,060 ....G 5
Reao (atoll), 255 ....N 7
Rennell (isl.), 900 ....F 7
Rimatara (isl.), 747 ....L 8
Rockhampton, 45,376 ....E 8
Roma, 5,996 ....E 8
Rongelap (atoll), 107 ....G 4

Rota (isl.), 1,344 ....E 4
Rotuma (isl.), 3,365 ....H 7
Rurutu (isl.), 1,546 ....L 8
Saipan, 9,590 ....E 4
Sala y Gómez (isl.) ....P 8
Samarai, 2,201 ....F 6
Samoa (isls.), 189,000 ....J 7
San Cristobal (isl.), 8,500 ....G 7
Santa Cruz (isls.), 2,800 ....G 6
Santa Isabel (isl.), 8,548 ....G 6
Satawal (isl.), 345 ....E 5
Savai'i (isl.), 36,159 ....J 7
Senyavin (isls.) ....F 5
Society (isls.), 81,487 ....L 7
Sohano, 877 ....F 6
Solomon (isls.), 234,186 ....F 6
Solomon (sea) ....F 6
Solomon Islands, 196,708 ....F 6
Sonsorol (isl.), 92 ....D 5
Sorol (atoll), 15 ....D 5
South (isl.), 798,681 ....G10
South Australia (state), 1,247,100 ...D 8
Starbuck (isl.) ....L 7
Stewart (isl.), 332 ....G10
Suva, 54,157 ....H 7
Suva, *80,248 ....H 7
Suwarrow (Suvarov) (atoll) ....K 7
Swains (isl.), 74 ....J 7
Sydney (isl.) (Manra) ....H 6
Sydney, *2,446,345 ....F 9
Tabiteuea (atoll), 4,419 ....H 6
Tahaa (isl.), 3,567 ....L 7
Tahiti (isl.), 61,519 ....L 7
Takaroa (atoll), 161 ....M 7
Tamworth, 21,680 ....E 9
Tanna (isl.), 10,500 ....H 7
Tarawa (atoll), 12,642 ....H 5

Tasman (sea) ....G 9
Tasmania (state), 410,800 ....E 10
Taveuni (isl.), 6,351 ....H 7
Tennant Creek, 1,001 ....D 7
Tikopia (isl.), 1,400 ....G 7
Timaru, 27,800 ....H10
Tinian (isl.), 696 ....E 4
Tobi (isl.), 80 ....D 5
Tokelau (isls.), 1,603 ....J 6
Tonga, 102,000 ....J 8
Tongareva (atoll), 545 ....L 6
Tongatapu (isl.), 47,606 ....J 8
Toowoomba, 52,139 ....E 8
Torres (isls.), 250 ....G 7
Townsville, 56,768 ....E 7
Trobriand (isls.), 10,199 ....F 6
Truk (isls.), 18,792 ....F 5
Tuamotu (archipelago), 6,148 ....M 7
Tubuai (isl.), 1,398 ....L 8
Tubuai (Austral) (isls.), 5,053 ....L 8
Tureia (atoll), 40 ....M 7
Tutuila (isl.), 25,557 ....J 7
Tuvalu, 5,887 ....H 6
Uahuka (isl.) ....N 6
Uapou (isl.), 1,414 ....M 6
Ujelang (atoll), 281 ....F 5
Ulithi (atoll), 523 ....D 5
Upolu (isl.), 94,691 ....J 7
Uturoa, 2,394 ....L 7
Uvéa (isl.) ....H 7
Vahitahi (atoll), 109 ....N 7
Vaitupu (atoll), 876 ....H 6
Vanua Levu (isl.), 71,933 ....H 7
Vava'u Group (isls.), 13,533 ....J 7
Victoria (state), 3,713,200 ....E 9
Vila, 7,000 ....G 7
Viti Levu (isl.), 341,784 ....H 7
Wagga Wagga, 25,819 ....E 9

Wake (isl.), 437 ....G 4
Wallis (isls.), 6,000 ....J 7
Wallis and Futuna, 9,000 ....J 7
Wanganui, 36,400 ....H 9
Warrnambool, 17,499 ....D 9
Washington (isl.), 437 ....L 5
Wau, 1,072 ....E 6
Wellington, 134,400 ....H10
Western Australia (state), 1,148,100 ...C 8
Western Samoa, 159,000 ....J 7
Wewak, 5,090 ....E 6
Whangarei, 29,600 ....H 9

Whyalla, 22,121 ....D 9
Willis (islets) ....F 7
Wiluna, 4219 ....C 8
Woleai (atoll), 586 ....E 5
Wollongong, *162,153 ....F 9
Wonthaggi, 4,026 ....D 9
Woomera, 4,745 ....D 9
Wotje (atoll), 976 ....H 5
Wyndham, 1,156 ....C 7
Yap (isl.), 4,380 ....D 5

*City and suburbs.
†Population of metropolitan area.
‡Population of sub-district.

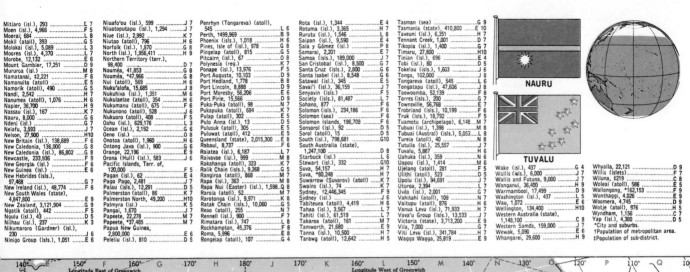

NAURU

TUVALU

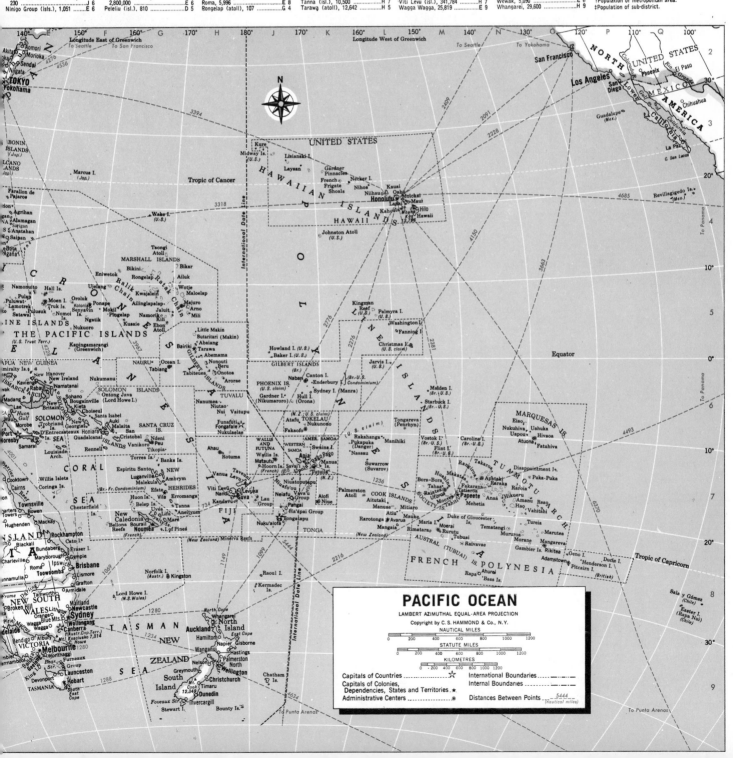

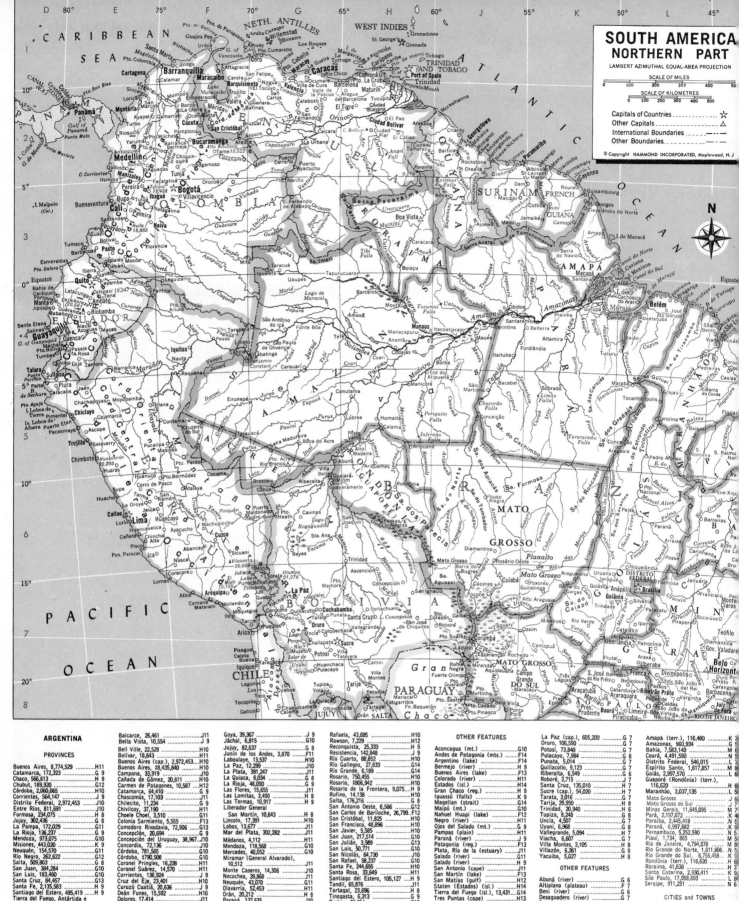

SOUTH AMERICA NORTHERN PART
LAMBERT AZIMUTHAL EQUAL-AREA PROJECTION

SCALE OF MILES
0 100 200 300 400 500

SCALE OF KILOMETRES
0 100 200 300 400 500

Capitals of Countries .... ☆
Other Capitals .... △
International Boundaries ...._._._
Other Boundaries ...._.._.._

© Copyright HAMMOND INCORPORATED, Maplewood, N.J

ARGENTINA

PROVINCES

Buenos Aires, 8,774,529	H11
Catamarca, 172,323	G 9
Chaco, 566,613	H 9
Chubut, 189,920	G12
Córdoba, 2,060,065	H10
Corrientes, 564,147	J 9
Distrito Federal, 2,972,453	J10
Entre Ríos, 811,691	J10
Formosa, 234,075	H 8
Jujuy, 302,436	G 8
La Pampa, 172,029	G11
La Rioja, 136,237	G 9
Mendoza, 973,075	G10
Misiones, 443,020	K 9
Neuquén, 154,570	G11
Río Negro, 262,622	G12
Salta, 509,803	G 8
San Juan, 384,284	G10
San Luis, 183,460	G10
Santa Cruz, 84,457	G13
Santa Fe, 2,135,583	H 9
Santiago del Estero, 495,419	H 9
Tierra del Fuego, Antártida e Islas del Atlántico Sur (terr.), 15,658	G14
Tucumán, 765,962	G 9

CITIES and TOWNS

Alta Gracia, 24,371	H10
Añatuya, 11,918	H 9
Andalgalá, 5,687	G 9
Ayacucho, 12,046	J11
Azul, 36,023	J11
Bahía Blanca, 182,158	H11
Balcarce, 26,461	J11
Bella Vista, 10,554	J 9
Bell Ville, 22,528	H10
Bolívar, 18,643	H11
Buenos Aires (cap.), 2,972,453	J10
Buenos Aires, 18,435,840	H10
Campana, 33,919	J10
Cañada de Gómez, 20,611	H10
Carmen de Patagones, 10,587	G12
Catamarca, 64,410	G 9
Chascomús, 17,103	J10
Chilecito, 11,234	G 9
Chivilcoy, 37,190	H10
Choele Choel, 3,510	G11
Colonia Sarmiento, 5,555	F13
Comodoro Rivadavia, 72,906	G13
Concepción, 20,694	G 9
Concepción del Uruguay, 38,967	J10
Concordia, 72,136	J10
Córdoba, 781,565	G10
Córdoba, 8790,508	G10
Coronel Pringles, 16,226	H11
Coronel Suárez, 14,570	H11
Corrientes, 136,924	J 9
Cruz del Eje, 23,401	H10
Curuzú Cuatiá, 20,636	J 9
Deán Funes, 15,592	H10
Dolores, 17,414	J11
Embarcación, 7,207	H 8
Empedrado, 4,269	J 9
Esperanza, 17,536	H10
Esquel, 13,771	F12
Formosa, 61,071	J 9
General Acha, 6,270	G11
General Alvear, 10,512	J11
General Alvear, 17,277	G11
General Juan Madariaga, 10,280	J11
General Pico, 21,897	H11
General Roca, 29,320	G11
Godoy Cruz, 112,481	G10

Goya, 39,367	J 9
Rawson, 7,229	H12
Jáchal, 6,815	G10
Jujuy, 82,637	G 8
Junín de los Andes, 3,870	F11
Laboulaye, 13,537	H10
La Paz, 12,299	J10
La Plata, 391,247	J11
La Quiaca, 6,034	G 8
La Rioja, 46,090	G 9
Las Flores, 15,655	J11
Las Lomitas, 3,490	H 8
Las Termas, 10,917	H 9
Liberador General San Martín, 10,643	H10
Lincoln, 17,391	H10
Lobos, 13,577	J11
Mar del Plata, 302,282	J11
Médanos, 4,112	H11
Mendoza, 118,568	G10
Mercedes, 44,630	G10
Miramar (General Alvarado), 10,512	J11
Monte Caseros, 14,306	J10
Necochea, 39,868	J11
Neuquén, 43,070	G11
Olavarría, 52,453	H11
Orán, 20,212	H 8
Paraná, 127,635	H10
Paso de los Libres, 17,341	J 9
Pergamino, 56,078	H10
Perico, 7,096	H 8
Plaza Huincul, 4,714	G11
Posadas, 97,514	J 9
Presidencia Roque Sáenz Peña, 38,620	H 9
Puerto Deseado, 3,735	G13
Puerto Madryn, 6,115	G12
Punta Alta, 36,926	H11
Quimilí, 4,076	H 9

Rafaela, 43,695	H10
Reconquista, 25,333	H 9
Resistencia, 142,848	J 9
Río Cuarto, 88,852	H10
Río Gallegos, 27,833	G14
Río Grande, 6,189	G14
Rosario, 750,455	H10
Rosario, 1806,942	H10
Rosario de la Frontera, 9,075	H 9
Rufino, 14,138	H10
Salta, 176,216	G 8
San Antonio Oeste, 6,566	G12
San Carlos de Bariloche, 26,799	F12
San Cristóbal, 11,825	H10
San Francisco, 48,896	H10
San Javier, 5,585	H10
San Juan, 217,514	G10
San Julián, 2,553	G13
San Luis, 50,771	G10
San Nicolás, 64,730	H10
San Rafael, 58,237	G10
Santa Fe, 244,655	H10
Santa Rosa, 33,649	H11
Santiago del Estero, 105,127	H 9
Tandil, 65,876	J11
Tartagal, 23,696	H 8
Tinogasta, 8,413	G 9
Trelew, 24,214	G12
Trenque Lauquen, 18,169	H11
Tres Arroyos, 37,991	H11
Tucumán, 321,567	G 9
Tunuyán, 10,813	G10
Uspallata, 5,373	G10
Venado Tuerto, 35,677	H10
Victoria, 17,046	H10
Victorica, 2,529	G11
Viedma, 12,888	H11
Villa Ángela, 17,091	H 9
Villa Dolores, 19,010	G10
Villa María, 56,067	H10
Zapala, 11,385	F11

OTHER FEATURES

Aconcagua (mt.)	G10
Andes de Patagonia (mts.)	F14
Argentino (lake)	F14
Bermejo (river)	H 9
Buenos Aires (lake)	F13
Colorado (river)	G11
Gran Chaco (reg.)	H 9
Iguassú (falls)	K 9
Magellan (strait)	G14
Maipú (mt.)	G10
Nahuel Huapi (lake)	F12
Negro (river)	G11
Ojos del Salado (mt.)	G 9
Pampas (plain)	H11
Paraná (river)	H 9
Patagonia (reg.)	F13
Plata, Río de la (estuary)	J11
Salado (river)	G11
Salado (river)	H 9
San Antonio (lake)	F13
San Martín (lake)	F13
San Matías (gulf)	H12
Staten (Estados) (isl.)	H14
Tierra del Fuego (isl.), 13,431	G14
Tres Puntas (cape)	G13
Uruguay (river)	J10
Valdés (pen.)	H12

BOLIVIA

CITIES and TOWNS

Achacachi, 3,621	G 7
Camiri, 4,969	G 7
Challapata, 2,529	G 7
Cobija, 3,010	F 5
Cochabamba, 169,930	G 7
Corocoro, 4,431	G 7

La Paz (cap.), 605,200	G 7
Oruro, 106,590	G 7
Potosí, 73,840	G 7
Pulacayo, 7,984	G 7
Punata, 5,014	G 7
Quillacollo, 9,123	G 7
Riberalta, 6,549	G 5
Roboré, 3,715	J 7
Santa Cruz, 135,010	H 7
Sucre (cap.), 54,020	G 7
Tarata, 3,016	G 7
Tarija, 29,950	G 7
Trinidad, 20,940	H 6
Tupiza, 8,248	G 7
Uncía, 4,507	G 7
Uyuni, 6,968	G 7
Vallegrande, 5,094	H 7
Viacha, 6,607	G 7
Villa Montes, 3,105	H 8
Villazón, 6,261	G 7
Yacuiba, 5,027	H 8

OTHER FEATURES

Abuná (river)	G 6
Altiplano (plateau)	G 6
Beni (river)	G 6
Desaguadero (river)	G 7
Grande (river)	H 7
Guaporé (river)	H 6
Illampu (mt.)	G 7
Mamoré (river)	H 6
Poopó (lake)	G 7
Real, Cordillera (mts.)	G 7
Titicaca (lake)	F 7

BRAZIL

STATES

Acre, 218,006	F 5
Alagoas, 1,606,174	N 5

Amapá (terr.), 116,480	K 3
Amazonas, 960,934	G 5
Bahia, 7,583,140	M 6
Ceará, 4,491,590	N 5
Distrito Federal, 546,015	L 7
Espírito Santo, 1,617,857	M 7
Goiás, 2,997,570	L 6
Guaporé (Rondônia) (terr.), 116,620	H 6
Maranhão, 3,037,135	L 5
Mato Grosso	J 6
Mato Grosso do Sul	K 7
Minas Gerais, 11,645,095	M 7
Pará, 2,197,072	K 4
Paraíba, 2,445,419	N 5
Paraná, 6,997,682	K 8
Pernambuco, 5,252,590	N 5
Piauí, 1,734, 865	M 5
Rio de Janeiro, 4,794,578	M 8
Rio Grande do Norte, 1,611,606	N 5
Rio Grande do Sul, 6,755,458	K 9
Rondônia (terr.), 116,620	H 6
Roraima, 41,638	H 3
Santa Catarina, 2,930,411	K 9
São Paulo, 17,958,693	L 8
Sergipe, 911,251	N 6

CITIES and TOWNS

Abaetetuba, 19,197	L 4
Alagoinhas, 53,891	N 6
Alegrete, 45,522	J 9
Anápolis, 89,405	L 7
Aquidauana, 16,534	J 7
Aracaju, 179,512	N 6
Aracati, 14,509	N 4
Araçatuba, 85,660	M 7
Araçuaí, 9,180	M 7
Arapiraca, 43,875	N 5
Araranguá, 12,261	L 9
Araraquara, 82,607	L 8

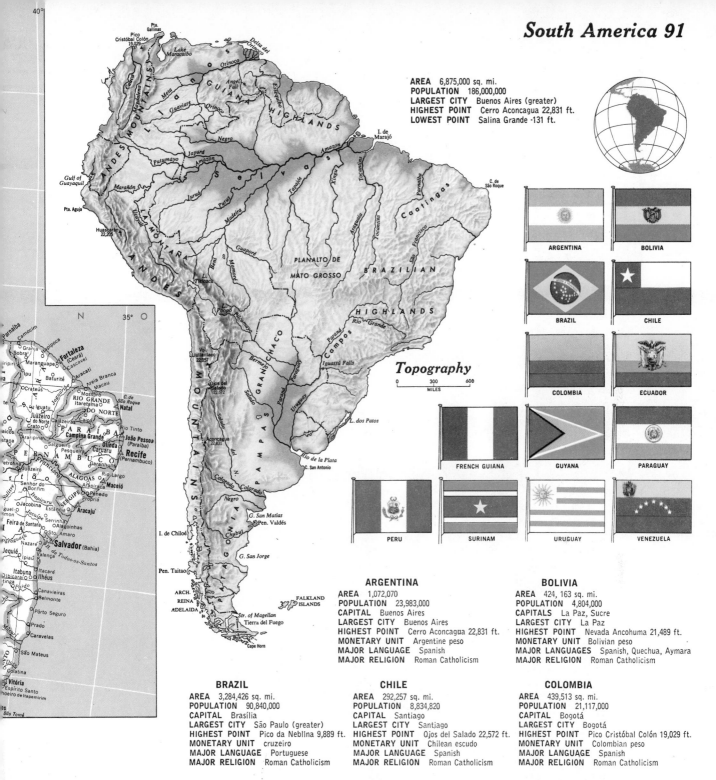

AREA 6,875,000 sq. mi.
POPULATION 186,000,000
LARGEST CITY Buenos Aires (greater)
HIGHEST POINT Cerro Aconcagua 22,831 ft.
LOWEST POINT Salina Grande -131 ft.

Topography

0   300   600
MILES

ARGENTINA

AREA 1,072,070
POPULATION 23,983,000
CAPITAL Buenos Aires
LARGEST CITY Buenos Aires
HIGHEST POINT Cerro Aconcagua 22,831 ft.
MONETARY UNIT Argentine peso
MAJOR LANGUAGE Spanish
MAJOR RELIGION Roman Catholicism

BOLIVIA

AREA 424, 163 sq. mi.
POPULATION 4,804,000
CAPITALS La Paz, Sucre
LARGEST CITY La Paz
HIGHEST POINT Nevada Ancohuma 21,489 ft.
MONETARY UNIT Bolivian peso
MAJOR LANGUAGES Spanish, Quechua, Aymara
MAJOR RELIGION Roman Catholicism

BRAZIL

AREA 3,284,426 sq. mi.
POPULATION 90,840,000
CAPITAL Brasília
LARGEST CITY São Paulo (greater)
HIGHEST POINT Pico da Neblina 9,889 ft.
MONETARY UNIT cruzeiro
MAJOR LANGUAGE Portuguese
MAJOR RELIGION Roman Catholicism

CHILE

AREA 292,257 sq. mi.
POPULATION 8,834,820
CAPITAL Santiago
LARGEST CITY Santiago
HIGHEST POINT Ojos del Salado 22,572 ft.
MONETARY UNIT Chilean escudo
MAJOR LANGUAGE Spanish
MAJOR RELIGION Roman Catholicism

COLOMBIA

AREA 439,513 sq. mi.
POPULATION 21,117,000
CAPITAL Bogotá
LARGEST CITY Bogotá
HIGHEST POINT Pico Cristóbal Colón 19,029 ft.
MONETARY UNIT Colombian peso
MAJOR LANGUAGE Spanish
MAJOR RELIGION Roman Catholicism

ECUADOR

AREA 109,483 sq. mi.
POPULATION 6,144,000
CAPITAL Quito
LARGEST CITY Guayaquil
HIGHEST POINT Chimborazo
MONETARY UNIT sucre
MAJOR LANGUAGES Spanish
MAJOR RELIGION Roman Cat

FRENCH GUIANA

AREA 35,135 sq. mi.
POPULATION 48,000
CAPITAL Cayenne
LARGEST CITY Cayenne
HIGHEST POINT 2,723 ft.
MONETARY UNIT French franc
MAJOR LANGUAGE French
MAJOR RELIGIONS Roman Catholicism, Protestantism

GUYANA

AREA 83,000 sq. mi.
POPULATION 763,000
CAPITAL Georgetown
LARGEST CITY Georgetown
HIGHEST POINT Mt. Roraima 9,094 ft.
MONETARY UNIT Guyana dollar
MAJOR LANGUAGES English, Hindi
MAJOR RELIGIONS Christianity, Hinduism, Islam

PARAGUAY

AREA 157,047 sq. mi.
POPULATION 2,314,000
CAPITAL Asunción
LARGEST CITY Asunción
HIGHEST POINT Amambay Range 2,264 ft.
MONETARY UNIT guaraní
MAJOR LANGUAGES Spanish, Guaraní
MAJOR RELIGION Roman Catholicism

PERU

AREA 496,222 sq. mi.
POPULATION 13,586,300
CAPITAL Lima
LARGEST CITY Lima
HIGHEST POINT Huascarán 22,205 ft.
MONETARY UNIT sol
MAJOR LANGUAGES Spanish, Quechua, Aymara
MAJOR RELIGION Roman Catholicism

SURINAM

AREA 55,144 sq. mi.
POPULATION 389,000
CAPITAL Paramaribo
LARGEST CITY Paramaribo
HIGHEST POINT Julianatop 4,200 ft.
MONETARY UNIT Surinam guilder
MAJOR LANGUAGES Dutch, Hindi, Indonesian
MAJOR RELIGIONS Christianity, Islam, Hinduism

URUGUAY

AREA 72,172 sq. mi.
POPULATION 2,900,000
CAPITAL Montevideo
LARGEST CITY Montevideo
HIGHEST POINT Mirador Nacional 1,644 ft.
MONETARY UNIT Uruguayan peso
MAJOR LANGUAGE Spanish
MAJOR RELIGION Roman Catholicism

VENEZUELA

AREA 352,143 sq. mi.
POPULATION 10,398,907
CAPITAL Caracas
LARGEST CITY Caracas
HIGHEST POINT Pico Bolívar 16,427 ft.
MONETARY UNIT bolívar
MAJOR LANGUAGE Spanish
MAJOR RELIGION Roman Catholicism

Agriculture, Industry and Resources

MAJOR MINERAL OCCURRENCES

Al	Bauxite
Ag	Silver
Au	Gold
Be	Beryl
C	Coal
Cr	Chromium
Cu	Copper
D	Diamonds
Em	Emeralds
Fe	Iron Ore
G	Natural Gas
Hg	Mercury
Id	Iodine
Mi	Mica
Mn	Manganese
Mo	Molybdenum
N	Nitrates
Na	Salt
Ni	Nickel
O	Petroleum
P	Phosphates
Pb	Lead
Pt	Platinum
Q	Quartz Crystal
S	Sulfur
Sb	Antimony
Sn	Tin
U	Uranium
V	Vanadium
W	Tungsten
Zn	Zinc

Water Power

Major Industrial Areas

AMUAY–PUNTA CARDÓN
Oil Refining

MEDELLÍN
Textiles, Clothing, Leather Goods

BOGOTÁ
Textiles, Leather Goods, Cement, Electrical Equipment

CARACAS
Textiles, Chemicals, Automobiles

CIUDAD GUAYANA
Iron & Steel, Aluminum

LIMA–CALLAO
Textiles, Chemicals, Leather Goods

CÓRDOBA
Automobiles, Aircraft, Food Processing, Chemicals, Cement

SANTIAGO–VALPARAÍSO
Textiles, Chemicals, Food Processing, Metal Products, Oil Refining, Leather Goods

CONCEPCIÓN
Iron & Steel, Food Processing, Textiles, Oil Refining

BUENOS AIRES–ROSARIO
Food Processing, Textiles, Machinery, Shipbuilding, Oil Refining, Chemicals

BELO HORIZONTE
Iron & Steel, Textiles, Cement, Metal Products

RIO DE JANEIRO
Iron & Steel, Chemicals, Food Processing, Textiles, Glass Products, Cement, Oil Refining

SÃO PAULO–SANTOS
Food Processing, Textiles, Chemicals, Iron & Steel, Machinery, Motor Vehicles, Oil Refining

DOMINANT LAND USE

- Wheat, Livestock
- Wheat, Corn, Livestock
- Cereals, Livestock
- Diversified Tropical Crops (chiefly plantation agriculture)
- Truck Farming, Horticulture, Special Crops
- Upland Cultivated Areas
- Intensive Livestock Ranching
- Upland Livestock Grazing, Limited Agriculture
- Extensive Livestock Ranching
- Forests
- Nonagricultural Land

South America 93

O'Higgins (lake) F13
Ojos del Salado (mt.) ....G 9
Penas (gulf) E13
Taitao (pen.) E13
Tierra del Fuego (isl.), 7,086....G14

COLOMBIA

CITIES and TOWNS

Aguadas, 9,449 ....E 2
Antioquia, 7,072 ....E 2
Arauca, 4,280 ....F 2
Ayapel, 8,094 ....E 2
Barbacoas, 4,653 ....E 3
Barrancabermeja, 82,171 ....F 2
Barranquilla, 664,533 ....F 1
Bogotá (cap.), 2,664,750 ....F 3
Bogotá, ‡3,182,013 ....F 3
Bolívar, 4,430 ....E 3
Bucaramanga 328,328 ....F 2
Buenaventura, 115,770 ....E 3
Buga, 71,016 ....E 3
Calamar, 5,923 ....F 1
Cali, 898,253 ....E 3
Cartagena, 289,649 ....E 1
Chiquinquirá, 37,504 ....F 2
Ciénaga, 43,048 ....F 1
Cúcuta, 216,509 ....F 2
El Banco, 20,708 ....F 2
Facatativá, 27,238 ....F 3
Florencia, 17,709 ....E 3
Gamarra, 5,082 ....F 2
Guapí, 5,005 ....E 3
Ibagué, 180,734 ....E 3
Ipiales, 30,871 ....E 3
Itsmina, 5,987 ....E 2
La Gloria, 2,684 ....F 2
Leticia, 4,013 ....F 4
Lorica, 17,586 ....E 2
Magangué, 40,613 ....E 2
Manizales, 197,246 ....E 2
Medellín, 1,064,741 ....E 2
Medellín, ‡1,244,893 ....E 2
Mocoa, 2,571 ....E 3
Mompós, 14,120 ....F 2
Montería, 89,552 ....E 2
Natagaima, 7,867 ....F 3
Neiva, 105,595 ....F 3
Ocaña, 37,935 ....F 2
Palmira, 140,481 ....E 3
Pamplona, 28,911 ....F 2
Pasto, 119,339 ....E 3
Pereira, 174,902 ....E 3
Popayán, 77,669 ....E 3
Puerto Berrío, 19,258 ....E 2
Puerto Colombia, 9,479 ....E 1
Puerto Leguízamo, 3,014 ....F 4
Puerto Wilches, 5,088, ...F 2
Quibdó, 27,318 ....E 2
Riohacha, 19,469 ....F 1
San Marcos, 10,890 ....E 2
Santa Marta, 126,719 ....F 1
Santander, 13,625 ....E 3
Sincelejo, 73,465 ....E 2
Sogamoso, 48,891 ....F 2
Sonsón, 15,206 ....E 2
Tame, 3,063 ....F 2
Tuluá, 86,736 ....E 3
Tumaco, 38,742 ....E 3
Tunja, 51,301 ....F 2
Turbo, 13,424 ....E 2
Uribia, 10,072 ....F 1
Villavicencio, 60,211 ....F 3
Yarumal, 18,849 ....E 2

OTHER FEATURES

Alto Ritacuva (mt.) ....F 2
Apaporis (river) ....F 3
Caquetá (river) ....F 4
Casanare (river) ....F 2
Cauca (river) ....E 2
Central, Cordillera (mts.) ....E 2
Guainía (river) ....G 3
Guajira (pen.) ....F 1
Guaviare (river) ....F 3
Huila (mt.) ....E 3
Inírida (river) ....G 3
Magdalena (river) ....F 2
Meta (river) ....G 2
Occidental, Cordillera (mts.) ....E 3
Oriental, Cordillera (mts.) ....F 2
Orinoco, Llanos del (plain) ......G 2
Putumayo (river) ....F 4
Tolima (mt.) ....E 3
Vaupés (river) ....F 3
Vichada (river) ....F 3

ECUADOR

CITIES and TOWNS

Alausí, 7,155 ....E 4
Ambato, 77,052 ....E 4
Azogues, 10,939 ....E 4
Babahoyo, 28,345 ....D 4
Bahía de Caráquez, 11,327 ....D 4
Cayambe, 11,042 ....E 4
Celica, 3,091 ....D 4
Cuenca, 104,667 ....E 4
Esmeraldas, 60,132 ....D 3
Guaranda, 11,387 ....E 4
Guayaquil, 814,064 ....D 4
Ibarra, 41,057 ....E 3
Jipijapa, 19,719 ....D 4
Latacunga, 22,106 ....E 4
Loja, 47,268 ....E 4
Machala, 68,379 ....D 4
Manta, 63,514 ....D 4
Otavalo, 13,848 ....E 3
Pasaje, 20,822 ....E 4
Portoviejo, 59,404 ....D 4
Quito (cap.), 597,133 ....E 4
Riobamba, 58,029 ....E 4
Salinas, 12,243 ....D 4
Santa Elena, 7,762 ....D 4
Santa Rosa, 18,846 ....E 4
Tulcán, 24,443 ....E 3
Zamora, 2,700 ....E 4

OTHER FEATURES

Chimborazo (mt.) ....E 4
Cotopaxi (mt.) ....E 4
Guayaquil (gulf) ....D 4
Morona (river) ....E 4
Napo (river) ....F 4
Occidental, Cordillera (mts.) ....E 4
Pastaza (river) ....E 4
Real, Cordillera (mts.) ....E 4
Santiago (river) ....E 4

FALKLAND ISLANDS

CITIES and TOWNS

Stanley (cap.), 1,079 ....J14

OTHER FEATURES

East Falkland (isl.), 1,577 ....J14
Falkland (sound) H14
West Falkland (isl.), 380 ....H14

FRENCH GUIANA

CITIES and TOWNS

Cayenne (cap.), 19,668 ....K 2
Saint-Laurent-du-Maroni, 3,486..K 2
Sinnamary, 1,355 ....K 2

OTHER FEATURES

Devils (isl.) ....K 2
Maroni (river) ....K 3
Oyapock (river) ....K 3

GUYANA

CITIES and TOWNS

Bartica, 2,352 ....J 2
Georgetown (cap.), ‡195,250 ......J 2
Mackenzie, †30,000 ....J 2
Mahaica, 8,646 ....J 2
New Amsterdam, 20,000 ....J 2
Rosignol, 1,204 ....J 2

OTHER FEATURES

Courantyne (river) ....J 3
Cuyuni (river) ....H 2
Essequibo (river) ....J 2
Kaieteur (falls) ....J 3
Mazaruni (river) ....H 2
Roraima (mt.) ....H 2
Rupununi (river) ....J 3

PARAGUAY

CITIES and TOWNS

Asunción (cap.), 392,753 ....J 9
Asunción, ‡563,681 ....J 9
Caapucú, 1,400 ....J 9
Caazapá, 3,117 ....J 9
Carapeguá, 3,418 ....J 9
Concepción, 19,200 ....J 8
Encarnación, 23,343 ....J 9
Fuerte Olimpo, 3,061 ....J 8
General Artigas, 3,547 ....J 9
Horquèta, 4,240 ....J 8
Luque, 13,932 ....J 8
Mariscal Estigarribia, 1,508 ......H 8
Paraguarí, 5,036 ....J 9
Pilar, 12,440 ....J 9
San Pedro, 3,158 ....J 8
Tacurupucú, 2,881 ....J 9
Villarrica, 17,448 ....J 9

OTHER FEATURES

Gran Chaco (reg.) ....H 8
Paraguay (river) ....J 8
Paraná (river) ....K 9
Pilcomayo (river) ....H 8

PERU

CITIES and TOWNS

Abancay, 12,172 ....F 6
Arequipa, 304,653 ....F 7
Ascope, 4,763 ....E 5
Atico, 3,053 ....F 7
Ayacucho, 34,593 ....F 6
Cajamarca, 37,608 ....E 5
Callao, 296,220 ....E 6
Camaná, 10,121 ....F 7
Cañete, 8,751 ....E 6
Catacaos, 19,155 ....D 5
Cerro de Pasco, 47,178 ....E 6
Chachapoyas, 10,418 ....E 5
Chiclayo, 189,685 ....E 5
Chimbote, 159,045 ....E 5
Chincha Alta, 28,785 ....E 6
Contamaná, 5,088 ....F 5
Coracora, 4,508 ....F 7
Cuzco, 120,881 ....F 6
Huacho, 36,697 ....E 6
Huancavelica, 15,916 ....E 6
Huancayo, 115,693 ....E 6
Huánuco, 41,123 ....E 6
Huarás, 29,719 ....E 5
Ica, 73,883 ....E 6
Ilo, 21,551 ....F 7
Iquitos, 111,327 ....F 4
Jaén, 13,912 ....E 5
Jauja, 13,936 ....E 6
Juli, 5,398 ....G 7
Juliaca, 38,475 ....F 7
La Oroya, 25,908 ....E 6
Lima (cap.), 2,836,374 ....E 6
Lima, ‡3,317,648 ....E 6
Lurín, 12,766 ....E 6
Mollendo, 15,373 ....F 7
Moquegua, 16,959 ....F 7
Moyobamba, 10,004 ....E 5
Nasca, 21,025 ....F 6
Nauta, 3,768 ....F 4
Pacasmayo, 15,381 ....D 5
Paita, 14,875 ....D 5
Pimentel, 7,742 ....D 5
Pisco, 41,429 ....E 6
Piura, 126,702 ....D 5
Pucallpa, 57,525 ....E 5
Puerto Eten, 2,521 ....D 5
Puerto Maldonado, 6,419 ....G 6
Puno, 41,166 ....F 7
Requena, 7,300 ....F 5
Salaverry, 5,316 ....E 5
San Ramón, 4,646 ....F 6
Sicuani, 12,956 ....F 6
Sullana, 60,112 ....D 4
Supe, 15,623 ....E 6
Tacna, 55,752 ....F 7
Talara, 29,884 ....D 4
Tarma, 28,100 ....E 6
Trujillo, 241,882 ....E 5
Tumbes, 32,972 ....D 4

OTHER FEATURES

Aguja (point) ....D 5
Altiplano (plateau) ....F 7
Apurímac (river) ....F 6
Central, Cordillera (mts.) ....E 5
Huascarán (mt.) ....E 5
Madre de Dios (river) ....G 6
Marañón (river) ....E 4
Misti, El (mt.) ....F 7
Montaña, La (reg.) ....F 5
Napo (river) ....F 4
Occidental, Cordillera (mts.) ....F 6
Oriental, Cordillera (mts.) ....E 5
Paracas (pen.), 1,213 ....E 6
Putumayo (river) ....F 4
Real, Cordillera (mts.) ....F 6
Sechura (bay) ....D 5
Titicaca (lake) ....F 7
Ucayali (river) ....E 5
Urubamba (river) ....F 6
Vilcanota (mt.) ....F 6

SURINAM

CITIES and TOWNS

Albina, 1,000 ....K 3
Moengo, 2,100 ....K 3
Nieuw-Nickerie, 7,400 ....J 2
Paramaribo (cap.), 135,000 ......K 2
Totness, 1,300 ....J 2

OTHER FEATURES

Coeroeni (river) ....J 3
Tapanahoni (river) ....J 3

URUGUAY

CITIES and TOWNS

Artigas, 23,781 ....J10
Bella Unión, 4,955 ....J10
Canelones, 14,180 ....J10
Carmelo, 12,707 ....J10
Colonia, 12,839 ....J10
Dolores, 12,483 ....J10
Durazno, 22,495 ....J10
Florida, 20,923 ....J10
Fray Bentos, 20,755 ....J10
Juan L. Lacaze, 11,022 ....J10
Maldonado, 15,361 ....K10
Melo, 33,378 ....K10
Mercedes, 31,352 ....J10
Minas, 31,388 ....K10
Montevideo (cap.), ‡1,500,000 ....J11
Paso de los Toros 11,008 ....J10
Paysandú, 52,472 ....J10
Rivera, 41,263 ....J10
Rocha, 19,063 ....K10
Salto, 57,958 ....J10
San José, 27,478 ....J10
Tacuarembó, 29,058 ....J10
Treinta y Tres, 22,422 ....K10
Trinidad, 15,460 ....J10

OTHER FEATURES

Mirim (lagoon) K10
Negro (river) J10
Plata, Río de la (estuary) J11
Uruguay (river) ....J 9

VENEZUELA

CITIES and TOWNS

Altagracia, 21,084 ....F 1
Aragua de Barcelona, 9,614 ......H 2
Barcelona, 76,410 ....H 2
Barinas, 56,329 ....G 2
Barquisimeto, 334,333 ....F 2
Caicara, 10,804 ....G 2
Calabozo, 37,282 ....G 2
Caracas (cap.), 1,035,499 ....G 1
Caracas, ‡2,183,935 ....G 1
Carora, 36,115 ....F 1
Carúpano, 50,935 ....H 1
Ciudad Bolívar, 103,728 ....H 2
Ciudad Guayana, 143,240 ....H 2
Coro, 68,701 ....G 1
Cumaná, 119,751 ....H 1
El Callao, 6,113 ....H 2
El Tigre, 49,801 ....H 2
El Tocuyo, 24,065 ....G 2
Encontrados, 12,502 ....F 2
Guanare, 37,715 ....G 2
La Asunción, 6,334 ....H 1
La Grita, 23,371 ....F 2
La Guaira, 20,344 ....G 1
La Urbana, 2,538 ....G 2
Maracaibo, 650,002 ....F 1
Maracaibo, ‡677,122 ....F 1
Maracay, 255,134 ....G 1
Maturín, 121,662 ....H 2
Mérida, 74,214 ....F 2
Nirgua, 21,003 ....G 2
Ocumare, 24,229 ....G 1
Puerto Ayacucho, 10,417 ....G 2
Puerto Cabello, 73,380 ....G 1
Puerto Cumarebo, 13,339 ....G 1
Puerto La Cruz, 63,276 ....H 1
Río Caribe, 21,387 ....H 1
Río Chico, 8,356 ....G 1
San Carlos, 21,029 ....G 2
San Cristóbal, 152,239 ....F 2
San Felipe, 43,801 ....G 1
San Fernando, 38,960 ....G 2
San Fernando de Atabapo, 3,568 ....G 3
Tinaquillo, 18,552 ....G 2
Trujillo, 25,921 ....F 2
Tucacas, 7,738 ....G 1
Tucupita, 21,417 ....H 2
Valencia, 367,154 ....G 2
Valera, 74,353 ....F 2
Valle de la Pascua, 36,809 ....G 2
Villa de Cura, 27,832 ....G 2

OTHER FEATURES

Angel (fall) ....H 2
Arauca (river) ....G 2
Apure (river) ....F 2
Bolívar (mt.) ....F 2
Caroní (river) ....H 2
Casiquiare, Brazo (river) ....G 3
Maracaibo (lake) ....F 2
Margarita (isl.), 113,967 ....H 1
Mérida, Cordillera de (mts.) ....F 2
Orinoco (river) ....G 2
Orinoco, Llanos del (plain) ......G 2
Paraguana (pen.), 134,401 ....F 1
Paria (gulf) ....H 1
Roques, Los (isls.), 438 ....G 1
Serpents Mouth (strait) ....H 2
Tortuga, La (isl.), 25 ....G 1
Venezuela (gulf) ....F 1

*Population of commune.
‡City and suburbs.
†Population of municipality.

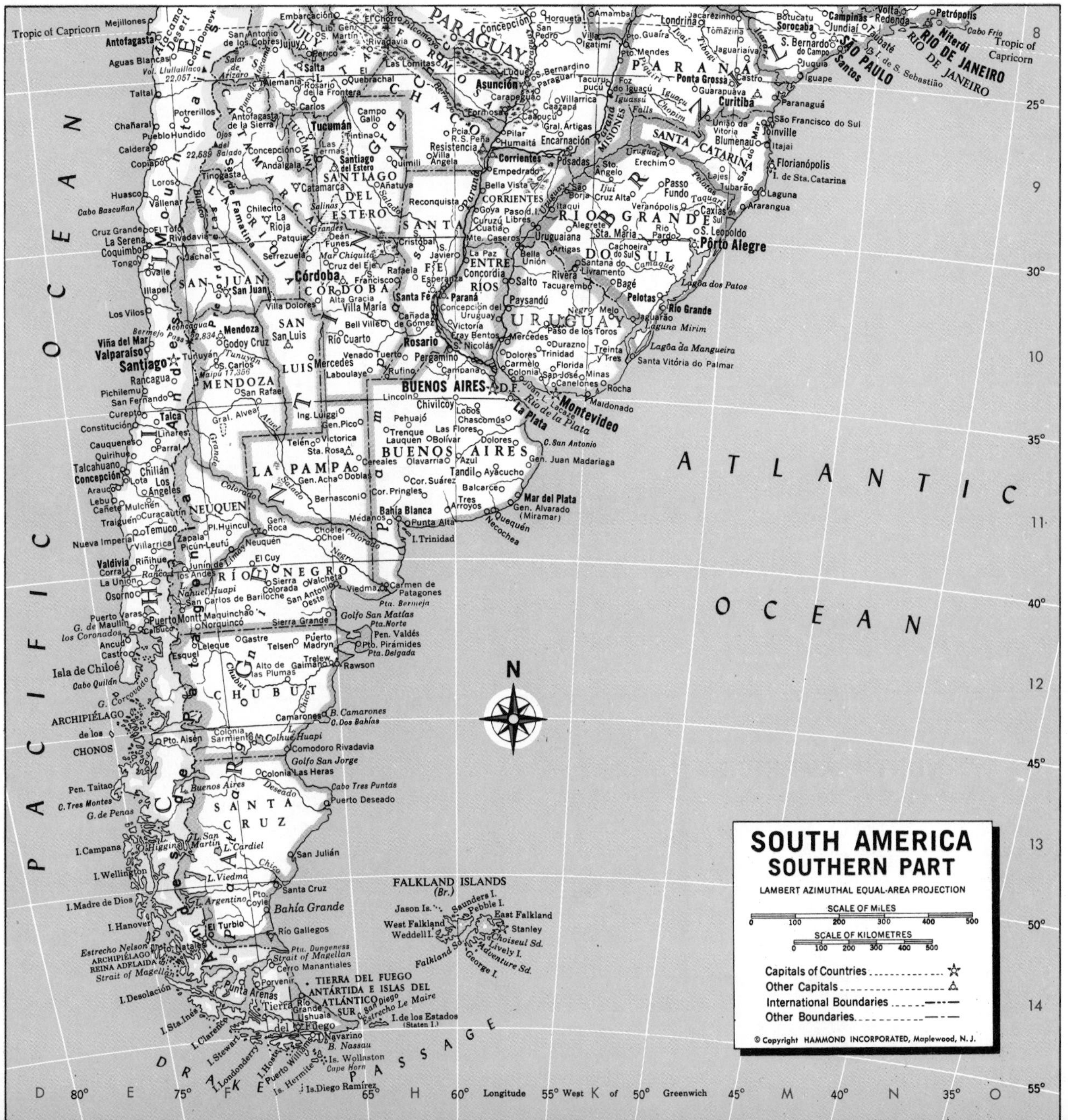

SOUTH AMERICA
SOUTHERN PART
LAMBERT AZIMUTHAL EQUAL-AREA PROJECTION
SCALE OF MILES
SCALE OF KILOMETRES
Capitals of Countries
Other Capitals
International Boundaries
Other Boundaries
© Copyright HAMMOND INCORPORATED, Maplewood, N. J.
PACIFIC OCEAN
ATLANTIC OCEAN

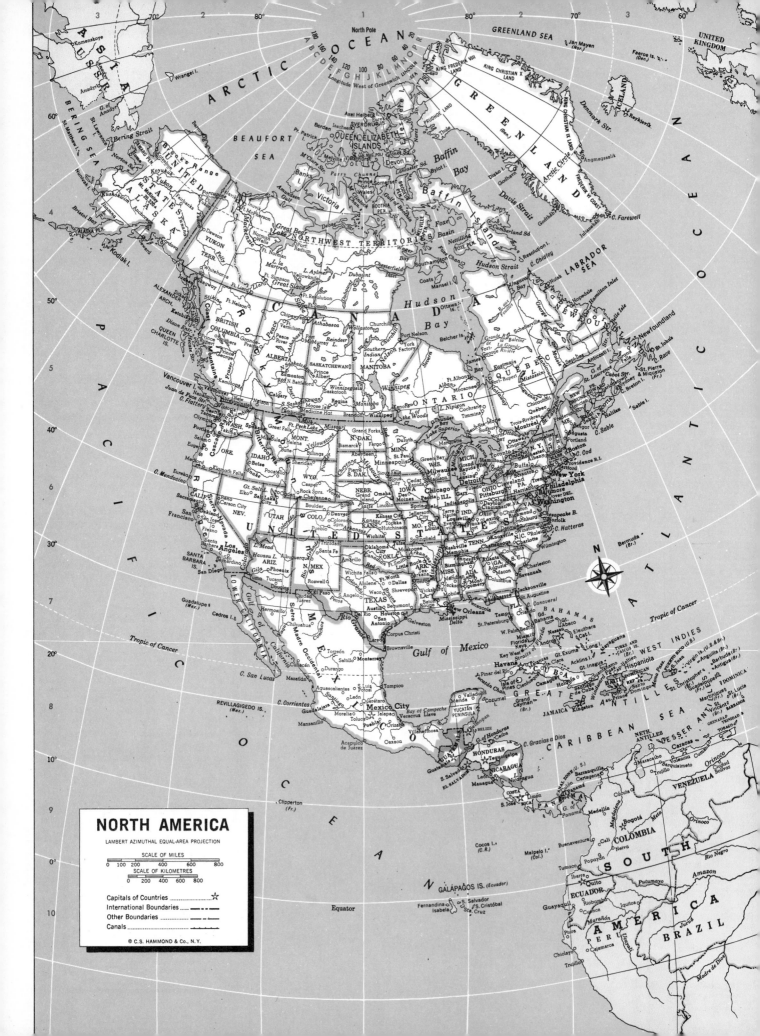

NORTH AMERICA

LAMBERT AZIMUTHAL EQUAL-AREA PROJECTION

SCALE OF MILES

0 100 200   400   600   800

SCALE OF KILOMETRES

0   200 400 600 800

Capitals of Countries .... ☆
International Boundaries ...... — ∙ — ∙ —
Other Boundaries .... — ∙ ∙ — ∙ ∙ —
Canals ....

© C.S. HAMMOND & Co., N.Y.

POPULATION DISTRIBUTION

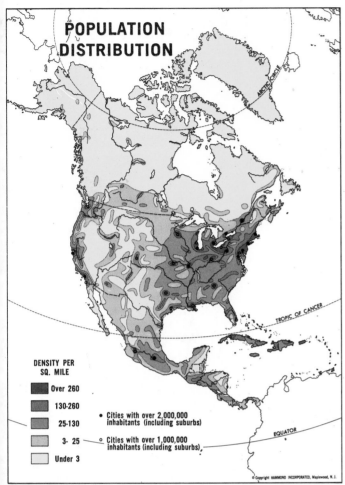

AREA 9,363,000 sq. mi.
POPULATION 314,000,000
LARGEST CITY New York
HIGHEST POINT Mt. McKinley 20,320 ft.
LOWEST POINT Death Valley 282 ft.

DENSITY PER SQ. MILE

- Over 260
- 130-260
- 25-130
- 3-25
- Under 3

• Cities with over 2,000,000 inhabitants (including suburbs)
○ Cities with over 1,000,000 inhabitants (including suburbs)

© Copyright HAMMOND INCORPORATED, Maplewood, N. J.

VEGETATION

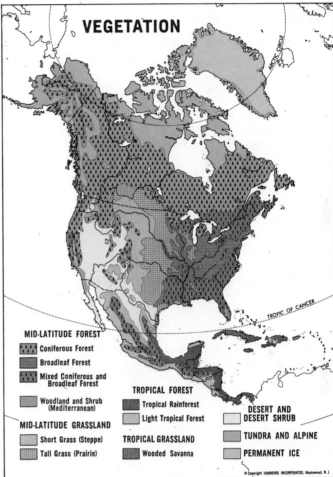

MID-LATITUDE FOREST
- Coniferous Forest
- Broadleaf Forest
- Mixed Coniferous and Broadleaf Forest
- Woodland and Shrub (Mediterranean)

MID-LATITUDE GRASSLAND
- Short Grass (Steppe)
- Tall Grass (Prairie)

TROPICAL FOREST
- Tropical Rainforest
- Light Tropical Forest

TROPICAL GRASSLAND
- Wooded Savanna

DESERT AND DESERT SHRUB

TUNDRA AND ALPINE

PERMANENT ICE

© Copyright HAMMOND INCORPORATED, Maplewood, N. J.

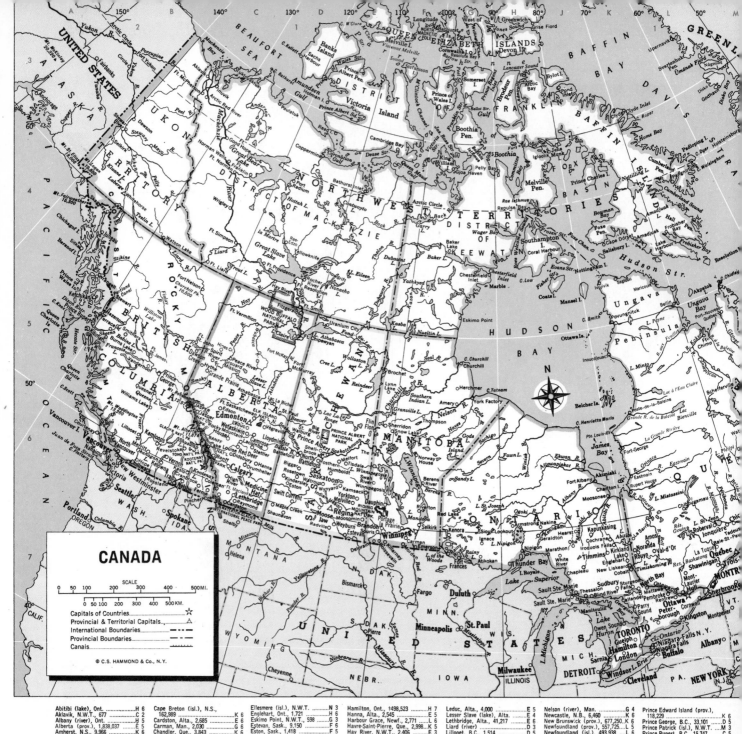

CANADA

SCALE

0 50 100 200 300 400 500 MI.

0 50 100 200 300 400 500 KM.

Capitals of Countries..........................☆
Provincial & Territorial Capitals...........△
International Boundaries.....................— ∙∙ — ∙∙ —
Provincial Boundaries.........................— ∙ — ∙ —
Canals...━┿━┿━┿━

© C.S. HAMMOND & Co., N.Y.

AREA 3,851,809 sq. mi.
POPULATION 23,388,100
CAPITAL Ottawa
LARGEST CITY Montréal
HIGHEST POINT Mt. Logan 19,850 ft.
MONETARY UNIT Canadian dollar
MAJOR LANGUAGES English, French
MAJOR RELIGIONS Protestantism, Roman Catholicism

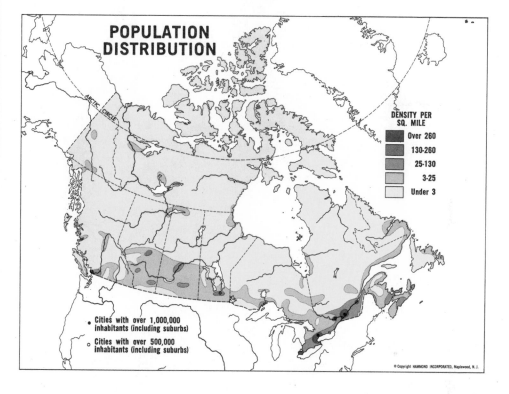

POPULATION DISTRIBUTION

DENSITY PER SQ. MILE

- Over 260
- 130-260
- 25-130
- 3-25
- Under 3

● Cities with over 1,000,000 inhabitants (including suburbs)
○ Cities with over 500,000 inhabitants (including suburbs)

© Copyright HAMMOND INCORPORATED, Maplewood, N.J.

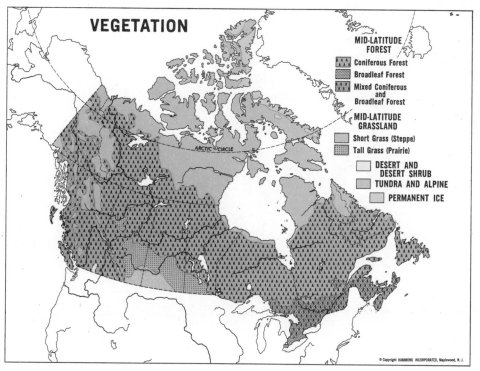

VEGETATION

MID-LATITUDE FOREST
- Coniferous Forest
- Broadleaf Forest
- Mixed Coniferous and Broadleaf Forest

MID-LATITUDE GRASSLAND
- Short Grass (Steppe)
- Tall Grass (Prairie)

- DESERT AND DESERT SHRUB
- TUNDRA AND ALPINE
- PERMANENT ICE

© Copyright HAMMOND INCORPORATED, Maplewood, N.J.

QUEEN ELIZABETH ISLANDS
0 50 100 200 MI.
0 50100 200 KM.

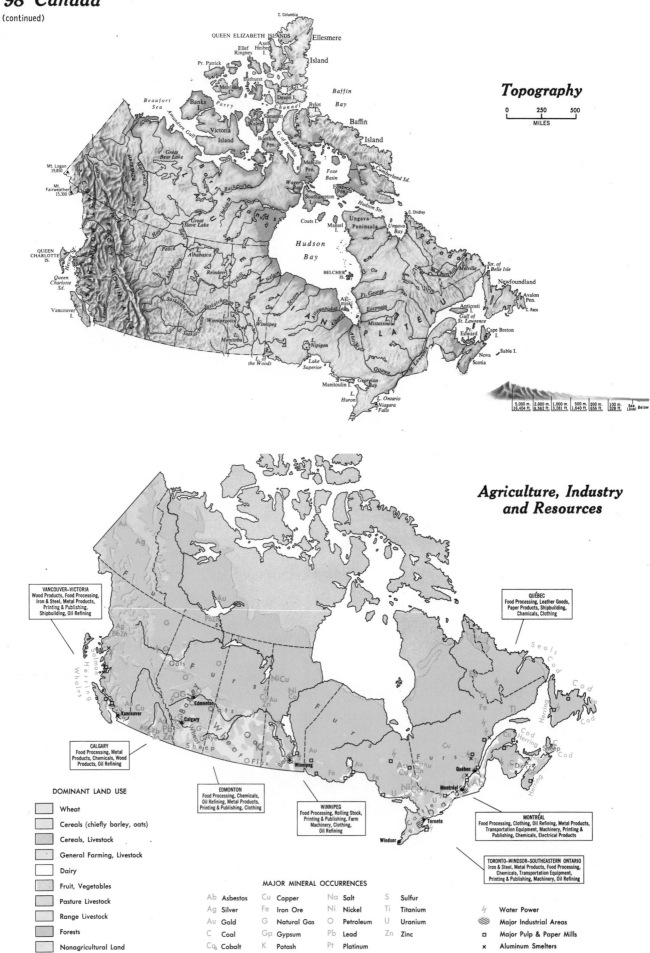

Topography

0   250   500
MILES

C. Columbia

QUEEN ELIZABETH ISLANDS   Ellesmere

Ellef
Ringnes   Axel
Heiberg
I.
Pr. Patrick   Island

Melville   Bathurst   Jones Sd.
Devon I.

Beaufort
Sea   Banks
I.   Parry   Channel   Bylot   Baffin
Bay

Amundsen Gulf   Pr.
of
Wales   Somerset   Bay

Mt. Logan
19,850   Victoria
Island   Boothia
Pen.   Gulf of Boothia   Baffin
Island

Mt.
Fairweather
15,300   Great
Bear Lake   Melville
Pen.   Foxe
Basin   Cumberland Sd.

Wager
Bay   Foxe
Pen.

QUEEN
CHARLOTTE
IS.   Great
Slave Lake   Coats I.   Southampton   C. Chidley

Queen
Charlotte
Sd.   Reindeer
L.   Mansel   Ungava
Peninsula   Ungava
Bay

Vancouver
I.   Peace   Athabasca   Churchill   Nelson   Severn   Hudson
Bay   BELCHER
IS.   Str. of
Belle Isle

N. Saskatchewan   Akimiski   Ft. George   Melville   Newfoundland
Churchill
Saskatchewan   Eastmain   Avalon
Pen.

S. Saskatchewan   L.
Winnipegosis   Winnipeg   Anguapiskat   Albany   Mistassini   Anticosti
I.   Gulf of
St. Lawrence   C. Race

L.
Manitoba   L.
Nipigon   PLATEAU   Pr.
Edward
I.   Cape Breton
I.

L. of
the Woods   Lake
Superior   Ottawa   Nova
Scotia   Sable I.

Manitoulin I.   Georgian
Bay   5,000 m. 2,000 m. 1,000 m. 500 m. 200 m. 100 m. Sea
L.   16,404 ft. 6,562 ft. 3,281 ft. 1,640 ft. 656 ft. 328 ft. Level Below
Huron   L. Ontario
Niagara
Falls

Agriculture, Industry
and Resources

VANCOUVER–VICTORIA
Wood Products, Food Processing,
Iron & Steel, Metal Products,
Printing & Publishing,
Shipbuilding, Oil Refining

QUÉBEC
Food Processing, Leather Goods,
Paper Products, Shipbuilding,
Chemicals, Clothing

CALGARY
Food Processing, Metal
Products, Chemicals, Wood
Products, Oil Refining

EDMONTON
Food Processing, Chemicals,
Oil Refining, Metal Products,
Printing & Publishing, Clothing

WINNIPEG
Food Processing, Rolling Stock,
Printing & Publishing, Farm
Machinery, Clothing,
Oil Refining

MONTRÉAL
Food Processing, Clothing, Oil Refining, Metal Products,
Transportation Equipment, Machinery, Printing &
Publishing, Chemicals, Electrical Products

TORONTO–WINDSOR–SOUTHEASTERN ONTARIO
Iron & Steel, Metal Products, Food Processing,
Chemicals, Transportation Equipment,
Printing & Publishing, Machinery, Oil Refining

DOMINANT LAND USE

- Wheat
- Cereals (chiefly barley, oats)
- Cereals, Livestock
- General Farming, Livestock
- Dairy
- Fruit, Vegetables
- Pasture Livestock
- Range Livestock
- Forests
- Nonagricultural Land

MAJOR MINERAL OCCURRENCES

Ab	Asbestos	Cu	Copper	Na	Salt	S	Sulfur
Ag	Silver	Fe	Iron Ore	Ni	Nickel	Ti	Titanium
Au	Gold	G	Natural Gas	O	Petroleum	U	Uranium
C	Coal	Gp	Gypsum	Pb	Lead	Zn	Zinc
Co	Cobalt	K	Potash	Pt	Platinum		

- ⚡ Water Power
- Major Industrial Areas
- ▫ Major Pulp & Paper Mills
- × Aluminum Smelters

AREA 156,185 sq. mi.
POPULATION 557,725
CAPITAL St. John's
LARGEST CITY St. John's
HIGHEST POINT Cirque Mtn. 5,160 ft.
SETTLED IN 1610
ADMITTED TO CONFEDERATION 1949
PROVINCIAL FLOWER Pitcher Plant

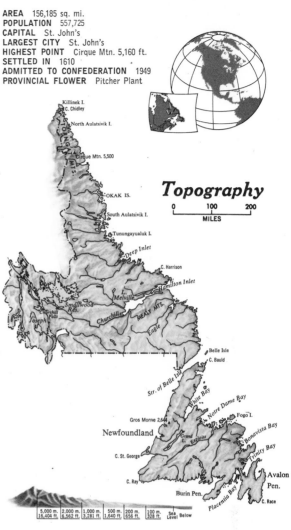

Topography

0   100   200
MILES

5,000 m. | 2,000 m. | 1,000 m. | 500 m. | 200 m. | 100 m. | Sea Level | Below
16,404 ft. | 6,562 ft. | 3,281 ft. | 1,640 ft. | 656 ft. | 328 ft.

NEWFOUNDLAND

SCALE
0 10 20 40 60 80 100MI.
0 1020 40 60 80 100KM.

Provincial Capital.....................⊕
Provincial Boundaries.........━ ━ ━

© C.S. HAMMOND & Co., Maplewood, N.J.

LABRADOR (PART OF NEWFOUNDLAND)

0 50 100 150 mi.
0 50 100 150 km.

Agriculture, Industry and Resources

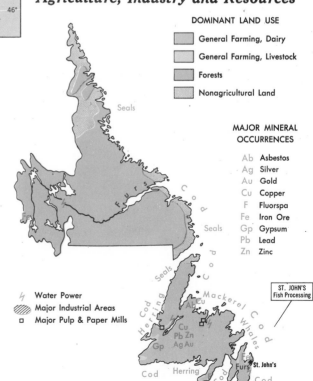

DOMINANT LAND USE

- General Farming, Dairy
- General Farming, Livestock
- Forests
- Nonagricultural Land

MAJOR MINERAL OCCURRENCES

Ab   Asbestos
Ag   Silver
Au   Gold
Cu   Copper
F   Fluorspa
Fe   Iron Ore
Gp   Gypsum
Pb   Lead
Zn   Zinc

ST. JOHN'S Fish Processing

⚡ Water Power
▨ Major Industrial Areas
▫ Major Pulp & Paper Mills

NOVA SCOTIA AND PRINCE EDWARD ISLAND

SCALE

0 10 20 30 40 50 MI.

0 10 20 30 40 50 KM.

Provincial Capitals ....⊛   Provincial Boundaries ....—..—
County Seats ....⊙   County Boundaries ....____

Copyright by C. S. HAMMOND & CO., N.Y.

PRINCE EDWARD ISLAND

AREA 2,184 sq. mi.
POPULATION 118,229
CAPITAL Charlottetown
LARGEST CITY Charlottetown
HIGHEST POINT 465 ft.
SETTLED IN 1720
ADMITTED TO CONFEDERATION 1873
PROVINCIAL FLOWER Lady's Slipper

NOVA SCOTIA

AREA 21,425 sq. mi.
POPULATION 828,571
CAPITAL Halifax
LARGEST CITY Halifax
HIGHEST POINT Cape Breton Highlands 1,747 ft.
SETTLED IN 1605
ADMITTED TO CONFEDERATION 1867
PROVINCIAL FLOWER Trailing Arbutus or Mayflower

Topography

0   30   60
MILES

Agriculture, Industry and Resources

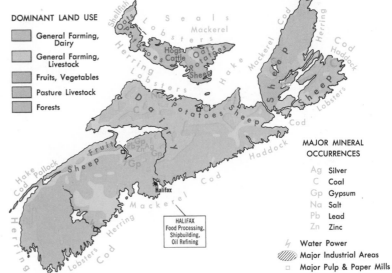

DOMINANT LAND USE

- General Farming, Dairy
- General Farming, Livestock
- Fruits, Vegetables
- Pasture Livestock
- Forests

HALIFAX
Food Processing,
Shipbuilding,
Oil Refining

MAJOR MINERAL OCCURRENCES

- Ag Silver
- C   Coal
- Gp Gypsum
- Na Salt
- Pb Lead
- Zn Zinc

⚡ Water Power
▨ Major Industrial Areas
□ Major Pulp & Paper Mills

COUNTIES

Albert, 16,307 ....F 3
Carleton, 24,428 ....C 2
Charlotte, 24,551 ....C 3
Gloucester, 74,752 ....E 1
Kent, 24,901 ....E 2
King's, 33,285 ....E 3
Madawaska, 34,976 ......A 1
Northumberland, 51,561 ...D 2
Queen's 12,486 ....D 3
Restigouche, 41,289 ......C 1
Saint John, 90,162 ....D 3
Sunbury, 21,268 ....D 3
Victoria, 19,796 ....C 2
Westmorland, 98,669 .....F 2
York, 64,126 ....C 3

CITIES and TOWNS

Acadie Siding, 112 ....E 2
Acadieville, 144 ....E 2
Adamsville, 119 ....E 2
Albert Mines, 130 ....F 3
Alcida, 222 ....E 1
Aldouane, 83 ....E 2
Allardville, 712 ....E 1

Alma, 425 ....F 3
Anagance, 109 ....E 3
Apohaqui, 352 ....E 3
Argyle, 63 ....C 2
Armstrong Brook, 321 ....E 1
Aroostook, 550 ....C 2
Arthurette, 299 ....C 2
Astle, 194 ....D 2
Atholville, 2,108 ....D 1
Aulac, 128 ....F 3
Back Bay, 567 ....D 3
Baie-Sainte-Anne, 735 ...F 1
Baie-Verte, 177 ....F 2
Bailey, 143 ....C 3
Bairdsville, 214 ....C 2
Baker Brook, 561 ....B 1
Balmoral, 896 ....D 1
Barker's Point, 1,882 ....D 3
Barnaby River, 87 ....E 2
Barnettville, 182 ....E 2
Bartibog Bridge, 163 .....E 1
Bas-Caraquet, 1,685 .....F 1
Bass River, 129 ....E 2
Bath, 920 ....C 2
Bathurst©, 16,674 ....E 1
Bathurst Mines, 45 ......E 1
Bayfield, 178 ....G 2
Bayside, 207 ....C 3
Beaver Brook Station, 276 .E 1
Beaver Harbour, 355 .....D 3

Beechwood, 349 ....C 2
Beersville, 85 ....E 2
Belledune, 784 ....E 1
Belledou, 145 ....E 1
Bellefond, 294 ....E 1
Belleisle Creek, 179 .....E 3
Benjamin, 65 ....E 1
Benton, 149 ....C 3
Beresford, 2,325 ....E 1
Berry Mills, 349 ....E 2
Bertrand, 1,094 ....F 1
Berwick, 130 ....E 3
Black Point, 150 ....D 1
Black River, 91 ....E 2
Black River Bridge, 335 ..E 2
Blacks Harbour, 1,771 ...D 3
Blackville, 915 ....E 2
Blissfield, 130 ....D 2
Bloomfield Ridge, 218 ...D 2
Blue Cove, 519 ....E 2
Bocabec, 59 ....C 3
Boiestown, 332 ....D 2
Bonny River, 134 ....D 3
Bosse, 134 ....B 1
Bourgeois, 306 ....F 2
Brantville, 1,072 ....E 2
Breau-Village, 249 ......F 2
Brest, 117 ....E 2
Bridgedale, 416 ....F 2
Briggs Corner, 138 ......E 2

Bristol, 771 ....C 2
Brockway, 68 ....C 3
Browns Flats, 262 ....D 3
Buctouche©, 1,964 ....F 2
Burnsville, 179 ....E 1
Burton©, 357 ....D 3
Burtts Corner, 487 ......D 2
Caissie-Village, 34 ......F 2
Cambridge-Narrows, 416 ..E 3
Campbellton, 10,335 .....D 1
Canaan Road, 130 ....E 2
Canaan Station, 102 .....E 2
Canterbury, 528 ....C 3
Cap-Bateau, 466 ....F 1
Cape Tormentine, 261 ...G 2
Cap Lumière, 305 ....F 2
Cap-Pelé, 2,081 ....F 2
Caraquet, 3,441 ....F 1
Caron Brook, 191 ....B 1
Carrolls Crossing, 188 ...D 2
Castalia, 199 ....D 4
Central Blissville (Bailey),
   143 ....D 3
Centre-Acadie, 151 ......E 2
Centre-Saint-Simon, 517 ..F 1
Centreville, 566 ....C 2
Chance Harbour, 181 ....D 3
Charlo, 1,621 ....D 1
Chartersville, 320 ....F 2
Chatham, 7,833 ....E 1

Chatham Head, 1,440 ....E 2
Chipman, 1,977 ....D 2
Clair, 704 ....B 1
Clarendon, 105 ....D 3
Cliffordvale, 110 ....C 2
Clifton, 231 ....D 1
Cloverdale, 133 ....C 2
Coal Branch, 89 ....E 2
Coal Creek, 71 ....D 2
Cocagne, 234 ....F 2
Cocagne Cape, 258 ......F 2
Codys, 67 ....E 3
Coldstream, 160 ....C 2
Coles Island, 121 ....E 3
College Bridge, 545 .....F 2
Collette, 178 ....E 2
Connell, 107 ....C 2
Connors, 231 ....B 1
Cork Station, 70 ....D 3
Cornhill, 83 ....E 3
Cross Creek, 241 ....D 2
Cumberland Bay, 246 ....E 2
Dalhousie©, 6,255 ......D 1
Dalhousie Junction, 275 ..D 1
Darlington, 585 ....D 1
Daulnay, 539 ....E 1
Dawsonville, 208 ....C 1
Debec, 222 ....C 2
Dieppe, 4,277 ....F 2
Dipper Harbour, 109 ....D 3

Doaktown, 938 ....D 2
Dorchester©, 1,199 .....F 2
Dorchester Crossing, 574 ..F 2
Douglas Harbour, 46 .....D 3
Douglastown, 637 ....E 1
Drummond, 637 ....C 1
Duguayville, 372 ....F 1
Dumbarton, 59 ....C 3
Dumfries, 257 ....C 3
Dupuis Corner, 218 ......F 2
Durham Bridge, 182 .....D 2
East Shediac, 585 ....F 2
Edmundston©, 12,365 ....B 1
Eel River Bridge, 487 ....F 1
Eel River Crossing, 1,075 ..D 1
Elgin, 283 ....E 3
Elmwood, 78 ....C 2
Enniskillen, 77 ....D 3
Evandale, 33 ....D 3
Evangeline, 298 ....F 1
Fairhaven, 118 ....C 4
Fairisle, 444 ....F 1
Fairvale, 2,050 ....D 3
Ferry Road, 520 ....E 2
Fielding, 215 ....C 2
Five Fingers, 148 ....D 1
Flatlands, 280 ....D 1
Florenceville, 584 ......C 2
Fontaine, 318 ....F 2
Forest City, 55 ....C 3

Fosterville, 71 ....C 3
Four Falls Corner, 97 ...C 2
Fox Creek, 488 ....F 2
Fredericton (cap.)©,
   24,254 ....D 3
Fredericton Junction, 615 ..D 3
Gagetown©, 609 ....D 3
Gardner Creek, 47 ......E 3
Geary, 1,023 ....D 3
Germantown, 71 ....F 3
Gillespie, 88 ....C 2
Glassville, 174 ....C 2
Glencoe, 143 ....D 1
Glenlivet, 231 ....D 1
Gloucester Junction, 167 ..E 1
Gondola Point, 850 .....D 3
Grafton, 359 ....C 2
Grand Bay, 1,066 ....D 3
Grande-Anse, 545 ....E 1
Grand Falls, 4,516 ......C 1
Grand Falls Hill, 559 ....C 1
Grand Harbour, 556 .....D 4
Gray Rapids, 307 ....D 2
Gunningville, 1,669 .....F 2
Hammondvale, 127 ......E 3
Hampstead, 118 ....D 3
Hampton©, 1,748 ....E 3
Harcourt, 163 ....E 2
Hardwicke, 93 ....E 1
Hardwood Ridge, 222 ...D 2

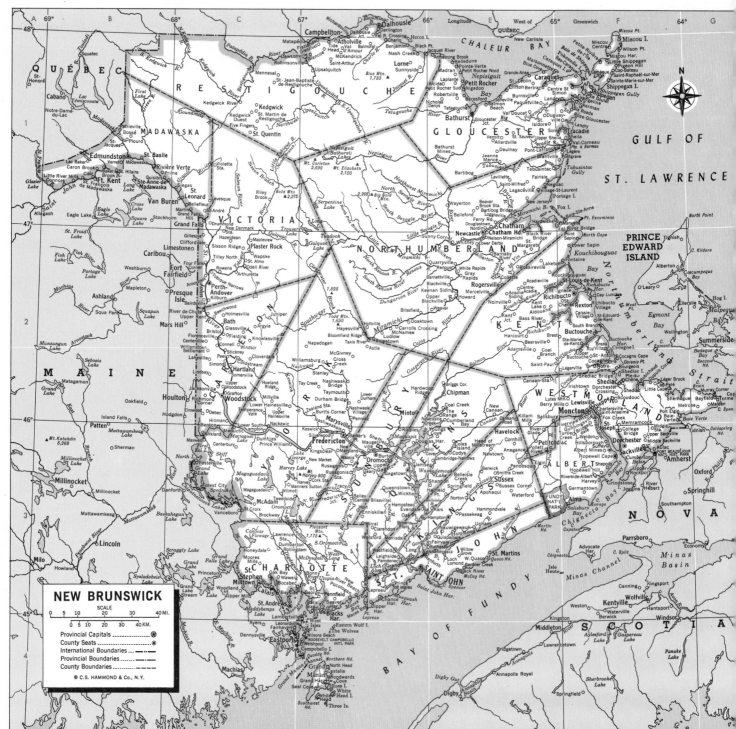

AREA 28,354 sq. mi.
POPULATION 677,250
CAPITAL Fredericton
LARGEST CITY Saint John
HIGHEST POINT Mt. Carleton 2,690 ft.
SETTLED IN 1611
ADMITTED TO CONFEDERATION 1867
PROVINCIAL FLOWER Purple Violet

OTHER FEATURES

◎ County seat.
‡ Population of metropolitan area.

Topography

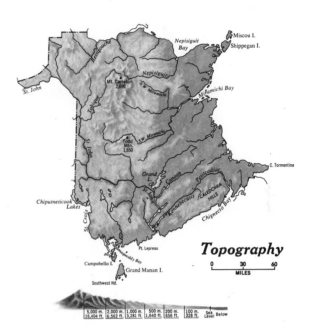

0 30 60
MILES

| 5,000 m. 16,404 ft. | 2,000 m. 6,562 ft. | 1,000 m. 3,281 ft. | 500 m. 1,640 ft. | 200 m. 656 ft. | 100 m. 328 ft. | Sea Level | Below |

Agriculture, Industry and Resources

SAINT JOHN
Food Processing, Shipbuilding, Pulp & Paper, Wood Products, Metal Products

DOMINANT LAND USE

- Cereals, Livestock
- Dairy
- Potatoes
- General Farming, Livestock
- Pasture Livestock
- Forests

MAJOR MINERAL OCCURRENCES

- Ag Silver
- C Coal
- Cu Copper
- Pb Lead
- Zn Zinc

- ⚡ Water Power
- ▨ Major Industrial Areas
- ▫ Major Pulp & Paper Mills

Topography

0 100 200
MILES

Below Sea Level | 100 m. 328 ft. | 200 m. 656 ft. | 500 m. 1,640 ft. | 1,000 m. 3,281 ft. | 2,000 m. 6,562 ft. | 5,000 m. 16,404 ft.

QUÉBEC

COUNTIES

Argenteuil, 31,319........C 4
Arthabaska, 51,524.......E 4
Bagot, 23,591............D 4
Beauce, 63,960...........G 3
Beauharnois, 52,137......C 4
Bellechasse, 23,517......G 3
Berthier, 27,288.........C 3
Bonaventure, 41,701......C 2
Brome, 15,311............D 4
Chambly, 231,590.........J 4
Champlain, 113,150.......E 2
Charlevoix-Est, 16,780...G 2
Charlevoix-Ouest, 13,650.G 2
Châteauguay, 53,737......D 4
Chicoutimi, 163,348......G 1
Compton, 21,367..........F 4
Deux-Montagnes, 52,369...C 4
Dorchester, 32,473.......G 3

Drummond, 64,144.........E 4
Frontenac, 27,293........G 4
Gaspé-Est, 41,727........D 1
Gaspé-Ouest, 18,754......C 1
Gatineau, 55,729.........B 3
Hull, 109,946............C 4
Huntingdon, 15,358.......C 4
Iberville, 20,400........D 4
Île-de-Montréal, 1,959,143.H 4
Île-Jésus, 228,010.......H 4
Joliette, 52,088.........C 3
Kamouraska, 26,264.......H 2
Labelle, 30,582..........B 3
Lac-Saint-Jean-Est,
  45,220................F 1
Lac-Saint-Jean-Ouest,
  57,074................E 1
Laprairie, 61,691........H 4
L'Assomption, 62,198.....D 4
Lévis, 62,776............G 3
L'Islet, 23,187..........G 2
Lotbinière, 27,373.......F 3

Maskinongé, 21,257.......D 3
Matane, 30,261...........B 1
Matapédia, 26,856........B 2
Mégantic, 58,020.........F 3
Missisquoi, 33,953.......D 4
Montcalm, 21,546.........C 3
Montmagny, 26,307........G 3
Montmorency No. 1,
  20,401................F 2
Montmorency No. 2, 5,435.G 3
Napierville, 12,067......D 4
Nicolet, 30,004..........E 3
Papineau, 51,540.........C 4
Pontiac, 19,570..........A 3
Portneuf, 51,540.........E 3
Québec, 423,162..........F 3
Richelieu, 47,093........D 4
Richmond, 41,044.........E 4
Rimouski, 64,263.........J 1
Rivière-du-Loup, 39,488..J 2
Rouville, 31,759.........D 4
Saguenay, 111,272........H 1

CITIES and TOWNS

Saint-Hyacinthe, 50,494..D 4
Saint-Jean, 45,892.......D 4
Saint-Maurice, 108,366...D 3
Shefford, 62,361.........E 4
Sherbrooke, 101,470......E 4
Soulanges, 11,449........C 4
Stanstead, 36,266........F 4
Témiscouata, 23,189......J 2
Terrebonne, 139,945......H 4
Vaudreuil, 36,593........C 4
Verchères, 35,273........J 4
Wolfe, 16,197............F 4
Yamaska, 15,206..........E 3

CITIES and TOWNS

Acton Vale, 4,564........E 4
Albanel, 788.............E 1
Alma◉, 22,622............F 1
Amqui◉, 3,797............B 2
Ancienne-Lorette, 8,304..H 3
Angers, 881..............B 4
Anjou, 33,886............H 4
Armagh, 987..............G 3
Arthabaska◉, 4,479.......E 3
Arvida, 18,448...........F 1
Asbestos, 9,749..........E 4
Ayer's Cliff◉, 873.......E 4
Aylmer, 7,198............B 4
Bagotville, 6,041........G 1
Baie-Comeau, 12,109......A 1
Baie-de-Shawinigan, 847..E 3
Baie-des-Sables, 638.....A 1
Baie-d'Urfé, 3,881.......H 4
Baie-Saint-Paul◉, 4,163..G 2
Baie-Trinité, 734........A 1
Beaconsfield, 19,389.....H 4
Beauceville, 2,098.......G 3
Beauceville-Est◉, 2,192..G 3
Beauharnois◉, 8,121......D 4
Beaulieu, 659............J 3
Beaumont, 630............F 3
Beauport, 14,681.........J 3
Beaupré, 2,862...........G 2
Bécancour◉, 8,182........E 3
Bedford◉, 2,786..........E 4
Beebe Plain, 1,236.......E 4
Bélair, 4,505............H 3
Beloeil, 12,274..........D 4
Bernierville, 2,415......E 3
Berthier◉, 4,080.........D 3
Bic, 1,157...............J 1
Black Lake, 4,123........F 3
Blainville, 9,630........H 4
Bois-des-Filion, 4,061...H 4
Bolduc, 1,496............G 4
Bonaventure, 1,079.......C 2
Boucherville, 19,997.....J 4
Breakeyville, 800........J 3
Bromont, 1,089...........E 4
Bromptonville, 2,771.....F 4
Brossard, 23,452.........H 4
Brownsburg, 3,481........C 4
Buckingham, 7,304........B 4
Cabano, 3,063............J 2
Calumet, 764.............C 4
Candiac, 5,185...........H 4
Cap-à-l'Aigle, 679.......G 2
Cap-Chat, 3,868..........B 1
Cap-de-la-Madeleine,
  31,463................E 3
Caplan, 693..............C 2
Cap-Rouge, 1,750.........H 3
Cap-Saint-Ignace, 1,338..G 2
Cap-Santé◉, 610..........F 3

Carignan, 3,340..........J 4
Carleton, 899............C 2
Caughnawaga, 3,982.......H 4
Causapscal, 2,965........B 2
Chambly, 11,469..........J 4
Chambord, 1,106..........E 1
Champlain, 632...........E 3
Chandler, 3,843..........D 1
Charlemagne, 4,111.......H 4
Charlesbourg, 33,443.....J 3
Charny, 5,175............J 3
Châteauguay, 15,797......H 4
Châteauguay-Centre,
  17,942................H 4
Château-Richer◉, 3,111...F 3
Chénéville, 718..........B 4
Chicoutimi◉, 33,893......G 1
Chicoutimi-Jonquière,
  ‡133,703..............G 1
Chicoutimi-Nord, 14,086..G 1
Chute-aux-Outardes,
  1,930.................A 1
Clermont, 3,386..........G 2
Coaticook, 6,569.........F 4
Coleraine, 1,474.........F 4
Contrecoeur, 2,694.......D 4
Cookshire◉, 1,484........F 4
Coteau-du-Lac, 838.......C 4
Coteau-Landing◉, 846.....C 4
Côte-Saint-Luc, 24,375...H 4
Courcelles, 679..........G 4
Courville, 6,222.........J 3
Cowansville, 11,920......D 4
Crabtree, 1,706..........D 4
Danville, 2,566..........E 4
Daveluyville, 998........E 3
Deauville, 761...........E 4
Dégelis, 3,046...........J 2
Delson, 2,941............J 4
Desbiens, 1,813..........E 1
Deschaillons-sur-Saint-
  Laurent, 1,176........E 3
Deschambault, 995........E 3
Deschênes, 1,806.........B 4
Deux-Montagnes, 8,631....H 4
Didyme, 720..............E 1
Disraëli, 2,934..........E 4
Dolbeau, 7,633...........E 1
Dollard-des-Ormeaux,
  25,217................H 4
Donnacona, 5,940.........F 3
Dorion, 6,209............C 4
Dorval, 20,469...........H 4
Douville, 3,267..........D 4
Drummondville◉, 31,813...E 4
Drummondville-Sud,
  8,989.................E 4
East Angus, 4,715........F 4
East Broughton, 1,380....F 3
East Broughton Station,
  1,127.................F 3
Escoumins, 1,968.........H 1
Farnham, 6,496...........D 4
Ferme-Neuve, 1,990.......B 3
Forestville, 1,606.......H 1
Frampton, 711............G 3
Francoeur, 1,186.........E 3
Gaspé, 17,211............D 1
Gatineau, 22,321.........B 4
Giffard, 13,135..........J 3
Girardville, 933.........E 1
Glenwood Domaine, 3,997..B 4
Godbout, 653.............A 1
Gracefield, 1,049........A 3
Granby, 34,385...........D 4
Grande-Rivière, 1,330....D 2
Grandes-Bergeronnes,
  802...................H 1
Grande-Vallée, 779.......H 1
Grand'Mère, 17,137.......E 3
Greenfield Park, 15,348..J 4
Grenville, 1,495.........C 4
Hampstead, 7,033.........H 4
Ham-Sud◉, 64.............E 4
Hauterive, 13,181........A 1
Hébertville-Station, 1,163.F 1
Hemmingford, 810.........D 4
Henryville, 666..........D 4
Hudson, 4,345............C 4
Hull◉, 63,580............C 4
Huntingdon◉, 3,087.......C 4
Iberville, 9,331.........D 4
Île-Bizard, 2,950........H 4
Île-Perrot, 4,021........H 4
Inverness◉, 362.........F 3
Joliette◉, 20,127........D 3
Jonquière, 28,430........F 1
Kénogami, 10,970.........F 1
Kirkland, 2,917..........H 4
Labelle, 1,492...........B 3
Lac-au-Saumon, 1,314.....B 2
Lac-aux-Sables, 844......E 3
Lac-Beauport, 42.........F 3
Lac-Bouchette, 954.......E 1
Lac-Brome◉, 4,063........E 4
Lac-Carré, 660...........C 3
Lac-Etchemin, 2,789......G 3
Lachine, 44,423..........H 4
Lachute◉, 11,813.........C 4
Lac-Mégantic◉, 6,770.....G 4
Lacolle, 1,254...........D 4
Lac-Saint-Charles, 1,693.H 3
Lafontaine, 2,980........C 4
La Guadeloupe, 1,934.....F 4
La Malbaie◉, 4,036.......G 2
Lambton, 767.............F 4
L'Ange-Gardien, 1,605....F 3
L'Annonciation, 2,162....C 3
Lanoraie, 1,151..........D 3
La Pérade, 1,123.........E 3
La Pocatière◉, 4,256.....G 2
La Prairie◉, 8,309.......H 4
La Providence, 4,709.....H 4
La Salle, 72,912.........H 4
L'Ascension, 1,034.......F 1
L'Assomption◉, 4,915.....D 4
La Station-du-Coteau, 885.C 4

La Tuque, 13,099.........E 2
Laurentides, 1,746.......D 4
Laurier-Station, 946.....F 3
Laurierville, 922........F 3
Lauzon, 12,809...........J 3
Laval, 228,010...........H 4
Lavaltrie, 1,261.........D 4
Le Moyne, 8,194..........J 4
Lennoxville, 3,859.......F 4
L'Épiphanie, 2,752.......D 4
Léry, 2,247..............H 4
Les Méchins, 792.........B 1
Lévis◉, 16,597...........J 3
Linière, 1,220...........G 3
L'Islet, 1,195...........G 2
L'Islet-sur-Mer, 772.....G 2
L'Isle-Verte, 1,360......G 1
Longueuil◉, 97,590.......J 4
Loretteville◉,
  11,644................H 3
Lorraine, 3,145..........H 4
Louiseville◉, 4,042......E 3
Luceville, 1,411.........J 1
Lyster, 879..............F 3
Magog, 13,281............E 4
Maniwaki◉, 6,689.........B 3
Manouane, 751............C 2
Manseau, 756.............E 3
Maple Grove, 1,708.......H 4
Maria, 1,157.............C 2
Marieville◉, 4,563.......D 4
Mascouche, 8,812.........H 4
Maskinongé, 996..........D 3
Masson, 2,336............B 4

Masseuville, 632.........E 4
Matane◉, 11,841..........B 1
Melocheville, 1,601......C 4
Mercier, 4,011...........H 4
Mistassini, 3,601........E 1
Mont-Carmel, 800.........G 2
Montebello, 1,285........B 4
Mont-Joli, 6,698.........J 1
Mont-Laurier◉, 8,240.....B 3
Mont-Louis, 815..........C 1
Montmagny◉, 12,432.......G 3
Montmorency, 4,949.......J 3
Montréal◉, 1,214,352.....H 4
Montréal-Est, 5,076......J 4
Montréal-Nord, 89,139....H 4
Mont-Rolland, 1,503......C 4
Mont-Royal, 21,561.......H 4
Mont-Saint-Hilaire, 5,758.D 4
Morin Heights, 710.......C 4
Murdochville, 2,891......C 1
Napierville◉, 1,987......D 4
Neuville, 798............F 3
New Carlisle◉, 1,384.....C 2
New Richmond, 3,957......C 2
Nicolet, 4,714...........E 3
Nitro, 1,827.............E 4
Nominingue, 699..........B 3
Normandin, 1,823.........E 1
North Hatley, 728........F 4
Notre-Dame-de-la-Doré,
  1,127................E 1
Notre-Dame-des-Anges,
  790..................E 4

Agriculture, Industry and Resources

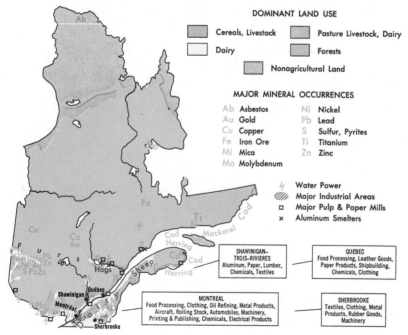

DOMINANT LAND USE

Cereals, Livestock
Pasture Livestock, Dairy
Dairy
Forests
Nonagricultural Land

MAJOR MINERAL OCCURRENCES

Ab Asbestos
Au Gold
Cu Copper
Fe Iron Ore
Mi Mica
Mo Molybdenum

Ni Nickel
Pb Lead
S Sulfur, Pyrites
Ti Titanium
Zn Zinc

Water Power
Major Industrial Areas
Major Pulp & Paper Mills
Aluminum Smelters

SHAWINIGAN–TROIS-RIVIÈRES
Aluminum, Paper, Lumber, Chemicals, Textiles

QUÉBEC
Food Processing, Leather Goods, Paper Products, Shipbuilding, Chemicals, Clothing

MONTRÉAL
Food Processing, Clothing, Oil Refining, Metal Products, Aircraft, Rolling Stock, Automobiles, Machinery, Printing & Publishing, Chemicals, Electrical Products

SHERBROOKE
Textiles, Clothing, Metal Products, Rubber Goods, Machinery

QUÉBEC SOUTHERN PART

SCALE
0 5 10 20 30 40 MI.
0 5 10 20 30 40 KM.

National Capital — ⊛
Provincial Capital — ⊛
County Seats — ◉
International Boundaries — — —
Provincial & State Boundaries
County Boundaries — — —

Notre-Dame-des-Laurentides, 5,080........H 3
Notre-Dame-des-Prairies, 3,541..........D 3
Notre-Dame-d'Hébertville, 1,506..........F 1
Notre-Dame-du-Bon-Conseil, 1,048........E 4
Notre-Dame-du-Lac◉, 2,107..............J 2
Nouvelle, 722..........................C 2
Omerville, 1,102.......................E 4
Ormstown, 1,517.......................D 4
Orsainville, 12,520....................H 3
Otterburn Park, 3,512..................D 4
Ouiatchouan, 1,217....................H 1
Outremont, 28,552.....................H 4
Pabos-Mills, 668......................D 2
Papineauville◉, 1,384..................C 4
Paspébiac, 1,317......................B 2
Percé◉, 5,617........................D 2
Petite-Matane, 668....................B 2
Petit-Saguenay (Saint-François-d'Assise), 691........G 1
Pierrefonds, 33,010...................H 4
Pierreville, 1,455.....................E 3
Pincourt, 5,899.......................H 4
Pintendre, 796........................J 3
Plaisance, 651........................C 4
Plessisville, 7,204....................F 3
Pointe-à-la-Croix, 753.................C 2
Pointe-au-Pic, 1,231..................G 2
Pointe-aux-Outardes, 836...............A 1

Pointe-aux-Trembles, 35,567............J 4
Pointe-Calumet, 2,214.................G 4
Pointe-Claire, 27,303..................H 4
Pointe-du-Lac, 1,314..................E 3
Pointe-Gatineau, 15,640................B 4
Pointe-Lebel, 756.....................A 1
Pont-Rouge, 3,272....................F 3
Port-Alfred, 9,228....................G 1
Portneuf, 1,347.......................F 3
Price, 2,740..........................B 2
Princeville, 3,829.....................F 3
Québec (cap.), 186,088.................H 3
Québec, ‡480,502......................H 3
Quyon, 879...........................C 4
Rawdon, 2,740.........................D 3
Repentigny, 19,520....................J 4
Restigouche, 1,155....................C 2
Richelieu, 1,777......................D 4
Richmond◉, 4,317.....................E 4
Rigaud, 2,138.........................C 4
Rimouski◉, 26,887.....................B 2
Rimouski-Est, 2,069...................J 1
Rivière-à-Pierre, 691..................F 3
Rivière-du-Loup◉, 12,760..............H 2
Rivière-du-Moulin, 4,393................G 1
Rivière-Portneuf, 987..................H 1
Robertsonville, 1,294..................E 4
Roberval◉, 8,330.....................E 1
Rock Forest, 793.....................E 4
Rock Island, 1,341....................E 4
Rosemère, 6,710.......................H 4
Rougemont, 853........................D 4
Roxboro, 7,633........................H 4

Roxton Falls, 1,139....................E 4
Sacré-Coeur-de-Jésus, 1,252...........H 1
Saint-Adelphe, 708....................E 3
Saint-Agapitville, 1,493................F 3
Saint-Alban, 770......................E 3
Saint-Alexandre-de-Kamouraska, 927.....H 2
Saint-Alexis-des-Monts, 1,905..........D 3
Saint-Amable, 1,051...................J 4
Saint-Ambroise, 1,629..................F 1
Saint-Anaclet, 955....................J 1
Saint-André-Avellin, 1,088.............B 4
Saint-André-Est, 1,201.................C 4
Saint-Anselme, 1,400..................F 3
Saint-Antoine, 5,831..................H 4
Saint-Antonin, 748....................H 2
Saint-Aubert, 952.....................G 2
Saint-Augustin-de-Québec, 688..........H 3
Saint-Basile-le-Grand, 4,402...........H 4
Saint-Basile-Sud, 1,731................F 3
Saint-Bernard-sur-Mer, 667.............G 2
Saint-Boniface-de-Shawinigan, 2,581.....D 3
Saint-Bruno-de-Montarville, 15,780......J 4
Saint-Camille-de-Bellechasse, 774.......G 3
Saint-Casimir, 1,239..................E 3

Saint-Césaire, 2,279..................D 4
Saint-Charles, 969....................G 3
Saint-Charles-de-Drummond, 2,266.......E 4
Saint-Charles-de-Mandeville, 900........D 3
Saint-Chrysostome, 1,077...............D 4
Saint-Coeur-de-Marie, 1,218............F 1
Saint-Côme, 914......................D 3
Saint-Constant, 4,139..................H 4
Saint-Cyprien 743.....................J 2
Saint-Cyrille, 1,125...................E 4
Saint-Damien-de-Buckland, 1,799........G 3
Saint-David-de-Falardeau, 770..........F 1
Saint-David-de-l'Auberivière, 3,818.....J 3
Saint-Denis, 899......................D 4
Saint-Dominique, 1,722.................E 4
Saint-Donat-de-Montcalm, 1,536.........C 3
Sainte-Adelaide-de-Pabos, 853..........D 2
Sainte-Adèle, 2,581...................C 4
Sainte-Agathe, 646....................F 3
Sainte-Agathe-des-Monts, 5,532.........C 3
Sainte-Angèle-de-Mérici, 688...........J 1
Sainte-Anne-de-Beaupré, 1,797..........F 2

Sainte-Anne-de-Bellevue, 4,976.........H 4
Sainte-Anne-des-Monts◉, 5,546..........C 1
Sainte-Anne-des-Plaines, 2,093.........H 4
Sainte-Blandine, 841..................J 1
Sainte-Catherine, 913..................F 3
Sainte-Claire-de-Joliette, 1,490........G 3
Sainte-Croix◉, 1,545..................F 3
Sainte-Famille-d'Orléans◉, 295.........G 3
Sainte-Félicité, 816...................H 1
Sainte-Foy, 68,385....................H 3
Sainte-Geneviève, 2,847................H 4
Sainte-Geneviève-de-Batiscan◉, 556.....E 3

Sainte-Hedwidge-de-Roberval, 641.......E 1
Sainte-Hélène-de-Kamouraska, 656.......H 2
Sainte-Hénédine◉, 533.................F 3
Sainte-Jeanne-d'Arc, 936...............E 1
Sainte-Julie-de-Verchères, 1,214........J 4
Sainte-Julienne◉, 839.................G 4
Sainte-Justine, 980...................G 3
Saint-Éleuthère, 1,083................H 2
Sainte-Marie, 4,307..................F 3
Sainte-Martine◉, 1,931................D 4
Saint-Émile, 2,645....................H 3
Sainte-Monique, 697...................F 1
Sainte-Perpétue-de-L'Islet, 1,048.......H 2

Saint-Éphrem-de-Tring, 954............G 3
Sainte-Pudentienne, 799...............E 4
Sainte-Scholastique◉, 14,787...........C 4
Saint-Esprit, 937.....................D 4
Sainte-Thècle, 1,725..................E 3
Sainte-Thérèse, 17,175................H 4
Sainte-Thérèse-Ouest, 7,278............H 4
Saint-Étienne-des-Grès, 870............E 3
Saint-Eugène, 656....................G 2
Saint-Eustache, 9,479.................H 4
Saint-Eustache-Est, 4,993..............H 4
Saint-Fabien, 1,537...................J 1
Saint-Félicien, 4,952.................E 1
Saint-Félix-de-Valois, 1,455............D 3

AREA 594,860 sq. mi.
POPULATION 6,234,445
CAPITAL Québec
LARGEST CITY Montréal
HIGHEST POINT Mt. Jacques Cartier 4,160 ft.
SETTLED IN 1608
ADMITTED TO CONFEDERATION 1867
PROVINCIAL FLOWER White Garden Lily

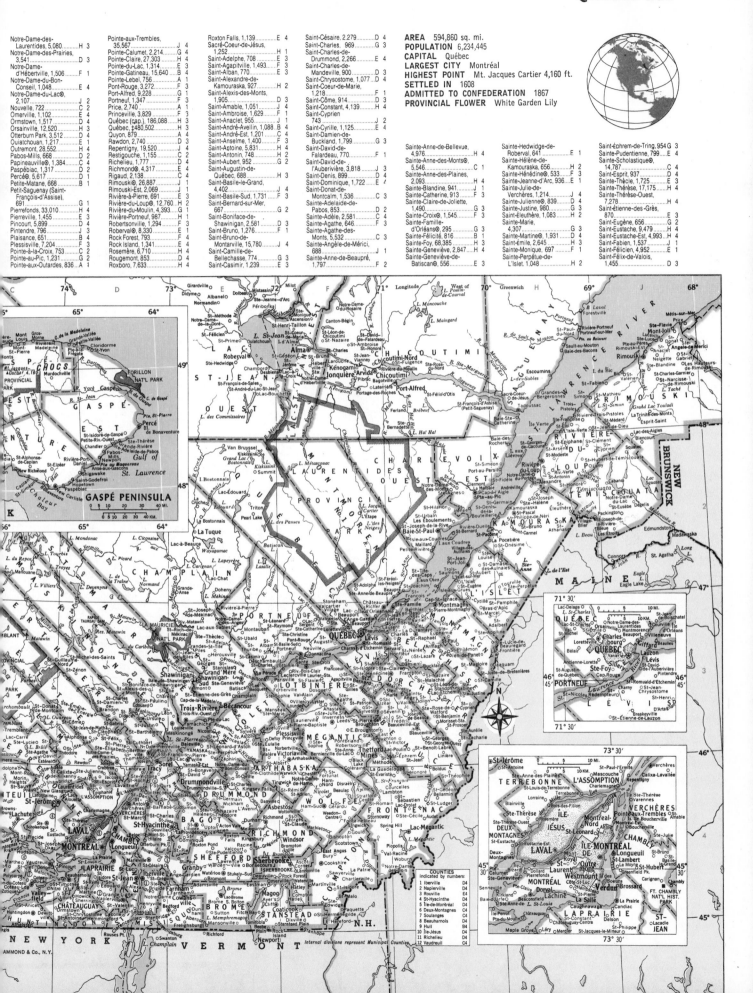

COUNTIES Referenced by numbers:
1 Iberville D4
2 Napierville D4
3 Rouville D4
4 St-Hyacinthe D4
5 Île-d'Orléans D4
6 Deux-Montagnes C4
7 Soulanges C4
8 Beauharnois D4
9 Hull B4
10 Laval H4
11 Richelieu D4
12 Vaudreuil C4

Internal divisions represent Municipal Counties

AMMOND & Co., N.Y.

Saint-Féréol-les-Neiges, 692 ....G 2
Saint-Flavien, 645 ....F 3
Saint-François-d'Assise, 691 ....G 1
Saint-François-du-Lac, 1,001 ....E 3
Saint-Fulgence, 999 ....G 1
Saint-Gabriel, 3,383 ....D 3
Saint-Gédéon, Frontenac, 1,174 ....G 4
Saint-Gédéon, Lac-St-Jean-E., 885 ....G 1
Saint-Georges, Beauce, 7,554 ....G 3
Saint-Georges, Champlain, 2,061 ....D 3
Saint-Georges-de-Cacouna, 1,001 ....H 2
Saint-Georges-Ouest, 6,000 ....G 3
Saint-Germain-de-Grantham, 1,104 ......E 4
Saint-Gilles, 694 ....F 3
Saint-Grégoire, 655 ....D 4
Saint-Grégoire-de-Greenlay, 694 ....E 4
Saint-Henri, 1,160 ....J 3
Saint-Honoré, Beauce, 1,045 ....G 4
Saint-Honoré, Chicoutimi, 1,055 ....F 1
Saint-Hubert, 36,851 ....J 4
Saint-Hubert-de-Témiscouata, 832 ......J 2
Saint-Hyacinthe, 24,562 ....D 4
Saint-Isidore, 736 ....F 3
Saint-Isidore-de-Laprairie, 749 ....D 4
Saint-Jacques, 1,975 ....D 4
Saint-Jean, 32,863 ....D 4
Saint-Jean-Chrysostome, 1,905 ....J 3
Saint-Jean-de-Boischatel, 1,685 ....J 3
Saint-Jean-de-Dieu, 1,148 ..J 1
Saint-Jean-de-Matha, 943 ...D 3
Saint-Jean-Port-Joli, 1,795 ....H 2
Saint-Jérôme, Lac-St-Jean-E., 1,910 ......F 1
Saint-Jérôme, Terrebonne, 26,524 .....H 4
Saint-Joachim, 920 ....G 2
Saint-Joachim-de-Tourelle, 1,021 ......C 1

Saint-Joseph, 4,945 ....E 4
Saint-Joseph-de-Beauce, 2,893 ....G 3
Saint-Joseph-de-la-Rivière-Bleue, 1,429 ...J 2
Saint-Joseph-de-Sorel, 3,296 ....D 3
Saint-Jovite, 3,132 ....C 3
Saint-Lambert, 18,616 ....J 4
Saint-Laurent, 62,955 ....H 4
Saint-Léonard, 52,040 ....H 4
Saint-Léonard-d'Aston, 995 ....E 3
Saint-Léon-de-Standon, 830 ....G 3
Saint-Léon-le-Grand, 695 ...B 2
Saint-Liboire©, 667 ....E 4
Saint-Louis-de-Terrebonne, 1,113 ....H 4
Saint-Louis-du-Ha! Ha!, 733 H 2
Saint-Luc, 4,850 ....D 4
Saint-Marc-des-Carrières, 2,650 ....E 3
Saint-Méthode-de-Frontenac, 793 ....E 4
Saint-Michel-de-Bellechasse, 967 ......G 3
Saint-Michel-des-Saints, 1,647 ....D 3
Saint-Nazaire-de-Chicoutimi, 884 ....F 1
Saint-Nicolas, 1,975 ....H 3
Saint-Noël, 910 ....B 1
Saint-Odilon, 818 ....G 3
Saint-Ours, 838 ....D 4
Saint-Pacôme, 1,180 ....G 2
Saint-Pamphile, 3,542 ......H 3
Saint-Pascal©, 2,513 ....H 2
Saint-Paul-de-Montminy, 746 ....G 3
Saint-Paulin,'809 ....D 3
Saint-Paul-l'Ermite, 3,165 ..J 4
Saint-Philippe-de-Néri, 701 ....H 2
Saint-Pie, 1,709 ....E 4
Saint-Pierre, 6,801 ....H 4
Saint-Prime, 2,350 ....E 1
Saint-Prosper-de-Dorchester, 1,696 .....G 3
Saint-Raphaël©, 1,216 ......G 3
Saint-Raymond, 4,036 ....F 3
Saint-Redempteur, 1,652 ....J 3
Saint-Régis, 1,247 ....C 4
Saint-Rémi, 2,282 ....D 4
Saint-Roch-de-l'Achigan, 962 ....D 4

Saint-Roch-de-Richelieu, 721 ....D 4
Saint-Romuald-d'Etchemin©, 8,394 .....J 3
Saint-Sauveur-des-Monts, 1,846 ....C 4
Saint-Siméon, 1,186 ....G 2
Saint-Thomas-de-Joliette, 728 ....D 4
Saint-Timothée, 1,613 ....D 4
Saint-Tite, 3,130 ....E 3
Saint-Ubald, 809 ....E 3
Saint-Ulric, 936 ....B 1
Saint-Urbain-de-Charlevoix, 1,172 ......G 2
Saint-Victor, 1,017 ....G 3
Saint-Zacharie, 1,390 ....G 3
Saint-Zotique, 1,243 ....C 4
Sault-au-Mouton, 951 ....H 1
Sawyerville, 864 ....F 4
Sayabec, 1,789 ....B 2
Scotstown, 917 ....F 4
Senneville, 1,412 ....A 4
Shawbridge, 969 ....C 4
Shawinigan, 27,792 ....E 3
Shawinigan-Sud, 11,470 ....E 3
Sherbrooke©, 80,711 ....E 4
Sillery, 13,932 ....J 3
Sorel©, 19,347 ....D 4
Squatec, 950 ....J 2
Stanstead Plain, 1,192 ......F 4
Sully, 776 ....H 2
Sutton, 1,684 ....E 4
Tadoussac©, 1,010 ....H 1
Templeton, 3,843 ....B 4
Terrebonne, 9,212 ....H 4
Thetford Mines, 22,003 .....F 3
Thurso, 3,219 ....B 4
Touraine, 6,978 ....B 4
Tourville, 678 ....H 2
Tracy, 11,842 ....D 3
Tring-Jonction, 1,283 ......F 3
Trois-Pistoles, 4,578 ....H 1
Trois-Rivières, 55,869 ......E 3
Trois-Rivières-Ouest, 8,057 ....E 3
Upton, 818 ....E 4
Val-Brillant, 690 ....B 1
Valcourt, 2,411 ....E 4
Val-David, 1,627 ....C 4
Vallée-Jonction, 1,295 ......G 3
Valleyfield, 30,173 ....C 4
Val-Saint-Michel, 2,050 .....H 3
Vanier, 9,717 ....J 3
Varennes, 2,382 ....J 4
Vaudreuil©, 3,843 ....C 4

Verchères©, 1,840 ....J 4
Verdun, 74,718 ....H 4
Victoriaville, 22,047 ....F 3
Villeneuve, 4,062 ....J 3
Warwick, 2,847 ....F 4
Waterloo©, 4,936 ....E 4
Waterville, 1,476 ....F 4
Weedon-Centre, 1,429 ......F 4
Westmount, 23,606 ....H 4
Windsor, 6,023 ....F 4
Wottonville, 683 ....F 4
Yamachiche©, 1,147 ....E 3

OTHER FEATURES

Alma (isl.) ....F 1
Aylmer (lake) ....B 4
Baskatong (res.) ....B 3
Batiscan (riv.) ....E 3
Bécancour (riv.) ....E 3
Bonaventure (co.) ....D 1
Bonaventure (riv.) ....C 2
Brome (lake) ....E 4
Brompton (lake) ....E 4
Cascapédia (riv.) ....C 1
Chaleur (bay) ....D 2
Champlain (lake) ....D 4
Chaudière (riv.) ....G 3
Chic-Chocs (mts.) ....C 1
Chicoutimi (riv.) ....G 2
Coudres (isl.), 1,522 ......G 2
Deschênes (lake) ....A 4
Deux Montagnes (lake) .....C 4
Ditton (riv.) ....F 4
Forillon Nat'l Park ....D 1
Fort Chambly Nat'l Hist. Park ....J 4
Gaspé (bay) ....D 1
Gaspé (cape) ....D 1
Gaspé (pen.) ....D 2
Gaspésie Prov. Park ....C 1
Gatineau (riv.) ....B 3
Îles (lake) ....E 4
Jacques-Cartier (mt.) ......F 2
Jacques-Cartier (riv.) ......F 2
Kénogami (lake) ....F 1
Kiamika (res.) ....C 3
La Maurice Nat'l Park ......E 3
Laurentides Prov. Park .....F 2
La Vérendrye Prov. Park ....A 2
Lièvre (riv.) ....B 4
Lièvres (isl.) ....H 2
Maskinongé (riv.) ....D 3
Matane (riv.) ....B 1
Matane Prov. Park ....B 1
Matapédia (riv.) ....C 2
Matawin (res.) ....D 3

Mégantic (lake) ....G 4
Memphrémagog (lake) .....E 4
Mercier (dam) ....A 3
Métabetchouane (riv.) ......F 1
Mille Îles (riv.) ....H 4
Montmorency (riv.) ....F 2
Mont-Tremblant Prov. Park .C 3
Nicolet (riv.) ....E 3
Nominingue (lake) ....C 3
Nord (riv.) ....C 4
Orléans (isl.), 5,435 ....F 2
Ottawa (riv.) ....B 4
Ouareau (riv.) ....D 3
Patapédia (riv.) ....D 2
Péribonca (riv.) ....F 1
Petite Nation (riv.) ....B 4
Prairies (riv.) ....H 4
Rimouski (riv.) ....J 1
Ristigouche (riv.) ....C 2
Saguenay (riv.) ....G 1
Sainte-Anne (riv.) ....F 2
Sainte-Anne (riv.) ....G 2
Saint-François (lake) ....E 4
Saint-François (riv.) ....E 4
Saint-Jean (lake) ....F 1
Saint Lawrence (gulf) ......D 2
Saint Lawrence (riv.) ......E 3
Saint-Louis (lake) ....H 4
Saint-Maurice (riv.) ....E 3
Saint-Pierre (lake) ....E 3
Shawinigan (riv.) ....F 1
Shipshaw (riv.) ....F 1
Soeurs (isl.) ....H 4
Témiscouata (lake) ....H 2
Tremblant (lake) ....C 3
Trente et un Milles (lake) ...B 3
Verte (isl.), 175 ....H 1
Yamaska (riv.) ....E 4
York (riv.) ....D 1

© County seat.
‡ Population of metropolitan area.

QUÉBEC, NORTHERN
INTERNAL DIVISIONS

Abitibi (co.), 112,244 ....B 2
Abitibi (terr.), 21,308 ....B 3
Chicoutimi (county), 163,348 ....C 2
Lac-Saint-Jean-Ouest (county), 57,074 .....C 2
Mistassini (terr.), 2,702 .B 2
Nouveau-Québec (terr.), 10,002 ......E 1

Pontiac (co.), 19,570 ....B 3
Saguenay (co.), 111,272 D 2
Témiscamingue (county), 54,656 ....B 3

CITIES and TOWNS

Aguanish, 442 ....E 2
Amos©, 6,984 ....E 3
Angliers, 404 ....B 3
Baie-du-Poste, 1,598 ......C 2
Barraute, 1,288 ....B 3
Belleterre, 614 ....B 3
Betsiamites, 1,574 ....D 3
Cadillac, 1,102 ....B 3
Chapais, 2,914 ....B 3
Chibougamau, 9,701 ......C 3
Clarke City, 750 ....D 2
Dolbeau, 7,633 ....C 2
Duparquet, 786 ....B 3
Dupuy, 439 ....B 3
Évain, 605 ....B 3
Forestville, 1,606 ....D 3
Fort-Chimo, 693 ....F 2
Fort-George, 1,280 ....B 2
Gagnon, 3,787 ....D 2
Godbout, 653 ....D 2
Hauterive, 13,181 ....D 3
Havre-St-Pierre, 2,999 ....E 2
Inoucdjouac, 525 ....E 1
La Reine, 450 ....B 3
La Sarre, 5,185 ....B 3
La Tabatière, 475 ....F 2
Lebel-sur-Quevillon, 2,936 ....B 3
Lorrainville, 906 ....B 3
Macamic, 1,705 ....B 3
Malartic, 5,347 ....B 3
Manicouagan, 500 ....D 2
Matagami, 2,411 ....B 3
Micoua, 851 ....D 3
Moisie, 570 ....D 2
Noranda, 10,741 ....B 3
Normétal, 1,851 ....B 3
Nouveau-Comptoir, 514..B 2
Obedjiwan, 712 ....C 3
Parent, 452 ....C 3
Port-Cartier, 3,730 ....D 2
Port-Cartier-Ouest, 500...D 2
Port-Menier, 244 ....D 2
Poste-de-la-Baleine, 987 B 1
Povungnituk, 676 ....E 1
Rivière-au-Tonnerre, 520 D 2
Rouyn, 17,821 ....B 3
Rupert House, 757 ....B 2

Saglouc, 402 ....E 1
Saint-Augustin, 916 ......F 2
Schefferville, 3,271 ....D 2
Sennetterre, 4,303 ....B 3
Sept-Îles, 24,320 ....D 2
Témiscaming, 2,428 ......B 3
Val-d'Or, 17,421 ....B 3
Ville-Marie©, 1,995 ......B 3

OTHER FEATURES

Anticosti (isl.), 419 ......E 2
Baleine, Grande Rivière de la (riv.) ....B 1
Betsiamites (riv.) ....C 2
Bienville (lake) ....C 2
Cabonga (res.) ....B 3
Caniapiscau (riv.) ....D 1
Daniel-Johnson (dam)...D 2
Dozois (res.) ....B 3
Eastmain (riv.) ....B 2
George (riv.) ....F 2
Gouin (res.) ....C 3
Grande Rivière, La (riv.) ....C 2
Guillaume-Delisle (lake) B 1
Harricana (riv.) ....B 3
Honguedo (passg.) ....E 3
Hudson (bay) ....A 1
Hudson (str.) ....E 1
Jacques-Cartier (passg.) ..D 2
James (bay) ....A 2
Koksoak (riv.) ....D 1
La Vérendrye Prov. Park ....B 3
Louis-XIV (pt.) ....B 2
Manicouagan (res.) ....D 2
Mistassibi (riv.) ....C 2
Mistassini (riv.) ....C 2
Moisie (riv.) ....D 2
Natashquan (riv.) ....E 2
Nottaway (riv.) ....B 2
Nouveau-Québec (crater) ....F 1
Otish (mts.) ....D 2
Ottawa (riv.) ....B 3
Reed (lake) ....D 2
Romaine (riv.) ....E 2
Saguenay (riv.) ....C 2
Saguenay Prov. Park .....E 2
Saint Lawrence (gulf)....E 2
Saint Lawrence (riv.) .....D 3
Ungava (bay) ....F 1
Ungava (pen.) ....E 1
Wolstenholme (cape) ....E 1
Wright (mt.) ....D 2

ONTARIO, NORTHERN

INTERNAL DIVISIONS

Algoma (terr. dist.), 121,937 D 3
Cochrane (terr. dist.), 95,836 D 2
Kenora (terr. dist.), 53,230 C 2
Manitoulin (terr. dist.), 10,931 D 3
Nipissing (terr. dist.), 78,867 E 3
Parry Sound (terr. dist.), 30,244 E 3
Rainy River (terr. dist.), 25,750 B 3
Renfrew (county), 90,875 E 3
Sudbury (reg. munic.), 168,224 D 3
Sudbury (terr. dist.), 198,079 D 3
Thunder Bay (terr. dist.), 145,390 C 3
Timiskaming (terr. dist.), 46,485 D 3

CITIES and TOWNS

Atikokan, 6,007 B 3
Blind River, 3,450 D 3
Capreol, 3,994 D 3
Chalk River, 1,094 E 3
Chapleau, 3,365 D 3
Cochrane ⊙, 4,965 D 3
Deep River, 5,671 E 3
Dryden, 6,939 B 3
Elliot Lake, 8,727 D 3
Espanola, 6,045 D 3
Fort Albany, 25 D 2
Fort Frances ⊙, 9,947 B 3
Geraldton, 3,178 C 3
Haileybury ⊙, 5,280 D 3
Hearst, 5,354 D 3
Huntsville, 9,784 E 3
Iroquois Falls, 7,055 D 3
Kapuskasing, 12,834 D 3
Kenora ⊙, 10,952 B 3
Kirkland Lake, 13,599 D 3
Manitouwadge, 3,258 C 3
Mattawa, 2,881 E 3
Moose Factory, 849 D 2
Moosonee, 1,793 D 2
New Liskeard, 5,488 E 3
Nickel Centre, 13,037 D 3
North Bay ⊙, 49,187 E 3
Onaping Falls, 7,511 D 3
Parry Sound ⊙, 5,842 D 3
Pembroke ⊙, 16,544 E 3
Renfrew, 9,173 E 3
Sault Sainte Marie ⊙, 80,332 D 3
Sturgeon Falls, 6,662 E 3
Sudbury, 99,512 D 3
Sudbury, ‡155,424 D 3
Thunder Bay ⊙, 108,411 C 3
Thunder Bay, ‡112,093 C 3
Timmins, 43,182 D 3
Valley East, 17,937 D 3
Walden, 10,788 D 3
Wawa, 4,375 C 3

OTHER FEATURES

Abitibi (lake) E 3
Abitibi (riv.) D 2
Albany (riv.) C 2
Algonquin Prov. Park, 337 E 3
Attawapiskat (riv.) C 2
Big Trout (lake) B 2
Caribou (isl.), 3 C 3
Eabamet (lake) C 2
Ekwan (riv.) C 2
English (riv.) B 2
Groundhog (riv.) D 3
Hannah (bay) D 2
Henrietta Maria (cape) D 1
Hudson (bay) D 1
James (bay) D 2
Kapuskasing (riv.) D 3
Kenogami (riv.) C 2
Lake of the Woods (lake) B 3
Lake Superior Prov. Park D 3
Manitoulin (isl.), 10,064 D 3
Mattagami (riv.) D 3
Michipicoten (isl.), 4 C 3
Mille Lacs (lake) B 3
Missinaibi (riv.) D 2
Nipigon (lake) C 3
North Caribou (lake) B 2
Ogidaki (mt.) D 3
Ogoki (riv.) C 2
Ottawa (riv.) E 3
Pipestone (riv.) B 2
Polar Bear Prov. Park D 2
Quetico Prov. Park B 3
Rainy (lake) B 3
Red (lake) B 2
Sachigo (riv.) B 2
Saint Joseph (lake) B 2
Sandy (lake) B 2
Seine (riv.) B 3
Seul (lake) B 2
Severn (riv.) B 2
Sibley Prov. Park, 2 C 3
Slate (isls.), 4 C 3
Superior (lake) C 3
Sutton (riv.) D 2
Thunder (bay) C 3
Timagami (lake) D 3
Timiskaming (lake) E 3
Winisk (riv.) C 2
Winnipeg (riv.) A 2
Woods (lake) B 3

ONTARIO

INTERNAL DIVISIONS

Algoma (terr. dist.), 121,937 J 5
Brant (county), 96,767 D 4
Bruce (county), 47,385 C 3
Cochrane (terr. dist.), 95,836 J 4
Dufferin (county), 21,200 D 3
Dundas (county), 17,457 J 2
Durham (reg. munic.), 221,503 F 4
Elgin (county), 66,608 C 5
Essex (county), 306,399 B 5
Frontenac (county), 101,692 H 3
Glengarry (county), 18,480 K 2
Grenville (county), 24,316 J 3
Grey (county), 66,403 D 3
Haldimand-Norfolk (reg. munic.), 86,772 D 5
Haliburton (county), 9,081 F 2
Hamilton-Wentworth (reg. munic.), 401,883 D 4
Halton (reg. munic.), 190,469 E 4
Hastings (county), 99,393 G 3
Huron (county), 52,951 C 4
Kenora (terr. dist.), 53,230 G 5
Kent (county), 101,118 B 5
Lambton (county), 114,314 B 5
Lanark (county), 42,259 H 3
Leeds (county), 50,093 H 3
Lennox and Addington (county), 28,359 G 3
Manitoulin (terr. dist.), 10,931 B 2
Middlesex (county), 282,014 C 4
Muskoka (dist. munic.) 31,938 E 3
Niagara (reg. munic.), 347,328 E 4
Nipissing (terr. dist.), 78,867 F 2
Northumberland (county), 60,102 G 3
Ottawa-Carleton (reg. munic.), 471,931 J 2
Oxford (county), 80,349 D 4
Parry Sound (terr. dist.), 30,244 D 2
Peel (reg. munic.), 259,402 E 4
Perth (county), 62,973 C 4
Peterborough (county), 92,417 F 3
Prescott (county), 27,832 K 2
Prince Edward (county), 20,640 G 3
Rainy River (terr. dist.), 25,750 G 5
Renfrew (county), 90,875 G 2
Russell (county), 16,287 J 2
Simcoe (county), 175,604 E 3
Stormont (county), 61,302 K 2
Sudbury (reg. munic.), 168,224 K 6
Sudbury (terr. dist.), 198,079 J 5
Thunder Bay (terr. dist.), 145,390 H 5
Timiskaming (terr. dist.), 46,485 K 5
Toronto (metro. munic.), 2,086,017 K 4
Victoria (county), 36,641 F 3
Waterloo (reg. munic.), 254,037 D 4
Wellington (county), 108,581 D 4
York (reg. munic.), 166,060 E 4

AREA 412,582 sq. mi.
POPULATION 7,707,000
CAPITAL Toronto
LARGEST CITY Toronto
HIGHEST POINT Ogidaki Mtn. 2,183 ft.
SETTLED IN 1749
ADMITTED TO CONFEDERATION 1867
PROVINCIAL FLOWER White Trillium

CITIES and TOWNS

Ailsa Craig, 608 C 4
Ajax, 15,052 E 4
Alban, 420 D 1
Alcona Beach, 659 E 3
Alexandria, 3,240 K 2
Alfred, 1,230 K 2
Alliston, 3,176 E 3
Almonte, 3,696 H 2
Alvinston, 702 B 5
Amherstburg, 5,169 A 5
Amherst View, 3,121 H 3
Ancaster, 15,326 D 4
Angus, 3,174 E 3
Apple Hill, 318 K 2
Arkona, 469 C 4
Armstrong, 574 H 4
Arnprior, 6,016 H 2
Arthur, 1,414 D 4
Athens, 1,071 J 3
Atherley, 392 E 3
Atikokan, 6,007 G 5
Atwood, 690 D 4
Aurora, 13,614 J 3
Avonmore, 287 K 2
Aylmer, 4,755 C 5
Ayr, 1,272 D 4
Ayton, 423 D 3
Baden, 959 D 4
Bala, 462 E 2
Bancroft, 2,276 G 2
Barrie ⊙, 27,676 E 3
Barry's Bay, 1,432 G 2
Batawa, 667 G 3
Batchawana Bay, 586 J 5
Bath, 810 H 3
Bayfield, 503 C 4
Bayside, 1,732 G 3
Baysville, 283 E 2
Beachburg, 549 H 2
Beachville, 995 D 4
Beardmore, 754 H 5
Beaverton, 1,485 E 3
Beeton, 1,061 E 3
Belle River, 2,877 B 5
Belleville ⊙, 35,128 G 3
Belmont, 798 C 5
Bethany, 325 F 3
Bewdley, 446 F 3
Bicroft, 576 F 2
Blackburn, 3,841 J 2
Blenheim, 3,490 C 5
Blind River, 3,450 J 5
Bloomfield, 730 G 4
Blyth, 814 C 4
Bobcaygeon, 1,518 F 3
Bonfield, 694 E 1
Bothwell, 810 C 5
Bourget, 855 J 2
Bracebridge ⊙, 6,903 E 2
Bradford, 3,401 E 3
Braeside, 522 H 2
Brampton ⊙, 73,570 J 4
Brantford ⊙, 64,421 D 4
Bridgenorth, 1,380 F 3
Brigden, 582 B 5
Brighton, 2,956 G 3
Brights Grove, 730 B 4
Britt, 500 D 2
Brockville ⊙, 19,765 J 3
Bruce Mines, 505 J 5
Brussels, 908 C 4
Burford, 1,291 D 4
Burgessville, 329 D 4
Burk's Falls, 891 E 2
Burlington, 87,023 E 4
Cache Bay, 727 D 1
Caesarea, 352 F 3
Calabogie, 299 H 2
Caledon, 13,480 E 4
Callander, 1,190 E 1
Cambridge, 64,114 D 4
Campbellford, 3,522 G 3
Cannington, 1,083 E 3
Cape Croker, 681 D 3
Capreol, 3,994 K 5
Caramat, 520 H 5
Cardinal, 1,865 J 3
Carleton Place, 5,020 H 2
Carlisle, 488 D 4
Carp, 516 H 2
Cartier, 740 J 5
Casselman, 1,337 J 2
Castleton, 289 F 3
Cedar Springs, 302 B 5
Chalk River, 1,094 G 1
Chapleau, 3,365 J 5
Charing Cross, 436 B 5
Chatham ⊙, 35,317 B 5
Chatsworth, 399 D 3
Chesley, 1,693 C 3
Chesterville, 1,252 J 2
Chute-a-Blondeau, 420 K 2
City View, 4,500 J 2
Clarence Creek, 411 J 2
Clarksburg, 389 D 3
Clifford, 555 D 4
Clinton, 3,154 C 4
Cobalt, 2,197 K 5
Cobden, 926 H 2
Coboconk, 477 F 3
Cobourg ⊙, 11,282 F 4
Cochrane ⊙, 4,965 K 5
Colborne, 1,588 G 4
Colchester, 752 B 6
Coldwater, 759 E 3
Collingwood, 9,775 D 3
Collins Bay, 2,089 H 3
Comber, 642 B 5
Consecon, 332 G 3
Cookstown, 847 E 3
Cornwall ⊙, 47,116 K 2
Corunna, 3,052 B 5
Cottam, 530 B 5
Courtland, 574 D 5
Courtright, 590 B 5
Coverdale, 670 F 4
Crediton, 409 C 4
Creemore, 978 D 3
Crysler, 481 J 2
Cumberland, 581 J 2
Cumberland Beach, 477 E 3
Dashwood, 434 C 4
Deep River, 5,671 G 1
Delaware, 627 C 5
Delhi, 3,894 D 5
Delta, 465 H 3
Deseronto, 1,863 G 3
Dorchester, 1,796 C 5
Douglas, 307 H 2
Drayton, 752 D 4
Dresden, 2,369 B 5
Drumbo, 460 D 4
Dryden, 6,939 G 4
Dublin, 314 C 4
Dubreuilville, 654 J 5
Dundalk, 1,022 D 3
Dundas, 17,208 D 4
Dunnville, 11,422 E 5
Durham, 2,448 D 3
Dutton, 878 C 5
East York, 104,784 J 4
Echo Bay, 493 J 5
Eganville, 1,395 G 2
Egmondville, 492 C 4
Elgin, 322 H 3
Elk Lake, 627 K 5
Elliot Lake, 8,727 B 1
Elmira, 4,730 D 4
Elmvale, 1,103 E 3
Elmwood, 345 C 3
Elora, 1,904 D 4
Embro, 703 C 4
Embrun, 1,452 J 2
Emeryville, 1,719 B 5
Emo, 768 F 5
Englehart, 1,721 K 5
Erieau, 509 C 5
Erin, 1,446 D 4
Espanola, 6,045 J 5
Essex, 4,002 B 5
Etobicoke, 282,686 J 4
Everett, 405 E 3
Exeter, 3,354 C 4
Fauquier, 643 J 5
Fenelon Falls, 1,616 F 3
Fergus, 5,433 D 4
Field, 655 E 1
Finch, 397 J 2
Fingal, 322 C 5
Fitzroy Harbour, 317 H 2
Flesherton, 524 D 3
Foleyet, 637 J 5
Fordwich, 325 C 4

(continued on following page)

NORTHERN ONTARIO
SCALE
0 25 50 100 150 200 MI.
0 25 50 100 150 200 KM.
Provincial Capital
Provincial and State Boundaries
County Seats
International Boundaries
County Boundaries
© C.S. HAMMOND & Co., N.Y.
Hudson Bay
James Bay
MANITOBA
KENORA
THUNDER BAY
COCHRANE
ALGOMA
SUDBURY
TIMISKAMING
NIPISSING
RAINY RIVER
MINNESOTA
MICHIGAN
Lake Superior
Longitude West of 85° Greenwich

Rockwood, 996 ....D 4
Rodney, 1,016 ....C 5
Rolphton, 418 ....G 1
Russell, 583 ....J 2
Ruthven, 461 ....B 6
Saint Catharines ⊙,
  109,722 ....E 4
Saint Catharines-Niagara,
  ‡303,429 ....E 4
Saint Charles, 468 ....D 1
Saint Clair Beach, 1,987 . .B 5
Saint-Eugène, 512 ....K 2
Saint George, 949 ....D 4
Saint Isidore de Prescott,
  615 ....K 2
Saint Jacobs, 787 ....D 4
Saint Mary's, 4,650 ....C 4
Saint Thomas ⊙, 25,545 . .D 5
Saint Williams, 437 ....D 5
Salem, 348 ....D 4
Sarnia ⊙, 57,644 ....B 5
Sauble Beach, 338 ....C 3
Sault Sainte Marie ⊙,
  80,332 ....J 5
Scarborough, 334,310 . .K 4
Schomberg, 677 ....J 3
Schreiber, 2,072 ....H 5
Scotland, 217 ....D 4
Seaforth, 2,134 ....C 4
Searchmont, 375 ....J 5
Sebringville, 571 ....C 4
Seeleys Bay, 406 ....H 3
Shallow Lake, 385 ....C 3
Shanty Bay, 316 ....E 3
Sharbot Lake, 461 ....H 3
Shedden, 277 ....C 5

Shelburne, 1,790 ....D 3
Simcoe ⊙, 10,793 ....D 5
Sioux Lookout, 2,530 . .G 4
Smithfield, 319 ....G 3
Smiths Falls, 9,585 ....H 3
Smithville, 1,418 ....E 4
Smooth Rock Falls, 1,239 . .J 5
Sombra, 685 ....B 5
Southampton, 2,036 ....C 3
South River, 1,052 ....E 2
Spanish, 1,257 ....J 5
Spencerville, 386 ....J 3
Springfield, 522 ....C 5
Springford, 296 ....D 5
Stayner, 1,937 ....E 3
Stirling, 1,500 ....G 3
Stittsville, 1,994 ....J 2
Stoney Creek, 27,373 . .E 4
Stoney Point, 749 ....B 5
Stratford ⊙, 24,508 . .C 4
Strathroy, 6,592 ....C 5
Stroud, 548 ....E 3
Sturgeon Falls, 6,662 . .E 1
Sudbury ⊙, 99,512 ....K 5
Sudbury, ‡155,424 ....K 5
Sultan, 343 ....J 5
Sunderland, 807 ....E 3
Sundridge, 723 ....E 2
Sutton, 2,500 ....E 3
Sydenham, 556 ....H 3
Tamworth, 375 ....H 3
Tara, 643 ....C 3
Tavistock, 1,490 ....D 4
Tecumseh, 5,165 ....B 5
Teeswater, 983 ....C 3

Terrace Bay, 1,819 ....H 5
Thamesford, 1,185 ....C 4
Thamesville, 1,028 ....C 5
Thedford, 719 ....C 4
Thessalon, 1,879 ....J 5
Thornbury, 1,220 ....D 3
Thorndale, 463 ....C 4
Thornton, 313 ....E 3
Thorold, 15,065 ....E 4
Thunder Bay ⊙, 108,411 . .H 5
Thunder Bay, ‡112,093 . .H 5
Tilbury, 3,580 ....B 5
Tillsonburg, 6,608 ....D 5
Timagami, 693 ....K 5
Timmins, 43,182 ....J 5
Tiverton, 567 ....C 3
Tobermory, 315 ....C 2
Toronto (cap.) ⊙, 712,786 K 4
Toronto (Metro.),
  2,086,017 ....K 4
Toronto, ‡2,628,043 . .K 4
Tottenham, 1,616 ....E 3
Trenton, 14,589 ....G 3
Trout Creek, 586 ....E 2
Turkey Point, 373 ....D 5
Tweed, 1,738 ....G 3
Uxbridge, 3,077 ....E 3
Vanier, 22,477 ....J 2
Vankleek Hill, 1,691 . .K 2
Vars, 395 ....J 2
Vaughan, 15,873 ....J 4
Vermilion Bay, 637 . .G 4
Verner, 1,011 ....D 1
Verona, 689 ....H 3
Victoria Harbour, 1,243 . .E 3
Vienna, 390 ....D 5
Vittoria, 455 ....D 5
Wabigoon, 312 ....G 5
Walden, 10,788 ....J 5
Walkerton ⊙, 4,479 . .C 3
Wallaceburg, 10,550 . .B 5
Wardsville, 388 ....C 5
Warkworth, 562 ....G 3
Warren, 613 ....D 1
Wasaga Beach, 1,923 . .D 3
Washago, 423 ....E 3
Waterdown, 2,146 ....D 4
Waterloo, 37,893 ....D 4
Watford, 1,400 ....C 5
Waubaushene, 718 ....E 3
Wawa, 4,375 ....J 5
Webbwood, 585 ....C 1
Welland, 44,397 ....E 5
Wellesley, 816 ....D 4
Wellington, 988 ....G 4
Wendover, 313 ....J 2
West Lorne, 1,094 ....C 5
Westport, 601 ....H 3
Wheatley, 1,657 ....C 5
Whitby ⊙, 25,324 ....F 4
Whitchurch-Stouffville,
  11,262 ....J 3
White River, 945 ....J 5
Whitney, 826 ....F 2
Wiarton, 2,222 ....C 3
Wikwemikong, 895 ....C 2
Williamsburg, 398 ....J 3
Williamstown, 312 ....K 2
Winchester, 1,575 ....J 2
Windsor ⊙, 203,300 . .B 5
Windsor, ‡258,643 ....B 5

Wingham, 2,913 ....C 4
Wolfe Island, 335 ....H 3
Woodstock ⊙, 26,173 . .D 4
Woodville, 473 ....F 3
Wroxeter, 291 ....C 4
Wyoming, 1,279 ....B 5
Yarker, 335 ....H 3
York, 147,301 ....J 4
Zephyr, 337 ....E 3
Zurich, 767 ....C 4

OTHER FEATURES

Abitibi (riv.) ....J 5
Algonquin Prov. Park, 337 F 2
Amherst (isl.), 367 ....H 3
Balsam (lake) ....F 3
Barrie (isl.), 109 ....B 1
Bays (lake) ....F 2

Big Rideau (lake) ....H 3
Black (riv.) ....E 3
Bruce (pen.) ....C 2
Buckhorn (lake) ....F 2
Cabot (head) ....C 2
Charleston (lake) ....J 3
Christian (isl.), 506 . .D 3
Clear (lake) ....F 2
Cockburn (isl.) ....A 2
Couchiching (lake) . .E 3
Croker (cape) ....D 3
Don (riv.) ....J 4
Douglas (pt.) ....C 3
Erie (lake) ....E 5
Flowerpot (isl.) ....C 2
French (riv.) ....D 1
Georgian (bay) ....D 2
Georgian Bay Is. Nat'l Park D 3

Georgina (isl.), 181 ....E 3
Grand (riv.) ....D 4
Humber (riv.) ....J 3
Hurd (cape) ....C 2
Huron (lake) ....B 3
Ipperwash Prov. Park, 32 C 4
Joseph (lake) ....E 2
Killbear Point Prov. Park . .D 2
Lake of the Woods (lake) . .F 5
Lake Superior Prov. Park . .J 5
Lonely (isl.), 3 ....C 2
Long (pt.) ....D 5
Long Point (bay) ....D 5
Madawaska (riv.) ....G 2
Magnetawan (riv.) ....D 2
Main (chan.) ....C 2
Manitou (lake) ....C 2
Manitoulin (isl.), 10,064 . .B 2
Mattagami (riv.) ....J 5
Michipicoten (isl.), 4 . .H 5
Missinaibi (riv.) ....J 5
Mississagi (riv.) ....A 1
Mississippi (lake) ....H 3
Muskoka (lake) ....E 2
Niagara (riv.) ....E 4
Nipigon (lake) ....H 5
Nipissing (lake) ....E 1
North (chan.) ....A 1
Nottawasaga (bay) ....D 3
Ogidaki (mt.) ....J 5
Ontario (lake) ....G 4
Opeongo (lake) ....F 2
Ottawa (riv.) ....H 2
Owen (sound) ....D 3
Panache (lake) ....C 1
Parry (isl.), 318 ....D 2
Parry (sound) ....D 2
Pelee (pt.) ....B 6

Petre (pt.) ....G 4
Point Pelee Nat'l Park, 202B 6
Presqu'île Prov. Park, 67 G 4
Quetico Prov. Park ....G 5
Rainy (lake) ....G 5
Rice (lake) ....F 3
Rideau (lake) ....H 3
Rondeau Prov. Park, 103 .C 5
Rosseau (lake) ....E 2
Saint Clair (riv.) ....B 5
Saint Lawrence (lake) . .K 3
Saint Lawrence (riv.) . .J 3
Saint Lawrence Is. Nat'l
  Park ....J 3
Saugeen (riv.) ....C 3
Scugog (lake) ....F 3
Seul (lake) ....G 4
Severn (riv.) ....E 3
Sibley Prov. Park, 2 . .H 5
Simcoe (lake) ....E 3
South (bay) ....C 2
Spanish (riv.) ....C 1
Stony (lake) ....G 3
Superior (lake) ....H 5
Sydenham (riv.) ....B 5
Thames (riv.) ....B 5
Theano (pt.) ....J 5
Thousand (isls.), 1,447 . .H 3
Timagami (lake) ....K 5
Trout (lake) ....E 1
Vernon (lake) ....E 2
Walpole (isl.), 1,420 . .B 5
Welland (canal) ....E 5
Woods (lake) ....F 5

⊙ County seat.
‡ Population of metropolitan
area.

Topography

MILES
0   100   200

C. Henrietta Maria

Below Sea Level | 100 m. 328 ft. | 200 m. 656 ft. | 500 m. 1,640 ft. | 1,000 m. 3,281 ft. | 2,000 m. 6,562 ft. | 5,000 m. 16,404 ft.

Agriculture, Industry and Resources

DOMINANT LAND USE

Cereals, Cash Crops, Livestock
Dairy
General Farming, Livestock
Fruits, Vegetables
Pasture Livestock
Forests
Nonagricultural Land

MAJOR MINERAL OCCURRENCES

Ab Asbestos   Mg Magnesium
Ag Silver   Mr Marble
Au Gold   Na Salt
Co Cobalt   Ni Nickel
Cu Copper   Pb Lead
Fe Iron Ore   Pt Platinum
G Natural Gas   U Uranium
Gr Graphite   Zn Zinc

⚡ Water Power
Major Industrial Areas
□ Major Pulp & Paper Mills

OTTAWA
Food Processing, Printing & Publishing, Wood Products, Machinery

THUNDER BAY
Pulp & Paper, Lumber, Machinery, Shipbuilding

SAULT STE.MARIE
Iron & Steel, Pulp & Paper, Lumber, Metal Products, Chemicals

SARNIA
Chemicals, Oil Refining, Rubber Products

WINDSOR
Motor Vehicles, Food Processing, Metal Products, Chemicals, Machinery

TORONTO–HAMILTON–NIAGARA
Iron & Steel, Metal Products, Food Processing, Electrical Products, Chemicals, Printing & Publishing, Machinery, Automobiles, Aircraft, Oil Refining

LONDON
Food Processing, Metal Products, Printing & Publishing, Locomotives, Chemicals, Machinery, Leather Goods

ONTARIO SOUTHERN PART

SCALE
0 10 20 30 40 50 MI.
0 10 20 30 40 50 KM.

National Capital ⊛
Provincial Capital ⊛
County Seats ⊙
International Boundaries ——

Provincial & State Boundaries ———
County Boundaries ----
Canals

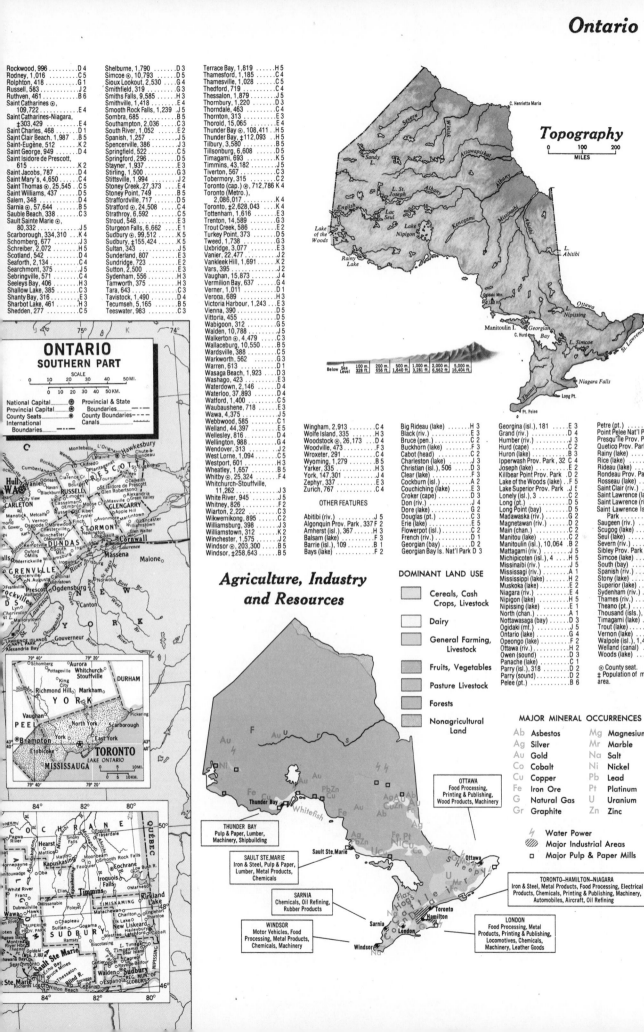

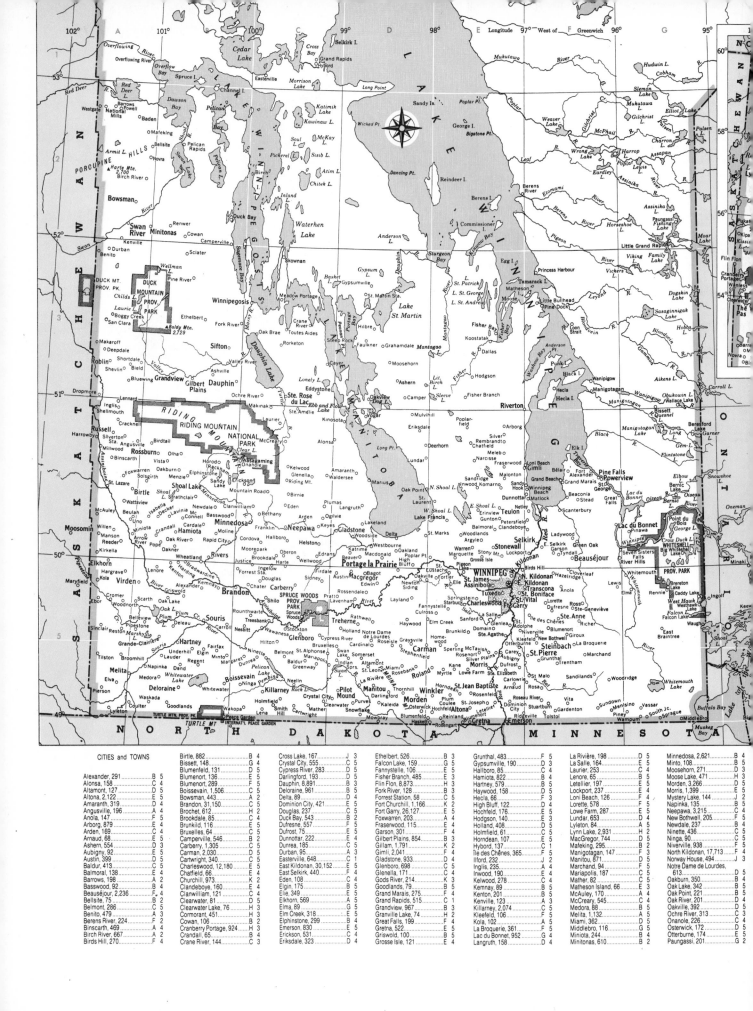

CITIES and TOWNS

MANITOBA NORTHERN PART

Scale: 0 40 80 120 MI. / 0 40 80 120 KM.

MANITOBA SOUTHERN PART

SCALE
0 5 10 20 40 60 MI.
0 5 10 20 40 60 KM.

Provincial Capital ⊛
International Boundaries
Provincial Boundaries

© C.S. HAMMOND & Co., N.Y.

AREA 251,000 sq. mi.
POPULATION 1,021,506
CAPITAL Winnipeg
LARGEST CITY Winnipeg
HIGHEST POINT Baldy Mtn. 2,729 ft.
SETTLED IN 1812
ADMITTED TO CONFEDERATION 1870
PROVINCIAL FLOWER Prairie Crocus

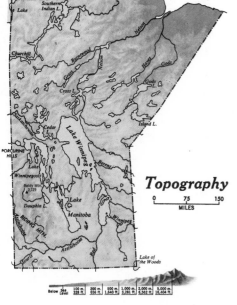

Topography

0 75 150
MILES

Below Sea Level / 100 m. 328 ft. / 200 m. 656 ft. / 500 m. 1,640 ft. / 1,000 m. 3,281 ft. / 2,000 m. 6,562 ft. / 5,000 m. 16,404 ft.

Agriculture, Industry and Resources

DOMINANT LAND USE

Cereals (chiefly barley, oats)
Cereals, Livestock
Dairy
Livestock
Forests
Nonagricultural Land

MAJOR MINERAL OCCURRENCES

Au Gold
Co Cobalt
Cu Copper
Na Salt

Ni Nickel
O Petroleum
Pb Lead
Pt Platinum
Zn Zinc

⚡ Water Power
▨ Major Industrial Areas
□ Major Pulp & Paper Mills

WINNIPEG
Food Processing, Rolling Stock, Printing & Publishing, Farm Machinery, Clothing, Oil Refining, Electrical Products

Topography

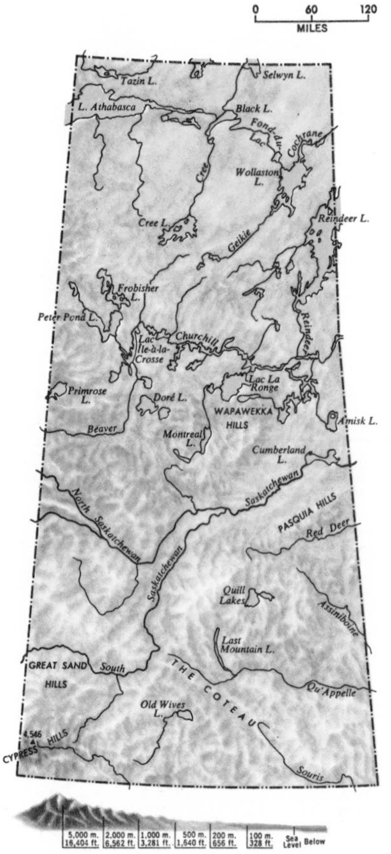
0 60 120
MILES
Tazin L.
Selwyn L.
L. Athabasca
Black L.
Fond-du-Lac
Cochrane
Wollaston L.
Cree L.
Reindeer L.
Geikie
Frobisher L.
Peter Pond L.
Lac Île-à-la-Crosse
Churchill
Reindeer
Lac La Ronge
Primrose L.
Doré L.
WAPAWEKKA HILLS
Amisk L.
Beaver
Montreal L.
Cumberland L.
Saskatchewan
PASQUIA HILLS
North Saskatchewan
Red Deer
Quill Lakes
Assiniboine
Last Mountain L.
GREAT SAND HILLS
South
THE COTEAU
Qu'Appelle
Old Wives L.
4,546
CYPRESS HILLS
Souris
5,000 m. 16,404 ft.
2,000 m. 6,562 ft.
1,000 m. 3,281 ft.
500 m. 1,640 ft.
200 m. 656 ft.
100 m. 328 ft.
Sea Level
Below

CITIES and TOWNS

Abbey, 246 C 5
Aberdeen, 288 E 3
Abernethy, 253 H 5
Air Ronge, 239 M 3
Alameda, 370 J 6
Alida, 230 K 6
Allan, 712 E 4
Alsask, 819 B 4
Alvena, 143 E 3
Aneroid, 163 D 6
Annaheim, 182 G 3
Antler, 115 K 6
Arborfield, 418 H 2
Archerwill, 302 H 3
Arcola, 539 J 6
Arran, 120 K 4
Asquith, 355 D 3
Assiniboia, 2,675 E 6
Avonlea, 391 G 5
Aylesbury, 88 F 5
Aylsham, 170 H 2
Balcarres, 678 H 5
Balgonie, 518 G 5
Batoche, 27 E 3
Battleford, 1,803 C 3
Beatty, 97 G 3
Beauval, 436 L 3
Beechy, 342 D 5
Bellevue, 122 F 3
Bengough, 650 F 6
Bethune, 291 F 5
Bienfait, 823 J 6
Biggar, 2,607 C 3
Big River, 836 D 2
Birch Hills, 696 F 3
Birsay, 123 D 4
Bjorkdale, 223 H 3
Black Lake, 471 M 2
Bladworth, 125 E 4
Blaine Lake, 671 D 3
Borden, 187 D 3
Bradwell, 100 E 4
Bredenbury, 472 K 5
Briercrest, 130 F 5
Broadview, 959 J 5
Brock, 205 C 4
Broderick, 115 E 4
Brownlee, 121 F 5
Bruno, 728 F 3
Buchanan, 442 J 4
Buffalo Narrows, 794 L 3
Bulyea, 109 G 5
Burstall, 507 B 5
Cabri, 737 C 5
Cadillac, 217 D 6
Calder, 186 K 4
Camsell Portage, 87 L 2
Cando, 193 C 3
Canoe Lake, 138 L 3
Canora, 2,603 J 4
Canwood, 325 E 2
Carievale, 229 K 6
Carlyle, 1,101 J 6
Carmel, 90 F 3
Carnduff, 1,075 K 6
Caron, 96 F 5
Carragana, 137 J 3
Carrot River, 953 H 2
Central Butte, 522 E 5
Ceylon, 279 G 6
Chamberlain, 161 F 5
Chaplin, 368 E 5
Chelan, 101 H 3
Chitek Lake, 131 D 2
Choiceland, 456 G 2
Christopher Lake, 143 F 2
Churchbridge, 973 J 5
Clair, 86 G 3
Climax, 341 C 6
Cochin, 163 C 2
Coderre, 161 E 5
Codette, 175 H 2
Coleville, 482 B 4
Colonsay, 526 F 4
Conquest, 261 D 4
Consul, 205 B 6
Coronach, 379 F 6
Craik, 503 F 4
Crane Valley, 84 F 6
Craven, 126 G 5
Creelman, 197 H 6
Creighton, 1,857 N 4
Crooked River, 106 H 3
Cudworth, 799 F 3
Cupar, 573 G 5
Cutbank, 217 E 4
Cut Knife, 560 B 3
Dalmeny, 417 E 3
Davidson, 1,043 E 4
Debden, 340 E 2
Delisle, 653 D 4
Delmas, 161 C 3
Denare Beach, 235 M 4
Denzil, 287 B 3
Deschambault Lake, 127 M 3
Dilke, 130 F 5
Dinsmore, 421 D 4
Dodsland, 404 C 4
Dollard, 92 C 6
Domremy, 208 F 3
Dorintosh, 87 L 4
Drake, 238 G 4
Drinkwater, 118 F 5
Dubuc, 153 J 5
Duck Lake, 584 E 3
Duff, 90 H 5
Dundurn, 354 E 4
Duval, 133 G 4
Dysart, 243 H 5
Earl Grey, 243 G 5
Eastend, 784 C 6
Eatonia, 610 B 4
Ebenezer, 140 J 4
Edam, 334 C 2
Edenwold, 129 G 5
Elbow, 361 E 4
Eldorado, 289 L 2
Elfros, 253 H 4
Elrose, 573 D 4
Elstow, 150 E 4
Endeavour, 193 J 3
Englefeld, 218 G 3
Ernfold, 100 D 5
Erwood, 94 J 3
Esterhazy, 2,896 K 5
Estevan, 9,150 J 6
Eston, 1,418 C 4
Eyebrow, 181 E 5
Fairlight, 127 K 6
Fenwood, 112 H 4
Ferland, 109 D 6
Fillmore, 396 H 6
Findlater, 96 F 5
Fiske, 85 C 4
Flaxcombe, 99 B 4
Fleming, 183 K 5
Flin Flon, 471 N 4
Foam Lake, 1,331 H 4
Fond du Lac, 328 L 2
Forget, 118 J 6
Fort Qu'Appelle, 1,606 H 5
Fosston, 119 H 3
Fox Valley, 489 B 5
Francis, 159 H 5
Frenchman Butte, 86 B 2
Frobisher, 245 J 6
Frontier, 249 C 6
Gainsborough, 375 K 6
Garrick, 120 G 2
Gerald, 174 K 5
Girvin, 86 F 4
Gladmar, 131 G 6
Glaslyn, 357 C 2
Glenavon, 340 J 5
Glen Ewen, 223 K 6
Glenside, 94 E 4
Glentworth, 126 E 6
Golden Prairie, 144 B 5
Goodeve, 169 H 4
Goodsoil, 219 L 4
Gorlitz, 94 J 4
Govan, 353 G 4
Grand Coulee, 131 G 5
Gravelbourg, 1,428 E 6
Grayson, 260 J 5
Green Lake, 450 L 4
Grenfell, 1,350 J 5
Griffin, 90 H 6
Gronlid, 138 G 2
Guernsey, 142 F 4
Gull Lake, 1,156 C 5
Hafford, 580 D 3
Hague, 431 E 3
Halbrite, 166 H 6
Hanley, 390 E 4
Harris, 254 D 4
Hawarden, 190 E 4
Hazel Dell, 105 H 4
Hazenmore, 127 D 6
Hazlet, 198 C 5
Hepburn, 305 E 3
Herbert, 1,024 D 5
Herschel, 89 C 4
Hitchcock, 91 J 6
Hodgeville, 399 E 5
Hoey, 95 F 3
Holdfast, 399 F 5
Hubbard, 119 H 4
Hudson Bay, 1,971 J 3
Humboldt, 3,881 F 3
Hyas, 215 J 4
Île-à-la-Crosse, 908 L 3
Imperial, 486 F 4
Indian Head, 1,810 H 5
Invermay, 412 J 4
Ituna, 960 H 4
Jansen, 241 G 4
Kamsack, 2,783 K 4
Kayville, 84 F 6
Kelliher, 460 H 4
Kelvington, 1,053 H 3
Kenaston, 402 E 4
Kendal, 90 H 5
Kennedy, 264 J 5
Kenosee Park, 103 J 6
Kerrobert, 1,180 C 4
Khedive, 91 G 6
Killaly, 139 J 5
Kincaid, 306 D 6
Kindersley, 3,451 B 4
Kinistino, 767 F 3
Kinoosao, 95 N 3
Kipling, 927 J 5
Kisbey, 260 J 6
Krydor, 136 D 3
Kuroki, 167 H 4
Kyle, 509 C 5
Lacadena, 84 C 5
Lac Vert, 111 G 3
Lafleche, 715 E 6
Laird, 218 E 3
Lake Alma, 173 G 6
Lake Lenore, 392 G 3
La Loche, 1,136 L 3
Lampman, 830 J 6
Lancer, 199 C 5
Landis, 297 C 3
Lang, 183 G 6
Langenburg, 1,236 K 5
Langham, 535 E 3
Lanigan, 1,430 F 4
La Ronge, 906 L 3
Lashburn, 494 B 2
Leader, 1,105 B 5
Leask, 439 E 2
Lebret, 278 H 5
Leipzig, 87 C 3
Lemberg, 409 H 5
Leoville, 399 D 2
Leross, 91 H 4
Leroy, 435 G 4
Leslie, 87 H 4
Lestock, 452 G 4
Liberty, 141 F 4
Limerick, 178 E 6
Lintlaw, 212 H 3
Lipton, 401 H 5
Livelong, 126 C 2
Lloydminster, 3,953 A 2
Lone Rock, 120 A 2
Loon Lake, 348 B 1
Loreburn, 252 E 4
Love, 133 G 2
Lucky Lake, 378 D 5
Lumsden, 900 G 5
Luseland, 728 B 3
Macdowall, 173 E 2
Macklin, 829 A 3
MacNutt, 184 K 4
Macoun, 172 H 6
Macrorie, 120 E 4
Maidstone, 691 B 2
Major, 164 B 4
Makwa, 126 C 2
Manitou Beach, 118 F 4
Mankota, 424 D 6
Manor, 409 K 6
Maple Creek, 2,268 B 6
Marcelin, 306 E 3
Marchwell, 129 K 5
Marengo, 133 B 4
Margo, 225 H 4
Marquis, 131 F 5
Marsden, 241 B 3
Marshall, 195 B 2
Martensville, 870 E 3
Maryfield, 408 K 6
Mayfair, 134 D 2
Maymont, 167 D 3
McKague, 91 G 3
McLean, 178 G 5
Meacham, 186 F 3
Meadow Lake, 3,435 C 1
Meath Park, 251 F 2
Medstead, 172 C 2
Melfort, 4,725 G 3
Melville, 5,375 J 5
Mendham, 163 B 5
Meota, 233 C 2
Mervin, 198 C 2
Meyronne, 142 E 6
Midale, 647 H 6
Middle Lake, 292 F 3
Mikado, 90 J 4
Milden, 239 D 4
Milestone, 483 G 5
Minton, 215 G 6
Mistatim, 165 H 3
Molanosa, 213 M 4
Montmartre, 510 H 5
Moose Jaw, 31,854 F 5
Moosomin, 2,407 K 5
Morse, 455 D 5
Mortlach, 310 E 5
Mossbank, 460 E 6
Mozart, 93 G 4
Muenster, 280 F 3
Naicam, 711 G 3
Neilburg, 298 B 3
Neuanlage, 107 E 3
Neudorf, 469 J 5
Neville, 154 D 6
Nipawin, 4,057 H 2
Nokomis, 533 F 4
Norquay, 513 J 4
North Battleford, 12,698 C 3
North Portal, 189 J 6
Odessa, 224 H 5
Ogema, 457 G 6
Ormiston, 173 F 6
Osler, 182 E 3
Outlook, 1,767 E 4
Oxbow, 1,380 J 6
Paddockwood, 230 F 2
Pambrun, 91 D 6
Pangman, 242 G 6
Paradise Hill, 344 B 2
Parkside, 112 E 2
Paynton, 204 B 2
Pelican Narrows, 265 N 3
Pelly, 426 K 4
Pennant, 215 C 5
Pense, 270 G 5
Perdue, 411 D 3
Piapot, 160 B 6
Pierceland, 271 K 4
Pilger, 109 F 3
Pilot Butte, 403 G 5
Pine House, 427 M 3
Pleasantdale, 153 G 3
Plenty, 208 C 4
Plunkett, 152 F 4
Ponteix, 786 D 6
Porcupine Plain, 830 H 3
Preeceville, 1,118 J 4
Prelate, 407 B 5
Prince Albert, 28,464 F 2
Prud'homme, 260 F 3
Punnichy, 451 G 4
Qu'Appelle, 451 H 5
Quill Lake, 566 G 3
Quinton, 195 G 4
Rabbit Lake, 206 D 2
Radisson, 416 D 3
Radville, 1,024 G 6
Rama, 188 H 4
Raymore, 523 G 4
Redvers, 846 K 6
Regina (cap.), 139,469 G 5
Regina, ‡140,734 G 5
Regina Beach, 334 F 5
Regway, 19 G 6
Reserve, 153 J 3
Rhein, 295 J 4
Rhineland, 84 D 5
Riceton, 112 G 5
Richmound, 208 B 5
Ridgedale, 169 H 2
Riverhurst, 264 E 5
Rocanville, 891 K 5
Roche Percée, 167 J 6
Rockglen, 550 F 6
Rosetown, 2,614 D 4
Rose Valley, 591 H 3
Rosthern, 1,431 E 3
Rouleau, 395 G 5
Rush Lake, 162 D 5
Saint Benedict, 193 F 3
Saint Brieux, 367 G 3
Saint Front, 94 G 3
Saint Gregor, 125 G 3
Saint Louis, 387 F 3
Saint Victor, 85 F 6
Saint Walburg, 656 B 2
Saltcoats, 509 J 4
Sandy Bay, 494 N 3
Saskatoon, 126,449 E 3
Saskatoon, ‡126,449 E 3
Sceptre, 234 B 5
Scott, 254 C 3
Sedley, 268 H 5
Semans, 331 G 4
Senlac, 94 B 3
Shamrock, 105 E 5
Shaunavon, 2,244 C 6
Sheho, 320 H 4
Shellbrook, 1,048 E 2
Shell Lake, 255 D 2
Simmie, 100 C 6
Simpson, 239 F 4
Sintaluta, 272 H 5
Smeaton, 315 G 2
Smiley, 124 B 4
Snowden, 87 G 2
Sonningdale, 106 D 3
Southey, 548 G 5
Sovereign, 91 D 4
Spalding, 329 G 3

Agriculture, Industry and Resources

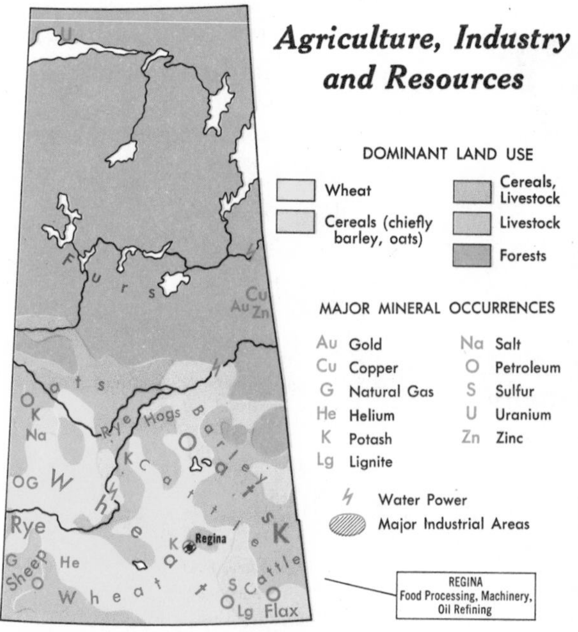
DOMINANT LAND USE
Wheat
Cereals (chiefly barley, oats)
Cereals, Livestock
Livestock
Forests
MAJOR MINERAL OCCURRENCES
Au Gold
Cu Copper
G Natural Gas
He Helium
K Potash
Lg Lignite
Na Salt
O Petroleum
S Sulfur
U Uranium
Zn Zinc
Water Power
Major Industrial Areas
REGINA
Food Processing, Machinery, Oil Refining
Furs
Oats
Rye
Hogs
Barley
Wheat
Cattle
Sheep
Flax
Regina

A
110°
B
109°
Meadow Lake
Lloydminster
Battleford
Wilkie
Kerrobert
Kindersley
Eston
Leader
Prelate
Maple Creek
Shaunavon
ALBERTA
North Battle River
South Saskatchewan
Red Deer R.
CYPRESS HILLS PROV. PARK
4,546
FT. WALSH NATIONAL HIST. PARK
M O

AREA 251,700 sq. mi.
POPULATION 921,323
CAPITAL Regina
LARGEST CITY Regina
HIGHEST POINT Cypress Hills 4,546 ft.
SETTLED IN 1774
ADMITTED TO CONFEDERATION 1905
PROVINCIAL FLOWER Prairie Lily

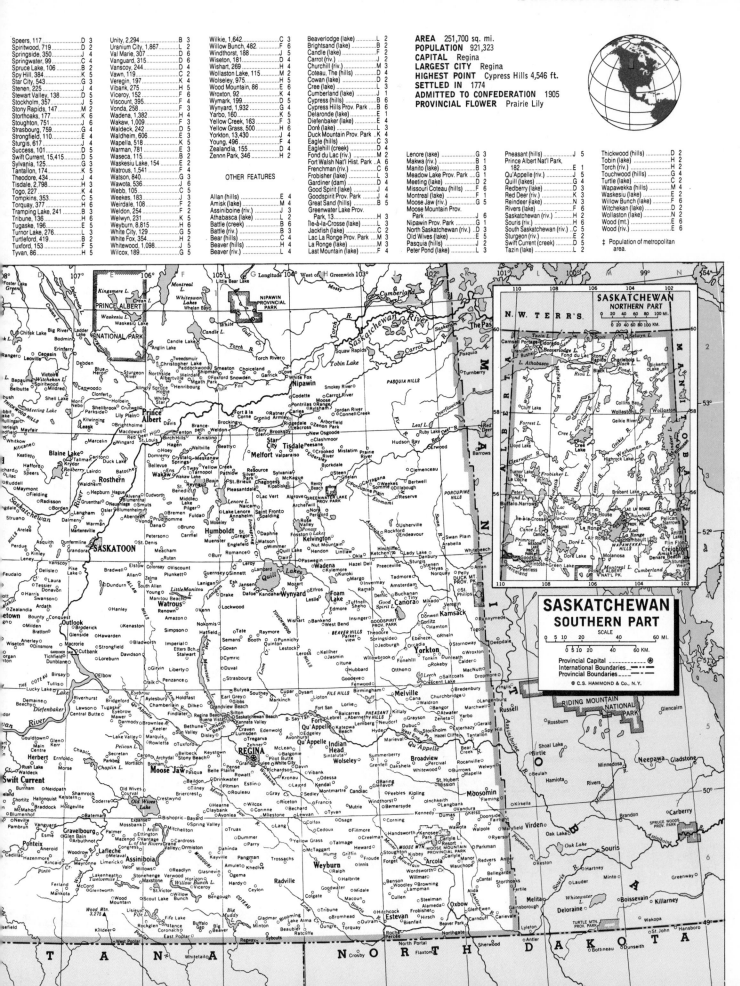

SASKATCHEWAN
NORTHERN PART

SASKATCHEWAN
SOUTHERN PART
SCALE

Provincial Capital ⊛
International Boundaries
Provincial Boundaries

© C.S. HAMMOND & Co., N.Y.

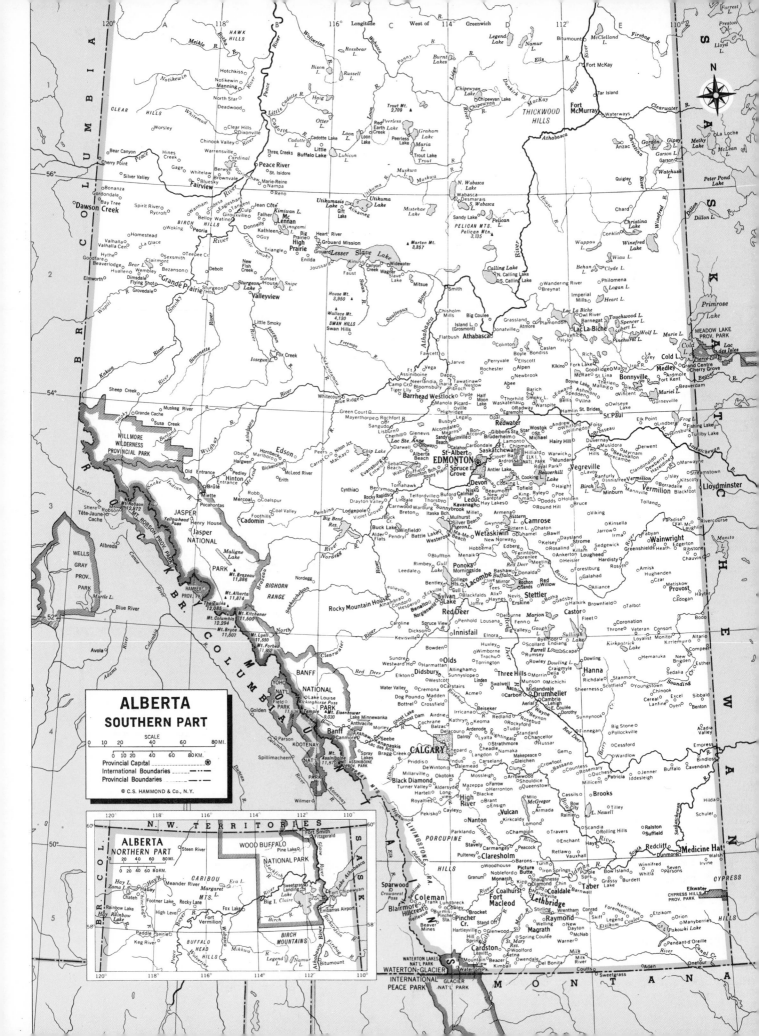

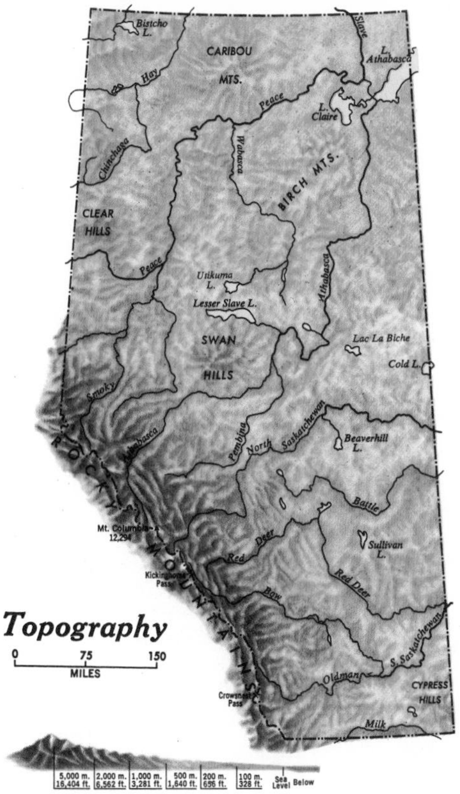
Bistcho L.
CARIBOU MTS.
Hay
Slave
L. Athabasca
Peace
L. Claire
Chinchaga
Wabasca
BIRCH MTS.
CLEAR HILLS
Peace
Utikuma L.
Lesser Slave L.
Athabasca
SWAN HILLS
Lac La Biche
Cold L.
Smoky
Pembina
North Saskatchewan
Beaverhill L.
Mt. Columbia 12,294
Battle
Sullivan L.
Red Deer
Kicking Horse Pass
Bow
Red Deer
Oldman
S. Saskatchewan
CYPRESS HILLS
Crowsnest Pass
Milk
5,000 m. 16,404 ft.
2,000 m. 6,562 ft.
1,000 m. 3,281 ft.
500 m. 1,640 ft.
200 m. 656 ft.
100 m. 328 ft.
Sea Level
Below

Topography

0 75 150 MILES

AREA 255,285 sq. mi.
POPULATION 1,838,037
CAPITAL Edmonton
LARGEST CITY Edmonton
HIGHEST POINT Mt. Columbia 12,294 ft.
SETTLED IN 1861
ADMITTED TO CONFEDERATION 1905
PROVINCIAL FLOWER Wild Rose

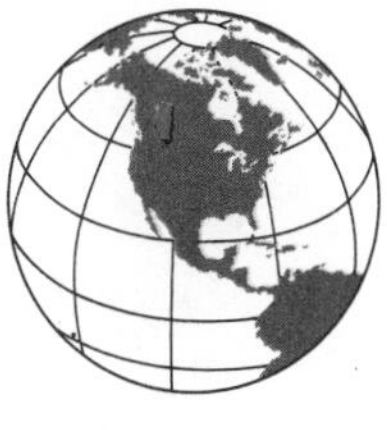

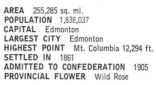

CITIES and TOWNS

Acadia Valley, 166	E	4
Acme, 300	D	4
Aerial, 151	D	4
Airdrie, 1,089	C	4
Alberta Beach, 320	C	3
Alder Flats, 133	C	3
Alix, 565	D	3
Alliance, 230	E	3
Amisk, 134	E	3
Andrew, 466	D	3
Anzac, 114	E	1
Ardmore, 230	E	2
Ardrossan, 137	D	3
Arrowwood, 166	D	4
Ashmont, 150	E	2
Athabasca, 1,765	D	2
Atikameg, 117	C	2
Banff, 3,219	C	4
Barnwell, 341	D	5
Barons, 237	D	4
Barrhead, 2,803	C	2
Bashaw, 757	D	3
Bassano, 861	D	4
Bawlf, 182	D	3
Beaumont, 337	D	3
Beaverlodge, 1,157	A	2
Beiseker, 414	D	4
Bellevue, 1,242	C	5
Bentley, 621	C	3
Berwyn, 474	B	1
Big Valley, 306	D	3
Black Diamond, 945	C	4
Blackfalds, 904	D	3
Blackfoot, 175	E	3
Blackie, 168	D	4
Blairmore, 2,037	C	5
Blue Ridge, 239	C	2
Bluesky, 124	A	1
Bon Accord, 332	D	3
Bonnyville, 2,587	E	2
Bowden, 560	C	4
Bow Island, 1,159	E	5
Boyle, 460	D	2
Bragg Creek, 203	C	4
Breton, 352	C	3
Brooks, 3,986	E	4
Brownvale, 161	B	1
Bruce, 110	E	3
Bruderheim, 350	D	3
Brûlé, 104	B	3
Buck Lake, 159	C	3
Burdett, 206	E	5
Cadomin, 109	B	3
Cadotte Lake, 192	B	1
Calgary, 403,319	C	4
Calgary, ‡403,319	C	4
Calmar, 799	D	3
Camrose, 8,673	D	3
Canmore, 1,538	C	4
Canyon Creek, 205	C	2
Carbon, 343	D	4
Carbondale, 115	D	3
Cardston, 2,685	D	5
Carmangay, 230	D	4
Caroline, 339	C	3
Carseland, 105	D	4
Carstairs, 884	D	4
Caslan, 117	D	2
Castor, 1,166	D	3
Cayley, 122	D	4
Cereal, 220	E	4
Champion, 335	D	4
Chateh, 400	A	5
Chauvin, 349	E	3
Chipewyan Lake, 118	D	1
Chipman, 181	D	3
Clairmont, 309	A	2
Clandonald, 119	E	3
Claresholm, 2,935	D	4
Clive, 247	D	3
Clyde, 233	D	2
Coaldale, 2,798	D	5
Coalhurst, 426	D	5
Cochrane, 1,046	C	4
Cold Lake, 1,309	E	2
Coleman, 1,534	C	5
Colinton, 125	D	2
College Heights, 331	D	3
Conklin, 119	E	2
Consort, 659	E	3
Cooking Lake, 196	D	3
Coronation, 877	E	3
Coutts, 407	D	5
Cowley, 201	D	5
Cremona, 186	C	4
Crossfield, 638	C	4
Czar, 196	E	3
Daysland, 593	D	3
Delburne, 383	D	3
Delia, 241	D	4
Derwent, 203	E	3
Desmarais, 258	D	2
Devon, 1,468	D	3
Dewberry, 160	E	3
Didsbury, 1,821	C	4
Dixonville, 113	B	1
Donalda, 232	D	3
Donnelly, 274	B	2
Drayton Valley, 3,900	C	3
Drumheller, 5,446	D	4
Duchess, 228	E	4
Eaglesham, 218	B	2
East Coulée, 312	D	4
Eckville, 660	C	3
Edberg, 145	D	3
Edgerton, 296	E	3
Edmonton (cap.), 438,152	D	3
Edmonton, ‡495,702	D	3
Edmonton Beach, 148	C	3
Edson, 3,818	B	3
Elk Point, 729	E	3
Elnora, 213	D	3
Empress, 266	E	4
Enilda, 201	B	2
Entwistle, 353	C	3
Erskine, 233	D	3
Evansburg, 528	C	3
Exshaw, 548	C	4
Fairview, 2,109	A	1
Falher, 918	B	2
Faust, 353	C	2
Fawcett, 141	C	2
Ferintosh, 127	D	3
Foremost, 568	E	5
Forestburg, 669	E	3
Fort Assiniboine, 173	C	2
Fort Chipewyan, 1,122	C	5
Fort Kent, 113	E	2
Fort Macleod, 2,715	D	5
Fort McKay, 200	E	1
Fort McMurray, 6,847	E	1
Fort Saskatchewan, 5,726	D	3
Fort Vermilion, 740	B	5
Fox Creek, 1,281	B	2
Frank, 224	C	5
Galahad, 179	E	3
Garden River, 134	B	5
Gibbons, 551	D	3
Gift Lake, 379	C	2
Girouxville, 347	B	2
Gleichen, 367	D	4
Glendon, 354	E	2
Glenwood, 200	D	5
Grand Centre, 2,088	E	2
Grande Cache, 2,525	A	3
Grande Prairie, 13,079	A	2
Granum, 324	D	5
Grassy Lake, 196	E	5
Grimshaw, 1,714	B	1
Grouard Mission, 277	C	2
Halkirk, 136	D	3
Hanna, 2,545	E	4
Hardieville, 473	D	5
Hardisty, 594	E	3
Hay Lakes, 211	D	3
Heisler, 199	D	3
High Level, 1,614	A	5
High Prairie, 2,354	B	2
High River, 2,676	D	4
Hillcrest, 613	C	5
Hill Spring, 213	D	5
Hines Creek, 438	A	1
Hinton, 4,911	B	3
Holden, 448	D	3
Hughenden, 267	E	3
Hussar, 170	D	4
Hythe, 487	A	2
Imperial Mills, 118	E	2
Innisfail, 2,474	D	3
Innisfree, 252	E	3
Irma, 423	E	3
Irricana, 139	D	4
Irvine, 194	E	5
Jarvie, 104	D	2
Jasper, 2,932	B	3
Joussard, 269	B	2
Kikino, 202	D	2
Killam, 851	E	3
Kinuso, 267	C	2
Kitscoty, 320	E	3
Lac La Biche, 1,791	E	2
Lacombe, 3,436	D	3
Lake Louise, 165	B	4
Lamont, 899	D	3
Langdon, 109	D	4
Lavoy, 114	E	3
Leduc, 4,000	D	3
Legal, 563	D	3
Leslieville, 159	C	3
Lethbridge, 41,217	D	5
Linden, 226	D	4
Little Buffalo Lake, 165	B	1
Lloydminster, 4,738	E	3
Lodgepole, 144	C	3
Lomond, 165	D	4
Longview, 189	C	4
Loon Lake, 135	C	1
Lougheed, 217	E	3
Lundbreck, 113	C	5
Magrath, 1,215	D	5
Mallaig, 190	E	2
Manning, 1,071	B	1
Mannville, 646	E	3
Marlboro, 156	B	3
Marwayne, 351	E	3
Mayerthorpe, 1,036	C	3
McLennan, 1,090	B	2
Meander River, 233	A	5
Medicine Hat, 26,518	E	4
Midlandvale, 392	D	4
Milk River, 775	D	5
Millet, 456	D	3
Milo, 117	D	4
Minburn, 106	E	3
Mirror, 365	D	3
Monarch, 102	D	5
Morinville, 1,475	D	3
Morrin, 197	D	4
Mulhurst, 139	D	3
Mundare, 511	D	3
Myrnam, 403	E	3
Nacmine, 350	D	4
Nampa, 283	B	1
Nanton, 991	D	4
Newbrook, 154	D	2
New Norway, 200	D	3
New Sarepta, 202	D	3
Nobleford, 401	D	5
North Calling Lake, 103	D	2
Okotoks, 1,247	C	4
Olds, 3,376	D	4
Onoway, 496	C	3
Oyen, 929	E	4
Paradise Valley, 144	E	3
Peace River, 5,039	B	1
Peerless Lake, 134	C	1
Peers, 129	B	3
Penhold, 452	D	3
Pibroch, 112	D	2
Picardville, 130	D	2
Picture Butte, 1,008	D	5
Pincher Creek, 3,227	D	5
Plamondon, 189	D	2
Pollockville, 29	E	4
Ponoka, 4,414	D	3
Provost, 1,489	E	3
Radway, 170	D	2
Rainbow Lake, 355	A	5
Ralston, 475	E	4
Ranfurly, 110	E	3
Raymond, 2,156	D	5
Redcliff, 2,255	E	4
Red Deer, 27,674	D	3
Redwater, 1,287	D	3
Rimbey, 1,450	C	3
Robb, 256	B	3
Rochester, 111	D	2
Rockyford, 286	D	4
Rocky Mountain House, 2,968	C	3
Rolling Hills, 127	E	4
Rosalind, 203	D	3
Rosemary, 208	E	4
Rycroft, 461	A	2
Ryley, 428	D	3
Saint Albert, 11,800	D	3
Saint Paul, 4,161	E	3
Sangudo, 360	C	3
Seba Beach, 165	C	3
Sedgewick, 730	E	3
Seebe, 108	C	4
Sexsmith, 559	A	2
Shaughnessy, 323	D	5
Sherwood Park, 14,282	D	3
Slave Lake, 2,052	C	2
Smith, 445	D	2
Smoky Lake, 881	D	2
Spirit River, 1,091	A	2
Spruce Grove, 3,029	D	3
Spruce View, 104	C	3
Standard, 267	D	4
Stavely, 351	D	4
Stettler, 4,168	D	3
Stirling, 436	D	5
Stony Plain, 1,770	C	3
Strathmore, 1,148	D	4
Strome, 226	E	3
Sundre, 933	C	4
Swan Hills, 1,376	C	2
Sylvan Lake, 1,597	C	3
Taber, 4,765	E	5
Thorhild, 509	D	2
Thorsby, 595	C	3
Three Hills, 1,354	D	4
Tilley, 270	E	4
Tofield, 924	D	3
Torrington, 118	D	4
Trochu, 739	D	4
Trout Lake, 162	C	1
Turin, 102	D	5
Turner Valley, 766	C	4
Two Hills, 979	E	3
Valleyview, 1,708	B	2
Vauxhall, 1,016	D	4
Vegreville, 3,691	E	3
Vermilion, 2,915	E	3
Veteran, 267	E	3
Viking, 1,178	E	3
Vilna, 303	E	2
Vulcan, 1,384	D	4
Wabamun, 336	C	3
Wabasca, 172	D	2
Wainwright, 3,872	E	3
Wanham, 268	A	2
Warburg, 464	C	3
Warner, 408	D	5
Warspite, 110	D	2
Waskatenau, 233	D	2
Waterton Park, 236	D	5
Wembley, 348	A	2
Westlock, 3,246	C	2
Westward Ho, 104	C	4
Wetaskiwin, 6,267	D	3
Whitecourt, 3,202	C	2
Whitelaw, 192	A	1
Widewater, 126	C	2
Wildwood, 386	C	3
Willingdon, 325	E	3
Winfield, 209	C	3
Youngstown, 305	E	4

OTHER FEATURES

Alberta (mt.)	B	3
Assiniboine (mt.)	C	4
Athabasca (lake)	C	5
Athabasca (riv.)	D	1
Banff Nat'l Park, 3,532	B	4
Battle (riv.)	D	3
Beaverhill (lake)	D	3
Belly (riv.)	D	5
Berry (creek)	E	4
Biche (lake)	E	2
Big Bend (res.)	C	3
Bighorn (range)	B	3
Birch (hills)	A	2
Birch (lake)	E	3
Birch (mts.)	B	5
Bow (riv.)	D	4
Boyer (riv.)	A	5
Brazeau (mt.)	B	3
Brazeau (riv.)	B	3
Buffalo (lake)	D	3
Buffalo Head (hills)	B	5
Cadotte (riv.)	B	1
Calling (lake)	D	2
Caribou (mts.)	B	5
Chinchaga (riv.)	A	5
Chip (lake)	C	3
Chipewyan (riv.)	D	1
Christina (riv.)	E	1
Claire (lake)	B	5
Clear (hills)	A	1
Clearwater (riv.)	C	4
Clearwater (riv.)	E	1
Cold (lake)	E	2
Columbia (mt.)	B	3
Crowsnest (pass)	C	5
Cypress (hills)	E	5
Cypress Hills Prov. Park	E	5
Eisenhower (mt.)	C	4
Elbow (riv.)	C	4
Elk Island Nat'l Park, 46	D	3
Etzikom Coulee (riv.)	E	5
Firebag (riv.)	E	1
Forbes (mt.)	B	4
Frog (lake)	E	3
Gordon (lake)	E	1
Gough (lake)	D	3
Graham (lake)	C	1
Gull (lake)	C	3
Hawk (hills)	B	1
Hay (riv.)	A	5
Highwood (riv.)	C	4
Iosegun (lake)	B	2
Jasper Nat'l Park, 3,064	A	3
Kickinghorse (pass)	B	4
Kimiwan (lake)	B	2
Kitchener (mt.)	B	3
Lesser Slave (lake)	C	2
Little Bow (riv.)	D	4
Little Smoky (riv.)	B	2
Livingstone (range)	C	4
Lyell (mt.)	B	4
Maligne (lake)	B	3
McGregor (lake)	D	4
McLeod (riv.)	B	3
Milk (riv.)	D	5
Muriel (lake)	E	2
Muskwa (riv.)	C	1
North Saskatchewan (riv.)	E	3
North Wabasca (lake)	D	1
Notikewin (riv.)	A	1
Oldman (riv.)	D	5
Pakowki (lake)	E	5
Peace (riv.)	B	1
Peerless (lake)	C	1
Pelican (mts.)	D	2
Pembina (riv.)	C	3
Pigeon (lake)	D	3
Porcupine (hills)	C	4
Red Deer (riv.)	D	4
Rocky (mts.)	C	4
Rosebud (riv.)	D	4
Sainte Anne (lake)	C	3
Saint Mary (riv.)	D	5
Saulteaux (riv.)	C	2
Slave (riv.)	C	5
Smoky (riv.)	A	2
Sounding (creek)	E	4
South Saskatchewan (riv.)	E	4
South Wabasca (lake)	D	2
Spray (mts.)	C	4
Sullivan (lake)	D	3
Swan (hills)	C	2
Temple (mt.)	B	4
The Twins (mt.)	B	3
Thickwood (hills)	D	1
Utikuma (lake)	C	2
Vermilion (riv.)	E	3
Wabasca (riv.)	C	1
Waterton-Glacier Int'l Peace Park, 259	C	5
Waterton Lakes Nat'l Park, 259	C	5
Whitemud (riv.)	A	1
Willmore Wilderness Prov. Park	A	3
Winagami (lake)	B	2
Winefred (lake)	E	2
Wood Buffalo Nat'l Park, 186	B	5
Yellowhead (pass)	A	3

‡ Population of metropolitan area.

Agriculture, Industry and Resources

DOMINANT LAND USE

- Wheat
- Cereals (chiefly barley, oats)
- Cereals, Livestock
- Dairy
- Pasture Livestock
- Range Livestock
- Forests
- Nonagricultural Land

MAJOR MINERAL OCCURRENCES

- C Coal
- G Natural Gas
- Na Salt
- O Petroleum
- S Sulfur

- Water Power
- Major Industrial Areas

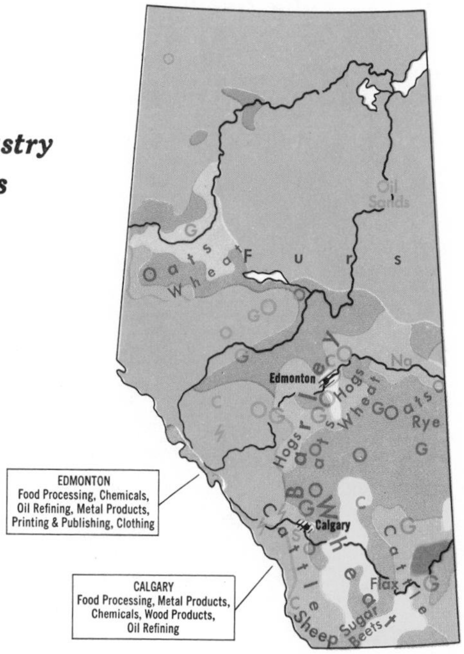
Oil Sands
Furs
Oats
Wheat
Edmonton
Hogs
Wheat
Oats
Rye
Calgary
Cattle
Sheep
Sugar Beets
Flax
EDMONTON
Food Processing, Chemicals, Oil Refining, Metal Products, Printing & Publishing, Clothing
CALGARY
Food Processing, Metal Products, Chemicals, Wood Products, Oil Refining

Topography

0   100   200
MILES

Below Sea Level | 100 m. 328 ft. | 200 m. 656 ft. | 500 m. 1,640 ft. | 1,000 m. 3,281 ft. | 2,000 m. 6,562 ft. | 5,000 m. 16,404 ft.

CITIES and TOWNS

Abbotsford, 706 ....L 3
Albert Head, 330 ....J 4
Alert Bay, 760 ....D 5
Alexandria, 168 ....K 4
Armstrong, 1,648 ....H 5
Ashcroft, 1,916 ....G 5
Ashton Creek, 318 ....H 5
Athalmer, 255 ....K 5
Atlin, 258 ....J 1
Avola, 265 ....H 4
Balfour, 195 ....J 5
Barrière, 829 ....H 4
Bear Lake, 302 ....F 3
Beaverdell, 241 ....H 5
Bella Coola, 273 ....D 4
Big Eddy, 654 ....H 4
Birch Island, 219 ....H 4
Blue River, 475 ....G 4
Boston Bar, 548 ....G 5
Bowen Island, 351 ....K 3
Bowser, 169 ....H 2

Brackendale, 692 ....F 5
Bralorne, 379 ....F 5
Britannia Beach, 738 ......K 2
Brouse, 446 ....J 5
Burnaby, ●125,660 ....K 3
Burns Lake, 1,259 ....D 3
Cache Creek, 1,013 ....G 5
Campbell River, ●10,000 ..E 5
Campbell River, 9,770 .....E 5
Canal Flats, 902 ....K 5
Cassiar, 1,073 ....K 2
Castlegar, 3,072 ....H 6
Cawston, 642 ....H 6
Caycuse, 297 ....J 3
Cedarside, 218 ....H 4
Celista, 178 ....H 4
Central Saanich, ●5,136 ..K 3
Charlie Lake, 214 ....G 2
Chase, 1,212 ....H 4
Chase River, 728 ....J 3
Chemainus, 2,129 ....J 3
Cherry Creek, 449 ....G 5
Cherryville, 284 ....H 5
Chetwynd, 1,260 ....F 2

Chilliwack, 9,135 ....M 3
Chilliwack, ●23,739 ....M 3
Clearbrook, 3,653 ....L 3
Clearwater, 513 ....G 4
Clinton, 905 ....G 4
Coal Harbour, 334 ....D 5
Cobble Hill, 280 ....K 3
Coldstream, ●3,602 ....H 5
Comox, 3,980 ....J 3
Coquitlam, ●53,073 ....K 3
Courtenay, 7,152 ....E 5
Cranbrook, 12,000 ....K 5
Crawford Bay, 244 ....J 5
Creston, 3,204 ....J 5
Crofton, 972 ....J 3
Cultus Lake, 554 ....M 3
Cumberland, 1,718 ....E 5
Dawson Creek, 11,885 .....G 2
Delta, ●45,860 ....K 3
Departure Bay, 3,744 .....J 3
Donald, 235 ....J 4
Duncan, 4,388 ....J 3
East Kelowna, 826 ....H 5
Eddontenajon, 180 ....K 2

Edgewater, 346 ....J 5
Elko, 196 ....K 5
Endako, 242 ....E 3
Enderby, 1,158 ....H 5
Errington, 464 ....J 3
Esquimalt, ●12,922 ....K 4
Extension, 181 ....J 3
Falkland, 375 ....H 5
Fernie, 4,422 ....K 5
Field, 358 ....J 4
Flood, ●295 ....M 3
Forest Grove, 238 ....G 4
Fort Fraser, 385 ....E 3
Fort Langley, 1,342 ....L 3
Fort Nelson, 2,289 ....M 2
Fort Saint James, 1,483 ..E 3
Fort Saint John, 8,264 ....G 2
Franklin River, 187 ....H 3
Fraser Lake, 1,292 ....E 3
Fraser Mills, ●157 ....K 3
Fruitvale, 1,379 ....H 6
Gabriola Island, 655 ....J 3
Galiano Island, 412 ....K 3
Ganges, 333 ....K 3
Gibsons, 1,934 ....K 3
Gillies Bay, 543 ....H 2
Giscome, 416 ....F 3
Golden, 3,012 ....J 4
Gold River, 1,896 ....D 5
Grand Forks, 3,173 ....H 6
Granisle, 451 ....D 3
Granthams Landing, 404 ..J 3
Greenwood, 868 ....H 6
Grindrod, 283 ....H 5
Hagensborg, 315 ....D 4
Haney, 3,221 ....L 3
Harrison Hot Springs, 598 ..M 3
Hatzic, 547 ....L 3
Hazelton, 351 ....D 2
Hedley, 385 ....G 5
Heffley Creek, 503 ....G 5
Hendrix Lake, 341 ....G 4
Heriot Bay, 187 ....E 5
Hixon, 385 ....F 3
Holberg, 333 ....C 5
Honeymoon Bay, 546 .....J 3
Hope, 3,153 ....M 3
Houston, ●2,232 ....D 3
Houston, 905 ....D 3
Hudson Hope, 1,116 ....F 2
Hudson's Hope, ●1,741 ...F 2
Huntingdon, 202 ....L 3
Invermere, 1,065 ....K 5
Ioco, 308 ....K 3
Jaffray, 193 ....K 5
Kaleden, 640 ....H 5
Kamloops, 26,168 ....G 5
Kaslo, 755 ....J 5
Kelly Lake, 231 ....G 4
Kelowna, 19,412 ....H 5
Kemano, 346 ....D 3
Kent, ●2,966 ....M 3
Keremeos, 605 ....G 5
Kimberley, 7,641 ....K 5
Kinnaird, 2,846 ....J 5
Kitimat, 11,824 ....C 3
Kitsault, 343 ....C 2
Kitwanga, 217 ....D 2
Kokish, 222 ....D 5
Lac La Hache, 417 ....G 4
Ladysmith, 3,664 ....J 3
Lake Cowichan, 2,364 ....J 3

Lang Bay, 285 ....E 5
Langley, ●21,936 ....L 3
Langley, 4,684 ....L 3
Lantzville, 565 ....J 3
Lillooet, 1,514 ....G 5
Lion's Bay, 396 ....K 3
Lone Butte, 206 ....G 4
Louis Creek, 289 ....H 4
Lower Nicola, 361 ....G 5
Lower Post, 206 ....K 1
Lumby, 940 ....H 5
Lytton, 494 ....G 5
Mackenzie, ●2,332 ....F 2
Mackenzie, 1,976 ....F 2
Madeira Park, 351 ....J 3
Maple Bay, 509 ....K 3
Maple Ridge, ●24,476 .....L 3
Masset, 975 ....B 3
Matsqui, ●23,554 ....L 3
Mayne Island, 293 ....K 3
McBride, 658 ....G 3
McConnell Creek, 233 ....D 2
McLure, 193 ....H 4
Merritt, 5,289 ....G 5
Merville, 227 ....E 5
Mesachie Lake, 266 ....J 3
Metchosin, 540 ....K 4
Mica Creek, 772 ....H 4
Midway, 502 ....H 6
Mill Bay, 347 ....C 2
Milnes Landing, 254 ......J 4
Mission, ●10,220 ....L 3
Mission City, 3,649 ....L 3
Moberly, 175 ....J 4
Monte Lake, 176 ....G 5
Montrose, 1,137 ....H 6
Nakusp, 1,163 ....H 5
Nanaimo, 14,948 ....J 3
Naramata, 461 ....H 5
Nelson, 9,400 ....J 5
New Denver, 644 ....J 5
New Hazelton, 475 ....D 2
New Westminster, 42,835 ..K 3
Nicholson, 619 ....J 4
Nicomen Island, 527 ......L 3
Nootka, 2 ....D 5
North Bend, 424 ....G 5
North Cowichan, ●12,170 ..J 3
North Pender Island, 407 ..K 3
North Saanich, ●3,601 ....K 3
North Vancouver, ●57,861 ..K 3
North Vancouver, 31,847 ..K 3
Nukko Lake, 182 ....F 3
Oak Bay, ●18,426 ....K 4
Ocean Falls, 1,085 ....D 4
Okanagan Centre, 266 ....H 5
Okanagan Falls, 621 ......H 5
Okanagan Landing, 656 ..H 5
Okanagan Mission, 857 ...H 5
Old Barkerville, 3 ....G 3
Oliver, 1,615 ....H 6
One Hundred Mile House, 1,120 ..G 4
Osoyoos, 1,285 ....H 6
Oyama, 326 ....H 5
Parksville, 2,169 ....J 3
Parson, 306 ....J 4
Peachland, 1,446 ....G 5
Penticton, 18,146 ....H 5
Pine Valley, 264 ....F 2
Pitt Meadows, ●2,771 .....L 3
Popkum, 286 ....M 3
Port Alberni, 20,063 ....J 3
Port Alice, 1,507 ....D 5
Port Clements, 406 ....B 3
Port Coquitlam, 19,560 ..L 3
Port Edward, 1,019 ....B 3
Port Hammond, 1,556 .....L 3
Port Hardy, ●1,761 ....D 5
Port McNeill, 934 ....D 5
Port Moody, 10,778 ....L 3
Port Renfrew, 362 ....J 3
Pouce-Coupé, 595 ....G 2
Powell River, ●13,726 .....E 5
Prince George, 33,101 ....F 3
Prince Rupert, 15,747 .....B 3
Princeton, 2,601 ....G 5
Procter, 183 ....J 5
Qualicum Beach, 1,245 ...J 3
Queen Charlotte, 665 .....A 3
Quesnel, 6,252 ....F 4
Radium Hot Springs, 393 ..J 5
Rayleigh, 652 ....G 5
Revelstoke, 4,867 ....J 5
Richmond, ●62,121 ....K 3
Riondel, 572 ....J 5
Robson, 1,046 ....J 5
Rossland, 3,896 ....H 6
Royston, 532 ....E 5
Rutland, 3,279 ....H 5
Saanich, ●65,040 ....K 3
Salmo, 872 ....J 5
Salmon Arm, ●7,793 ....H 5
Salmon Arm, 1,981 ....H 5
Saltair, 1,008 ....J 3
Sandspit, 459 ....B 3
Sardis, 1,194 ....M 3
Saseenos, 574 ....J 4
Saturna Island, 174 ....K 3
Savona, 670 ....G 5
Sayward, 465 ....D 5
Sechelt, 590 ....J 3
Seventy Mile House, 225 ..G 4
Shawnigan Lake, 213 .....J 3
Shoreacres, 345 ....J 5
Sicamous, 814 ....H 5
Sidney, 4,868 ....K 3
Silverton, 246 ....J 5
Slocan, 346 ....J 5
Slocan Park, 360 ....J 5
Smithers, 3,864 ....D 3
Sointula, 575 ....D 5
Sooke, 836 ....J 4
Sorrento, 269 ....H 5
South Fort George, 1,282 ..F 3
South Hazelton, 483 ....D 2
South Slocan, 278 ....J 5

South Wellington, 460 ....J 3
Sparwood, 2,990 ....K 5
Sparwood, 2,154 ....K 5
Spences Bridge, 199 ......G 5
Sproat Lake, 321 ....H 3
Squamish, ●6,121 ....F 5
Squamish, 1,597 ....F 5
Stewart, ●1,357 ....C 2
Stoner, 182 ....F 3
Summerland, ●5,551 ....G 5
Surrey, ●98,601 ....K 3
Tahsis, 1,351 ....D 5
Tasu, 331 ....A 4
Taylor, 605 ....G 2
Telkwa, 712 ....D 3
Terrace, ●9,991 ....C 3
Terrace, 7,820 ....C 3
Thrums, 365 ....J 5
Tofino, 461 ....E 5
Trail, 11,149 ....J 6
Ucluelet, 1,018 ....E 6
Union Bay, 407 ....H 2
Upper Fraser, 339 ....G 3
Valemount, 693 ....H 4
Valleyview, 3,787 ....G 5
Vananda, 497 ....E 5
Vancouver, 426,256 ....K 3
Vancouver, ‡1,082,352 ...K 3
Vancouver (Greater),
●1,028,334 ....K 3
Vanderhoof, 1,653 ....E 3
Vavenby, 331 ....H 4
Vernon, 13,283 ....H 5

Victoria (cap.), 61,761 ....K 4
Victoria, ‡195,800 ....K 4
Warfield, 2,132 ....J 6
Wasa, 355 ....K 5
Wells, 409 ....G 3
Westbank, 747 ....H 5
West Vancouver, ●36,440 ..K 3
Westwold, 434 ....G 5
White Rock, 10,349 ....K 3
Williams Lake, 4,072 ......F 4
Willow River, 422 ....F 3
Wilmer, 200 ....J 5
Wilson Creek, 408 ....J 3
Windermere, 421 ....K 5
Winfield, 875 ....H 5
Winlaw, 383 ....J 5
Woodfibre, 408 ....F 5
Woss Lake, 394 ....D 5
Wynndel, 579 ....J 5
Yahk, 192 ....J 5
Yale, 224 ....M 2
Yarrow, 1,039 ....L 3
Ymir, 292 ....J 5
Youbou, 1,109 ....J 3
Zeballos, 186 ....D 5

OTHER FEATURES

Adams (riv.) ....H 4
Alberni (inlet) ....H 3
Alsek (riv.) ....H 1

Agriculture, Industry and Resources

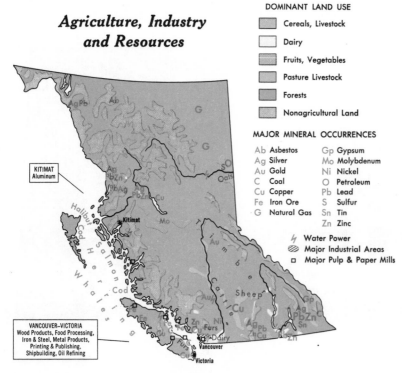

KITIMAT
Aluminum

VANCOUVER–VICTORIA
Wood Products, Food Processing,
Iron & Steel, Metal Products,
Printing & Publishing,
Shipbuilding, Oil Refining

DOMINANT LAND USE

- Cereals, Livestock
- Dairy
- Fruits, Vegetables
- Pasture Livestock
- Forests
- Nonagricultural Land

MAJOR MINERAL OCCURRENCES

Ab	Asbestos	Gp	Gypsum
Ag	Silver	Mo	Molybdenum
Au	Gold	Ni	Nickel
C	Coal	O	Petroleum
Cu	Copper	Pb	Lead
Fe	Iron Ore	S	Sulfur
G	Natural Gas	Sn	Tin
		Zn	Zinc

Water Power
Major Industrial Areas
Major Pulp & Paper Mills

BRITISH COLUMBIA

SCALE
0 15 30   60   90   120 MI.
0 15 30   60   90   120 KM.

Provincial Capital .... ⊛
State Capital .... ⊛
International Boundaries .... — — —
Provincial Boundaries .... — · — ·

Ⓒ C.S. HAMMOND & Co., N.Y.

Aristazabal (isl.)	C 4	Douglas (chan.)	C 3	Kickinghorse (pass)	J 5	Nanika (dam)	D 3
Assiniboine (mt.)	K 5	Duncan (riv.)	J 5	King (isl.)	D 4	Nass (riv.)	C 2
Atlin (lake)	J 1	Dundas (isl.)	B 3	Klinaklini (riv.)	E 4	Nechako (riv.)	E 3
Babine (lake)	E 3	Elk (riv.)	K 5	Knight (inlet)	E 5	Nootka (isl.)	D 5
Babine (riv.)	D 2	Eutsuk (lake)	D 3	Knox (cape)	A 3	Nootka (sound)	D 5
Banks (isl.)	B 3	Fairweather (mt.)	H 1	Kokanee Glacier Prov.		North Thompson (riv.)	G 4
Barkley (sound)	E 6	Finlay (riv.)	E 1	Park	J 5	Observatory (inlet)	C 2
Bennett, W.A.C. (dam)	F 2	Flores (isl.)	D 5	Koocanusa (lake)	K 5	Okanagan (lake)	H 5
Bowron Lake Prov. Park	G 3	Fort Nelson (riv.)	M 2	Kootenay (lake)	J 5	Okanogan (riv.)	H 6
Bryce (mt.)	J 4	François (lake)	D 3	Kootenay (riv.)	K 5	Omineca (mts.)	E 2
Burke (chan.)	D 4	Fraser (riv.)	F 4	Kootenay Nat'l Park	J 4	Ootsa (lake)	D 3
Burnaby (isl.)	B 4	Galiano (isl.)	K 3	Kunghit (isl.)	B 4	Pacific Rim Nat'l Park	E 6
Bute (inlet)	E 5	Gardner (canal)	D 3	Kyuquot (sound)	D 5	Parsnip (riv.)	F 2
Caamaño (sound)	C 4	Garibaldi Prov. Park	F 5	Langara (isl.)	A 3	Peace (riv.)	G 2
Calvert (isl.)	C 4	Georgia (str.)	J 3	Liard (riv.)	L 2	Pine (riv.)	G 2
Canoe (riv.)	H 4	Glacier Nat'l Park	J 4	Lillooet (riv.)	F 5	Pitt (isl.)	C 3
Cariboo (mts.)	G 3	Golden Ears Prov. Park	L 2	Lower Arrow (lake)	H 5	Pitt (riv.)	L 3
Cassiar (mts.)	K 2	Graham (isl.)	A 3	Malaspina (str.)	J 3	Porcher (isl.)	B 3
Chatham (sound)	B 2	Grenville (chan.)	C 3	Manning Prov. Park, 23	G 5	Portland (canal)	B 2
Chilcotin (riv.)	E 4	Hamber Prov. Park	H 4	Masset (inlet)	A 3	Portland (inlet)	B 2
Chilko (riv.)	E 4	Harrison (lake)	M 2	Milbanke (sound)	C 4	Princess Royal (isl.)	C 3
Chilkoot (pass)	J 1	Hazelton (mts.)	C 2	Monashee (mts.)	H 5	Principe (chan.)	C 3
Churchill (peak)	K 2	Hecate (str.)	B 3	Moresby (isl.)	B 4	Prophet (riv.)	M 2
Clayoquot (sound)	D 5	Howe (sound)	F 5	Morice (riv.)	D 3	Purcell (mts.)	J 5
Clearwater (riv.)	G 4	Hunter (isl.)	C 4	Mount Assiniboine Prov.		Quatsino (sound)	C 5
Coast (mts.)	D 3	Iskut (riv.)	J 2	Park	K 5	Queen Charlotte (isls.),	
Columbia (lake)	K 5	Jervis (inlet)	E 5			2,390	B 3
Columbia (mt.)	J 4	Johnstone (str.)	D 5	Mount Edziza Prov. Park		Queen Charlotte (sound)	C 4
Columbia (riv.)	H 4	Juan de Fuca (str.)	J 4	and Rec. Area	B 1	Queen Charlotte (str.)	D 5
Cowichan (lake)	J 3	Kates Needle (mt.)	A 1	Mount Revelstoke Nat'l		Quesnel (lake)	H 4
Crowsnest (pass)	K 5	Kechika (riv.)	L 2	Park	H 5	Rivers (inlet)	D 4
Dean (chan.)	D 4	Kenney (dam)	E 3	Mount Robson Prov. Park	H 3	Robson (mt.)	H 3
Dease (lake)	K 2	Kettle (riv.)	H 5	Muncho Lake Prov. Park	L 2	Rocky (mts.)	F 2
Dixon Entrance (chan.)	A 3			Muskwa (riv.)	M 2		

Rose (pt.)	B 3	Smith (sound)	C 4	Tweedsmuir Prov. Park	D 3
Saint James (cape)	B 4	Stave (lake)	L 3	Upper Arrow (lake)	H 5
Salmon (riv.)	F 3	Stikine (riv.)	B 1	Valdes (isl.)	K 3
Scott (cape)	C 5	Stone Mountain Prov. Park	L 2	Vancouver (isl.), 381,297	E 4
Seechelt (inlet)	J 2	Strathcona Prov. Park	E 5	Waddington (mt.)	E 4
Seechelt (pen.)	J 2	Stuart (lake)	E 3	Wells Gray Prov. Park	H 4
Selkirk (mts.)	J 4	Tagish (lake)	J 1	Whitesail (lake)	D 3
Seymour (inlet)	D 4	Tahtsa (lake)	D 3	Williston (lake)	F 2
Shuswap (lake)	H 4	Takla (lake)	D 2	Work (chan.)	C 3
Sikanni Chief (riv.)	M 2	Taku (riv.)	K 1	Yellowhead (pass)	H 4
Sir Sandford (mt.)	H 4	Teslin (lake)	K 1	Yoho Nat'l Park	J 4
Skeena (mts.)	C 2	Tetachuck (lake)	D 3	
Skeena (riv.)	C 3	Texada (isl.)	J 3	
Skidegate (inlet)	B 4	Thompson (riv.)	G 5	
Slocan (lake)	J 5	Tiedemann (mt.)	E 4	

‡ Population of metropolitan area.
● Population of municipality.

AREA 366,255 sq. mi.
POPULATION 2,466,608
CAPITAL Victoria
LARGEST CITY Vancouver
HIGHEST POINT Mt. Fairweather 15,300 ft.
SETTLED IN 1806
ADMITTED TO CONFEDERATION 1871
PROVINCIAL FLOWER Dogwood

Topography

0   150   300
MILES

C. San Lucas

TRES MARÍAS ISLANDS

C. Corrientes

• REVILLAGIGEDO IS.

Yucatán Pen.

Bay of Campeche

Lag. de Términos

Isthmus of Tehuantepec

Gulf of Tehuantepec

| 5,000 m. 16,404 ft. | 2,000 m. 6,562 ft. | 1,000 m. 3,281 ft. | 500 m. 1,640 ft. | 200 m. 656 ft. | 100 m. 328 ft. | Sea Level | Below |

MEXICO

CONIC PROJECTION

SCALE OF MILES

0   100   200

SCALE OF KILOMETRES

0   100   200   300

National Capitals .... ☆   State Capitals .... ◉
International Boundaries ----   State Boundaries ----

AREA 761,601 sq. mi.
POPULATION 48,313,438
CAPITAL Mexico City
LARGEST CITY Mexico City
HIGHEST POINT Citlaltépetl 18,855 ft.
MONETARY UNIT Mexican peso
MAJOR LANGUAGE Spanish
MAJOR RELIGION Roman Catholicism

States Indicated by Numbers
1 Tlaxcala
2 Morelos
3 Distrito Federal
4 México
5 Hidalgo
6 Querétaro
7 Guanajuato
8 Aguascalientes
9 Nayarit
10 Colima

San Gabriel Chilac, 7,303 ....K 7
San Ignacio, 22,116 ....F 5
San Javier, 390 ....D 2
San Juan del Cabo, 9,382 ....D 5
San Juan, Jalisco, 31,389 ....H 6
San Juan, Querétaro,
  53,332 ....K 6
San Juan de Guadalupe,
  8,877 ....H 4
San Juan del Río,
  14,639 ....G 4
San Juan Ixtenco, 4,894 ....N 1
San Juan Xiutetelco,
  11,771 ....O 1
San Luis de la Paz, 26,819........J 6
San Luis del Cordero,
  3,155 ....H 4
San Luis Potosí, 274,320 ....J 6
San Luis Río Colorado,
  63,644 ....B 1
San Marcos, 33,954 ....K 8
San Martín Texmelucan,
  50,071 ....M 1
San Martín Xaltocan,
  6,142 ....N 1
San Miguel, 63,937 ....J 6
San Nicolás, 1,023 ....K 4
San Nicolás Terrenate,
  7,160 ....K 4
San Pedro, 70,407 ....H 4
San Pedro del Gallo, 3,843........G 4
Santa Ana, 10,416 ....D 1
Santa Bárbara, 20,117 ....F 3
Santa Cruz, 1,659 ....D 1
Santa Inés Zacatelco,
  19,972 ....M 1
Santa María, 6,260 ....M 1
Santa María del Río, 30,072 ......J 6
Santa María del Tule ....K 8
Santander Jiménez, 5,323 ....K 4
Santa Rosalía ....C 3
Santiago, Baja California,
  4,978 ....E 5
Santiago, Nayarit, 84,167 ....K 8
Santiago Jamiltepec,
  104,275 ....K 8
Santiago Juxtlahuaca,
  37,095 ....K 8
Santiago Papasquiaro,
  35,828 ....F 4
Santiago Tuxtla, 33,471 ....M 7
Saucillo, 30,781 ....G 6
Sayula, 18,878 ....H 7
Sierra Mojada, 5,517 ....H 3
Silao, 69,866 ....J 6
Simojovel, 14,896 ....N 8
Sinaloa de Leyva, 53,639 ....E 4
Soledad de Doblado,
  19,467 ....Q 2
Soledad Díez Gutiérrez,
  28,337 ....J 5
Sombrerete, 48,411 ....J 5
Sotuta, 5,417 ....P 6
Soyopa, 2,314 ....E 2
Suaqui, 1,061 ....E 2
Tacámbaro de Codallos,
  23,690 ....J 7
Tacotalpa, 20,912 ....N 8
Tala, 33,369 ....G 6
Talpa de Allende, 13,027 ....G 6
Tamazunchale, 60,976 ....L 6
Tamiahua, 23,689 ....L 5
Tampico, 196,147 ....L 5
Tapachula, 108,464 ....N 9
Taxco de Alarcón, 64,368 ....K 7
Teapa, 19,787 ....N 8

Tecamachalco, 21,688 ....O 2
Tecate, 17,917 ....A 1
Tecomán, 45,933 ....H 7
Tecpan de Galeana,
  44,820 ....J 8
Tecuala, 41,129 ....H 6
Tehuacán, 67,520 ....P 2
Tehuantepec, 100,176 ....M 8
Tehuipango, 7,163 ....P 2
Tekax, 16,370 ....P 6
Teloloapan, 48,458 ....J 7
Temascalapa, 9,428 ....M 1
Temax, 5,821 ....P 6
Temósachic, 8,378 ....F 2
Tenabo, 3,992 ....P 6
Tenango de Río Blanco,
  27,266 ....K 7
Tenosique de Pino Suárez,
  26,954 ....O 2
Teocaltiche, 29,330 ....H 6
Teocelo, 7,441 ....P 1
Teotihuacán de Arista,
  15,704 ....L 1
Teotitlán, 103,209 ....L 8
Tepatitlán, 53,683 ....H 6
Tepatlaxco de Hidalgo,
  8,768 ....N 1
Tepeaca, 26,334 ....N 2
Tepeapulco, 26,254 ....M 1
Tepehuanes, 16,361 ....G 4
Tepeji, 24,107 ....K 6
Tepetlaoxtoc, 6,987 ....L 1
Tepexi de Rodríguez,
  12,655 ....O 2
Tepeyahualco, 9,504 ....N 1
Tepic, 111,344 ....H 6
Tepoztlán, 12,835 ....L 1
Tequisquiapan de Mora,
  67,220 ....M 1
Tequila, 41,502 ....L 6
Ticul, 16,537 ....P 6
Tierra Blanca, 48,733 ....L 7
Tihuatlán, 53,447 ....L 6
Tijuana, 333,125 ....A 1
Tixtla, 19,735 ....K 8
Tizayuca, 8,717 ....L 1
Tizimín, 29,895 ....O 5
Tlachichuca, 15,225 ....O 1
Tlacolula, 78,684 ....L 8
Tlacotalpan, 13,404 ....M 7
Tlacotepec de Mejía,
  1,948 ....P 1
Tlahualilo de Zaragoza,
  21,646 ....H 3
Tlalixcoyan, 28,625 ....L 7
Tlalmanalco de Velásquez,
  20,420 ....L 1
Tlalnepantla de Comonfort,
  373,657 ....K 1
Tlalpan, 115,528 ....L 1
Tlaltenango, 19,145 ....L 6
Tlaltizapán, 20,716 ....L 2
Tlapacoyan, 23,623 ....P 1
Tlapa de Comonfort,
  23,261 ....K 8
Tlaquiltenango, 16,335 ....L 2
Tlaxcala, 21,424 ....M 1
Tlaxco de Morelos,
  16,128 ....N 1
Tlaxiaco, 85,929 ....L 8
Tlayacapan, 1,249 ....L 2
Todos Santos, 4,506 ....D 5
Tolimán, 12,017 ....K 6
Toluca, 220,195 ....M 1
Tomatlán, 17,201 ....G 6

Tonalá, 41,562 ....N 8
Topolobampo ....E 4
Torreón, 257,045 ....H 4
Tula, 21,201 ....K 5
Tulancingo, 45,449 ....K 7
Tulcingo de Valle, 6,718 ....M 2
Tultepec, 13,693 ....L 1
Tuxpan, Jalisco, 23,569 ....H 7
Tuxpan, Nayarit, 26,345 ....G 6
Tuxpan de Rodríguez Cano,
  65,211 ....L 6
Tuxtepec, 184,757 ....L 7
Tuxtla Gutiérrez, 69,326 ....N 8
Umán, 14,258 ....P 6
Ures, 10,368 ....D 2

Úrsulo Galván, 16,772 ....Q 1
Uruáchic, 7,565 ....E 3
Uruapan, 104,475 ....H 7
Valladolid, 25,367 ....P 6
Valle de Bravo, 23,591 ....J 7
Valle de Santiago, 80,504 ....J 6
Valle Hermoso, 41,546 ....L 4
Vanegas, 6,384 ....J 5
Venado, 12,147 ....J 6
Venustiano Carranza, 32,131 ....N 8
Veracruz Llave, 242,351 ....Q 1
Vicente Guerrero, Durango,
  13,529 ....G 5
Vicente Guerrero, Puebla,
  10,207 ....M 2

Viesca, 15,046 ....H 4
Villa de Cos, 18,012 ....H 5
Villa de Guadalupe, 12,436 ......H 5
Villa de Seris ....J 3
Villa Frontera, 31,055 ....J 3
Villa García, 9,116 ....J 5
Villagrán, 10,338 ....K 4
Villahermosa, 162,678 ....N 8
Villaldama, 4,639 ....J 3
Villa Matamoros, 5,928 ....G 3
Villanueva, 35,553 ....H 5
Villa Unión, 20,002 ....H 5
Xicoténcatl, 21,144 ....K 5
Xicotepec de Juárez,
  27,372 ....K 6

Xochihuehuetlán, 6,046 ....K 8
Xochimilco, 117,083 ....L 1
Xochitlán, 8,166 ....N 2
Yajalón, 29,497 ....N 8
Yautepec, 26,182 ....L 2
Yécora, 4,898 ....E 2
Yecuatla, 10,382 ....P 1
Zaachila, 22,739 ....L 8
Zacapoaxtla, 25,479 ....O 1
Zacapu, 52,649 ....J 7
Zacatecas, 56,829 ....H 5
Zacatlán, 37,261 ....N 1
Zacoalco, 21,929 ....H 6
Zamora, 82,712 ....H 7
Zaragoza, 8,955 ....J 3
Zimatlán de Álvarez,
  40,302 ....L 8
Zitácuaro, 67,173 ....J 7
Zongolica, 24,372 ....P 2
Zumpango, 35,035 ....L 1
Zumpango del Río, 21,894 ....J 8

OTHER FEATURES

Agiabampo (bay) ....E 3
Aguanaval (river) ....H 4
Amistad (res.) ....J 2
Angel de la Guarda
  (island) ....C 2
Antigua (river) ....Q 1
Arena (point) ....E 5
Arenas (cay) ....N 2
Atoyac (river) ....J 7
Atoyac (river) ....N 2
Babía (river) ....J 3
Bacalar (lake) ....P 7
Ballenas (bay) ....C 7
Balsas (river) ....J 7
Banderas (bay) ....G 6
Bavispe (river) ....E 1
Blanco (river) ....Q 2
Bravo (river) ....J 3
Burro, Sierra del (mts.) ....J 2
California (gulf) ....D 3
Campeche (bank) ....N 5
Campeche (bay) ....N 7
Candelaria (river) ....N 8
Carmen (island) ....D 7
Casas Grandes (river) ....F 1
Catoche (cape) ....P 5
Cedros (island) ....B 4
Cerralvo (island) ....E 4
Chamela (bay) ....G 6
Chapala (lake) ....H 6
Chetumal (bay) ....P 8
Chichén-Itzá (ruins) ....P 6
Chixoy (river) ....N 8
Citlaltépetl (mt.) ....P 1
Clarión (island) ....B 8
Colorado (river) ....B 1
Conchos (river) ....F 3
Corrientes (cape) ....F 6
Coyuca (river) ....J 8
Cresciente (island) ....D 5
Cuitzeo (lake) ....J 7
Delgada (point) ....P 1
Dzibilchaltún (ruins) ....P 6
El Azúcar (res.) ....L 4
Espíritu Santo (island) ....D 4
Falcón (res.) ....K 4
Falso (cape) ....D 5
Fuerte (river) ....E 3
Giganta, Sierra de la
  (mts.) ....D 4
Grande (river) ....N 8
Grande (river) ....G 2
Grande de Santiago
  (river) ....G 6
Grijalva (river) ....N 8
Guzmán (lake) ....E 1
Herrero (point) ....Q 7
Holbox (island) ....P 5
Hondo (river) ....P 7
Jesús María, Barra
  (inlet) ....L 4
La Boquilla (res.) ....G 3
La Paz (bay) ....D 5
Lobos (cape) ....C 2
Lobos (point) ....D 3

Lower California (pen.),
  980,559 ....B 3
Madre (lagoon) ....L 4
Madre del Sur, Sierra
  (mts.) ....J-L 8
Madre Occidental, Sierra
  (mts.) ....F 3
Madre Oriental, Sierra
  (mts.) ....J 4
Magdalena (bay) ....C 4
Maldonado (point) ....K 8
Mapimí, Bolsón de
  (depression) ....G 3
María Cleófas (island) ....F 6
María Madre (island) ....F 6
María Magdalena (island) ....F 6
Mexico (gulf) ....N 4
Mezquital (river) ....G 5
Mita (point) ....K 8
Mitla (ruins) ....M 8
Moctezuma (river) ....K 6
Monserrate (isl.) ....D 4
Montague (isl.) ....B 1
Muerto, Mar (lagoon) ....N 9
Nauhcampatépetl (mt.) ....O 1
Nayarit, Sierra (mts.) ....G 4
Nazas (river) ....G 4
Nuevo (cay) ....O 6
Orizaba (Citlaltépetl)
  (mt.) ....O 2
Palenque (ruins) ....O 8
Palmito de la Virgen (isl.) ......F 5
Palmito del Verde (isl.) ....F 5
Pánuco (river) ....K 5
Paricutín (vol.) ....J 7
Pátzcuaro (lake) ....J 7
Pérez (isl.) ....O 5
Petacalco (bay) ....H 8
Popocatépetl (mt.) ....M 1
Ramos (river) ....G 4
Revillagigedo (isls.) ....C 7
Río Grande (river) ....J 3
Roca Partida (isl.) ....B 7
Sabinas (river) ....J 3
Salada (lagoon) ....A 1
San Antonio, Barra de
  (inlet) ....L 4
San Benedicto (isl.) ....B 7
San Benito (isl.) ....B 4
San Blas (river) ....D 1
San Jorge (bay) ....C 1
San José (isl.) ....D 4
San Lázaro (cape) ....C 4
San Lucas (cape) ....D 5
San Marcos (isl.) ....D 3
San Rafael, Barra de
  (inlet) ....L 4
Santa Ana, Barra de
  (inlet) ....N 7
Santa Catalina (isl.) ....D 4
Santa Cruz (isl.) ....D 4
Santa Eugenia (point) ....B 3
Santa Inés (bay) ....D 3
Santa Margarita (isl.) ....C 5
Santa María (river) ....F 1
Santiaguillo (lake) ....G 4
Sebastián Vizcaíno (bay) ....B 3
Socorro (isl.) ....B 7
Sonora (river) ....D 2
Superior (lagoon) ....M 9
Teacapán, Boca (inlet) ....F 5
Tehuantepec (gulf) ....M 8
Tehuantepec (isthmus) ....M 1
Teotihuacán (ruins) ....M 1
Términos (lagoon) ....O 7
Tiburón (isl.) ....C 2
Tres Marías (isls.) ....F 6
Triángulo Este (isl.) ....N 6
Triángulo Oeste (isl.) ....N 6
Urique (river) ....E 3
Usumacinta (river) ....N 8
Uxmal (ruins) ....P 6
Valsequillo, Presa (res.) ....N 2
Verde (river) ....J 6
Verde (river) ....L 8
Yaqui (river) ....E 2

*City and suburbs.

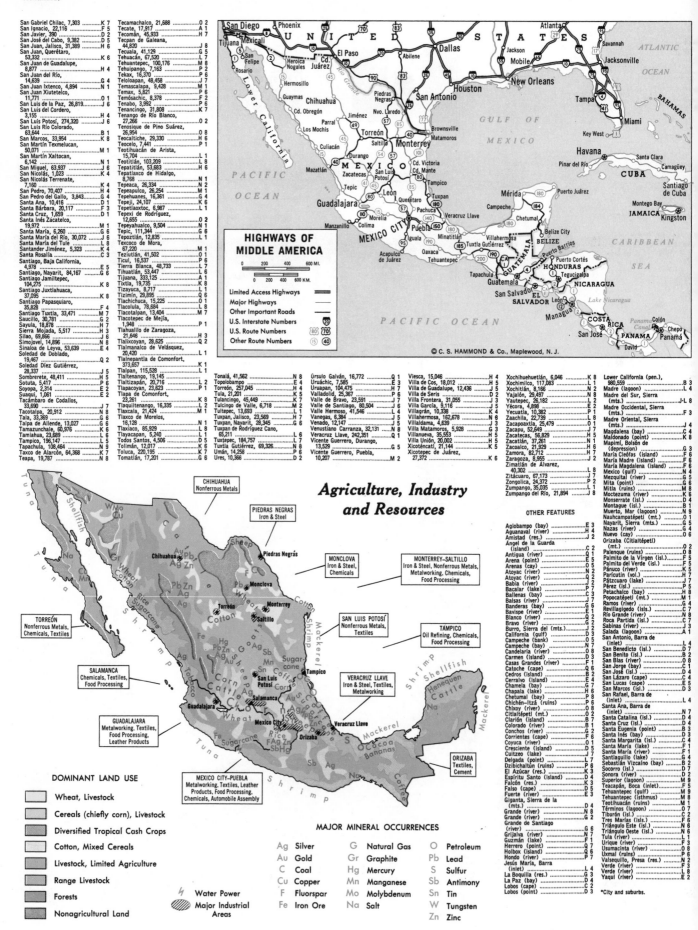

HIGHWAYS OF MIDDLE AMERICA

0   200   400   600 MI.
0 200 400 600 KM.

Limited Access Highways
Major Highways
Other Important Roads
U.S. Interstate Numbers
U.S. Route Numbers
Other Route Numbers

© C. S. HAMMOND & Co., Maplewood, N.J.

Agriculture, Industry and Resources

CHIHUAHUA
Nonferrous Metals

PIEDRAS NEGRAS
Iron & Steel

MONCLOVA
Iron & Steel,
Chemicals

MONTERREY–SALTILLO
Iron & Steel, Nonferrous Metals,
Metalworking, Chemicals,
Food Processing

SAN LUIS POTOSÍ
Nonferrous Metals,
Textiles

TAMPICO
Oil Refining, Chemicals,
Food Processing

TORREÓN
Nonferrous Metals,
Chemicals, Textiles

SALAMANCA
Chemicals, Textiles,
Food Processing

VERACRUZ LLAVE
Iron & Steel, Textiles,
Metalworking

GUADALAJARA
Metalworking, Textiles,
Food Processing,
Leather Products

ORIZABA
Textiles,
Cement

MEXICO CITY–PUEBLA
Metalworking, Textiles, Leather
Products, Food Processing,
Chemicals, Automobile Assembly

DOMINANT LAND USE

Wheat, Livestock
Cereals (chiefly corn), Livestock
Diversified Tropical Cash Crops
Cotton, Mixed Cereals
Livestock, Limited Agriculture
Range Livestock
Forests
Nonagricultural Land

Water Power
Major Industrial Areas

MAJOR MINERAL OCCURRENCES

Ag Silver
Au Gold
C Coal
Cu Copper
F Fluorspar
Fe Iron Ore

G Natural Gas
Gr Graphite
Hg Mercury
Mn Manganese
Mo Molybdenum
Na Salt

O Petroleum
Pb Lead
S Sulfur
Sb Antimony
Sn Tin
W Tungsten
Zn Zinc

GUATEMALA
AREA 42,042 sq. mi.
POPULATION 5,200,000
CAPITAL Guatemala
LARGEST CITY Guatemala
HIGHEST POINT Tajumulco 13,845 ft.
MONETARY UNIT quetzal
MAJOR LANGUAGES Spanish, Quiché
MAJOR RELIGION Roman Catholicism

BELIZE
AREA 8,867 sq. mi.
POPULATION 122,000
CAPITAL Belmopan
LARGEST CITY Belize City
HIGHEST POINT Victoria Peak, 3,681 ft.
MONETARY UNIT Belize dollar
MAJOR LANGUAGES English, Spanish, Mayan
MAJOR RELIGIONS Protestantism, Roman Catholicism

EL SALVADOR
AREA 8,260 sq. mi.
POPULATION 3,418,455
CAPITAL San Salvador
LARGEST CITY San Salvador
HIGHEST POINT Santa Ana 7,825 ft.
MONETARY UNIT colón
MAJOR LANGUAGE Spanish
MAJOR RELIGION Roman Catholicism

HONDURAS
AREA 43,277 sq. mi.
POPULATION 2,495,000
CAPITAL Tegucigalpa
LARGEST CITY Tegucigalpa
HIGHEST POINT Las Minas 9,347 ft.
MONETARY UNIT lempira
MAJOR LANGUAGE Spanish
MAJOR RELIGION Roman Catholicism

NICARAGUA
AREA 45,698 sq. mi.
POPULATION 1,984,000
CAPITAL Managua
LARGEST CITY Managua
HIGHEST POINT Cerro Mocotón 6,913 ft.
MONETARY UNIT córdoba
MAJOR LANGUAGE Spanish
MAJOR RELIGION Roman Catholicism

COSTA RICA
AREA 19,575 sq. mi.
POPULATION 1,800,000
CAPITAL San José
LARGEST CITY San José
HIGHEST POINT Chirripó Grande 12,530 ft.
MONETARY UNIT colón
MAJOR LANGUAGE Spanish
MAJOR RELIGION Roman Catholicism

PANAMA
AREA 29,209 sq. mi.
POPULATION 1,425,343
CAPITAL Panamá
LARGEST CITY Panamá
HIGHEST POINT Vol. Chiriquí 11,401 ft.
MONETARY UNIT balboa
MAJOR LANGUAGE Spanish
MAJOR RELIGION Roman Catholicism

CANAL ZONE
AREA 647 sq. mi.
POPULATION 44,650
CAPITAL Balboa Heights

Agriculture, Industry and Resources

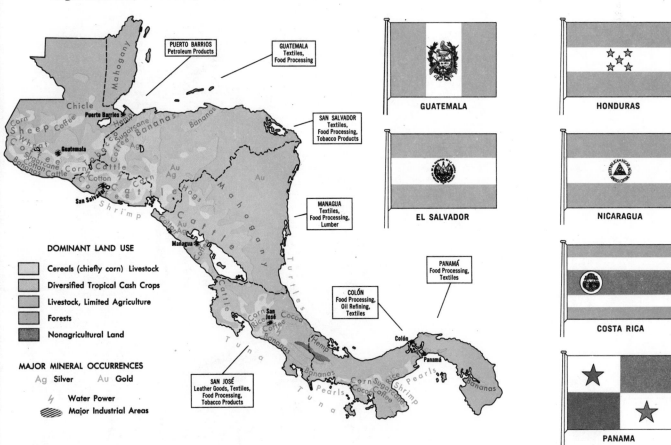

DOMINANT LAND USE

Cereals (chiefly corn) Livestock

Diversified Tropical Cash Crops

Livestock, Limited Agriculture

Forests

Nonagricultural Land

MAJOR MINERAL OCCURRENCES

Ag Silver   Au Gold

⚡ Water Power

▨ Major Industrial Areas

GUATEMALA

HONDURAS

EL SALVADOR

NICARAGUA

COSTA RICA

PANAMA

BELIZE

CITIES and TOWNS

Belize City, 37,000 .... C 2
Belize City, *48,421 .... C 2
Belmopan (capital) .... C 2
Benque Viejo, 1,607 .... C 2
Cayo, 1,890 .... C 2
Corozal Town, 3,171 .... C 1
Hill Bank, 78 .... C 2
Monkey River Town, 417 .... C 2
Orange Walk Town, 2,157 .... C 1
Punta Gorda, 1,789 .... C 2

San José, 365 .... C 2
San Pedro, 170 .... D 2
Stann Creek Town, 5,287 .... C 2

OTHER FEATURES

Ambergris (cay), 1572 .... D 1
Belize (river) .... D 2
Bokel (cay) .... D 2
Cockscomb (mts.) .... C 2
Corker (cay), 1360 .... D 2
Glovers (reef) .... D 2
Half Moon (cay) .... D 2
Hondo (river) .... C 1

Honduras (gulf) .... D 2
Mauger (cay) .... D 2
New (river) .... D 2
Saint Georges (cay), 134 .... D 2
Sarstún (river) .... C 3
Turneffe (isls.), 99 .... D 2

CANAL ZONE

CITIES and TOWNS

Balboa, 2,568 .... H 6
Cristóbal, 817 .... G 6

COSTA RICA

CITIES and TOWNS

Alajuela, 25,195 .... E 6
Atenas, 963 .... E 6
Atlanta .... F 6
Bagaces, 1,175 .... E 5
Beverly .... F 6
Boruca, ‡1,049 .... E 6
Buenos Aires, ‡4,624 .... E 6
Cañas, 2,991 .... E 5
Carmen .... F 6
Cartago, 19,038 .... F 6
Chomes, ‡1,991 .... E 6

Ciudad Quesada, 3,696 .... E 5
El Salvador .... F 5
Esparta, 2,860 .... E 6
Filadelfia, 1,574 .... E 5
Golfito, 6,859 .... F 6
Grecia, 4,862 .... E 6
Guácimo, 5,731 .... F 5
Guápiles, 983 .... F 5
Heredia, 20,523 .... E 6
Las Juntas, 827 .... E 5
Liberia, 11,171 .... E 5
Limón, 30,676 .... F 6
Miramar, 1,122 .... E 6
Nicoya, 3,196 .... E 5
Orotina, 1,749 .... E 6

Palmares, 1,529 .... F 6
Paquera .... E 6
Paraíso, 4,427 .... F 6
Pejivalle .... F 6
Platanilla .... F 6
Playa Bonita .... F 6
Puerto Cortés, 1,757 .... F 6
Puntarenas, 27,527 .... E 6
Quepos, 1,858 .... E 6
San Ignacio, 315 .... F 6
San José (cap.), 182,961 .... F 5
San José, *408,000 .... F 5
San Marcos, 411 .... E 6
San Ramón, 6,444 .... E 5
Santa Cruz, 3,849 .... E 5

Santa Rosa, ‡1,750 .... E 5
Santo Domingo, 3,333 .... F 6
Sibube .... F 5
Siquirres, 2,157 .... F 5
Turrialba, 8,629 .... F 6
Vesta .... F 6

OTHER FEATURES

Blanca (point) .... F 5
Blanco (cape) .... E 6
Blanco (mt.) .... F 6
Burica (point) .... F 6
Cahuita (point) .... F 6
Caño (isl.) .... F 6

(continued on following page)

COSTA RICA (continued)

Carreta (point)	F 6
Chirripó Grande (mt.)	F 6
Coronada (bay)	F 6
Cuilapa Miravalles (volcano)	E 5
Dulce (gulf)	F 6
Góngora (mt.)	F 6
Guiones (point)	E 6
Irazú (mt.)	F 6
Judas (point)	F 6
Llerena (point)	F 6
Matapalo (cape)	F 6
Nicoya (gulf)	E 6
Nicoya (pen.)	E 6
Papagayo (gulf)	E 5
Salinas (bay)	D 5
San Juan (river)	E F 5
Santa Elena (cape)	E 5
Talamanca (range)	F 6
Velas (cape)	D 5

EL SALVADOR

CITIES and TOWNS

Acajutla, 5,310	B 4
Ahuachapán, 16,180	B 4

Atiquizaya, 7,878	C 3
Chalatenango, 7,209	C 3
Chinameca, 7,020	C 4
Cojutepeque, 16,084	C 4
Estanzuelas, 2,785	C 4
Ilobasco, 6,432	C 4
Intipucá, 3,683	D 4
Jucuarán, 1,600	D 4
La Libertad, 7,015	C 4
La Palma, 1,992	C 3
La Unión, 16,459	D 4
Metapán, 4,896	C 3
Nueva San Salvador (Santa Tecla), 36,944	C 4
Puerto de la Concordia	C 4
San Francisco Gotera, 4,638	C 4
San Miguel, 50,668	D 4
San Salvador (cap.), 349,725	C 4
Santa Ana, 102,301	B 4
Santa Rosa de Lima, 6,297	D 4
Santa Tecla, 36,944	C 4
San Vicente, 19,887	C 4
Sensuntepeque, 6,791	C 4
Sonsonate, 32,675	C 4
Suchitoto, 5,758	C 4
Texistepeque, 1,723	C 3
Usulután, 17,796	C 4
Zacatecoluca, 16,189	C 4

OTHER FEATURES

Fonseca (gulf)	D 4
Güija (lake)	C 3
Lempa (river)	C 4
Remedios (point)	C 4
Santa Ana (mt.)	C 4

GUATEMALA

CITIES and TOWNS

Amatitlán, 12,225	B 3
Antigua, 13,576	B 3
Asunción Mita, 6,341	C 3
Cahabón, 939	C 2
Chahal, 323	C 2
Chajul, 4,187	B 3
Champerico, 3,823	A 3
Chichicastenango, 2,099	B 3
Chimaltenango, 9,077	B 3
Chinaja	B 2
Chiquimula, 14,760	C 3
Chisec, 812	C 2
Coatepeque, 13,657	A 3
Cobán, 9,073	B 3
Comalapa, 9,202	B 3

Cubulco, 1,676	B 3
Cuilapa, 3,657	B 3
Cuilco, 728	A 3
Dolores, 630	C 2
El Cambio	C 2
El Porvenir	C 2
El Progreso, 3,458	B 3
Escuintla, 24,832	B 3
Flores, 1,503	C 2
Gualán, 4,425	C 3
Guatemala (cap.), 700,000	B 3
Huehuetenango, 10,185	B 3
Ipala, 3,190	C 3
Izabal	C 2
Iztapa, 751	B 4
Jacaltenango, 3,873	A 3
Jalapa, 10,035	B 3
Jutiapa, 7,747	C 3
La Gomera, 1,397	B 3
La Libertad, 770	B 2
Livingston, 3,453	C 2
Los Amates, 1,131	C 3
Masagua, 1,100	B 3
Matías de Gálvez	C 3
Mazatenango, 19,506	B 3
Momostenango, 3,148	B 3
Morales, 1,710	C 3
Nejapa	C 3

Ocós, 576	A 3
Panzós, 1,803	C 2
Puerto Barrios, 22,242	C 2
Quezaltenango, 45,195	A 3
Quezaltepeque, 2,578	C 3
Rabinal, 4,155	B 3
Retalhuleu, 14,366	B 3
Río Hondo, 1,300	C 3
Sacapulas, 1,407	B 3
Salamá, 4,442	B 3
San Andrés, 939	C 2
San Felipe, 2,916	B 3
San Juan de Dios	B 2
San José, 5,771	B 3
San Luis, 763	C 2
San Luis Jilotepeque, 5,795	C 3
San Marcos, 5,569	B 3
San Martín Jilotepeque, 2,806	B 3
San Mateo Ixtatán, 2,892	B 3
San Miguel	C 2
San Pedro Carchá, 3,966	C 3
Santa Ana, 239	C 2
Santa Ana Mixtán	B 3
Santa Cruz del Quiché, 6,472	B 3
Santa Rosa de Lima, 734	C 3
Sipacate	B 3
Solalá, 3,957	B 3
Tacaná, 900	A 3

Tejutla, 973	B 3
Totonicapán, 7,292	B 3
Yaloch	C 2
Zacapa, 11,173	C 3

OTHER FEATURES

Atitlán (lake)	B 3
Atitlán (volcano)	B 3
Azul (river)	C 2
Chixoy (river)	B 2
Dulce (Izabal) (lake)	C 2
Güija (lake)	C 3
Honduras (gulf)	D 2
Izabal (lake)	C 2
Minas (mts.)	C 3
Motagua (river)	C 3
Pasión (river)	B 2
Petén-Itzá (lake)	C 2
San Pedro (river)	B 2
Sarstun (river)	C 2
Tacaná (volcano)	A 3
Tajumulco (volcano)	A 3
Tres Puntas (cape)	C 2
Usumacinta (river)	B 2

HONDURAS

CITIES and TOWNS

Ahuás	E 3
Amapala, 3,491	C 4
Balana	E 3
Balfate, 602	D 3
Belén, 201	D 4
Brus Laguna, 1,247	E 3
Carataska	E 3
Catacamas, 4,751	D 3
Cedros, 1,177	C 3
Chichicaste	D 3
Choloma, 6,678	C 3
Choluteca, 17,350	D 4
Colorado	D 3
Comayagua, 11,247	C 3
Comayagüela	C 3
Concepción de María, 653	C 4
Concordia, 644	C 3
Copán, 1,177	B 3
Corquín, 2,817	C 3
Cruta	E 3
Danlí, 8,242	C 3
Donel	E 3
El Dulce Nombre, 145	D 3

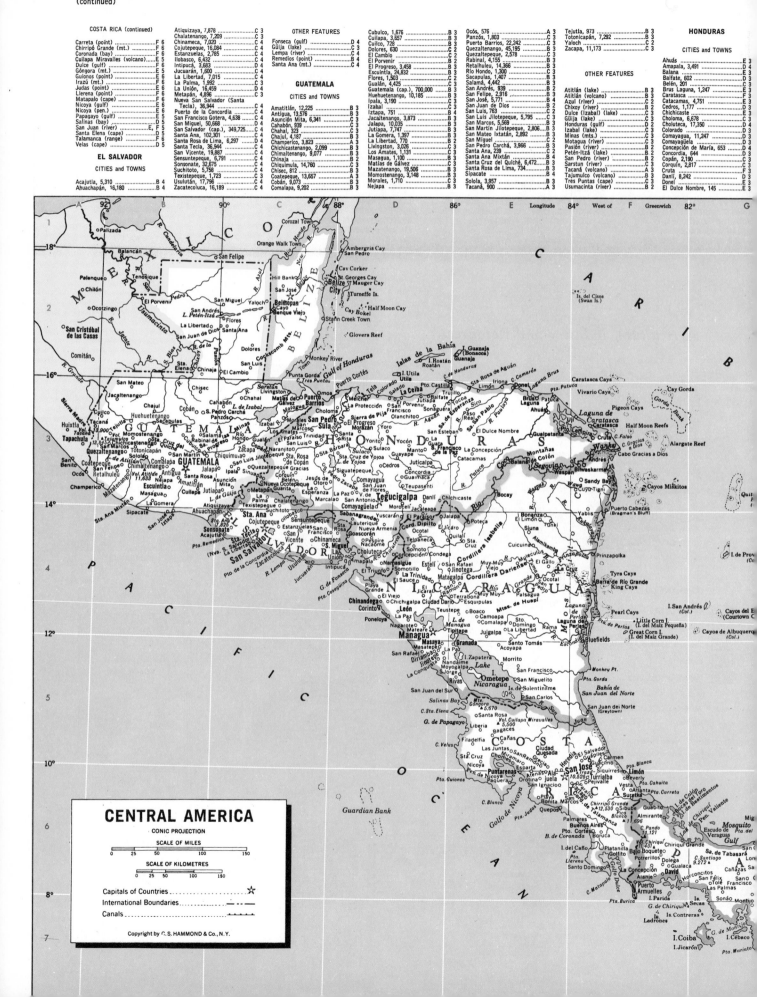

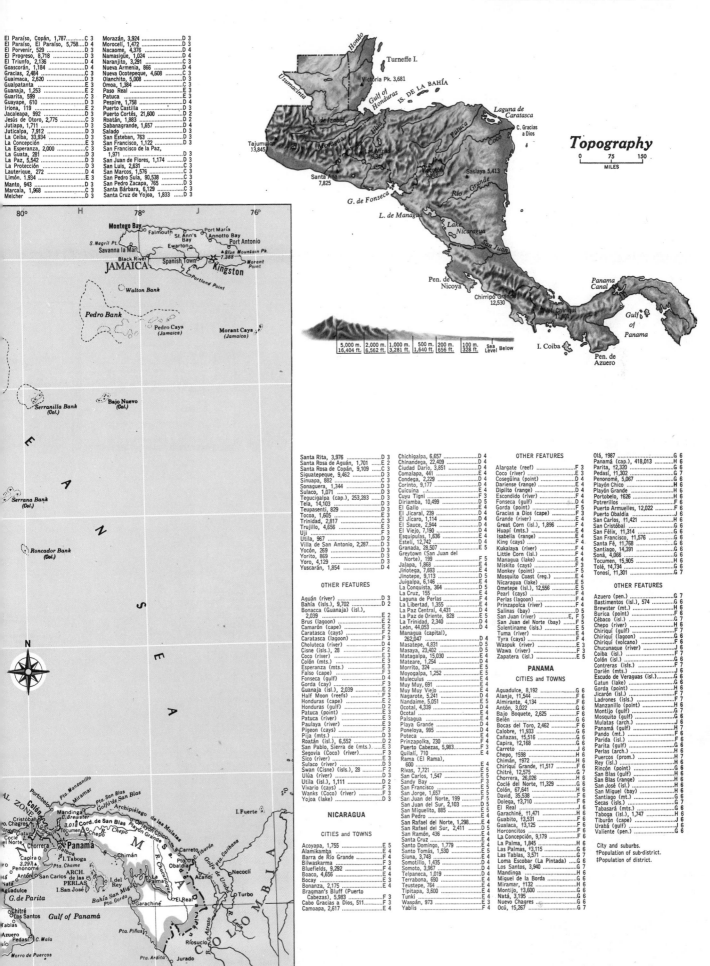

Topography

| 0 | 75 | 150 |
MILES

5,000 m. 16,404 ft. | 2,000 m. 6,562 ft. | 1,000 m. 3,281 ft. | 500 m. 1,640 ft. | 200 m. 656 ft. | 100 m. 328 ft. | Sea Level | Below

El Paraíso, Copán, 1,787....C 3
El Paraíso, El Paraíso, 5,758..D 4
El Porvenir, 529....D 3
El Progreso, 8,718....D 3
El Triunfo, 2,136....D 4
Goascorán, 1,184....C 3
Gracias, 2,484....C 3
Guaimaca, 2,620....D 3
Gualpatanta....E 3
Guanaja, 1,253....E 2
Guarita, 599....C 3
Guayape, 610....D 3
Iriona, 119....E 2
Jacaleapa, 992....D 3
Jesús de Otoro, 2,775....C 3
Jutiapa, 1,711....D 3
Juticalpa, 7,912....D 3
La Ceiba, 33,934....D 2
La Concepción....E 3
La Esperanza, 2,000....C 3
La Guata, 281....D 3
La Paz, 5,542....D 3
La Protección....D 3
Lauterique, 272....C 3
Limón, 1,934....E 3
Manto, 943....D 3
Marcala, 1,968....C 3
Melcher....D 3

Morazán, 3,924....D 3
Morocelí, 1,472....D 3
Nacaome, 4,376....D 4
Namasigüe, 1,024....D 4
Naranjito, 3,291....C 3
Nueva Armenia, 866....D 4
Nueva Ocotepeque, 4,608....C 3
Olanchito, 5,008....D 3
Omoa, 1,384....C 2
Paso Real....E 3
Patuca....E 3
Pespire, 1,758....D 4
Puerto Castilla....E 2
Puerto Cortés, 21,600....D 2
Roatán, 1,883....D 2
Sabanagrande, 1,857....D 4
Salado....E 3
San Esteban, 763....D 3
San Francisco, 1,122....D 3
San Francisco de la Paz, 1,971....D 3
San Juan de Flores, 1,174....D 3
San Luis, 2,631....C 3
San Marcos, 1,576....C 3
San Pedro Sula, 90,538....C 3
San Pedro Zacapa, 765....C 3
Santa Bárbara, 6,129....C 3
Santa Cruz de Yojoa, 1,833....D 3

Santa Rita, 3,976....D 3
Santa Rosa de Aguán, 1,701....E 2
Santa Rosa de Copán, 9,109....C 3
Siguatepeque, 9,462....C 3
Sinuapa, 882....C 3
Sonaguera, 1,344....D 3
Sulaco, 1,071....D 3
Tegucigalpa (cap.), 253,283....D 3
Tela, 14,103....D 2
Teupasenti, 829....D 3
Tocoa, 1,605....E 3
Trinidad, 2,817....C 3
Trujillo, 4,656....E 3
Uji....F 3
Utila, 967....D 2
Villa de San Antonio, 2,287....D 3
Yocón, 269....D 3
Yorito, 869....D 3
Yoro, 4,129....D 3
Yuscarán, 1,854....D 4

OTHER FEATURES

Aguán (river)....D 3
Bahía (isls.), 9,702....D 2
Bonacca (Guanaja) (isl.), 2,039....E 2
Brus (lagoon)....E 2
Camarón (cape)....E 2
Caratasca (cays)....F 2
Caratasca (lagoon)....F 2
Choluteca (river)....D 4
Cisne (isls.), 28....F 2
Coco (river)....E 3
Colón (mts.)....E 3
Esperanza (mts.)....E 3
Falso (cape)....F 2
Fonseca (gulf)....D 4
Gorda (cay)....F 3
Guanaja (isl.), 2,039....E 2
Half Moon (reefs)....F 2
Honduras (gulf)....D 2
Patuca (point)....E 2
Patuca (river)....E 3
Paulaya (river)....E 3
Pigeon (cays)....F 3
Pija (mts.)....D 3
Roatán (isl.), 6,552....D 2
San Pablo, Sierra de (mts.)....E 3
Segovia (Coco) (river)....E 3
Sico (river)....E 3
Swan (Cisne) (isls.), 28....F 2
Ulúa (river)....D 3
Utila (isl.), 1,111....D 2
Vivario (cays)....F 3
Wanks (Coco) (river)....F 3
Yojoa (lake)....D 3

NICARAGUA

CITIES and TOWNS

Acoyapa, 1,755....E 5
Alamikamba....E 4
Barra de Río Grande....F 4
Bilwaskarma....F 3
Bluefields, 9,292....F 4
Boaco, 4,656....E 4
Bocay....E 4
Bonanza, 2,175....E 4
Bragman's Bluff (Puerto Cabezas), 5,983....F 3
Cabo Gracias a Dios, 511....F 3
Camoapa, 2,617....E 4

Chichigalpa, 6,657....D 4
Chinandega, 22,409....D 4
Ciudad Darío, 3,851....D 4
Comalapa, 441....E 4
Condega, 2,229....D 4
Corinto, 9,177....D 4
Culcuina....E 4
Cuyu Tigni....F 3
Diriamba, 10,499....D 5
El Gallo....F 4
El Jicaral, 239....D 4
El Jícaro, 1,114....D 4
El Sauce, 2,944....D 4
El Viejo, 7,190....D 4
Esquipulas, 1,636....E 4
Estelí, 12,742....D 4
Granada, 28,507....E 5
Greytown (San Juan del Norte), 199....F 5
Jalapa, 1,868....E 4
Jinotega, 7,693....D 4
Jinotepe, 9,113....D 5
Juigalpa, 6,146....E 4
La Conquista, 364....D 5
La Cruz, 155....E 4
Laguna de Perlas....F 4
La Libertad, 1,355....E 4
La Paz Central, 4,431....D 4
La Paz de Oriente, 828....D 5
La Trinidad, 2,340....D 4
León, 44,053....D 4
Managua (capital), 262,047....D 4
Masatepe, 4,831....D 5
Masaya, 23,402....D 5
Matagalpa, 15,030....E 4
Mateare, 1,254....D 4
Morrito, 324....E 5
Moyogalpa, 1,252....E 5
Muleculus....E 4
Muy Muy, 691....E 4
Muy Muy Viejo....E 4
Nagarote, 5,241....D 4
Nandaime, 5,051....E 5
Ocotal, 4,339....D 4
Ocotal....E 4
Palsagua....E 4
Playa Grande....D 4
Poneloya, 995....D 4
Poteca....E 4
Prinzapolka, 230....F 4
Puerto Cabezas, 5,983....F 3
Quilalí, 710....E 4
Rama (El Rama), 600....E 4
Rivas, 7,721....D 5
San Carlos, 1,547....E 5
Sandy Bay....F 3
San Francisco....E 5
San Jorge, 1,657....D 5
San Juan del Norte, 199....F 5
San Juan del Sur, 2,103....D 5
San Miguelito, 885....E 5
San Pedro....E 4
San Rafael del Norte, 1,298....E 4
San Rafael del Sur, 2,411....D 5
San Ramón, 436....E 4
Santa Cruz....E 4
Santo Domingo, 1,779....E 4
Santo Tomás, 1,530....E 4
Siuna, 3,743....D 4
Somotillo, 1,435....D 4
Somoto, 3,967....D 4
Telpaneca, 1,019....D 4
Terrabona, 690....E 4
Teustepe, 764....E 4
Tipitapa, 3,600....D 4
Tunki....E 4
Waspán, 973....F 3
Yablis....F 4

OTHER FEATURES

Alargate (reef)....F 3
Coco (river)....E 3
Coseguina (point)....D 4
Dariense (range)....E 4
Dipilto (range)....D 4
Escondido (river)....F 4
Fonseca (gulf)....D 4
Gorda (point)....F 5
Gracias a Dios (cape)....F 3
Grande (river)....F 4
Great Corn (isl.), 1,896....F 4
Huapí (mts.)....E 4
Isabella (range)....E 4
King (cays)....F 4
Kukalaya (river)....F 4
Little Corn (isl.)....F 4
Managua (lake)....D 4
Miskito (cays)....F 3
Monkey (point)....F 4
Mosquito Coast (reg.)....F 4
Nicaragua (lake)....E 5
Ometepe (isl.), 12,556....E 5
Pearl (cays)....F 4
Perlas (lagoon)....F 4
Prinzapolca (river)....F 4
Salinas (bay)....D 5
San Juan (river)....E, F 5
San Juan del Norte (bay)....F 5
Solentiname (isls.)....E 5
Tuma (river)....E 4
Tyra (cays)....F 4
Waspuk (river)....E 4
Wawa (river)....F 3
Zapatera (isl.)....E 5

PANAMA

CITIES and TOWNS

Aguadulce, 8,192....G 6
Alanje, 11,544....F 6
Almirante, 4,134....F 6
Antón, 3,022....G 6
Bajo Boquete, 2,625....F 6
Belén....G 6
Bocas del Toro, 2,462....G 6
Calobre, 11,933....G 6
Cañazas, 15,516....G 6
Capira, 12,168....G 6
Carreto....J 6
Chepo, †598....H 6
Chimán, 1972....H 6
Chiriquí Grande, †1,517....F 6
Chitré, 12,575....G 7
Chorrera, 26,026....H 6
Coclé del Norte, 11,329....G 6
Colón, 67,641....H 6
David, 35,538....F 6
Dolega, 13,710....F 6
El Real....J 6
Garachiné, 11,471....H 6
Guabito, 13,531....F 6
Gualaca, 13,125....F 6
Horconcitos....F 6
La Concepción, 9,179....F 6
La Palma, 1,845....H 6
Las Palmas, †3,115....G 6
Las Tablas, 3,571....G 7
Loma Escobar (La Pintada)....G 6
Los Santos, 3,940....G 7
Mandinga....H 6
Miguel de la Borda....H 6
Miramar, †132....H 6
Montijo, 13,600....G 6
Natá, 3,195....G 6
Nuevo Chagres....G 6
Ocú, 15,267....G 7

Olá, 1987....G 6
Panamá (cap.), 418,013....H 6
Parita, 12,320....G 6
Pedasí, †1,302....G 7
Penonomé, 5,067....G 6
Playón Chico....H 6
Playón Grande....H 6
Portobelo, 1626....H 6
Potrerillos....F 6
Puerto Armuelles, 12,022....F 6
Puerto Obaldía....J 6
San Carlos, 11,421....G 6
San Cristóbal....H 6
San Félix, †1,314....F 6
San Francisco, 11,576....G 6
Santa Fé, 11,768....G 6
Santiago, 14,391....G 6
Soná, 4,066....G 6
Tocumen, 15,905....H 6
Tolé, 14,734....F 6
Tonosí, †1,301....G 7

OTHER FEATURES

Azuero (pen.)....G 7
Bastimentos (isl.), 574....H 6
Brewster (mt.)....H 6
Burica (point)....F 7
Cébaco (isl.)....G 7
Chepo (river)....H 6
Chiriquí (gulf)....F 7
Chiriquí (lagoon)....F 6
Chiriquí (volcano)....F 6
Chucunaque (river)....J 6
Coiba (isl.)....F 7
Colón (isl.)....F 6
Contreras (isls.)....G 7
Darién (mts.)....J 6
Escudo de Veraguas (isl.)....G 6
Gatun (lake)....H 6
Gorda (point)....H 6
Jicarón (isl.)....G 7
Ladrones (isls.)....F 7
Manzanillo (point)....H 6
Montijo (gulf)....G 6
Mosquito (gulf)....G 6
Mulatas (arch.)....H 7
Panamá (gulf)....H 6
Pando (mt.)....F 6
Parida (isl.)....F 6
Parita (gulf)....G 6
Perlas (arch.)....H 7
Puercos (prom.)....H 7
Rey (isl.)....H 6
Rincón (point)....G 6
San Blas (gulf)....H 6
San Blas (range)....H 6
San José (isl.)....H 6
San Miguel (bay)....H 6
Santiago (mt.)....G 7
Secas (isls.)....G 7
Tabasará (mts.)....G 6
Taboga (isl.), 1,747....H 6
Tiburón (cape)....J 6
Urabá (gulf)....J 6
Valiente (pen.)....G 6

*City and suburbs.
†Population of sub-district.
‡Population of district.

124 West Indies

BAHAMAS
AREA 4,404 sq. mi.
POPULATION 168,838
CAPITAL Nassau
LARGEST CITY Nassau
HIGHEST POINT Mt. Alvernia (Cat. I.) 206 ft.
MONETARY UNIT Bahaman dollar
MAJOR LANGUAGE English
MAJOR RELIGIONS Roman Catholicism,
Protestantism

BAHAMAS

CUBA

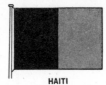
HAITI

DOMINICAN REPUBLIC

JAMAICA

CUBA
AREA 44,206 sq. mi.
POPULATION 8,553,395
CAPITAL Havana
LARGEST CITY Havana
HIGHEST POINT Pico Turquino 6,561 ft.
MONETARY UNIT Cuban peso
MAJOR LANGUAGE Spanish
MAJOR RELIGION Roman Catholicism

JAMAICA
AREA 4,411 sq. mi.
POPULATION 1,972,000
CAPITAL Kingston
LARGEST CITY Kingston
HIGHEST POINT Blue Mountain Peak, 7,402 ft.
MONETARY UNIT Jamaican pound
MAJOR LANGUAGE English
MAJOR RELIGIONS Protestantism, Roman
Catholicism

GRENADA
AREA 133 sq. mi.
POPULATION 96,000
CAPITAL Saint George's
LARGEST CITY Saint George's
HIGHEST POINT Mt. St. Catherine
2,757 ft.
MONETARY UNIT East Caribbean dollar
MAJOR LANGUAGES English, French patois
MAJOR RELIGIONS Roman Catholicism,
Protestantism

DOMINICA
AREA 290 sq. mi.
POPULATION 70,302
CAPITAL Roseau
HIGHEST POINT Morne Diablotin 4,747
MONETARY UNIT East Caribbean dollar
MAJOR LANGUAGES English,
French patois
MAJOR RELIGIONS Roman Catholicism,
Protestantism

BARBADOS

GRENADA

HAITI
AREA 10,694 sq. mi.
POPULATION 4,867,190
CAPITAL Port-au-Prince
LARGEST CITY Port-au-Prince
HIGHEST POINT Pic La Selle 8,793 ft.
MONETARY UNIT gourde
MAJOR LANGUAGES Creole French, French
MAJOR RELIGION Roman Catholicism

TRINIDAD AND TOBAGO
AREA 1,980 sq. mi.
POPULATION 1,040,000
CAPITAL Port of Spain
LARGEST CITY Port of Spain
HIGHEST POINT Mt. Aripo 3,084 ft.
MONETARY UNIT Trinidad and Tobago dollar
MAJOR LANGUAGES English, Hindi
MAJOR RELIGIONS Roman Catholicism, Prot.
Hinduism, Islam

DOMINICAN REPUBLIC
AREA 18,704 sq. mi.
POPULATION 4,011,589
CAPITAL Santo Domingo
LARGEST CITY Santo Domingo
HIGHEST POINT Pico Duarte 10,417 ft.
MONETARY UNIT Dominican peso
MAJOR LANGUAGE Spanish
MAJOR RELIGION Roman Catholicism

BARBADOS
AREA 166 sq. mi.
POPULATION 253,620
CAPITAL Bridgetown
LARGEST CITY Bridgetown
HIGHEST POINT Mt. Hillaby 1,104 ft.
MONETARY UNIT East Caribbean dollar
MAJOR LANGUAGE English
MAJOR RELIGION Protestantism

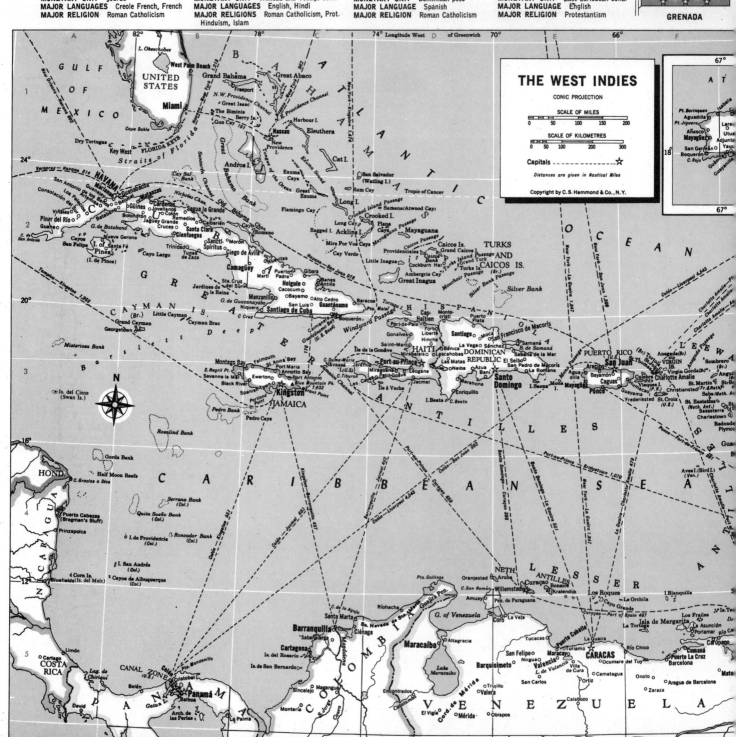

THE WEST INDIES
CONIC PROJECTION
SCALE OF MILES
0   50   100   150   200
SCALE OF KILOMETRES
0 50 100   200   300
Capitals - - - - - - - - - - ☆
Distances are given in Nautical Miles
Copyright by C.S. Hammond & Co., N.Y.

Agriculture, Industry and Resources

DOMINANT LAND USE

- Diversified Tropical Cash Crops
- Tobacco
- Fruit
- Livestock, Limited Agriculture
- Forests
- Nonagricultural Land

TRINIDAD & TOBAGO

DOMINICA

HAVANA
Tobacco Products, Food Processing, Sugar Refining, Distilling, Textiles

SANTIAGO DE CUBA
Sugar Refining, Distilling, Tanning, Metal Products

SAN JUAN
Clothing, Metal Products, Sugar Refining, Chemicals, Food Processing

⚡ Water Power
▨ Major Industrial Areas

KINGSTON
Food Processing, Tanning, Woodworking

PORT-AU-PRINCE
Food Processing

SANTO DOMINGO
Food Processing, Distilling, Textiles

ORANJESTAD–WILLEMSTAD
Oil Refining

MARABELLA–PT. FORTIN
Oil Refining, Chemicals

MAJOR MINERAL OCCURRENCES

Al Bauxite	Cr Chromium	Gp Gypsum	Ni Nickel
At Asphalt	Cu Copper	Mn Manganese	O Petroleum
Co Cobalt	Fe Iron Ore	Na Salt	P Phosphates

PUERTO RICO

BERMUDA ISLANDS

Topography

UNITED STATES

POLYCONIC PROJECTION

SCALE

0 50 100 200 300 400MI.

0 50 100 200 300 400KM.

Capitals of Countries............☆
State Capitals.....................△
International Boundaries.........—·—·—
State Boundaries..................—··—··—

© C.S. HAMMOND & Co., N.Y.

AREA 3,615,123 sq. mi.
POPULATION 217,739,000
CAPITAL Washington
LARGEST CITY New York
HIGHEST POINT Mt. McKinley 20,320 ft.
MONETARY VALUE U.S. dollar
MAJOR LANGUAGE English
MAJOR RELIGIONS Protestantism, Roman Catholicism, Judaism

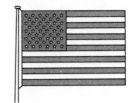

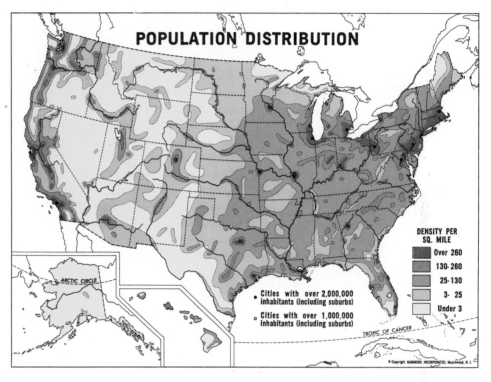

POPULATION DISTRIBUTION

DENSITY PER SQ. MILE
Over 260
130-260
25-130
3-25
Under 3

● Cities with over 2,000,000 inhabitants (including suburbs)
○ Cities with over 1,000,000 inhabitants (including suburbs)

ARCTIC CIRCLE

TROPIC OF CANCER

© Copyright HAMMOND INCORPORATED, Maplewood, N. J.

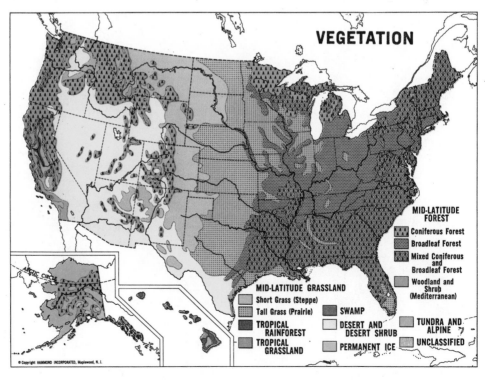

VEGETATION

MID-LATITUDE FOREST
Coniferous Forest
Broadleaf Forest
Mixed Coniferous and Broadleaf Forest
Woodland and Shrub (Mediterranean)

MID-LATITUDE GRASSLAND
Short Grass (Steppe)
Tall Grass (Prairie)

TROPICAL RAINFOREST
TROPICAL GRASSLAND

SWAMP
DESERT AND DESERT SHRUB
PERMANENT ICE

TUNDRA AND ALPINE
UNCLASSIFIED

ARCTIC CIRCLE

© Copyright HAMMOND INCORPORATED, Maplewood, N. J.

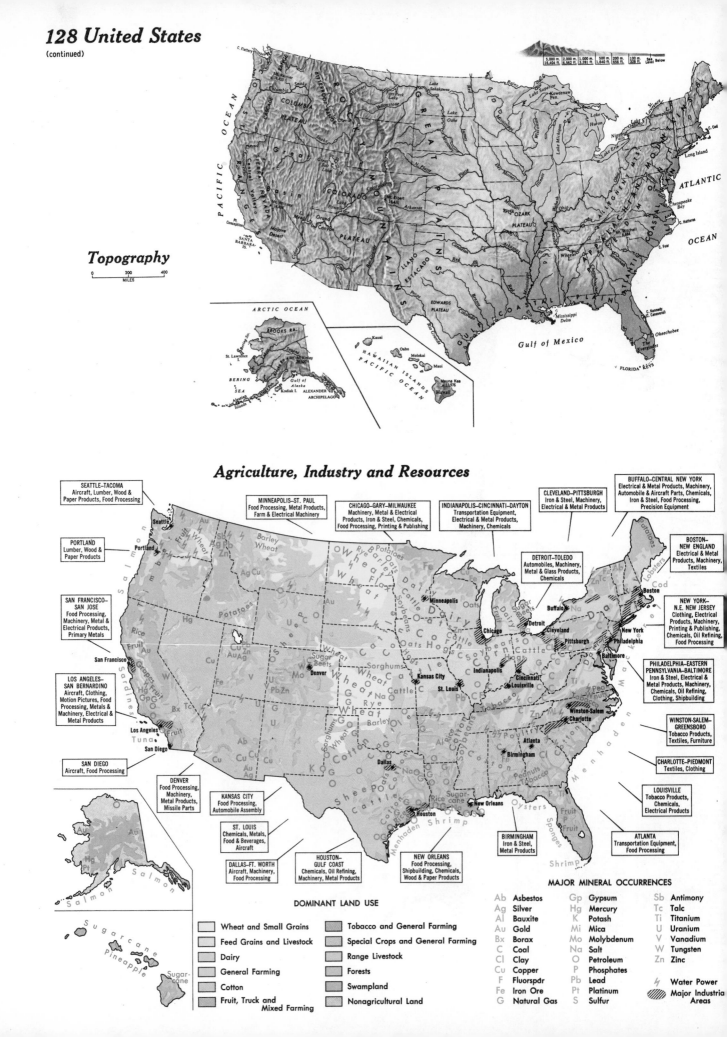

Topography

Agriculture, Industry and Resources

SEATTLE–TACOMA
Aircraft, Lumber, Wood &
Paper Products, Food Processing

MINNEAPOLIS–ST. PAUL
Food Processing, Metal Products,
Farm & Electrical Machinery

CHICAGO–GARY–MILWAUKEE
Machinery, Metal & Electrical
Products, Iron & Steel, Chemicals,
Food Processing, Printing & Publishing

INDIANAPOLIS–CINCINNATI–DAYTON
Transportation Equipment,
Electrical & Metal Products,
Machinery, Chemicals

CLEVELAND–PITTSBURGH
Iron & Steel, Machinery,
Electrical & Metal Products

BUFFALO–CENTRAL NEW YORK
Electrical & Metal Products, Machinery,
Automobile & Aircraft Parts, Chemicals,
Iron & Steel, Food Processing,
Precision Equipment

PORTLAND
Lumber, Wood &
Paper Products

DETROIT–TOLEDO
Automobiles, Machinery,
Metal & Glass Products,
Chemicals

BOSTON–
NEW ENGLAND
Electrical & Metal
Products, Machinery,
Textiles

SAN FRANCISCO–
SAN JOSE
Food Processing,
Machinery, Metal &
Electrical Products,
Primary Metals

NEW YORK–
N.E. NEW JERSEY
Clothing, Electrical
Products, Machinery,
Printing & Publishing,
Chemicals, Oil Refining,
Food Processing

LOS ANGELES–
SAN BERNARDINO
Aircraft, Clothing,
Motion Pictures, Food
Processing, Metals &
Machinery, Electrical &
Metal Products

PHILADELPHIA–EASTERN
PENNSYLVANIA–BALTIMORE
Iron & Steel, Electrical &
Metal Products, Machinery,
Chemicals, Oil Refining,
Clothing, Shipbuilding

WINSTON-SALEM–
GREENSBORO
Tobacco Products,
Textiles, Furniture

SAN DIEGO
Aircraft, Food Processing

CHARLOTTE–PIEDMONT
Textiles, Clothing

DENVER
Food Processing,
Machinery,
Metal Products,
Missile Parts

KANSAS CITY
Food Processing,
Automobile Assembly

LOUISVILLE
Tobacco Products,
Chemicals,
Electrical Products

ST. LOUIS
Chemicals, Metals,
Food & Beverages,
Aircraft

DALLAS–FT. WORTH
Aircraft, Machinery,
Food Processing

HOUSTON–
GULF COAST
Chemicals, Oil Refining,
Machinery, Metal Products

NEW ORLEANS
Food Processing,
Shipbuilding, Chemicals,
Wood & Paper Products

BIRMINGHAM
Iron & Steel,
Metal Products

ATLANTA
Transportation Equipment,
Food Processing

DOMINANT LAND USE

Wheat and Small Grains

Feed Grains and Livestock

Dairy

General Farming

Cotton

Fruit, Truck and
Mixed Farming

Tobacco and General Farming

Special Crops and General Farming

Range Livestock

Forests

Swampland

Nonagricultural Land

MAJOR MINERAL OCCURRENCES

Ab	Asbestos	Gp	Gypsum	Sb	Antimony
Ag	Silver	Hg	Mercury	Tc	Talc
Al	Bauxite	K	Potash	Ti	Titanium
Au	Gold	Mi	Mica	U	Uranium
Bx	Borax	Mo	Molybdenum	V	Vanadium
C	Coal	Na	Salt	W	Tungsten
Cl	Clay	O	Petroleum	Zn	Zinc
Cu	Copper	P	Phosphates		
F	Fluorspar	Pb	Lead		Water Power
Fe	Iron Ore	Pt	Platinum		Major Industrial
G	Natural Gas	S	Sulfur		Areas

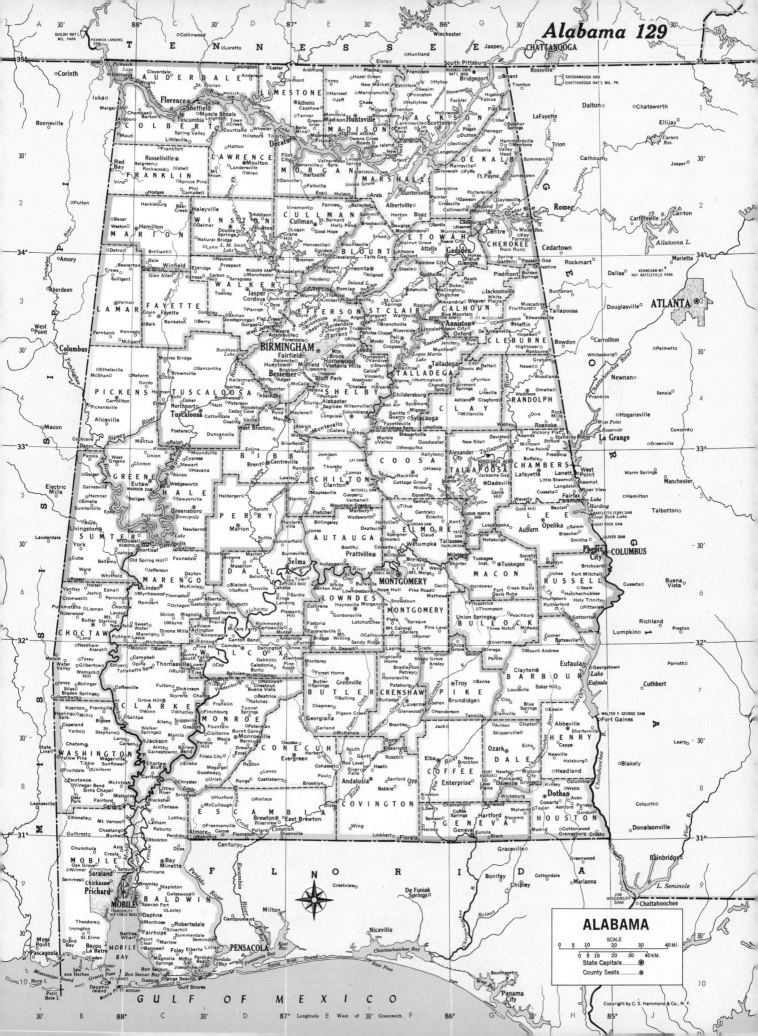

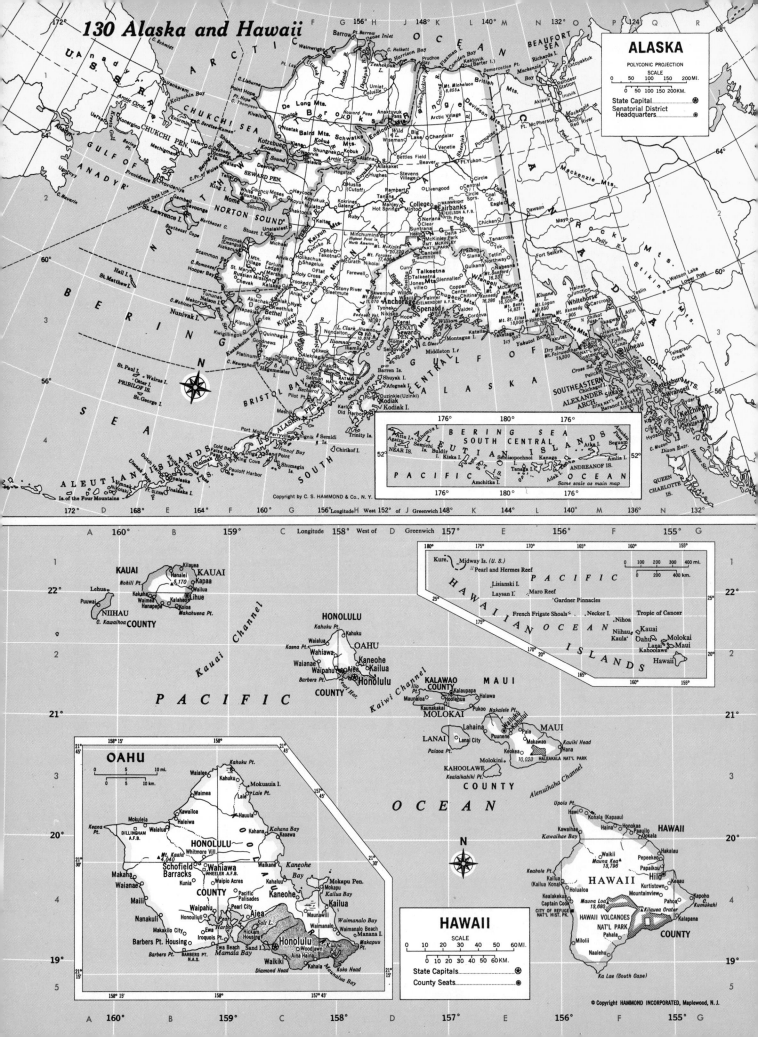

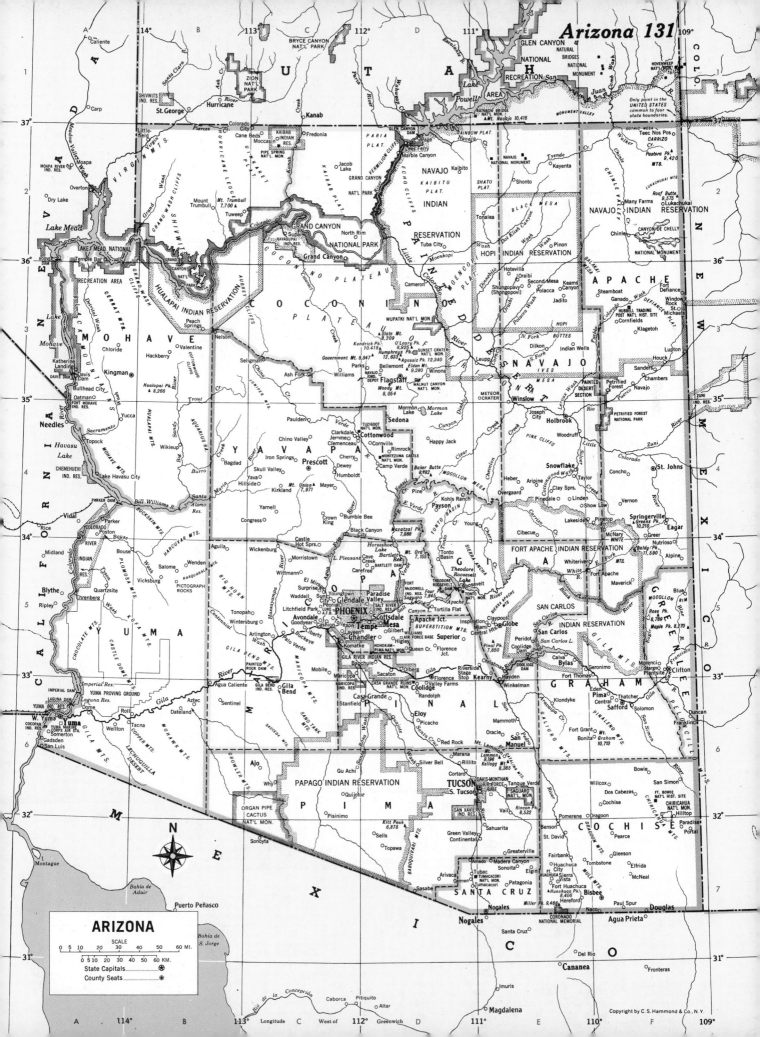

ARIZONA

SCALE
0 5 10 20 30 40 50 60 MI.
0 5 10 20 30 40 50 60 KM.

State Capitals .... ⊛
County Seats .... ⊚

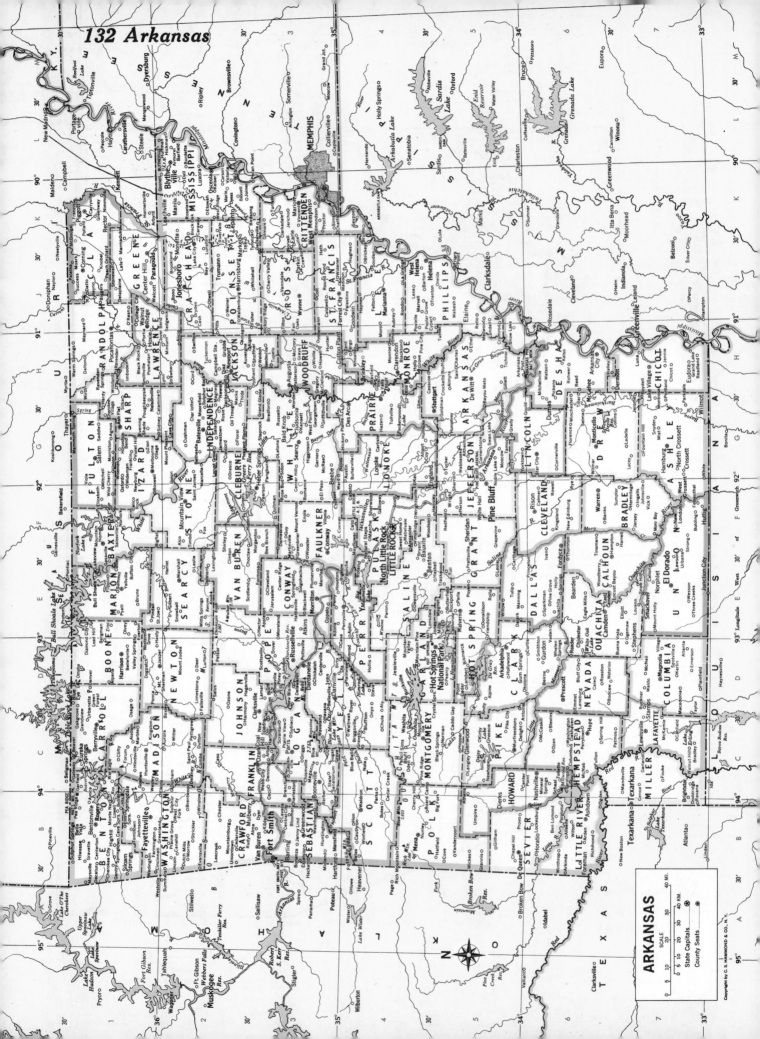

ARKANSAS

SCALE
5 0 10 20 30 40 MI.
5 0 10 20 30 40 KM.

State Capitals .... ⊛
County Seats .... ◉

Copyright by C. S. HAMMOND & CO., N.Y.

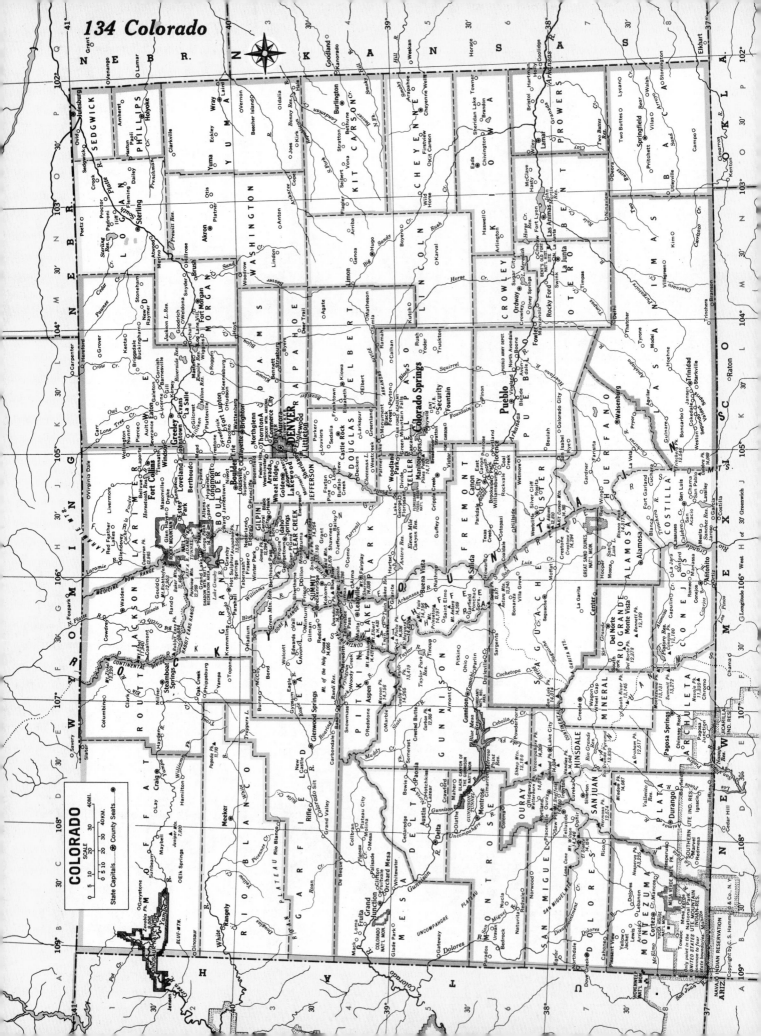

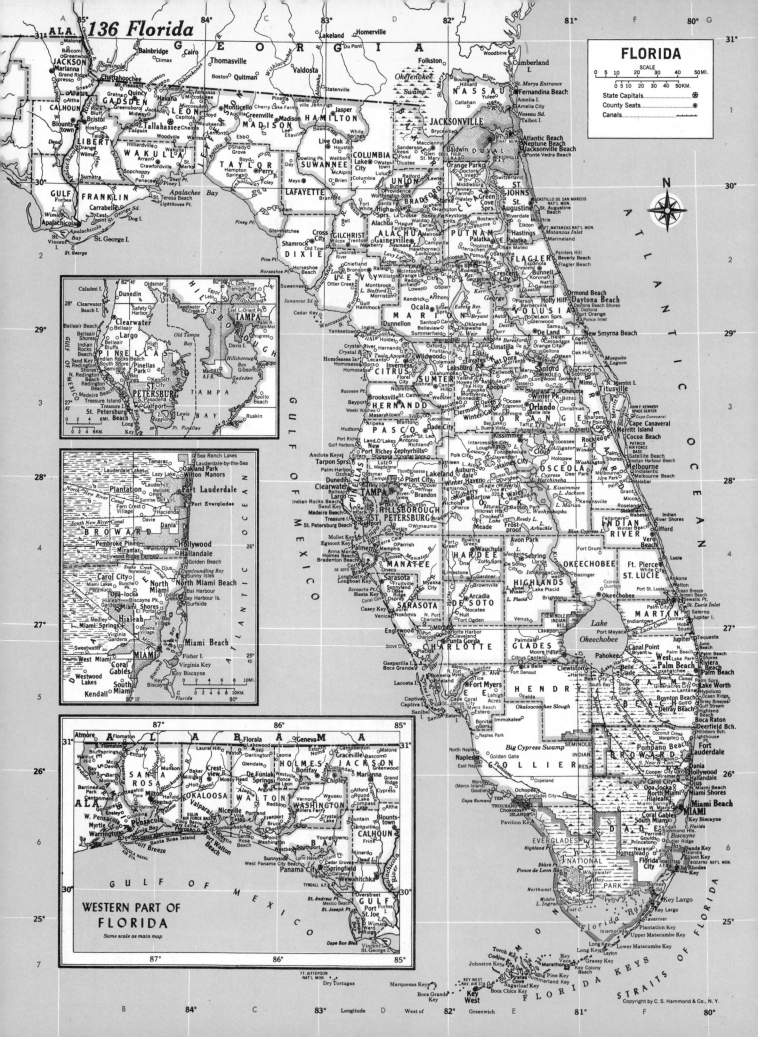

136 Florida

Georgia 137

GEORGIA

SCALE

0 5 10 20 30 40 MI.

0 5 10 20 30 40 KM.

State Capitals .... ⊛

County Seats .... ○

© Copyright HAMMOND INC., Maplewood, N. J.

IDAHO

SCALE

0 5 10 20 30 40 50 60 MI.

0 5 10 20 30 40 50 60 KM.

State Capitals .... ⊛

County Seats .... ⊚

Copyright by C. S. Hammond & Co., N.Y.

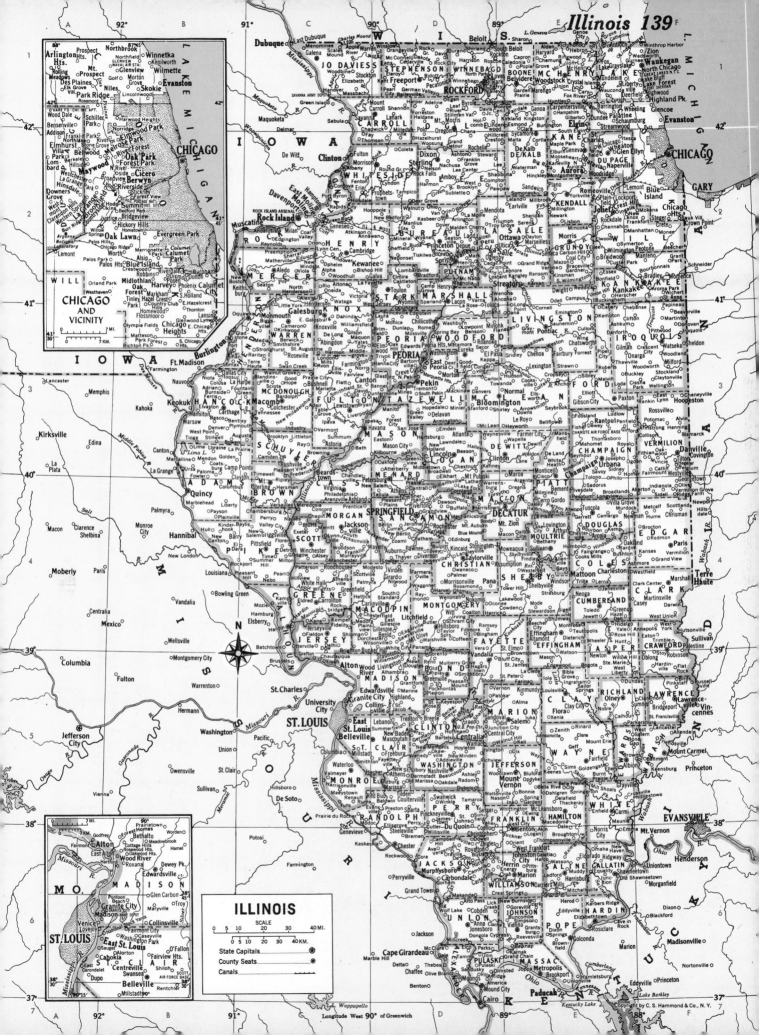

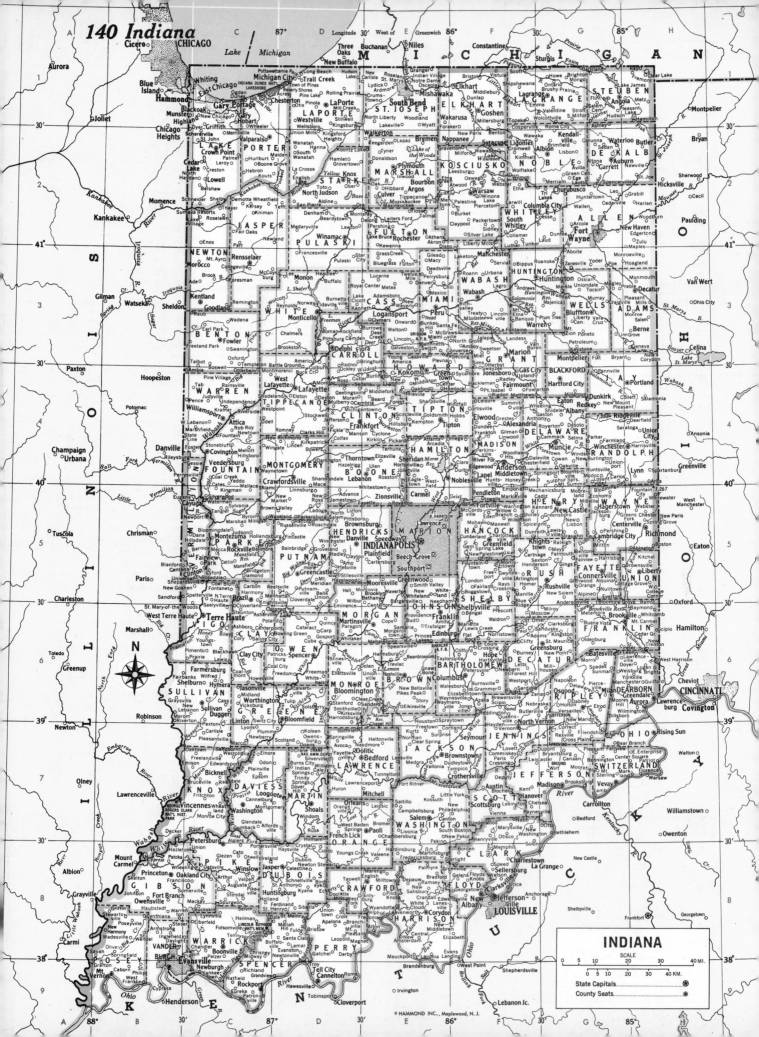

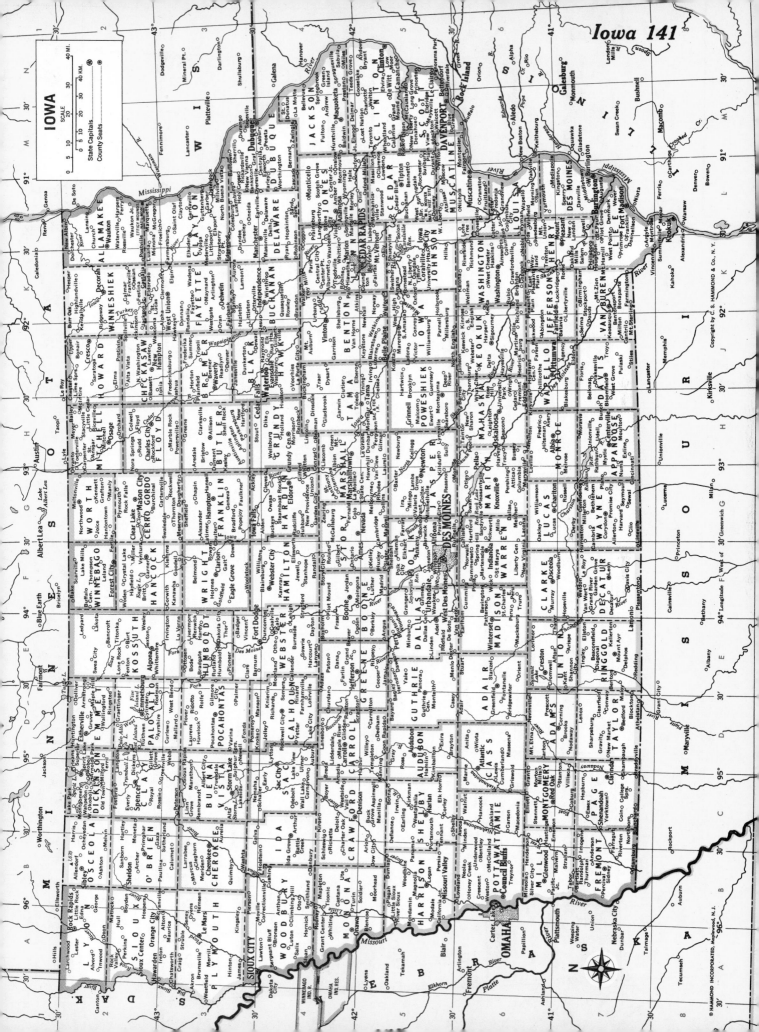

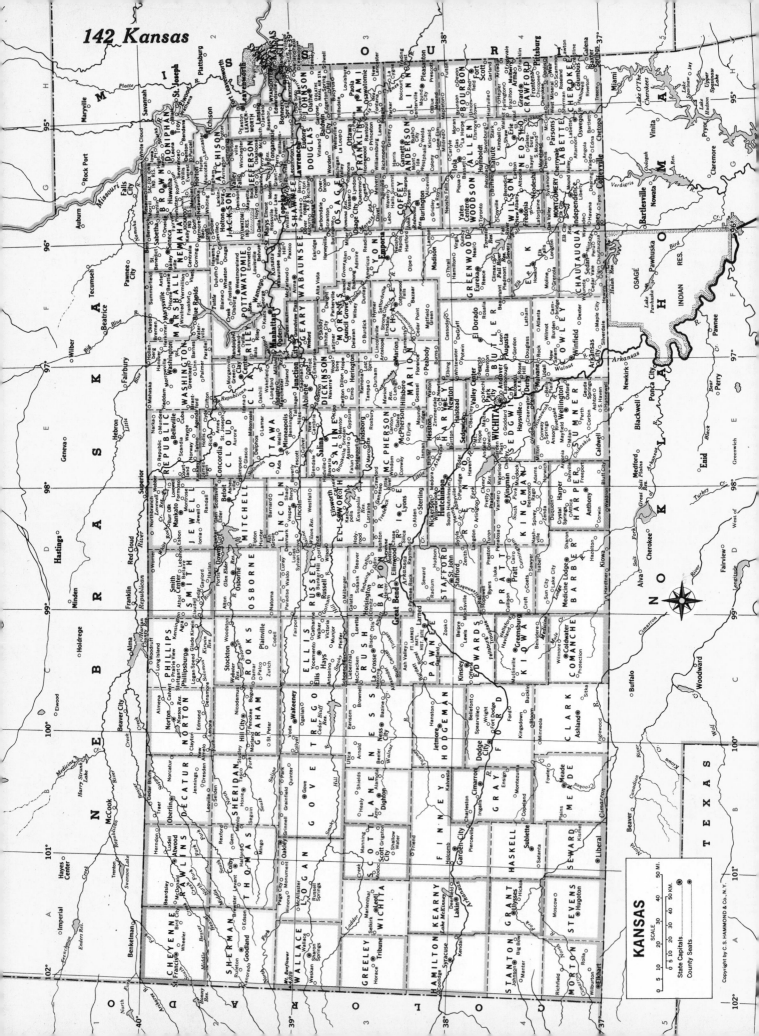

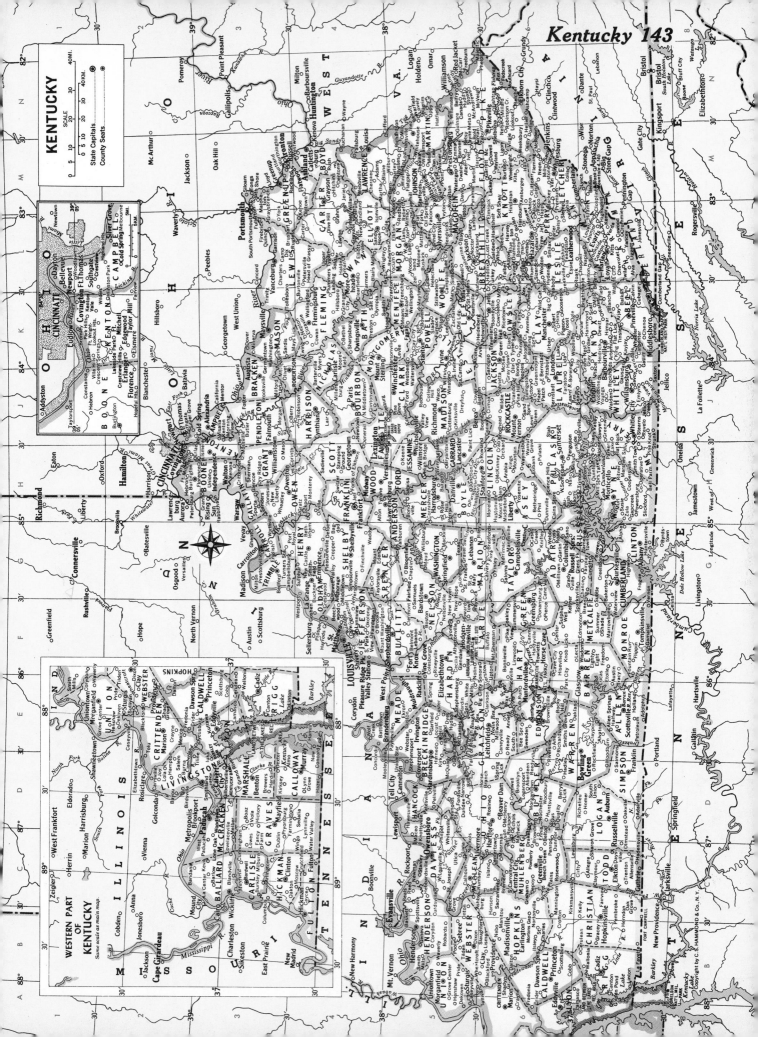

144 Louisiana

NEW ORLEANS, BATON ROUGE AND VICINITY

LOUISIANA

SCALE

State Capitals .... ⊛

Parish Seats .... ⊙

Canals.

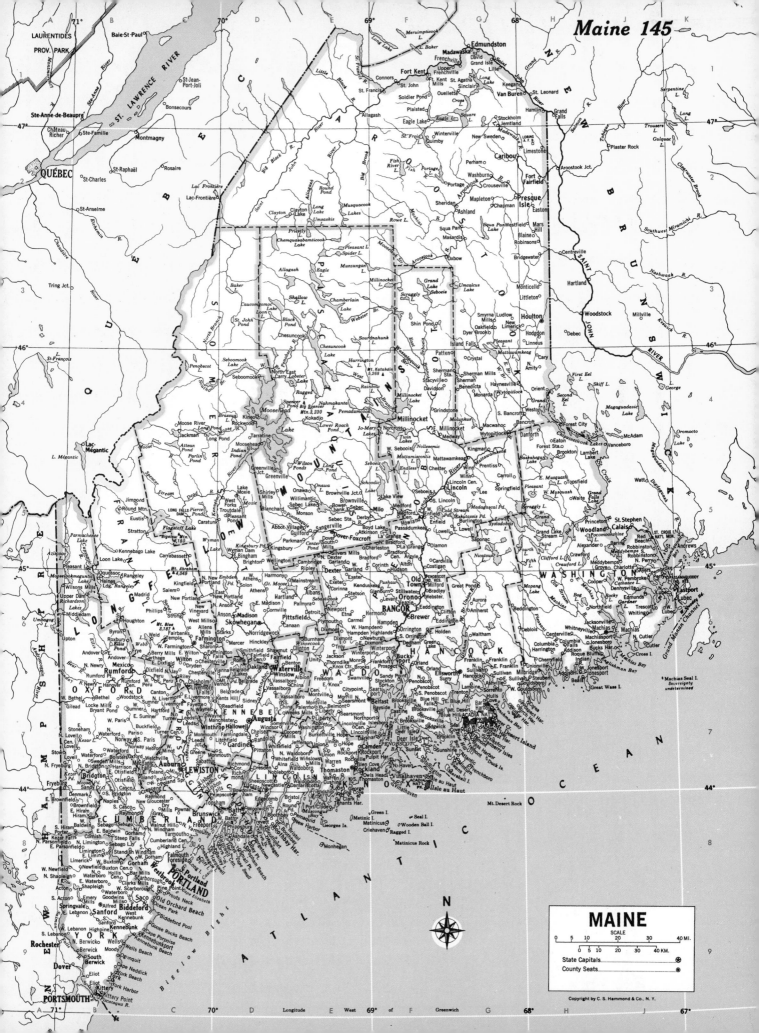

Maine 145

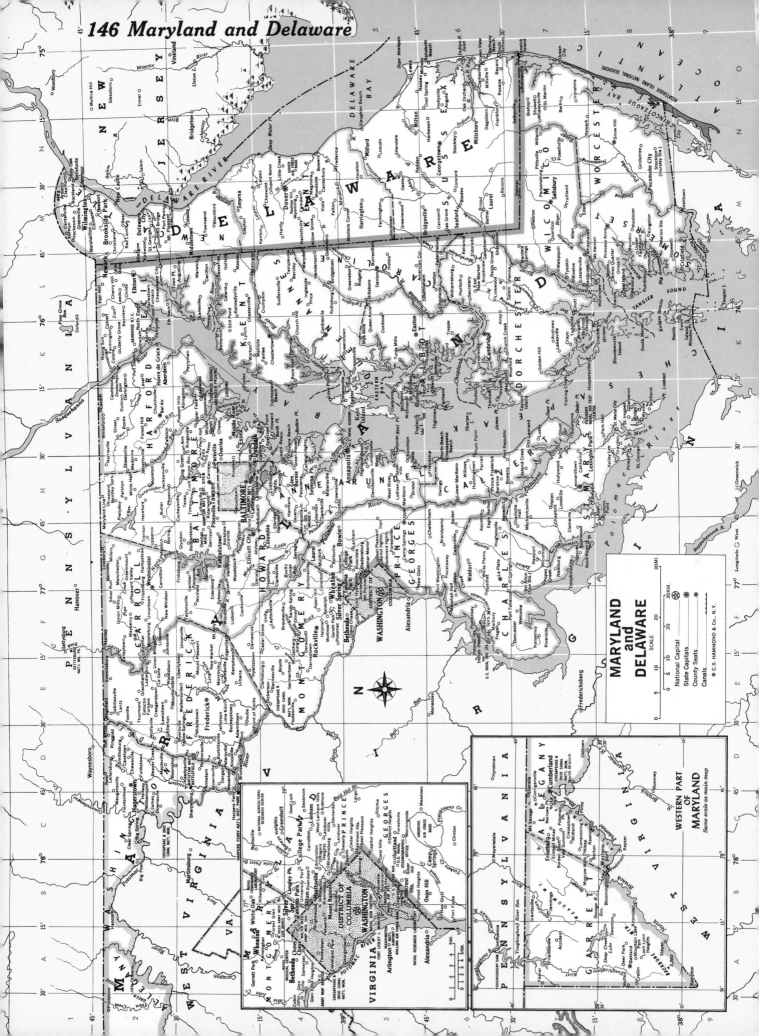

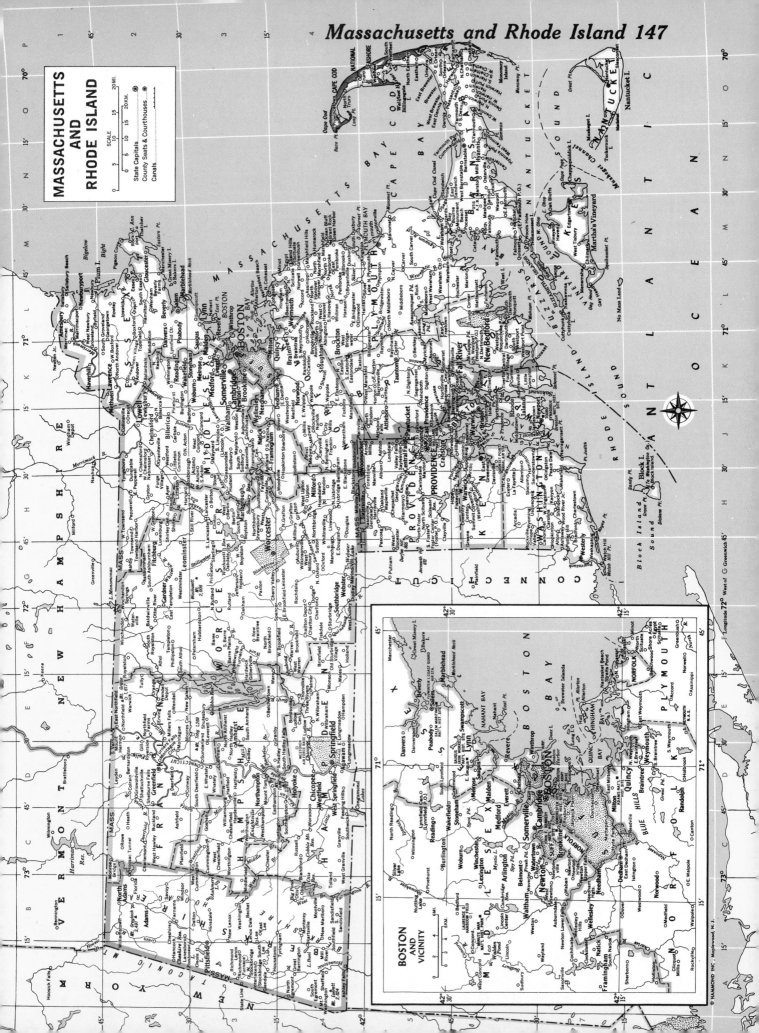

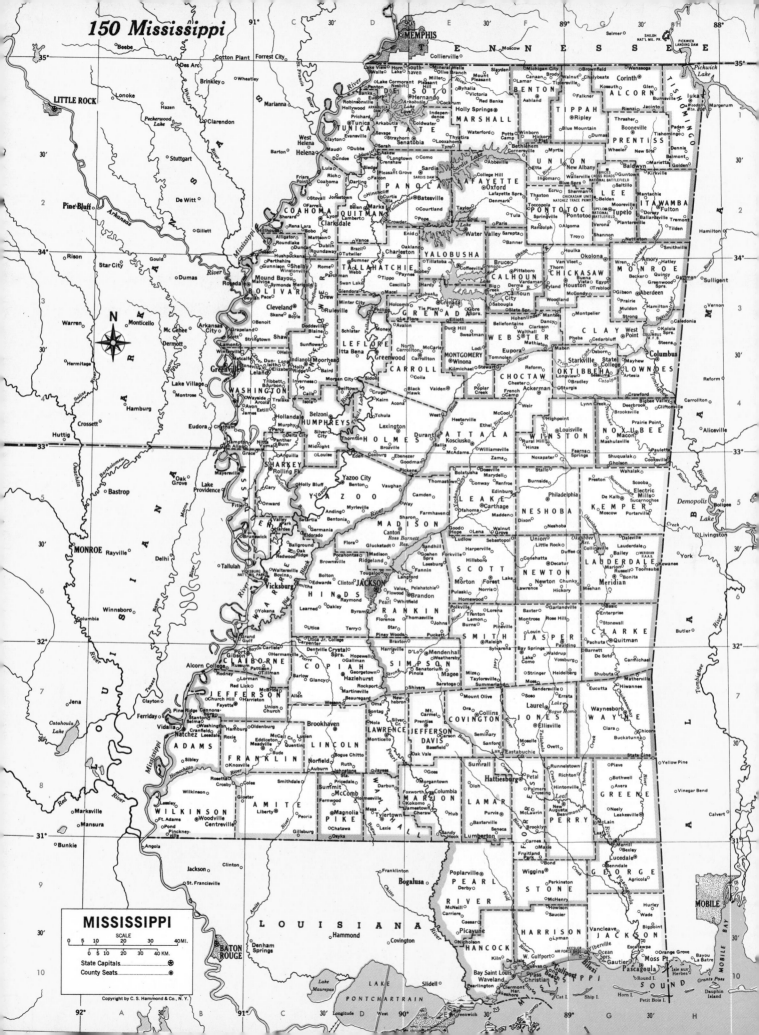

150 Mississippi

MISSISSIPPI

SCALE
0 5 10 20 30 40 MI.
0 5 10 20 30 40 KM.

State Capitals .... ⊛
County Seats .... ◉

Copyright by C. S. Hammond & Co., N.Y.

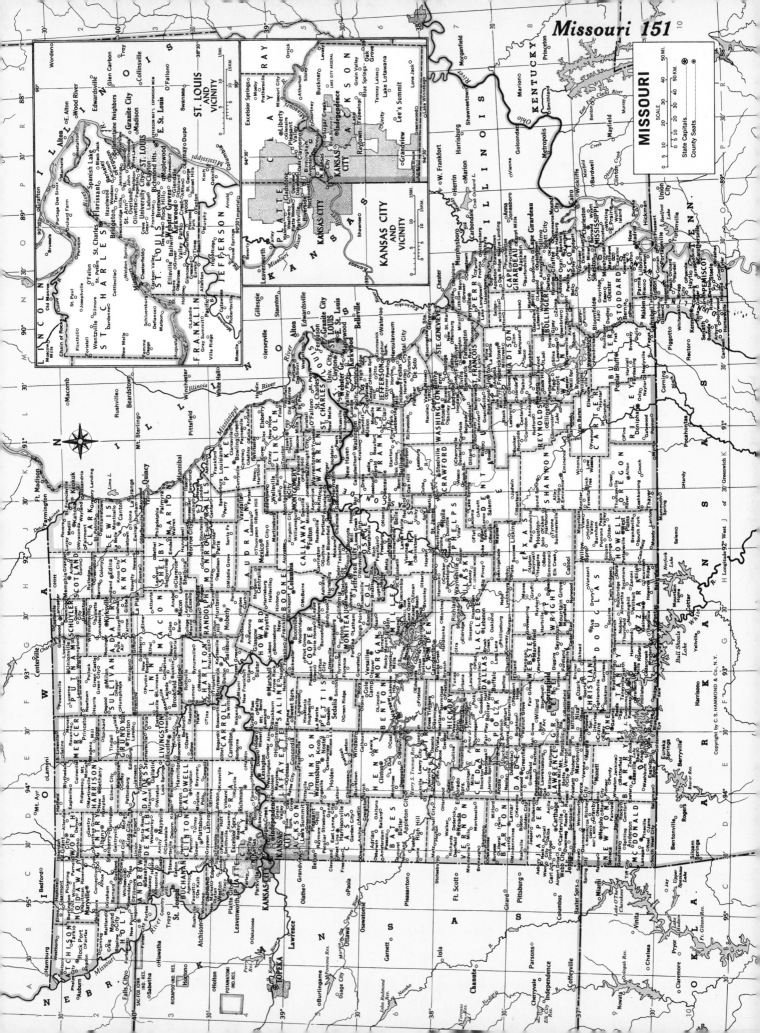

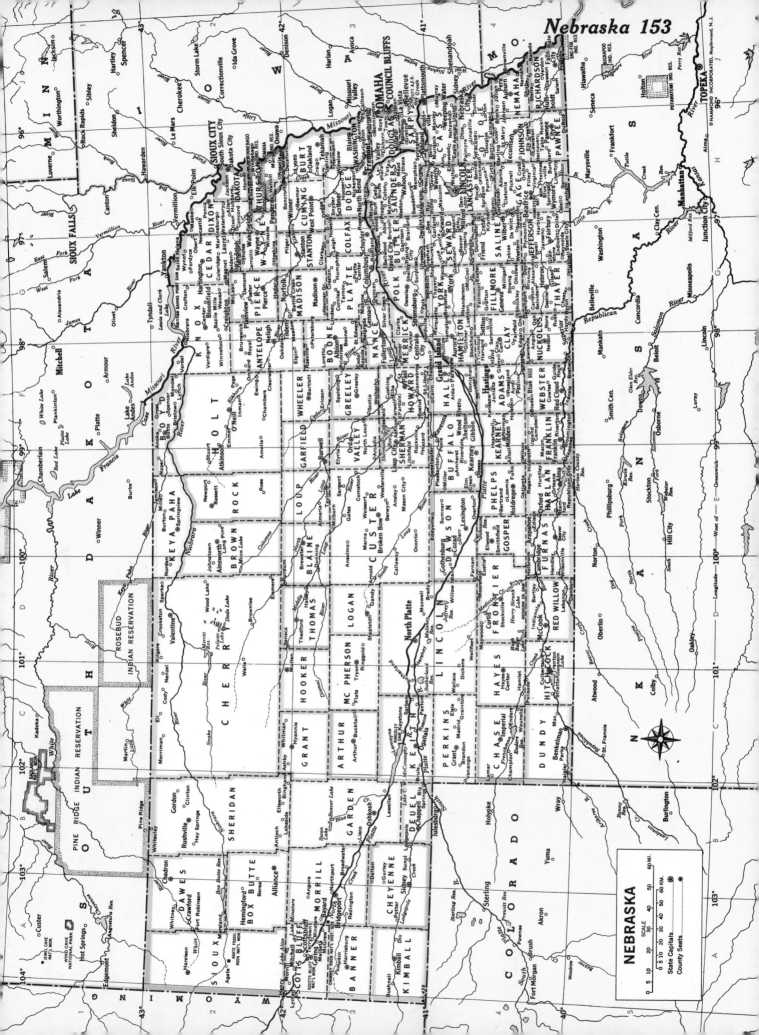

154 Nevada

NEW HAMPSHIRE
and VERMONT

SCALE
0   5   10   15   20   25MI.
0   5   10   15   20   25KM.

State Capitals .... ⊛
County Seats .... ⊛

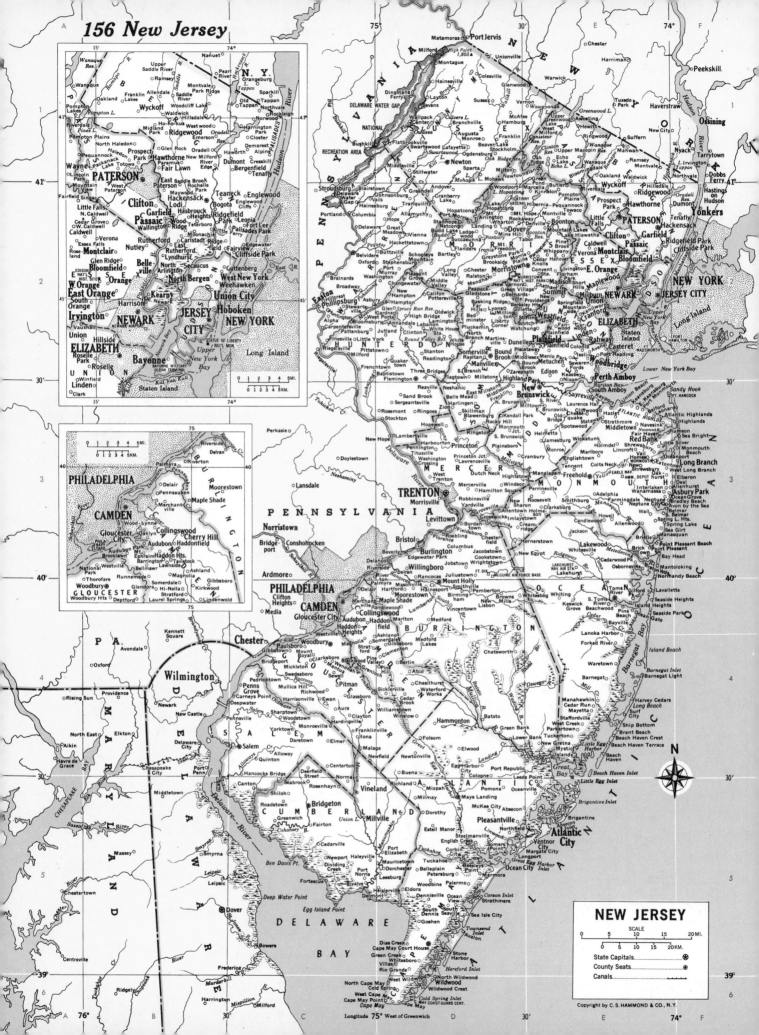

156 New Jersey

NEW JERSEY

SCALE

| 0 | 5 | 10 | 15 | 20 MI. |

| 0 | 5 | 10 | 15 | 20 KM. |

State Capitals .... ⊛
County Seats .... ◉
Canals ....

Copyright by C. S. HAMMOND & CO., N.Y.

Longitude 75° West of Greenwich

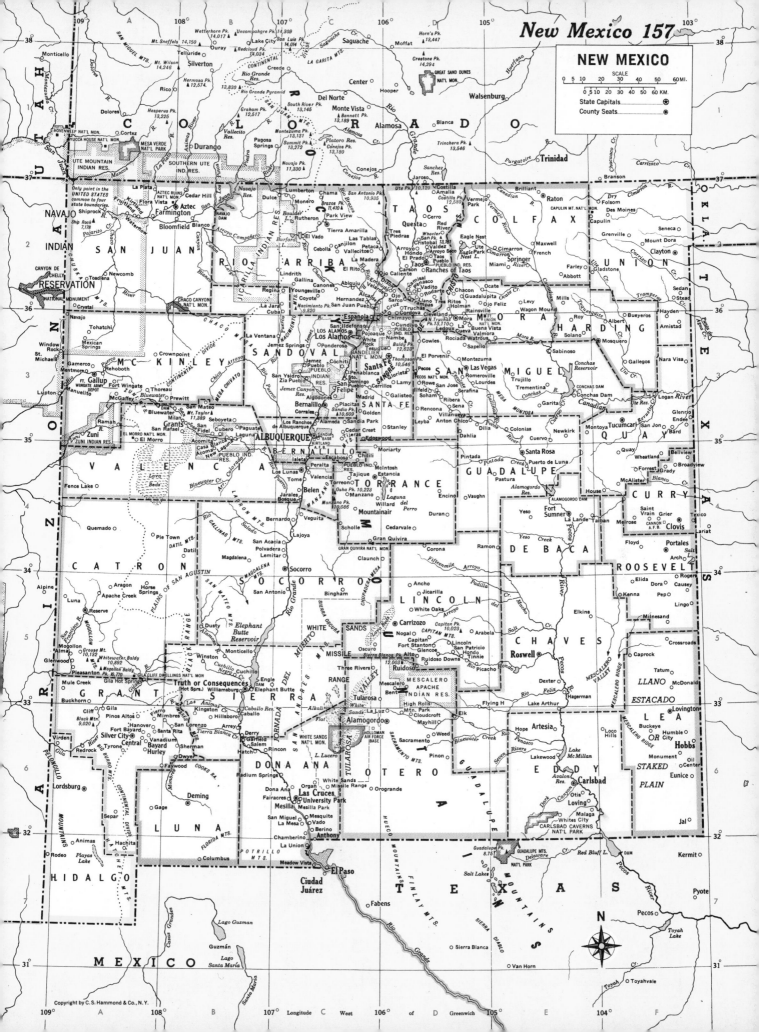

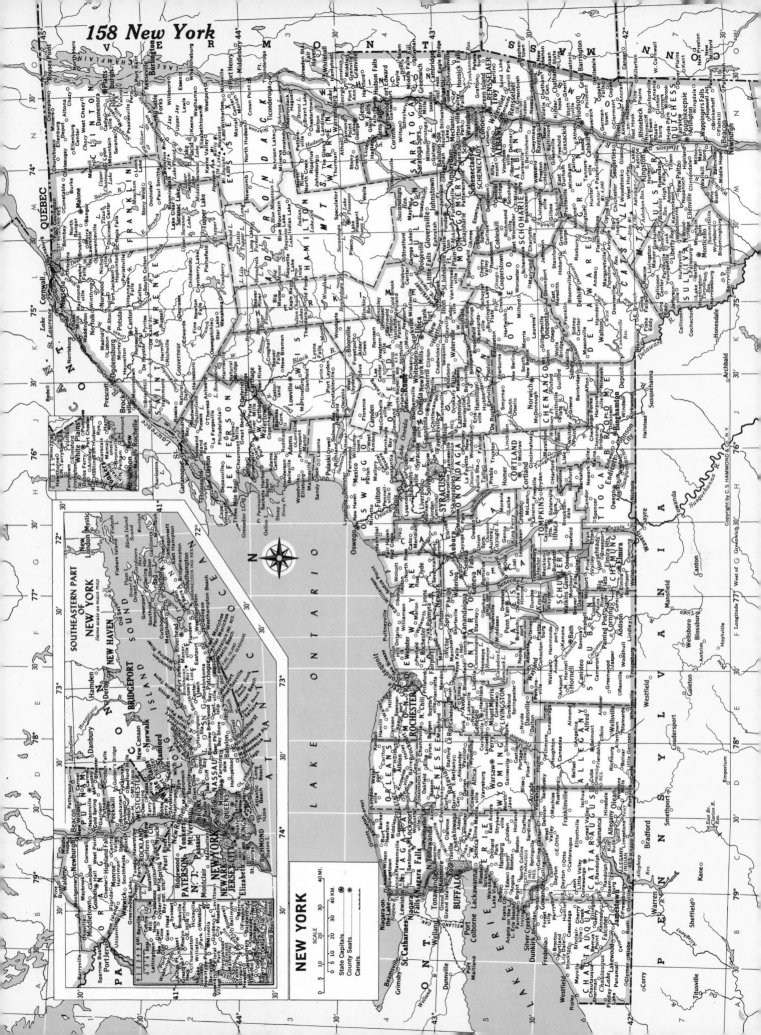

NEW YORK

SCALE

0 10 20 30 40 MI.

0 5 10 20 30 40 KM.

State Capitals.
County Seats.
Canals.

SOUTHEASTERN PART
of
NEW YORK
Same scale as main map

Copyright by C. S. HAMMOND & CO., N.Y.

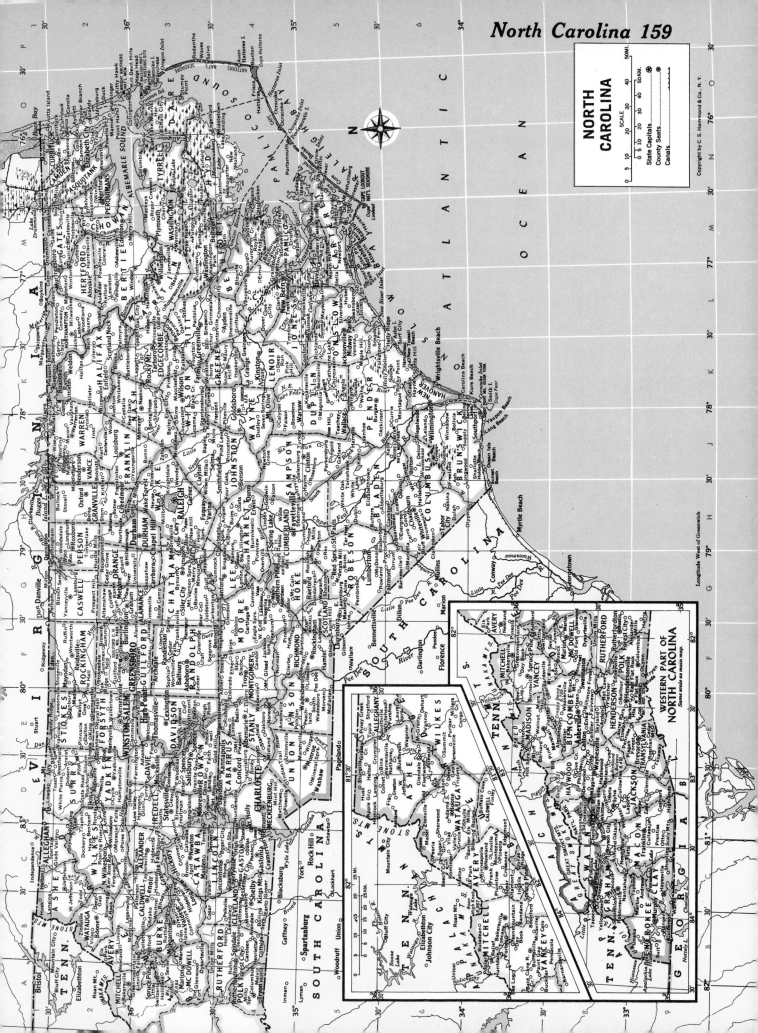

NORTH CAROLINA

SCALE

State Capitals
County Seats
Canals

WESTERN PART OF
NORTH CAROLINA
Same scale as main map.

Longitude West of Greenwich

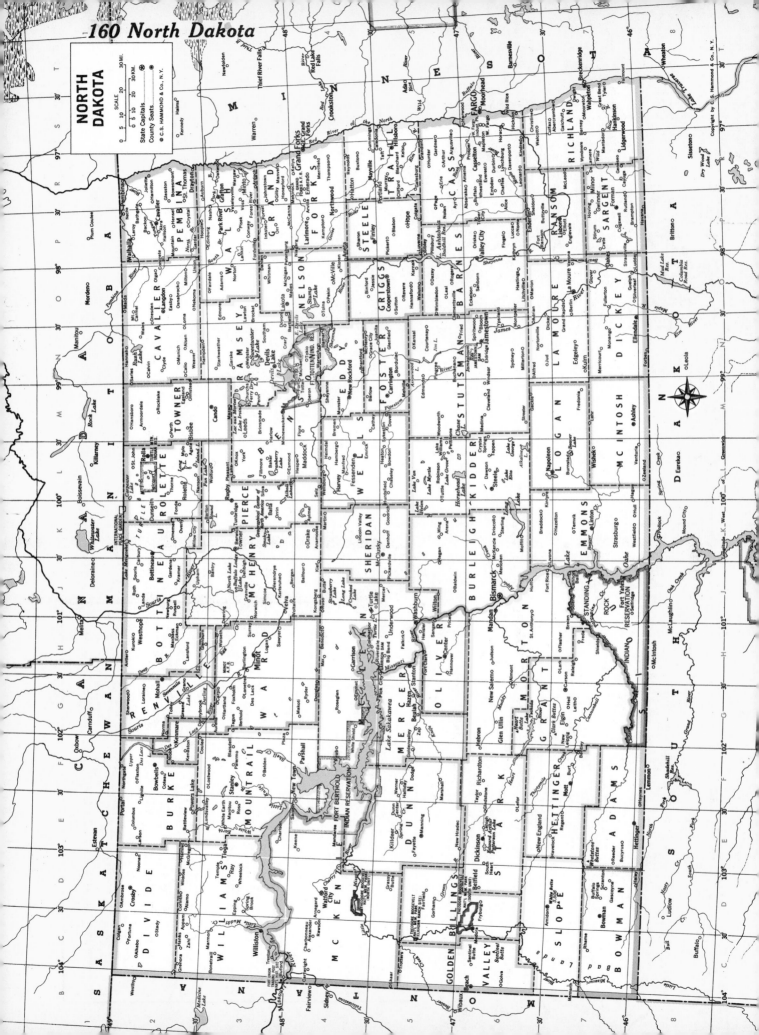

160 North Dakota

OHIO

SCALE

0   5   10   20   40 MI.

0 5 10   20   30   40 KM.

State Capitals..................⊛

County Seats...................⊙

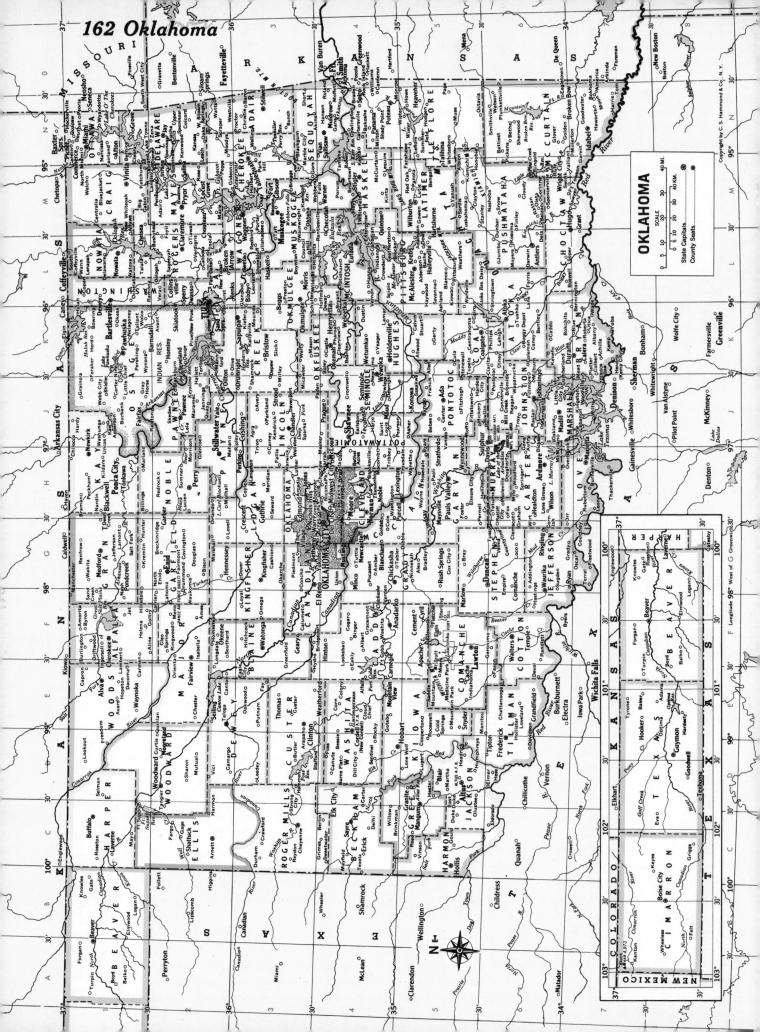

OKLAHOMA

SCALE
0 5 10 20 30 40 MI.
0 5 10 20 30 40 KM.
State Capitals ⊛
County Seats ●

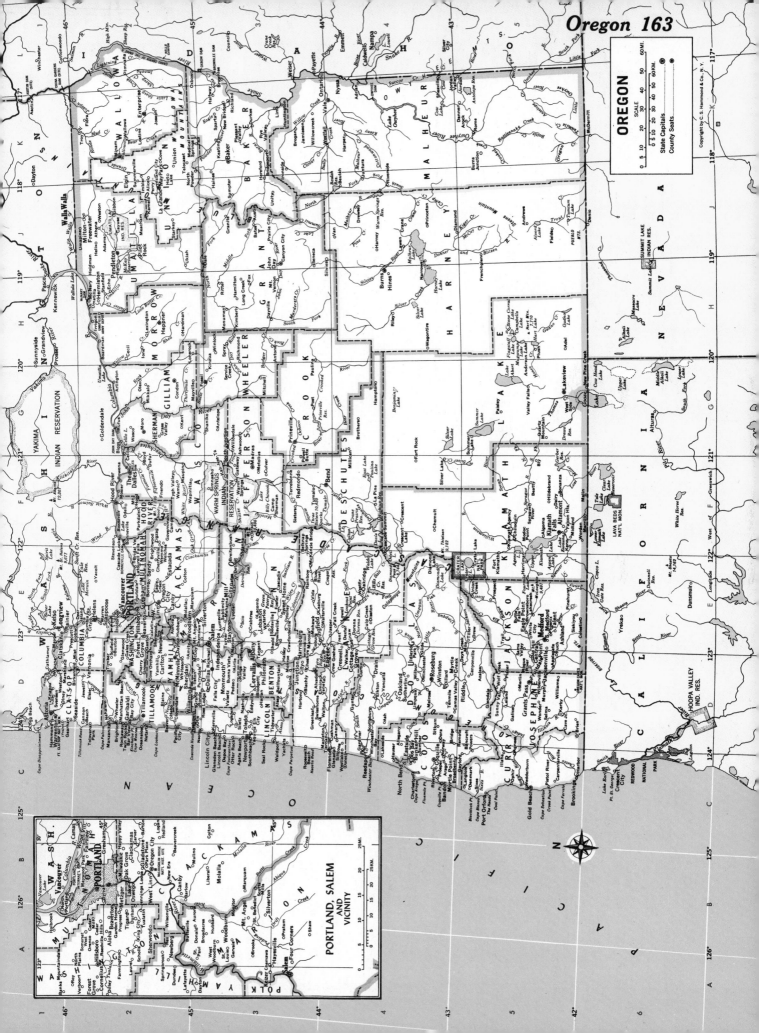

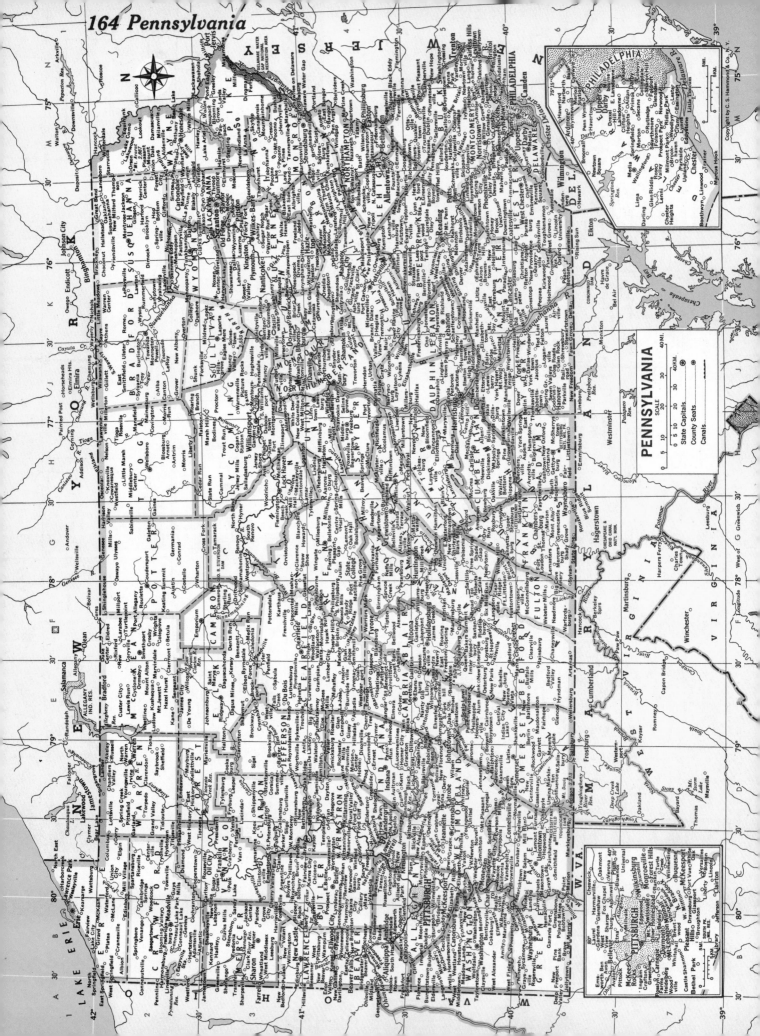

PENNSYLVANIA
SCALE
0   5   10   20   30   40 MI.
0 5 10   20   30   40KM.
⊛ State Capitals
◉ County Seats
····· Canals

Copyright by C. S. Hammond & Co., N.Y.

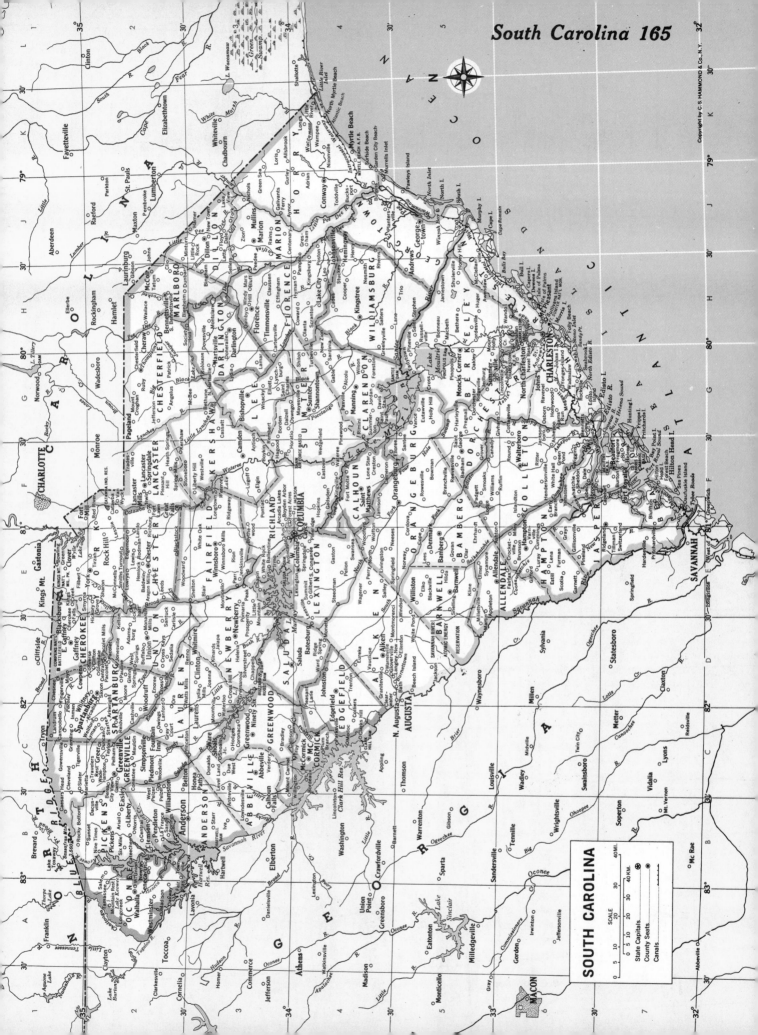

SOUTH CAROLINA

SCALE
5 10   20   30   40 MI.
0 5 10 20 30 40 KM.

State Capitals............⊕
County Seats.............◉
Canals....................

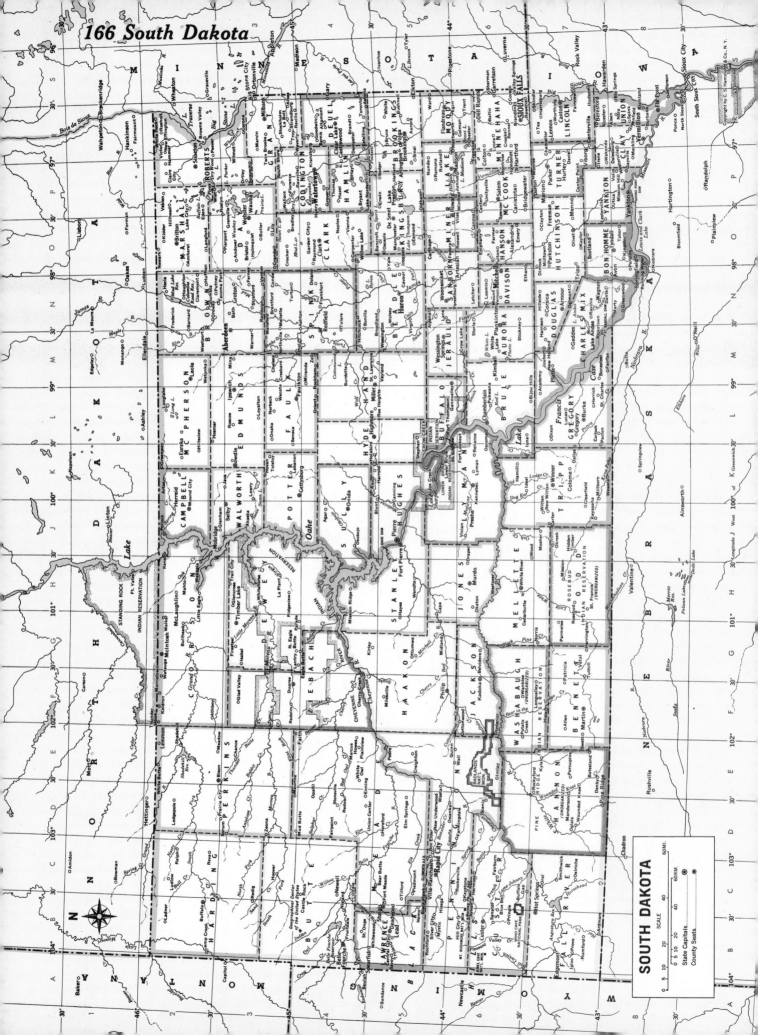

TENNESSEE

SCALE
0 5 10 20 30 40 MI.
0 5 10 20 30 40 KM.

State Capitals ⊛
County Seats ⊙

Copyright by C.S. HAMMOND & CO., N.Y.

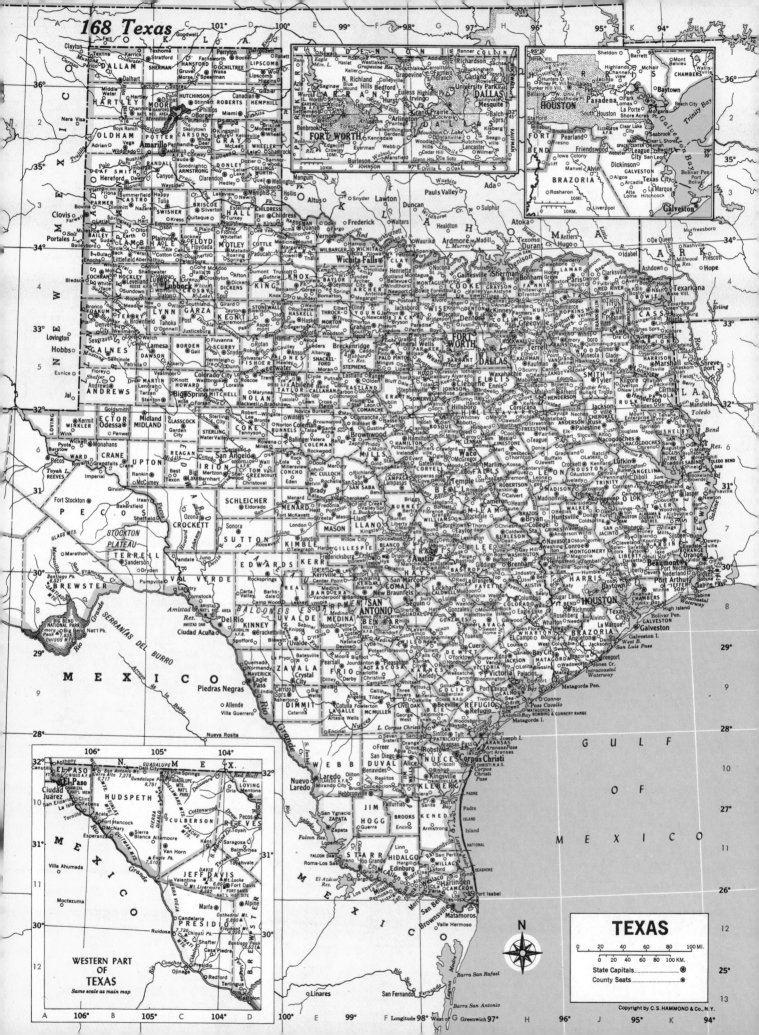

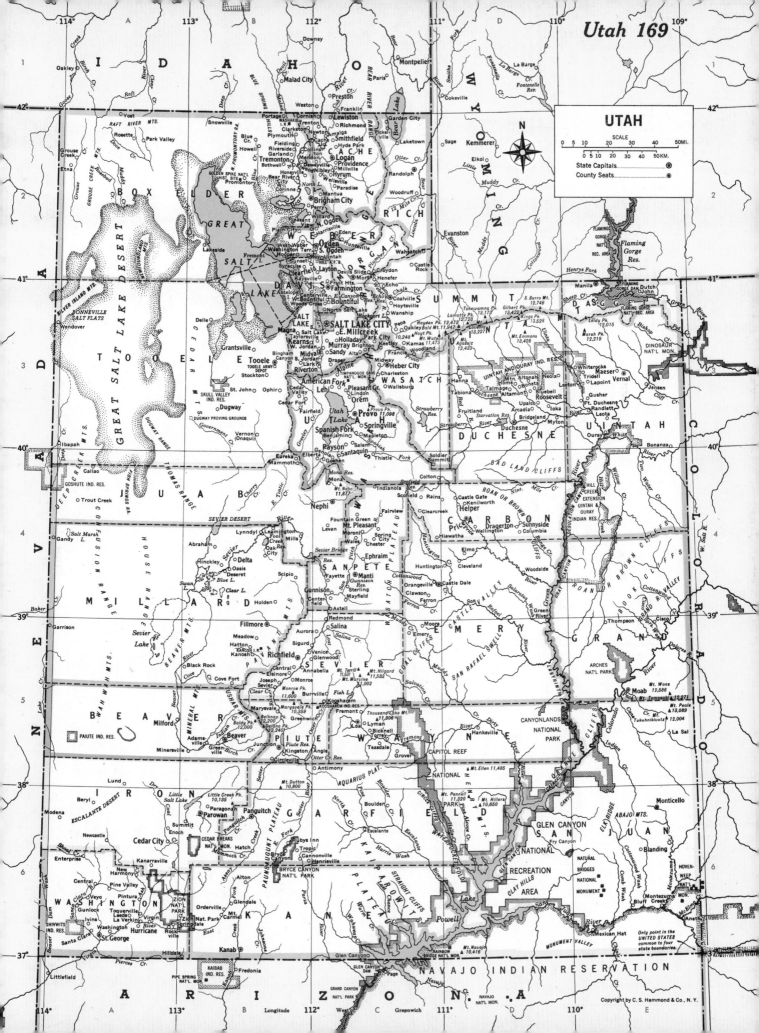

UTAH

SCALE

0 5 10   20   30   40   50MI.

0 5 10 20 30 40 50KM.

State Capitals.............⊛

County Seats.............◉

Copyright by C. S. Hammond & Co., N.Y.

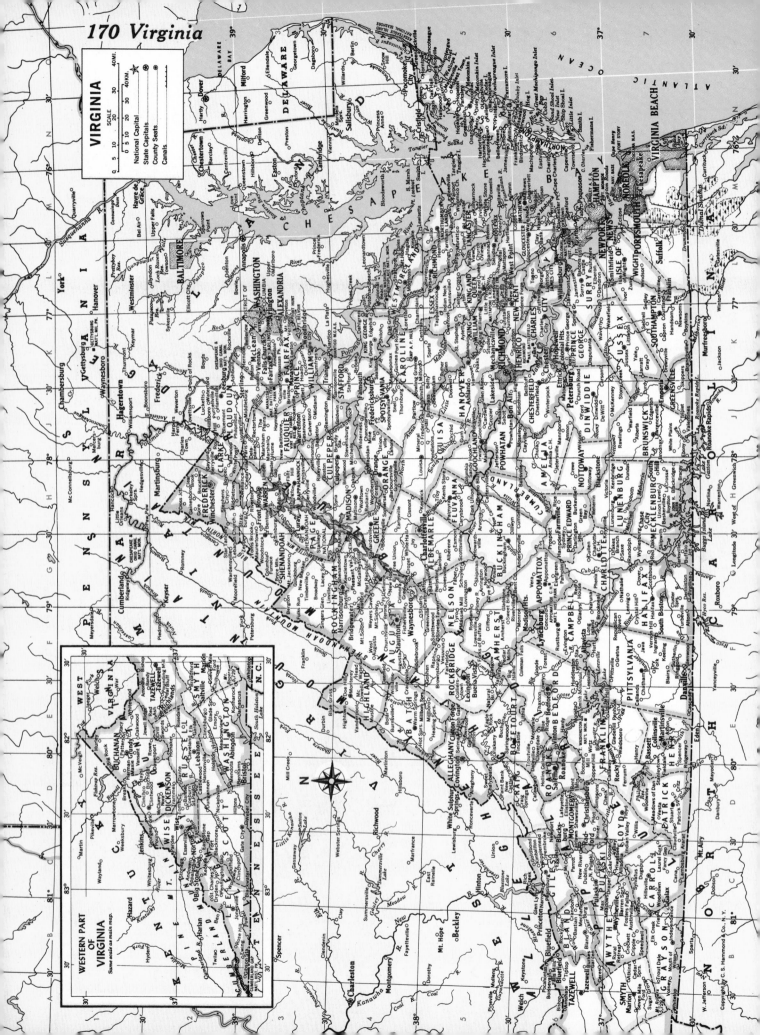

VIRGINIA

SCALE
0 5 10   20   30   40 MI.
0 5 10 20 30 40 KM.

National Capitals
State Capitals
County Seats
Canals

WESTERN PART
OF
VIRGINIA
Same scale as main map.

Copyright by C. S. Hammond & Co., N.Y.

WASHINGTON
SCALE
0 5 10 20 30 40 MI.
0 5 10 20 30 40 KM.
⊛ State Capitals
◉ County Seats

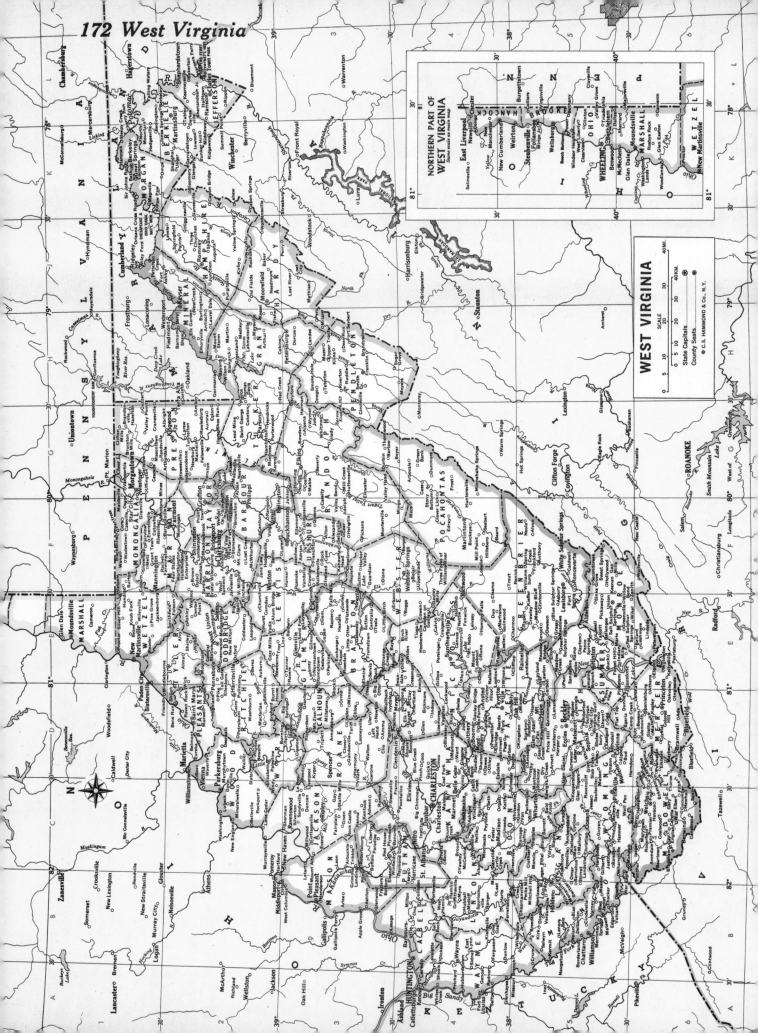

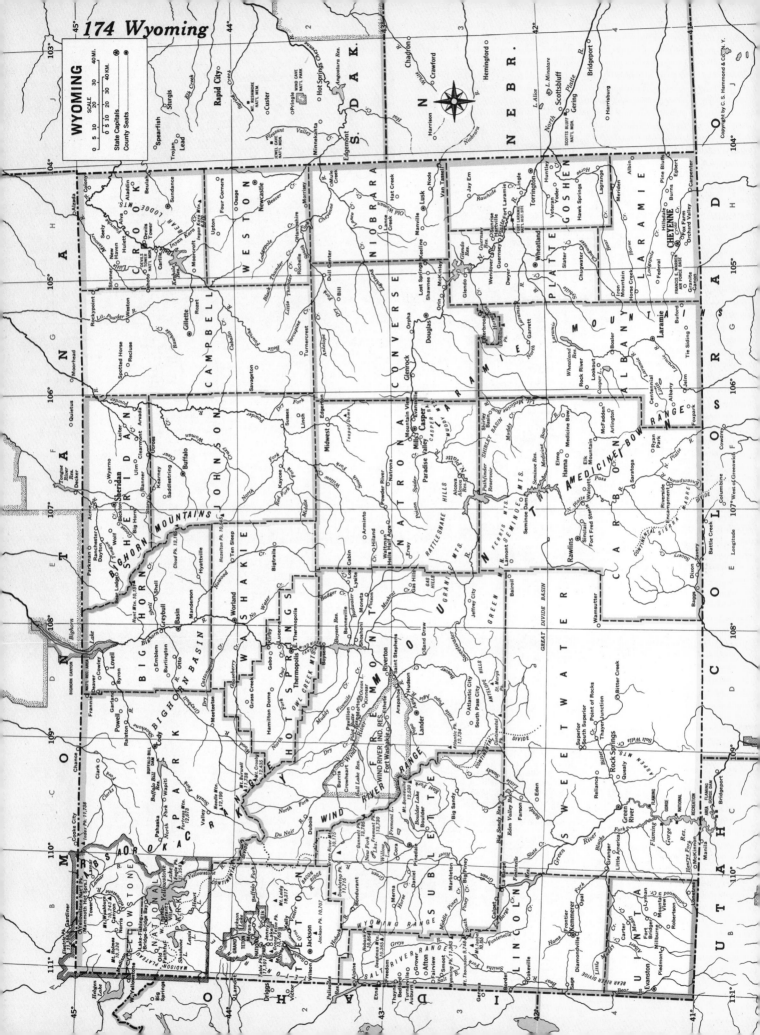

WYOMING

SCALE

State Capitals ⊛

County Seats ◉

MAJOR CITIES OF THE UNITED STATES

This section lists the major cities and all state capitals and territorial capitals of the United States. Listings for the states and territories can be found on pages 4 and 5. Population figures are derived from the 1970 U.S. Final Census, as revised.